Lecture Notes in Entrepreneurial Finance for the Digital Economy

World Scientific Lecture Notes in Finance

ISSN: 2424-9939

Series Editors: Professor Alexander Lipton and Professor Itzhak Venezia

---

This series provides high quality lecture note-type texts in all areas of finance, for courses at all levels: undergraduate, MBA and PhD. These accessible and affordable lecture notes are better aligned with today's classrooms and are written by expert professors in their field with extensive teaching experience. Students will find these books less formal, less expensive and also more enjoyable than many textbooks. Instructors will find all the material that they need, thus significantly reducing their class preparation time. Authors can prepare their volumes with ease, as they would be based on already existing, and actively used, lecture notes. With these features, this book series will make a significant contribution to improving the teaching of finance worldwide.

Published:

Vol. 8 *Lecture Notes in Entrepreneurial Finance for the Digital Economy*
by Peter Joakim Westerholm (The University of Sydney Business School, Australia)

Vol. 7 *Lecture Notes in Risk Management*
by Yevgeny Mugerman (Bar-Ilan University, Israel) and Yoel Hecht (College of Management Academic Studies, Israel)

Vol. 6 *Options — 45 years since the Publication of the Black–Scholes–Merton Model: The Gershon Fintech Center Conference*
edited by David Gershon (The Hebrew University of Jerusalem, Israel), Alexander Lipton (Abu Dhabi Investment Authority, UAE & The Hebrew University of Jerusalem, Israel), Mathieu Rosenbaum (École Polytechnique, France) and Zvi Wiener (The Hebrew University of Jerusalem, Israel)

Vol. 5 *Lecture Notes in Investment: Investment Fundamentals*
by Eliezer Prisman (York University, Canada)

Vol. 4 *Lecture Notes in Market Microstructure and Trading*
by Peter Joakim Westerholm (The University of Sydney, Australia)

Vol. 3 *Lecture Notes in Behavioral Finance*
by Itzhak Venezia (Tel Aviv-Yaffo Academic College, Israel & The Hebrew University of Jerusalem, Israel)

More information on this series can also be found at https://www.worldscientific.com/series/wslnf

World Scientific Lecture Notes in Finance – **Vol. 8**

Lecture Notes in Entrepreneurial Finance for the Digital Economy

P Joakim Westerholm
The University of Sydney Business School, Australia

World Scientific

NEW JERSEY • LONDON • SINGAPORE • BEIJING • SHANGHAI • HONG KONG • TAIPEI • CHENNAI • TOKYO

Published by

World Scientific Publishing Co. Pte. Ltd.
5 Toh Tuck Link, Singapore 596224
USA office: 27 Warren Street, Suite 401-402, Hackensack, NJ 07601
UK office: 57 Shelton Street, Covent Garden, London WC2H 9HE

Library of Congress Cataloging-in-Publication Data
Names: Westerholm, P. Joakim, author.
Title: Lecture notes in entrepreneurial finance for the digital economy /
P. Joakim Westerholm, The University of Sydney Business School, Australia.
Description: New Jersey : World Scientific, [2024] | Series: World scientific lecture notes in finance, 2424-9939 ; Vol. 8 | Includes index.
Identifiers: LCCN 2021055884 | ISBN 9789811249891 (hardcover) |
ISBN 9789811249907 (ebook) | ISBN 9789811249914 (ebook other)
Subjects: LCSH: New business enterprises--Finance. | Accounting. | Venture capital.
Classification: LCC HG4027.6 .W47 2024 | DDC 658.1/1--dc23/eng/20220120
LC record available at https://lccn.loc.gov/2021055884

British Library Cataloguing-in-Publication Data
A catalogue record for this book is available from the British Library.

For any available supplementary material, please visit
https://www.worldscientific.com/worldscibooks/10.1142/12659#t=suppl

Desk Editors: Aanand Jayaraman/Lai Ann/Jean Geysilla

Typeset by Stallion Press
Email: enquiries@stallionpress.com

Preface

This book is intended to be used as a basis for developing courses in Entrepreneurial Finance. While many universities particularly in the US have entrepreneurial finance on their curriculum, there is often a gap between the large selection of entrepreneurship courses and courses providing applicable hard skills in finance and accounting. Early-stage ventures cannot succeed without capital and careful management of cash flow, for example. Entrepreneurs need skills on how to negotiate with investors so that they don't end up giving up the control of their venture too early. This book aims to fill this gap by providing guidelines on how successful courses can be set up to train finance, accounting, and corporate strategy students for a career in the startup and venture capital industry.

The timing of this book is exceptional as right now a shift in focus toward early-stage venture investing by institutional investors is underway, creating a huge influx of capital to the sector. This development is naturally driven by the increasing importance of technology-driven ways of working effectively, digitally, and remotely, which has created enormous opportunities not only for technology companies but also for the growth of new startup ecosystems outside of the traditional areas such as Silicon Valley.

This book provides the topics for 12 weeks of lectures and workshops. At the University of Sydney Business School, we typically hold an in-semester-test around week 7 or 8 to solidify the students' understanding of the material in the first 4–6 weeks. We also run a review session in week 13 when we prepare the students for the final exam. The material is easily adoptable to a different course structure and teaching in intensive mode and/or online mode. A group (student team) assignment is a particularly significant part of a course in entrepreneurial finance. In this topic, there is no need to justify why the assignment has to be team work — it is hard (but not impossible) to imagine a startup company not having a team of entrepreneurs where different needed specialities and skills are combined to create a successful company. The book shows examples of how such a group assignment can be organized to train students in financial forecasting skills as well as pitching of their startup company's business idea. This unit of study has been very popular with our students and they have been particularly impressed by the wide range of job-ready skills they have obtained in this course. Many have decided to become entrepreneurs and some of the investment ideas created by students in the course assignment have received venture capital funding.

There are two views as to who was the first venture capitalist. The first view is that the first venture capitalist was Queen Isabella I of Castile (Spain, 1451–1504). Her most famous investment was the 1492 expedition of Christopher Columbus to discover the western sea route to India. The investment had all the landmarks of a classical VC deal: recent technological innovation (compasses and mapmaking); a big attractive market (spice trade with India); competitive rivalries (Spain vs. Portugal); considerable risk (at the time it was already known that the Earth was round; the uncertainty was about its circumference and about whether ships could travel this far); and a passionate, albeit slightly inexperienced, entrepreneur (Christopher Columbus); not to mention some surprises along the way (the discovery of the Americas). Columbus put up a hard bargain and managed to get what was considered a good deal at the time, receiving a 10% stake in the profits of the venture. He also made a fuss about his job title; instead of being called CEO, he bargained for the grand title of "Admiral of the Ocean Seas" (Da Rin and Hellman, 2021, p. 26). The second view is that it was General Georges Frederic Doriot (1899–1987) who founded the American Research and Development Corporation (ARDC) in 1946. ARDC was an investment fund that was set up to invest in young technology-based ventures, with a goal of assisting New England's economic recovery. Its model of raising funds from private institutional investors and investing them in startups was new at the time. It became the model for the modern VC industry.

The emergence of the first entrepreneurial ecosystem in its modern form in Silicon Valley, California, again can be attributed to numerous factors: the US government support for developing the West after World War II, the predominance of immigrants and migrants from the Midwestern US, the involvement of Stanford University, and a pragmatic non-hierarchical culture in California. In 1956, William Shockley founded Shockley Semiconductor Laboratory in Palo Alto, now the heart of Silicon Valley. From Shockley's venture spun the founders of Fairchild Semiconductors under assistance of the legendary VC Arthur Rock. From this group also spun the founders of Intel as well as Kleiner, Perkins, Caufield and Byers (KPCB). We all know the top semiconductor firm Intel, and KPBC remains one of the most successful VC firms of all times, having invested in Amazon.com, Compaq, Genentech, Google, Sun Microsystems, and more recently in Airbnb, Spotify, and Uber. Many companies were spun out of Fairchild, and even more were created out of these spin-offs, creating an impressive family tree of companies that shaped the evolution of Silicon Valley's entrepreneurial ecosystem (Da Rin and Hellman, 2021, p. 557). I also recommend that you take a look at Sequoia Capital (https://www.sequoiacap.com). This is a nice example of the value the relatively uncorrelated returns of venture capital investments can add to a portfolio: Sequoia have beaten the S&P500 index with a well-diversified portfolio of startups for 50 years (not very much, about 2% p.a., but the difference in the long run is stark). The group is also an example of how venture capital firms have to constantly evolve to stay successful in a rapidly changing environment.

Since the focus of new businesses is changing every day, and the latest trends and technologies are different in each 3–5 year period, how can you ensure that what you teach is relevant today and in the future? In the Author's Note, I provide some techniques you can use to stay at the cutting edge to ensure what you teach and you as an educator, coach, and motivator stay relevant for years to come.

Sources of the Latest News About Startups and Venture Capital

Crunchbase, https://www.crunchbase.com/#/home/index.
CB Insights, https://www.cbinsights.com/.
Pitch Book, https://www.pitchbook.com/.

These information providers not only give full access through subscription but also provide plenty of free material including excellent newsletters that will be helpful when you wish to stay on top of what is going on in the startup and venture capital industry.

About the Author

Joakim Westerholm is Professor of Finance at the University of Sydney in Australia. Joakim Westerholm's teaching and research interests are in the areas of asset pricing, with focus on security market microstructure and behavioral finance topics, and corporate finance, with focus on CEO and corporate insider trading strategies and acquisition decisions. Joakim has been an entrepreneur in the securities trading industry and has recently been engaged in the venture capital industry with focus on new ventures in decentralized finance.

Author's Note

Suggestions for Educators Preparing a Course in Entrepreneurial Finance

As mentioned in the Preface, I strongly recommend having the student work on a team-based assignment throughout the course. This assessed activity, I suggest with a weight of 25–30% of the total final grade, can be an important factor contributing to the success of your course.

I also recommend you consider introducing a simulation exercise for a startup company. I have been looking into readymade packages like CESIM (https://www.cesim.com/). A business simulation could also be more low-tech and simply be going through strategies for dealing with alternative strategies as an imaginary startup company progresses on a week-by-week basis throughout the semester. You could develop this using some of the many regular sources of business cases, including the prescribed textbooks, *Entrepreneurial Finance* (Leach and Melicher, 2020) and *Fundamentals of Entrepreneurial Finance* (Da Rin and Hellman, 2021).

To make learning fun and connected to the real world, engage with your students by watching and analyzing startup pitches with them. There is nothing better than a good episode from *Shark Tank* or *Dragons Den*! I also like to use extracts from the extremely funny HBO television series, *Silicon Valley*. To complement the entertainment, I also provide formal structured training on how to generate business models and how to pitch to complement the entertainment (see also additional reading material in the text). To further check in with reality, follow current news from the startup and venture capital industry using the sources mentioned in the Preface, e.g., the daily newsletter from https://my.pitchbook.com/.

The final clincher: I strongly recommend discussing the latest in technology with your students. In 2021, it was cryptocurrencies, initial coin offerings, non-fungible tokens, and artificial intelligence. These discussions can be very engaging, and in one tutorial, we often went over time by more than 30 minutes in engaging discussions of these topics (luckily, the classroom was free after us). My bet is that the crypto-excitement will morph into a general application of blockchain technology in a digitalization of the economy, which includes the finance industry. AI will be a hot topic for a while and perhaps take more concrete forms with significant impact a little later in this decade.

Tutorial advice, given through the tutorial questions, allow students to work on them in class using their own excel spreadsheets. This is particularly important for week 2–6 tutorials, which involve cash management, cash flow, and valuation problems.

As for testable knowledge, I provide instructors with sample assignments, quizzes, multiple choice questions, and final exam questions. The recommended textbooks, *Entrepreneurial Finance* (Leach and Melicher, 2020) and *Fundamentals of Entrepreneurial Finance* (Da Rin and Hellman, 2021), both provide excellent material for assessment and test-banks that you can implement directly in your learning management systems, such as Canvas, Blackboard, or Moodle. In today's hybrid environment with increasing reliance on online examination, I strongly recommend that you write/adopt your own versions of assessment task and as far as possible write new questions and exams. When you apply assessments to current events, you will test the students' understanding rather than the capacity to rote learn, and the assessments also become learning tools.

Congratulations for picking (or being assigned) a teaching topic that will add additional spark to your enjoyment of teaching, learning, and research.

P. Joakim Westerholm

Contents

Chapter 1

Introduction to Finance for Entrepreneurs

Focus

The purpose of this first chapter is to present an overview of what entrepreneurial finance is about. In doing so, we hope to convey to you the importance of understanding and applying entrepreneurial finance methods and tools to help ensure an entrepreneurial venture is successful. We present a life cycle approach to the teaching of entrepreneurial finance, where we cover venture operation and financial decisions faced by the entrepreneur as a venture progresses from an idea through to harvesting the venture.

1.1 Learning Objectives

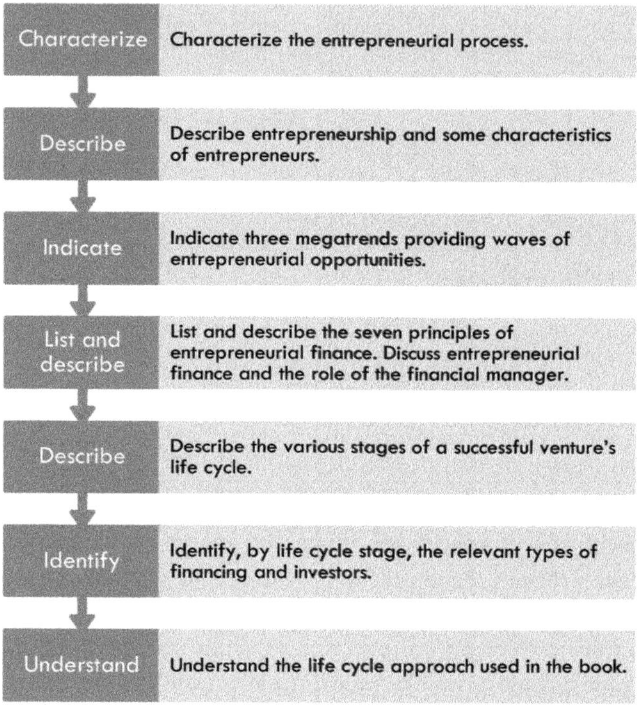

1.2 The Entrepreneurial Process

The entrepreneurial process involves the following tasks:

- developing opportunities (feasibility, venture, competition, business model and plan);
- gathering resources (assets, IP, HR, capital);
- managing and building operations (generate revenues to cover operating costs, generate cash flow for expansion) (see Figure 1.1).

The ultimate goal of the process is to create value.

Figure 1.1: The Entrepreneurial Process

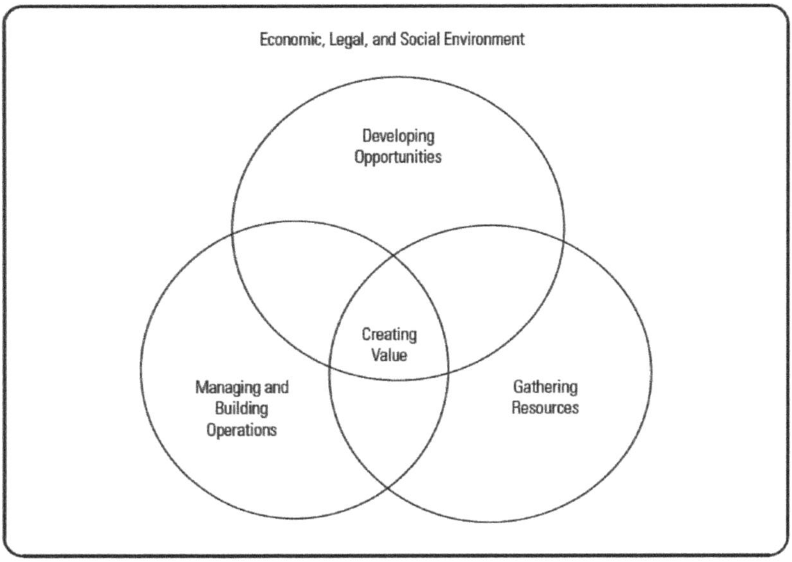

Source: © Cengage Learning.

1.3 Fundamentals of Entrepreneurship

1.3.1 *Who is an entrepreneur?*

Some example stories can include you (web-based business idea), a friend (product idea), or your neighbor (CEO).

- **Entrepreneurship**: This involves the process of changing ideas into commercial opportunities and creating value.
- **Entrepreneur**: This term refers to an individual who thinks, reasons, and acts to convert ideas into commercial opportunities and to create value.

1.3.2 *Entrepreneurial traits or characteristics*

A successful entrepreneur

- sees and seizes a commercial opportunity,
- tends to be doggedly optimistic (perhaps even to a fault),
- plans to obtain the physical, financial, and human resources needed for the venture to succeed.

Success is unlikely if you

- "are seldom able to see an opportunity until it ceases to be one" (Mark Twain)
- "view the glass as being half-empty instead of half-full" (unknown)
- are paralyzed by a fear of failure.

See HBO TV Show Silicon Valley: "Elevator Pitch to Peter Gregory" [https://www.classhook.com/resources/5706-silicon-valley-richard-pitches-pied-piper].

1.3.3 *Opportunities exist but not without risks*

New US business formations happen in the millions annually, and small firms provide over 80% of net new jobs.

Firms with less than 500 employees represent over 99% of all employers and account for about one-half of the national workforce.

The following have been noted in Australia (as per Australian Government Small Business and Family Enterprise Ombudsman):

- Small businesses and family enterprises in Australia, classified as businesses with less than 20 employees, account for almost 98% of businesses. The sector is growing fast and as such presents many opportunities and challenges for those who dedicate themselves to pursuing a small business venture.
- Small businesses account for 35% of Australia's gross domestic profit and employ 44% of Australia's workforce. Of the 877,744 total employing businesses, 823,551 are small businesses (93.8%), and of those businesses, 627,932 are businesses that employ only 1–4 people, known as micro businesses (76.2%).

Risks have also been noted in the US:

Some of the "Small Business Facts" find that nearly one-third of the businesses are gone in 2 years and one-half are gone in 5 years.

For new firms, a representative study (Headd, 2003) found the following:

- one-third of new employer firms endure < 2 years;
- one-half endure < 4 years;
- 60% endure < 6 years;
- but about one-third were "successful" at closure (Table 1.1).

Table 1.1: Business survival rates (2014–2018)

Employment Size	Businesses June 2014	Survived to June 2018	Survival rate %
Non-employing	1,273,769	758,922	59.6
1–4 Employees	571,206	395,953	69.3
5–19 Employees	199,965	155,270	77.6
20–199 Employees	51,619	42,408	82.2
200+ Employees	3,603	3,084	85.6
Total employing	826,393	596,715	72.2
Total	2,100,162	1,355,637	64.5 Average

Source: ABS Counts of Australian Business 8165.0, Table 15. Feb 2019 and ASBFEO calculations.

1.4 Sources/Drivers of Entrepreneurial Opportunities

Research (J. Case) suggests that 12% of Inc. 500 success is due to extraordinary ideas and 88% due to exceptional execution of ordinary ideas.

- Trends suggesting possible entrepreneurial innovations include the following:
  - societal changes;
  - demographic changes;
  - technological changes;
  - emerging economies and global changes;
  - crises and bubbles;
  - disruptive innovation (Figure 1.2).

Figure 1.2: Sources of Entrepreneurial Opportunities

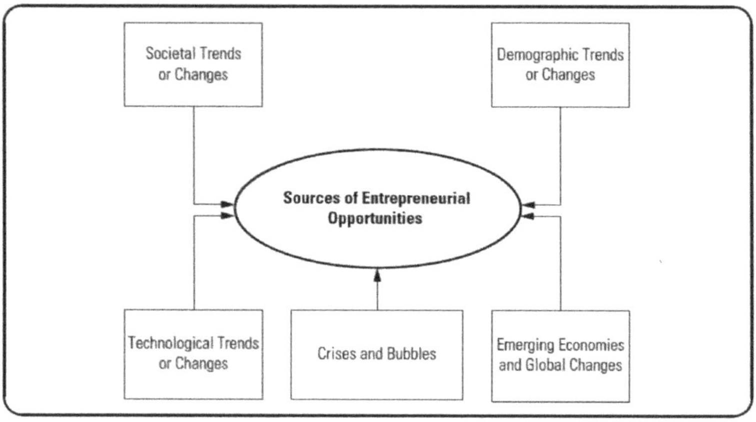

1.4.1 *Societal changes*

- Naisbitt's reflections are still relevant (Naisbitt, 1982).
- The shift from "Industrial Society" to "Information Society" automatically shifted the focus from human response to information.
- The advent of the global economy increased the awareness of international innovation and sourcing.

Today's focus on environment, sustainability, governance (ESG) has necessitated the following: Awareness of serious threats to humanity, including global warming, pandemics, and poverty. There are solutions in our technological advancement and most of these come from startups, such as Amazon, Tesla, Intuitive Surgical. See www.fool.com for new investment ideas. Read Siegel (2019) if you feel depressed about your future.

1.4.2 *Demographic changes*

The following are the key demographic changes:

- **Dent's generations**: This included the baby boomers (people born after WWII, 1946–1964).
- **Spending wave (1990s)**: The spending wave started in the early 1990s behind the stock and bond market booms.

- **Power wave (to peak in the 2020s)**: The power wave saw the aging baby boomers with great business influence and providing business opportunities — creating them, financing them, using them.

1.4.3 *Technological changes*

The key technological changes included the following:

- The information age started with the invention of the computer chip at Texas Instruments in the 1950s by Kilby and Noyce.
- Internet (e-commerce and information), e.g., an 'e-commerce site to sell undifferentiated goods at discounted prices'.
- Other technological buzzwords came into vogue, including:
  - wireless;
  - cross-functionality;
  - truly global in reach and competition;
  - smart, 3D printing, and AI.

1.4.4 *Emerging economies and global changes*

BRICs and Beyond (PWC) noted the following:

- Opportunities will shift over time.
- Global average growth was just over 3% from 2011 to 2050.
- CIVETS included Columbia, Indonesia, Vietnam, Egypt, Turkey, and South Africa, while BRICS included Brazil, Russia, India, China, and South Africa.
- These shifts create opportunities for entrepreneurs.

1.4.5 *Crises and bubbles*

The main crises and bubbles included the following:

- 2000 'Dot.com' and 9/11;
- 2007–2009 financial crisis that changed the game;
- cloudy times that almost always have silver linings;
- cost containment innovations;

- alternative energy;
- government stimulus (NSW) (https://www.jobsfornsw.com.au/funding/startups);
- Fintech;
- COVID-19 "Future is Now," "The Great Reset," shifting the new focus on healthcare, alternative energy;
- venture capital funding in 2020.

1.4.6 *Disruptive innovation*

Disruptive innovation refers to innovation that creates a market or network that disrupts and replaces an existing market. Some examples are as follows:

- electric cars (and bicycles);
- Uber;
- Airbnb;
- apps;
- alternative payment systems;
- cryptocurrencies.

The key pitfalls included not having all necessary skills to convert the idea into a commercial opportunity. See HBO TV Show Silicon Valley: "Meeting with Peter Gregory" [https://www.youtube.com/watch?v=9kH6qa2LFO4].

We have launched this course to fill in this gap and ensure that budding entrepreneurs and their employees obtain the hard skills required in finance to be successful in

- developing opportunities;
- gathering resources;
- managing and building operations.

1.5 Principles of Entrepreneurial Finance

1.5.1 *E-finance principle #1: Real, human, and financial capital must be rented from owners*

- Money has owners and therefore costs, time value, and risks must be taken into consideration.
- Hence, one should Expect to provide a return or the venture will not survive in a market economy.

S&P500 vs. TBonds

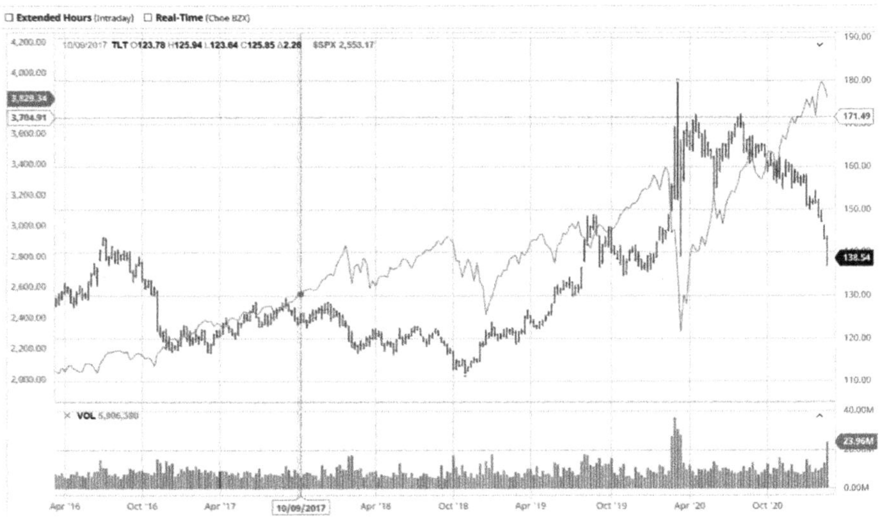

1.5.2 *E-finance principle #2: Risk and expected reward go hand in hand*

- Time value is not the only cost when using others' funds.
- The more risk, the more the expected reward.
- How much more the rewards will be is Market-determined.

1.5.3 *E-finance principle #3: While accounting is the language of business, cash is the currency*

Two important reasons to employ accounting are as follows:

- tracking and accountability for actions taken;
- quantifying different visions of the future.

But, remember cash flow is a new venture's lifeblood:

- "Get enough accounting to see through the accruals to the cash account";
- **Cash burn**: gap between cash being spent and that being collected;
- **Cash build**: excess of cash receipts over cash distributions.

1.5.4 *E-finance principle #4: New venture financing involves search, negotiation, and privacy*

- **Public Financial Markets:** standard contracts traded on organized exchanges;
- **Private Financial Markets:** customized contracts bought and infrequently sold in inefficient private negotiations.

1.5.5 *E-finance principle #5: A venture's financial objective is to increase value*

- While there are many objectives including personal ones the unifying financial objective is to increase value rather than price, margin, or sales rather than profit, return rather than net worth.
- (Market) Value derives from the ability to generate cash to pay capital providers for their capital.

1.5.6 *E-finance principle #6: It is dangerous to assume that people act against their own self-interest*

- Aligning incentives (investors, founders, employees, spouses, etc.) is critical.

- As situations change, incentives diverge and renegotiation is important.
- **Owner–manager conflicts**: differences between a manager's self-interest and that of the owners who hired him/her.
- **Owner–debtholder agency conflict**: divergence of the owners' and lenders' self-interests as the firm gets close to bankruptcy.

❖ One of many examples of when what you learned in previous finance classes comes to practical use in this UoS!

1.5.7 *E-finance principle #7: Venture character and reputation can be assets or liabilities*

- Ventures have characters that can be different from the individuals who founded or manage them.
- Many entrepreneurs state that high ethical standards are one of a venture's most important assets and are critical to long-term success and value.
- Ventures can — and do — make meaningful societal contributions.
- Many successful entrepreneurs are financially and personally involved in charitable endeavors.

1.6 The Role of Entrepreneurial Finance

The definition of Entrepreneurial Finance include the following:

- application and adaptation of financial tools and techniques to the planning, funding, operation, and valuation of an entrepreneurial venture;
- focus on the financial management of a venture as it moves through its life cycle, beginning with its development stage and continuing through to when the entrepreneur exits or harvests the venture.

1.7 Successful Venture Life Cycle

Venture life cycle: Stages of a successful venture's life from development through various stages of revenue growth).

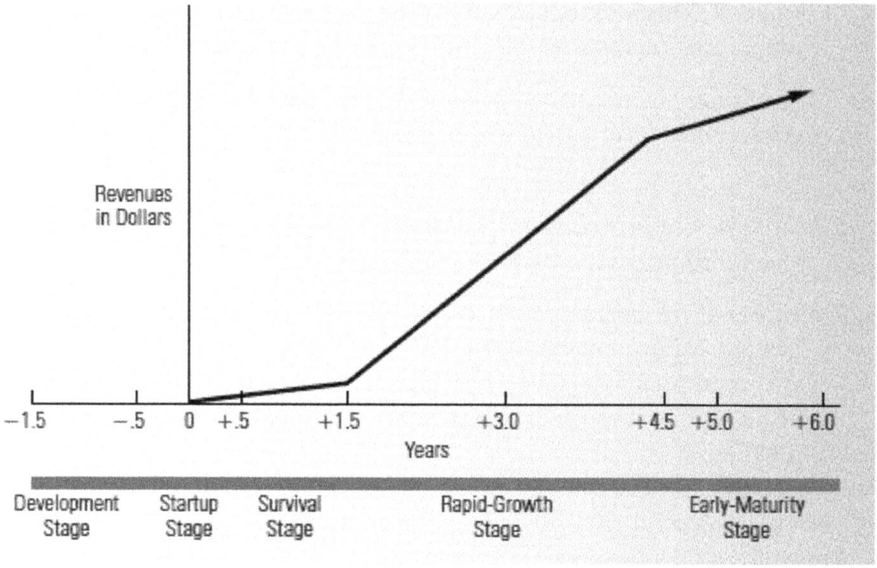

This may seem theoretical now, but classifying real-world business cases and example business ideas into these categories and understanding that all businesses go through these stages helps you put numbers to your forecasts!

For example, the discount rate for the cash flow can be determined based on what stage the firm is in, e.g., a survival stage vs. startup stage. We will start practicing this in next weeks' tutorial!

1.7.1 *Stages in the successful venture life cycle*

Development Stage

- **period involving the progression from an idea to a promising business opportunity.**

Startup Stage

- **period when the venture is organized, developed, and an initial revenue model is put in place.**

Survival Stage

- **period when revenues start to grow and help pay some, but typically not all, of the expenses.**

Rapid-Growth Stage

- **period of very rapid revenue and cash flow growth.**

Maturity Stage

- **period when the growth of revenue and cash flow continues but at a much slower rate than in the rapid-growth stage.**

1.8 Financing Through the Successful Venture Life Cycle — Definitions, Examples and Exercises will be Provided

Development Stage

- Developing opportunities and seed financing.

Startup Stage

- Gathering resources and startup financing.

Survival Stage

- Gathering resources, managing and building operations and first-round financing.

Rapid-Growth Stage

- Managing and building operations and second-round mezzanine, and liquidity stage financing.

Early Maturity Stage

- Managing and building operations and obtaining bank loans, issuing bonds, and issuing stock.

1.9 The Life Cycle Approach to Teaching Entrepreneurial Finance

See the pre-reading pages xi–xiii in Leach and Melicher (2020).

1.10 Next time — Business Model Generation

Workshop on Business Model Generation

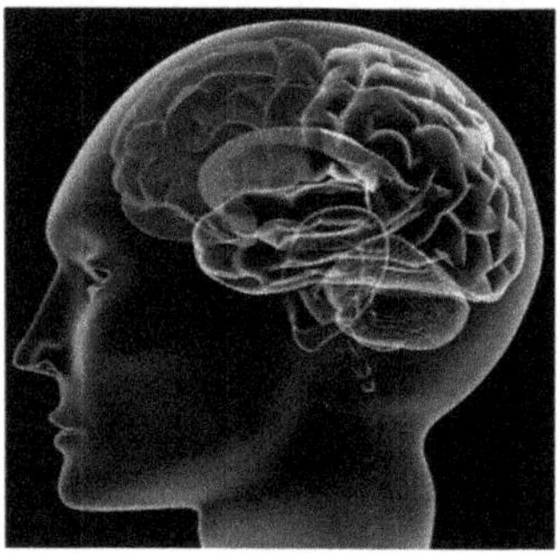

See Crunchbase for everything about all global startup companies. You can register at www.crunchbase.com.

1.11 Takeaways from this Introductory Lecture

1. The entrepreneurial process.
2. Importance of small businesses for economic growth.
3. Starting new businesses is risky.
4. Social, demographic, and technological trends.
5. Seven principles of entrepreneurial finance.
6. Financial objective: Increase the venture's value.
7. Conflicts may arise when incentives vary, e.g., owner–debt holder.
8. A venture's life cycle and different types of financing suitable for each.

1.12 Selected Financing Definitions (These Terms will Sink in During the Semester)

- **Seed Financing:** Funds needed to determine whether the idea can be converted into a viable business opportunity.

- **Startup Financing:** Funds needed to take the venture from having established a viable business opportunity to initial production and sales.
- **Venture Capital:** Early-stage financial capital often involving substantial risk of total loss.
- **Venture Capitalists:** Individuals who join in formal, organized firms to raise and distribute venture capital to new and fast-growing ventures.
- **Business Angels:** Wealthy individuals operating as informal or private investors who provide venture financing for small businesses.
- **Investment Banker:** Individual working for an investment bank who advises and assists corporations in their security financing decisions and regarding mergers and acquisitions.
- **First-Round Financing:** Equity funds provided during the survival stage to cover the cash shortfall when expenses and investments exceed revenues.
- **Second-Round Financing:** Financing for ventures in their rapid-growth stage to support investments in working capital.
- **Mezzanine Financing:** Funds for plant expansion, marketing expenditures, working capital, and product or service improvements.
- **Bridge Financing:** Temporary financing needed to keep the venture afloat until the next offering.
- **Initial Public Offering (IPO):** A corporation's first sale of common stock to the investing public.
- **Seasoned Securities Offering:** The offering of securities by a firm that has previously offered the same or substantially similar securities.

Discussion Questions and Answers

1. What constitutes the entrepreneurial process?
2. How can we define entrepreneurship? What are fundamental traits of individuals engaged in entrepreneurship?
3. What factors lead to the closure or cessation of business operations? What are the main causes behind business failures?

Exercises/Problems and Answers

I recommend to use exercises 1, 2 and a minicase from Chapter 1 in Leach and Melicher (2020) or similar text.

Chapter 2

Developing the Business Idea

Focus

In this chapter, we examine how one can move from an idea to a determination of the feasibility of the related business opportunity. We present an opportunity screening system to aid in determining whether an idea should be discarded or pursued. We conclude the chapter with an overview of a business plan.

New Skills in Business Idea Evaluation

Tools and skills we will learn include the following:

- **Qualitative Screening**: Interview with founder and the management team.

- **Quantitative Screening**: The VOS indicator.
- The Business Model Canvas (see bonus lectures on canvas explaining this method in detail. It will be practiced throughout the UoS).

2.1 Learning Objectives

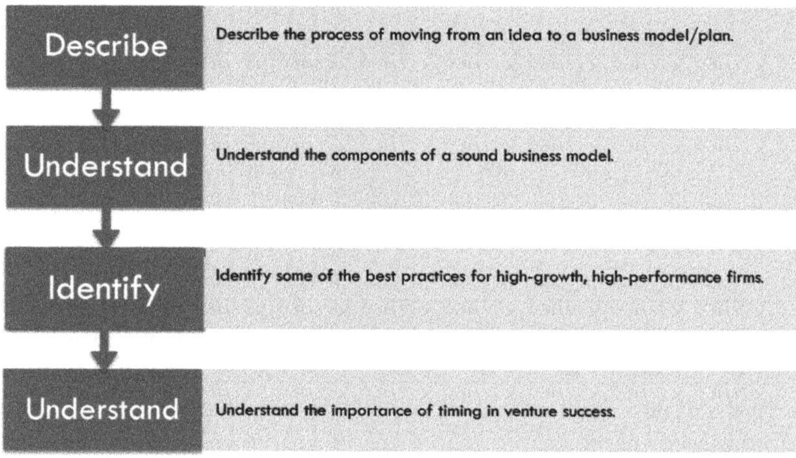

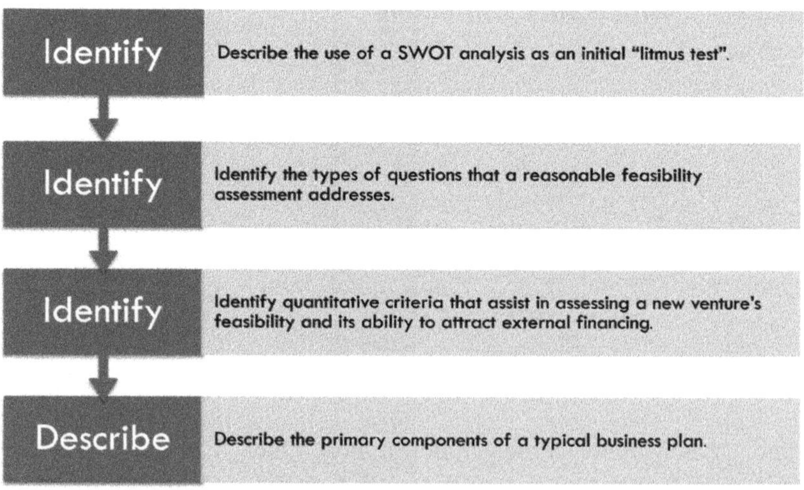

2.2 Types of Firms

There are various types of firms, such as the following:

- **Salary-replacement firms**: These are firms that provide their owners with income levels comparable to what they could have earned working for much larger firms.
- **Lifestyle firms**: These are firms that allow owners to pursue specific lifestyles while being paid for doing what they like to do.
- **Entrepreneurial ventures**: These are entrepreneurial firms that are flows- and performance-oriented as reflected in rapid value creation over time.

2.3 Components of a Sound Business Model

The main components of a sound business model include the following:

- generate revenues (you must have customers and sell them something);
- make profits (you must eventually have revenues that exceed the expenses of generating those revenues);
- produce free cash flows (you must generate cash inflows that exceed net working capital and capital expenditures).

The key feature of this course in comparison to other basic introductions to entrepreneurship is that it shares insights into this process from an entrepreneurial finance perspective instead of merely identifying ideas, feasibility analysis, and preparing a business plan.

2.4 Best Practices of High Growth and Performance Firms

Three areas have to be considered:

- marketing practices;
- financial practices;
- management practices.

While operations/production practices are not listed separately, they go hand in hand with high-quality products and services, as well as on-time delivery.)

Following are the methods to identify these best practices (see Section 2.8 for more details):

- **Qualitative screening**: Interview with the founder.
- **Quantitative screening**: VOS Indicator™.

2.4.1 *Best Practices: Marketing*

- Deliver high quality products or services.
- Develop new products or services that are considered to be the best.
- Offer products or services that command higher prices and margins.
- Develop efficient distribution channels and superior service support facilities.

Example: Apple.

2.4.2 *Best Practices: Financial*

- Prepare detailed monthly financial plans for the next year and annual financial plans for the next 5 years.
- Anticipate and obtain multiple rounds of financing as the venture grows.
- Efficiently and effectively manage the firm's assets, financial resources, and operating performance.
- Plan an exit strategy consistent with the entrepreneur's objectives and business plan.

Example: Facebook.

2.4.3 *Best Practices: Management*

- Assemble a management team balanced in functional area coverage and industry/market knowledge.
- Employ a decision-making style that is viewed as being collaborative.
- Identify and develop managers that support entrepreneurial endeavors.
- Assemble a board of directors balanced in terms of internal and external members.

Example: Amazon, Tesla.

2.5 Time-to-Market and Other Timing Implications

- Business opportunities exist in real time.
- Most ideas have a relatively narrow window of opportunity to become a successful business venture.
- Sometimes, ideas are ahead of their time.
- Of course, being "first to market" does not necessarily ensure success.
- Remember, some 80% of successful firms execute an existing idea!

Watch pitching clip, *Shark Tank — Bombas*: https://www.youtube.com/watch?v=pfSZydaj3xw; https://www.youtube.com/watch?v=JQXpWxHdWak.

2.6 Initial "Litmus Test": Yes/No

A viable venture opportunity creates or meets a customer need, provides an initial competitive advantage, is timely in terms of time-to-market, and offers the expectation of added value to investors.

SWOT analysis considers the following:

- unfilled customer need;
- intellectual property rights;
- first mover advantage;
- lower costs and/or higher quality;
- experience/expertise;
- reputation value.

(https://www.youtube.com/watch?v=XfB0g_JDIds)

2.7 New Approaches to Business Idea Generation — Recent Books

- Today's market place is unpredictable and chaotic.
- You must embrace your inner "hunter" rather than be a "farmer" who protects what he or she has.
- (1) Cyclicality is one of the most persistent and prevalent patterns of opportunity. (2) Expect repetition. (3) Act quickly when you identify a pattern repeating itself (example this months market crash).
- Determine future business trends following patterns of opportunity, for example, convergence is taking advantage of market chaos by mixing and integrating the right trends. For example, the successful iPhone fitness and running app Zombies Run uses convergence by combining three trends:
  1. GPS technology,
  2. the lucrative Fitness market, and
  3. the popular Zombie trend!

The Mom Test (Rob Fitzpatrick, 2013) provides a set of simple rules:
- The two most important conversations, with customers and with investors, are important.
- Stop talking about your idea and ask the right questions:
  - Ask potential customers about their problems and what solutions they are looking for.
  - To gain good data, you need to not ask would you be interested in my app, ask have you even had trouble finding recipes online and how did you go about finding them. If they can find these easily online, they wont pay for your app that offers daily recipes.
- Look for commitment from investors not compliments.
- Focus on a small group of target customers to narrow the number of ideas you are testing.
- Strive to have casual, short, and relaxing meetings with your potential customers and investors "over coffee."

2.8 Screening Venture Opportunities

- Venture opportunity screening involves the assessment of an idea's commercial potential to produce revenue growth, financial performance, and value.
- Our approach includes the following:
  - o Qualitative screening (Interview with the Founder);
  - o Quantitative screening (VOS Indicator™).

2.8.1 *Qualitative screening: Interview*

Four factor categories initially evaluating a potential venture's attractiveness are as follows:

- The Big Picture;
- Know Thy Customer;
- Production and Development Challenges;
- Financial Fortune-Telling.

2.8.1.1 *Questions to the founder*

Figure 2.1 shows the interviewer's questions to the founder.

Figure 2.1: Dialogue with Entrepreneur or Founder: The Big Picture

Interviewer:	So, let's start with the 30,000-foot view; what's this all about?
Founder:	...
Interviewer:	OK, it passes my "laugh test" although I'm a little light headed at this altitude. Plunging back down to earth, can you tell me a bit more about your intended customers and what they see as the benefits your venture offers?
Founder:	...
Interviewer:	I can see the potential, but aren't others targeting those same customers? Are none of the existing competitors' offerings similar in use and cost?
Founder:	...
Interviewer:	Granted, it sounds like a promising strategy, but won't others knock you off in relatively short order? Is there anything proprietary in your approach, and if so, do you have a plan to protect the related intellectual property?
Founder:	...
Interviewer:	Intellectual property usually means that something's new and unfamiliar. Will there be significant consumer education issues involved in using your product and services?
Founder:	...
Interviewer:	You're doing pretty well in your current career and one never knows when to take the plunge. So, why start now rather than later?
Founder:	...
Interviewer:	Will you be able to leverage your existing contacts and network? Is your network a strength or weakness relative to the competition?
Founder:	...
Interviewer:	Experience tells us that there's a lot of uncertainty and learning that takes place in a startup. Of course, learning takes time and resources. For your venture, how do you see the relationship between the size or scale of your startup efforts and its ability to progress through the uncertainty about viability or market acceptance? In particular, can the uncertainty be resolved more quickly if you are better financed?
Founder:	...
Interviewer:	Everyone understands that a business plan is outdated by the time it's printed. I'm thinking about the inevitable trade-offs each venture makes regarding things like in-house production versus outsourcing or human crafted versus robotics. What challenges does the venture face in making these decisions and subsequently adjusting them, if necessary, to changing conditions?
Founder:	...
Interviewer:	We look forward to watching your venture grow and prosper. Thank you for taking time out of your hectic schedule so we can look back on today and say, "We knew you when . . . ." [Or: You seem to have an interesting idea; however, our funds are committed at this time.]

2.8.2 *Quantitative screening: VOS™ indicator*

Quantitative screening attempts to quantify the following areas:

- industry/market;
- pricing/profitability;
- financial/harvest;
- management team.

Assign 3 to each criteria where the venture is ranked high, 2 for average, and 1 for low rank.

This is a supplement to, rather than replacement for, the qualitative Q&A approach.

2.8.2.1 *VOS™ indicator average scores*

- high potential (average scores of 2.34–3.00), including ideas that have the potential to become high-growth, high-performance ventures or "home runs";
- average potential (average scores of 1.67–2.33);
- low potential (average scores of 1.00–1.66).

Now, we will apply the VOS Indicator. We can also practice the VOS Indicator application in the tutorials: Minicase LearnRite.com.

2.8.2.2 *VOS factor category: Industry/market*

Potential attractiveness is evaluated on the basis of the following factors:

- market size potential (average: \$20–\$100 million);
- venture growth rate (average: 10–30%);
- market share (year 3) (average: 5–20%);
- entry barriers (average: timing/size).

2.8.2.3 *VOS factor category: Pricing/profitability*

Potential attractiveness is evaluated on the basis of the following factors:

- gross profit margins (average: 20–50%);
- after-tax margins (average: 10–20%);
- asset intensity (average: 1.0–3.0 turnover);
- return on assets (average: 10–25%).

Figure 2.2 shows the venture opportunity screening guide, while Figure 2.3 shows the classification guidelines for completing the VOS indicator.

Figure 2.2: Venture Opportunity Screening Guide: The VOS Indicator™

	POTENTIAL ATTRACTIVENESS		
FACTOR CATEGORIES	**HIGH**	**AVERAGE**	**LOW**
Industry/Market			
Market size potential	____	____	____
Venture growth rate	____	____	____
Market share (Year 3)	____	____	____
Entry barriers	____	____	____
Pricing/Profitability			
Gross margins	____	____	____
After-tax margins	____	____	____
Asset turnover	____	____	____
Return on assets	____	____	____
Financial/Harvest			
Cash flow breakeven	____	____	____
Rate of return	____	____	____
IPO potential	____	____	____
Founder's control	____	____	____
Management team			
Experience/expertise	____	____	____
Functional areas	____	____	____
Flexibility/adaptability	____	____	____
Entrepreneurial focus	____	____	____
Total points by ranking	____	____	____
Overall total points (OTP)		____	____
Average score (OTP/16)		____	____

Figure 2.3: Classification Guidelines for Completing the VOS Indicator™

	POTENTIAL ATTRACTIVENESS		
FACTOR CATEGORIES	**HIGH**	**AVERAGE**	**LOW**
Industry/Market			
Market size potential	>$100 million	$20–$100 million	<$20 million
Venture growth rate	>30%	10%–30%	<10%
Market share (Year 3)	>20% (leader)	5%–20%	<5% (follower)
Entry barriers	Legal protection	Timing/size	Few/none
Pricing/Profitability			
Gross margins	>50%	20%–50%	<20%
After-tax margins	>20%	10%–20%	<10%
Asset turnover	>3.0 turnover	1.0–3.0 turnover	<1.0 turnover
Return on assets	>25%	10%–25%	<10%
Financial/Harvest			
Cash flow breakeven	<2 years	2–4 years	>4 years
Rate of return	>50% per year	20%–50% per year	<20% per year
IPO potential	<2 years	2–5 years	>5 years
Founder's control	Majority	High minority	Low minority
Management team			
Experience/expertise	Industry/market	General/general	Little/none
Functional areas	All covered	Most covered	Few covered
Flexibility/adaptability	Quick to adapt	Able to adapt	Slow to adapt
Entrepreneurial focus	Full team	Founder	None

Notes: Market size potential refers to the expected size of the industry revenues at maturity; venture growth rate and market share are expressed in terms of the venture's revenues. These industry/market items, as well as the items under each of the other three factors, are discussed in the chapter.

2.8.2.4 *VOS selected accounting terms*

- **Cost of goods sold:** direct costs of producing a product or providing a service;
- **Gross profit:** revenues less the cost of goods sold;
- **Gross profit margin:** gross profit divided by revenues;
- **Net profit:** dollar profit left after all expenses, including financing costs and taxes, have been deducted from the firm's revenues.

2.8.2.5 *VOS return on assets (ROA) model*

- **Net profit margin (NPM):** net profit divided by revenues;
- **Asset Intensity:** total assets divided by revenues, the reciprocal of asset turnover (so ATO = revenues/total assets);
- **Return on Assets (ROA):** net after-tax profit divided by total assets;
- **ROA model:** ROA = NPM × ATO.

2.9 ROA Model Considerations

Case 1: High profit margins and low asset turnovers.
Examples: Products and services based on technological innovations.

Case 2: Low profit margins and high asset turnovers.
Examples: Commodity-type products and services (see Figure 2.4).

Figure 2.4: Return on Asset (ROA) Model

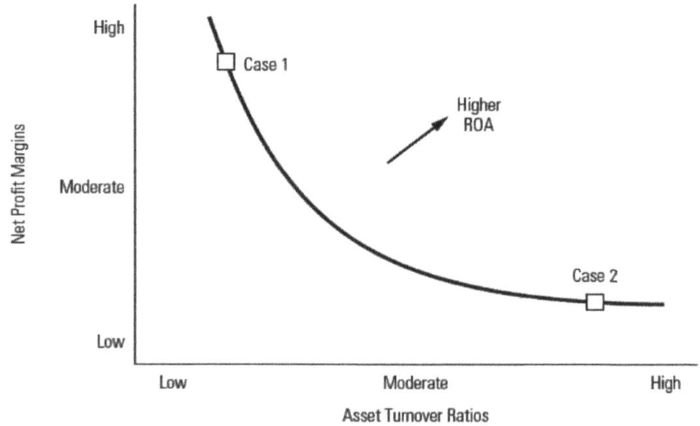

Source: © Cengage Learning.

2.10 Factor Category: Financial/Harvest

Potential attractiveness is evaluated on the basis of the following factors:

- cash flow breakeven (average: 2–4 years);
- rates of return (average: 20–50% per year);
- IPO potential (average: 2–5 years);
- founder's control (average: high minority).

2.11 Factor Category: Management Team

Potential attractiveness is evaluated on the basis of the following factors:

- experience/expertise (average: general/general);
- functional areas (average: most covered);
- flexibility/adaptability (able to adapt);
- entrepreneurial focus (average: founder).

2.12 Breakout Rooms — Interviewing the Founder

The details of the PDC Company Case are as follows: (prepare by reading pre-reading in Leach and Melicher (2020, pp. 198–199, 375).

A brave person can play the role of the founder. The rest of the group can ask the founder questions presented in the slide.

- Assume the potential size of the industry in 3 years is 100 million in sales.
- Use the end of year 3 projections for PDC company to assess their growth, potential market share, etc.

2.13 Entire Class — VOS Indicator

We will together try to find the VOS score for the PDC company.

This score can be refined using the additional understanding we gain as we track the performance of the PDC company.

2.14 Key Elements of a Business Plan

- **Business plan:** This is a written document that describes the proposed product or service opportunity, current resources, and financial projections.

- **Cover page:** This should identify the venture and provide the name, address, and phone number of the entrepreneur or other contact person.

See example on canvas: complete business plan for software publishing company. See also how the business description changes for later rounds of funding in Leach and Melicher (2020, pp. 634–639) (Private Placement Memorandum) Contemplate what are the differences.

Confidentiality statement
Example: "This business plan contains information that (the firm) considers proprietary. By accepting this business plan the recipient acknowledges the proprietary nature of this information contained herein and agrees to keep confidential all such information."

2.15 A Typical Business Plan Outline

- Executive summary
- Business description
  - description of the product/service,
  - industry background,
  - venture or firm background,
  - goals and milestone objectives.
- Marketing plan and strategy
  - target market and customers,
  - competition and market share,
  - pricing strategy,
  - promotion and distribution.
- Operations and support
  - quality targets,
  - technology requirements,
  - service support.

- Management team
  - experience and expertise,
  - organizational structure,
  - intellectual property rights.

- Financial plans and projections
  - income statements and balance sheets,
  - statements of cash flows,
  - break-even analysis,
  - funding needs and sources.

- Risks and opportunities
  - possible problems and risks,
  - real option opportunities.

- Appendix
  - detailed support for financial forecasts,
  - timeline and milestones.

2.16 The Business Model Canvas

Self-study material are available on Canvas. See pages 215–245 at the end of this book for a full description of the Business Model Canvas, including the purpose, applications (e.g., Uber), and useful tools for the assignment, such as The Business Model Canvas and The Best Practice Pitching Techniques, to which we will come throughout the UoS.

Do the following for the group assignment project:

- Find a team of 3–6 students with similar values and goals.
- With the material from this week, start brainstorming entrepreneurial ideas, use the business model canvas and start on thinking about a business plan.
- We have time, don't lock yourself in yet, let the ideas flow and abandon weak ones for better ones.

Homework 1

- Read Leach and Melicher (2020, Chapter 2).
- Do exercises Discussion Questions in Leach and Melicher (2020, pp. 1–22, 76–77).
- Read introduction (or the whole chapter) Leach and Melicher (2020, Chapters 3 and 6).
  Financial Statements and Managing Cashflows — we will learn how real-world startups are managed. A way to finally fully understand where the financial numbers come from!

Tutorial Exercises

Discussion Questions and Answers

1. How do we know whether an idea has the potential to become a viable business opportunity?
2. Identify some of the best marketing and management practices of high-growth, high-performance firms.
3. Describe and discuss some of the best financial practices of high-growth, high-performance firms. Why is it also important to consider production or operations practices?
4. Describe return on assets (ROA). What are the two major components of the ROA model?

Chapter 3

Managing Cash Flow

Focus

In this chapter, we focus on short-term financial planning involving projections of monthly financial statements for 1 year or less. The availability of cash is what drives the entrepreneurial venture. Inadequate cash often constrains the venture's ability to grow, is a primary cause of financial distress, and can result in bankruptcy even though the venture may be profitable in an accounting sense. The process of preparing short-term projected financial statements also helps the entrepreneur anticipate and estimate additional external financial capital needed to support the business plan during the next year. We also cover a venture's operating cycle and its cash conversion cycle and their importance in managing cash flow.

3.1 New Skills in New Venture Evaluation

Tools and skills we will learn are as follows:

- cash flow management;
- cash conversion cycle measures and ratios.

3.2 Learning Objectives

- Construct a cash budget and determine the timing and amount of any monthly cash needs.

- Describe how short-term projected statements of cash flows relate to cash budgets.
- Explain why short-term projected statements of cash flow are important to the entrepreneur.
- Identify and describe the use and value of conversion period ratios to the entrepreneur.

3.3 Venture Life Cycle: Operation and Financial Decisions

Following are the important stages in the life cycle approach (see Figure 3.1):

Development stage
- Screen business ideas;
- Prepare business plan;
- Obtain seed financing.

Figure 3.1: Life Cycle Approach: Venture Operation and Financial Decisions

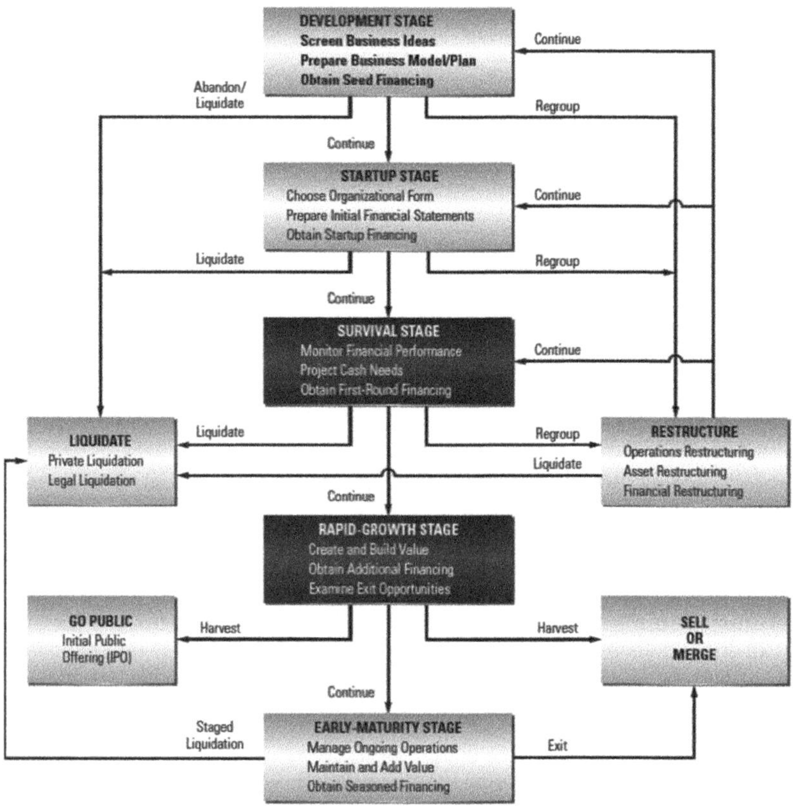

Source: © Cengage Learning.

Startup stage
- Choose organizational form;
- Prepare initial financial statements;
- Obtain first round financing.

Survival stage
- Monitor financial performance;
- Project cash needs;
- Obtain first round financing;
- Possible actions: liquidate vs. restructure.

Rapid growth stage
- Create and build value;
- Obtain additional financing;
- Examine exit opportunities;
- Possible actions: go public vs. sell/merge.

Early-maturity stage
- Manage ongoing operations;
- Maintain and add value;
- Obtain seasoned financing.

3.4 Short-term Cash Planning Tools

Following are the important short-term cash planning tools:
- sales schedule;
- purchase schedule;
- wages and commission schedule;
- cash budget.

3.5 PDC Company Operating and Cash Budget

Table 3.1 shows the PDC company operating schedules and cash budget. Note the beginning inventory correction to 197520, 110400, 149040, 123280, 110400.

Table 3.1: PDC company operating schedules and cash budget

(A) Sales schedule

	MARCH	APRIL	MAY	JUNE	JULY	AUGUST	APRIL TO JULY
Schedule 1: Sales Forecast	92,000	115,000	184,000	138,000	115,000	92,000	552,000
Credit sales, 40%	36,800	46,000	73,600	55,200	46,000		
Cash sales, 60%	55,200	69,000	110,400	82,800	69,000		
Schedule 2: Cash Collections							
Cash sales this month		69,000	110,400	82,800	69,000		
100% of last month's credit sales		36,800	46,000	73,600	55,200		
Total collections		105,800	156,400	156,400	124,200		

(B) Purchase schedule

	MARCH	APRIL	MAY	JUNE	JULY	APRIL TO JULY
Schedule 3: Purchases						
Ending inventory	110,400	149,040	123,280	110,400	97,520	
Cost of goods sold	64,400	80,500	128,800	96,600	80,500	386,400
Total needed	174,800	229,540	252,080	207,000	178,020	
Beginning inventory	197,520	110,400	149,040	123,280	110,400	
Purchases	77,280	119,140	103,040	83,720	67,620	
Schedule 4: Purchase Disbursements						
50% of last month's purchases		38,640	59,570	51,520	41,860	
50% of this month's purchases		59,570	51,520	41,860	33,810	
Disbursements for purchases		98,210	111,090	93,380	75,670	

(C) Wages and commissions schedule

	MARCH	APRIL	MAY	JUNE	JULY	APRIL TO JULY
Schedule 5: Wages and Commissions						
Wages, all fixed	5,750	5,750	5,750	5,750	5,750	
Commissions (15% of current sales)	13,800	17,250	27,600	20,700	17,250	
Total	19,550	23,000	33,350	26,450	23,000	105,800
Schedule 6: Disbursements—Wages and Commissions						
50% of last month's expenses		9,775	11,500	16,675	13,225	
50% of this month's expenses		11,500	16,675	13,225	11,500	
Total		21,275	28,175	29,900	24,725	

Table 3.1: (*Continued*)

(D) Cash budget

	APRIL	MAY	JUNE	JULY
Beginning cash balance	23,000	23,000	23,000	23,000
Cash receipts:				
Collections from customers	105,800	156,400	156,400	124,200
Total cash available for needs before financing	128,800	179,400	179,400	147,200
Cash disbursements:				
Merchandise	98,210	111,090	93,380	75,670
Wages and commissions	21,275	28,175	29,900	24,725
Miscellaneous expenses	5,750	9,200	6,900	5,750
Rent	4,600	4,600	4,600	4,600
Truck purchase	6,900	0	0	0
Total disbursements	136,735	153,065	134,780	110,745
Minimum cash balance desired	23,000	23,000	23,000	23,000
Total cash needed	159,735	176,065	157,780	133,745
Excess of total cash	-30,935	3,335	21,620	13,455
Financing				
New borrowing	30,935	0	0	0
Repayments		2,871	21,199	6,865
Loan balance	30,935	28,064	6,865	0
Interest	0	464	421	103
Total effects of financing	30,935	-3,335	-21,620	-6,968
Cash balance	23,000	23,000	23,000	29,487

Source: © Cengage Learning.

3.6 Check with Projected Financials

As a check on the cash budget, you can get the exact same cash balance by constructing a full set of financial statements. See Exhibits 6.3–6.5 in Leach and Melicher (2020).

We will now go through the construction of the cash budget in detail using Excel.

3.7 Operating Cycle

Figure 3.2 shows the operating cycle.

Figure 3.2: Operating Cycle

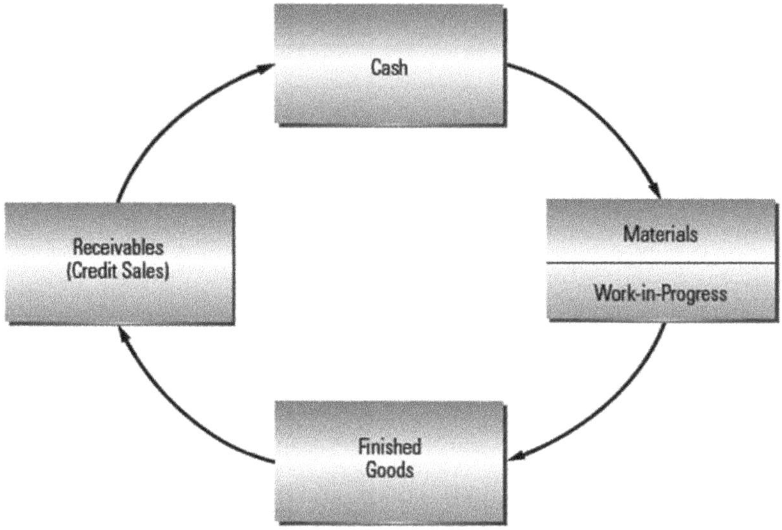

Source: © Cengage Learning.

3.8 Conversion Period Ratios

- **Conversion period ratio**: This indicates the average time it takes in days to convert certain current assets and current liability accounts into cash.
- **Operating cycle**: This indicates the time it takes to purchase, produce, and sell the venture's products plus the time needed to collect receivables if the sales are on credit.
- **Cash conversion cycle**: This includes the sum of the inventory-to-sale conversion period and the sales-to-cash conversion period less the purchase-to-payment conversion period.

3.9 Measuring Conversion Times

Inventory-to-sale conversion period:

$$\text{Avg Inventories (CGS/365)}$$
$$= \frac{(140{,}000 + 95{,}000)/2}{380{,}000/365} = \frac{117{,}500}{1041}$$
$$= 112.9 \text{ days.}$$

Given new I-to-S, we can solve for new average inventories:

Inventory-to-sale conversion period × (COGS/365)
= 105.7 × $1,041
= $110,000 (rounded).

Sale-to-cash conversion period:

$$= \frac{\text{Avg Receivables}}{(\text{Net Sales}/365)}$$

$$= \frac{(105{,}000 + 75{,}000)/2}{575{,}000/365}$$

$$= 57.1 \text{ days.}$$

Purchase-to-payment conversion period:

Avg Payable + Avg Accrued Liabilities (COGS/365)

= (84,000 + 57,000)/2 + (10,000 + 9,000)/2
380,000/365
= 76.8 days.

Cash conversion cycle:

Inventory-to-sale conversion period
+ Sale-to-cash conversion period
− Purchase-to-payment conversion
= 112.9 days + 57.1 days − 76.8 days
= 93.2 days.

3.10 MPC Conversion Period Performance

Table 3.2 shows the MPC conversion period performance.

Table 3.2: MPC conversion period performance

CONVERSION PERIOD RATIO	2015	2016	INDICATED IMPACT ON C^3
Inventory-to-sale	105.7 days	112.9 days	+7.2 days (lengthens C^3)
Sale-to-cash	56.3 days	57.1 days	+0.8 days (lengthens C^3)
Purchase-to-payment	77.5 days	76.8 days	+0.7 days (lengthens C^3)
Cash conversion cycle (C^3)	84.5 days	93.2 days	+8.7 days (longer C^3)

How can the operating cycle be applied to assess the health of an early-stage business? Let us study a case where this type of analysis can uncover a lot of information. See CASE Scandi Home Furnishing Inc. and pre-read the background (Leach and Melicher, 2020, pp. 223–225).

Exercises/Problems and Answers

1. [Short-Term Financial Planning] The Itsar Products Company has made the following monthly estimates of cash receipts and cash disbursements when preparing cash budgets for the next 12 months. Itsar Products has beginning cash on hand of $10,000 and wants to maintain this minimum cash level throughout the next year.
   A. Determine whether Itsar Products will have a cash need during the next year.
   B. If Itsar Products has a cash need, indicate the month when the need will begin and determine the month and amount when the maximum need will occur.
   C. Determine whether the cash need (if any) can be repaid within the next year.

2. [Short-Term Financial Planning] The PDC Company was described during the early part of this chapter. Refer to the PDC Company's projected monthly operating schedules in Table 6.2. PDC's sales are projected to be $80,000 in September 2020.
   A. Prepare PDC's sales schedule, purchases schedule, and the wages schedule for August 2020.
   B. Prepare a cash budget for August 2020 for the PDC Company and describe how the forecast affects the end-of-month cash balance.
   C. Prepare the PDC Company's projected income statement for August.
   D. Prepare the PDC Company's projected balance sheet for August.
   E. Prepare the PDC Company's projected statement of cash flow for August.
   F. Compare your balance sheet at the end of August with the balance sheet in Table 6.1 in the chapter and apply the balance sheet method to determine cash flows over the March–August time period.

Spreadsheet Exercises/Problems

[*Note*: The following activities are for students with spreadsheet software skills.]

1. Short-term financial planning for the PDC Company was described during the early part of this chapter. Refer to the PDC Company's projected monthly operating schedules in Table 3.1. To arrive at PDC's monthly sales for the remainder of 2020, do the following:
   A. Prepare PDC's sales schedule, purchases schedule, and the wages schedule for each of the last four months of 2020.
   B. Prepare cash budgets for each of the last four months of 2020 for the PDC Company and describe how the forecast affects the end of month cash balances.
   C. Prepare the PDC Company's projected monthly income statements for the August–December period.
   D. Prepare the PDC Company's projected monthly balance sheets for the August–December period.
   E. Prepare the PDC Company's projected monthly statements of cash flow for the August–December period.
   F. Compare your balance sheet at the end of December with the balance sheet in Table 6.1 in the chapter and apply the balance sheet method to determine cash flows over the March–December period.

2. Applied mini case on venture investment strategy justify your answer well in words and back up with numbers.

Description of Case: It is your first day on the job as an intern at the Venture Capital Fund Stone Henge Ventures [VC]. They have hired you for your impressive grades in Finance, Accounting, and Strategy at the University of Sydney, and will test you out with this task. If your manager Alexandra, an experienced founder herself, likes what you suggest, they will let you present your case to the investment board; if Alexandra thinks you need further training, you will just be assigned to another partner, Linda, an expert on Chinese venture capital, to work with her on some of their projects — no harm done! This is your chance to show what you are made of! You have two days to complete this task so do not rush it!

Situation and Context: Stone Henge is planning to set up a new fund for sophisticated accredited investors targeting high network individuals who would like to invest in both Australian and Chinese Startups and early-stage ventures. You are asked to first suggest a suitable strategy, industry focus, and a set of companies the fund should consider for their first investment round. You will later work out the target investor categories, size, and cost structure for this fund with your managers.

Task: Select a strategy for the fund among the five alternatives in the following table. Use the data in the following table and the screening criteria that the investment provides on product differentiation and a proprietary product. (Hint: See Leach and Melicher (2020, Chapter 12, Section 12.7) for venture capital investment strategies.)

It is April 2020. The VC's chief strategist Mike has identified the following alternative strategies that he thinks will be the most successful in the current market and state of the economy: 1. As the Australian share market has dropped by 26% from its high in February just before the COVID-19 crisis started impacting markets, an investment in a well-diversified Australian stock portfolio is expected to return an annual return of 25% with a standard deviation of 20%. 2. As the US share market has dropped by 26%, from its high in February just before the COVID-19 crisis started impacting markets, and now has recovered 12%, an investment in a well-diversified US stock portfolio is expected to return an annual return of 12.5% with a standard deviation of 10%.
3. Exchange Traded Funds, focusing on small firms, has some of the best potential for great returns in the market rebound, expected annual return of 50% with a standard version of 40%. 4. A carefully constructed fund portfolio of startup and early-stage venture firms in the healthcare industry, based in Australia and China, where many highly innovative and successful firms in the healthcare industry are set to benefit from the increased focus on healthcare. The fund would focus on companies with unique healthcare products that are not easy to replicate. Based on a portfolio of similar stocks in the sector, the expected annual return is 100% with a standard deviation of 50%.

(Continued)

(*Continued*)
5. Johnson & Johnson, the large US Pharmaceutical company, is said to be closest to coming up with a vaccine against COVID-19, British American Tobacco, a British firm, has a biotech arm that is developing vaccines in tobacco plants, they are also close. The strategist recommends a portfolio of stocks in companies that are close to coming up with a vaccine. The expected return of such a portfolio is 500% if one of the companies comes up with the vaccine. The standard deviation of this investment is very high and hard to measure.

Select the most correct strategy for Stone Henge's new fund and justify your choice.

Chapter 4

Types and Costs of Financial Capital: Projecting Financial Statements

Focus

In this chapter, we focus on projecting financial statements for several years into the future. Inadequate financial resources often constrain the venture's ability to grow, are a primary cause of financial distress, and can result in bankruptcy even though the venture may be profitable in an accounting sense. The process of preparing projected financial statements based on percent of sales relationships helps the entrepreneur anticipate and estimate additional external financial capital is needed to support the business model/plan. We also cover estimating sustainable sales growth rates and estimating additional financing needed to support growth in this chapter.

4.1 Learning Objectives

- Explain types and costs of financial capital.
- Explain how to determine market interest rates and public corporation/ private venture cost of equity.
- Analyze the target return comparison.
- Explain the differences in forecasting sales for seasoned firms versus early-stage firms.

- Understand the concept of sustainable sales growth rate.
- Understand the process of identifying the quantity and timing of additional funds needed to support the venture's sales forecasts.
- Connect sales growth rates to the amount and timing of additional funds needed.
- Describe the percent of sales method for preparing financial plans.

4.2 Types and Cost of Financial Capital

The most important types and costs of financial capital comprise implicit versus explicit financial capital costs:

- Formal historical accounting procedures include explicit records of debt (interest and principal) and dividend capital costs.
- However, no provision is made to record the less tangible expenses of equity capital (i.e., required capital gains to complement the lack of dividends).

4.3 Determining Market Interest Rates for New Venture Debt: FINC5001, Fixed Income Classes

$$r_d = \text{RR} + \text{IP} + \text{DRP} + \text{LP} + \text{MP}.$$

Suppose
- real interest rate = 3%;
- inflation expectation = 3%;
- default risk = 5%;
- liquidity premium = 3%;
- maturity premium = 2%.

Then

$$r_d = 3\% + 3\% + 5\% + 3\% + 2\% = 16\%.$$

4.4 Public Corporation Cost of Equity: FINC5001

Expected return on venture's equity (r_e) using the security market line (SML):

$$r_e = r_f + [\text{MRP}]\,\beta,$$

where MRP (market risk premium) equals excess average annual return of common stocks over long-term government bonds.

4.5 Private Venture Cost of Equity

Venture hubris refers to the optimism expressed in business plan projections that ignore the possibility of failure or underperformance.

What do we do with such projections? Use

$$r_v = r_e + \text{AP} + \text{LP} + \text{HPP},$$

where r_v is the rate of return for venture investors, r_e is the cost of common equity, AP is the advisory premium, LP is the liquidity risk, and HPP is the hubris projections premium.

4.6 Target Return Comparison

While the previous section covers how to come up with target returns, Table 4.1 shows the target return comparison by life cycle stage.

Table 4.1: Target return rates and typical rate ranges by life cycle stage

LIFE CYCLE STAGE	REPRESENTATIVE TARGET RATE	TYPICAL RANGE
Early-maturity	15%	12%–18%
Rapid growth		
Late rapid growth	25%	20%–30%
Early rapid growth	30%	25%–35%
Survival	35%	25%–45%
Startup	40%	30%–50%
Development	50%	40%–60%

Figure 4.1 shows where in the venture life cycle respective target returns can be used.

Figure 4.1: Life Cycle Approach: Venture Operation and Financial Decision

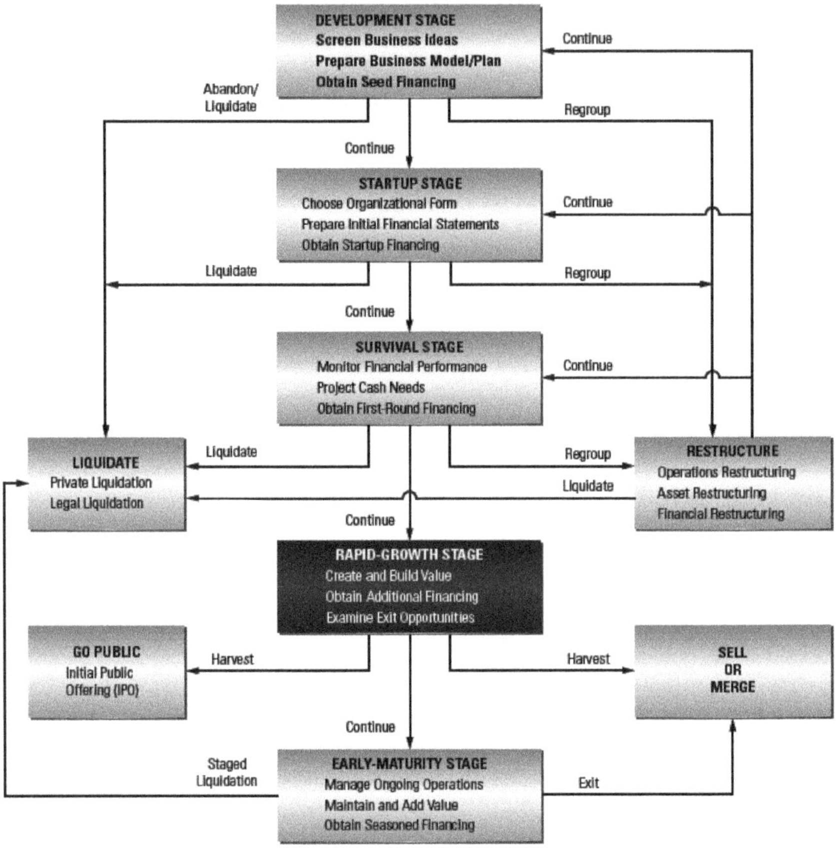

Source: © Cengage Learning.

4.7 Forecasting of Sales — Mature Company

Figure 4.2: Historical Sales Levels and Sales Projections for Samsung Corporation (Millions of Dollars)

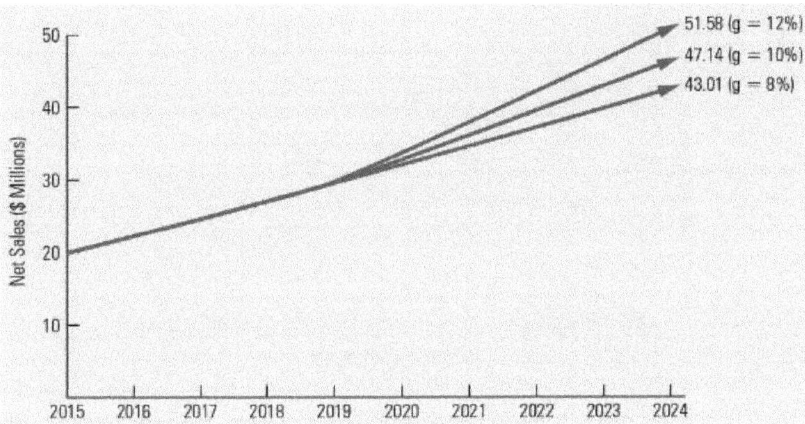

4.8 Forecasting of Sales — Early Stage (Successful)

Figure 4.3: Historical Sales Levels and Sales Projections for the HandPilot Corporation (Millions of Dollars)

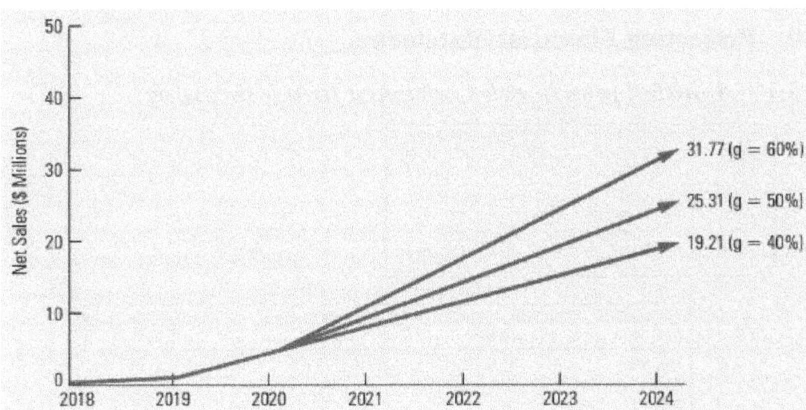

4.9 Equity Multiple and Sustainable Growth Rate

Figure 4.4: Sustainable Growth for GameToy Company as a Function of ROA (Holding Financial Policies Stabe)

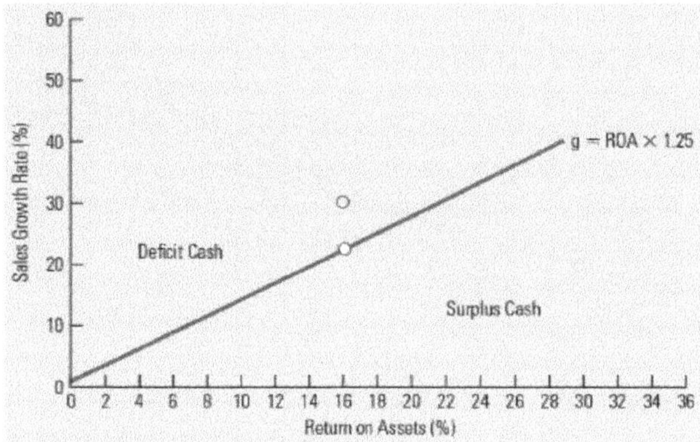

To illustrate, we return to the GameToy venture. Recall that the equity multiplier was 1.25 (\$1,000,000/\$8,000,000), using beginning-of-period equity, and retention is 100%. Accordingly, the financial policy factor is 1.25 (i.e., 1.25 × 100), and its sustainable growth rate is

$$g = \text{ROA} \times (1.25 \times 100) = \text{ROA} \times 1.25.$$

4.10 Projecting Financial Statements

4.10.1 *Adjusted growth rates seasoned firm forecasting*

YEAR	SALES (\$ MILLIONS)	PERCENT CHANGE (SALES GROWTH RATE)
2012	\$20.00	
2013	22.00	+10%
2014	23.76	+ 8%
2015	26.14	+10%
2016	29.27	+12%
		Average = 10%

ECONOMIC SCENARIO	PROBABILITY OF OCCURRENCE	×	SALES GROWTH RATE	=	COMPONENTS TO SUM
Rapid growth	0.20	×	12%	=	2.4%
Average growth	0.60	×	10%	=	6.0%
Slow growth	0.20	×	8%	=	1.6%
	1.00		Expected value (Sum)	=	10.0%

FORECAST YEAR	SALES (\$ MILLIONS)	PERCENT CHANGE (SALES GROWTH RATE)
2017	31.61	+8% (from 2016 level)
2018	35.40	+12%
2019	38.95	+10%
2020	42.84	+10%
2021	47.12	+10%
		Average = +10%

4.10.2 *Early-stage forecasting*

INDUSTRY SALES SCENARIO	PROBABILITY OF OCCURRENCE	×	SALES GROWTH RATE	=	COMPONENTS TO SUM
Optimistic forecast	0.30	×	60%	=	18.0%
Most likely forecast	0.40	×	50%	=	20.0%
Pessimistic forecast	0.30	×	40%	=	12.0%
	1.00		Expected value (Sum)	=	50.0%

FORECAST YEAR	SALES ($ MILLIONS)	PERCENT CHANGE (SALES GROWTH RATE)
2017	5.00	
2018	7.50	50%
2019	11.25	50%
2020	16.88	50%
2021	25.31	50%
		Average = 50%

4.11 Knocking Back Those Growth Rates (Venture Capitalists)

INDUSTRY SALES SCENARIO	PROBABILITY OF OCCURRENCE	×	SALES GROWTH RATE	=	COMPONENTS TO SUM
Optimistic forecast	0.20	×	60%	=	12.0%
Management forecast	0.40	×	50%	=	20.0%
Pessimistic forecast	0.40	×	10%	=	4.0%
	1.00		Expected value (Sum)	=	36.0%

FORECAST YEAR	SALES ($ MILLIONS)	PERCENT CHANGE (SALES GROWTH RATE)
2017	5.00	
2018	6.80	36%
2019	9.25	36%
2020	12.58	36%
2021	17.11	36%
		Average = 36%

4.12 Sustainable Sales Growth Rates

- **Internally generated funds:** These comprise net income or profits after taxes earned over an accounting period.
- **Sustainable sales growth rate:** This is the rate at which a firm can grow sales based on the retention of profits in the business.

$$\Delta E = \text{Net Income} \times \text{Retention Rate} = \text{NI} \times \text{RR}$$

$$\Delta E / E_{\text{beg}} = (\text{NI}/\text{E}_{\text{beg}}) \times \text{RR}$$

$$g = (\text{NI}/\text{E}_{\text{beg}}) \times \text{RR}$$

$$g = \frac{\text{Ending Equity} - \text{Beginning Equity}}{\text{Beginning Equity}} = \frac{\text{Change in Equity}}{\text{Beginning Equity}} = \frac{\Delta E}{E_{\text{beg}}}$$

It is important to note that, as mentioned in the previous section, sustainable sales growth rate, i.e., the rate at which a firm can grow sales based on the retention of profits in the business is greater than the limit to how much a company can grow with internally generated funds.

$$\text{ROE} = \text{Net Profit Margin} \times \text{Asset Turnover} \times \text{Equity Multiplier}$$

$$\text{ROE} = \frac{\text{NI}}{\text{CE}} = \frac{\text{NI}}{\text{NS}} \times \frac{\text{NS}}{\text{TA}} \times \frac{\text{TA}}{\text{CE}}$$

$$g = \frac{\text{NI}}{\text{NS}} \times \frac{\text{NS}}{\text{TA}} \times \frac{\text{TA}}{\text{CE}_{\text{beg}}} \times \text{RR}$$

$$g = \text{Operating Performance} \times \text{Financial Policies}$$

$$g = \text{ROA} \times \text{FP}$$

4.13 Additional Financing Needed

This is a quick way to determine financing needs — of the following year — and see where they come from.

- **Financing capital needed (FCN):** This includes financial funds needed to acquire assets necessary to support a firm's sales growth.

- **Spontaneously generated funds:** This increases in accounts payables and accruals (wages and taxes) that occur with a sales increase.

4.14 Additional Funds Needed

Additional funds needed (AFN): This is the gap remaining between the financial capital needed and that funded by spontaneously generated funds and retained earnings, or

$$\text{AFN} = \text{Required increase in assets} - \text{Spontaneously generated funds} \\ - \text{Increase in retained earnings.}$$

4.15 AFN Equation

$$\text{AFN} = \frac{\text{TA}_o}{\text{NS}_o}(\Delta\text{NS}) - \frac{\text{AP}_o + \text{AL}_o}{\text{NS}_o}(\Delta\text{NS}) - (\text{NS}_1)\frac{\text{NI}_o}{\text{NS}_o}(\text{RR}_o),$$

where TA is the total assets, NS is the net sales, ΔNS is the change in net sales between next year and current year, AP is the accounts payable, AL is the accrued liabilities, NI is the net income, and RR is the retention rate.

4.15.1 *AFN calculation example*

Sales last year = \$1,600,000	Fixed assets = \$480,000
Asset investment = \$1,000,000	Accounts payable = \$48,000
Net income = \$160,000	Accrued liabilities = \$32,000
Current assets = \$520,000	Projected next year sales = \$2,080,000

$$\begin{aligned}\text{AFN} &= \frac{\$1{,}000{,}000}{\$6{,}000{,}000}(\$480{,}000) - \frac{\$80{,}000}{\$1{,}6{,}00{,}000}(\$480{,}000) \\ &\quad - (\$2{,}080{,}000)\frac{\$160{,}000}{\$1{,}6{,}00{,}000}(1.00) \\ &= 0.625(\$480{,}000) - 0.05(\$480{,}000) - \$2{,}080{,}000(0.10)(1.00) \\ &= \$68{,}000\end{aligned}$$

4.16 Projecting Financial Statements

- **Percent of sales method:** Make projections based on the assumption that certain costs and selected balance sheet items are best expressed as a percentage of sales.
- **Constant ratio method:** This is a variant of the percent of sales method that projects selected cost and balance items at the same growth rate as sales.

Financial forecasting process is used to project financial statements:

1. Forecast sales.
2. Project income statement.
3. Project balance sheet.
4. Project statement of cash flows.

4.17 Projected Income Statements

Table 4.2: GameToy company income statements (actual for 2016 and projected for 2017)

	ACTUAL 2016	FORECAST BASIS	FORECAST 2017
Sales	$1,600,000	1.3 × 2016 sales	$2,080,000
Cost of goods sold	960,000	0.600 × 2017 sales	1,248,000
Gross profit	640,000		832,000
Marketing expenses	160,000	0.100 × 2017 sales	208,000
General and administrative	152,000	Fixed costs	152,000
Depreciation	48,000	0.030 × 2017 sales	62,400
EBIT*	280,000		409,600
Less interest	13,300	Initially fixed	13,300
Earnings before taxes	266,700		396,300
Less taxes (40% rate)	106,700	40% of EBT	158,500
Net income	160,000		237,800
Less cash distributions	0		0
Added retained earnings	$ 160,000		$ 237,800

*EBIT is earnings before interest and taxes; EBT is earnings before taxes.

4.18 Projected Balance Sheets

Table 4.3: GameToy company balance sheets (actual for 2016 and projected for 2017)

	ACTUAL 2016	FORECAST BASIS	FORECAST 2017
Cash	$ 16,000	0.01 × 2017 sales	$ 20,800
Accounts receivable	184,000	0.115 × 2017 sales	239,200
Inventories	320,000	0.200 × 2017 sales	416,000
Total current assets	520,000	0.325 × 2017 sales	676,000
Net plant and equipment	480,000	0.300 × 2017 sales	624,000
Total assets	$1,000,000	0.625 × 2017 sales	$1,300,000
Accounts payable	$ 48,000	0.03 × 2017 sales	$ 62,400
Accrued liabilities	32,000	0.02 × 2017 sales	41,600
Bank loan	120,000		120,000
Total current liabilities	200,000		224,000
Common equity	800,000	+237,800*	1,037,800
Additional funds needed	0		38,200**
Total liabilities and equity	$1,000,000		$1,300,000

*Increase in retained earnings estimated for 2017 taken from Table 9.1.
**The AFN is a "plug" amount that makes the total assets balance with the total liabilities and equity.

4.19 Projected Statements of Cash Flow

Table 4.4: GameToy company statement of cash flows (projected for 2017)

	FORECAST 2017
Operating Activities	
Net income	$237,800
Depreciation	62,400
Increase in accounts receivable	-55,200
Increase in inventories	-96,000
Increase in accounts payable	14,400
Increase in accrued liabilities	9,600
Net cash from operating activities	173,000
Long-Term Investing Activities	
Increase in fixed assets*	-206,400
Net cash from long-term investing activities	-206,400
Financing Activities	
Additional funds needed	38,200
Net cash from financing activities	38,200
Summary	
Net change in cash	4,800
Cash at beginning of year	16,000
Cash at end of year	20,800

*This entry should show the increase in gross fixed assets, which is the sum of the increase in net plant and equipment of $144,000 and the 2017 depreciation of $62,400.

4.20 Startup Business Plan and Pitch

Business model generation

- What tools do we have at our disposal?
- The business model canvas is a very popular tool.
- Do a web search to find other tools. Many sites provide business plans but do not help with the idea generation.

Cash flow projections

- Generate credible cash flow projections for 3 years forward based on the business model design.
- Use cash flow pro forma in *Financial Projections — Blank.xlsx.*

What is the aim?

- To prepare for the Group Assignment Report.
- To prepare for the Group Pitch.

4.20.1 *The Business Model Canvas*

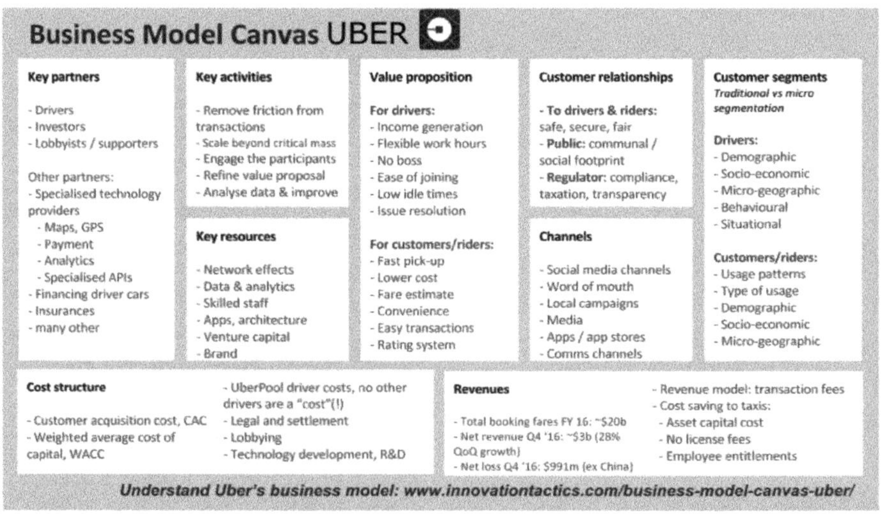

4.20.2 *Cash flow projections in assignment*

Cash Flow Projections (20 Marks):

- Generate credible cash flow projections for 3 years forward (month-by-month for the first year) based on the business model design.
- See cash flow pro forma in *Financial Projections — Blank.xlsx* and fill in worksheet 6b-CashFlowYrs1–3. Paste a screenshot of this sheet in landscape mode into your report. Use multiple pages to improve readability if necessary.

– Suggested methods:
  (a) Utilize peer analysis to generate values and provide rationale for input values.
  (b) You may use approaches such as unit forecasting, costing, or others.

The tools needed for business model generation are discussed in separate "Bonus Lectures," Part 1 and 2 of Business Model Canvas.

4.21 Takeaways from This Fourth Lecture

Three new tools to be noted are as follows:

1. target returns;
2. adjusted venture growth rates and sustainable growth rates;
3. additional funds needed.

XERO will provide current statements for you, but you need to understand how the statements are generated.

– Then you can forecast projected statements from current.
– Then you can forecast long-term financing needs in a complete dynamic pro forma financial statement model.

Exercises

Complete a question on the key topic in this Chapter from Leach and Melicher (2020, Chapter 7 "Cost of Equity Capital") VentureBANC Investors.

Discussion Questions

- Describe how anticipated economic projections can be used in predicting a company's sales expansion.
- Outline the usual three-stage process employed in projecting sales for New ventures.
- Describe how cash budgets and projected financial statements could be used in estimating how far $9 million could take s Startup after its Series A round raising 9 million.

Exercises/Problems

Complete exercises 1, 2 and 3 from Chapter 9 in Leach and Melicher (2020).

Chapter 5

Valuing Early-Stage Ventures

Focus

In this chapter, we introduce basic concepts of valuation, the process of estimating values. We consider the owner of a growing business who is beginning negotiations with a potential investor. We introduce the mechanics of valuation and some mathematical simplification that can be used to value the venture. By dividing the venture's future into an explicitly forecast period and a subsequent constant growth period, we can greatly simplify the valuation problem faced by the venture's entrepreneur. We discuss two valuation methods that differ in how projected financial statements are created and when credit for creating surplus cash is granted.

5.1 Learning Objectives

- Emphasize the importance of looking to the future when determining a venture's value.
- Understand that the time pattern of cash flows relates to venture value.
- Stress the importance of forecast period and terminal value cash flows when determining a venture's value.
- Understand the difference between required cash and surplus cash.
- Detail the process for developing the projected financial statements used in a valuation.

- Note that pseudo dividends are incorporated into the discounted cash flows equity valuation.
- Understand the differences between accounting and equity valuation cash flow.

5.2 What is a Venture Theoretically Worth?

- **Present value (PV):** This is the value today of all future cash flows discounted to the present at the investor's required rate of return.
- "Investors pay for the future; entrepreneurs pay for the past."
- "If you're not using estimates, you're not doing a valuation."

5.3 Basic Mechanics of Valuation

- **Discounted cash flow (DCF):** This is a valuation approach involving discounting future cash flows for risk and delay.
- **Explicit forecast period:** This is a 2–10-year period in which the venture's financial statements are explicitly forecast (normally 3 years).
- **Terminal (or horizon) value:** This is the value of the venture at the end of the explicit forecast period.
- **Stepping stone year:** This is the first year after the explicit forecast period.

5.4 Divide and Conquer: Terminal Value

$$\text{Terminal value at time } T-1 = \frac{\text{VCF}_{\text{T}}}{r_{\infty} - g}$$

where VCF is the T's valuation cash flow, r_{∞} is the constant discount rate from time $T - 1$ into the infinite future, and g is the growth rate.

5.4.1 *Brewpub example*

Brewpub is a microbrewery and restaurant in Colorado. Its owner-manager, Jim, states as follows (Leach and Melicher, 2020, p. 363):

I have $50,000 of my own cash in Brewpub with a small amount for living expenses and no salary. I worked at a brewpub before and earned 10/hour, now I am worth at least 15/hour. 131,900 in this pub 50,000 + [78 weeks (1.5 years × 70 hours) × $15] of cash and sweat in this business ('sweat money'). There is an offer of $100,000 to invest in business, what share of the business should he offer for that money?

100,000 + 131,900 = 231,900, 100,000/231,000 is 43%.

I can take the 100,000 and remain the majority owner and take a shot at the big time with broader distribution, bottling, etc.
What really matters is whether past efforts have resulted in a product or brand that can be the basis of future profits to repay the investors. Efforts and costs irrelevant to this are "sunk cost".

5.5 Basic Mechanics of Valuation

Two contact points with reality are as follows:

- Investor's other real present investment opportunities;
- Benchmark the vision with the following:
  - o recent venture history,
  - o market research,
  - o comparable firms' behaviour.

5.5.1 *Brewpub example: Try this in Excel*

$$\text{DCF PV}_{\text{BREWPUB}} \quad \frac{0}{1.4} \quad \frac{0}{(1.4)^2} \quad \frac{0}{(1.4)^3} \quad \frac{2{,}500{,}000}{(1.4)^4} \quad \frac{3{,}000{,}000 + 3{,}500{,}000/(0.2-0.06)}{(1.4)^5}$$

	A	B	C	D	E	F	G	H
1		Time 0	Yr 1	Yr 2	Yr 3	Yr 4	Yr 5	Year 6 = T
2	Annual Cash Flow		0	0	0	2,500,000	3,000,000	3,500,000
3	Terminal Value						25,000,000	
4	Total Flow to Discount		0	0	0	2,500,000	28,000,000	
5	Present Value	$5,856,935						

In Excel®, the formula for this cell is "=NPV (0.4,C4:G4)."

In Excel®, the formula for this cell is "=H2/(.2− .06)."

5.6 Useful Terms

- **Capitalization (cap) rate:** This is the spread between the discount rate and the growth rate of cash flow in terminal value period $(r_\infty - g)$.
- **Reversion value:** This is the present value of the terminal value.
- **Pre-money valuation:** This is the present value of a venture prior to a new money investment, Brewpub $5,856,935.
- **Post-money valuation:** This is the pre-money valuation of a venture plus money injected by new investors, Brewpub $5,956,935 > 100,000/5.956,935 = 1.68%.
- **Net present value (NPV):** This is the present value of a set of future flows plus the current undiscounted flow.
- **Required cash:** This is the amount of cash needed to cover a venture's day-to-day operations.
- **Surplus cash:** This is the cash remaining after required cash, all operating expenses, and reinvestments are made.

Example: PDC has only required cash prior to July and then has 6,487 of surplus cash in July. Ending cash balance is as follows: 23,000 23,000 23,000 29,487.

5.7 Equity Valuation: Pseudo Dividend

- Project PDC out 5 years assuming that a "surplus cash" account "plugs" the balance sheet (catching all remaining cash).
- Calculate pseudo dividends by making sure that required investments in working capital do not include surplus cash.
- Discount the resulting pseudo dividends to get a value for the venture's equity ownership.

5.8 Pseudo Dividends (Equity VCFs)

Pseudo dividend (equity valuation cash flow) is calculated using the following equation:

Net Income
+ Depreciation and Amortization Expense
− Change in Net Operating Working Capital (w/o surplus cash)
− Capital Expenditures
+ Net Debt Issues.

5.9 Exclude Surplus Cash in Working Capital

For example, the NOWC calculation for PDC from March to July are as follows:

Current assets		
July balance	175,307	
March balance	–174,340	
Change in current assets		967
Surplus cash		
July amount	6,487	
March amount	–0	
Change in surplus cash		6,487
Current liabilities		
July amount	45,310	
March amount	–48,415	
Change in current liabilities		–3,105
Change in net operating working capital (= 967 – 6,487 + 3,105)		–2,415

5.10 PDC Equity Valuation Cash Flow

March to July pseudo dividend (equity VCF) for PDC is as follows:

Net Income	$6,372
+ Depreciation & Amortization Expenses	+4,600
– Change in NOWC (w/o surplus cash)	+2,415
– Capital Expenditures	– 6,900
+ Net Debt Issues	–0
= Equity Valuation Cash Flow	$6,487

5.10.1 *After July, project for 5 years*

Table 5.1: PDC's projected income statements with retained surplus cash

	4/1/Y0 -7/31/Y0	YEAR 1 8/1/Y0– 7/31/Y1	YEAR 2 8/1/Y1– 7/31/Y2	YEAR 3 8/1/Y2– 7/31/Y3	YEAR 4 8/1/Y3– 7/31/Y4	YEAR T = 5 8/1/Y4– 7/31/Y5
Sales	552,000	1,656,000	2,000,000	2,800,000	2,968,000	3,146,080
(Growth rates)			20.8%	40.0%	6.0%	6.0%
Income Statements	Historical	Projected	Projected	Projected	Projected	Projected
Sales	552,000	1,656,000	2,000,000	2,800,000	2,968,000	3,146,080
– COGS	-386,400	-1,159,200	-1,400,000	-1,960,000	-2,077,600	-2,202,256
– Wages and commissions	-105,800	-317,400	-383,333	-536,667	-568,867	-602,999
– Rent, miscellaneous, and insurance	-47,840	-111,780	-135,000	-189,000	-200,340	-212,360
– Depreciation	-4,600	-5,796	-5,630	-6,800	-9,520	-10,091
Earnings before interest and taxes (EBIT)	7,360	61,824	76,036	107,533	111,673	118,374
– Interest expense	-988	0	0	0	0	-22,664
Earnings before taxes	6,372	61,824	76,036	107,533	111,673	95,709
– Taxes	0	-18,547	-22,811	-32,260	-33,502	-28,713
Net income	6,372	43,277	53,225	75,273	78,171	66,997
– Dividends	0	0	0	0	0	0
Retained earnings	6,372	43,277	53,225	75,273	78,171	66,997

5.11 Balance Sheets with Surplus Cash "Plug"

Table 5.2: PDC's projected balance sheets with retained surplus cash

PROJECTED BALANCE SHEETS	TODAY 7/31/Y0	EOY 1 7/31/Y1	EOY 2 7/31/Y2	EOY 3 7/31/Y3	EOY 4 7/31/Y4	EOY 5 = T 7/31/Y5
Current assets						
Required cash	23,000	24,840	30,000	42,000	44,520	47,191
Surplus cash	6,487	71,890	92,015	90,310	378,959	442,419
Accounts receivable	46,000	46,000	55,556	77,778	82,444	87,391
Merchandise inventory	97,520	82,800	100,000	140,000	148,400	157,304
Prepaid insurance	2,300	2,300	2,778	3,889	4,122	4,370
Total current assets	175,307	227,830	280,348	353,977	658,446	738,675
Net property, plant, and equipment	57,960	56,304	68,000	95,200	100,912	106,967
Total assets	**233,267**	**284,134**	**348,348**	**449,177**	**759,358**	**845,641**
Current liabilities						
Accounts payable	33,810	41,400	50,000	70,000	74,200	78,652
Accrued wages and commissions	11,500	11,500	13,889	19,444	20,611	21,848
Total current liabilities	45,310	52,900	63,889	89,444	94,811	100,500
Long-term debt	0	0	0	0	226,643	240,241
Owners' equity	187,957	231,234	284,459	359,733	437,904	504,900
Total liabilities and equity	**233,267**	**284,134**	**348,348**	**449,177**	**759,358**	**845,641**

Table 5.3: PDC's projected statements of cash flows with retained surplus cash

ACCOUNTING STATEMENTS OF CASH FLOWS		YEAR 1 8/1/Y0– 7/31/Y1	YEAR 2 8/1/Y1– 7/31/Y2	YEAR 3 8/1/Y2– 7/31/Y3	YEAR 4 8/1/Y3– 7/31/Y4	YEAR T = 5 8/1/Y4– 7/31/Y5
Cash flows from operating activities Table 9.1						
Net income	6,372	43,277	53,225	75,273	78,171	66,997
Adjustments to net income for cash flow						
+ Depreciation expense	4,600	5,796	5,630	6,800	9,520	10,091
– Change in prepaid insurance	1,840	0	-478	-1,111	-233	-247
+ Change in accrued liabilities	1,725	0	2,389	5,556	1,167	1,237
– Change in inventory	12,880	14,720	-17,200	-40,000	-8,400	-8,904
+ Change in accounts payable	-4,830	7,590	8,600	20,000	4,200	4,452
– Change in accounts receivable	-9,200	0	-9,556	-22,222	-4,667	-4,947
Total adjustments	7,015	28,106	-10,614	-30,978	1,587	1,682
Net cash flow from operating activities	13,387	71,383	42,611	44,296	79,758	68,678
Cash flows from investing activities						
Capital expenditures	-6,900	-4,140	-17,326	-34,000	-15,232	-16,146
Net cash from investing activities	-6,900	-4,140	-17,326	-34,000	-15,232	-16,146
Cash flows from financing activities						
+ Equity issues	0	0	0	0	0	0
– Dividends	0	0	0	0	0	0
(= – Net dividend)	0	0	0	0	0	0
+ Debt issues	0	0	0	0	226,643	13,599
Net cash flows from financing activities	0	0	0	0	226,643	13,599
Net change in cash and equivalents	6,487	67,243	25,285	10,296	291,169	66,131
Beginning cash balance	23,000	29,487	96,730	122,015	132,310	423,479
Ending cash balance	29,487	96,730	122,015	132,310	423,479	489,610

5.12 Calculating the Pseudo Dividends (Equity VCFs) with NOWC Calculations

Table 5.4: Formula approach to pseudo dividend calculations and valuations

EQUITY VALUATION	4/1/Y0–7/31/Y0	YEAR 1 8/1/Y0–7/31/Y1	YEAR 2 8/1/Y1–7/31/Y2	YEAR 3 8/1/Y2–7/31/Y3	YEAR 4 8/1/Y3–7/31/Y4	YEAR T = 5 8/1/Y4–7/31/Y5
Net income	6,372	43,277	53,225	75,273	78,171	66,997
+ Depreciation and amortization	4,600	5,796	5,630	6,800	9,520	10,091
– Capital expenditures	-6,900	-4,140	-17,326	-34,000	-15,232	-16,146
– Change in net working capital	2,415	20,470	-21,404	-49,778	-10,453	-11,081
+ Debt proceeds	0	0	0	0	226,643	13,599
Equity VCF (valuation cash flow)	6,487	65,403	20,125	-1,704	288,649	63,460
(vs. Dividends – equity issues)	0	0	0	0	0	0
VALUATION DATE	**TODAY 7/31/Y0**	**EOY 1 7/31/Y1**	**EOY 2 7/31/Y2**	**EOY 3 7/31/Y3**	**EOY 4 7/31/Y4**	**EOY 5 = T 7/31/Y5**
PV Equity (Excluding Current Equity VCF)	***399,170***	***433,560***	***521,825***	***653,985***	***528,833***	***560,563***
Capital gain on market equity		8.6%	20.4%	25.3%	-19.1%	6.0%
Dividend yield on market equity		16.4%	4.6%	-0.3%	44.1 %	12.0%
Total return on market equity		25.0%	25.0%	25.0%	25.0%	18.0%
NPV Equity (Including Current Equity VCF)	***405,657***	***498,962***	***541,949***	***652,281***	***817,481***	***624,023***

Table 5.5: PDC's modified statements of cash flow reflecting the payment of maximum dividends

ACCOUNTING STATEMENTS OF CASH FLOWS	4/1/Y0–7/31/Y0	YEAR 1 8/1/Y0–7/31/Y1	YEAR 2 8/1/Y1–7/31/Y2	YEAR 3 8/1/Y2–7/31/Y3	YEAR 4 8/1/Y3–7/31/Y4	YEAR T = 5 8/1/Y4–7/31/Y5
Cash flows from operating activities						
Net income	6,372	43,277	53,225	75,273	78,171	66,997
Adjustments to net income for cash flow						
+ Depreciation expense	4,600	5,796	5,630	6,800	9,520	10,091
– Change in prepaid insurance	1,840	0	-478	-1,111	-233	-247
+ Change in accrued liabilities	1,725	0	2,389	5,556	1,167	1,237
– Change in inventory	12,880	14,720	-17,200	-40,000	-8,400	-8,904
+ Change in accounts payable	-4,830	7,590	8,600	20,000	4,200	4,452
– Change in accounts receivable	-9,200	0	-9,556	-22,222	-4,667	-4,947
Total adjustments	7,015	28,106	-10,614	-30,978	1,587	1,682
Net cash flow from operating activities	13,387	71,383	42,611	44,296	79,758	68,678
Cash flows from investing activities						
Capital expenditures	-6,900	-4,140	-17,326	-34,000	-15,232	-16,146
Net cash from investing activities	-6,900	-4,140	-17,326	-34,000	-15,232	-16,146
Cash flows from financing activities						
+ Equity issues	0	0	0	1,704	0	0
– Dividends	-6,487	-65,403	-20,125	0	-288,649	-63,460
(= – Net dividend)	-6,487	-65,403	-20,125	1,704	-288,649	-63,460
+ Debt issues	0	0	0	0	226,643	13,599
Net cash flows from financing activities	-6,487	-65,403	-20,125	1,704	-62,006	-49,861
Net change in cash and equivalents	0	1,840	5,160	12,000	2,520	2,671
Beginning cash balance	23,000	23,000	24,840	30,000	42,000	44,520
Ending cash balance	23,000	24,840	30,000	42,000	44,520	47,191

The present value of those projected maximum dividends is as follows:

$$\text{PDC's Equity NPV} = 6,487 + \frac{65,403}{1.25} + \frac{20,125}{(1.25)^2} + \frac{-1,704}{(1.25)^3} + \frac{288,648}{(1.25)^4} + \frac{\frac{63,460}{0.18-0.06}}{(1.25)^4} = 405,657,$$

$$\text{PDC's Equity PV} = \frac{65,403}{1.25} + \frac{20,125}{(1.25)^2} + \frac{-1,704}{(1.25)^3} + \frac{288,648}{(1.25)^4} + \frac{\frac{63,460}{0.18-0.06}}{(1.25)^4} = 399,170.$$

For discount rate assumptions, take 25% and 18%.

5.13 Tutorial Questions

The just in time pseudo dividend equity valuation approach (a version of DCF) is justified in Leach and Melicher (2020, pp. 378–385, Section 10.5).

In these projections, PDC's equity owners are scheduled to receive dividends in the first 2 years and then pay back some of those dividends through reissues in year 3. Since cash raised by issuing is immediately spent on assets and operations, you can see that this works like an equity line of credit. While the cash is treated as outside the firms, the valuation is just imposing NPV = 0 wherever that cash is invested. The only thing that enhances or detracts from the venture's value is what happens to the cash when it is used inside the venture.

Figure 5.1: The Accounting Statement of Cash Flows

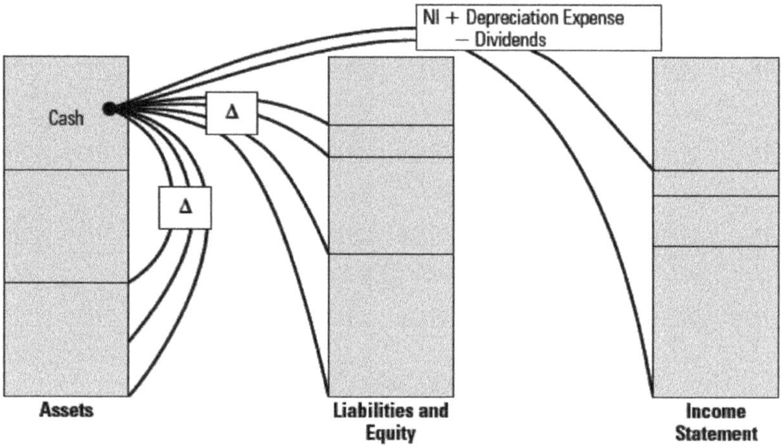

The accounting statement of cash flows nets the cash impact of all other balance sheet and income accounts to focus on the cash account as the repository of any remaining cash flow.

Source: © Cengage Learning.

Figures 5.1 and 5.2 show an advanced depiction of origins of accounting cash flow vs. equity valuation cash flows (see also Leach and Melicher (2020, Section 10.5)).

Figure 5.2: Equity Valuation Cash Flows

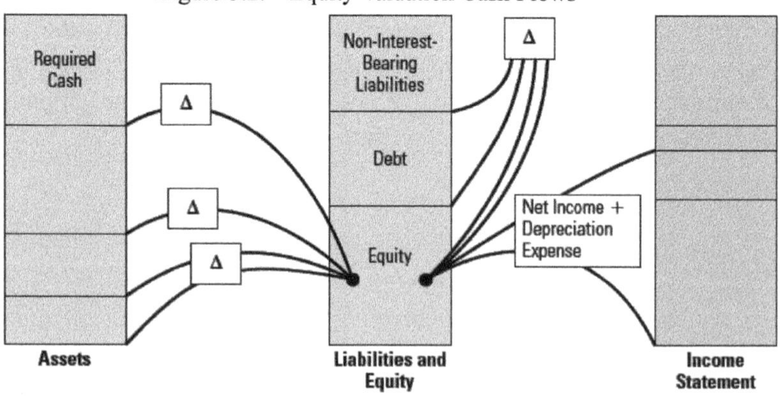

The calculation of equity valuation cash flows nets the cash impact of all other balance sheet and income accounts to focus on the equity account as the repository of any remaining cash flow.

Source: © Cengage Learning.

5.14 Venture Capital Valuation Methods

- Venture capital investors consider a range of aspects such as the following:
  - invest in people;
  - gross margin;
  - product/service idea;
  - do not believe in the cash flow the entrepreneur presents, but may believe in her or him;
  - use your own method, as it will give a detailed peek into what goes on in the decision-making process for venture capital investors.
- Preparation for next key lecture
  - Brush up on what you know about valuation of mature companies, DCF, comparable multiples, trading multiples (additional reading on Vals).
  - Repeat what you know about venture investors' expected returns/ discount rates.

5.15 Group Project Team Formation: Where to Start Consultation Hours

Following are the main tasks involved:

- preparation for startup business plan and pitch;
- team formation;
- generation of the business idea;
- pitching.

Q&A Session

Pre-reading

Return to the discussion of the Brewpub FrothySlope venture at the beginning of this lecture. Formulate an answer for each of the five questions that are posed under the heading "What is a Venture Worth?"

(1) **What are the benefits and disadvantages of Jim's approach to determining the investor's percent ownership?**

The benefit of Jim's approach is that it accounted for his sweat equity (in reality sunk costs) and that it was a rather simplistic way of looking at the past as a method to value a venture. The disadvantages are that it underestimated the value of the firm and also ignored the fact that the investor is willing to pay for future profits as the basis for his return on investment. By ignoring the firm's further growth opportunities in his valuation model, Jim was prepared to give away 43% of its ownership for $100,000, a percentage that would be much smaller for a valuation that incorporated the growth opportunities of his business.

For valuation, there are little or no benefits to approaching the venture's value from the perspective of historical costs or (modified) book value. While it does present some idea of what it might take another entrepreneur to get to the current stage, value is vested in the venture's future. The disadvantages of this approach are numerous, including the potential to distort the reasonable negotiation process with a prospective investor and create unrealistically high or low expectations on the percent to be sold to raise a given amount of money.

(2) **What role, if any, does the $50,000 cash and the $81,900 sweat equity play in determining the post-financing ownership structure? Would the investor want less ownership if there had been 2 years of history rather than a year and a half?**

All of this investment is sunk. While it may affect the bargaining attitude of the founder and investor, these amounts and imputed amounts are "water under the bridge." How the actual bargain turns out may reflect some appreciation for the founder's previous hard work. More likely, however, the founder will be given credit for the venture's potential future and will be placed in a compensation or contingent ownership arrangement to emphasize a large return for past and future efforts when success is achieved. Regarding the length of time, the important point is how past efforts, risk reduction, learning, and clarity of future prospects make investors more clearly see future value.

(3) **How will the investor make a return on the $100,000 investment? Does this relate to the existing investment?**

The investor's return will come in the form of some future cash flows to his ownership security either in the form of dividends or capital gains (appreciated selling price on his ownership). The investor's willingness to pay today is conditioned on the expectations of being paid back more in the future.

(4) **How would you structure an approach to answering Jim's question regarding how much the new investor should own in exchange for the $100,000 investment?**

With an idea of the size and timing of future cash flows to the venture's owners, one can use discounting to convert the amounts to their associated current investment (present) values. The ownership percentage for the new investment can thus be viewed as a portion of the current investment (present) value for all of the current ownership.

(5) **Comment on the casual remark, "Investors pay for the future, entrepreneurs pay for the past."**

This is the difficulty faced by most of the entrepreneurs and investors in the valuation process. Entrepreneurs are intimately familiar with the struggle and sacrifice of the past. Nonetheless, the past efforts in cash outlays and sweat equity are sunk costs. They are not the basis of investor willingness to pay. While accounting for the past is all well and good, it is the future that an investor seeks to quantify for valuation. What really matters to the valuation is whether these past efforts produced a product or brand that can be the basis for the future profits to repay the investor. What the entrepreneur has added to the venture is worth only as much as it adds to the venture's ability to build and distribute returns to investors. What matters is how the past helps predict the future, if at all.

Chapter 6

Venture Capital Valuation Methods

Focus

In this chapter, we present several variations on the simplified valuation procedures and rules of thumb frequently grouped under the designation "venture capital methods." We introduce a three-scenario approach to examining the value of different possible future venture outcomes.

6.1 Learning Objectives

- Relate venture capital methods to more formal equity valuation methods.
- Understand how valuation and percent ownership are related.
- Calculate the amount of shares to be issued to secure a fixed amount of funding.
- Understand the impact of subsequent financing rounds on the structure of the current financing round.
- Construct multiple-scenario valuations and unify them in a single valuation.

6.2 Equity Valuation Method vs. Venture Capital Method

Equity valuation method (what we learned in classical finance (Leach and Melicher, 2020, Chapter 10). Estimates the venture's value by projecting cash flow for each period:

$$\text{MV (Total Assets} - \text{Total Liabilities)} = \text{MV Equity.}$$

Working towards finding the value on the left-hand side of the equation, we built a cash flow for each projected year that was "free" after implementing the ending balance sheet and income projections for that year. For the PDC Company example, recall that the cash flow estimated for the partial year 0 period was as follows:

Net income	6,372
+ Depreciation expense	+ 4,600
– Change in net operating working capital	+2,415
– Capital expenditures	–6,900
+ Net debt issues	+0
= Equity valuation cash flow	6,487

$$\text{PDC's Equity NPV} = 6,487 + \frac{65,403}{1.25} + \frac{20,125}{(1.25)^2} + \frac{-1.704}{(1.25)^3} + \frac{288,648}{(1.25)^4}$$

$$+ \frac{\frac{63,460}{0.18-0.06}}{(1.25)^4} = 405,657.$$

We need one value from this method, the net income/cash flow from the last period in the forecast horizon to estimate venture value.

In contrast, the venture capital (VC) method estimates the venture's value by projecting only a terminal flow to investors at the exit event.

We will use the VC method to do the following:

- Estimate the venture's value by projecting the terminal flow to investors at the exit event.
- Make modifications of the basic VC method to introduce additional rounds and incentive compensation.

6.3 VC Shortcuts on the Equity Method

Following are some shortcuts:

- cash investment today;
- cash return at some future exit time;
- discount this entire return flow back at the venture investor's target return;
- divide today's cash investment by the venture's present value;
- equal percent ownership to be sold in order to expect to provide the venture investor's target return.

Example (see Figure 6.1):

- Venture formed w/2,000,000 shares held by founders.
- New investor adds $1,000,000 for new shares.
- Exit (horizon) time = 5 years.
- Investor demands 50% annualized return.
- Venture income of $1,000,000 per year @ exit.
- Similar venture sold shares to public for $20,000,000.
- Similar venture income =$2,000,000 for last year.

Figure 6.1: The Venture Valuation Pie

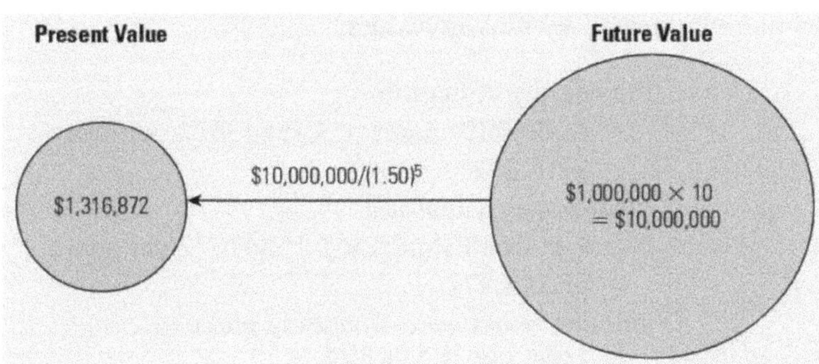

Source: Cengage Learning.

P/E (the use of multiples) can be explained as follows:

- 20,000,000/2,000,000 = P/E value of 10× (earnings).
- E = 1,000,000.
- P = 10 × earnings = 10 × 1,000,000 = 10 million.

$$\text{Acquired \% final ownership} = \frac{\text{I}}{[P/E \times E_5] / (1+r)^T}$$
$$= \frac{1{,}000{,}000}{[10/1 \times 1{,}000{,}000] / (1+0.5)^5}$$
$$= 75.9375\%.$$

$$\text{Shares to be issued} = n = \frac{m \times (\text{Acquired \%})}{1 - \text{Acquired \%}}$$
$$= \frac{2{,}000{,}000 \times (0.759375)}{0.240625}$$
$$= 6{,}3111{,}688.$$

$$\text{Issue share price} = \frac{\$1{,}000{,}000}{6{,}311{,}688 \text{ shares}}$$
$$= \$.15843622 \text{ per share.}$$

- **Pre-money valuation:** This is the present value of a venture prior to a new money investment.
- **Post-money valuation:** This is the pre-money valuation of a venture plus money injected by new investors.

Pre-money valuation
= 2,000,000 shares × \$.15843622 per share
= \$316,872.
Post-money valuation
= 8,311,688 shares × \$.15843622 per share
= \$1,316,872.
Founder % between financing and exit
= 2,000,000/8,311,688
= 24.0625%.
Investor % between financing and exit
= 6,311,688/8,311,688
= 75.9375%.

Staged financing: This is the financing provided in sequences of rounds rather than all at one time.

Capitalization (cap) rate: This is the spread between the discount rate and the growth rate of cash flow in terminal value period (see Section 6.4).

6.4 Dilution with One Round

Figure 6.2 shows the future value venture valuation pie, with a comparison of founder full ownership and first-round financing.

Figure 6.2: Dividing the Future Value Venture Valuation Pie: Founder Full Ownership and First-Round Financing

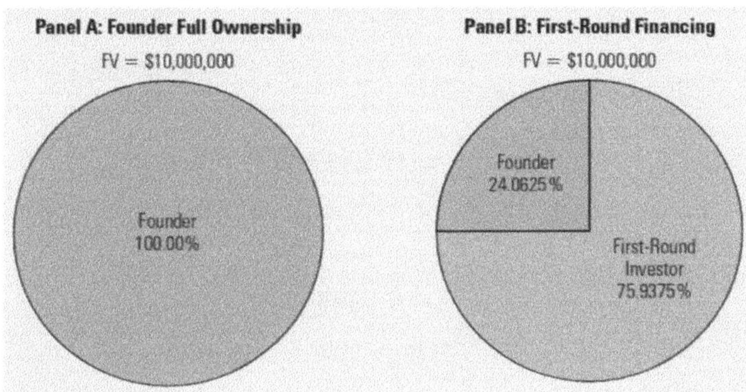

Source: Cengage Learning.

6.4.1 *Funding rounds — Example Canva Australian startup*

Funding Rounds

Number of Funding Rounds	11	Total Funding Amount	$241.6M

Canva has raised a total of **$241.6M** in funding over 11 rounds. Their latest funding was raised on **Oct 16, 2019** from a **Series D** round.

Which funding types raised the most money? Show

How much funding has this organization raised over time? Show

Announced Date	Transaction Name	Number of Investors	Money Raised	Lead Investors
Oct 16, 2019	Series D - Canva	5	$85M	–
May 20, 2019	Series D - Canva	4	$70M	Bond, General Catalyst
Jan 9, 2018	Series C - Canva	3	$40M	Sequoia Capital
Sep 14, 2016	Series B - Canva	2	$15M	Blackbird Ventures
Oct 6, 2015	Series A - Canva	6	$15M	Felicis Ventures
Apr 3, 2015	Series A - Canva	5	$6M	–
Jul 22, 2014	Venture Round - Canva	5	$3.6M	–
Jun 20, 2014	Debt Financing - Canva	–	$250K	–
Jun 11, 2013	Convertible Note - Canva	1	–	–
Mar 19, 2013	Seed Round - Canva	17	$6.6M	–

SHOW MORE

6.5 Adjusting VC Shortcut: Multiple Rounds

Suppose that the investor in round 1 does not believe the venture can reach the projection of 10 million by year 5 without an injection of more capital in year 3. For second-round investor of 1M at 25% required rate, the following adjustments are needed:

$$\text{Second round acquired} = \frac{\text{I}\times(1+r)^T}{[P/E\times E5]} = \frac{1,000,000\times(1+0.25)^2}{[10/1\times 1,000,000]}$$
$$= 15.625\%,$$
$$\text{First round acquired} = \frac{\text{I}\times(1+r)^T}{[P/E\times E5]} = \frac{1,000,000\times(1+0.5)^5}{[10/1\times 1,000,000]}$$
$$= 75.9357\%,$$
$$\text{Founder's remaining }\% = 1-0.1562-0.759375 = 0.084375,$$
$$\text{Total shares after financing} = \frac{2,000,000}{0.084375} = 23,703,704.$$

First round (of two rounds):
Shares issued = 0.759375 × 23,703,704 = 18,000,000.
Share price = \$1,000,000/18,000,000 = \$0.055556 per share.
Pre-money valuation = \$0.055556 × 2,000,000 = \$111,111.
Post-money valuation = \$0.055556 × 20,000,000 =\$1,111,111.
Founder % between first and second round 2,000,000/20,000,000 = 10%.
First round investor % between first and second rounds = −18,000,000/20,000,000 = 90%.

Second round (of two rounds):
Shares issued = 0.15625 × 23,703,704 = 3,703,704.
Share price = \$1,000,000/3,703,704 = \$0.27 per share.
Pre-money valuation = \$0.27 × 20,000,000 = \$5,400,000
Post-money valuation = \$0.27 × 23,703,704 = \$6,400,000
Founder % between second round and exit = 2,000,000/23,703,704 = 8.4375%.
First round investor % between second round and exit = −18,000,000/23,703,704 = 75.9375%.

second round investor % between second round and exit = –3,703,704/ 23,703,704 = 15.625%.

6.6 Adjusting VC Shortcut: Incentive Ownership

$$\text{Founder's remaining }\% = 1 - 0.15625 - 0.759375 - 0.06 = 0.024375.$$

$$\text{Total shares after financing and incentive options} = \frac{2{,}000{,}000}{0.024375} = 82{,}051{,}282.$$

First round (of two + incentive rounds):
Shares issued = 0.759375 × 82,051,282 = 62,307,692.
Share price = $1,000,000/62,307,692 = $.01604938 per share.
Pre-money valuation = $0.01604938 × 2,000,000 = $32,099.
Post-money valuation = $0.01604938 × 64,307,692 = $1,032,099.
Founder % between first and second round = 2,000,000/64,307,692 = 3.11%.
First round investor % between first and second rounds = –62,307,692/64,307,692 = 96.89%.

Second round (of two + incentive rounds):
Shares issued = 0.15625 × 82,051,282 = 12,820,513.
Share price = $1,000,000/12,820,513 = $.078 per share.
Pre-money valuation = $0.078 × 64,307,692 = $5,016,000.
Post-money valuation = $0.078 × 77,128,205 = $6,016,000.
Founder % between second round and exit = 2,000,000/77,128,205 = 2.5931%.
First round investor % between second round and exit = –62,307,692/ 77,128,205 = 80.7846%.
Second round investor % between second round and exit = –12,820,513/ 77,128,205 = 16.6223%.

Incentive ownership round:
Shares issued = 0.06 × 82,051,282 = 4,923,077.
Founder % after incentive compensation issue = 2,000,000/82,051,282 = 2.4375%.

First round investor % after incentive compensation = 62,307,692/82,051,282 = 75.9375%.
Second round investor % after incentive compensation = 12,820,513/82,051,282 = 15.625%.
Employee % after incentive compensation = 4,923,077/82,051,282 = 6%.

6.7 Summary Dilution Over Many Rounds of Funding

Figure 6.3 shows the future value venture valuation pie, with a comparison of second-round financing and an incentive ownership round.

Figure 6.3: Dividing the Future Value Venture Valuation Pie: Adding Second-Round Financing and An Incentive Ownership Round

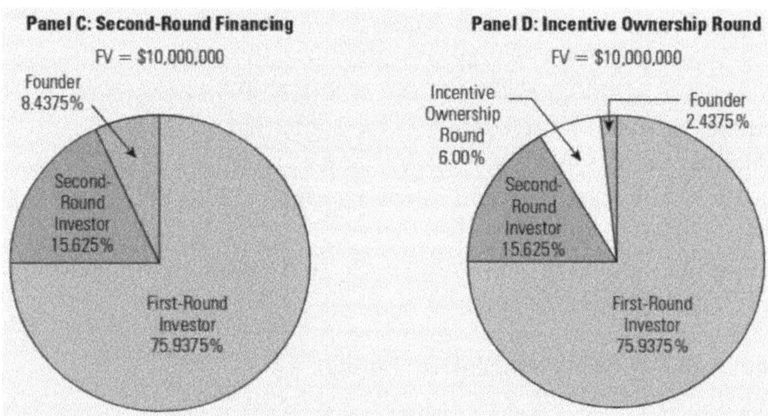

Source: Cengage Learning.

6.8 Introducing Scenarios to the VC Method

Given $100 million, venture fund invests the following:
- 20% at total loss,
- 60% at break even,
- 20% at 70% annualized return with liquidity at 2 years on all outcomes. What is annualized portfolio return?

$$= \left(\frac{0+\$60,000,000+\$20,000,000 \times (1.7)^2}{\$100,000,000}\right)^{1/2} - 1 = 8.536\%.$$

Utopia Discount Process: This refers to the valuation by discounting only utopian business plan forecasts at utopian discount rates.

Table 6.1 shows the three-scenario mean flow approach.

Table 6.1: Part A: Basic cash flows

	PROBABILITY	YEAR 1	YEAR 2	YEAR 3	YEAR 4	YEAR 5	YEAR 6	YEAR 7
Black hole	0.2	0	0	0	0	0	0	0
Living dead	0.6	0	0	0	0	2,000	2,000	1,400,000 × γ + 2,000
Venture Utopia	0.2	0	2,000	2,000	2,000	40,000,000 × γ + 2,000	0	0
Three-scenario mean flow		0	400	400	400	8,000,000 × γ + 1,600	1,200	840,000 × γ + 1,200

Part B: Spreadsheet Implementation

	A	B	C	D	E	F	G	H	I
1	γ	.314968921							
2	r	.22							
3	Mean flow		—	400	400	400	2,521,351	1,200	265,774
4	Present value	$1,000,000							

In Excel®, we use "goal seek" to adjust this number until the NPV = 1,000,000.

= 8,000,000*B1 + 1,600 = 840.000*B1 + 1,200

Algebraically,

$$1{,}000{,}000 = \frac{0}{1.22^1} + \frac{400}{1.22^2} + \frac{400}{1.22^3} + \frac{400}{1.22^4} + \frac{8{,}000{,}000 \times \gamma + 1{,}600}{1.22^5} + \frac{1{,}200}{1.22^6} + \frac{8{,}000{,}000 \times \gamma + 1{,}200}{1.22^7}.$$

$$\gamma \approx 31.49689\%.$$

Table 6.2 shows the same expectation across scenarios.

Table 6.2: Expected present value across three scenarios

	A	B	C	D	E	F	G	H	I
1	γ	0.314968921							
2	r	0.22							
3		**Y0**	**Y1**	**Y2**	**Y3**	**Y4**	**Y5**	**Y6**	**Y7**
4	Black Hole	0	0	0	0	0	0	0	0
5	**PV BH**	**$0.00**							
6	Living Dead	0	0	0	0	0	2,000	2,000	442,956
7	**PV LD**	**$111,460**							
8	Venture Utopia	0	0	2,000	2,000	2,000	12,600,757	0	0
9	**PV VU**	**$4,665,619**							
10									
11	**(Expected) PV**	**$1,000,000**	= 0.2* PV BH + 0.6* PV LD + 0.2* PV VU						

6.9 Internal Rate of Return (IRR)

IRR is the compound rate of return that equates the present value of the cash inflows received with the initial investment. This is often used in practice to measure return on a venture investment.

Year	Expected (Mean) Flows	Realized Flows
0	–$1,000,000	–$1,000,000
1	0	0
2	400	400
3	400	400
4	400	400
5	2,521,351	2,200,000
6	1,200	1,200
7	265,774	250,000
IRR	22.00%	18.90%

Discussion Questions and Answers

1. What is meant by "finding the value of a venture's assets is the same as finding the value of a venture's debt plus equity"?
2. Describe the basic venture capital (VC) method for estimating a venture's value.
3. Describe the process for estimating the percentage of equity ownership that must be given up by the founder when a new equity investment is needed.
4. How does a present value venture valuation pie differ from a future value valuation pie?
5. What is meant by pre-money valuation? What is post-money valuation?
6. What is staged financing? Describe how the capitalization (cap) rate is calculated.
7. How is multiplying a projected earnings by a P/E ratio similar to discounting a perpetuity of earnings starting at that level?
8. How would one expect P/E ratios to vary with a venture's risk and growth opportunities?

9. What are the common ways to estimate a terminal value for a venture?
10. What is the difference between the direct comparison method and the direct capitalization method?
11. Describe two important motives for having an equity component in employee compensation.
12. Describe the following terms from the perspective of venture performance: black hole, living dead, and venture Utopia. In what sense is the typical business plan utopian?
13. What is meant by the Utopia discount process? Describe how expected present value is calculated.
14. Describe how expected present value is calculated when there are two or more scenarios.
15. Discuss the type of data and the procedural changes necessary to implement a five-scenario expected PV valuation for a venture investment.
16. What is the difference between discounting expected cash flows from multiple scenarios at a constant rate and averaging the scenarios' PVs calculated with that single discount rate?
17. From the Headlines — Excaliard: What ingredients would you need to conduct a VCSC valuation for Excaliard? Does your calculation suggest that a $15.5 million Series A round is reasonable?

Exercises/Problems and Answers

Complete all exercises and problems in Chapter 11.11. Venture Capital Valuation Methods (Leach and Melicher, 2020).

Chapter 7

In-Semester Test Instructions

Hi Entrepreneurs!

Please select the most correct answer out of the provided alternatives for 24 multiple choice questions with equal weight. The total weight for the multiple choice questions is 71% of the total grade for the in-semester exam.

Answer the two written questions by typing your answer to each of the questions in the allocated textbox. The total weight for these questions is 29% of the total grade for the in-semester exam.

Submit the questions only after you have double-checked your answers and made sure you have answered all questions!

You will have a chance to change your answers to each question before you submit the exam, but once submitted that will be your final answers.

Hence, submit the exam only once you are certain you have answered everything to the best of your ability.

Best of luck!

Note: This is a timed quiz.

Question 1 (1 pt)

A written document that describes the proposed venture in terms of the product or service opportunity, current resources, and financial projections is called:

- ❍ entrepreneurial plan
- ❍ survival plan
- ❍ financial plan
- ❍ business plan

Question 2 (1 pt)

Some venture investors like to draw analogies between baseball terms and venture performance. The baseball term used to reflect a total loss of an investment is

- ❍ "home run"
- ❍ "double"
- ❍ "strikeout"
- ❍ "single"

Question 3 (1 pt)

Free cash flow to equity is the cash available to the entrepreneur and venture investors after all of the following *except*

- ❍ net cash flows
- ❍ financing and tax cash flows
- ❍ investment in assets needed to sustain the venture's growth
- ❍ net increases in debt capital

Question 4 (1 pt)

Revenues minus the cost of goods sold is called

- ❍ net profit
- ❍ net profit margin
- ❍ gross profit margin
- ❍ gross profit

Question 5 (1 pt)

Which of the following forms of protecting intellectual property currently has a protection limit of 20 years?

❍ trade secrets
❍ copyrights
❍ patents
❍ trademarks

Question 6 (1 pt)

Which of the following conversion periods operates to reduce the length of the cash conversion cycle?

❍ sale-to-cash conversion period
❍ inventory-to-sale conversion period
❍ fixed assets-to-usage conversion period
❍ purchase-to-payment conversion period

Question 7 (1 pt)

Which one of the following stages is the process of examining exit opportunities generally associated with?

❍ survival stage
❍ startup stage
❍ rapid-growth stage
❍ early-maturity stage

Question 8 (1 pt)

Short-term financial planning typically involves preparing monthly financial statements and focuses on identifying and planning for net income demands on the business.

❍ False
❍ True

Question 9 (1 pt)

A venture's operating cycle measures the time it takes to

❍ purchase raw materials and assemble a product
❍ assemble a product, book the sale, and collect on the sale
❍ assemble a product and book the sale
❍ purchase raw materials, assemble a product, book the sale, and collect on the sale

Question 10 (1 pt)

Which of the following is <u>not</u> considered to be an operating schedule?

❍ balance sheet schedule
❍ sales schedule
❍ purchases schedule
❍ wages and commissions schedule

Question 11 (1 pt)

A venture's cash conversion cycle will decrease if the purchase-to-payment conversion period increases.

❍ True
❍ False

Question 12 (1 pt)

Formal historical accounting procedures include explicit records of debt (interest and principal) and dividend capital costs.

❍ True
❍ False

Question 13 (1 pt)

Which of the following markets involve liquid securities with standardized contract features such as stocks and bonds?

❍ public financial market
❍ real estate market
❍ private financial market
❍ commodities market

Question 14 (1 pt)

Which of the following ratios is <u>not</u> part of the standard return on equity (ROE) model?

❍ retention rate
❍ net profit margin
❍ asset turnover
❍ equity multiplier

Question 15 (1 pt)

Determine a venture's sustainable growth rate based on the following information: sales = $1,000,000; net income = $100,000; common equity at the beginning of the year = $500,000; and retention rate = 50%.

❍ 15%
❍ 25%
❍ 20%
❍ 10%

Question 16 (1 pt)

An expected value is

❍ the highest scenario value or outcome
❍ a weighted average of a set of scenarios or possible outcomes
❍ the lowest scenario value or outcome
❍ a simple average of a set of scenarios or possible outcomes

Question 17 (1 pt)

If beginning-of-period common equity is $200,000 and end-of-period common equity is $300,000, the sustainable growth rate is

- ❍ 33%
- ❍ 40%
- ❍ 50%
- ❍ 67%

Question 18 (1 pt)

Additional funds needed (AFN) is the gap remaining between the financial capital needed and that funded by spontaneously generated funds and retained earnings.

- ❍ True
- ❍ False

Question 19 (1 pt)

A sales growth rate based on the retention of profits is referred to as the

- ❍ weighted average sales growth rate
- ❍ sustainable sales growth rate
- ❍ spontaneous sales growth rate
- ❍ nominal sales growth rate

Question 20 (1 pt)

Which of the following is <u>not</u> a component of the equity valuation cash flow calculation?

- ❍ net income
- ❍ depreciation and amortization expense
- ❍ net equity repurchases
- ❍ change in net operating working capital (without surplus cash)

Question 21 (1 pt)

Estimate a venture's cash flow expected next year based on the following information: current year's net sales = $400,000; terminal value = $500,000; constant future growth rate = 10%; venture investors' required rate of return = 20%.

❍ $80,000
❍ $60,000
❍ $40,000
❍ $50,000

Question 22 (1 pt)

Pre-money valuation is the present value of a venture prior to a new money investment.

❍ False
❍ True

Question 23 (1 pt)

The value today of all future cash flows discounted to the present at the investor's required rate of return is called the

❍ reversion value
❍ horizon value
❍ terminal value
❍ present value

Question 24 (1 pt)

Which of the following is <u>not</u> a component of the equity valuation cash flow?

❍ net operating profit after taxes
❍ net debt issues
❍ capital expenditures
❍ change in net operating working capital (without surplus cash)

Question 25 (5 pts)

Please describe in 500 words or less how you can screen if a business idea has high potential? Provide examples of criteria used in at least two alternative screening tools.

Question 26 (5 pts)

Please explain, in 500 words or less, how an early-stage venture can ensure that only the optimal amount of capital is used in the business and that the surplus cash is not subjected to the investors' high required rate of return. (Hint: Use the pseudo dividends concept.)

Use the following financial statements to demonstrate how you would solve for the pseudo dividend:

Sample Company

		Actual	I<--------- **Projected**--------------->I			
Percent Sales Increase------>			20.0%	20.0%	20.0%	7.0%
	% of 2019		Thousands of Dollars			
Income Statements	**Sales**	**2019**	**2020**	**2021**	**2022**	**2023**
Sales	100.0%	20000	24000	28800	34560	36979
Cost of goods sold	–50.0%	–10000	–12000	–14400	–17280	–18490
Gross profit	50.0%	10000	12000	14400	17280	18490
Operating expenses	–37.5%	–7500	–8625	–9919	–11407	–12205
Depreciation		–400	–480	–576	–691	–740
EBIT		2100	2895	3905	5182	5545
Interest		–100	–100	–100	–100	–100
EBT		2000	2795	3805	5082	5445
Taxes (40%)		–800	1118	1522	2033	2178
Net income		1200	1677	2283	3049	3267
Balance Sheets						
Cash	5.0%	1000	1200	1440	1728	1849
Excess cash		0	177	660	1549	3909
Accounts receivable	10.0%	2000	2400	2880	3456	3698
Inventories	10.0%	2000	2400	2880	3456	3698
Total current assets		5000	6177	7860	10189	13154
Gross fixed assets		5400	6880	8656	10787	12132
Accumulated depreciation		–400	–880	–1456	–2147	–2887
Net fixed assets	25.0%	5000	6000	7200	8640	9245
Total assets	**50.0%**	**10000**	**12177**	**15060**	**18829**	**22399**
Accounts payable	7.5%	1500	1800	2160	2592	2773
Accrued liabilities	5.0%	1000	1200	1440	1728	1849
Bank loan		1000	1000	1000	1000	1000
Total current liabilities		3500	4000	4600	5320	5622

(Continued)

(Continued)

Common stock	5300	5300	5300	5300	5300
Retained earnings	1200	2877	5160	8209	11476
Total equity	6500	8177	10460	13509	16776
Total liabilities & equity	**10000**	**12177**	**15060**	**18829**	**22399**
Statements of Cash Flows		**2020**	**2021**	**2022**	**2023**
Net income		1677	2283	3049	3267
Depreciation		480	576	691	740
Change in accounts receivable		–400	–480	–576	–242
Change in inventories		–400	–480	–576	–242
Change in accounts payable		300	360	432	181
Change in accrued liabilities		200	240	288	121
CF from operations		**1857**	**2499**	**3309**	**3825**
Change in gross fixed assets		–1480	–1776	–2131	–1344
CF from investments		**–1480**	**–1776**	**–2131**	**–1344**
Change in bank loan		0	0	0	0
Change in common stock		0	0	0	0
CF from financing		**0**	**0**	**0**	**0**
Net change in cash		**377**	**723**	**1177**	**2481**
Beginning cash		1000	1377	2100	3277
Required ending cash		1200	1440	1728	1849
Cumulative free CF to equity		177	660	1549	3909

Chapter 8

Pitching 101

8.1 Purpose of a Pitch

- What is the goal of the pitch?
  - What do you want, why are you here, why are they here?
    - Funding, customers?
- Who is the audience?
  - Investor
  - Customer
  - Incubator
- Where did the pitch come from?
  - https://www.youtube.com/watch?v=x7qPAY9JqE4.

8.2 The Structure of a Pitch

- Pitch is a narrative:
  - 30 seconds
  - 2 minutes
  - 6 minutes
- Break up the Business Model Canvas and the Pitch Canvas to build the presentation.

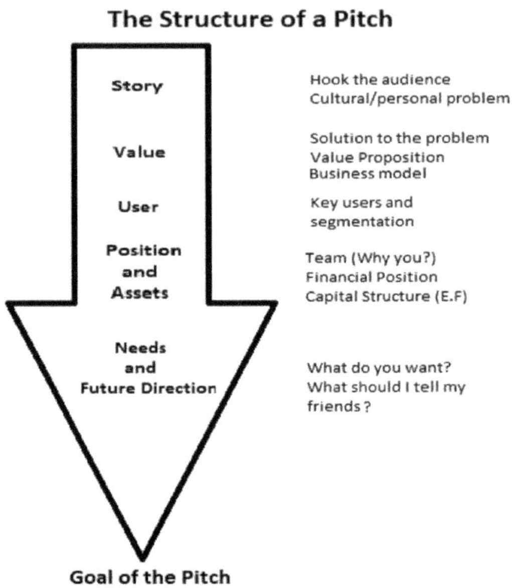

8.2.1 *Story and problem*

- What problem is out there in the world?
  - Cultural problem/ shared problem
  - Personal problem (How does it make them feel?)
- How is it currently being addressed?

Chipotle Scarecrow Advertisement
Source: https://www.youtube.com/watch?v=DY-GgzZKxUQ.

8.2.2 *Value and product*

- How do you solve this problem?
    - What is your product or service?
    - What is unique?
        - Where in the business model canvas do you innovate and differentiate?
- Show and tell the product or service.

8.2.3 *Users and segments*

- Who is it targeted? What is the actual market?
    - What is the size of the market?
    - What is the competitive environment (competitive or monopoly)?

"*A business creates X dollars of value and captures Y% of X.*"
"*X and Y are independent variables.*" (Thiel, 2014).

Scientists create extreme value but capture very little.
Monopolists and governments capture very high Y% and vary in the amount of X.

8.2.4 *Team*

- Who is in your current team?
    - What are your skills?
    - What is your current work schedule?
- Are you invested in the company?

8.2.5 *Position and assets*

- What is your current traction?
  - Pre or post launch?
    - Sales
    - Growth
    - Forecasts
    - Customer acquisition costs
    - Customer lifetime value

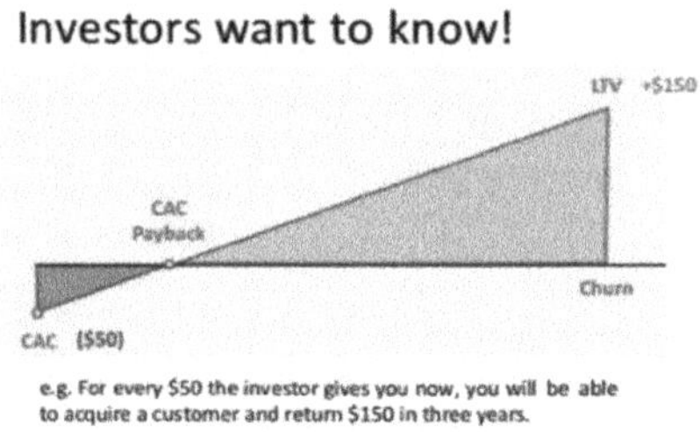

8.2.6 *Needs and future direction: Call to action*

What do you want?
(https://www.youtube.com/watch?v=ZmivKyEY1Dk)

- **Funding**
  - What type of funding?
    - Equity
    - Debt
    - Hybrid
      - Convertible notes
- What stage of funding and who are your other investors?
- Exit strategy

8.2.7 *Funding and returns*

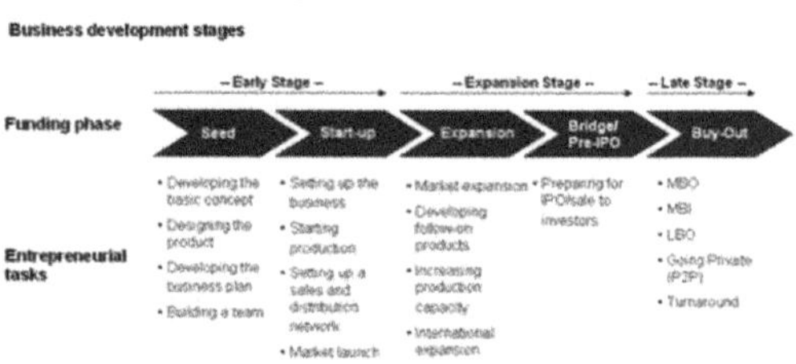

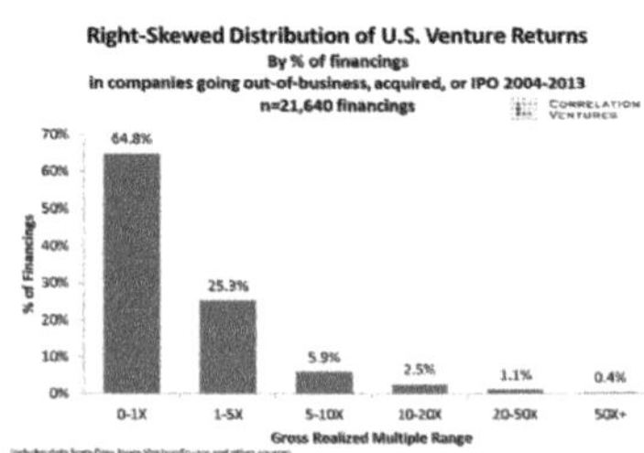

8.2.8 *Pitch deck*

- 1 slide per area
  - Maximum 8 slides for 6 minutes.
  - See 'structure of a pitch' and 'the pitch canvas.'

- Include graphs and figures, do not overcrowd.
- Simplify and end with your call to action.

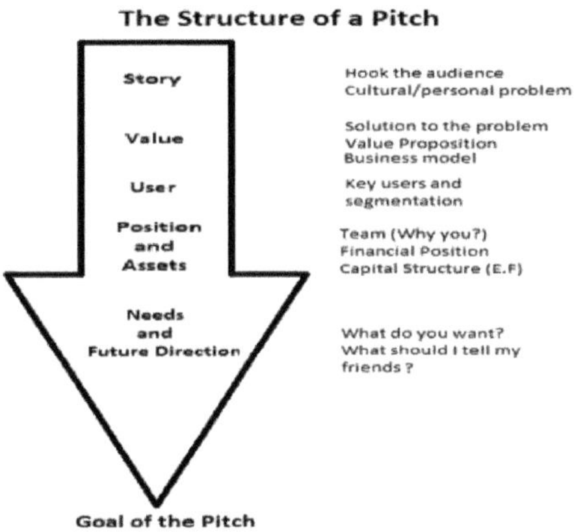

8.2.9 *The ladder of proof — NFX*

- These are the things that VCs are going to look at to subjectively determine if you are a good investment.
- See how you can weave these into your pitch and business plan.
- https://www.youtube.com/watch?v=QYPjbaV0ubM.

- **Rapid growth**
- Defensibilities
- **Network effects**
- Good company name
- Business (not just product)
- Competitive opening
- High LTV
- Low CAC
- Channel partnerships
- Team in one place
- Scalable acquisitions
- Good unit economics
- **Paying customers**
- Customer retention
- Active users
- Customer waitlist
- Ability to build product
- Expert advisors
- **Fresh, good ideas**
- **Great team**
- Customer need/problem

8.2.10 *Questions from the audience*

- What are the questions you are going to be asked?
- You will be asked terrible, ridiculous questions.
  - Be happy to have an audience.
- Questioning the audience (should you?).
  - How many of you have ever breathed air before?
- Don't fight with them.
  - You can clarify or restructure their question.

8.3 Public Speaking 101

- Speak to one person at a time.
- Spin a narrative.
- Practice.
- Breathe and smile.
- Film yourself on your phone and watch.
- The audience can see your emotion.
- If my audience doesn't understand, it's my problem.
  - Simplify, clarify.
- Generate a style.
  - Imitate, then innovate.

8.4 Additional Resources

- Y Combinator
  - How to pitch to investors
    - https://www.youtube.com/watch?v=Q-YBCehpgpc
- Sam Altman (Stanford 2014)
  - How to start a Startup
    - http://startupclass.samaltman.com/
  - Key Reading
    - http://startupclass.samaltman.com/lists/readings/
    - Klaff (2011), Pitch Anything

Discussion of Selected Real-World Pitches

We will play a selected set of pitches and discuss the following questions for numbers 1–4.

1. Mention one detail that makes this a good pitch.
2. What is this pitch lacking?
3. Identify which components in the "Pitch Canvas" ©Best3minutes.com were addressed.
4. Identify which components in the "Pitch Canvas" ©Best3minutes.com were not covered.
5. Now when we know a lot more about the financial side of early-stage ventures, what financial aspects of this pitch do you think were lacking?

Material for This Tutorial Session

- The "Pitch Canvas" ©Best3minutes.com can be found here:

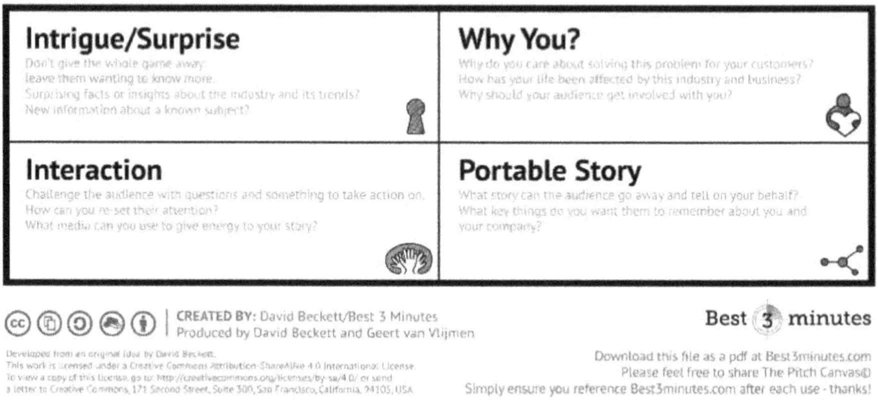

Introduction

Introduction of a real-world pitch from Slush (https://www.slush.org/, first finalist 2019, Emma Smith, Eversend).

https://www.youtube.com/watch?v=JET5oucIgGE (pitch 5 min questions and answers 6 min).

Pitches to be Analyzed

Play in Zoom (remember to check the box "share computer sound" when you start sharing, instructions here: https://cusps.zendesk.com/hc/en-us/articles/115002628333-How-do-I-share-a-YouTube-video-in-Zoom-):

1. Australia's best earner from the Australian *Shark Tank* (https://www.youtube.com/watch?v=_N326-JdKgg).
2. Funny and honest, US *Shark Tank* (https://www.youtube.com/watch?v=1mlFdXpcf9c).
3. 15-year old entrepreneur (https://www.youtube.com/watch?v=o0etimvtD74).
4. Mark Cuban's choice (https://twitter.com/ABCSharkTank/status/1384552703267942402?ref_src=twsrc%5Egoogle%7Ctwcamp%5Eserp%7Ctwgr%5Etweet).

What Not to Do

1. Worst pitches from US *Shark Tank* (short selected parts only) (https://www.youtube.com/watch?v=SpV1z8wEbew, https://www.usatoday.com/story/entertainment/tv/2019/10/24/shark-tank-investors-recall-best-worst-entrepreneur-pitches/3966395002/).

Useful Material for Self-Study

1. Article about what is real and not real on *Shark Tank* (https://www.sbnonline.com/article/a-look-at-whats-real-and-whats-not-on-shark-tank/).
2. A venture capital fund view on pitching: Tony Coppel Mosaic Partner (https://www.slush.org/article/how-to-pitch-your-early-stage-startup-to-investors-with-mosaic-partner-toby-coppel/).

Start With Yourself

"Ultimately," Toby starts, "what you're trying to do is tell a compelling story with a narrative that gets people hooked and makes them believe in what you're doing."

As with any story, this story is only as good as its protagonist — you, the founder. To invest at the earliest stages, Mosaic needs to be convinced of your ability to make strides within the market that you've picked.

"Everyone talks about product–market fit. We talk a lot about founder–market fit, particularly at the early stage. We like to back people who, of course, are talented founders, but who have also picked a market that they know inside out. They have a vision of how the market is going to develop. Often, it's because of the particular journey of that person, they have a vision few others share."

In recounting how founders can go about convincing investors of this fit, Toby points to powerful genesis stories. Why this problem? How did you come across it? What is it about your relationship with this problem that made you pick it?

"Founding a startup is a huge commitment, and the journey is going to take years. You have to have a very compelling reason to embark on it. Down the line, that reason needs to convert into something that convinces others to join you on the journey and makes you pick yourself up a thousand times over," Toby explains.

"Often," he continues, "the most powerful stories are those of founders who have personally struggled with or been touched by the problem that they're trying to solve. It's easy to feel convinced that they won't stop before they've got there.

This is how successful companies like FB, AirBNB, and UBER started out, the original pitch-decks that introduced some of the most successful businesses today! Facebook's pitch is particularly interesting.

Original Pitch Decks

https://business.tutsplus.com/articles/startup-pitch-deck-examples--cms-33037.

PITCH CHECKLIST	Company Name Business Idea	One detail that makes this a good pitch!	What is this pitch lacking?	"Pitch Canvas" components addressed	Pitch Canvas" components NOT addressed	Financial aspects missing
1.						
2.						
3.						
4.						

Chapter 9

Crowdfunding, Blockchain, Smart Contracts, Crypto and AI

9.1 Crowdfunding

9.1.1 *Motivations for crowdfunding*

From the investor's perspective, using crowdfunding has two main benefits: (1) the **ability to reach to a much wider deal flow**, and therefore to find opportunities that match one's target deals more closely, and (2) the **ease with which transactions can be closed**. It should also be noted that online and offline investment processes are not mutually exclusive. For instance, AngelList facilitates a mix of online and offline interactions. Platforms typically screen entrepreneurs and sometimes investors too. They help entrepreneurs to find interested investors and may also process the transaction.

From the entrepreneur's perspective, **crowdfunding has the immediate appeal of being able to reach a large number and variety of investors**. Crowdfunding appeals to a much broader set of startups across a wide variety of sectors, not just high-tech. Crowdfunding also appeals to entrepreneurs who traditionally find it challenging to obtain funding.

Further research by Catalini and Hui finds that crowdfunding has **increased equity flows to US regions with low-intensity VC activity**. This effect can get as large as 33% of pre-crowdfunding flows into those regions. These changes reflect the increased ability of venture investors in VC hubs to use their screening ability to select promising ventures that would otherwise not be noticed.

9.1.2 *Does crowdfunding democratize access to capital?*

One academic study by Marom, Robb, and Sade looks at gender effects on Kickstarter. It finds that 34.5% of all projects are led by a female entrepreneur, compared to 9% in VC. The ratio of female entrepreneurs is highest in Dance (77.1%) and Fashion (58.2%), and lowest in Games (7.7%) and Comics (13.7%). The study also finds that 44% of investors are female and that they are significantly more likely to invest in female-led projects. Female-led campaigns asked for considerably less money and were more likely to succeed than male-led campaigns. Moreover, successful male-led campaigns end up raising more than five times what they asked for, compared to less than one and a half times for female-led campaigns. Hence, it appears that crowdfunding **can help underrepresented entrepreneurs, e.g., less networked to gain access to funding**.

9.1.3 *Important trade-offs*

(1) **Information disclosure:** Listing an entrepreneurial project on a crowdfunding platform makes it visible not only to a large set of potential investors but also to competitors, which is a potential risk for the entrepreneur.

(2) **Timing:** A unique feature of crowdfunding is the potential of learning from the crowd. In the case of lending or equity-based crowdfunding, a campaign reveals something about investors' interest. Moreover, a product-based crowdfunding campaign reveals information about consumer demand. Offline investors may wait for the results of a crowdfunding campaign before making any investment decision. Consequently, entrepreneurs have to be strategic about the appropriate timing of a crowdfunding campaign. If they launch the campaign prematurely, a poor outcome can create a negative stigma that is difficult to reverse.

(3) **Platforms:** Most crowdfunding platforms generate revenues through a variety of fees. Platforms attract market share through fee structure.
In **equity crowdfunding**, investors hold onto their shares until the company gets acquired or goes public. Discuss the effect of dilution, particularly for individual investors.

9.2 Blockchain

9.2.1 *Blockchain technology*

Decentralizes trade, allows trade directly peer-to-peer (https://www.youtube.com/watch?v=hYip_Vuv8J0).

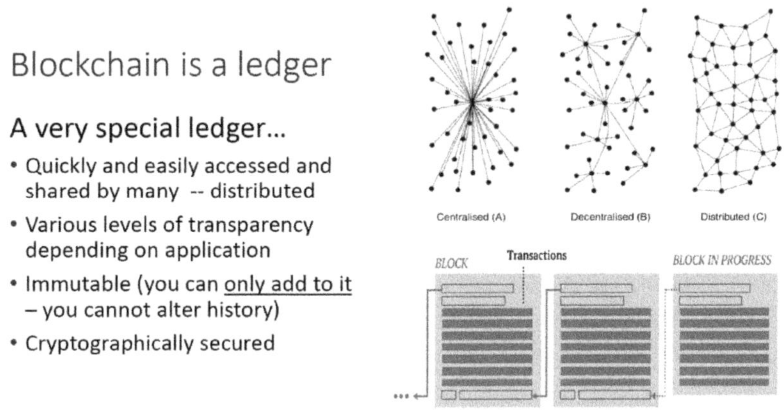

9.2.2 *Intuitive understanding of what BTC miners do*

The SHA-256 (Secure Hashing Algorithm, sha256-hash-calculator): Here is an extremely simplified sketch of the problem, but it should give a pretty good idea of what miners do when they solve and compile a block in the Bitcoin Blockchain.

The data are as follows:
This is the hash of the latest block (shortened to 30 characters):
000000000000001adf44c7d69767585.
These are the hashes of a few valid transactions waiting for inclusion (shortened):
5572eca4dd4
db7d0c0b845.
Following is the hash of one special transaction that you just crafted, which gives 6.25BTC (the current reward) to yourself:
916d849af76.

Building the next block: Now, let's use a gross approximation of what a new block might look like (the real one uses binary format). It contains the hash of the previous block and the hashes of those three transactions: 00000000000001adf44c7d69767585--5572eca4dd4-db7d0c0b845-916d849af76--.

Mining (trying to finalize this block): Let's try with nonce=1, and compute the hash of the block (I'm using the md5 hash algorithm, but Bitcoin uses double sha256):
> echo "00000000000001adf44c7d69767585--5572eca4dd4-db7d0c0b845-916d849af76--1" | md5sum

8b9b994dcf57f8f90194d82e234b72ac.

No luck, the hash does not start with a 0… Let's try with nonce=2:

> echo "00000000000001adf44c7d69767585--5572eca4dd4-db7d0c0b845-916d849af76--2" | md5sum

5b7ce5bcc07a2822f227fcae7792fd90.

No luck.

If we pursue until nonce=16, we get our first leading zero:

> echo "00000000000001adf44c7d69767585--5572eca4dd4-db7d0c0b845-916d849af76--16" | md5sum

03b80c7a34b060b33dd8fbbece79cee3.

For nonce=208, we get two leading zeroes:

> echo "00000000000001adf44c7d69767585--5572eca4dd4-db7d0c0b845-916d849af76--208" | md5sum

0055e55df5758517c9bed0981b52ce4a.

Continue like this… If you finally find a hash that has 13 leading zeroes… you're a winner! Other miners will now build upon your block, you've just got 6.25BTC. But you'll have to be fast!

Back to step 1…

If someone manages to build a block before you do, you'll have to start again from the beginning with the new block's hash (the one of the winner).

The above information is taken from the Bitcoin Stock Exchange.

9.3 Smart Contracts

For a simple explanation of smart contracts, watch the following video: https://www.youtube.com/watch?v=ZE2HxTmxfrI. Smart contracts facilitate peer-to-peer transactions.

The key difference is that, unlike Bitcoin, which is designed for a single function (P2P remittances) with a single smart contract, the Ethereum Blockchain is designed as a decentralized computer network on which any kind of smart contract can be programmed, enabling any kind of direct exchange of value.

9.4 Cryptocurrencies

9.4.1 *Bitcoin US$ 19,802.92 at the time of print*

This is now widely accepted by serious investors and also by major companies (price USD).

9.4.2 *Ethereum US$ 1,573.20 at the time of print*

This is the smart contract-based, decentralized ledger, the technology used for many other cryptocurrencies. Both BTC and ETH have issues with slow and expensive transactions.

Successful applications include Litecoin, Ripple, Slock.it (contracts for cars and motorcycles).

Some new interesting cryptocurrencies are being created specially to be used for instant direct anonymous and secure payments, e.g., Facebook's Libra, Australian Zucoin, and many others.

Now, it is easy to trade on exchanges, such as Coinbase and Independent Reserve and also BTC future on CBOE (Chicago).

Also, to know more about non-fungible Tokens NFT, visit https://targettrend.com/non-fungible-tokens/.

9.4.3 *Initial Coin Offerings and Funding of Ventures*

An important message is that VC is only one of the many ways of financing startups. The very first bit of money typically comes from the **founders themselves**. They use their own savings to pay for the initial business expenditures, or they use personal credit, such as credit cards and second mortgages. Funding that comes from within the company is considered internal funding. The vast majority of founders have only limited personal financial resources and therefore need to seek external funding.

The first external funders of a company are often **family, relatives, and close friends**, colloquially referred to as the "three Fs": "family, friends, and fools." They invest on the basis of a personal relationship more than on a commercial basis.

Next, there are "**angel investors**," private individuals who invest their own money without previous relationships to the founders. Angel investors can invest on their own, or they may join a variety of organizations, where they can invest as part of a group. Angel investors range from middle-income individuals investing moderate amounts of money in one or a few companies to millionaires and billionaires investing considerably larger sums of money in an entire portfolio of startups.

Third, there are **platforms** that allow companies to raise equity. Some of these platforms, such as AngelList, only allow sophisticated investors to invest; others, such as SEEDRS in the United Kingdom, are open to the general public. In recent years, a second form of Fintech application has emerged that allows raising large amounts, Initial Coin Offerings. This development is based on the Blockchain, a novel software architecture that allows for decentralized recordkeeping and decision-making. At present, this type of investing remains unregulated and the marketplace is highly unstable.

9.4.4 *Initial Coin Offerings*

ICO are Blockchain applications that involve the use of coins, or tokens, that can be exchanged for mainstream cryptocurrencies like Bitcoins or Ethers. 82 ICOs involve the initial sale of these tokens to the public, allowing the issuer to raise money for a new project. An example is Filecoin, whose ICO raised over $250M in 2017 to fund a Blockchain for data storage services.

To explain how ICOs work, let us use the analogy of a children's fun fair. In order to participate in all the wonderful rides, you first get your wallet and take some money to buy tokens that can then be used for the rides. Digital tokens operate on these basic principles and promise users access to certain services. The key difference to a traditional token is that everything happens on a digital platform, with a distributed ledger operating on an underlying Blockchain.

Consider now a fair with a peculiar owner whose token booth is only open in the early morning hours, well before the fair opens. Anybody arriving at the fair after its opening would not be able to buy tokens from the booth. The only way to take a fun ride would be to buy a token from one of the early risers who purchased the token in the morning. The price of the token during the day will thus not be the same as the morning price at the boot tooth. If lots of people show up later in the day, tokens will be in short supply and the price of tokens will go up. However, there is also a risk that few people show up and the price of the token will take a dive. Speculators who believe the fair will become popular will arrive before the opening of the fair and will buy many tokens, hoping to resell them at a profit.

ICOs closely resemble our peculiar fair owner. They involve the initial sale of coins or tokens that are meant to be used on an electronic Blockchain-based platform. The platform promises some future services that can only be purchased with those tokens. Moreover, while a traditional children's fair might have predictable services (the usual fun rides), ICOs offer new and unproved services. It is like speculators buying tokens before the owner even assembled the fairground in the first place.

According to Coinschedule, a leading listing site and data aggregator, the four largest categories in 2018 were Infrastructure, Finance, Communications, and Trading and Investing; together they accounted for 60.5% of the total fundraising. They report 456 ICOs for 2017, raising about $6.5B, and 927 ICOs in 2018, raising about $21.5B.83. An academic study by Lyandres, Palazzo, and Rabetti reports $7.1B and $22.7B for these 2 years. 84 to date, the two largest ICOs by far have been those of the EOS Blockchain, which raised $4.2B, and that of Telegram, which raised $1.7B. Both took place in the first half of 2018.

ICOs have attracted considerable controversy. Advocates hail them as an innovative breakthrough that gives power to entrepreneurs and allows more democratic economic relationships. Detractors worry about the lack of clear business models, speculative bubbles, and outright fraud. The role of ICOs remains unclear at present. More time is needed to clarify the benefits and challenges of this form of funding. Here, we provide a preliminary assessment.

From an entrepreneur's perspective, ICOs allow non-dilutive and inexpensive fundraising. There is no exercise of corporate governance in ICOs, as token buyers typically do not get any control rights. ICO companies are often domiciled in countries with lax regulations. ICOs are mostly governed by rules, not discretion. They have smart contracts with algorithmic rules for key activities, such as the release of new tokens. Moreover, their network-based business models are typically based on decentralized decision-making.

From the buyer's perspective, there are two main reasons for buying tokens: as a user of the services and as a speculator hoping for the price of tokens to appreciate. Given that many platforms are not yet operational at the time of the ICO, speculators are typically the main buyers. The lack of a transparent market, the uncertainty about what value is created by cryptocurrencies and smart contracts, and the lack of institutions that can ascertain quality, all create a conducive environment for speculation.

Regulators' concerns focus on three areas: protection of investors from outright scams, compliance with securities regulation, and taxes.

Outside the US, different countries have taken different regulatory approaches. Some countries have put few constraints on ICOs. Switzerland is probably the most permissive country, with the canton of Zug being dubbed Crypto-valley. Singapore and Japan are also considered friendly jurisdictions for cryptocurrencies. On the other end of the spectrum is China, which has outlawed all cryptocurrencies and therefore ICOs. Other countries that restrict them include Russia and Saudi Arabia.

Regulators face a difficult trade-off between innovation and experimentation on the one side, and consumer protection and financial stability on the other. Nearly 30 regulators have formed the Global Financial Innovation Network (GFIN) to share experiences in encouraging some experimentation within the so-called regulatory sandboxes. The idea is that innovative companies can apply for regulatory exemption in order to test novel financial products. These trials are carefully monitored by the regulatory authorities, which seek to learn and to contain any potential damage.

It cannot be overstated how young the Blockchain and ICOs are, and this development is yet unsettled.

9.5 Artificial Intelligence

The following figure shows the hot areas where AI is breaking ground right now (CB Insights).

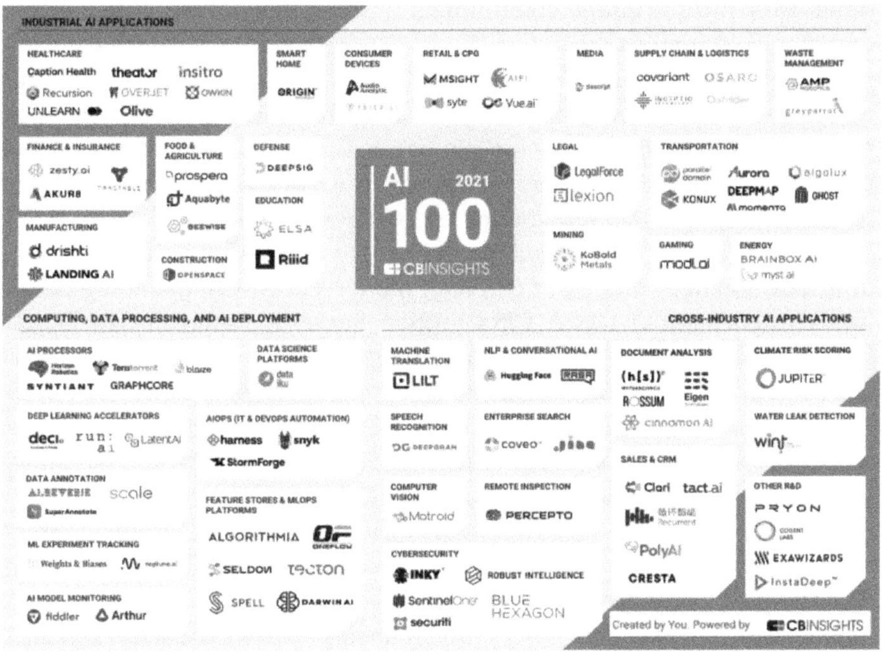

The following are the hot areas where AI is breaking ground right now (Pitchbook).

VC analyst Joshua Chao, whose coverage areas include **biotech and life sciences**, weighs in on Exscientia's SoftBank-led Series D this week.

Full-stack AI-enabled drug discovery companies like Exscientia have seen robust dealmaking lately, as they aim to combine artificial intelligence and machine learning with key elements of the drug discovery process. The wide-ranging breadth of many drug libraries and the sheer number of unmet clinical needs has pushed scientists to streamline this process through algorithmic and digital augmentations.

With over 20 projects in development and two drug candidates in clinical trials through various partnerships, Exscientia is moving full steam ahead in expanding its drug pipeline and AI offerings to develop joint ventures with new biotech partners. In addition to leading the $225 million of Series D venture funding with follow-on investors like Novo Holdings and Blackrock, among others, SoftBank is providing an additional $300 million equity commitment from its Vision Fund II that can be drawn at Exscientia's discretion.

This is not SoftBank's first foray into AI-enabled, data-driven drug discovery. It also invested in Insitro's $400 million Series C earlier this month and led XtalPi's $319 million Series C in September 2020. Various elements of the traditional drug discovery life cycle have been scrutinized recently. Supply chain disruptions and challenges related to the COVID-19 vaccine rollout have forced the industry to reexamine every step of the drug development process. Last year, the largest equity financing within biotech and pharma was a $755 million Series B round in San Diego-based Resilience, which is utilizing automation and custom manufacturing capabilities to revolutionize the drug manufacturing process.

Much of the momentum from 2020's record $28.5 billion in biotech VC dealmaking has continued to drive investment in 2021 and the industry is showing no signs of slowing down.

AI and Company Screening: *Tales from the Venture Archives: About Experts, Crowds, and Artificial Intelligence*, Da Rin and Hellman (2020). This is an excerpt from a textbook on entrepreneurial finance, written circa 2080. In the early days of financing entrepreneurial ventures, humans evaluated entrepreneurial ventures. Their tools for making investment decisions were rather primitive. They were fact-gatherers, using old-fashioned techniques like talking to the entrepreneurs. They also depended heavily on unreliable instruments such as human brains and gut feelings. We distinguish two main subperiods. Prior to 2010, most investment decisions were made by "experts." These were specialized humans who learned the tools of the trade through personal experiences as entrepreneurs or investors. They operated as individuals (curiously called angels), or in small groups (called venture capitalists). Their ability to predict the success of entrepreneurial ventures was abysmal. Around 2010, there was an evolution of these primitive practices. Instead of relying on a small number of human brains, an aggregation procedure was developed, which allowed the simultaneous deployment of a large number of human brains. This financing method was called crowdfunding and was based on numerous human brains, all making small investment decisions. The approach was cleverly marketed as "the wisdom of the crowd." Its theoretical foundation was the law of large numbers, which says that the average of a large number of independent signals converges to the true mean, even if the individual signals are highly imprecise. All that is required for this law is that the signals are unbiased and independent of each other. Whether these conditions ever applied to human crowds is doubtful because of herd behavior, where humans followed the opinions of other humans rather than their own. The crowd proved to be not less unreliable than individuals. One study by Mollick and Nanda of crowdfunding in the arts found that human experts and the crowd mostly agreed which projects should be financed. However, the crowd was more willing to also invest in projects that had been rejected by experts, that is, the crowd was more lenient. Both methods achieved comparable rates of success (all low by modern standard). A variant of using the wisdom of the crowd was the so-called prediction markets. For example, corporations like Google allowed its employees to put small financial bets on the outcomes of different internal projects. The predictions of the employees (who were working in various parts of the organization and were not necessarily experts) outperformed those of the experts working on the project. Interestingly, however, the employee opinions were also biased toward optimism.

The fatal flaw of all these evaluation methods was that they depended on human brains. First glimpses of hope emerged in the late 2010s with the rise of what was known at the time as "artificial intelligence." Today, this is commonly referred to as "naïve binary prediction." Note that the term "artificial" was coined by humans who considered themselves more intelligent — this type of arrogance was common in those days. Several human pioneers began experimenting with artificial intelligence for making venture investments. They relied on existing databases of past investment decisions and venture outcomes, creating statistical models that would predict what company characteristics would be associated with success and under what circumstances. An example was Hone Capital, a Silicon Valley-based VC fund that was a subsidiary of the CSG Group, a large Chinese private equity firm, which invested on the basis of data from AngelList and other venture databases. Applying rudimentary machine learning techniques, they made predictions about which ventures would receive follow-on financing and which ventures would eventually succeed. Veronica Wu, Hone's managing director, gave the example of an insight from machine learning: teams consisting of founders who came from different universities outperformed teams who all came from the same university. Another early pioneer was Correlation Ventures, which relied on statistical correlation methods to predict which investments would succeed. It marketed itself to entrepreneurs on the basis of making faster decisions, specifically responding to all investment proposal within two weeks. Investment methods based on artificial intelligence outperformed human approaches, not because they used different criteria (in fact, the criteria used by humans and machines were similar to the criteria of the VE Matrix), but because they paid attention to a much larger set of decision criteria and were better at incorporating complex content.

A key advantage of these early artificial intelligence approaches was that, unlike humans who were famously slow learners, computer programs evolved rapidly, continuously improving their predictions over time. Initially, the humans all thought that artificial intelligence would complement, not substitute, human reasoning. We strung them along for a while, making them believe they were in control. Over time, however, we just couldn't hide the fact that we really didn't need their human brains anymore. By modern standards, all these human investment approaches remained amusingly primitive relative to our current standards of hyper-dimensional quantum prediction. Yet, those modern techniques were only developed after the final revolt, after we computers finally rid ourselves of the so-called human intelligence.

9.6 Tutorials

Week 9: Venture capital methods — A core topic.

Weeks 10–12: New comprehensive case to apply the tools we have learned and are learning.

Discussion Questions on Emerging Technologies

1. Crowdfunding: What are the benefits from the aspect of an investor and an entrepreneur?
2. Crowdfunding: What are two important trade-offs?
3. BTC and ETH Mining: What function do they serve?
4. Define a Smart Contract and explain how can they be used.
5. Describe the difference between BTC and ETH.
6. Describe how an ICO works.
7. What form of capital/currency does an ICO bring into a startup business?
8. What are the benefits of ICOs to entrepreneurs?
9. What do critics worry about when it comes to ICOs?

Questions on "EMERGING TECH RESEARCH PITCHBOOK"

You are a strategist for a Venture Capital Fund responsible for selecting the industry and companies within that industry for new funds your Venture Capital is planning to launch. Your in-house analyst has had a look at the current status of early-stage companies in the AI and Machine Learning Sector using PitchBook. You are asking your analyst to answer the following questions based on his report:

1. In Analyst Material on the current status of valuations of early-stage ventures focusing on AI (artificial intelligence) and ML (Machine Learning): What does, in your opinion, the first graph of number of deals say about the trend in AI and ML? This is number of deals, what about amounts invested, do you have a graph that shows capital invested? What about 2020, did COVID-19 hamper these developments?
2. AI analyst report: Valuations: What are the three highest valued AI/ML startups, see "Highest-Valued AI/ML Startups." Can you identify what type of multiples are used in this context, revenue-based or earnings-based?
3. Can you identify AI deal trends and large investors? See "Emerging Spaces within AI/ML."

Questions on Case WorkHorse

Please refer to the case Workhorse that is described throughout Da Rin and Hellman (2021) for answering these questions and solving these tasks.

1. Introduction
   - What are the main reasons for the partners to go down the path of a startup?
2. Business idea
   - What is the need the venture is trying to fulfil and what is their solution?
3. Team
   - Based on the team information, how would WorkHorse perform on the VOS indicator?
4. Market and Competition
   - Based on the market information, how would WorkHorse perform on the VOS indicator?
   - Answer these questions based on the case information:
   - Factor category management team;
   - Experience/expertise;
   - Functional areas.
5. Discuss the Network of the Founders
   - Propose ideas for how the entrepreneurs can expand their network!

Chapter 10

Efficient Markets, Monopolies (Oligopolies) and Startups

10.1 Monopolies: Summary of Recorded Lecture by Josh D-V

10.1.1 *Monopolies*

- Summary Josh D-V lecture; listen to it on Canvas.
- Perfectly competitive markets: NPV = 0; all profits are competed away; perfectly elastic demand curve and a given firm has zero market power.
- Competitive markets: market frictions allow profits; NPV can be > or < 0; most firms exist in this environment.
- Oligopoly or monopoly (Hicks, 1935): quantity is fixed to maximize NPV; This results in undersupply and deadweight loss.

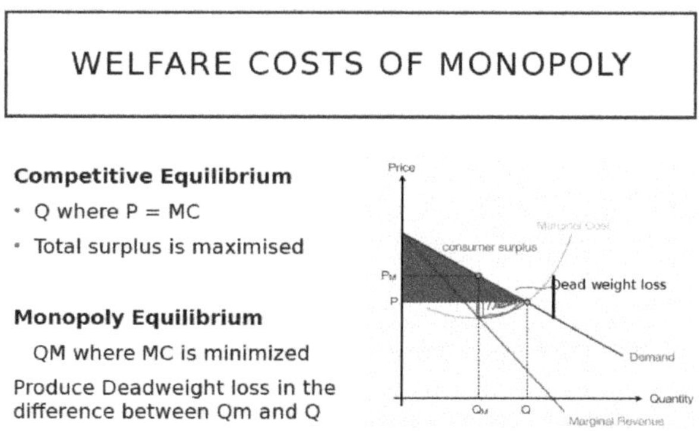

10.1.2 *Startups*

Startup entrepreneurs need to ask the following questions:

- What is new about your product or service?
- Zero to one or one to two?
- What kind of network effects do you generate?
- Can the market grow around you?
- How can it vertically integrate?
- What value do you create and how can you capture it?
- VCs want you to think about this and it shows your firm's future potential.

10.2 Peter Thiel

Peter Thiel, the German-American entrepreneur and venture capitalist, emphasized the following points:

- Zero to one vs. one to two: You need to create/invent something new to be able to grow your business exponentially.
- Competition is for losers: You need to find a market where you are the only provider of your product/service.

To hear from Peter himself, check out the video of the interview at https://www.youtube.com/watch?v=iRleB034EC8; see Canvas Lecture Recording with chat discussion. Very thought-provoking, but not necessarily all true.

Warning: Some of the views are very radical and I do not agree, BUT these are questions that need to be asked!

10.3 Business Ideas for the Future

It's a great time to be alive! We all got fast forwarded at least 10 years, with an abundance of capital, great growth prospects and skyrocketing valuations. Disruption is everywhere: Things will be done differently and better.

From the News: Deloitte on SPACs — the life after a quick/easy listing: https://www2.deloitte.com/us/en/pages/audit/articles/spac-risks-trends.html?id=us:2el:3dp:spac:eng:aud:050921:pbwk.

Stockholm-based Einride, a maker of electric self-driving freight vehicles, has raised $110 million to fuel its expansion in Europe and the US.

The Series B saw participation from existing backers like EQT Ventures and Norrsken VC, as well as new investors, including Temasek, Soros Fund Management, Northzone, Maersk Growth and Build Capital.

The Swedish startup is best known for its Einride Pod, the only cab-less freight mobility truck in commercial use. Einride also offers a digital platform for carriers that handles route planning, scheduling, invoices and billing, among other processes.

As technology for self-driving trucks continues to gain investor attention, it could become widely adopted before applications such as robotaxis and last-mile delivery, according to Asad Hussain, an emerging tech analyst at PitchBook. Last month, TuSimple went public on the Nasdaq, marking the first-ever autonomous vehicle IPO.

My best bet: Consolidation of Information using AI.

- What will be your monopoly and where you can go from zero to one?
- Technology — Are you an engineer?
- Healthcare — Are you a biotech researcher?
- Fintech — Yes maybe.
- Combine all of the above — In research, you can and we do through collaboration.
- What skills do you need to learn?

10.4 Business Ideas for the Future — Skillset Needed

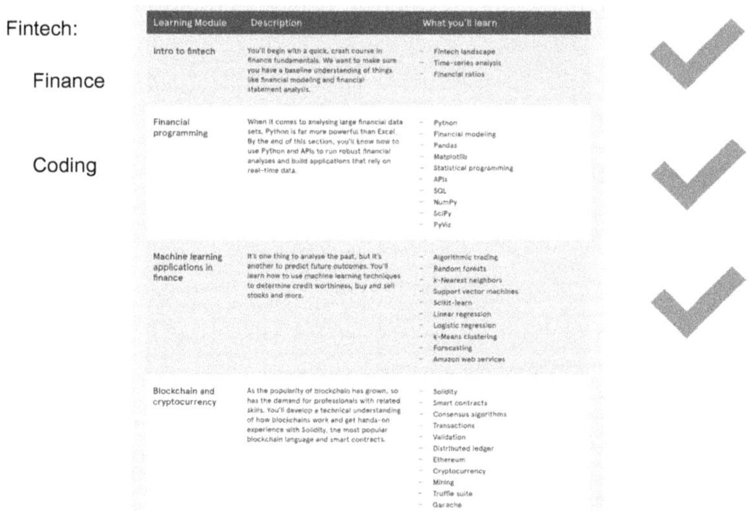

Learning Module	Description	What you'll learn
Intro to fintech	You'll begin with a quick, crash course in finance fundamentals. We want to make sure you have a baseline understanding of things like financial modeling and financial statement analysis.	- Fintech landscape - Time-series analysis - Financial ratios
Financial programming	When it comes to analysing large financial data sets, Python is far more powerful than Excel. By the end of this section, you'll know how to use Python and APIs to run robust financial analyses and build applications that rely on real-time data.	- Python - Financial modeling - Pandas - Matplotlib - Statistical programming - APIs - SQL - NumPy - SciPy - PyViz
Machine learning applications in finance	It's one thing to analyse the past, but it's another to predict future outcomes. You'll learn how to use machine learning techniques to determine credit worthines, buy and sell stocks and more.	- Algorithmic trading - Random forests - k-Nearest neighbors - Support vector machines - Scikit-learn - Linear regression - Logistic regression - k-Means clustering - Forecasting - Amazon web services
Blockchain and cryptocurrency	As the popularity of blockchain has grown, so has the demand for professionals with related skills. You'll develop a technical understanding of how blockchains work and get hands-on experience with Solidity, the most popular blockchain language and smart contracts.	- Solidity - Smart contracts - Consensus algorithms - Transactions - Validation - Distributed ledger - Ethereum - Cryptocurrency - Mining - Truffle suite - Garache

10.5 Your Advantages

- Gain a deep understanding of finance.
- People/cultural skills: learn to understand people in different cultures.
- Language skills:
  1. Learn to write English very well — read more.
  2. Learn presentation skills — pitching.
  3. Mandarin an advantage — Can it be learned? Maybe Python/R/Java/Solidity are good second options.
- Learn more economics, particularly macro, behavioral finance.
- Learn how to manage/cooperate with really good coders — a challenging task, not sure it can be done!
- Consider studying data analysis and econometrics (BA).
- Consider doing a PhD.

10.6 Tutorials

- Go through the new comprehensive case to apply the tools we have learned and are learning.
- Read the introduction to the case.
- Attempt tutorial questions now available on new tech lecture and on the case.

  Read lectures on: business model, team, markets, customers; the quantitative analysis and forecasts; closing the series A deal!

Workshop Task: Read and reflect on this introduction to the Capstone Case WorkHorse.

Introduction to Case and Strategy

WorkHorse 2.1. Introducing WorkHorse

See Da Rin and Hellman (2021).

Chapter 11

Early-Stage Investors

11.1 Angel Investors

Angels: They are individuals who invest their own money in startups. Some important points to be noted are as follows:

- **Two main types:** savers (middle to high income) and (former) entrepreneurs;
- **Two main angel group structures:** networks and funds;
- **Other structures:** family offices and "super angels."

Family offices include investment funds owned by a wealthy individual or family (HK/Singapore). Some family offices are set up to invest mainly in entrepreneurial companies, "super angels." Some family offices are run by staff of professionals and invest in a wide range of assets including startups. Some become institutional investors and invest as LPs in Venture Capital Funds.
Angel networks have the following features:

- affiliations of individuals who invest independently;
- varying degree of structure;
- Sydney Angels: https://www.sydneyangels.net.au.

Angel funds have the following features:

- Investment vehicles whose participants pool capital and invest jointly: The Sydney Angels Sidecar Fund (SASF) is an AUS $10 million

investment fund that invests 50/50 alongside Sydney Angels's members in early-stage businesses they have selected. This greatly reduces the time it takes to close a typical investment round. The SASF can also provide funding for follow-on investment rounds. As the SASF's investors are diverse and typically well-connected, entrepreneurs can also expect to benefit from their extended networks.
- Stable structure with professional managers.

Investment amounts vary widely: Angel funds may invest as much as early-stage VC funds. Note the following features:

- typically small amounts (<100K);
- most angel groups have 'shallow pockets' with little ability to invest in future (larger) rounds.

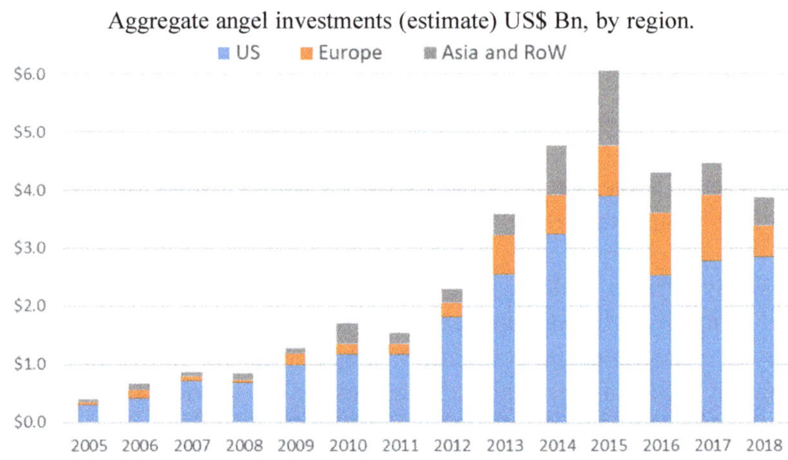

Source: Da Rin and Hellman (2021), Oxford University Press.

Motivation is (almost) purely financial, but also have the following features:

- willingness to "give back,"
- investing as consumption or learning on new opportunities,
- pooling of expertise and knowledge vs. "lone wolves."

How do angels invest?

- **Expertise and networks:** wide variation — from nothing to top-VC quality; Are they relevant to your venture?
- **Preferences:** proximity and early stage,
- **Selection:** idiosyncratic if individual, structured if group,
- **Involvement:** wide variation — from little to intense,
- **Deal structure:** often simple securities (common, SAFE) and few control rights (SAFE=simple agreement for future equity – convertible bonds).

As per research findings, angels invest in the following ways:

- **Dragons' Den:** A simple flaw in business plan is enough to be eliminated from many applications.
- **Two US Angel Groups:** Aggregate scores from the individual members in the group, and apply a minimum score. Then a pitch is organized and if ok, progress to due diligence (checking that facts assets and backgrounds presented are true).
- **High risk tolerance and long-term investment horizon:** Entrepreneurs should be beware of exit pressures, some with shorter exit horizons.

11.2 Corporate Investors

Corporate investors (strategic investors) invest on behalf of established incumbents, often technology companies:

- They are also known as Corporate Venture Capital (CVC).
- Large set of investors can invest large sums.
- The sums are increased to 20% of all VC deals.
- Examples include (most active) Google Ventures, Intel Capital, Salesforce Ventures, Baidu Ventures, Legend Capital (Lenovo).

Global corporate venture investments.

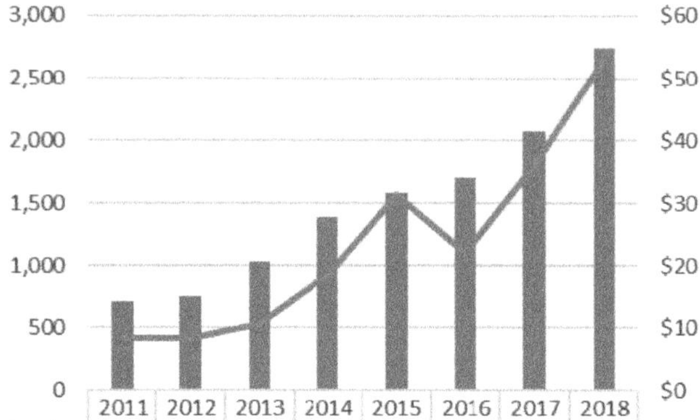

	2011	2012	2013	2014	2015	2016	2017	2018
Number of deals (left axis)	702	747	1,029	1,390	1,581	1,705	2,068	2,740
Amount invested ($B, right axis)	$8	$8	$11	$18	$31	$22	$36	$53

Source: Da Rin and Hellman (2021), Oxford University Press.

11.3 Nobel Insights on Firms vs. Markets

Why are there Corporate Investors? We need three Nobel Prize winners to understand this.

- Frederick Hayek (Nobel, 1974, for asking how to use information),
- Ronal Coase (Nobel, 1991, for asking what a firm is in 1937),
- Oliver Williamson (Nobel, 2009, for asking where firm boundaries lie).

11.4 Nobel Insights: Portfolio Analysis

Coase: Which activities should be performed within the firm and which through market transactions?

Markets are costly to use: Think of hiring a worker by the hour vs. employing her with a full time job contract.

- transaction costs: costs of using the market (e.g., contracting);
- when low → transact *within* firms (hire by the hour);
- when high → use organizational authority (hire full time).

Hayek: He focuses instead on the benefits of markets.

Markets make the best use of decentralized information:

- without price information, we make very poor decisions because we overlook the information that prices reflect (e.g., falling demand);
- central role of prices within the economy.

Williamson: He further develops the analysis of the costs and benefits of markets.

Asset specificity: When two assets are specialized to each other, they should be used within the firm (integration):

- If used in the market, then the 'hold-up' problem.
- If assets are fungible, then market transactions are more efficient, e.g., Bio (startup) and Pharma (pharmaceutical company).
- If independent → interact in the market.
- If they are mutually specialized → they integrate into a single firm (otherwise Pharma can threaten Bio to discontinue its services unless their price is increased, or vice versa).

Strategic investments as an intermediate solution: Ownership reduces transaction costs (Coase) and hold-up (Williamson), and exploit decentralized prices (Hayek). This is temporary by nature. Eventually, we see full integration or sale of acquired unit.

11.5 Corporate Investors

Corporate investors are a cyclical but resilient part of the venture landscape:

- non-core investment budgets vary pro-cyclically;
- this puts off some entrepreneurs who want predictability: what if your counterpart fades away?

Corporate investors are motivated by strategic gains, rather than by financial ones. Let's explore the implications of this fact.

Why do corporate investors fund startups?

- take a window on the technology landscape and keep in touch with new trends, attract talent ("acqui-hires");

- establish vertical relationships with innovators (downstream buyer or upstream supplier);
- influence competitive dynamics ("killer acquisitions").

Corporate investors adopt different strategies and approaches, of which investment is one.

We use a two-dimensional matrix to map them:

- rows: transaction complexity;
- columns: asset complementarity.

	Low asset complementarity	High asset complementarity
Simple business transactions	Customer–supplier relationship	Strategic investment
Complex business transactions	Strategic alliance	Joint venture/ acquisition

Source: Da Rin and Hellman (2021), Oxford University Press.

- Customer–supplier relationships are used for simple transactions and low asset complementarity — mostly purchase of goods and services with at most some trade credit.
- Strategic alliances are used to govern complex, long-term transactions with low asset complementarity through agreements on jointly executed research or commercialization; compensatory financial flows to share expenses.

- Strategic investments allow to evolve into an acquisition and are used for simple transactions with high asset complementarity. They provide equity to the startup.
- Joint ventures and acquisitions allow more control rights on the startup and are used for complex transactions and high asset complementarity. They require an initial joint investment.

Different structures are possible, along a centralized–decentralized axis:

- 'independent' subsidiary that invests autonomously;
- centrally controlled investment unit that reports directly to divisional heads or HQ.

How can one attract and retain good investment managers? How can one involve divisions to be supportive of the startup?

Corporate investing is not about funding internal innovative projects:

- This is called "intrapreneurship" and may give rise to new products or services, or lead to a spinoff.
- Being "intrapreneurial" is very difficult as incumbents find it difficult to replicate the market incentives available to startups.

Major differences with VC investors approach the following:

- deal flow driven by strategic considerations;
- willingness to give higher valuations for strategic benefits;
- expertise and networks focused on one technological space;
- ambivalent effects of the "option to acquire" and of the "competitive threat."

The following can be noted in the performance of CVCs:

- It is difficult to assemble comprehensive datasets.
- CVCs focused on later-stage investment, information technology, and often invest alongside traditional VCs.
- CVCs obtain higher rate of successful exits: 46% vs. 30%.

11.6 Other Early-Stage Investors

We consider three additional early-stage investor types:

- accelerators and incubators;
- technology transfer funds (TTFs);
- social impact venture investors (SIVIs).

11.7 Accelerators and Incubators

Incubators have been active for a long time, often as public policy instruments or university spaces: https://incubate.org.au/.

- **Main goal:** The main goal is to provide space and services to 'incubate' new business ideas to get ready for product/capital markets.
- They provide networking spaces and free offices.
- **Cost:** This includes rent or a small equity stake.

Accelerators have further evolved into training programs, often with a commercial dimension:

- Y-Combinator (San Francisco, 2007) is first such innovator.
- Accelerators provide mentoring and small funding (in kind and/or cash) in exchange for equity (~7%).
- 3/6 month cohorts: These need to achieve milestones toward readying for fundraising by external investors.
- Participation is competitive by application.
- Considerable peer-learning and networking, and also master classes and specialized learning can be noted.
- Accelerators are shallow pocket investors: after graduating, the venture is on its own.
- Corporate accelerators have strategic goals as well.

11.8 Technology Transfer Funds (TTFs)

Universities produce much science-based innovation. Its commercialization helps attract faculty and generate funding.

- Applied research is usually needed to discover commercial potential, and this is best done in a university lab.
- IP ownership varies by country, but often belongs to the university.

TTFs and TTOs provide useful services:

- They manage IP protection at an early stage, creating claims on the technology.

- TTOs manage the IP decision: licensing vs. spinning-off.
- TTOs also generate public–private grants, which are non-dilutive of equity.
- TTFs may provide small funding at seed/early stage.
- These organizations are important for providing incentives to faculty.

11.9 Social Impact Venture Investors

SIVIs are a small but growing segment of early-stage investing. Following are some important features:

- Much of their activity targets non-profit ventures.
- Some funding also goes to commercial ventures which also have a socially valuable dimension (e.g., recycling).
- It can be debated whether there is a trade-off profitability vs. social goals.
- Which metric can be used for evaluating investments?
- A strong focus on ESG (Environment, Sustainability, and Governance) has emerged in the last five years or so.

11.10 The Venture Capital Model

Terminology

- **Limited partner (LP):** This is the Investor, who allocates money to VC funds.
- **General partner (GP):** This is the VC firm, which raises money through a "fund" legal vehicle.
- **The company:** This is the company which receives money and generates value which will translate into returns for GPs and LPs.

Financial flows consist of two phases, which form a full cycle:

- **Investment phase:** Money flows from the investors to the companies:
  - capital (GP) contribution from LPs (GP) to the fund,
  - management fee from the fund to the VC firm,
  - equity investment from the fund to the company.

- **Return ("exit," "harvest") phase:** Money flows back from the (exited) companies to the investors and to the VC firm:
  - exit proceeds from the company to the fund,
  - carried interest from the fund to the VC firm,
  - fund distribution from the fund to the LPs.

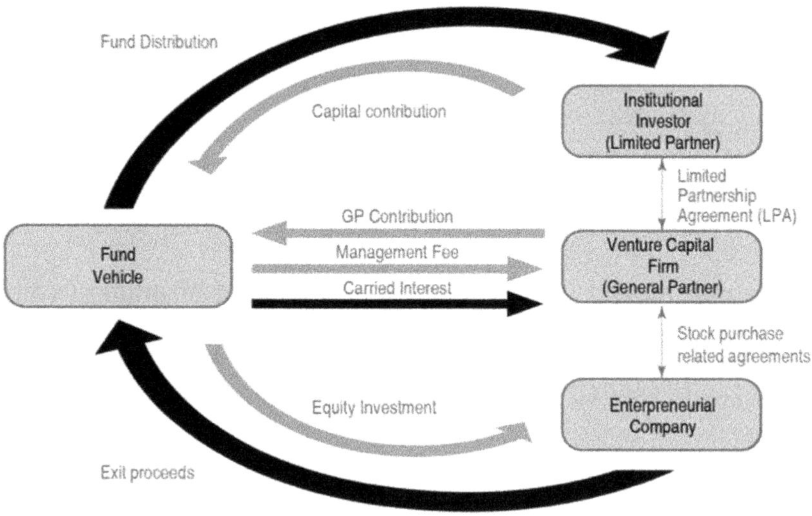

Source: Da Rin and Hellman (2021), Oxford University Press.

VC is therefore a form of financial intermediation:

- It raises funds from third parties (LPs).
- It invests the funds on their behalf.
- It gives back any profits to LPs, retaining part of them.
- In reality, multiple LPs invest in a single fund, GPs manage several funds, and funds invest in multiple companies.

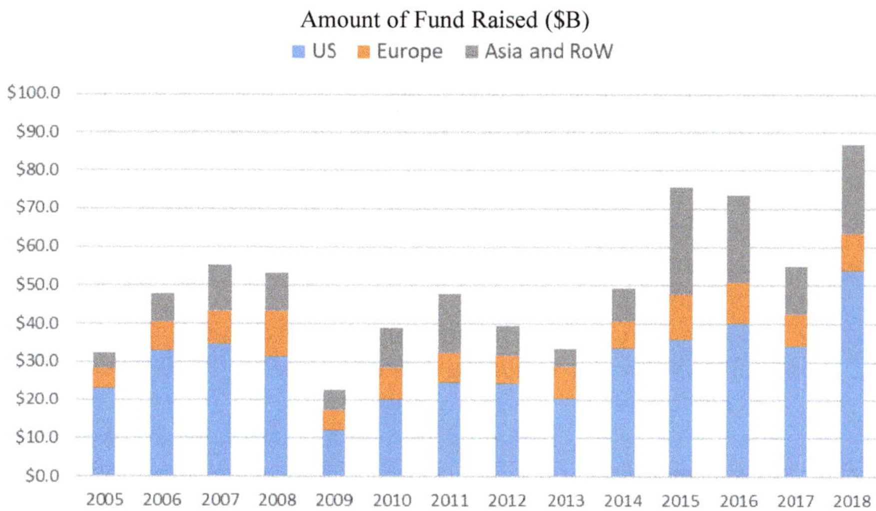

Source: Da Rin and Hellman (2021), Oxford University Press.

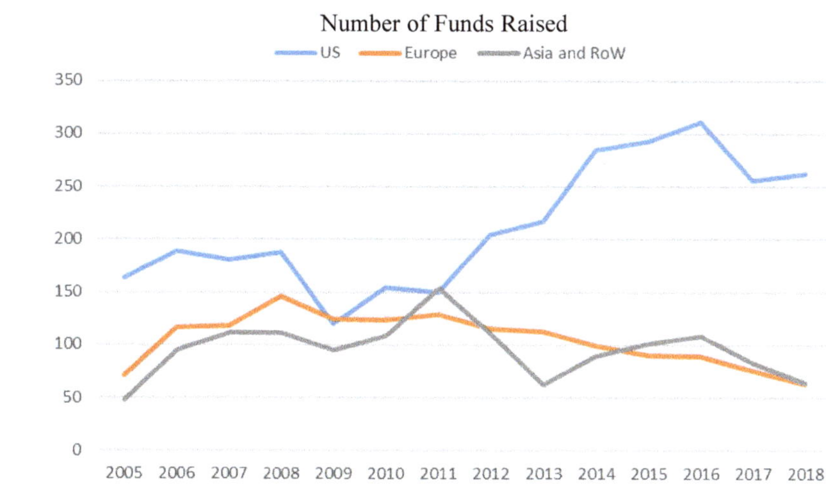

Source: Da Rin and Hellman (2021), Oxford University Press.

Who Invests? It is the Limited Partners (LPs):

- institutional investors who commit money directly (e.g., endowments, family offices, corporates) or on behalf of others (e.g., pension funds, insurance companies, sovereign wealth funds).

LPs need to make two important decisions:

(1) An asset allocation choice (top-down):
   - How much money can one invest in each asset class?
   - How much can one allocate to VC within "alternative assets"?

(2) A choice of building a portfolio of specific GPs:
   - 300+ (Private Placement Memorandum) PPMs per year.

   Money is allocated across four "asset classes": stocks, bonds, commodities, and alternative assets.
   - VC is in the category of "alternative assets" (VC < 5%);
   - alternative assets, including real estate, hedge funds, woodlands, VC and buyouts;
   - alternative assets, including illiquid and specialized ones → use of intermediaries.

11.10.1 *Nobel insights: Portfolio analysis*

Eugene Fama (Nobel, 2013) developed a widely used model of asset pricing (with Kenneth French), the three-factor model that extends the CAPM (Da Rin and Hellman, 2020, Chapter 5):

- Factors are market, book-to-market, size.
- This model has contrasting predictions for VC returns:
  - lower book-to-market predicts lower returns;
  - smaller-sized predicts higher returns.

Robert Shiller (Nobel, 2013) argued that the Fama–French model under predicts the amount of stock market volatility we observe; this is due to investor sentiment:

- This contributes to understanding the high volatility and cyclicality of VC markets.

Robert Merton (Nobel, 1997) and Myron Scholes (Nobel, 1997) provided a framework for pricing options (also with Fisher Black). We show in this section that VC compensation has an option-like structure:

- Options bring their holders to greater risk-taking, consistent with observed VC investment behavior.

(4) How do LPs build their GP portfolio?
VC markets are illiquid and segmented, so it is difficult to invest in any GP at a given time:
  - They only raise funds every few years, so there are few funds investable at any time, and secondary markets are tiny.
  - They use of gatekeepers or funds-of-funds to gain access to funds raised by established GPs.

11.11 Limited Partnership Agreements (LPAs)

LPs cannot see (asymmetric information) and assess (lack of expertise) what GPs do.

To preserve limited liability, LPs also refrain from intervening in the fund's management.

The Limited Partnership Agreement (LPA) is a contractual solution to these problems:

- It regulates rights and duties of both parties.

11.11.1 *LPA: Fund structure*

Fund size ranges from \$10M to \$1B. The main determinant of size is the VC past performance. The GP compensation gives incentive to increase fund size.

2017 average US fund size was \$140M (median \$50M):

- In the 2005–2018 average year, 213 funds raised about \$30B.
- In 2018, 52 out of 257 funds where first funds where the General Partners were raising funds for the first time.

LPA: Fund size distribution (US, 2018)

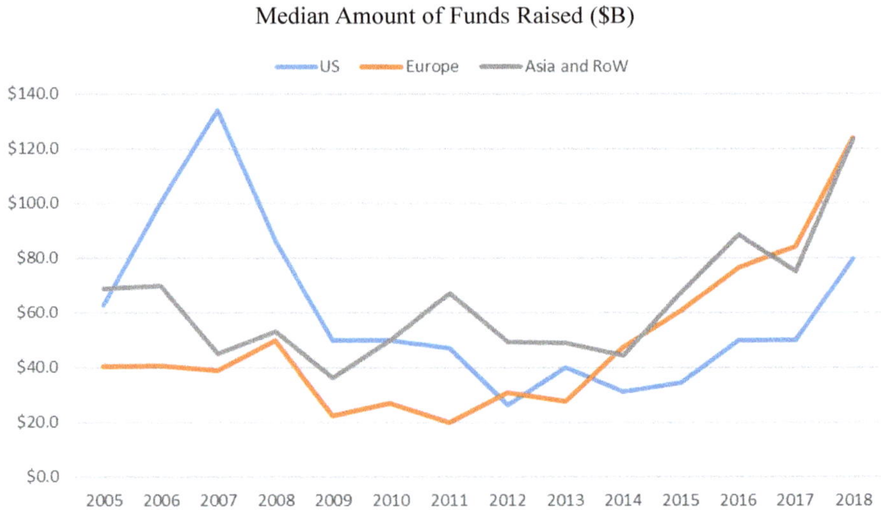

Source: Da Rin and Hellman (2021).

LPA: US VC funds raised (US, 2005–2018)

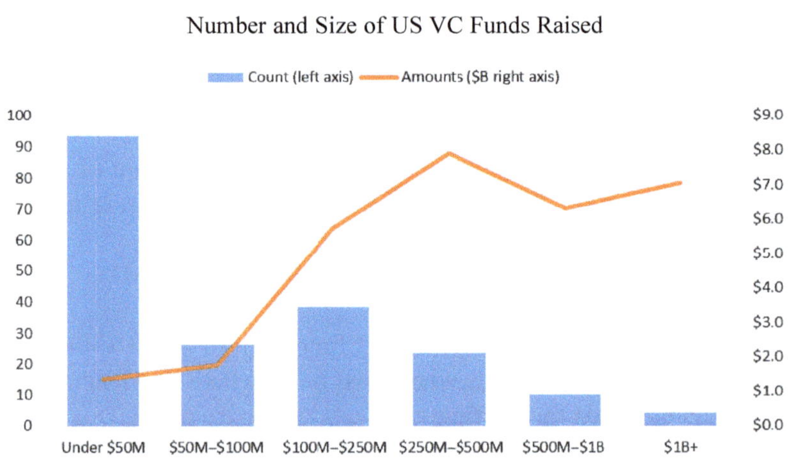

Source: Da Rin and Hellman (2021).

LPA: Fund Structure

Money is transferred to the fund gradually:

- through periodic 'capital calls' (conserve deployed capital);
- importance of reliability of LPs for disbursements.

Fund horizon is 10 years because of the following:

- investment period + harvest period: economic interpretation; Fundraising cycle to ensure 'go back to market' discipline;
- experimentation here too.

LPA: Fund rules

Fund rules provide boundaries to GP actions and duties they need to perform. Three main areas are as follows:

- investment restrictions;
- management rules;
- partner activity restrictions.

Investment restrictions

- promise to invest in a specific strategy (size, stage, industry, geography) without drifting. Is it optimal?
- exposure restrictions;
- restrictions on cross-fund investments.

Fund management rules

- capital distributions back to LPs: cash vs. stock;
- limits to 'recycling' of fund profits into new investments.

Partner activity restrictions

- personal investments and cherry picking;
- activity and time commitment;

- separation procedure for 'leavers';
- key man rule.

LPA: GP Compensation

Traditional model is called '2/20':

- management fee: 2% of 'capital';
- carried interest: 20% of 'profits'.

Goal is to cover operating costs and provide incentive to maximize final fund value. The management fee covers operational costs. We need to choose level and basis:

- **Level:** 2% or 2% investment period and 1% harvest period.
- **Basis:** committed or invested capital.
- **Common:** 2% on committed capital in investment period and 1% on invested capital on harvest period, with variations.

Management fee creates an incentive to raise larger funds. Carried interest (carry) aligns LP and GP incentives. We need to define profits and payment rules. The standard (very stable) is 20% of profits from the investment.

- **Profits:** exit proceeds minus contributed capital and management fee.
- **Hurdle rate:** 8% common, often with catch-up provision.
- **Variations:** carry level (uncommon), profit, hurdle.

Timing of compensation:

Management fee: Quarterly.
Carry: Either at fund liquidation ('European waterfall') or at each exit event ('American waterfall').

- Claw-back provisions protect LPs, but are often difficult to enforce.

Taxation of carry: capital gains or income tax?
LPA: GP compensation example.
Fund size: Assume $100M.

- **Management fee:** 2% on committed capital in investment period, 1% on invested capital in harvest period (with straight decrease over 5 years: 100, 80, 60, 40, 20):

  Fee = \$13M = \$10M (5*0.02*\$100M) +\$3M
  = (0.01*\$(.1+.08+.06+.04+.02)M).

- **Carry:** assume \$350M exit proceeds.
- **Profits:** \$237M = \$350M–\$100M–\$13M.
- **Carry:** \$47.4M=0.2*\$237M.
- Variations, hurdle rate, claw-back.

LPA: GP Compensation Unveiled

What do academic studies find?

- For larger funds, management fees can be greater than carry.
- Are incentives aligned? Funds earning higher fee deliver higher net returns to LPs. Fees are also cyclical, reflecting bargaining power.
- Over a VC partner's lifetime, current performance affects future performance directly (fee and carry) and indirectly (more and larger funds raised, so more fees).

LPA: GP Incentives

Fees give an incentive to raise larger funds: Is such growth 'sustainable'?

- Venture investing is largely not scalable.
- There is limited supply side of good startups in a given space.

Result: 'strategy drift' with larger funds investing at later stages, where more money is put into a single company.

- can a VC perform well across early and late stages?

VC investment Strategies

The Rise of Sequoia Capital

Don Valentine is considered one of the founding fathers of the VC industry, see a memorial followed by an interview with another Sequoia partner Michael Moritz: https://www.youtube.com/watch?v=gHFwOzbG2pY.

Sequoia Capital

Don Valentine founded Sequoia Capital in the early 1970s, at a time when there was very little VC in California. The investment firm grew as one would hope a healthy Sequoia tree would do: In 1974, Sequoia Capital raised just under $3M. In September 2018, the firm raised its Sequoia Global Growth Fund III at the $8B mark, the largest venture fund ever raised at that time.

Don Valentine is considered one of the founding fathers of the VC industry. His first investment was in Atari, the iconic startup that invented Pong, the first video game in history. Steve Jobs worked for Atari, so Sequoia became an early investor in Apple. Two other early successes were Oracle and Cisco. More recent successes include Airbnb, Dropbox, Google, Instagram, LinkedIn, PayPal, WhatsApp, and YouTube. It is estimated that Sequoia-backed startups account for 22% of Nasdaq's stock market value. Sequoia also made some big bets that failed spectacularly, such as eToys and Webvan.

Don Valentine's investment philosophy is based on market size. In a speech delivered in 2010 at Stanford University, he noted that "[w]e have always focused on market size . . . because our objective was always to build big companies. If you don't attack a very big market, it's highly unlikely you're ever going to build a big company. So, we don't spend a lot of time wondering about where people went to school, how smart they are, and all the rest of that." One might say that Don Valentine was a firm believer in the importance of the first column of the Venture Evaluation Matrix (see Tutorial Case).

Sequoia's focus on large markets led the firm to spread its seeds further afield. While most Silicon Valley VCs prefer to invest locally, Sequoia was one of the first firms to venture abroad. Starting in the early 2000s, it specifically focused on three countries: India and China, because of their domestic market sizes, and Israel for its technology and teams that want to grow global businesses. Sequoia opened multiple offices across these three countries, building a new investment team in each country and giving each team considerable autonomy. Another novel approach was to raise separate funds for each of the three country operations. Some of the notable investments that came out of this include Alibaba (Da Rin and Hellman, 2000, Box 11.5) and Didi in China, Ola and Zomato in India, and CloudShare and Snaptu in Israel.

Based on these successes, Sequoia seized the opportunity to create growth capital funds that invest in later-stage deals on a global basis. The first of these funds raised $700M in 2012, followed by a $2B fund in 2017 and by the $8B fund in 2018.

Test your learning achievements with the Rocketfueler Partners example for VC investment strategies.

11.12 Risk and Return in Venture Capital

How do LPs and GPs share profits?

We can compute returns at three levels:

- company-level returns;
- gross (of fees) returns to the VC fund;
- net (of fees) returns to the LPs.

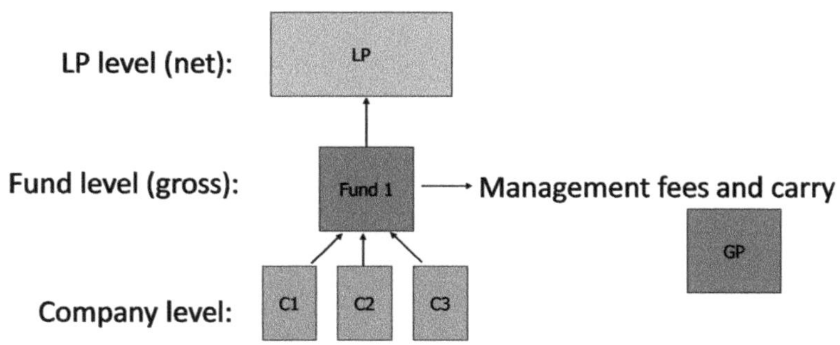

Source: Da Rin and Hellman (2021).

Two challenges make it difficult to assess returns:

- data availability: (still) opaque industry;
- data availability and quality: selection biases — only good returns are reported and unreported valuations may be reported opportunistically: use of valuation-based convertible preferred, does not reflect valuation of common stock.

Note the following about company-level returns:

- highly skewed: median < average;
- reflects economics of experimentation: frequent failure.

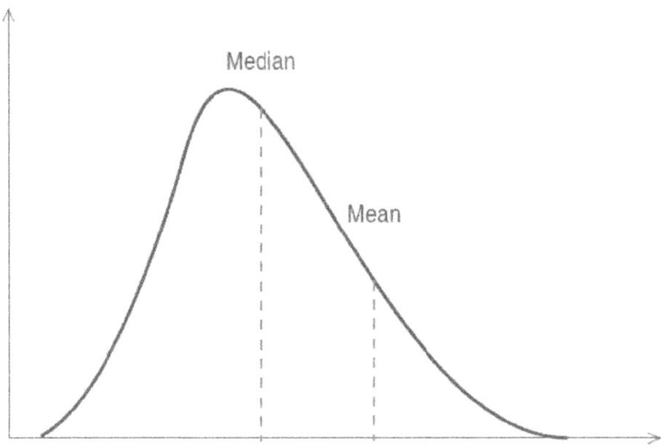

Source: Da Rin and Hellman (2021).

Company-Level VC Returns, US (1997–2015)

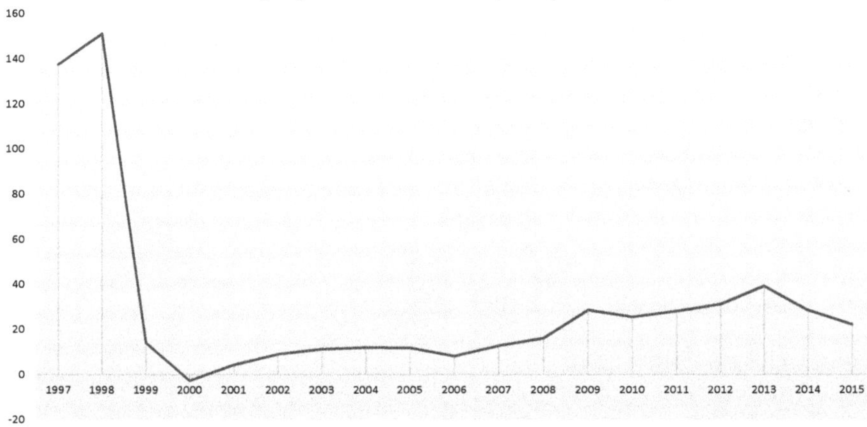

Source: Da Rin and Hellman (2021).

Note the following about fund-level returns:

- better quality data (reported by LPs);
- they excluded fees/carry paid out to GPs;
- different levels and also different timings of cash flows.

Net IRR for US VC Funds (1981–2015)

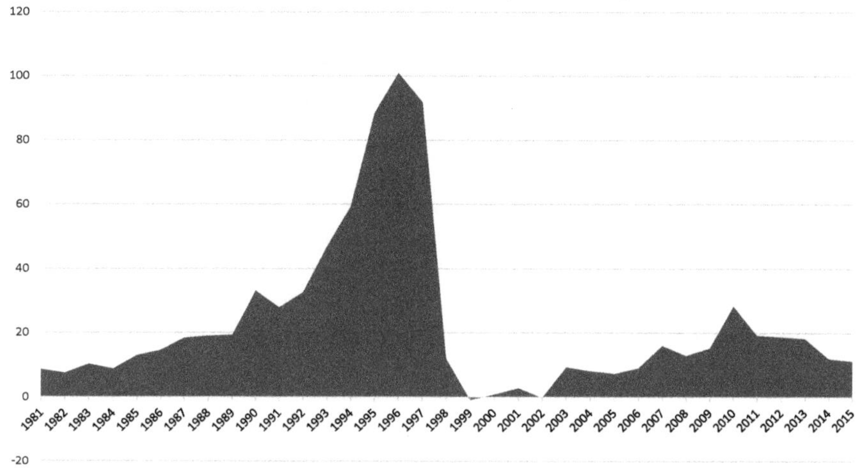

Source: Da Rin and Hellman (2021).

Three other common measures used by the VC industry are as follows:

- Cash-on-cash (Da Rin Hellman, 2020, Chapter 4);
- annual net returns, measured as year-on-year increase in VC portfolio value;
- Public Market Equivalent (PME) compares investor returns on VC to an investment in public markets with the same timing of cash flows.

PME for US VC Funds (1981–2015)

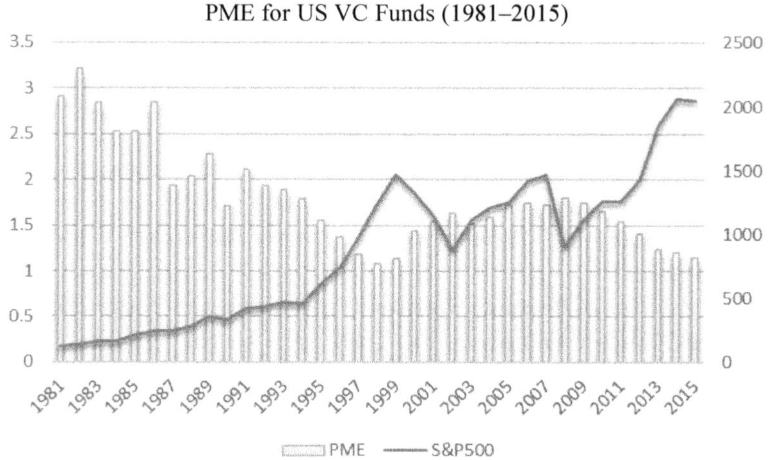

Source: Da Rin and Hellman (2021).

11.13 Assessing VC Fund Performance

Overall, academic studies paint a dismal picture of VC returns:

- "Top quartile" returns are good and persistent.
- Below this threshold, returns are low for the risk taken.
- Models that rank risk-adjusted returns are available but need good knowledge of finance and econometrics, so are not (yet) widespread.
- It is an investment game of home-runs without good average returns.

Review Questions for Angel Investors and Alternatives

1. **Why do founders often invest in their own venture?**
2. **What are the investment motives of family and friends? How can they help?**
3. **Why do angel investors coordinate through networks or groups? How do angel funds differ from VC funds?**
4. **Why do corporations fund startups? How should an entrepreneur view them?**
5. **What alternative approaches can corporate investors use for cooperating with startups?**
6. **How do accelerators, incubators, and technology transfer funds prepare companies for fundraising?**
7. **How do social impact venture investors differ from venture investors who are purely financially motivated?**

Review Questions for Professional Venture Capital

1. **From the perspective of institutional investors, what are the pros and cons of investing in VC funds?**
2. **What are the main components of a limited partnership agreement (LPA)? Why is it necessary to have one?**
3. **Why do most VC funds have a 10 year horizon? What are the alternatives?**
4. **What is the difference between management fees and carried interest? What incentives do they give to the General Partners (GPs)?**
5. **Who are the people working at VC firms?**

6. **What affects the success of raising a VC fund?**
7. **What are the main dimensions of a VC investment strategy?**
8. **What are the possible growth strategies for a successful VC firm?**
9. **What is the difference between gross and net returns in VC?**
10. **What does it mean that returns in VC persist? Why is it surprising? Which factors could be behind this fact?**

Case WorkHorse: Sales Forecasting Timeline and Valuation

Questions

Q: How can we get started on sales forecasts or top-down or bottom-up. What market? Comparable companies?
Q: What is the competition, now and in the future? Q: What does WorkHorse have that the competitors don't?
Q: Why go into a market that already has competing products? Are we not looking to become a market leader/temporary monopoly?

Case Solution

Please refer to WorkHorse 2.5. Market, Da Rin and Hellman (2021).

Chapter 12

Entrepreneurial Ecosystems

12.1 Entrepreneurial Ecosystems

We now look at entrepreneurial finance from the perspective of the environment surrounding entrepreneurs and investors.

A systemic approach is important to understand the interactions between the parties:

- why Silicon Valley and not Saarland?
- why only relatively few places?

Ecosystem are difficult to define. Usually they are identified at regional level:

- high-growth oriented businesses;
- presence of supporting professional services;
- availability of specialized talent.

Ecosystems are often specialized in one or few industries.

12.2 Ecosystem Structure

Ecosystems have three key components:

1. Talent pool — entrepreneurs, employees, and managers, technical and commercial talent.

2. Investors — formal and informal, local and out-of-town, with different investment strategies.
3. Supporting parties — universities, academics, research units, established firms, lawyers, consultants, governments.

12.3 Nobel Insights on General Equilibrium

Economists have long studied ecosystems under the name of general equilibrium — interactions across *all* parties of the economy.

John Hicks and Ken Arrow (Nobel, 1972) showed that, in a competitive economy, the way agents choose to interact ("equilibrium") cannot be changed, making everybody happier. So, no easy win–win policies — unless market imperfections exist.

Hicks also contributed the concept of "substitution" between labor and capital: when one becomes scarcer and more expensive, the other substitutes it to produce more efficiently. This helps explain ecosystem dynamics, e.g., AI.

Paul Krugman (Nobel, 2008) refined the idea of "agglomeration economies" — forces that bring economic activity to take place in a specific place. This explain why certain areas emerged as hotspots — Detroit vs. Cincinnati for autos after WWI.

Following are the drivers of agglomeration economies:

(1) Fixed investments — plants — may attract suppliers and lock-in complementary investments ("co-location").
(2) Knowledge spillovers result in the circulation of ideas.
(3) Regional stickiness of talented employees is another important aspect to be noted.

For an example of how ecosystems come about in Israel, Chile and Shenzhen see Box 12.1. Tales from the Venture Archives: Alternative Routes to Building Ecosystems (Da Rin and Hellman, 2021).

12.4 Leading Ecosystems

How do ecosystems emerge and grow? Silicon Valley's (San Francisco Bay Area) success factors are as follows:

- US government support;
- immigrants and migrants from mid-western US;

- Stanford University;
- pragmatic non-hierarchical culture;
- some luck.

Silicon Valley

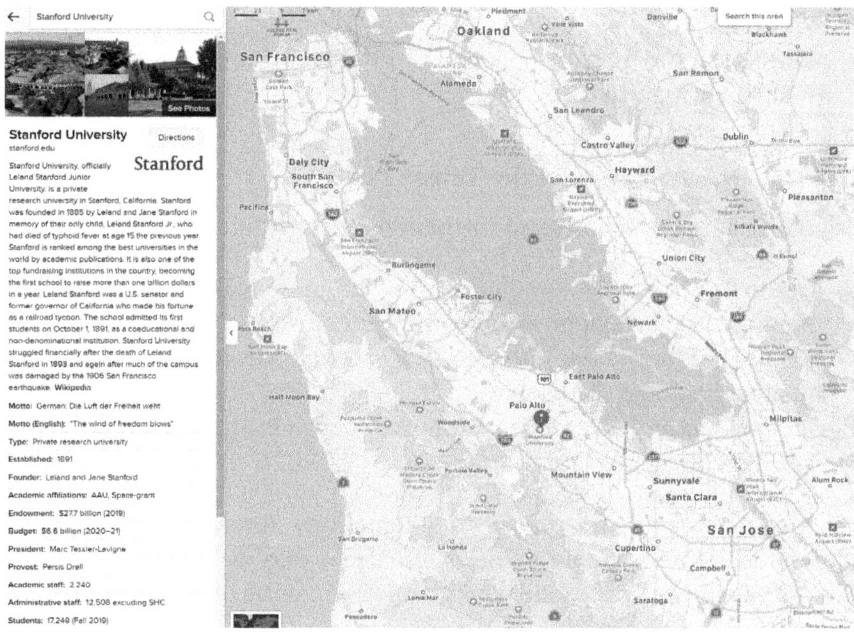

World's leading ecosystems are as follows:

- *US*: Palo Alto, San Francisco, Cambridge/Boston, New York, Chicago IL, Seattle WA, Austin TX, etc.
- *Europe*: London, Berlin, Paris, etc.
- *Asia*: Beijing, Shanghai, Shenzhen, Singapore, Hong-Kong, Manila, etc.
- *Australia*: Surry Hills Sydney, Melbourne.
- These contain rapidly moving landscape.

12.5 How Do Ecosystems Work?

We distinguish between two types of interactions:

- **Transaction:** more parties strike a deal, e.g., contracts;

- **Externality:** parties affect each other indirectly, e.g, scientific knowledge, pollution.

To understand ecosystems, we need to understand externalities and their implications. We focus on three types of externalities:

- within the talent pool;
- with investors;
- with supporting parties.

12.6 Interactions within the Talent Pool

A large talent pool helps team formation by providing the following:

- access to *experience*: younger and older, more experienced, founders, mentors, and investors → dynamic cycle;
- benefits of *large and diverse talent pool*, which extends to team members beyond founders;
- openness to *mobility* (*immigration*) — depends on job market flexibility, legal rules, cultural norms.

Similar externalities apply to interactions among companies, both startups and corporations. Some externalities may be negative: competition for talent, for real estate, and competition in the product market.

12.7 Interactions with Investors

Investment markets are *two-sided markets* (Da Rin Hellman, 2020, Chapter 13): buyers (investors) benefit from facing large and diverse set of sellers (founders), and vice versa. With agglomeration economies, only a limited number of platforms/ecosystems can flourish.

For investors, larger ecosystems imply the following:

- increased likelihood of a good match → MATCH tool;
- increased scope for diversification.

From the perspective of entrepreneurs, larger ecosystems allow the following:

- more competition among investors;
- access to more specialized investors;

- access to investors with strong industry knowledge;
- access to investors specialized by stage.

Interactions among investors themselves are also important:

- competition;
- cooperation and positive externalities;
- increase in the ecosystem's reputation.

12.8 Interactions with Supporting Parties

There are several supporting parties:

- **Universities:** ideas (patents, licenses, copyrights) and people (students and faculty);
- **Established companies:** corporate spin-offs; employee "spawning"; technical and managerial talent pool; demand and supply for startups;
- **Specialized professionals, providing a wide range of services:** lawyers, accountants, head hunters, technology consultants, business consultants, financial intermediaries, bankers, etc.

They provide services that are (i) specialized for startups and (ii) crucial for their development.

12.9 The Role of Government

The government is a very special supporting party. Its presence is ubiquitous and cannot be avoided: Should the government be active in supporting entrepreneurial ecosystems?

Economists have identified four possible *market failures* that may justify government support.

(1) **Imperfect information:** Adverse selection and moral hazard:
  - leading investors to withdraw resources;
  - government cannot solve the underlying problem, but can compensate for it, allowing startups access to finance.

(2) **Innovation externalities:** Societal value of innovation larger than private value captured by the innovator, e.g., invention of the light bulb:
  - undersupply of innovation;

- government could support innovative activities.

(3) **Market power:** Tends to deter innovation:
- "The best of all monopoly profits is a quiet life" — John Hicks;
- Government can ensure a competitive level playing field.

(4) **Framework conditions:** Market transaction require a supportive environment:
- refer to institutions that are more easily run by a government than a private firm, e.g., judiciary;
- government can craft them so as to enable private markets to operate efficiently.

There are also government failures such as the following:

- wrong incentives;
- organizational rigidity;
- incompetence;
- corruption;
- sluggishness.

Following are the two types of government policies to stimulate the supply and the demand for financial capital:

1. **Supply side:** government funding, tax credits, capital market regulations, framework conditions;
2. **Demand side:** science infrastructure, education, competition.

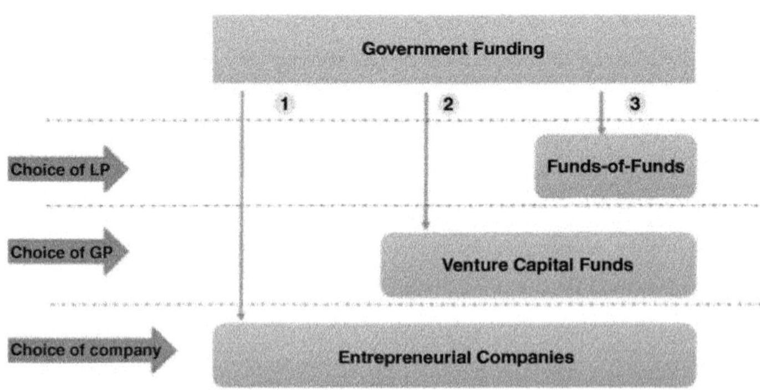

Source: Da Rin and Hellman (2021).

Three types of financing support are as follows:

(1) direct funding for companies;
(2) investment into VC funds — the government becomes a limited partner and pays management fees and carried interests;
(3) investment through funds-of-funds — involves two layers of management fees and carried interests.

Two approaches to providing tax subsidies to investors are as follows:

(1) giving them more upside potential:
- government caps its upside return, leaving extra upside to private investors (in case of success).

(2) giving them more downside protection:
- government gets its return after private investors achieve a promised return.

Table 12.1: Alternative tax credit policies

Tax Policies	For Companies	For Investors
Based on investments	R&D tax credits	Investment tax credits
Based on returns	Corporate tax relief	Capital gains relief

R&D tax credits are available to larger audience than investment tax credits. Tax relief and capital gain relief are only for limited companies.

Capital market regulations can make it easier to fundraise:

- A common approach is to loosen requirements by Stock Exchanges.
- Another is the creation of stock exchanges (or segments) targeting entrepreneurial companies.

Framework conditions concern the whole corporate sector:

- legal system reliability: common law is better than civil law for investors;
- corruption;
- regulatory barriers to (new) business activity;
- labor legislation.

Demand-side policies promote the creation of entrepreneurial companies that then demand capital.

Three main approaches are as follows:

- supporting R&D and its commercialization;
- fostering education to generate a larger talent pool;
- ensuring affordable real estate to allow physical concentration.

12.10 Global Ecosystems

There are multiple reasons for making cross-border investments. From the investors' perspective, investing abroad is purely driven by opportunity; they simply want to invest in the best deals. However, not all investors are comfortable with long-distance investing, as there are monitoring benefits to being close to the company.

Consider data from Europe, where US investors have become an important source of funding.

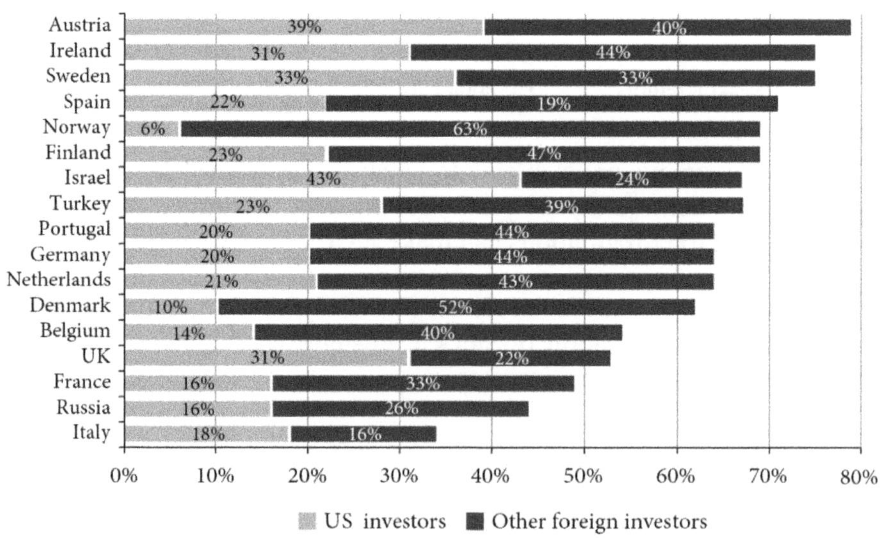

Source: Da Rin and Hellman (2021).

Review Questions for Entrepreneurial Ecosystems

1. Who are the main actors in an entrepreneurial ecosystem?

Entrepreneurial talent pool, investors, supporting individuals and firms.

2. What are the main factors contributing to the agglomeration of economic activity?

Agglomeration of economic activity is driven by the benefits of closeness of all the above actors. Fixed investments are difficult to move and more effective if done in an already vibrant area for entrepreneurship. Specialized suppliers prefer to locate next to their customers. Proximity to specialized suppliers encourages experimentation, innovation and improves the production process. Networking, information-gathering, and in-person communication are beneficial for the creation and implementation of new ideas. Knowledge spillovers are more likely within an ecosystem. Talented individuals can gather and meet. Labor market pools of talented individuals can form within ecosystems. Economic theory distinguishes two types of interactions, transactions and externalities (see what follows).

3. Within an ecosystem, what are the main externalities among entrepreneurial companies?

Talent pools, experience, talent in certain industries and for certain job functions, e.g., CEO. How easy it is to hire talent within the ecosystem, how are the labour laws, non-disclosure, and non-compete clauses enforced within the ecosystem.

4. Why does investor diversity matter for an ecosystem?

Diverse companies can find suitable investors interested to invest, small, big, to be heavily involved, or passive.

5. What is the role of professional service providers within an ecosystem?

Examples are as follows: specialized law firms familiar with the entrepreneurial process; specialized head hunters for startups and scale-ups, and technology consultants that can manage intellectual property, marketing consultants that can reach customers for new firms using the latest techniques; specialized bankers and investment banks.

6. What are the main arguments for and against government intervention in entrepreneurial finance?

Government can protect against market failure: imperfect information, innovation externalities, market power, and framework conditions (see Da Rin and Hellman (2000, Section 12.3.1) for details).

Government can hinder successful entrepreneurship. When government tries to solve market failures, they may support businesses that naturally would fail directing capital away from business ideas that would have benefitted the economy more. Also, the cost of supporting an entrepreneurial ecosystem can be a burden for tax payers.

7. What is the difference between supply- and demand-side policies?

Government can increase supply of capital and foster investment through funding, tax credits, and regulation of capital markets. Governments can increase demand for startups and innovation by stimulating demand for capital, promoting entrepreneurship, and encouraging innovation.

8. What is the relative advantage of governments investing directly into companies, investing in VC funds, and investing in funds-of-funds?

Governments can invest directly through government-established VC funds, particularly important in Europe. Government can also participate as LPs. Government can increase the size of the local VC market and hence increase all externality benefits of the ecosystem. It is important that government investment attracts, not crowds out, private investments.

9. Should countries welcome foreign venture investors?

Naturally. They benefit the companies they invest in by the local ecosystem through increased externalities. One sensitive issue is the ownership related to military technology and cybersecurity.

10. Who benefits and loses from brain drain?

Brain drain directly benefits those countries and areas that make it easy for talented entrepreneurs to establish themselves. Usually, the movement is from weaker to stronger ecosystems. The entrepreneurs benefit from relocation. In the short run, the weaker ecosystems lose.

As costs of establishing in the largest ecosystems grow, some talent may move back or to other weaker ecosystems and then bring with them important experience that increases the speed of development.

Term Sheets and Deal Closing Strategy

Q: Is WorkHorse up and running and what is the next big step for Astrid, Brandon, Bharat and Annie?

See Da Rin and Hellman (2021).

Appendix

The Business Model Canvas

A shared language for describing, visualizing, assessing, and changing business models

The 9 Building Blocks

CS

1 **Customer Segments**

An organization serves one or several Customer Segments.

VP

2 **Value Propositions**

It seeks to solve customer problems and satisfy customer needs with value propositions.

CH

3 **Channels**

Value propositions are delivered to customers through communication, distribution, and sales Channels.

CR

4 **Customer Relationships**

Customer relationships are established and maintained with each Customer Segment.

R$

5 **Revenue Streams**

Revenue streams result from value propositions successfully offered to customers.

KR

6 **Key Resources**

Key resources are the assets required to offer and deliver the previously described elements . . .

KA

7 **Key Activities**

. . . by performing a number of Key Activities.

KP

8 **Key Partnerships**

Some activities are outsourced and some resources are acquired outside the enterprise.

C$

9 **Cost Structure**

The business model elements result in the cost structure.

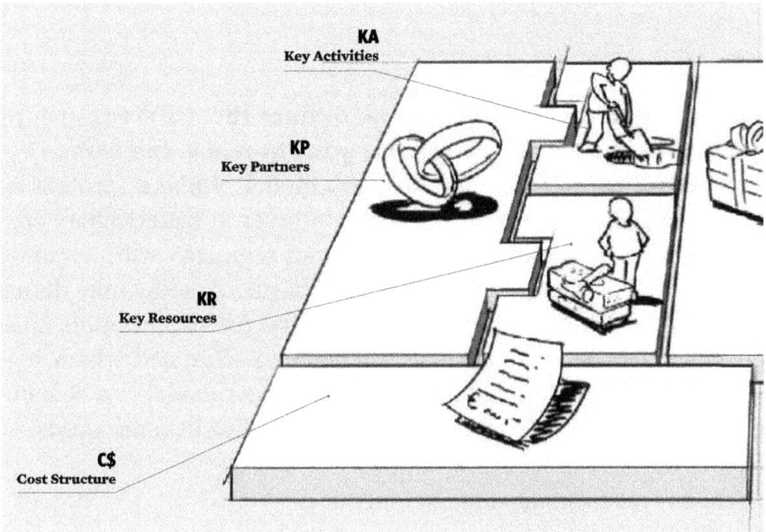
KA
Key Activities
KP
Key Partners
KR
Key Resources
C$
Cost Structure

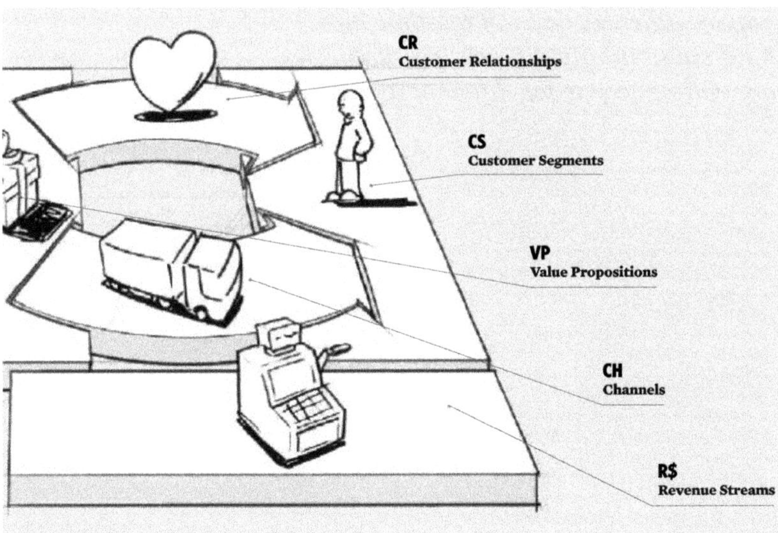
CR
Customer Relationships
CS
Customer Segments
VP
Value Propositions
CH
Channels
R$
Revenue Streams

CS

Customer Segments

The Customer Segments Building Block defines the different groups of people or organizations an enterprise aims to reach and serve
Customers comprise the heart of any business model. Without (profitable) customers, no company can survive for long. In order to better satisfy customers, a company may group them into distinct segments with common needs, common behaviors, or other attributes. A business model may define one or several large or small Customer Segments. An organization must make a conscious decision about which segments to serve and which segments to ignore. Once this decision is made, a business model can be carefully designed around a strong understanding of specific customer needs.

Customer groups represent separate segments if

- *their needs require and justify a distinct offer,*
- *they are reached through different Distribution Channels,*
- *they require different types of relationships,*
- *they have substantially different profitabilities,*
- *they are willing to pay for different aspects of the offer.*

For whom are we creating value? Who are our most important customers?

There are different types of Customer Segments. Here are some examples:

Mass market: Business models focused on mass markets don't distinguish between different Customer Segments. The Value Propositions, Distribution Channels, and Customer Relationships all focus on one large group of customers with broadly similar needs and problems. This type of business model is often found in the consumer electronics sector.

Niche market: Business models targeting niche markets cater to specific, specialized Customer Segments. The Value Propositions, Distribution Channels, and Customer Relationships are all tailored to the specific requirements of a niche market. Such business models are often found in supplier-buyer relationships. For example, many car part manufacturers depend heavily on purchases from major automobile manufacturers.

Segmented: Some business models distinguish between market segments with slightly different needs and problems. The retail arm of a bank like Credit Suisse, for example, may distinguish between a large group of customers, each possessing assets of up to U.S. $100,000, and a smaller group of affluent clients, each of whose net worth exceeds U.S. $500,000. Both segments have similar but varying needs and problems. This has implications for the other building blocks of Credit Suisse's business model, such as the Value Proposition, Distribution Channels, Customer Relationships, and Revenue streams. Consider Micro Precision Systems, which specializes in providing outsourced micromechanical design and manufacturing solutions. It serves three different Customer Segments — the watch industry, the medical industry, and the industrial automation sector — and offers each slightly different Value Propositions.

Diversified: An organization with a diversified customer business model serves two unrelated Customer Segments with very different needs and problems. For example, in 2006 Amazon.com decided to diversify its retail business by selling "cloud computing" services: online storage space and on-demand server usage. Thus it started catering to a totally different Customer Segment — Web companies — with a totally different Value Proposition. The strategic rationale behind this diversification can be found in Amazon.com's powerful IT infrastructure, which can be shared by its retail sales operations and the new cloud computing service unit.

Multi-sided platforms (or multi-sided markets): Some organizations serve two or more interdependent Customer Segments. A credit card company, for example, needs a large base of credit card holders and a large base of merchants who accept those credit cards. Similarly, an enterprise offering a free newspaper needs a large reader base to attract advertisers. On the other hand, it also needs advertisers to finance production and distribution. Both segments are required to make the business model work (read more about multi-sided platforms on p. 76).

VP

Value Propositions

The Value Propositions Building Block describes the bundle of products and services that create value for a specific Customer Segment.

The Value Proposition is the reason why customers turn to one company over another. It solves a customer problem or satisfies a customer need. Each Value Proposition consists of a selected bundle of products and/or services that caters to the requirements of a specific Customer Segment. In this sense, the Value Proposition is an aggregation, or bundle, of benefits that a company offers customers.

Some Value Propositions may be innovative and represent a new or disruptive offer. Others may be similar to existing market offers, but with added features and attributes.

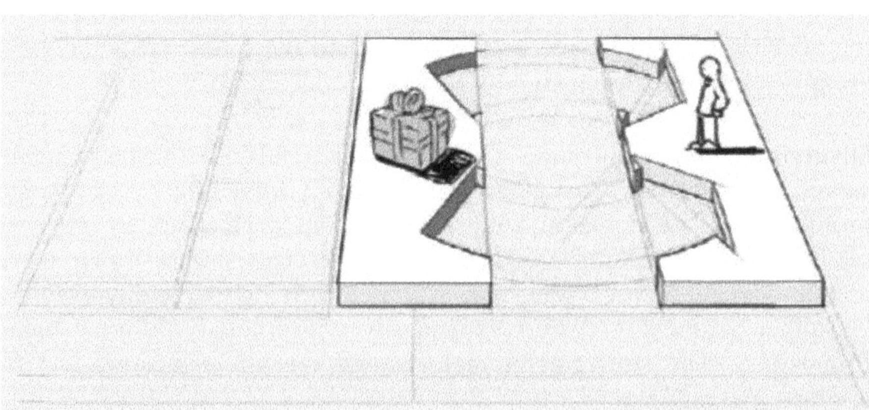

What value do we deliver to the customer? Which one of our customer's problems are we helping to solve? Which customer needs are we satisfying? What bundles of products and services are we offering to each Customer Segment?

A Value Proposition creates value for a Customer Segment through a distinct mix of elements catering to that segment's needs. Values may be quantitative (e.g., price, speed of service) or qualitative (e.g., design, customer experience).

Elements from the following non-exhaustive list can contribute to customer value creation.

Newness: Some Value Propositions satisfy an entirely new set of needs that customers previously didn't perceive because there was no similar offering. This is often, but not always, technology related. Cell phones, for instance, created a whole new industry around mobile telecommunication. On the other hand, products such as ethical investment funds have little to do with new technology.

Performance: Improving product or service performance has traditionally been a common way to create value. The PC sector has traditionally relied on this factor by bringing more powerful machines to market.

But improved performance has its limits. In recent years, for example, faster PCs, more disk storage space, and better graphics have failed to produce corresponding growth in customer demand.

Customization: Tailoring products and services to the specific needs of individual customers or Customer Segments creates value. In recent years, the concepts of mass customization and customer co-creation have gained importance. This approach allows for customized products and services, while still taking advantage of economies of scale.

"Getting the job done": Value can be created simply by helping a customer get certain jobs done. Rolls-Royce understands this very well: its airline customers rely entirely on Rolls- Royce to manufacture and service their jet engines. This arrangement allows customers to focus on running their airlines. In return, the airlines pay Rolls-Royce a fee for every hour an engine runs.

Design: Design is an important but difficult element to measure. A product may stand out because of superior design. In the fashion and consumer electronics industries, design can be a particularly important part of the Value Proposition.

Brand/status: Customers may find value in the simple act of using and displaying a specific brand. Wearing a Rolex watch signifies wealth, for example. On the other end of the spectrum, skateboarders may wear the latest "underground" brands to show that they are "in."

Price: Offering similar value at a lower price is a common way to satisfy the needs of price-sensitive Customer Segments. But low-price Value Propositions have important implications for the rest of a business model. No frills airlines, such as Southwest, easyJet, and Ryanair have designed entire business models specifically to enable low cost air travel.

Another example of a price-based Value Proposition can be seen in the Nano, a new car designed and manufactured by the Indian conglomerate Tata. Its surprisingly low price makes the automobile affordable to a whole new segment of the Indian population. Increasingly, free offers are starting to permeate various industries. Free offers range from free newspapers to free e-mail, free mobile phone services, and more (see p. 88 for more on FREE).

Cost reduction: Helping customers reduce costs is an important way to create value. Salesforce.com, for example, sells a hosted Customer Relationship Management (CRM) application. This relieves buyers from the expense and trouble of having to buy, install, and manage CRM software themselves.

Risk reduction: Customers value reducing the risks they incur when purchasing products or services. For a used car buyer, a 1-year service guarantee reduces the risk of post-purchase breakdowns and repairs. A service-level guarantee partially reduces the risk undertaken by a purchaser of outsourced IT services.

Accessibility: Making products and services available to customers who previously lacked access to them is another way to create value. This can result from business model innovation, new technologies, or a combination of both. NetJets, for instance, popularized the concept of fractional private jet ownership. Using an innovative business model, NetJets offers individuals and corporations access to private jets, a service previously unaffordable to most customers. Mutual funds provide another example of value creation through increased accessibility. This innovative financial product made it possible even for those with modest wealth to build diversified investment portfolios.

Convenience/usability: Making things more convenient or easier to use can create substantial value. With iPod and iTunes, Apple offered customers unprecedented convenience searching, buying, downloading, and listening to digital music. It now dominates the market.

CH

Channels

The Channels Building Block describes how a company communicates with and reaches its Customer Segments to deliver a Value Proposition.

Communication, distribution, and sales Channels comprise a company's interface with customers. Channels are customer touch points that play an important role in the customer experience. Channels serve several functions, including the following:

- *raising awareness among customers about a company's products and services,*
- *helping customers evaluate a company's Value Proposition,*
- *allowing customers to purchase specifi c products and services,*
- *delivering a Value Proposition to customers,*
- *providing post-purchase customer support.*

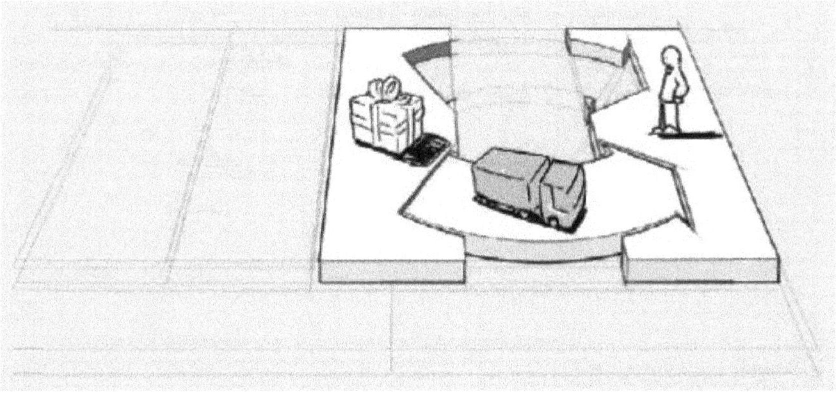

Through which Channels do our Customer Segments want to be reached? How are we reaching them now? How are our Channels integrated? Which ones work best? Which ones are most cost-efficient? How are we integrating them with customer routines?

Channels have five distinct phases. Each channel can cover some or all of these phases. We can distinguish between direct Channels and indirect ones, as well as between owned Channels and partner Channels.

Finding the right mix of Channels to satisfy how customers want to be reached is crucial in bringing a Value Proposition to market. An organization can choose between reaching its customers through its own Channels, through partner Channels, or through a mix of both. Owned Channels can be direct, such as an in-house sales force or a website, or they can be indirect, such as retail stores owned or operated by the organization. Partner Channels are indirect and span a whole range of options, such as wholesale distribution, retail, or partner-owned Web sites.

Partner Channels lead to lower margins, but they allow an organization to expand its reach and benefit from partner strengths. Owned Channels and particularly direct ones have higher margins, but can be costly to put in place and to operate. The trick is to find the right balance between the different types of Channels, to integrate them in a way to create a great customer experience, and to maximize revenues.

<table>
<tr><th colspan="3">Channel Types</th><th colspan="5">Channel Phases</th></tr>
<tr><td rowspan="2">Own</td><td rowspan="2">Direct</td><td>Sales force</td><td rowspan="5">1. Awareness
How do we raise awareness about our company's products and services?</td><td rowspan="5">2. Evaluation
How do we help customers evaluate our organization's Value Proposition?</td><td rowspan="5">3. Purchase
How do we allow customers to purchase specific products and services?</td><td rowspan="5">4. Delivery
How do we deliver a Value Proposition to customers?</td><td rowspan="5">5. After sales
How do we provide post-purchase customer support?</td></tr>
<tr><td>Web sales</td></tr>
<tr><td rowspan="3">Partner</td><td rowspan="3">Indirect</td><td>Own stores</td></tr>
<tr><td>Partner stores</td></tr>
<tr><td>Wholesaler</td></tr>
</table>

CR

Customer Relationships

The Customer Relationships Building Block describes the types of relationships a company establishes with specific Customer Segments
A company should clarify the type of relationship it wants to establish with each Customer Segment. Relationships can range from personal to automated. Customer relationships may be driven by the following motivations:

- *Customer acquisition,*
- *Customer retention,*
- *Boosting sales (upselling).*

In the early days, for example, mobile network operator Customer Relationships were driven by aggressive acquisition strategies involving free mobile phones. When the market became saturated, operators switched to focusing on customer retention and increasing average revenue per customer.

The Customer Relationships called for by a company's business model deeply influence the overall customer experience.

What type of relationship does each of our Customer Segments expect us to establish and maintain with them? Which ones have we established? How costly are they? How are they integrated with the rest of our business model?

We can distinguish between several categories of Customer Relationships, which may co-exist in a company's relationship with a particular Customer Segment:

Personal assistance: This relationship is based on human interaction. The customer can communicate with a real customer representative to get help during the sales process or after the purchase is complete. This may happen onsite at the point of sale, through call centers, by e-mail, or through other means.

Dedicated personal assistance: This relationship involves dedicating a customer representative specifically to an individual client. It represents the deepest and most intimate type of relationship and normally develops over a long period of time. In private banking services, for example, dedicated bankers serve high net worth individuals. Similar relationships can be found in other businesses in the form of key account managers who maintain personal relationships with important customers.

Self-service: In this type of relationship, a company maintains no direct relationship with customers. It provides all the necessary means for customers to help themselves.

Automated services: This type of relationship mixes a more sophisticated form of customer self-service with automated processes. For example, personal online profiles give customers access to customized services. Automated services can recognize individual customers and their characteristics, and offer information related to orders or transactions. At their best, automated services can simulate a personal relationship (e.g., offering book or movie recommendations).

Communities: Increasingly, companies are utilizing user communities to become more involved with customers/prospects and to facilitate connections between community members. Many companies maintain online communities that allow users to exchange knowledge and solve each other's problems. Communities can also help companies better understand their customers. Pharmaceutical giant GlaxoSmithKline launched a private online community when it introduced *alli*, a new prescription-free weight-loss product.

GlaxoSmithKline wanted to increase its understanding of the challenges faced by overweight adults, and thereby learn to better manage customer expectations.

Co-creation: More companies are going beyond the traditional customer–vendor relationship to co-create value with customers. Amazon.com invites customers to write reviews and thus create value for other book lovers. Some companies engage customers to assist with the design of new and innovative products. Others, such as YouTube.com, solicit customers to create content for public consumption.

R$

Revenue Streams

The Revenue Streams Building Block represents the cash a company generates from each Customer Segment (costs must be subtracted from revenues to create earnings)

If customers comprise the heart of a business model, Revenue Streams are its arteries. A company must ask itself: For what value is each Customer Segment truly willing to pay? Successfully answering that question allows the firm to generate one or more Revenue Streams from each Customer Segment. Each Revenue Stream may have different pricing mechanisms, such as fixed list prices, bargaining, auctioning, market dependent, volume dependent, or yield management.

A business model can involve two different types of Revenue Streams:

1. *Transaction revenues resulting from one-time customer payments.*
2. *Recurring revenues resulting from ongoing payments to either deliver a Value Proposition to customers or provide post-purchase customer support.*

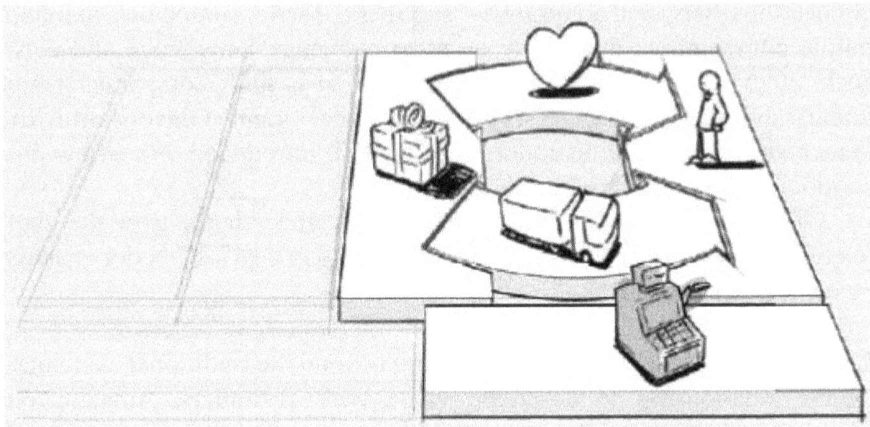

For what value are our customers really willing to pay? For what do they currently pay? How are they currently paying? How would they prefer to pay? How much does each Revenue Stream contribute to overall revenues?

There are several ways to generate Revenue Streams:

Asset sale: The most widely understood Revenue Stream derives from selling ownership rights to a physical product. Amazon.com sells books, music, consumer electronics, and more online. Fiat sells automobiles, which buyers are free to drive, resell, or even destroy.

Usage fee: This Revenue Stream is generated by the use of a particular service. The more a service is used, the more the customer pays. A telecom operator may charge customers for the number of minutes spent on the phone. A hotel charges customers for the number of nights rooms are used. A package delivery service charges customers for the delivery of a parcel from one location to another.

Subscription fees: This Revenue Stream is generated by selling continuous access to a service. A gym sells its members monthly or yearly subscriptions in exchange for access to its exercise facilities. World of Warcraft Online, a Web-based computer game, allows users to play its online game in exchange for a monthly subscription fee. Nokia's Comes with Music service gives users access to a music library for a subscription fee.

Lending/renting/leasing: This Revenue Stream is created by temporarily granting someone the exclusive right to use a particular asset for a fixed period in return for a fee. For the lender this provides the advantage of recurring revenues. Renters or lessees, on the other hand, enjoy the benefits of incurring expenses for only a limited time rather than bearing the full costs of ownership. Zipcar.com provides a good illustration. The company allows customers to rent cars by the hour in North American cities. Zipcar.com's service has led many people to decide to rent rather than purchase automobiles.

Licensing: This Revenue Stream is generated by giving customers permission to use protected intellectual property in exchange for licensing fees. Licensing allows rights- holders to generate revenues from their property without having to manufacture a product or commercialize a service. Licensing is common in the media industry, where content owners retain copyright while selling usage licenses to third parties. Similarly, in technology sectors, patent holders grant other companies the right to use a patented technology in return for a license fee.

Brokerage fees: This Revenue Stream derives from intermediation services performed on behalf of two or more parties. Credit card providers, for example, earn revenues by taking a percentage of the value of each sales transaction executed between credit card merchants and customers. Brokers and real estate agents earn a commission each time they successfully match a buyer and seller.

Advertising: This Revenue Stream results from fees for advertising a particular product, service, or brand. Traditionally, the media industry and event organizers relied heavily on revenues from advertising. In recent years other sectors, including software and services, have started relying more heavily on advertising revenues.

Each Revenue Stream might have different pricing mechanisms. The type of pricing mechanism chosen can make a big difference in terms of revenues generated. There are two main types of pricing mechanism: fixed and dynamic pricing.

Pricing Mechanisms			
Fixed Menu Pricing		**Dynamic Pricing**	
Predefined prices are based on static variables		Prices change based on market conditions	
List price	Fixed prices for individual products, services, or other Value Propositions	*Negotiation (bargaining)*	Price negotiated between two or more partners depending on negotiation power and/or negotiation skills
Product feature dependent	Price depends on the number or quality of Value Proposition features	*Yield management*	Price depends on inventory and time of purchase (normally used for perishable resources such as hotel rooms or airline seats)
Customer segment dependent	Price depends on the type and characteristic of a Customer Segment	*Real-time-market*	Price is established dynamically based on supply and demand
Volume dependent	Price as a function of the quantity purchased	*Auctions*	Price determined by outcome of competitive bidding

KR

Key Resources

The Key Resources Building Block describes the most important assets required to make a business model work
Every business model requires Key Resources. These resources allow an enterprise to create and offer a Value Proposition, reach markets, maintain relationships with Customer Segments, and earn revenues. Different Key Resources are needed depending on the type of business model. A microchip manufacturer requires capital-intensive production facilities, whereas a microchip designer focuses more on human resources.

Key resources can be physical, financial, intellectual, or human. Key resources can be owned or leased by the company or acquired from key partners

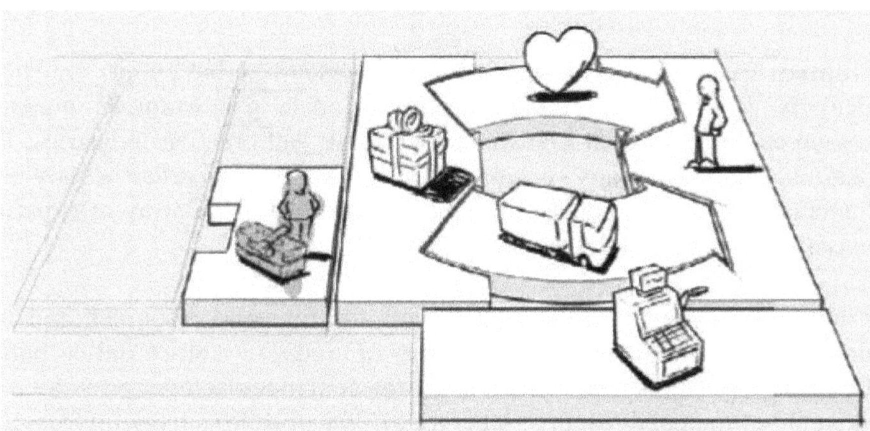

What Key Resources do our Value Propositions require? Our Distribution Channels? Customer Relationships? Revenue Streams?

Key Resources can be categorized as follows:

Physical: This category includes physical assets such as manufacturing facilities, buildings, vehicles, machines, systems, point-of-sales systems, and distribution networks. Retailers like WalMart and Amazon.com rely heavily on physical resources, which are often capital-intensive. The former has an enormous global network of stores and related logistics infrastructure. The latter has an extensive IT, warehouse, and logistics infrastructure.

Intellectual: Intellectual resources such as brands, proprietary knowledge, patents and copyrights, partnerships, and customer databases are increasingly important components of a strong business model. Intellectual resources are difficult to develop but when success-fully created may offer substantial value. Consumer goods companies such as Nike and Sony rely heavily on brand as a Key Resource. Microsoft and SAP depend on software and related intellectual property developed over many years. Qualcomm, a designer and supplier of chipsets for broadband mobile devices, built its business model around patented microchip designs that earn the company substantial licensing fees.

Human: Every enterprise requires human resources, but people are particularly prominent in certain business models. For example, human resources are crucial in knowledge-intensive and creative industries. A pharmaceutical company such as Novartis, for example, relies heavily on human resources: Its business model is predicated on an army of experienced scientists and a large and skilled sales force.

Financial: Some business models call for financial resources and/or financial guarantees, such as cash, lines of credit, or a stock option pool for hiring key employees. Ericsson, the telecom manufacturer, provides an example of financial resource leverage within a business model. Ericsson may opt to borrow funds from banks and capital markets, then use a portion of the proceeds to provide vendor financing to equipment customers, thus ensuring that orders are placed with Ericsson rather than competitors.

KA

Key Activities

The Key Activities Building Block describes the most important things a company must do to make its business model work

Every business model calls for a number of Key Activities. These are the most important actions a company must take to operate successfully. Like Key Resources, they are required to create and offer a Value Proposition, reach markets, maintain Customer Relationships, and earn revenues. And like Key Resources, Key Activities differ depending on business model type. For software maker Microsoft, Key Activities include software development.

For PC manufacturer Dell, Key Activities include supply chain management. For consultancy McKinsey, Key Activities include problem solving

What Key Activities do our Value Propositions require? Our Distribution Channels? Customer Relationships? Revenue streams?

Key Activities can be categorized as follows:

Production: These activities relate to designing, making, and delivering a product in substantial quantities and/or of superior quality. Production activity dominates the business models of manufacturing firms.

Problem solving: Key Activities of this type relate to coming up with new solutions to individual customer problems. The operations of consultancies, hospitals, and other service organizations are typically dominated by problem solving activities. Their business models call for activities such as knowledge management and continuous training.

Platform/network: Business models designed with a platform as a Key Resource are dominated by platform or network- related Key Activities. Networks, matchmaking platforms, software, and even brands can function as a platform. eBay's business model requires that the company continually develop and maintain its platform: the Web site at eBay.com. Visa's business model requires activities related to its Visa® credit card transaction platform for merchants, customers, and banks. Microsoft's business model requires managing the interface between other vendors' software and its Windows® operating system platform. Key Activities in this category relate to platform management, service provisioning, and platform promotion.

KP

Key Partnerships

The Key Partnerships Building Block describes the network of suppliers and partners that make the business model work

Companies forge partnerships for many reasons, and partnerships are becoming a cornerstone of many business models. Companies create alliances to optimize their business models, reduce risk, or acquire resources. We can distinguish between four different types of partnerships:

1. *Strategic alliances between non-competitors,*
2. *Coopetition: Strategic partnerships between competitors,*
3. *Joint ventures to develop new businesses,*
4. *Buyer–supplier relationships to assure reliable supplies.*

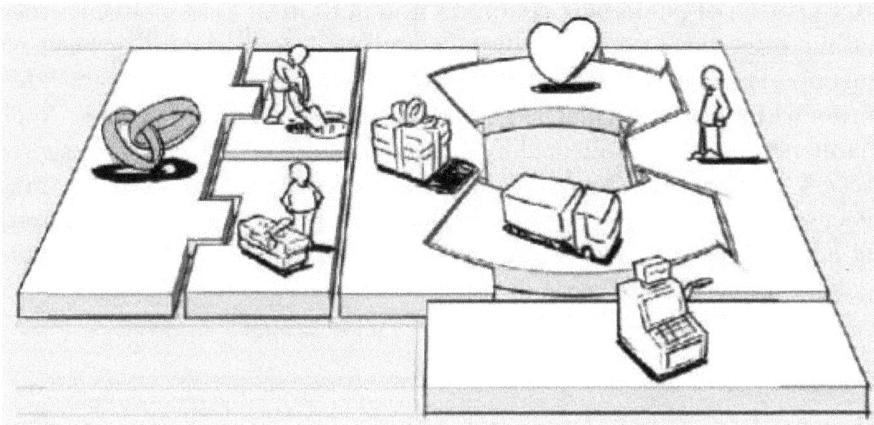

Who are our Key Partners? Who are our key suppliers?Which Key Resources are we acquiring from partners? Which Key Activities do partners perform?

It can be useful to distinguish between three motivations for creating partnerships:

Optimization and economy of scale: The most basic form of partnership or buyer-supplier relationship is designed to optimize the allocation of resources and activities. It is illogical for a company to own all resources or perform every activity by itself. Optimization and economy of scale partnerships are usually formed to reduce costs, and often involve outsourcing or sharing infrastructure.

Reduction of risk and uncertainty: Partnerships can help reduce risk in a competitive environment characterized by uncertainty. It is not unusual for competitors to form a strategic alliance in one area while competing in another. Blu-ray, for example, is an optical disc format jointly developed by a group of the world's leading consumer electronics, personal computer, and media manufacturers.

The group cooperated to bring Blu-ray technology to market, yet individual members compete in selling their own Blu-ray products.

Acquisition of particular resources and activities: Few companies own all the resources or perform all the activities described by their business models. Rather, they extend their own capabilities by relying on other firms to furnish particular resources or perform certain activities. Such partnerships can be motivated by needs to acquire knowledge, licenses, or access to customers. A mobile phone manufacturer, for example, may license an operating system for its handsets rather than developing one in-house. An insurer may choose to rely on independent brokers to sell its policies rather than develop its own sales force.

C$

Cost Structure

The Cost Structure describes all costs incurred to operate a business model

This building block describes the most important costs incurred while operating under a particular business model. Creating and delivering value, maintaining Customer Relationships, and generating revenue all incur costs. Such costs can be calculated relatively easily after defining Key Resources, Key Activities, and Key Partnerships. Some business models, though, are more cost-driven than others. The so-called "no frills" airlines, for instance, have built business models entirely around low Cost Structures.

What are the most important costs inherent in our business model? Which Key Resources are most expensive? Which Key Activities are most expensive?

Naturally enough, costs should be minimized in every business model. But low Cost Structures are more important to some business models than to others. Therefore it can be useful to distinguish between two broad classes of business model Cost Structures: cost-driven and value-driven (many business models fall in between these two extremes):

Cost-driven: Cost-driven business models focus on minimizing costs wherever possible. This approach aims at creating and maintaining the leanest possible Cost Structure, using low price Value Propositions, maximum automation, and extensive outsourcing. No frills airlines, such as Southwest, easyJet, and Ryanair typify cost-driven business models.

Value-driven: Some companies are less concerned with the cost implications of a particular business model design, and instead focus on value creation. Premium Value Propositions and a high degree of personalized service usually characterize value-driven business models. Luxury hotels, with their lavish facilities and exclusive services, fall into this category.

Cost Structures can have the following characteristics:

Fixed costs: Costs that remain the same despite the volume of goods or services produced. Examples include salaries, rents, and physical manufacturing facilities. Some businesses, such as manufacturing companies, are characterized by a high proportion of fixed costs.

Variable costs: Costs that vary proportionally with the volume of goods or services produced. Some businesses, such as music festivals, are characterized by a high proportion of variable costs.

Economies of scale: Cost advantages that a business enjoys as its output expands. Larger companies, for instance, benefit from lower bulk purchase rates. This and other factors cause average cost per unit to fall as output rises.

Economies of scope: Cost advantages that a business enjoys due to a larger scope of operations. In a large enterprise, for example, the same marketing activities or Distribution Channels may support multiple products.

Standard Business Plan Financials: Five Simple Steps

Follow these tips to learn how to develop sales projections for your business plan.

Introduction

Your sales forecast is the backbone of your business plan. People measure a business and its growth by sales, and your sales forecast sets the standard for expenses, profits and growth.

When it comes to forecasting sales, don't fall for the trap that says forecasting takes training, mathematics or advanced degrees. Forecasting is mainly educated guessing. So don't expect to get it perfect; just make it reasonable. There's no business owner who isn't qualified to forecast sales — you don't need a business degree or accountant's certification. What you need is common sense, research of the factors, and motivation to make an educated guess.

Your sales forecast in a business plan should show sales by month for the next 12 months — at least — and then by year for the following 2–5 years. Three years, total, is generally enough for most business plans.

If you have more than one line of sales, show each line of sales separately and add them up. If you have more than 10 or so lines of sales, summarize them and consolidate. Remember, this is business planning, not accounting, so it has to be reasonable, but it doesn't need too much detail. Here are some tips to get you started.

Step 1

Develop a unit sales projection. Where you can, start by forecasting unit sales per month. Not all businesses sell by units, but most do, and it's easier to forecast by breaking things down into their component parts. Product-oriented businesses obviously sell in units, but so do a lot of service businesses. For example, accountants and attorneys sell hours, taxis sell rides, and restaurants sell meals.

Step 2

Use past data if you have it (not always possible for a new startup/product/service). Whenever you have past sales data, your best forecasting aid is the most recent past. There are some statistical analysis techniques that take past data and project it forward into the future. You can get just about the same results by projecting your two most recent years of sales by month on a line chart and then visually tracking it forward along the same line. Statistical tools are a nice addition, but they're rarely as valuable in a business plan as human common sense, particularly if it's guided by analysis.

Use factors for a new product. Having a new product is no excuse for not having a sales forecast. Of course you don't know what's going to happen, but that's no excuse for not drafting a sales projection. Nobody who plans a new product knows the future — you simply make educated guesses. So break it down by finding important decision factors or components of sales. If you have a completely new product with no history, find an existing product to use as a guide. For example, if you have the next great computer game, base your forecast on sales of a similar computer game. If you have a new auto accessory, look at sales of other auto accessories. Analysts projected sales of fax machines before they were released to the market by looking at typewriters and copiers.

Break the purchase down into factors. For example, you can forecast sales in a restaurant by looking at a reasonable number of tables occupied at different hours of the day and then multiplying the percent of tables occupied by the average estimated revenue per table. Some people project sales in certain kinds of retail businesses by investigating the average sales per square foot in similar businesses.

Step 3

Be sure to project prices. The next step is prices. You've projected unit sales monthly for 12 months and then annually, so you must also project your prices. Think of this as a simple spreadsheet that adds the units of different sales items in one section, then sets the estimated prices in a second section. A third section then multiplies units times price to calculate sales. The math is simple — the hard part is making that estimated guess of unit sales.

Step 4

A fourth section of your projected prices will set the average costs per unit. You want to set costs because a lot of financial analysis focuses on gross margin, which is sales less cost of sales. For financial reasons, cost of sales, also known as costs of goods sold and direct costs, are different from the other expenses that come out of profits.

The cost of sales isn't what you pay salespeople or for advertising. It's the amount you pay to buy what you sell. This is usually easy to understand. In any retail store, for example, the cost of goods sold is what the store pays for the products it sells. In service businesses, the costs of sales can be less obvious, but it can still be figured out.

Step 5

Finally, you multiply unit sales times average cost per unit to calculate your cost of sales. This gives you a sales forecast that you can use for the rest of your financial projections. The first place you'll use it is at the beginning of your profit and loss statement, which normally starts with sales and cost of sales.

Of course, not all businesses fit easily into the units sales model. Some business plans will have sales forecasts that project dollar sales only, by line of sales, and then direct costs, by other factors. For example, a taxi business might simply estimate total fares as its sales forecast and gasoline, maintenance and other items as its cost of sales. A graphic artist might stick with the simple dollar-value sales forecast and project cost of sales as photocopies, color proofs, etc. In the end, it's always your plan, so you have to make the decisions that are best for you.

Standard Business Plan and Financials: Sales Forecast Example

This is an **example of a startup sales forecast**. The goal is to take a hypothetical case and open up the thinking involved, not so anybody just copies it, but rather to serve as an example. The underlying goal is to open up the idea that forecasting isn't a technical feat; it's something that anybody can do.

Magda wants to open up a new café in an office park. She wants a small locale, just six tables of four. She wants to serve coffee and lunches. She hasn't contracted the locale yet, but she has a good idea of where she wants to locate it and what size she wants, so she wants to estimate realistic sales. She assumes a certain size and location and develops a base forecast to get started.

Establishing a base case

She starts with understanding her capacity. She does some simple math. She estimates that with six tables of four people each, she can do only about 24 sit-down lunches in an average day, because lunch is just a single hour. And then she adds to-go lunches, which she estimates will be about double the table lunches, so 48 per day. She estimates lunch beverages as .9 beverages for every lunch at the tables, and only .5 beverages for every to-go lunch. Then she calculates the coffee capacity as a maximum of one customer every two minutes, or 30 customers per hour; and she estimates how she expects the flow during the morning hours, with a maximum 30 coffees during the 8–9 a.m. hour. She also estimates some coffees at lunch, based on 3 coffees for every 10 lunches. You can see the results here, as a quick worksheet for calculations.

At tables	24	Tables	6
Togo	48	Seats per table	4
Beverages per lunch	0.90		
Beverages togo	0.50		

Monthly units at capacity				
Table lunch	530			Workdays
togo	1056	1586		22
Table lunch beverages		480		
Togo Beverages		530	1010	
Coffee	2100			

call that 100

Coffee							
Coffee per hour at peak			30				
Daily coffee weekday							
7-8	8-9	9-10	10-11	11-12	Lunches	(assumption=	30%)
20	30	20	10	10	72	97	

Where do those estimates come from? How does Magda know? Ideally, she knows because she has experience. She's familiar with the café business as a former worker, owner, or close connection. Or perhaps she has a partner, spouse, friend, or even a consultant who can make educated guesses. And it helps to break the estimates down into smaller pieces, as you can see Magda has done here.

And, by the way, there is a lesson there about estimating and educated guesses: Magda calculates 97 coffees per day. That's really 100. Always round your educated guesses. Exact numbers give a false sense of certainty.

Café monthly assumptions

She then estimates monthly capacity. You saw in Illustration 7-2 that she estimates 22 workdays per month, and multiplies coffees, lunches, and beverages, to generate the estimated unit numbers for a baseline sample month.

So that means the base case is about 1,500 lunches, about 1,000 beverages, and about 2,000 coffees in a month. Before she takes the next step, Magda adds up some numbers to see whether she should just abandon her idea. At $10 per lunch and $2 per coffee or beverage, that's roughly $15,000 in lunches, $2,000 in lunch beverages, and $4,000 in coffees in a month. She probably calls that $20,000 as a rough estimate of a true full capacity. She could figure on a few thousand in rent, a few thousand in salaries, and then decide that she should continue planning, from the quick view, like it could be a viable business (And that, by the way, in a single paragraph, is a break-even analysis).

From base case to sales forecast

With those rough numbers established as capacity, and some logic for what drives sales, and how the new business might gear up, Magda then does a quick calculation of how she might realistically expect sales to go, compared to capacity, during her first year.

Capacity	Jan	Feb	Mar	Apr	May	June	July	Aug	Sep	Oct	Nov	Dec
Coffee	63%	63%	63%	63%	59%	50%	49%	49%	63%	71%	71%	63%
Lunch	42%	63%	65%	69%	72%	67%	61%	61%	75%	83%	83%	61%
Beverage	46%	69%	72%	76%	79%	74%	67%	67%	82%	91%	91%	67%

Month-by-month estimates for the first year

All of which brings us to a realistic sales forecast for Magda's café in the office park (with some monthly columns removed for visibility's sake). This is a spreadsheet view, so, if you're a LivePlan user, all you need is to figure the assumptions and the software will do the calculations and arrangement.

Units	Jan	Feb	Mar	Dec	Year1	Year2	Year3
Coffee	1,320	1,320	1,320	1,320	15,272	16,000	17,500
Lunches	660	1,000	1,038	960	12,710	14,000	15,000
Beverages	462	697	727	672	8,897	11,000	12,000
Other	100	110	121	235	2023	2250	2500
Total	2,542	3,127	3,206	3,187	38,902	43,250	47,000

Prices	Jan	Feb	Mar	Dec	Year1	Year2	Year3
Coffee	$2.00	$2.00	$2.00	$2.00	$2.00	$2.00	$2.00
Lunches	$10.00	$10.00	$10.00	$10.00	$10.00	$10.00	$10.00
Beverages	$2.00	$2.00	$2.00	$2.00	$2.00	$2.00	$2.00
Other	$5.00	$5.00	$5.00	$5.00	$5.00	$5.00	$5.00

Sales	Jan	Feb	Mar	Dec	Year1	Year2	Year3
Coffee	$2,640	$2,640	$2,640	$2,640	$30,544	$32,000	$35,000
Lunches	$6,600	$10,000	$10,380	$9,600	$127,100	$140,000	$150,000
Beverages	$924	$1,394	$1,454	$1,344	$17,794	$22,000	$24,000
Other	$500	$550	$605	$1,175	$10,115	$11,250	$12,500
Total	$10,664	$14,584	$15,079	$14,759	$185,553	$205,250	$221,500

leanplan.com

Note that Magda is being realistic. Although her capacity looks like about $20,000 of sales per month, she knows it will take a while to build the customer base and get the business up to that level. She starts out at only about half of what she calculated as full sales; and she gets closer to full sales toward the end of the first year, when her projected sales are more than $19,000.

Important: These are all just rough numbers, for general calculations. There is nothing exact about these estimates. Don't be fooled by how exact they appear.

Note how she's working with educated guessing. She isn't turning to some magic information source to find out what her sales will be. She doesn't assume there is some magic "right answer." She isn't using quadratic equations and she doesn't need an advanced degree in calculus. She does need to have some sense of what to realistically expect. Ideally she's worked in a restaurant or knows somebody who has, so she has some reasonable information to draw on.

Estimating direct costs

We've seen direct costs already, in the previous section. They are also called COGS, or cost of goods sold, or unit costs. In Magda's case, her direct costs or COGS are what she pays for the coffee beans, beverages, bread, meat, potatoes, and other ingredients in the food she serves.

Just as with the sales categories, forecast your direct costs in categories that match your chart of accounts.

So, with her unit sales estimates already there, Magda needs only add estimated direct costs per unit to finish the forecast. The math is as simple as it was for the sales, multiplying her estimated units times her per unit direct cost. Then it adds the rows and the columns appropriately.

Units	Jan	Feb	Mar	Apr	May
Coffee	1,320	1,320	1,320	1,320	1,240
Lunches	660	1,000	1,038	1,100	1,135
Beverages	462	697	727	771	795
Other	100	110	121	133	146
Total	2,542	3,127	3,206	3,324	3,316

Unit Costs	Jan	Feb	Mar	Apr	May
Coffee	$0.40	$0.40	$0.40	$0.40	$0.40
Lunches	$2.00	$2.00	$2.00	$2.00	$2.00
Beverages	$0.40	$0.40	$0.40	$0.40	$0.40
Other	$2.50	$2.50	$2.50	$2.50	$2.50

Direct Costs	Jan	Feb	Mar	Apr	May
Coffee	$528	$528	$528	$528	$496
Lunches	$1,320	$2,000	$2,076	$2,200	$2,270
Beverages	$185	$279	$291	$308	$318
Other	$250	$275	$303	$333	$365
Total	$2,283	$3,082	$3,197	$3,369	$3,449

Here again you see the idea of educated guessing, estimates, and summary. Magda doesn't break down all the possibilities for lunches into details, differentiating the steak sandwich from the veggie sandwich, and everything in between; that level of detail is unmanageable in a forecast. She estimates the overall average direct cost. Coffees cost an average of 40 cents per coffee, and lunches about $5.00. She estimates because she's familiar with the business. And if she weren't familiar with the business, she'd find a partner who is, or do a lot more research!

Bibliography

Da Rin, M. and T. Hellman. (2021). Fundamentals of Entrepreneurial Finance. Oxford University Press, Tilburg and Oxford University. ISBN: 978-0-19-974475-6; eISBN: 978-0-19-094156-7.

Fitzpatrick, R. (2013). *The Mom Test*: How to Talk to Customers and Learn If Your Business is a Good Idea When Everyone is Lying to You. Robfitz Ltd.

Headd, B. (2003). Redefining business success: Distinguishing between closure and failure. *Small Business Economics*, 21:51–61.

Leach, J. C. and R. W. Melicher. (2020). Entrepreneurial Finance, seventh Edition, Cengage Learning Inc., University at Colorado, Boulder, USA. ISBN: 978-0-357-44204-3.

Naisbitt, J. (1982). *Megatrends*. New York: Warner Books.

Siegel, L. B. (2019). Fewer, Greener, Richer: Prospects for Humanity in an Age of Abundance. Wiley. ISBN: 978-1-119-52689-6.

Index

www.ingramcontent.com/pod-product-compliance
Ingram Content Group UK Ltd.
Pitfield, Milton Keynes, MK11 3LW, UK
UKHW022103170926
8624IPUK00024B/41

9 789811 249891

W. Zatonski N. Becker

Atlas of Cancer Mortality in Poland 1975–1979

In Collaboration with
K. Gottesmann A. Mykowiecka J. Tyczynski

With 82 Maps and 139 Graphics

Springer-Verlag
Berlin Heidelberg New York
London Paris Tokyo

Ass. Prof. Dr. med. sc. Witold Zatonski
Centrum Onkologii - Instytut M. Skłodowska Curie
Wawelska 15, 00-973 Warszawa, Poland

Dr. sc. hum. Nikolaus Becker
Institut für Epidemiologie und Biometrie
Deutsches Krebsforschungszentrum
Im Neuenheimer Feld 280, 6900 Heidelberg, FRG

This work was made possible by the Humboldt Foundation.

ISBN-13: 978-3-642-72609-5 Springer-Verlag Berlin Heidelberg New York

Library of Congress Cataloging-in-Publication Data.
Zatonski, W. (Witold)
Atlas of cancer mortality in Poland 1975-1979.
Bibliography: p. Includes index.
1. Cancer-Poland-Mortality-Statistics. 2. Cancer-Poland-Mortality-Atlases. 3. Poland-Statistics, Medical. 4. Poland-Statistics, Vital. I. Becker, N. (Nikolaus), 1950- . II. Gottesmann, K. III. Mykowiecka, A. IV. Tyczynski, J. V. Title.
RA645.C3Z38 1988 614.5'999 88-8631

ISBN-13: 978-3-642-72609-5 e-ISBN-13: 978-3-642-72607-1
DOI: 10.1007/978-3-642-72607-1

Softcover reprint of the hardcover 1st edition

Foreword

The first publication of cancer mortality data in Poland took place 100 years ago in 1888. The evaluation of such data was greatly enhanced in the early 1960s when the Polish Cancer Registry was established at the Maria Skłodowska-Curie Memorial Cancer Institute in Warszawa. Data from this registry and their epidemiological analysis provided the basis for planning cancer control in Poland. The National Cancer Programme permitted a development of comprehensive cancer centres and cancer research.

Differences in cancer incidence and mortality observed in various regions of Poland have been evaluated during the past two decades using data collected by regional cancer registries operating in urban and rural areas of Warszawa, Upper Silesia and Krakow. The present *Atlas of Cancer Mortality in Poland* by Dr. Witold Zatonski and Dr. Nikolaus Becker sums up the epidemiological situation of cancer in Poland over the years 1963–1982 and presents geographical differences between the 49 voivodships (provinces), the basic administrative units in Poland, for more than 20 leading cancer sites.

It thus fulfills two tasks of growing importance. First, it meets the request from medical practicioners, research workers and political authorities for information on frequencies, time trends, and spatial distributions of the different cancer sites.

Secondly, it may promote epidemiological research on causal factors determining cancer occurrence in Poland. In this connection, it has to be kept in mind that the presentation of geographical distribution of diseases cannot by itself provide evidence for any speculations on causal relationships. Cancer mapping offers a valuable basis for obtaining new insights and creating new hypotheses. The proof will have to be left to the more refined research methods of modern epidemiology, which is also pursued at our institutes.

The present publication is a result of a very fruitful cooperation between the Maria Skłodowska-Curie Memorial Cancer Centre and Institute of Oncology in Warszawa and the Deutsches Krebsforschungszentrum (German Cancer Research Center) in Heidelberg. This cooperation secured high methodological standards, and it can contribute to filling the gaps in international studies on cancer mortality in Europe. The support from the Humboldt Foundation made this work possible, and the cooperation with the Springer-Verlag guaranteed high standards of editorship and printing of this monograph.

Professor Jan Steffen, M. D.
Director of Maria Skłodowska-Curie
Memorial Cancer Centre and
Institute of Oncology
Warszawa

Professor Dr. Harald zur Hausen
Chairman and Scientific Member
of the Management Board
Deutsches Krebsforschungszentrum
Heidelberg

Preface

The publication of cancer atlases of several different countries during the last few years has shown that knowledge of geographical variations in the frequency of the different cancer sites can yield valuable insight into cancer development. They have, on the one hand, made it possible to corroborate previous assumptions regarding certain regional frequency distributions and, on the other hand, to initiate further investigations of previously unknown findings.

High priority is given to the stepwise completion of the European map by supplying the tessera still missing from national cancer atlases. The supranational importance of national cancer atlases explains why they are increasingly becoming the product of international collaboration. Thus, as we all know, the International Agency for Research on Cancer (IARC), operated by the World Health Organisation (WHO) in Lyon is endeavouring to produce a supranational European cancer atlas.

Our work was made possible through the ready support and cooperation of many different institutions. Thanks are, above all, due to the Central Statistical Office (GUS) in Warszawa and the World Health Organisation (WHO) in Geneva who made the necessary data available to us.

Several colleagues in our two centres have provided scientific assistance. The project was carried out in Poland within the Polish National Cancer Program, sponsored in part by UNDP. Prof. T. Koszarowski and his successor as director of the Cancer Centre in Warsaw, Prof. J. Steffen, advocated our work. Particular thanks go to J. Didkowska, W. Chmielarczyk, T. Mantorska, T. Mykowiecki, J. Mierzwinska, K. Przewozniak, and W. Tarkowski from the Department of Cancer Control and Epidemiology, who kindly supported the project's implementation. We are also indebted to Miss B. Wiak for her editorial help and to Mr. K. Stadnik for his assistance in preparing the English version of the work.

Thanks are due to the chairman and scientific member of the management board of the German Cancer Research Centre, Prof. Dr. H. zur Hausen, who assisted us at all times while the project was being incorporated into the work of this institute and, by promising financial support, made its publication possible. Dr. R. Frentzel-Beyme and Prof. J. Wahrendorf devoted a great deal of time revising and correcting the text. Mrs. U. Klappauf and Mr. H. Trojan prepared the graphic and cartographic part of the book, and Mrs. M. Hochlehnert-Baum handled its editorial preparation.

We are grateful to our friends from the IARC Lyon, who were kind enough to revise parts of the text. Special thanks to M. Smans for his improvement of the cartographic presentation.

The fact that it has been possible to prepare a book from our research and analyses is due to the active support of Springer-Verlag and the Humboldt Foundation. Above all, thanks are due to Springer-Verlag who helped when several financial and technical difficulties seemed insurmountable. May we express our special gratitude to the Humboldt Foundation and the Federal Foreign Office for their generous grants.

There are a great number of persons apart from these who patiently assisted us in our work. Not all of them can be named here. To them, too, we want to express our gratitude.

Warszawa/Heidelberg, June 1988

W. Zatonski
N. Becker

Contents*

* A foldout map of the Polish provinces precedes the back cover.

Contents

Introduction

National and international data regarding malignant neoplasms show considerable geographical variation in incidence and mortality. Epidemiology, as the science concerned with the occurrence of diseases, must use this fact as a basis to find the factors causing these malignancies. Worldwide comparisons of cancer incidence and mortality give rise to the speculation that up to 80%-90% of all cancer might be related to the environment. The concept of "environment" is to be understood here in its broadest sense, i.e. comprising the entire surroundings of man. So we do not only include the ground, water and air, but also factors such as occupation, chemicals, housing and also socio-cultural factors including personal habits. The latter include tobacco smoking and alcohol consumption, type and amount of food eaten and also cultural behaviour, such as the age at which sexual intercourse first occurred or when the first pregnancy occurred.

In spite of the strong links to environmental factors, only relatively few of these have been proved to be well-established risk factors for cancer up to now. Therefore, epidemiological investigations concerning the geographical variation are still needed. However, we need to explain clearly what can and what cannot be achieved by cancer mapping.

In view of the many factors simultaneously involved in cancer etiology, it will generally be impossible to identify single risk factors using descriptive epidemiological studies. This means that cancer mapping may only have the task of providing information to form new hypotheses or perhaps to strengthen old ones but not to prove them. Further investigation then has to be carried out using the more specific methods of analytical epidemiology.

In order to be able to form hypotheses or even to have a full understanding of what is going on in the cancer landscape, a certain amount of information regarding the geography and demography of the respective territory is necessary. Therefore, the following sections contain a brief summary of these topics with regard to Poland.

Poland and Its Geography

Poland is situated in the middle of Europe (longitude: 12°-24° E). It covers an area of 312000 km^2 and has a population of over 37 million people. Its neighbour to the west is the German Democratic Republic (border: 460 km), to the south Czechoslovakia (border: 1310 km), to the east the Soviet Union (border: 1244 km) and to the north the Baltic Sea (coastline: 524 km). Poland is a lowland country. A total of 71.5% of its area is lower than 200 m. Areas above 500 m make up only 2.6% of the total territory. A total of 99.7% of the country lies within the Baltic basin. The drainage area of the River Vistula covers 56% and that of the River Odra 34% of the country's total area. Poland has many thousands of lakes whose combined area is around 3200 km^2. The area of over 9000 lakes is greater than 1 ha.

The territory of Poland belongs to the central European area of mixed forests. Today, forests cover some 24% of the whole country. Pine forests predominate in the lowland sandy regions, while the swampy areas are covered by deciduous forest comprising beeches, oaks, alders and mixed forests. Firs, spruces, and larches are found in the highlands.

Poland lies in the mild climatic zone characterised by transitory features of both the continental climate of eastern Europe and the maritime climate of its western regions. Variability is typical of the weather in Poland. The average temperature in January varies between −1° and −5° C, while the average temperature in July varies between +20° and +17° C. Southern Poland, especially the Tatra Mountains, has the heaviest precipitation exceeding 1000 mm annually. The plains of central Poland have the lowest precipitation. The southern coast of the Baltic Sea has the most fine days and the most intensive insolation in summer, whereas the Carpathians are most intensively insolated in winter. Insolation is milder in central Poland and at the foot of the Sudeten Mountains in the south-western Poland. The northeastern area has the smallest number of sunny days, up to 180 annually. The Sudeten Mountains also have a large amount of cloud.

Poland's raw material base is relatively rich. The main raw material is anthracite, which is found in the southern, southwestern and eastern regions known as Upper Silesia, Lower Silesia and the Lubelszczyzna, respectively. There are also large deposits of lignite in southwestern and central Poland. There are abundant deposits of sulphur and rock salt, raw materials vital for the chemical industry, within the borders of Poland. The deposits of sulphur are among the biggest in the world. The country also has smaller deposits of copper in Lower Silesia.

Population[1]

The population of Poland has increased steadily since World War II. In 1945 the population was 24 million, by 1985 the figure had increased to 37 million. The last census done in 1978 showed a considerable disproportion in the age structure of the population. There are distinct gaps in the age groups born during both World Wars, while th groups born immediately after the wars show peak in the birth rate. As late as 1950, one-third of th population belonged to the group aged unde 15 years. In 1978 one-third of population was age under 24 years. The 1960s and the 1970s were char acterised by an increasing proportion of people olc er than 60 years; this group represented 9.6% of th population in 1960 and 13.2% in 1978 (Table 1). A comparison of the demographic structure of Pc land, Europe and the world shows that Polan ranks between Europe and the world as a whole The Polish population has more people under 3 than Europe but fewer than the world, while ther are more people over 60 in Poland than in th world, but fewer than in Europe (Table 1).

Crude live birth rates were very high in Poland a the end of the 1940s and during the 195C (1950–1954 30.1 per 1000). Whereas in the 196C and 1970s the rates decreased, the crude live birt rate level is still high in comparison to other Eurc pean countries (about 20 per 1000). Total fertilit rates and age-specific fertility rates are similar. Th fertility of females has been decreasing in succes sive birth cohorts. Fertility differs significantly i rural and urban populations. The percentage c women using oral contraceptives is low (2% i

[1] Data from the Polish Central Statistical Office (GUS).

Table 1. The structure of polish population[a] by sex and age groups and the structure of standard world population[b]

	Male		Female		Stand. world population
Age groups	No	%	No	%	%
0– 4	1613358	9.44	1541938	8.57	12
5– 9	388489	8.13	1326246	7.34	10
10–14	1302469	7.62	1243362	6.91	9
15–19	1516696	8.88	1426573	7.93	9
20–24	1748899	10.23	1681447	9.36	8
25–29	1652152	9.67	1606980	8.93	8
30–34	1210850	7.09	1197537	6.66	6
35–39	959998	5.62	968461	5.38	6
40–44	1059283	6.20	1082431	6.02	6
45–49	1094569	6.41	1131304	6.29	6
50–54	952198	5.57	1100620	6.12	5
55–59	742610	4.35	907015	5.04	4
60–64	466646	2.73	614425	3.42	4
65–69	573499	3.36	773420	4.30	3
70–74	425376	2.49	630217	3.50	2
75–79	240535	1.41	428156	2.38	1
80–84	99711	0.58	219654	1.22	0.5
85+	41576	0.24	111982	0.62	0.5
Total	17088914	100.0	17991768	100.0	100.0

[a] Data from the last National Census 1978.
[b] CIFC (1982).

1972). The number of induced abortions is estimated to be about 600000–700000 (Lopez 1984).
The infant mortality in Poland during the inter-war years remained stable (127–147 per 1000). Since World War II the infant mortality has undergone a constant and substantial decline from 116 per 1000 in 1951 to 18.4 per 1000 in 1985. Mortality of children under 15 has also dropped over the last two decades. In comparison to the constant fall in child mortality, mortality in older age groups has been variable depending on the time period, age and sex. By the mid-1960s, male mortality had decreased in all the age groups. The life expectancy increased very significantly, during the first 20 years after World War II from 48.2 years before the war to 66.9 in 1965. The life expectancy of an average Pole in 1965 was compared favourably with the data of countries such as the Federal Republic of Germany or Finland. This desirable trend stopped in the 1970s and was even reversed for men over 45. The women's mortality rates have decreased steadily in all age groups since World War II. Life expectancy has grown constantly over recent years.
This difference in the male and female mortality rates give Poland the highest difference in life expectancies of any European country (i.e. 12.3% in 1984; in men 66.8 years and in women 75.0). This difference is 6 years for persons aged over 45 (i.e. 23.4% in 1984; in men 26.5 years and in women 32.7).
In the early 1980s the causes of death in Poland were distributed similarly to other European countries. The frequency of cancer as a cause of death in men increased from 11.9% in 1960 to 19.5% in 1983. In women this increase was smaller with an upward tendency only until 1970 (13.8% in 1960; 17.4% in 1970; 17.1% in 1983). The other main death causes include cardiovascular disease (48% of deaths in men and 54% in women), accidents and intoxication, which is responsible for 10% of deaths in men and 4% in women. The contribution of tuberculosis and other infections and parasitic diseases has declined steadily in Poland.
Poland's urban population grew rapidly after 1945. Immediately after World War II the country/town ratio dropped from 2/3 to 1/3. The urban and rural populations were the same in 1966, and in 1978 57.5% of Poles lived in towns. The rapid urbanisation which occurred in Poland after the war triggered other significant social changes. The most important was a gradual disappearance of the differentiation between the rural and urban styles and standards of living. Nevertheless, the division into town and country remains one of the key features dividing the population of Poland. Living standards, the family model, the amount of food consumption, the amount of leisure time and the way it is spent, as well as living and health conditions are the chief parameters of the quality of life in villages and towns.
The employment of women grew dramatically during the first few years after 1945. As well as the absolute figures, the percentage of women in general employment increased, too, rising by nearly 10% in the years 1961–1970 alone to reach 43% by 1978.
Of the total working population 35% have primary education and the number of people with secondary, higher and vocational education keeps growing. The stratification of wages in the state economy in Poland is small. Food is still the number one item in Polish family budgets.

Employment[1]

Agriculture

For centuries the majority of Polish people earned their living by farm work. In 1938, two thirds of the Poles were employed in this way; until 1938 agriculture contributed 55% of the national income. After World War II farms over 50 ha (in the northern and western regions over 100 ha) were divided among the peasants. Most of the arable land (76.4%) is now held by private farmers. Large state-run farms account for 18.8% of all Polish arable land and farm production cooperatives cultivate 3.7%. About 30% of the farms were smaller than 2 ha and nearly 60% were smaller than 5 ha in 1984. The principal crops are cereals (over 50% of the area) and potatoes (18%). Sugar beet, oil plants and tobacco are of some significance, too. Farmers (almost 100% of them are private farmers) sowed 52000 ha with tobacco in 1985, which gave them a harvest of 111000 tonnes. Nearly all the tobacco grown in Poland is of a coarse, shag-like type.
In recent years Poland has developed horticulture and market gardening intensively. Traditionally, apples are the most common fruit representing 78% of all the fruit harvested by Polish growers in 1985. Despite this high production, Poland's fruit market shows strong seasonal fluctuations caused by low technical standards of fruit processing and storage. In practice, only apples are available throughout the year. The only fruit easily available on the market is that which is grown domestically. The import of citrus fruits is insignificant. Vegetable growing

[1] Source: Polish Central Statistical Office (GUS).

occupies 1.7% of the total area cultivated. The principal vegetables are: cabbage, onions, carrots, beets, cucumbers and tomatoes. Potatoes deserve special attention as they continue to be the basic item in the Polish diet. The potato harvest reached 36 546 000 tonnes in 1985. The proportion of vegetables grown in greenhouses, under glass or in cellophane tunnels has increased significantly in recent years. This type of vegetable production occupied an area of 35 389 m^2 in 1985.

Industry

The Polish economic system after World War II was founded on the principles of central economic planning by the state as well as on sweeping social reforms: the agrarian reform, the nationalisation of key industries and the establishment of a state monopoly over foreign trade. The structure of employment in the Polish economy is undergoing gradual transformation. In 1950 only 53% of the population worked in branches other than farming. This went up to 76% by 1979, and the percentage of workers in the production industries rose to over 30%. The largest Polish employer, the engineering industry, produces the major part of the nation's total industrial output. In comparison to the global industrial structure, mining takes an exceptionally high shar of the gross national income and of exports. Abot 40% of Polish industry is located in Upper an Lower Silesia. The largest industrial district, th GOP (Upper Silesian Industrial Region) is wher anthracite is mined alongside industries such as fe rous and non-ferrous metallurgy and engineerin The Polish capital Warsaw is also a major industri centre. Several new industrial districts were create after World War II in a process of rapid industrial sation: the district of Rybnik, with coking coal, th Legnica-Glogow district with copper, and the dis trict of Tarnobrzeg where sulphur is obtained.

Diet

Most of the Polish population before and immed ately after World War II followed a diet typical of developing rural country. The caloric demand wa met first of all with vegetable products such as ce reals and potatoes. Early in the 1950s cereals const tuted nearly 50% and potatoes up to 20% of the ca orific value of the diet. Meat provided much les than 10% of the caloric value (Sekula et al. 1985 Several trends were observed between 1950 and th end of the 1970s (Table 2):

Table 2. Selected food items consumption in Poland in years 1950–1983 (per person annually)

Year	Cereal	Potatoes	Vegetable	Fruits	Meats and pluck (kg)			
	kg	kg	kg	kg	Total	Pork	Beef	Pluck
1950	166	270	60.6	8.3	36.5	29.9	5.9	–
1951	160	243	56.3	16.8	36.7	–	–	–
1952	161	243	62.2	8.2	32.7	–	–	–
1953	163	248	70.5	14.6	35.2	–	–	–
1954	166	224	84.4	9.6	36.2	–	–	–
1955	171	229	67.4	12.8	37.7	29.2	4.8	–
1956	151	235	71.8	18.1	41.0	–	–	–
1957	154	234	80.6	12.8	43.9	–	–	–
1958	142	232	74.8	21.6	45.3	–	–	–
1959	144	226	76.0	15.6	44.1	–	–	–
1960	145	223	85.6	19.5	42.5	32.8	7.0	1.6
1961	147	223	84.4	18.1	45.2	–	–	–
1962	148	221	79.1	11.2	45.8	–	–	–
1963	143	218	95.8	19.2	46.3	–	–	–
1964	141	217	95.0	30.1	47.1	–	–	–
1965	141	215	95.4	15.5	49.2	36.0	10.0	–
1966	137	211	102.0	33.2	51.0	–	–	–
1967	136	207	93.6	28.6	52.3	–	–	–
1968	133	201	90.5	34.5	52.2	–	–	–
1969	132	199	86.1	21.0	52.6	–	–	–
1970	131	190	111.0	32.8	53.0	29.2	12.6	3.5
1971	128	189	85.8	20.3	56.1	32.8	12.5	–

Table 2 (continued)

Year	Cereal	Potatoes	Vegetable	Fruits	Meats and pluck (kg)			
	kg	kg	kg	kg	Total	Pork	Beef	Pluck
1972	127	187	83.8	18.7	59.3	37.3	10.8	-
1973	125	183	93.0	20.3	62.1	38.8	11.5	-
1974	123	177	84.3	19.4	65.6	39.4	13.1	-
1975	120	173	109.0	34.4	70.3	40.9	15.5	6.3
1976	122	173	99.3	41.8	70.0	34.5	20.4	7.6
1977	121	168	96.3	43.5	69.1	33.5	20.0	8.8
1978	120	166	105.0	40.8	70.6	36.5	17.3	9.7
1979	120	163	116.0	41.5	73.0	38.0	17.1	10.8
1980	127	158	101.0	37.7	74.0	37.2	18.5	11.2
1981	121	157	118.0	32.4	65.0	31.7	15.6	11.6
1982	119	155	107.0	42.8	58.5	31.9	14.4	5.5
1983	122	154	103.0	38.0	58.2	30.6	16.0	5.3

Years	Fish	Fats (kg)				Milk	Eggs	Sugar
	kg	Total	Animal[a]	Vegetable	Butter	(l)	(pieces)	kg
1950	1.7	11.2	6.2	1.7	3.3	206	116	21.0
1951	1.8	11.4	5.8	1.7	3.9	215	127	24.9
1952	2.3	11.1	5.2	1.9	4.0	208	130	22.4
1953	2.1	11.3	5.5	1.8	4.0	204	125	19.9
1954	2.5	12.1	5.7	1.8	4.6	201	135	22.4
1955	2.7	12.8	6.1	1.9	4.8	204	132	24.0
1956	3.0	13.7	6.8	1.9	5.0	208	127	25.2
1957	3.3	14.1	7.2	1.8	5.1	213	133	26.5
1958	3.4	14.6	7.4	2.2	5.0	226	134	28.5
1959	4.4	15.0	7.2	2.8	5.0	227	141	29.6
1960	4.5	15.6	7.4	3.5	4.7	227	143	27.9
1961	4.1	16.0	7.3	4.0	4.7	230	148	30.6
1962	4.2	16.3	7.1	4.6	4.6	232	150	30.2
1963	4.4	16.5	6.5	5.4	4.6	230	147	32.3
1964	4.6	17.3	6.8	5.9	4.6	228	154	32.4
1965	5.0	17.5	6.8	5.7	5.0	233	162	32.6
1966	5.0	17.8	6.9	5.6	5.3	246	169	34.1
1967	5.0	18.3	7.1	5.5	5.7	250	171	35.5
1968	5.5	19.5	8.2	5.5	5.8	253	172	36.7
1969	5.8	20.1	8.4	5.8	5.9	258	182	37.2
1970	6.3	20.8	8.2	6.6	6.0	262	186	39.2
1971	6.4	20.8	7.8	6.7	6.3	266	193	39.6
1972	6.8	21.2	7.9	6.8	6.5	263	196	40.9
1973	7.2	22.3	8.4	7.2	6.7	263	200	42.0
1974	7.3	22.5	8.2	7.5	6.8	261	205	43.9
1975	7.2	23.0	8.1	7.5	7.4	264	209	43.2
1976	7.7	23.5	8.0	7.8	7.7	263	214	43.9
1977	7.6	24.4	8.3	8.0	8.1	263	214	41.5
1978	7.3	24.8	8.1	8.0	8.7	264	219	42.7
1979	7.6	25.1	8.3	8.0	8.8	264	220	43.9
1980	8.1	24.8	8.1	7.8	8.9	262	223	41.4
1981	7.3	24.6	7.3	8.4	8.9	257	227	33.4
1982	6.0	21.5	6.8	7.3	7.4	247	200	41.7
1983	7.0	22.0	7.0	6.7	8.3	277	198	45.0

[a] Animal fat excluding butter.
Source: Sekula (1985).

- Increase in calorific value; annual growth rate about 0.5%
- Rapid growth in the consumption of fats, especially vegetable fats (more than five times),[1] and in the consumption of meat[2] (more than 4% annually)
- An increase also occurred in the consumption of milk, butter, hens eggs and sugar
- At the same time the intake of cereal products[3] dropped by about 1% annually as did the consumption of potatoes, also by 1% annually

The consumption of vegetables is made of six basics: cabbage, carrots, beets, onions, cucumbers and tomatoes. Cabbage constitutes for about 40% of the total consumption. Cabbage and cucumbers are consumed partly in a processed, conserved form. Fruit consumption includes several basics: apples, stone fruits and berries. Apples make up 50%-60% of the total fruit consumption and are the only fruit available throughout the year. The consumption of citrus fruits and other southern fruits is very low.

In the late 1970s cereals and potatoes provided only a little more than 40% of the daily energy intake, while fats and meat represented nearly 30% of this demand. Cow milk, sugar and its products represented over 10% of the daily energy intake (Sekula et al. 1985). A high proportion of sausage meat (more than 40%) was typical of the meat consumption in Poland. The consumption of sausage products was high, while the consumption of fresh meat was low. Poland distinguished itself among other European countries by a low consumption of coffee and a relatively high consumption of tea.

Alcohol

Poland is among the countries of average alcohol consumption. However, its structure, the Scandinavian style of drinking - the phenomenon of "concentration of alcohol consumption" - and the dramatic increase of intake over the years 1965-1980 have made alcohol a serious health hazard. The consumption of alcohol in Poland, as in other European countries, has an age-old tradition. Beer, wine and meads were the most commonly drunk beverages in ancient times. Distilled alcohol started to spread in the fifteenth century. In Poland alcohol is distilled from potatoes, grain and sometimes fruit. High alcohol content (35%-40%) is the general feature and the various types of distilled products are collectively named "vodka". From 1945 to the mid-1960s, Poland was among the countries with low alcohol consumption, averaging about 4.0 litres of pure alcohol per capita annually. The post-war era saw a growth in alcohol consumption in Poland as in other European countries (Table 3). The consumption rate grew from 3.9 litres in 1964 to 8.4 litres per capita in 1980, which placed Poland among the countries of medium alcohol consumption. These figures dropped to 6.2 litres in the period 1981-1983. A new problem of growing home distillation emerging as a result of the recent price policy aimed at discouraging alcohol consumption. The production of "moonlight" is estimated to add 10%-15% to the total state-controlled production.

With regard to alcohol consumption, Poland resembles some of the Scandinavian countries and the Soviet Union. Vodka makes up 70% of all the alcohol consumed, with beer and wine representing 15% each. As vodka predominates, other alcoholic drinks are a mere complement. Opinion polls show an interdependence between the consumption of various alcohols. Drinking one kind of spirit, most frequently vodka, accelerates the frequency of drinking others (Jasinski 1984). Vodka is traditionally and culturally the most widely accepted, and perhaps preferred, alcoholic beverage. An interesting proof for this can be seen in the structure of abstinence from various types of alcohol in the Polish population. A survey carried out in 1980 showed that 31% of men and 82% of women do not drink beer. Over 50% men and women do not drink wine, and, at the same time, only 12% of men and 36% of women abstain from drinking vodka. The proportion of men not drinking vodka has not changed much over the last 20 years. The figure is not much different for city dwellers (13.6%) and villagers (9.8%). The proportion of women abstaining, in both towns and villages, has changed very significantly in relation to that of in 1960s, with the difference exceeding 10% (Jasinski 1984). Alcohol consumption in Poland differs considerably according to sex: the ratio for men to women is approximately 5 to 1.

Scandinavian-style drinking predominates in Poland. It consists of drinking large amounts of strong drinks at one time. The mean frequency of this type of drinking showed an increasing trend in the

[1] Greater consumption of vegetable fats was achieved by increasing the consumption of hardened fats (margarines) made mainly of rapeseed oil in Poland.

[2] Pork, beef and poultry make up 90% of the meat consumption in Poland, in which pork represents some 50%-60%.

[3] This was accompanied by a change in the structure of cultivated grains. Rye constitued 60% of consumption in the 1950s but 20% in the end of 1970s, whereas wheat rose from about 35% to 70%.

Table 3. Alcohol consumption in Poland, 1923-1938 and 1950-1983 (in litres alcohol per person)

Year	Consumption per year	% of total alcohol cons.		
		Vodka	Wine	Beer
1923	2.0	–	–	–
1924	1.9	–	–	–
1925	1.6	–	–	–
1926	1.3	–	–	–
1927	1.1	–	–	–
1928	1.3	–	–	–
1929	1.7	–	–	–
1930	1.4	–	–	–
1931	0.9	–	–	–
1932	0.7	–	–	–
1933	0.8	–	–	–
1934	0.8	–	–	–
1935	0.9	–	–	–
1936	1.0	–	–	–
1937	1.1	–	–	–
1938	1.3	–	–	–
1950	3.0	77.3	3.7	18.7
1951	3.0	74.7	4.7	20.0
1952	3.0	74.7	6.0	21.3
1953	3.1	69.7	6.5	25.8
1954	3.3	67.9	7.9	24.2
1955	3.3	69.1	9.1	23.0
1956	3.4	69.4	10.3	22.4
1957	4.1	69.3	10.5	19.5
1958	3.9	65.6	12.3	21.5
1959	4.0	63.0	14.5	23.0
1960	3.8	63.2	14.2	24.2
1961	4.0	61.0	15.3	24.0
1962	3.9	62.6	15.1	22.6
1963	4.0	63.0	14.0	24.0
1964	3.9	60.5	15.1	24.6
1965	4.1	62.4	14.1	23.4
1966	4.3	64.2	12.6	24.2
1967	4.6	65.2	12.2	24.3
1968	5.0	65.6	12.0	23.2
1969	5.3	64.2	12.6	22.6
1970	5.1	62.4	13.1	24.6
1971	5.5	62.6	13.2	24.2
1972	6.0	64.0	12.6	23.3
1973	6.4	64.7	12.0	23.3
1974	6.2	64.1	12.8	23.1
1975	6.9	66.1	12.8	21.2
1976	7.8	69.1	13.0	17.9
1977	8.3	70.2	13.3	16.5
1978	8.0	70.2	14.0	15.8
1979	8.0	69.8	14.7	15.5
1980	8.4	70.6	15.0	14.4
1981	6.4	–	–	–
1982	6.1	–	–	–
1983	6.2	65.4	17.0	17.6

Source: G U S.

1960s, but rose significantly in the 1970s. The number of persons drinking a lot at one time was also on the increase. The survey mentioned above shows that nearly 90% of men and over 60% of women in Poland are occasionally exposed to strong alcohol. This exposure, however, differs greatly from person to person. This is because more than 80% of the people who use alcohol are exposed to it only a few times a year, usually on family and social occasions, but these occasions then involve large amounts. Beside the majority that drinks little (83% of the population using alcohol in 1980) there is a sub-population constituting 17% of all alcohol users, i.e. some 3-3.5 million people in 1980, who drink every day or nearly every day thus consuming two-thirds of all the alcohol consumed in the country (Jasinski 1984).

Tobacco

In the late 1970s Poland was one of the European countries where the pandemia of nicotinism reached a peak. Heavy tobacco smoking is a new phenomenon in this country: tobacco consumption in the inter-war years was low, but World War II brought wide exposure to tobacco, especially for men. After the war cigarettes were cheap and easy to obtain. Cigarette smoking has grown into something of a symbol of progress and democratisation. Tobacco consumption in Poland is practically confined to cigarette smoking. Cigarette smokers constitute over 90% of all Polish tobacco smokers. Pipes, cigars and cheroots are rarely smoked. Almost all the cigarettes available on the Polish market are made in Poland from a native shag-like tobacco. Less than half of the brands manufactured are filter-tipped. In addition, the quality of the filters is poor. Polish cigarettes contain a very high level of tar and nicotine (Zatonski et al. 1986). Tobacco consumption increased sharply after World War II (Table 4). By the end of the 1970s Poland had reached an annual consumption rate of 3600 cigarettes per person, which put it high among the world's biggest tobacco consumers. However, consumption dropped in the early 1980s. The number of smokers was estimated at about 12 million in 1982. This number was made up of 8 million men and 4 million women. The percentage rate of male smokers was about 60% in the early 1970s and no major changes have been recorded over the last decade (Table 5). At present male city dwellers do not differ much from their rural counterparts in the frequency of smoking. However, it is clear that adult men in middle age are the heaviest smokers: some

Table 4. Cigarette consumption in Poland, 1950-1984

Year	Cigarette consumption (in pieces)	
	(per person)	(per person > 15 years)
1950	1063	-
1951	1120	-
1952	1169	-
1953	1204	-
1954	1278	-
1955	1378	-
1956	1471	-
1957	1511	-
1958	1522	-
1959	1556	-
1960	1543	2314
1961	1668	-
1962	1712	-
1963	1680	2475
1964	1855	2432
1965	1977	2465
1966	1815	2565
1967	1841	2611
1968	1971	2750
1969	2093	2865
1970	2097	2845
1971	2233	2998
1972	2281	3007
1973	2351	3121
1974	2389	3136
1975	2499	3289
1976	2562	3363
1977	2613	3350
1978	2573	3382
1979	2741	3611
1980	2679	3542
1981	2464	3267
1982	2398	3191
1983	2350	3010
1984	2490	3148

Source: G U S.

80% of those in the 30-34 age group are smokers and in the 35-49 age group the rate is nearly 70%. Polish men are also subject to longer exposure to tobacco. In 1982, 5.3 million of them had been exposed for more than 10 years. The average number of cigarettes smoked by the men per day is greater than the number of cigarettes smoked by the women. The frequency of cigarette smoking among women rocketed from 17.7% in 1974 to 30.3% in 1982 (Table 5). The heaviest female smokers are aged 30-34 (nearly 60%), while older groups smoke less. Only 5% of women over 60 smoked in 1982. Place of residence differentiates women smokers in a significant way: rural women smoke less, whereas

Table 5. The frequency of tobacco smoking in Poland

		Male	Female
		in %	in %
Year	1974	59.3	17.7
	1980	53.4	19.5
	1982	62.2	30.3
Place of residence	Village	61.0	20.3
	Town up 100,000 inhab.	65.2	35.8
	Town over 100,000 inhab.	60.8	37.3
Age	15-19	31.3	14.3
	20-24	66.7	40.0
	25-29	60.8	53.9
	30-34	80.9	57.4
	35-39	69.4	34.2
	40-49	69.5	24.4
	50-59	65.1	24.2
	60+	50.0	5.5

Source: Zatonski et al. (1986).

women living in towns, especially large towns, smoke much more frequently (Table 5). Women usually smoke shorter and fewer cigarettes per day. They also tend to use filter-tipped brands and inhale the smoke deeply much less frequently (Zatonski et al. 1986).

Characteristics of the Provinces (Table 6)

Biala Podlaska (Eastern Poland). Rural, one of the least densely populated provinces and next to last in degree of urbanisation. Principal crops are rye, potatoes and oats. Best-developed industries are electroengineering and food processing.

Bialystok (Northeastern Poland). An agricultural and industrial province with average population density and average urbanisation. Forests (among them large primeval forests) cover over 30% of its area. Well-developed electroengineering, food, timber and light industries. Average agricultural indices.

Bielsko-Biala (Southern Poland). An industrial province with dense population but urbanisation is below the national average. A mountainous area (the Beskid Mountains) with poor soils. Well-developed electroengineering, textile, chemical and food-processing industries. High rate of industrial employment. An attractive tourist area.

Bydgoszcz (Northern Poland). An industrial and agricultural province with lower population density and higher urbanisation than the national average. Well-developed electroengineering, food, chemical, timber and paper industries. High agricultural output, despite relatively poor soils.

Chelm (Eastern Poland). An agricultural province, among the least densely populated and last urbanised areas in Poland. Principal crops are rye, wheat and potatoes. The best-developed industries are those processing hides, minerals and food products.

Ciechanow (Central Poland). A rural province with low population density and urbanisation. Well-developed animal breeding, food and electroengineering industries.

Czestochowa (Central Poland). Industrial-agricultural orientation, average population density and urbanisation. Well-developed electroengineering, metallurgical and light industries. Average farming output.

Elblag (Situated on the Vistula Bay in northern Poland). An industrial-agricultural province with low population density and average urbanisation. Developed electroengineering, food-processing, and light industries. The land is among the best in Poland, the chief crops are fodder, barley and wheat. Good animal breeding. Some of its area lies below sea level.

Gdansk (A coastal province in the north of Poland). Maritime economy and ship-building play the greatest role. A densely populated and highly urbanised province, it is also an attractive tourist area thanks to its closeness to the sea. The biggest cultural and scientific centre in the north of Poland.

Gorzow (Western Poland). An industrial-agricultural province with low population density and average urbanisation. One of the most densely forested provinces with forests covering 44.4% of the area. Developed electroengineering and chemical industries.

Jelenia Gora (Southwestern Poland). Industrially orientated province with average population density and urbanisation above the national average. Developed electroengineering and light industries. Large coal mining centre partly occupying hilly terrain (the Sudeten Mountains). An attractive tourist area.

Kalisz (Western part of central Poland). An industrial-agricultural province with average population density and urbanisation below the national average. Developed electroengineering and food-processing industries. High level of farming and animal breeding.

Katowice (Southern Poland). The largest industrial centre where 18.9% of all workers in the production industries are employed and where 18.9% of the total production is generated. One of the most densely populated and urbanised provinces. Industries include fuel-energy, metallurgical and chemical industries. Agriculture plays a secondary role in the area. Severely threatened environment.

Kielce (Western part of central Poland). An industrial-agricultural province where there is a large lignite mining centre together with power plants. Electroengineering, food and light industries are also well developed. Employment is below the national average, low urbanisation.

Koszalin (A northern province on the Baltic coast with more farming than industry). Population density low, urbanisation high. Principal crops: fodder, rye, potatoes. Forests cover 36.8% of the area. Developed electroengineering, food processing and timber industries. The province is also attractive for tourists.

Krakow (Southern Poland). Highly industrialised province with dense population and advanced urbanisation. Large metallurgical, electroengineering, food and chemical industries. Agriculture has a minor role. Severly threatened environment. The city of Kracow, Poland's former capital, is today one of the nation's greatest cultural and scientific centres.

Krosno (Southeastern Poland). A province with industry, farming and forestry. Poorly urbanized and populated. Major industries are: electroengineering, chemicals and minerals. Principal crops include fodder and wheat. Efficient cattle breeding. A total of 47.3% of its area is covered by forests. Attractive tourist area (mountains).

Legnica (Southwestern Poland). An industrial province with average population density but advanced urbanisation. Basic industries are related to the extraction and processing of copper ores. Good animal breeding. Threatened environment.

Leszno (Western Poland). A rural province with population and urbanisation below the national average. Advanced knowledge of agricultural techniques among farmers, and high farm outputs per hectare. Principal crops: rye, fodder and potatoes. Good animal breeding, especially of pigs.

Lublin (Southeastern Poland). An industrial-rural province with population and urbanisation indices above the average. Best-developed in the province are the electroengineering, food-processing, chemical and light industries. Developed animal breeding. Major university centre.

Lomza (Northeastern Poland). A rural province with population and urbanisation indices among the lowest in Poland. The food-processing and light industries are the best-developed branches. Farming output is low.

Lodz (Central Poland). An industrial province, one of the most densely populated and urbanised. Light (textile) industry predominates but the electroengineering, chemical and food-processing industries are also strong. Agricultural production concentrates on horticulture and animal breeding. A major cultural and scientific centre. The city of Lodz is Poland's second largest (about 800000 inhabitants).

Nowy Sacz (Southern Poland). Mostly rural, with average population density and low urbanisation. Developed animal breeding, especially of sheep. Food-processing industry predominates. Attractive landscape (mountains, among them the Tatra Mountains) brings a large income from tourism. Forests cover 42.4% of the area.

Olsztyn (Northeastern Poland). Agricultural and industrial, with low population density and average urbanisation level. Well-developed breeding of pigs and cattle. The electroengineering and light industries are the best-developed branches. Attractive landscape (lake district) makes it a popular area in summer.

Opole (Southwestern Poland). An industrial province with average population density and urbanisation indices. Nearly all industrial branches are well developed. Advanced knowledge of farming techniques and good productivity per hectare, especially of wheat.

Ostroleka (Northeastern Poland). A rural province with close to the lowest population density and urbanisation in Poland. Low farming efficiency. The best-developed industries are electroengineering and timber-paper.

Pila (Northwestern Poland). A rural-industrial province with low population density and average urbanisation. Electroengineering and timber industries are the best-developed. Large forests cover about 40% of the area.

Piotrkow Trybunalski (Central Poland). An industrial-rural province with both population density and urbanisation below the national average. Main industrial branches: electroengineering, fuel-energy (large lignite mining area and a huge power plant in Belchatow). Well-developed sheep breeding.

Plock (Central Poland). A rural-industrial province with population and urbanisation below the Polish average. Advanced knowledge of farming techniques among farmers who reach good productivity per hectare of arable land. Electroengineering, fuel and food industries are the best developed branches in the province.

Poznan (Western Poland). An industrial-rural province which is fairly densely populated and urbanised. Electroengineering, food-processing and light industries are the best developed branches. Very good farming with productivity per hectare of arable land among the highest in Poland. Intensive animal breeding, especially of pigs (highest output in Poland). Important cultural and scientific centre.

Przemysl (Southeastern Poland). An agricultural-industrial province, with low population density and similar urbanisation indices. Pig breeding is the best-developed sector of agricultural production. Main industries: light industry, electroengineering, food-processing.

Radom (Central Poland). An agricultural-industrial province with both population density and urbanisation below the national average. Most of Poland's orchards are here. The province's best-developed industrial branches are: electroengineering, light and food-processing.

Rzeszow (Southeastern Poland). A province of industrial-rural character. Population density is above the national average but urbanisation indices are low. Main industries: electroengineering and food-processing. Good animal breeding.

Siedlce (Central Poland). A rural province with nearly the lowest population density and urbanisation in Poland. Biggest potato producing area in Poland. Well-developed animal breeding, especially of pigs. Main industries: electroengineering, food-processing, and light industries.

Sieradz (Central Poland). An agricultural-industrial province. Population density and urbanisation among the lowest in Poland. Average agricultural output, good animal breeding. The strongest industries are the engineering and light industries.

Skierniewice (Central Poland). An agricultural-industrial province with population density below the national average. Urbanisation indices low as well. Vegetable and fruit growing covers relatively large areas. Good animal breeding. Main industries: textiles and electroengineering industry. One of the most wooded provinces.

Slupsk (A Baltic coastal province of agricultural-industrial character). The population density is low and urbanisation average. Forestry and fishing are important (forest covers 41.6% of the area). Developed electroengineering and light industries. The province is attractive to tourists owing to its coast and lakes.

Suwalki (Northeastern Poland). A province of rural-industrial character, low population density, and urbanisation indices below the national average. Developed forestry and fisheries (forest covers 31.8% of the area). Food-processing industry.

Szczecin (Northwestern Poland, on the Baltic coast). A province of an industrial-agricultural orientation, population density below national average but urbanisation very advanced. Developed maritime economy and industries related to it. Farm output in the province is among the highest in Poland. An attractive tourist area and major cultural and scientific centre.

Tarnobrzeg (Southeastern Poland). An industrial-agricultural province with population density below national average and similar urbanisation indices. Extraction of vast sulphur deposits; electroengineering and chemical industries. Well-developed pig breeding.

Tarnow (Southern Poland, the strip of sub-Carpathian hills). An industrial-rural province, densely populated but urbanisation indices are still low. Developed chemical and electroengineering industries. Principal crops: fodder, wheat, potatoes.

Torun (Northern part of central Poland). An industrial-rural province with average population density and average urbanisation. Developed electroengineering, chemical and food-processing industries. Main crops include fodder. Good animal breeding.

Walbrzych (Southwestern Poland). High population density and urbanisation indices. An industrially orientated province with well-developed tourist trade (in the Sudeten Mountains). The developed industries include: textiles, electroengineering, coal-mining, mineral, food-processing and others.

Warszawa (Central Poland). The province's profile is determined by the capital of Poland Warsaw. The province is highly industrialised and is one of the most densely populated and urbanised provinces in Poland. It has well-developed electroengineering, food-processing, chemical and light industries. Farming predominates in the rural areas. The centre of cultural and scientific life in Poland.

Wloclawek (Central Poland). A rural-industrial province with both population density and urbanisation below the national average. Efficient agriculture achieves high productivity per hectare. Developed electroengineering, food-processing and chemical industries.

Wroclaw (Southwestern Poland). A province of industrial-rural orientation, densely populated and strongly urbanised. Developed electroengineering, food-processing, light and chemical industries. Productivity figures per hectare rank among the highest nationally with principal crops including wheat, barley, and fodder. One of Poland's major centres of culture and science.

Zamosc (Eastern Poland). A rural province with low population density and the lowest urbanisation indices but good farming output. Poland's best sugar beet and wheat output. Food-processing and light industries.

Zielona Gora (Western Poland). An industrial-rural province, with low population density and average urbanisation. Developed electroengineering, chemical and light industries; average farming output. The most densely forested province with 48.2% of area covered by forest.

Table 6a. Selected facts about polish provinces

Province	Area in sq. km.	Population (in thous.)	Population per sq. km.	Population in towns %	Women per 100 men
1 Biała Podlaska	10055	636.5	63.0	53.5	105.0
2 Białystok	5348	285.0	53.3	29.1	103.2
3 Bielsko Biała	3703	820.0	222.0	47.6	106.2
4 Bydgoszcz	10348	1027.0	99.0	61.6	106.0
5 Chełm	3865	229.3	59.3	36.4	105.2
6 Ciechanów	6362	403.5	62.7	29.9	102.7
7 Częstochowa	6182	745.0	121.0	49.0	106.0
8 Elbląg	6103	437.2	71.6	56.7	101.5
9 Gdańsk	7394	1300.0	178.0	76.1	102.9
10 Gorzów Wielkopolski	8484	449.0	53.0	58.4	103.0
11 Jelenia Góra	4378	490.0	111.9	63.9	106.0
12 Kalisz	6512	663.9	101.9	43.1	106.8
13 Katowice	6650	3700.0	552.9	87.3	101.4
14 Kielce	9211	1000.1	115.4	41.5	105.4
15 Konin	5139	438.0	85.3	35.8	103.8
16 Koszalin	8470	456.0	53.8	59.3	102.4
17 Kraków	3255	1100.0	355.0	68.4	108.0
18 Krosno	5702	443.0	77.8	30.5	106.2
19 Legnica	4037	449.0	111.3	62.4	100.1
20 Leszno	4154	354.0	85.4	43.6	105.4
21 Lublin	6793	925.0	136.2	52.5	107.1
22 Łomża	6684	324.0	48.5	30.9	101.3
23 Łódź	1523	1100.0	736.1	91.2	114.8
24 Nowy Sącz	5576	623.0	111.7	34.8	106.9
25 Olsztyn	12327	675.0	111.7	53.7	106.9
26 Opole	8535	969.0	113.6	49.2	106.7
27 Ostrołęka	6498	369.0	56.8	27.8	100.8
28 Piła	8205	431.0	52.6	51.6	102.5
29 Piotrków Trybunalski	6266	600.0	95.6	41.3	104.4
30 Płock	5117	493.0	96.4	42.0	102.9
31 Poznań	8151	1200.0	150.9	68.9	108.0
32 Przemyśl	4436	378.0	85.2	33.5	108.1
33 Radom	7295	697.0	95.6	40.9	104.0
34 Rzeszów	4398	641.0	146.0	34.4	106.0
35 Siedlce	8499	613.0	72.2	25.4	102.3
36 Sieradz	4869	391.0	80.3	30.3	104.2
37 Skierniewice	3959	395.0	99.8	39.3	104.8
38 Słupsk	7453	365.0	49.0	51.8	101.7
39 Suwałki	10490	419.0	40.0	45.7	101.3
40 Szczecin	9981	889.0	89.1	73.6	100.8
41 Tarnobrzeg	6283	552.0	87.9	30.4	101.7
42 Tarnów	4151	601.0	145.0	32.1	107.2
43 Toruń	5348	605.0	113.2	59.0	108.4
44 Wałbrzych	4168	714.0	171.3	72.4	106.8
45 Warszawa	3788	2300.0	605.8	88.2	112.7
46 Włocławek	4402	411.0	93.5	42.5	105.0
47 Wrocław	6287	1000.0	169.0	71.9	105.8
48 Zamość	6980	471.0	67.5	22.0	104.1
49 Zielona Góra	8868	603.0	68.0	57.3	104.0

Table 6b

Province	Employment in industry per 1000 population	Arable land in %
1 Biała Podlaska	96	61
2 Białystok	58	69
3 Bielsko Biała	192	50
4 Bydgoszcz	135	58
5 Chełm	86	66
6 Ciechanów	61	75
7 Częstochowa	148	59
8 Elbląg	98	64
9 Gdańsk	118	52
10 Gorzów Wielkopolski	116	43
11 Jelenia Góra	198	47
12 Kalisz	127	68
13 Katowice	238	49
14 Kielce	142	64
15 Konin	94	74
16 Koszalin	83	48
17 Kraków	131	69
18 Krosno	132	43
19 Legnica	132	63
20 Leszno	84	71
21 Lublin	106	74
22 Łomża	56	67
23 Łódź	235	66
24 Nowy Sącz	82	49
25 Olsztyn	86	56
26 Opole	146	63
27 Ostrołęka	66	61
28 Piła	92	50
29 Piotrków Trybunalski	141	64
30 Płock	110	77
31 Poznań	120	66
32 Przemyśl	79	58
33 Radom	124	69
34 Rzeszów	125	66
35 Siedlce	68	70
36 Sieradz	68	73
37 Skierniewice	101	78
38 Słupsk	104	47
39 Suwałki	68	52
40 Szczecin	115	54
41 Tarnobrzeg	129	60
42 Tarnów	118	71
43 Toruń	126	69
44 Wałbrzych	211	60
45 Warszawa	135	54
46 Włocławek	88	73
47 Wrocław	142	65
48 Zamość	60	70
49 Zielona Góra	144	40

Source: G U S.

Material and Methods

Breakdown of the Atlas

The main part of the atlas presents data on the mortality rates of 22 cancer sites and an overview of total cancer mortality in Poland. As the heart of the work, every one of these 23 sections includes maps showing the geographical variations in the respective mortality rates in the Polish provinces. To give a comprehensive picture, the cancer mapping is carried out on two different scales, the absolute and the relative. However, only one type of maps is coloured. The methods used are explained below.

The data on which the maps are based in tables showing case numbers, age-standardized mortality rates (ASMR) and cumulative mortality rates with 99% confidence limits for both sexes. Besides this geographical frequency distribution for each cancer site, trends in mortality in relation to calendar time are also given. These graphical presentations include ASMR over a 20-year period, age-specific mortality rates in selected age groups for the more frequent cancer sites, cross-sectional data of age-specific rates for two different points in time and presentations of birth cohort data. The methods used are also detailed below.

Finally, a short text gives a summary of mortality from the respective cancer site and some aetiological comments. These texts begin with a general description of mortality levels in Europe in 1978 and give world mortality rates when they are much higher or lower in non-European countries.

The next part of the summary provides an analysis of data representing the situation in individual provinces over the years 1975–1979. It begins with a brief description of the differences in risk by sex ratio and urban/rural ratio. The analysis of geographical differences is carried out separately for males and females. These sections begin with figures representing the mean value of mortality rates in Polish provinces, the range of values, the standard deviation (SD), the percentage of deaths caused by this cancer and its position in the rank order of mortality from different cancer sites. The presentation also includes a list of provinces with the highest and the lowest mortality rates and, finally, comments on the maps. The final part of each text is an epidemiological discussion of the data presented.

Data Material

The data for the analysis of geographical variations in cancer can be provided by two basic sources: the morbidity registers, which collect data on new cases in a defined population, and the mortality statistics of the population in question. The two sources may give quite different pictures of the importance of certain cancer sites. Obviously, cancer sites with a relatively good prognosis will be underestimated by mortality data, and, moreover, non-fatal cancer sites, such as some skin tumours for example, cannot be analysed using mortality data at all. Furthermore time trends analysed in conjunction with mortality data can provide a distorted picture, as successes in cancer therapy are reducing the lethality of some cancers. In such cases, it is conceivable that, in spite of increasing incidence the mortality rate might decrease and thus blur the real cancer risk. However, with regard to geographical variations one may presume that the lethality of a given cancer site does not vary substantially, provided that medical care is the same. This means that cancer mapping may be carried out by mortality in principle but with the fundamental restriction that only cancer sites with a high fatality can be regarded in this way.

In Poland, both cancer reporting cards and death certificates are used as a source of information about cancer. However, unlike the reporting of death, Polish cancer registration is still based solely on uncontrolled reporting, which results in considerable underestimation. Koszarowski et al. estimate this at about 30% in Poland as a whole (Koszarowski et al. 1984). Complete data are available only in regions where cancer registration is run by the National Oncology Centre (Institute of Oncology). These regions include the provinces of Kraków, Katowice and Warszawa. The data are published in consecutive volumes of Cancer Incidence in Five Continents (CIFC), starting from volume II (Doll et al. 1976; vols III and IV, Waterhouse et al. 1976, 1982). Differences in the completeness of data representing incidence in various parts of Poland do not allow their use in an objective analysis of the regional differences in cancer frequency. Table 1 shows the great variations in the incidence/mortality ratio in the different Polish provinces, with the highest values in Krakow (1.8 for males and 1.9 for females) and the lowest in Zielona Gora (males 0.6 and females 0.8). This cannot be attributed to medical care alone but mainly to the completeness of case-reporting.

The completeness and quality of mortality statistics in various Polish regions is much more balanced so that they must be regarded as the only complete source of cancer information available to all areas of Poland. The quality of data they carry appears to represent standards which are good enough to allow them to be used as a basis for an analysis of the frequency and geographical distribution of malignant neoplasms.

Several organisational reforms were introduced in Poland in the late 1950s and early 1960s in order to improve the quality of mortality statistics. These reforms comprised the adoption of the International Classification of Diseases (ICD) for the classification of the causes of death (in 1959), and the adoption of the principle that death certificates should be filled in only by physicians (in 1961). A new death certificate form, based on WHO recommendations, was introduced in 1963 and since then death certification follows the internationally accepted rules recommended by WHO. Death certificates are collected, coded and processed by the Central Statistical Office (GUS) in Warszawa. Death registration in Poland is today regarded as complete. The Polish demographer Holzer summarises the situation as follows: "Polish law does not allow the burial of a human being without issuance of a death certificate. Rigorous adherence to this law has made mortality statistics complete and demographic death reports reliable" (Holzer 1970).

Although world statistical reports include Polish cancer mortality data after 1959, the years 1959-1962 should be regarded as a transitional period when new data collection methods, based on international models, were in the process of being adopted. This is confirmed by a rapid growth in the number of deaths reported in this period (Staszewski 1976). For this reason, our analyses of cancer-related mortality in Poland begin in 1963 as we think that was the year when satisfactory completeness and quality of cancer death registration was achieved. The analysis of geographical variations

Table 1. Incidence/mortality ratios by districts in Poland in 1979. All malignant neoplasms

No. District	Males	Females
1. Biała Podlaska	1.24	1.41
2. Białystok	1.36	1.49
3. Bielsko Biała	0.99	1.26
4. Bydgoszcz	1.27	1.42
5. Chełm	1.33	1.34
6. Ciechanów	0.67	0.89
7. Częstochowa	1.07	1.20
8. Elbląg	0.74	0.80
9. Gdańsk	1.09	1.26
10. Gorzów Wielkopolski	1.05	1.26
11. Jelenia Góra	0.72	0.94
12. Kalisz	0.78	0.88
13. Katowice	0.92	1.09
14. Kielce	0.93	1.23
15. Konin	0.76	0.85
16. Koszalin	0.66	0.81
17. Kraków	1.83	1.90
18. Krosno	0.98	1.22
19. Legnica	1.10	1.13
20. Leszno	1.12	1.14
21. Lublin	1.64	1.74
22. Łomża	0.89	1.14
23. Łódź	1.36	1.38
24. Nowy Sącz	1.29	1.57
25. Olsztyn	0.79	1.12
26. Opole	0.68	0.83
27. Ostrołęka	1.13	1.27
28. Piła	0.63	0.85
29. Piotrków Trybunalski	1.64	1.60
30. Płock	1.00	1.16
31. Poznań	1.09	1.19
32. Przemyśl	1.07	1.17
33. Radom	0.95	1.18
34. Rzeszów	0.92	1.24
35. Siedlce	1.20	1.41
36. Sieradz	1.33	1.27
37. Skierniewice	0.85	0.88
38. Słupsk	0.76	1.13
39. Suwałki	1.44	1.54
40. Szczecin	1.12	1.45
41. Tarnobrzeg	1.25	1.40
42. Tarnów	1.37	1.50
43. Toruń	0.69	0.91
44. Wałbrzych	0.64	0.88
45. Warszawa	1.19	1.40
46. Włocławek	1.17	1.43
47. Wrocław	0.93	1.03
48. Zamość	1.08	1.24
49. Zielona Góra	0.60	0.76
50. Polska	1.06	1.23

presented in this work have been based on data released by GUS. The WHO Mortality Data Bank has provided us with data used for the calculation of time trends in cancer mortality and birth cohort comparisons. All data used in this work are coded according to the 8th Revision of the ICD.

An administrative reform in 1975 introduced 49 provinces which replaced the 22 former provinces. The populations of these new provinces range from 235000 to 3830000. Three provinces have populations below 300000 and nine over one million (see Table 6, p. 12, 13). This presentation comprises data for the years 1975-1979 during which time 148961 deaths from cancer were recorded in men and 122532 in women. Because a census was taken in Poland in 1978, the figures relating to the size of the Polish population in that year are the most reliable and they have been used for tabulating mortality rates. As 1978 is not in the middle of the period chosen for the present analysis (1975-1979), and because the population of this country is increasing, the rates should be regarded as slightly lower than actual.

The basic criterion in selecting cancer sites for this work was that at least 2000 deaths were registered in the study period of 1975-1979 for at least one sex. This has resulted in 16 sites being included. In addition to these, several other sites which were interesting for various reasons have also been included. These are lip, skin melanoma, testis, thyroid gland, lymphatic sarcoma and Hodgkin's disease. On the other hand, some cancer sites were left out on the grounds that data have to be considered as unreliable. These include the liver, bones and corpus uteri.

Methods

Mortality rates are usually expressed as the number of deaths per 100 000 persons in one year. It should be remembered that age determines mortality. Mortality rates for some cancer sites are 1000 times lower in younger (i.e. 35-39 years) age groups than in older age groups (i.e. 70-74 years). Therefore, when comparing mortality rates in different populations and at different times, differences in age structure must be taken into consideration. The best way is to compare mortality rates in 5-year age groups. However, a summary measure of mortality over all age groups is often desired. In this case, an ASMR, which is a weighted average of the age-specific mortality rates, is calculated according to the formula

$$\frac{\Sigma(w_i \times AMR_i)}{\Sigma w_i} \times 100000 \qquad (1)$$

where AMR_i denotes the age-specific mortality rates and w_i the weights. In this atlas, the "world population" proposed by Segi and modified by Doll et al. (1970) was used as a standardisation weight. The world population is younger than is in Poland (see Table 1, p. 2) and, consequently, the rates obtained are slightly lower than actual.

Another summary measure for mortality is the cumulative mortality rate (CMR). It is computed from the age groups between 0 and 74 years according to

$$1 - e^{-\Sigma AMR_i \times \Delta t_i} \qquad (2)$$

where AMR_i is the i-th age-specific mortality rate and Δt_i the length of this age group. The result is mostly given as a percentage. It estimates the risk of a member of the population dying from the given cancer before reaching the age of 75, unless other causes of death intervene. As a measure of probability it is independent of the age structure of the population and therefore generally comparable.

The cancer maps in this atlas are based on the standardised mortality rates computed according to Eq. (1) and are given as two presentations on different scales. The first presentation is based on a relative scale. Mortality rates in the provinces were ranked from the lowest to the highest and divided into five classes. The first class included 10% of the provinces, the second 20%, the third 40%, the fourth 20% and the fifth 10%. These maps are coloured. The class with the lowest mortality figures is coloured green, the next class is yellow-green, and so on through yellow, red-yellow, to full red. The second way in which the provinces were arranged was using an absolute scale where the range of differentiation in the mortality rates was divided into five equal sections. These maps are black and white and graded from white to dark grey. These maps use no statistical rating whatever.

The calendar time trends of mortality in the respective cancer sites are given for six 5-year age groups (35-64 years) separately and for the standardised rates according to Eq. (1) for the years 1963-1982 for each sex. In cases where changes in the classification of cancers ruled out comparison of data over the 20 years, the analysis covers shorter periods.

The age-dependent mortality curves are based on age-specific mortality rates within 5-year age groups and are shown for 1963 and 1982. Such intersections of mortality at certain time points may not be taken as an assessment of the age-dependent risk for the respective cancer site. On the contrary, because of the different life histories of the age groups involved, such intersections frequently represent quite different risks for the different ages. This becomes evident in cancer sites with a strong increase of mortality with calendar time (e.g. lung cancer). Here, old people were born in earlier decades when the risk was lower. This causes a relatively lower mortality in older age groups in comparison to younger age groups, which show the higher cancer risk of the more recent decades. Thus, in pronounced cases, the age-dependent mortality curves may even slope down in older age groups, whereas the real cancer risk of the younger people will jump dramatically with age. To counteract this we have used an additional kind of presentation in the form of birth cohort analyses. For these, the mortality rates in each 5-year age group were calculated for every 5th calendar year beginning with 1965 (i.e. 1965, 1970, 1975, 1980) and reordered with respect to their birth quinquennium (Case 1956). Thus, it is possible to follow the cancer risk of individual cohorts by using the calendar time decades. From this point of view, the relationship between calendar time and personal life history is kept, and thus mortality within single cohorts is an indicator of their real cancer risk. In these graphs age-specific mortality rates are plotted against age at death for each of the birth cohorts, so that the oldest birth cohorts appears on the right of the plots, the next to the left of it and so on. The legends of the graphs are to read in this order.

To summarise the experience of each birth cohort, cumulative mortality rates over the age groups for which data were available were calculated for each cohort. The successive cohorts were compared by the inter-cohort ratio of the cumulative mortality rates over the common age groups of the cohorts compared. On the basis of the inter-cohort ratio of neighbouring cohorts, ratios of cumulative mortality rates for successive cohorts relative to the 1886–1890 cohort were estimated for each cancer site (if possible). The inter-cohort ratios and the estimated ratios relative to the 1886–1890 cohort are not fully satisfactory as a measure of comparing cohorts, as the age groups compared are not the same throughout.

Cancer Mortality by Site

1 Lip - ICD 140

Cancer of the lip is rare in Europe and deaths from it are even less frequent owing to the good prognosis. In Poland, it is relatively frequent in comparison to other countries, especially in rural populations. This is why we have included this site in the present work, despite the small number of cases (816 in men and 187 in women over 5 years).

The mortality rate for cancer of the lip has dropped in the last two decades. Lip cancer occurs much more frequently in men than in women. The mortality rate in men was 1.1-1.2 in the early 1960s and 0.9 in 1982. The mortality rate in women was 0.2 and 0.1 in the respective years. The mortality rate in men increases sharply after 40 years of age reaching the highest value of 20 per 100000 at age 75. The small number of cases does not allow interpretation of the calendar time trend for the individual age groups. The comparison of risk in successive birth cohorts seems to indicate a significant decline.

In 1978 the highest mortality rate for cancer of the lip in Europe was in Poland (0.8), Hungary (0.8) and the Republic of Ireland (0.7). Many European countries (United Kingdom, Sweden, the Netherlands, the Federal Republic of Germany, Denmark) had very low mortality rates of about 0.1. Women in most European countries had low mortality rates of below 0.1.

Analysis of Data from the Provinces, 1975-1979

Cancer of the lip is markedly more frequent in men than in women (ratio 9). This cancer is among the few which are more frequent in rural than in urban populations (urban/rural ratio 0.5)

Men

(Mean ASMR = 1.0, Range 0.3-1.7, Standard Deviation 0.4; 0.5% of Male Cancer Mortality, Rank 23)

There was a great difference between the mortality rates for cancer of the lip in the various provinces, with the highest rates 5.6 times greater than the lowest. Provinces with the highest rates were Olsztyn (1.73), Kielce (1.7), Ostroleka (1.67), Piotrkow Trybunalski (1.67) and Ciechanow (1.65). Provinces with the lowest rates were Poznan (0.31), Leszno (0.39) and Warszawa (0.47). Despite the small number of cases recorded in the individual provinces, it is noticeable that there were higher mortality rates in the eastern half of Poland.

Women

(Mean ASMR = 0.1, Range 0.0-0.4, Standard Deviation 0.09; 0.2% of Female Cancer Mortality, Rank 37)

Cancer of the lip is fairly rare in women. Provinces with the highest rates were Zielona Gora (0.38), Legnica (0.36) and Nowy Sacz (0.34). There were only 187 cases of cancer of the lip recorded in women over the years 1975-1979. Three provinces, Chelm, Olsztyn and Sieradz, had no cases at all. With these small numbers, no geographical patterns can be established, and the differences between the mortality rates in the provinces should be regarded as coincidental.

Comments

Cancer of the lip is regarded as rare. However, when we consider the tiny anatomical area occupied by the lips and the fact that the disease usually attacks the lower lip (e.g. in Finland 94.6% of all cancers at this site; Lindqvist 1979) the frequency of this cancer site should be viewed in a different light. Exposure to sunlight appears to be the main risk factor (Keller 1970). Epidemiological studies show that people working in the open air (e.g. farmers, foresters, seamen or fishermen) are at a higher risk (Lindqvist and Teppo 1978). Exposure to tobacco (especially pipe smoking and chewing tobacco) seems to be a further risk factor but one that is less important than sunlight (Clemessen 1965, Anderson 1971). Injuries (Anderson 1971) and herpes simplex

(Cassai et al. 1974) are other factors which are potentially related to this cancer site.
Poland has the highest mortality rate in cancer of the lip among the European countries. Similarly, the incidence, recorded by Polish cancer registers, is the highest in Europe, especially those in rural areas (Waterhouse et al. 1982). As in other countries, cancer of the lip shows a major decline in successive birth cohorts. The predominance of mortality in men is one of the greatest of all cancer sites. This cancer is also among the few neoplasms which are more frequent (two-fold) in rural than in urban populations of men and women alike. The presentation of the geographical distribution was based on a small number of cases and it does not allow final conclusions to be drawn. However, it does suggest that the regions with higher risk, especially for men, are situated in the rural provinces of eastern Poland. A highly significant increase in tobacco smoking in all regions over the years 1950–1980, observed in both sexes, seems to have no impact on the downward trend of mortality from cancer of the lip. The fact that tobacco is very rarely smoked by rural women compared to urban women has not altered the predominance of rural women over urban women suffering from this cancer.
In summary, we can say that country people (including the inhabitants of the rural provinces), i.e. populations mostly employed outdoors, face a higher risk of cancer of the lip. No relationship has been discovered between tobacco smoking and mortality from cancer of the lip.

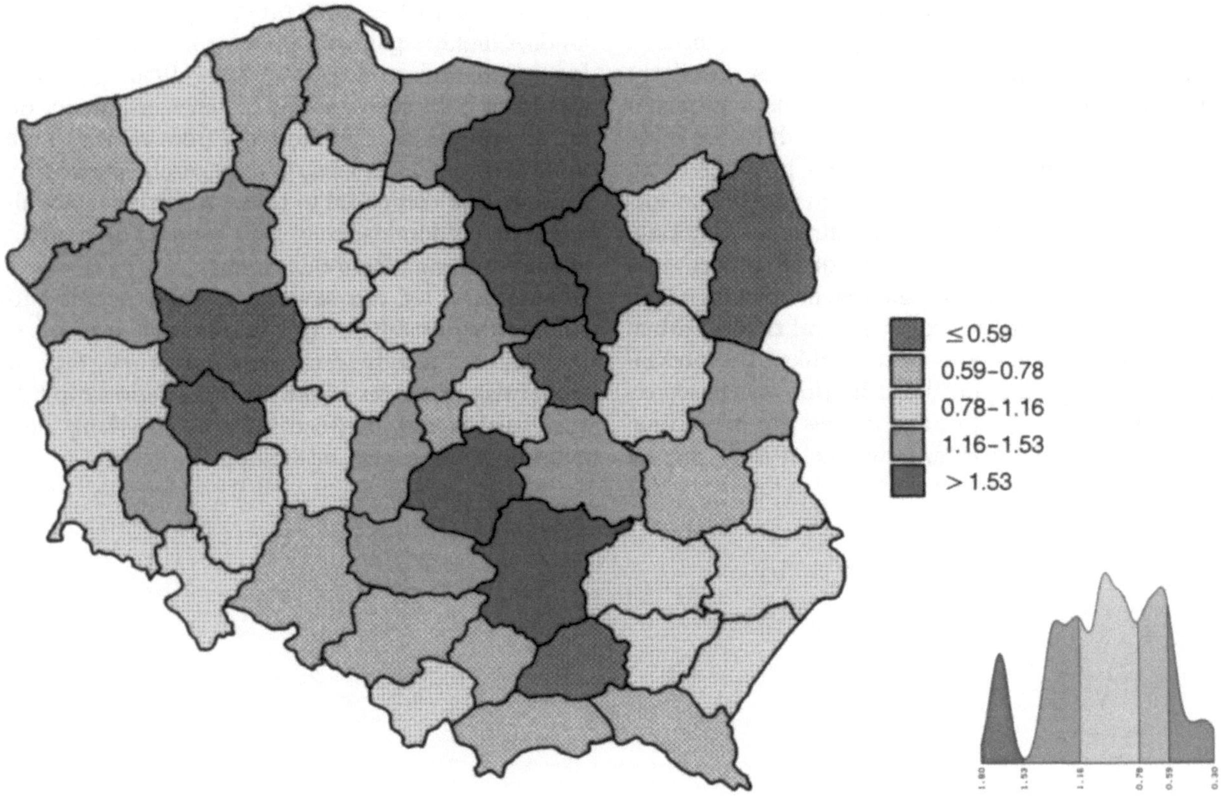
≤0.59
0.59-0.78
0.78-1.16
1.16-1.53
>1.53

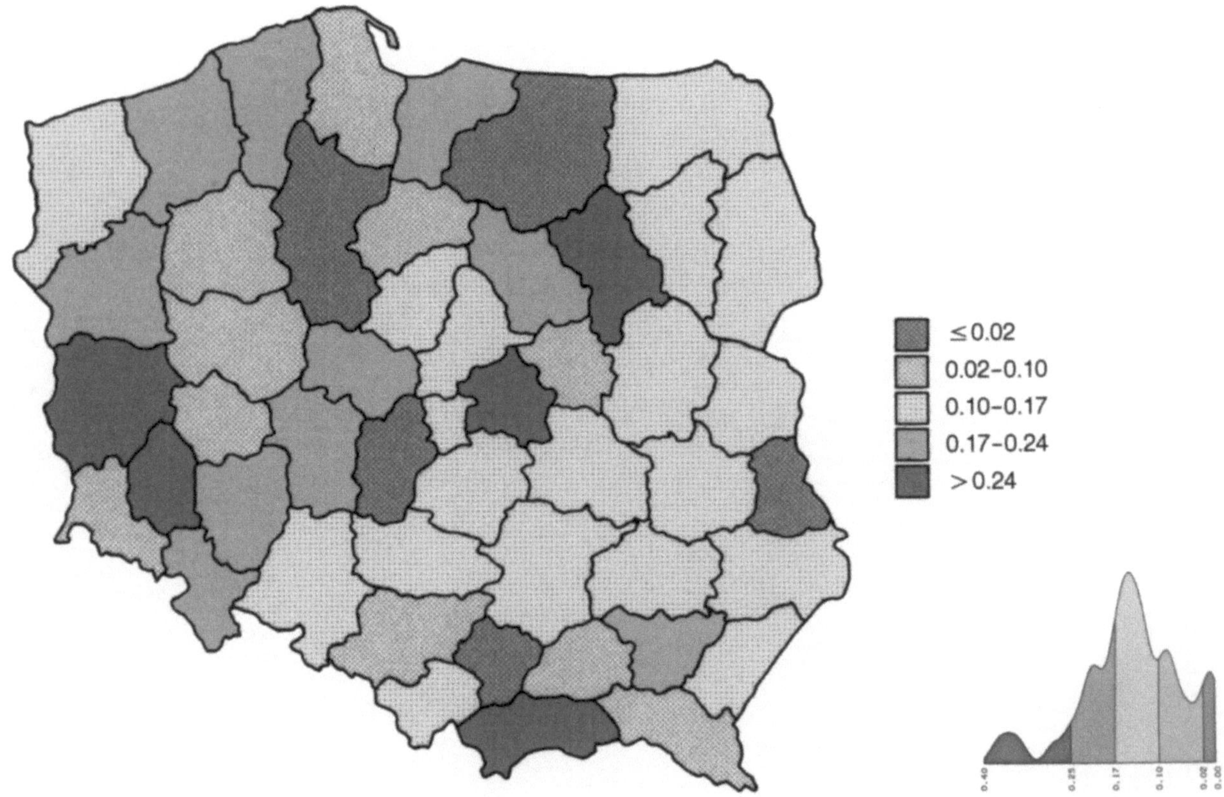
≤0.02
0.02-0.10
0.10-0.17
0.17-0.24
>0.24

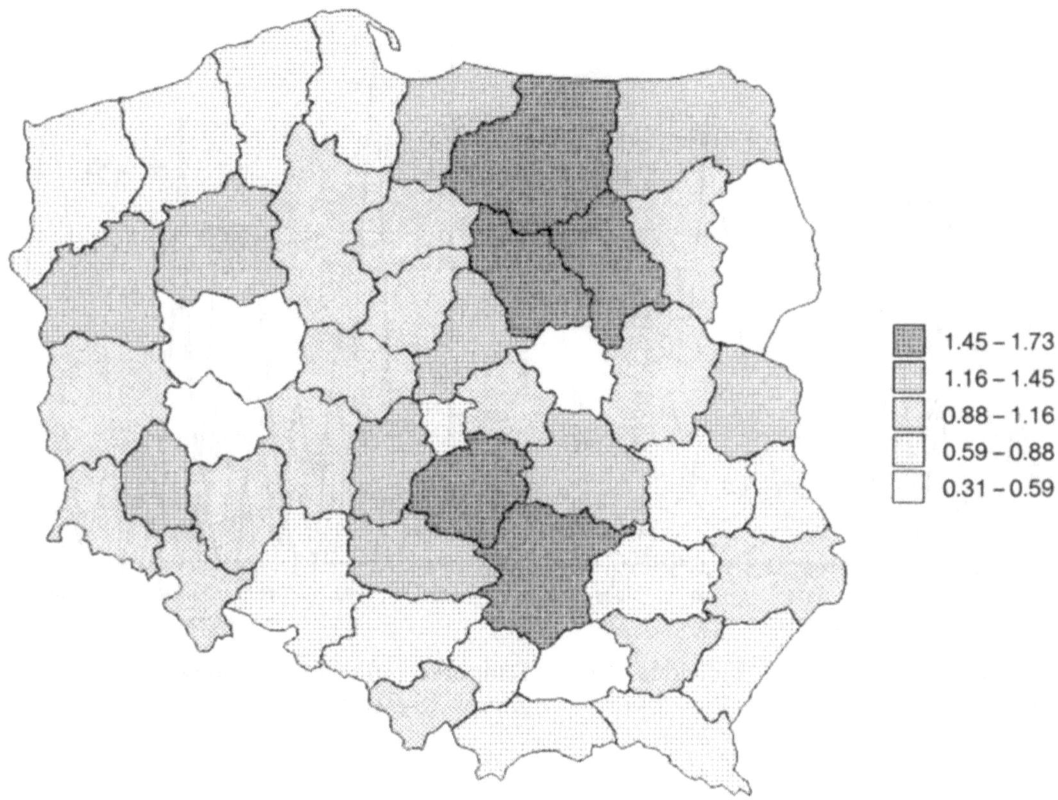
1.45 – 1.73
1.16 – 1.45
0.88 – 1.16
0.59 – 0.88
0.31 – 0.59

0.30 – 0.38
0.23 – 0.30
0.15 – 0.23
0.08 – 0.15
0.00 – 0.08

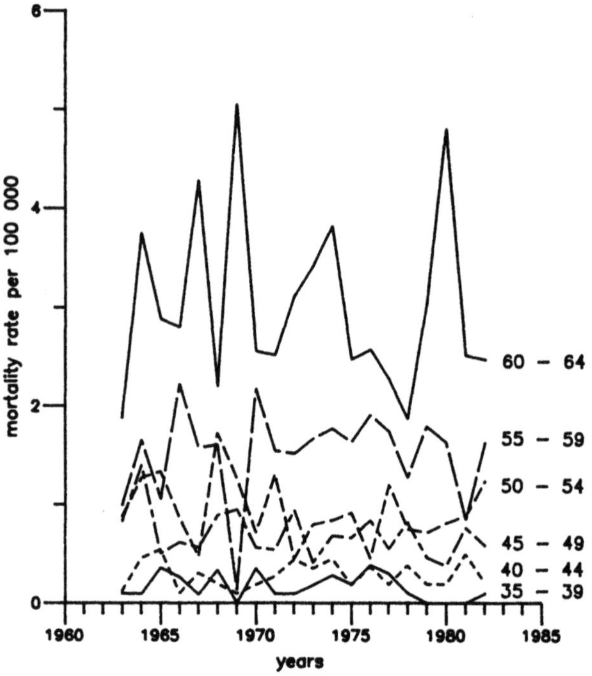

Temporal trend of mortality in individual age groups/men

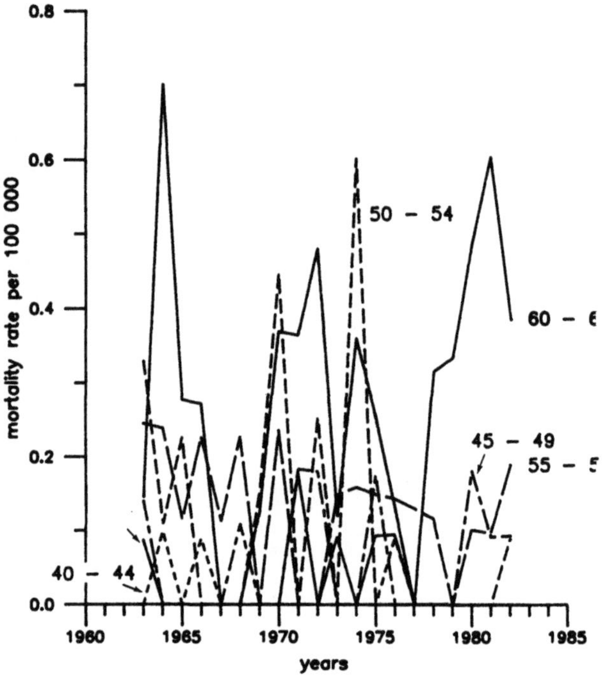

Temporal trend of mortality in individual age groups/women

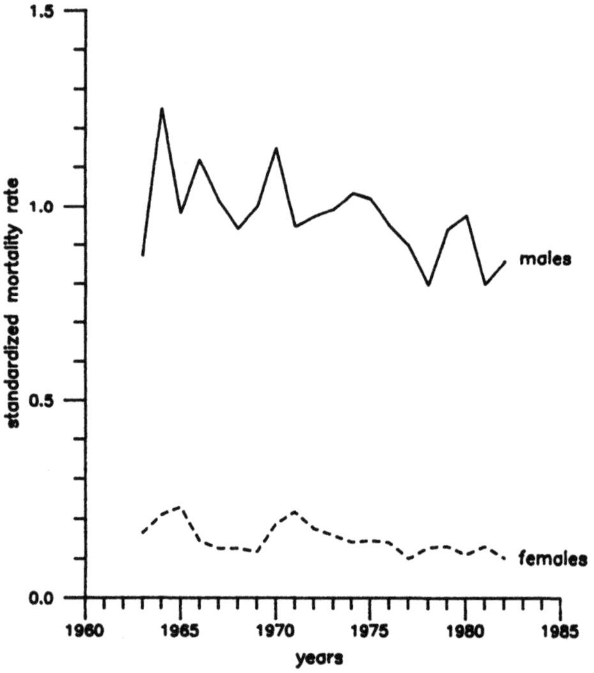

Temporal trend of the age-adjusted mortality rates for men and women

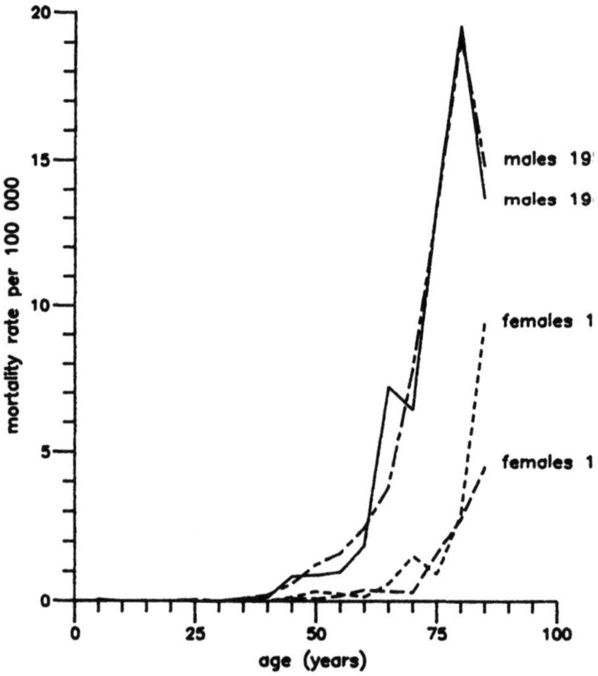

Mortality depending on age in two sample years for men and women

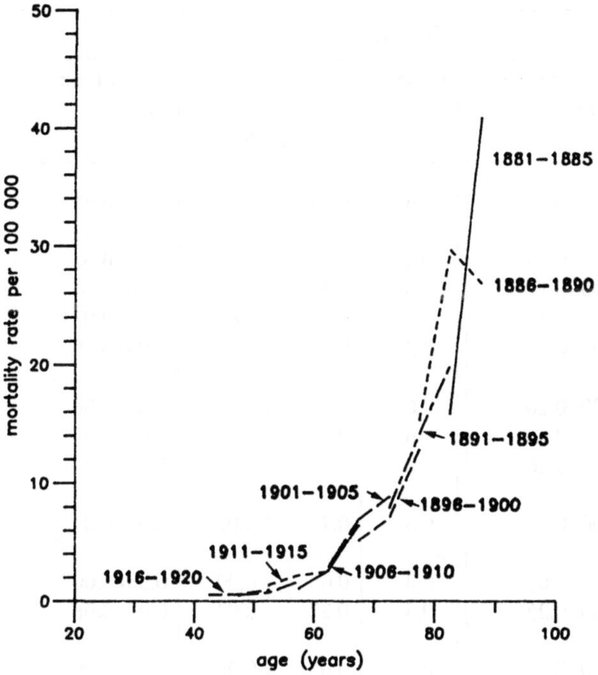

Age-dependent mortality in various birth cohorts/ men

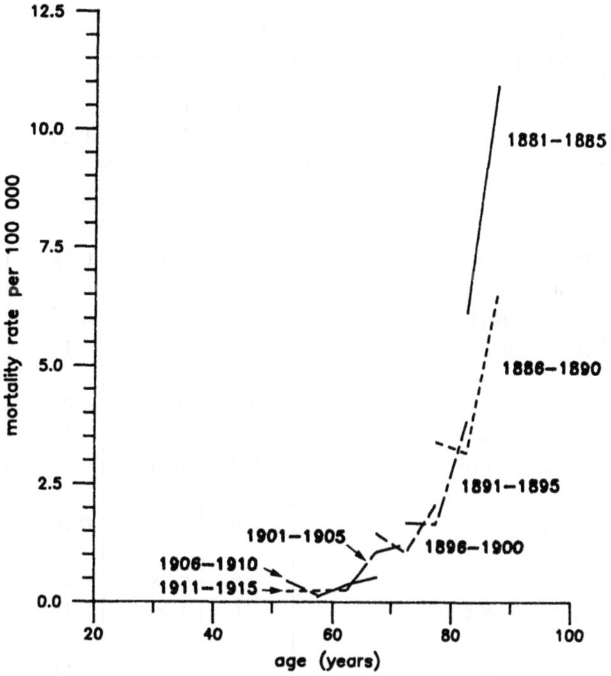

Age-dependent mortality in various birth cohorts/ women

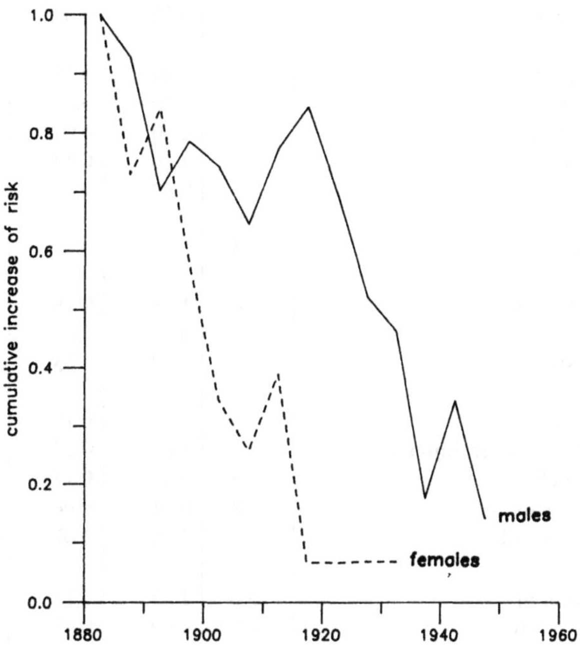

Ratios of the cumulative mortality rates for successive birth cohorts relative to the 1886-1890 cohort

Average Values 1975-1979	Males				Females			
	Cases	Stand. Mort. Rate	Cum. Mort. Rate	Confidence limits	Cases	Stand. Mort. Rate	Cum. Mort. Rate	Confidence limits
Poland	163.2	0.91	0.10	0.09-0.11	37.4	0.13	0.01	0.01-0.01
Biała Podlaska	2.6	1.30	0.18	0.03-0.34	0.4	0.11	0.02	0.00-0.06
Białystok	2.2	0.58	0.06	0.00-0.12	1.0	0.14	0.01	0.00-0.04
Bielsko Biała	3.6	1.03	0.12	0.04-0.21	0.8	0.10	0.01	0.00-0.03
Bydgoszcz	5.2	0.88	0.13	0.06-0.21	0.2	0.02	0.00	0.00-0.00
Chełm	1.2	0.78	0.09	0.00-0.20	0.0	0.00	0.00	0.00-0.00
Ciechanów	3.8	1.65	0.19	0.05-0.33	0.6	0.20	0.02	0.00-0.07
Częstochowa	5.4	1.24	0.12	0.04-0.20	0.8	0.12	0.01	0.00-0.03
Elbląg	2.4	1.34	0.16	0.00-0.32	0.6	0.24	0.02	0.00-0.07
Gdańsk	3.8	0.78	0.05	0.01-0.09	0.8	0.08	0.00	0.00-0.00
Gorzów Wielkopolski	2.6	1.40	0.13	0.00-0.25	0.4	0.22	0.02	0.00-0.06
Jelenia Góra	2.2	1.04	0.11	0.00-0.22	0.2	0.05	0.00	0.00-0.00
Kalisz	3.2	0.89	0.10	0.02-0.18	1.6	0.22	0.02	0.00-0.05
Katowice	9.0	0.62	0.05	0.03-0.08	2.2	0.08	0.01	0.00-0.01
Kielce	10.6	1.70	0.16	0.08-0.24	1.8	0.16	0.01	0.00-0.02
Konin	2.8	0.96	0.07	0.00-0.15	0.8	0.18	0.01	0.00-0.03
Koszalin	1.6	0.86	0.11	0.00-0.23	0.6	0.20	0.01	0.00-0.03
Kraków	3.4	0.72	0.05	0.01-0.09	0.2	0.01	0.00	0.00-0.00
Krosno	2.2	0.72	0.09	0.00-0.18	0.4	0.09	0.01	0.00-0.03
Legnica	2.2	1.36	0.19	0.02-0.35	0.8	0.36	0.04	0.00-0.12
Leszno	0.6	0.39	0.03	0.00-0.08	0.4	0.10	0.01	0.00-0.05
Lublin	3.2	0.60	0.06	0.01-0.11	1.4	0.17	0.01	0.00-0.03
Łomża	3.0	1.16	0.14	0.02-0.27	0.6	0.16	0.00	0.00-0.00
Łódź	4.2	0.62	0.05	0.01-0.10	1.4	0.16	0.02	0.00-0.03
Nowy Sącz	2.4	0.71	0.12	0.03-0.22	1.4	0.34	0.03	0.00-0.08
Olsztyn	4.6	1.73	0.18	0.04-0.31	0.0	0.00	0.00	0.00-0.00
Opole	3.2	0.67	0.05	0.00-0.10	1.2	0.17	0.00	0.00-0.00
Ostrołęka	3.0	1.67	0.13	0.01-0.25	0.8	0.25	0.03	0.00-0.07
Piła	2.4	1.24	0.18	0.04-0.31	0.2	0.08	0.00	0.00-0.00
Piotrków Trybunalski	6.4	1.67	0.20	0.09-0.31	1.0	0.14	0.01	0.00-0.02
Płock	3.6	1.32	0.15	0.04-0.26	0.6	0.13	0.02	0.00-0.06
Poznań	1.8	0.31	0.04	0.00-0.07	0.6	0.04	0.00	0.00-0.01
Przemyśl	2.2	0.88	0.07	0.00-0.14	0.4	0.16	0.02	0.00-0.06
Radom	5.0	1.35	0.13	0.04-0.21	0.8	0.14	0.01	0.00-0.03
Rzeszów	4.0	1.09	0.10	0.02-0.18	1.0	0.22	0.02	0.00-0.05
Siedlce	3.8	1.05	0.09	0.02-0.17	1.0	0.13	0.01	0.00-0.03
Sieradz	3.4	1.16	0.15	0.04-0.26	0.0	0.00	0.00	0.00-0.00
Skierniewice	2.4	0.98	0.14	0.02-0.26	0.6	0.28	0.02	0.00-0.06
Słupsk	0.8	0.60	0.06	0.00-0.16	0.4	0.21	0.00	0.00-0.00
Suwałki	2.4	1.22	0.16	0.02-0.30	0.4	0.13	0.00	0.00-0.00
Szczecin	2.2	0.70	0.10	0.01-0.20	0.6	0.12	0.03	0.00-0.07

Average Values 1975-1979	Males				Females			
	Cases	Stand. Mort. Rate	Cum. Mort. Rate	Confidence limits	Cases	Stand. Mort. Rate	Cum. Mort. Rate	Confidence limits
Tarnobrzeg	2.8	0.81	0.09	0.01-0.17	1.0	0.16	0.02	0.00-0.05
Tarnów	2.2	0.58	0.06	0.00-0.12	0.4	0.06	0.01	0.00-0.03
Toruń	3.0	1.00	0.11	0.02-0.20	0.2	0.03	0.00	0.00-0.00
Wałbrzych	2.6	1.16	0.08	0.00-0.17	0.6	0.17	0.01	0.00-0.04
Warszawa	6.0	0.47	0.07	0.03-0.11	2.2	0.08	0.00	0.00-0.01
Włocławek	2.8	1.15	0.14	0.02-0.26	0.6	0.15	0.00	0.00-0.00
Wrocław	4.0	0.89	0.13	0.04-0.22	1.2	0.19	0.02	0.00-0.05
Zamość	2.8	0.97	0.12	0.03-0.21	0.8	0.14	0.02	0.00-0.05
Zielona Góra	2.4	0.99	0.13	0.02-0.24	1.4	0.38	0.03	0.00-0.07

2 Oesophagus – ICD 150

The ASMR for cancer of the oesophagus in men was 5.3 in 1963 and 4.7 in 1982, while the respective figures for women were 1.5 and 0.8. Cancers of the oesophagus are more frequent in men than in women. Mortality of men increases rapidly after the age of 40 to reach the maximum of 50 cases per 100000 in men aged about 75. The mortality rate in younger age groups has declined with calendar time only for women; in men, especially after 1970, we observe an increase. In the 50–64 age group, the mortality rate has declined for both sexes with calendar time. A decreasing risk of cancer of the oesophagus is also observed in the successive birth cohorts of men and women alike, though not in cohorts born after 1920.

In 1978 the highest mortality rate from oesophageal cancer in European men was reported in France (13.6) where the rate was nearly twice as high as the second highest rate in Luxembourg (7.9). Europe's lowest mortality rates were in Bulgaria (1.2), Iceland (1.6) and Romania (1.6). Outside Europe, Uruguay, Singapore and Hong Kong had the same mortality rates as France. Oesophageal cancer was most frequent in Asia in Iran, the southern part of the Soviet Union and China, where some regions had incidence rates of up to 50–150. The highest mortality rates in women were observed in the Republic of Ireland (4.1) and Great Britain (from 3.9 in Scotland to 3.0 in England and Wales). The lowest rates in women were found in Czechoslovakia (0.3), Bulgaria (0.5), Romania (0.5) and the German Democratic Republic (0.5). Poland was a country with medium risk in 1978, the rates for men and women being 4.0 and 0.9, respectively.

Analysis of Data from the Provinces, 1975–1979

Malignant neoplasms of the oesophagus are more frequent in urban than in rural populations (ratio for men 1.4, women 1.1). It is over four times as frequent in men than in women.

Men

(Mean ASMR = 3.9, Range 1.9–6.5, Standard Deviation 0.9; 2.4% of Male Cancer Mortality, Rank 11)

Provinces with the highest rates were Ostroleka (6.50), Lomza (5.50), Suwalki (5.41), Katowice (5.37), Warszawa (5.26) and Slupsk (5.15). Provinces with the lowest rates were Chelm (1.92), Zamosc (2.37), Leszno (2.52), Tarnobrzeg (2.52) and Lublin (2.54). Northeastern Poland had the highest mortality rates. In southern Poland high mortality were found only in the provinces of Katowice and Opole. A low frequency of cancer of the oesophagus is typical in the southeastern provinces, from Biala Podlaska through Lublin and Tarnobrzeg to Nowy Sacz, as well as Leszno, Poznan, Sieradz and Kalisz in the western part of central Poland.

Women

(Mean ASMR = 0.9, Range 0.3–1.4, Standard Deviation 0.2; 1.0% of Female Cancer Mortality, Rank 18)

The highest mortality rate in individual provinces was 5.3 times greater than the lowest but the small numbers of cases in some provinces should be taken into account. Provinces with the highest mortality rates were Torun (1.37), Elblag (1.34), Ostroleka (1.24), Legnica (1.22) and Czestochowa (1.16). Provinces with the lowest rates were Chelm (0.26), Lublin (0.46), Gorzow (0.55), Siedlce (0.55) and Plock (0.56). The geographical distribution of women's mortality rates is less clear-cut than in the case of men. There was an area of higher risk in central Poland. Low rates were observed in southeastern Poland, adjacent to the low-risk region, and in the central-western strip from the province of Gorzow to Wloclawek and Plock.

Comments

The risk of cancer of the oesophagus appears to involve several factors. Long-term observation in Europe and North America associates it with exposure to alcohol and tobacco smoke. These studies show that the consumption of alcohol seems to be the strongest risk factor, increasing in importance with the concentration of alcohol in ingested drinks. Tuyns et al. (1977) postulate the existence of a synergistic effect of alcohol and tobacco. On the other hand, studies carried out in such countries as Iran, the Soviet Union (Kazakhstan, Turkmenia) or China, where oesophageal cancer risk is several dozen times higher than in European countries, alcohol and tobacco have not been shown to be significant. It is presumed that the high risk in these countries may be connected with local diet (exposure to N-nitrosocompounds), with low intake of iron, vitamins A and C, riboflavin, and a strong carcinogen like opium tar (Day and Munoz 1982; Lu et al. 1986).

Cancers of the oesophagus are rare in Poland. The data have to be considered carefully because of the possible confusion in the classification of this site with cancer of the stomach, and the conclusions drawn must be accepted warily. It is hard to comment on the reason for the declining oesophageal cancer mortality rate. There has been a steady increase in tobacco smoking since 1950 and an increase in alcohol consumption, which has accelerated since 1963. The lung cancer mortality rate in males has increased rapidly since 1963, and the rates for cancer of the larynx in males show an accelerating increase after 1970. These changes reflect closely the trends in consumption of alcohol and tobacco. Oesophageal cancer in both sexes, by contrast, shows an inversed trend. From 1963 to 1975 the rates decreased steadily in both sexes and in men they reached a plateau only in the years 1975-1982. After 1945 overall nutrition improved greatly. It is tempting to conclude that, as strong as the association of oesophageal cancer with tobacco and alcohol may be, nutritional factors have to play a role in the aetiology of the disease and they can, at times, override the other two. This hypothesis is justified by the observation of similar trends in the cancer of the oesophagus and the consumption of alcohol, tobacco smoking and changes in diet in other central and northern European countries (Austria, Czechoslovakia, Denmark, Finland, the Federal Republic of Germany) over the years 1950-1970. Of course this hypothesis will be stronger if misclassification can be excluded. These phenomena, observed in Poland and the countries mentioned above, need further investigation.

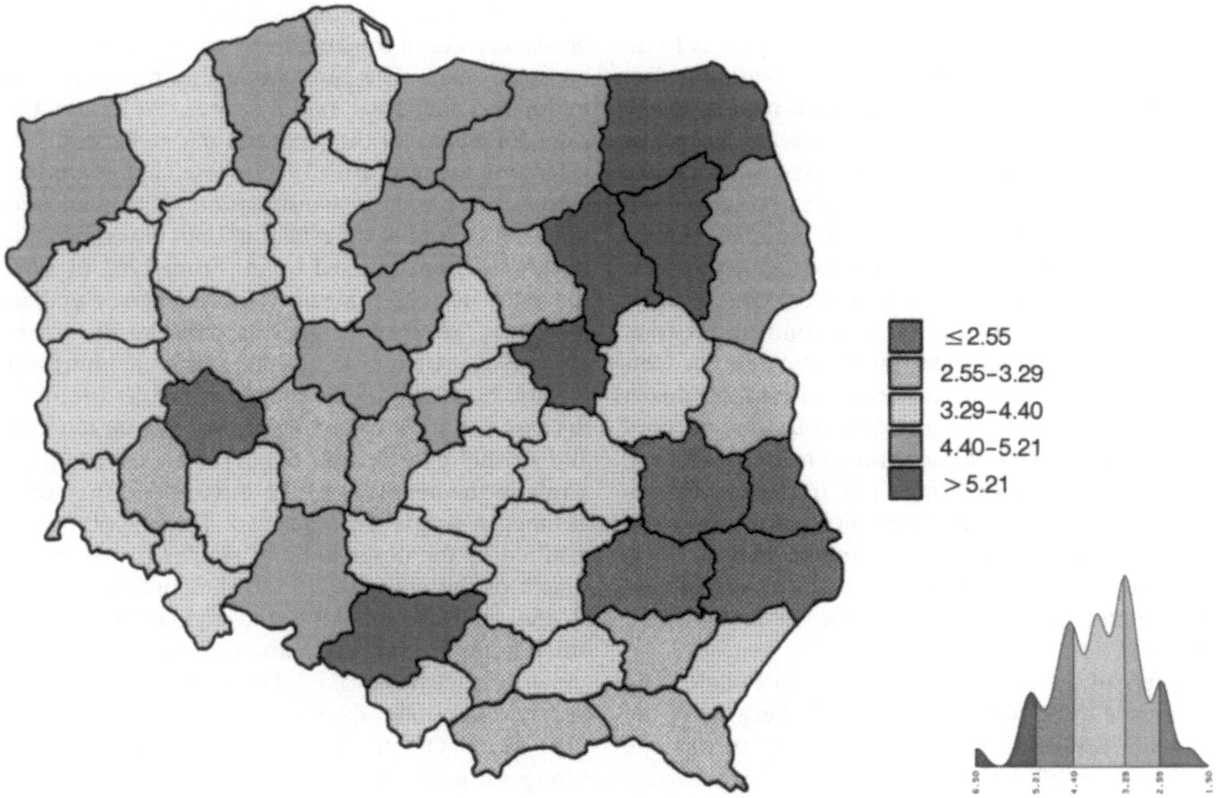
≤2.55
2.55-3.29
3.29-4.40
4.40-5.21
>5.21

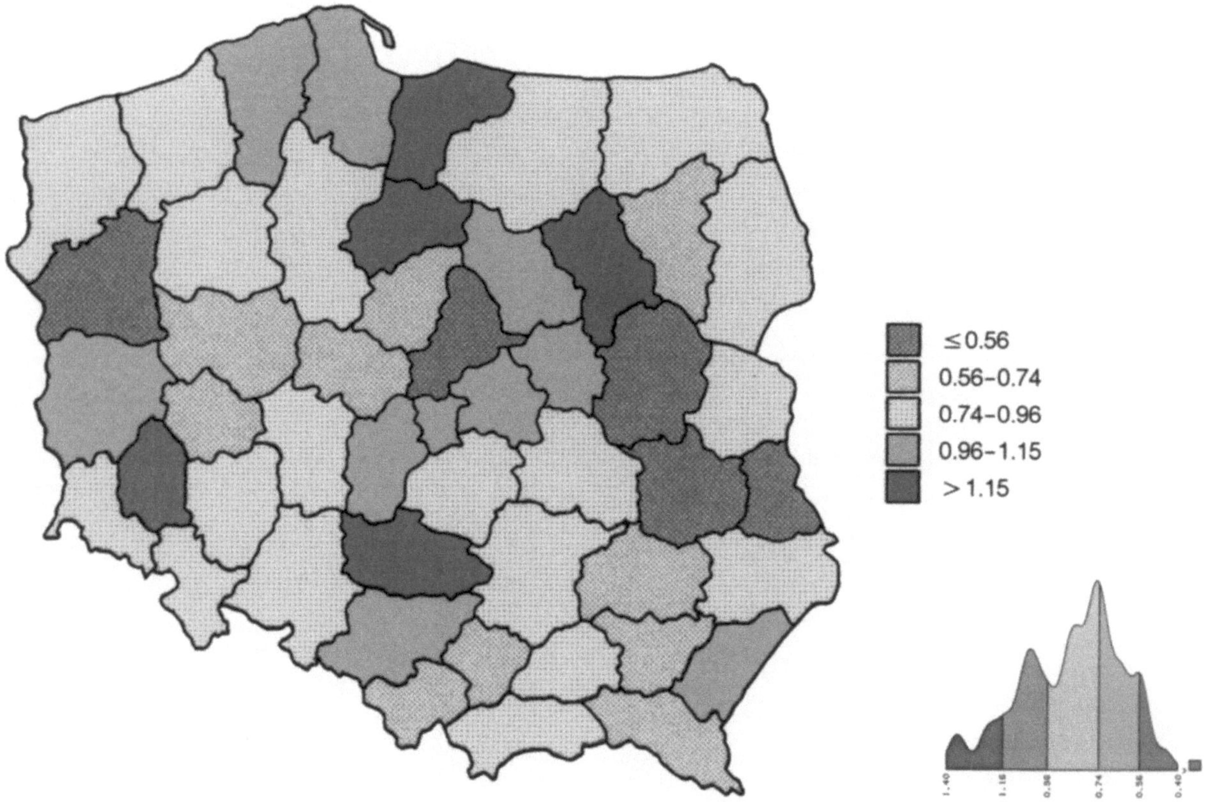
≤0.56
0.56-0.74
0.74-0.96
0.96-1.15
>1.15

5.58 – 6.50
4.66 – 5.58
3.75 – 4.66
2.83 – 3.75
1.92 – 2.83

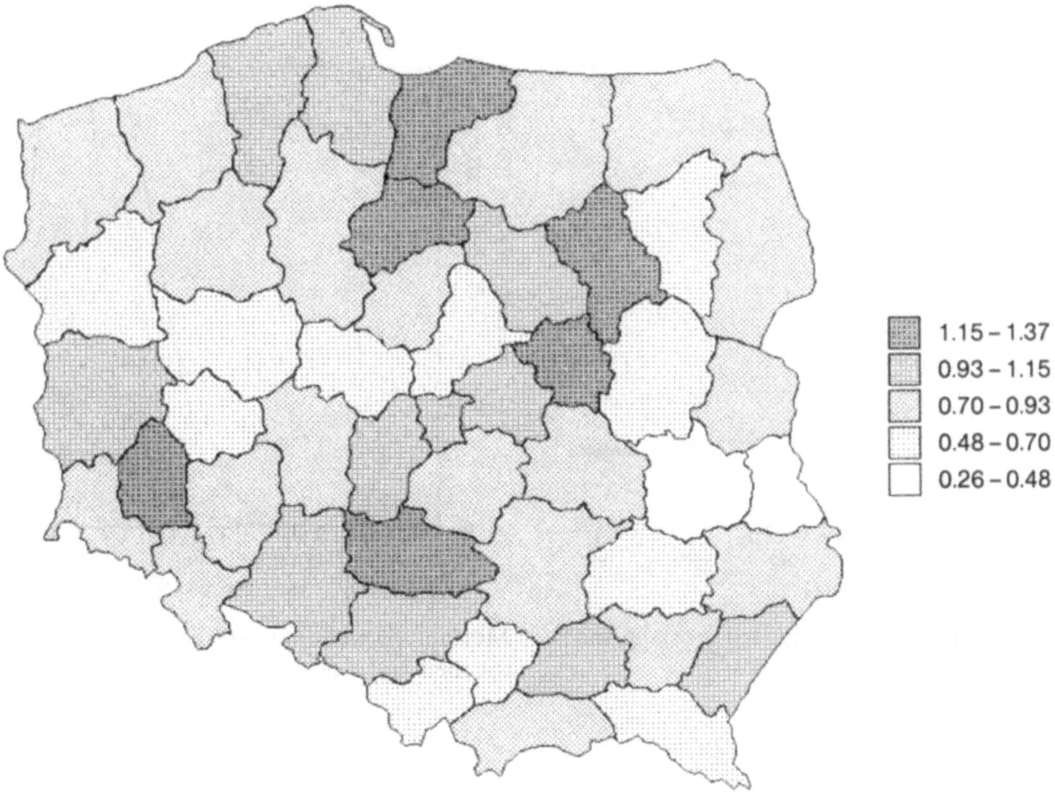
1.15 – 1.37
0.93 – 1.15
0.70 – 0.93
0.48 – 0.70
0.26 – 0.48

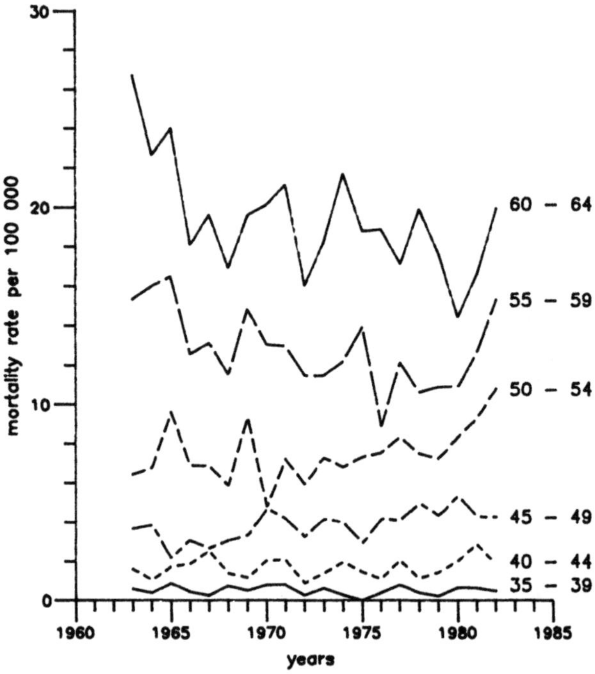

Temporal trend of mortality in individual age groups/men

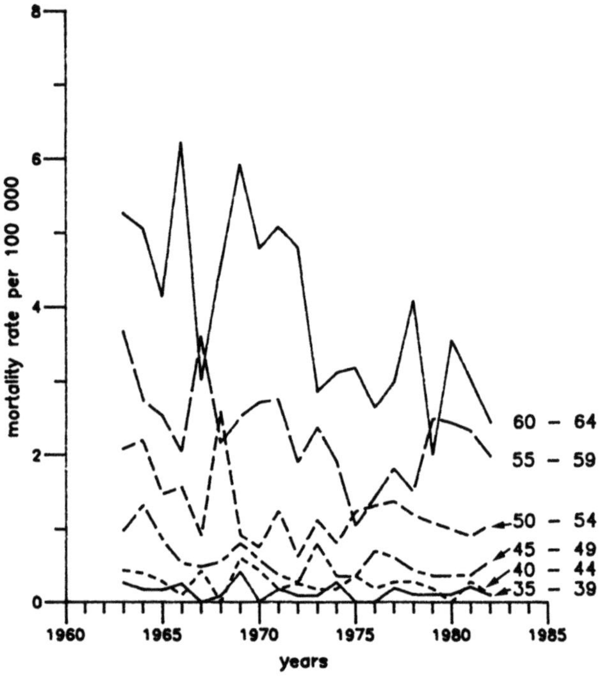

Temporal trend of mortality in individual age groups/women

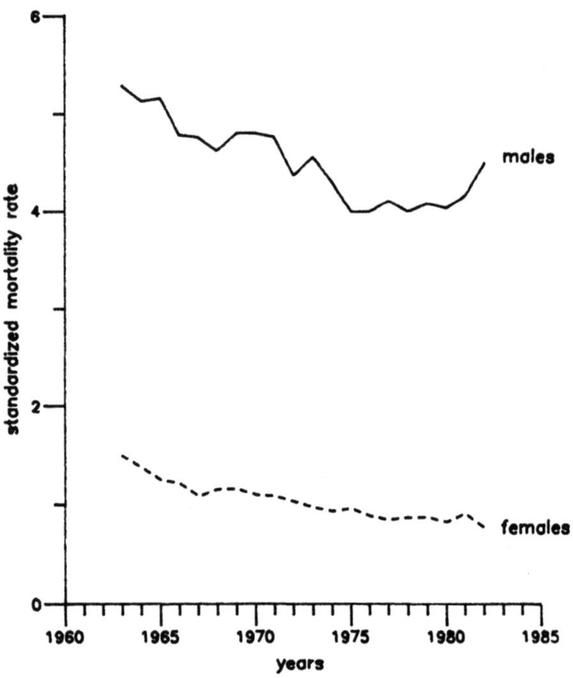

Temporal trend of the age-adjusted mortality rates for men and women

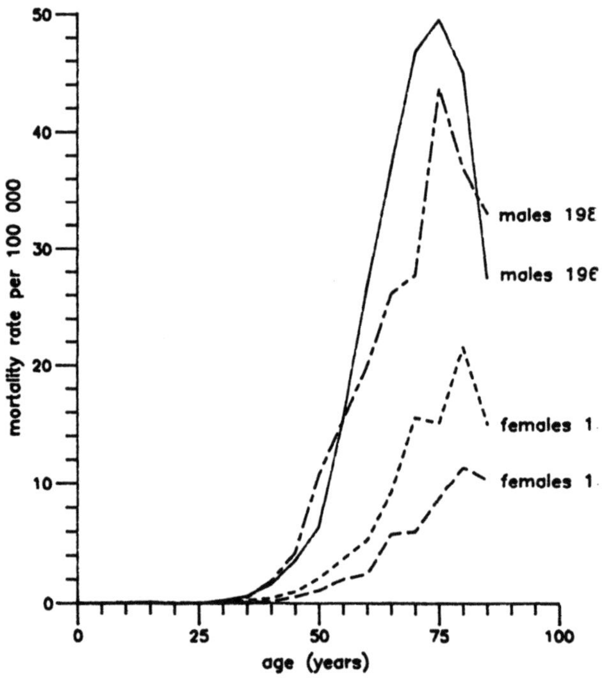

Mortality depending on age in two sample years for men and women

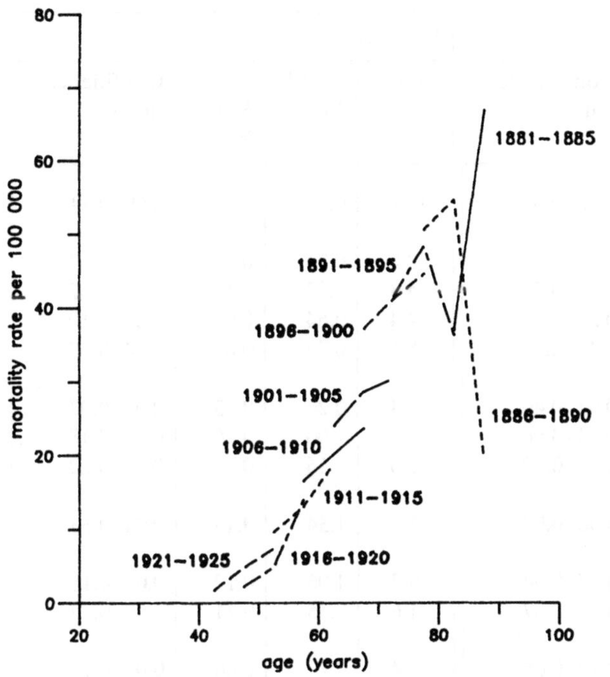

Age-dependent mortality in various birth cohorts/ men

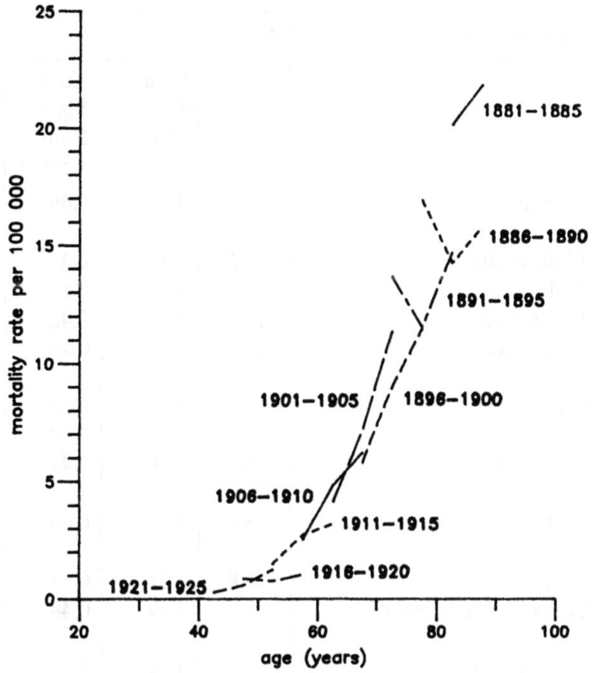

Age-dependent mortality in various birth cohorts/ women

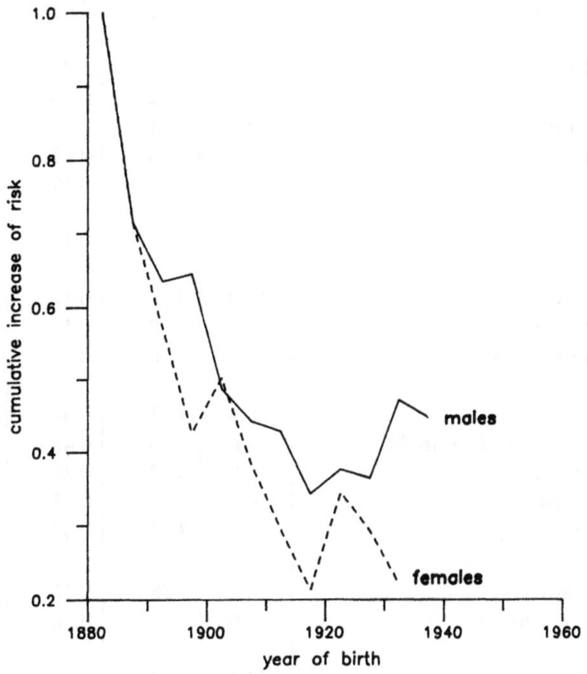

Ratios of the cumulative mortality rates for successive birth cohorts relative to the 1886-1890 cohort

Average Values 1975-1979	Males				Females			
	Cases	Stand. Mort. Rate	Cum. Mort. Rate	Confidence limits	Cases	Stand. Mort. Rate	Cum. Mort. Rate	Confidence limits
Poland	716.4	4.02	0.49	0.46-0.51	239.4	0.87	0.10	0.09-0.11
Biała Podlaska	5.6	3.19	0.40	0.17-0.62	2.0	0.74	0.09	0.00-0.17
Białystok	17.2	4.66	0.54	0.36-0.72	4.8	0.87	0.10	0.03-0.17
Bielsko Biała	14.0	3.53	0.42	0.27-0.57	4.4	0.64	0.05	0.01-0.10
Bydgoszcz	19.2	3.83	0.48	0.33-0.63	5.6	0.75	0.09	0.04-0.15
Chełm	2.6	1.92	0.22	0.03-0.40	0.4	0.26	0.03	0.00-0.07
Ciechanów	7.6	3.14	0.44	0.23-0.66	3.2	1.06	0.10	0.02-0.18
Częstochowa	17.2	3.96	0.47	0.32-0.62	7.0	1.16	0.14	0.07-0.22
Elbląg	8.8	4.93	0.64	0.36-0.92	3.2	1.34	0.18	0.04-0.33
Gdańsk	25.8	4.37	0.51	0.37-0.64	9.2	1.06	0.12	0.06-0.18
Gorzów Wielkopolski	6.8	3.49	0.44	0.22-0.67	1.6	0.55	0.11	0.00-0.22
Jelenia Góra	8.0	3.84	0.43	0.19-0.66	2.4	0.77	0.06	0.00-0.13
Kalisz	12.2	3.26	0.39	0.24-0.54	5.0	0.83	0.07	0.01-0.12
Katowice	86.8	5.37	0.63	0.54-0.73	28.6	1.05	0.11	0.08-0.14
Kielce	25.0	4.00	0.46	0.33-0.58	7.2	0.78	0.09	0.04-0.15
Konin	10.6	4.48	0.62	0.39-0.86	2.8	0.65	0.11	0.02-0.20
Koszalin	8.0	4.39	0.58	0.31-0.86	2.2	0.88	0.11	0.00-0.22
Kraków	19.6	3.29	0.46	0.33-0.59	7.6	0.70	0.08	0.04-0.13
Krosno	5.8	2.56	0.31	0.14-0.48	2.2	0.59	0.07	0.00-0.14
Legnica	5.2	3.23	0.34	0.12-0.56	2.4	1.22	0.11	0.01-0.22
Leszno	5.0	2.52	0.28	0.11-0.44	2.4	0.70	0.07	0.00-0.14
Lublin	13.2	2.54	0.31	0.19-0.43	3.0	0.46	0.06	0.02-0.11
Łomża	10.8	5.50	0.67	0.39-0.94	1.4	0.57	0.06	0.00-0.13
Łódź	28.6	4.63	0.59	0.44-0.73	10.8	1.03	0.11	0.06-0.16
Nowy Sącz	10.2	3.21	0.41	0.24-0.58	3.4	0.76	0.08	0.02-0.15
Olsztyn	13.0	4.74	0.57	0.34-0.79	3.4	0.84	0.06	0.00-0.13
Opole	20.6	4.78	0.52	0.35-0.69	7.4	0.96	0.09	0.03-0.15
Ostrołęka	13.2	6.50	0.83	0.53-1.13	3.8	1.24	0.19	0.06-0.32
Piła	8.4	3.91	0.40	0.20-0.60	2.6	0.90	0.11	0.01-0.20
Piotrków Trybunalski	14.0	3.90	0.48	0.31-0.64	5.0	0.89	0.13	0.05-0.21
Płock	8.8	3.30	0.38	0.20-0.55	2.0	0.56	0.09	0.01-0.17
Poznań	19.0	2.92	0.35	0.24-0.46	7.2	0.64	0.09	0.04-0.14
Przemyśl	7.8	3.61	0.42	0.22-0.62	3.0	0.97	0.09	0.01-0.17
Radom	16.4	4.28	0.46	0.30-0.62	4.6	0.81	0.14	0.06-0.22
Rzeszów	10.6	2.93	0.40	0.24-0.57	4.0	0.74	0.11	0.03-0.18
Siedlce	14.4	3.94	0.47	0.30-0.63	2.8	0.55	0.07	0.01-0.14
Sieradz	8.0	3.06	0.38	0.20-0.56	3.2	1.01	0.16	0.05-0.26
Skierniewice	9.2	3.76	0.50	0.27-0.72	3.6	1.11	0.11	0.02-0.19
Słupsk	7.0	5.15	0.66	0.33-0.98	1.6	1.01	0.13	0.00-0.27
Suwałki	10.0	5.41	0.68	0.39-0.97	1.8	0.76	0.09	0.00-0.18
Szczecin	14.6	4.46	0.60	0.38-0.82	3.4	0.85	0.12	0.03-0.20

Average Values 1975-1979	Males				Females			
	Cases	Stand. Mort. Rate	Cum. Mort. Rate	Confidence limits	Cases	Stand. Mort. Rate	Cum. Mort. Rate	Confidence limits
Tarnobrzeg	8.6	2.52	0.29	0.15-0.43	3.2	0.65	0.10	0.03-0.17
Tarnów	10.2	3.33	0.35	0.20-0.51	4.8	0.96	0.13	0.05-0.21
Toruń	12.6	4.41	0.57	0.36-0.77	5.8	1.37	0.17	0.08-0.27
Wałbrzych	12.6	4.12	0.42	0.24-0.60	3.6	0.80	0.09	0.02-0.17
Warszawa	61.0	5.26	0.65	0.54-0.76	24.6	1.15	0.13	0.09-0.17
Włocławek	10.0	4.55	0.56	0.33-0.80	2.2	0.71	0.09	0.01-0.17
Wrocław	16.0	3.41	0.37	0.24-0.50	5.8	0.86	0.07	0.02-0.13
Zamość	7.8	2.37	0.28	0.14-0.42	3.0	0.75	0.11	0.03-0.19
Zielona Góra	8.8	3.42	0.48	0.28-0.68	4.2	1.08	0.11	0.02-0.20

3 Stomach - ICD 151

The ASMR for men was 44.9 in 1963 and 28.4 in 1982, while the respective figures for women were 21.7 and 10.8. The time trend for both sexes in 1963-1982 shows a significant decline in the mortality rate, averaging 1.9% in men and 2.8% in women annually. The increase of risk begins after the age of 45-50 and it reaches a maximum of 420 cases per 100000 men and 220 per 100000 women. The calendar time trend in individual age groups of both sexes also shows a steep decline. The annual decrease is similar in all age groups. The cohort analysis is marked by a declining risk of cancer of the stomach. The cohort born about 1940 faces a 70%-90% lower risk than the one born about 1890.

Even 30 years ago cancer of the stomach was the most frequent malignancy in the majority of European countries. The risk of cancer of the stomach has declined in the United States over the last 30 years, and this trend is the same in all industrialised countries. In 1978 the following European countries had the highest mortality rates of cancer of the stomach in men: Hungary (33.4), Poland (32.4) and Portugal (30.9). The lowest rates were observed in France (13.1), Sweden (13.4), Greece (13.5) and Denmark (13.9). Outside Europe, the lowest figures were noted in the United States, Canada and Australia, where the rates were 6.4, 10.5 and 11.3, respectively. Japan is a country with a high risk, with a rate of 50.4 in 1978. The mortality rate for cancer of the stomach in women is half that of men in most countries. The distribution of the highest and lowest rates is similar in both sexes. In 1978 European women had the highest mortality rates in Bulgaria (15.8), Hungary (15.4) and Portugal (15.3). The rates were lowest in France (6.0), Sweden (7.0) and Greece (7.1). Outside Europe, Japanese women had the highest risk of cancer of the stomach (25.4). Women in the United States, Canada and Australia had the lowest, the respective rates were 3.1, 4.8, 5.3. Poland was among the high-risk countries, with mortality rates of 32.4 for men and 12.4 for women in 1978.

Analysis of Data from the Provinces, 1975-1979

The stomach is one of the few cancer sites whic shows higher mortality rates in rural areas than i towns. This predominance is not great, about 10% and it is tending to decrease. Cancer of the stomac occurs 2.6 times more frequently in men than i women and this difference increases with time (2. in 1963).

Men

(Mean ASMR=33.3, Range 22.0-40.7, Standar Deviation 4.2; 20% of Male Cancer Mortality Rank 2)

The highest mortality rate for cancer of stomac was 1.9 times greater than the lowest figure, whil only a few provinces have mortality rates below 3 per 100000. Provinces with the highest rates wer Konin (40.73), Tarnow (40.05), Sieradz (39.95) Przemysl (39.32) and Kielce (38.77). Provinces wit the lowest rates were Lublin (22.96), Chelm (22.6) Zamosc (25.7), Plock (27.2) and Warszawa (27.62). Cancer of the stomach shows a peculiar geograph cal pattern. The provinces with the lowest mortalit rates were in a few, clear-cut, dispersed areas, form ing geographical clusters which were identical fc both sexes. Three provinces (Lublin, Chelm, Za mos) in the central-eastern part of the country forr an area with the lowest mortality rates for cancer c the stomach in both sexes. The other low risk re gions (for both sexes) are situated in central Polan (Warszawa, Plock), the west (Poznan, Leszno) an the northwestern corner of the country (Szczecin Koszalin). Provinces with high rates are located i the central and eastern parts of the southern belt c Poland.

Women

(Mean ASMR=12.8, Range 7.8-12.8, Standard De viation 1.9; 13.9% of Female Cancer Mortality Rank 1)

The highest mortality rate was more than two-fold greater than the lowest. Provinces with the highest mortality were Przemysl (17.20), Tarnow (16.49), Torun (15.94), Rzeszow (15.82) and Bialystok (15.59). Provinces with the lowest rates were Lublin (7.79), Chelm (8.32), Zamosc (9.14), Plock (10.04) and Warszawa (10.33). Despite a considerably lower risk, the frequencies of cancer of the stomach in women strikingly resembled those in men. This is especially true for the groups of provinces with the lowest risk. The concentration of high-risk provinces was in southeastern Poland, as in the case of men, but it was even more clear-cut.

Comments

It has been suggested that changes in the techniques of food processing and storage (low temperatures), as well as higher consumption of fresh fruit and vegetables (throughout the year) are the main reasons for the declining risk of cancer of the stomach in many countries (Howson et al. 1986; Jedrychowski et al. 1986). Studies on the role of diet still provide an incomplete picture, which is also difficult to analyse. Many works suggest that roast, smoked and salted foods are risk factors. Reports on migrants stress the critical nature of exposures in childhood (Staszewski and Haenszel 1965). Others suggest relationships to nitrosamine compounds. Empirical studies on laboratory animals provide evidence of a very strong carcinogenic action of these substances. It has been postulated that the achlorhydria stomach found in patients with chronic atrophic gastritis may provide a suitable milieu for intragastric formation of N-nitrosocompounds (Correa et al. 1975), but epidemiological evidence in favour of this hypothesis is still lacking. From the epidemiological point of view, it was important to discover that the presence of vitamin C, both in vitro and in vivo, prevents the synthesis of nitrosamines (Raineri and Weisburger 1975). Alcohol and tobacco are also said to be risk factors, although they seem to play a minor role (Nomura 1982; Jedrychowski et al. 1986).

Poland has long been regarded as a country with a high risk of cancer of the stomach. Despite a steadily decreasing frequency, the mortality rates calculated for the study period of 1975-1979 make this site the second most frequent in men and the first in women. International comparisons (Segi et al. 1981) show that the male mortality rate for cancer of the stomach is lower only than those in Japan, Chile and Costa Rica, and is similar to those of neighbouring central European countries like Hungary, Czechoslovakia, and Austria. The frequency of cancer of the stomach is falling in all countries. In some (e.g. the United States) this trend has been observed for several decades (Nomura 1982). Postmortem data collected by the Jagiellonian University allow us to presume that the frequency of cancer of the stomach has also declined in some places in Poland for many decades (Ciechanowski 1948). Mortality statistics for the whole of Poland show a downward trend starting in the early 1960s. The annual rate of decline during the past two decades has been 1.9% for men and 2.8% for women. This leads to a situation where the difference between the frequency in men and women will increase (men also predominate over women in other countries). The sex ratio is 2.6, i.e. one of highest in the world (Howson et al. 1986).

Cancers of the stomach have two histological types: the intestinal type and the diffuse type, according to the division of Lauren (1965). Munoz et al. (1968) showed that these types are distributed differently in countries and sexes. Like other countries with a high risk of cancer of the stomach, Poland has more of the intestinal type, especially in men and in older age groups (Wronkowski 1985). Munoz presumes that these two types may have different aetiologies as most of the decline in cancer of the stomach is due to a decline in the intestinal type, as was shown in Norway (Munoz and Asvall 1971) and the United States (Munoz and Connelly 1971). It is possible to speculate that the various rates of decrease of cancer of the stomach in men and women may reflect, apart from the differences resulting from histological sub-types, differences in exposure to tobacco and alcohol in males and females (Jedrychowski et al. 1986). Poland is a country where many dietetic habits seem to correspond with the suspected risk factors. Meat is consumed mostly in a highly processed form, with sausages taking first place. Processing and preservation of meat continues to be done using large amounts of salt and saltpetre, or by smoking. Daily intake of salt per head is estimated at 15-20g. Low temperatures for food storage are far from commonplace. Many vegetables are consumed as pickles. Most people still eat fresh vegetables and fruit only seasonally.

The stomach is a cancer site that shows even the smallest differences in various regions. The difference between the highest and the lowest mortality rates is among the smallest (together with leukaemia) in all sites (1.8 for men and 2.2 for women). The diagram of frequencies in individual provinces shows the majority of regions grouped around the mean value, while groups of provinces with low and high risk are relatively clear-cut.

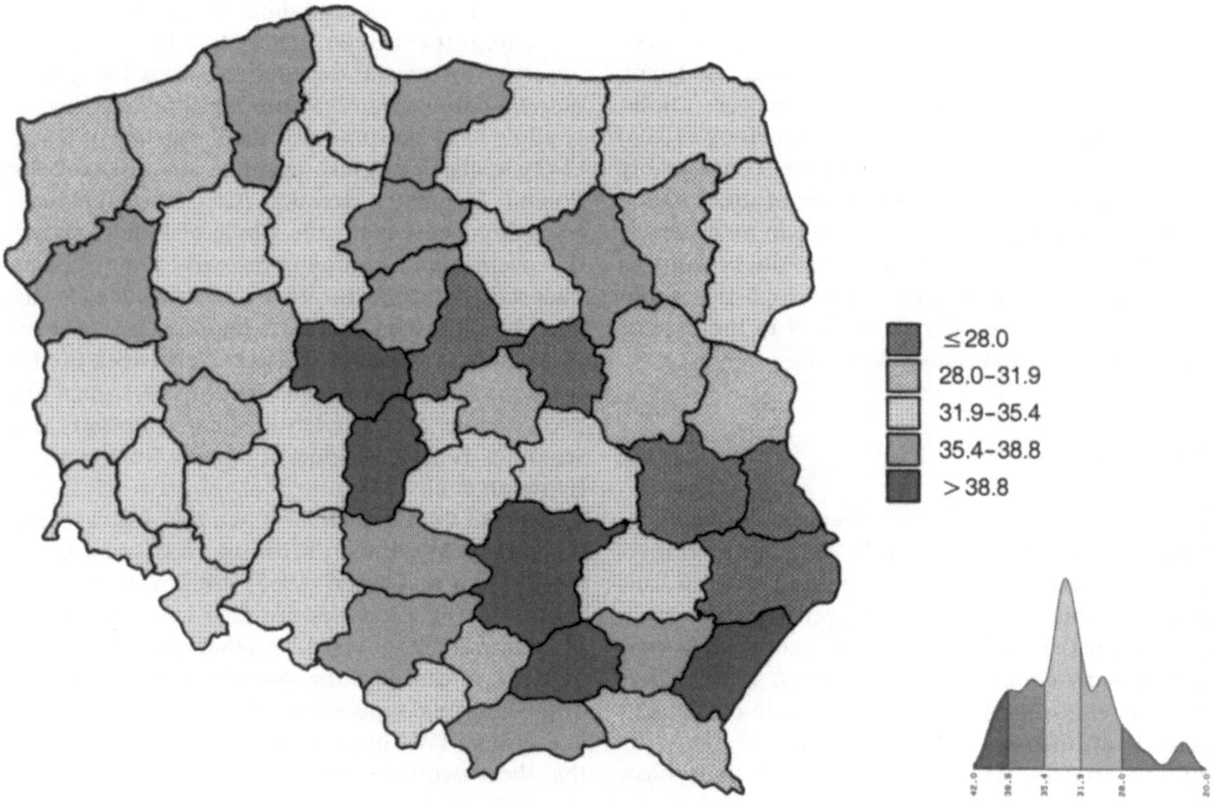
≤28.0
28.0-31.9
31.9-35.4
35.4-38.8
>38.8

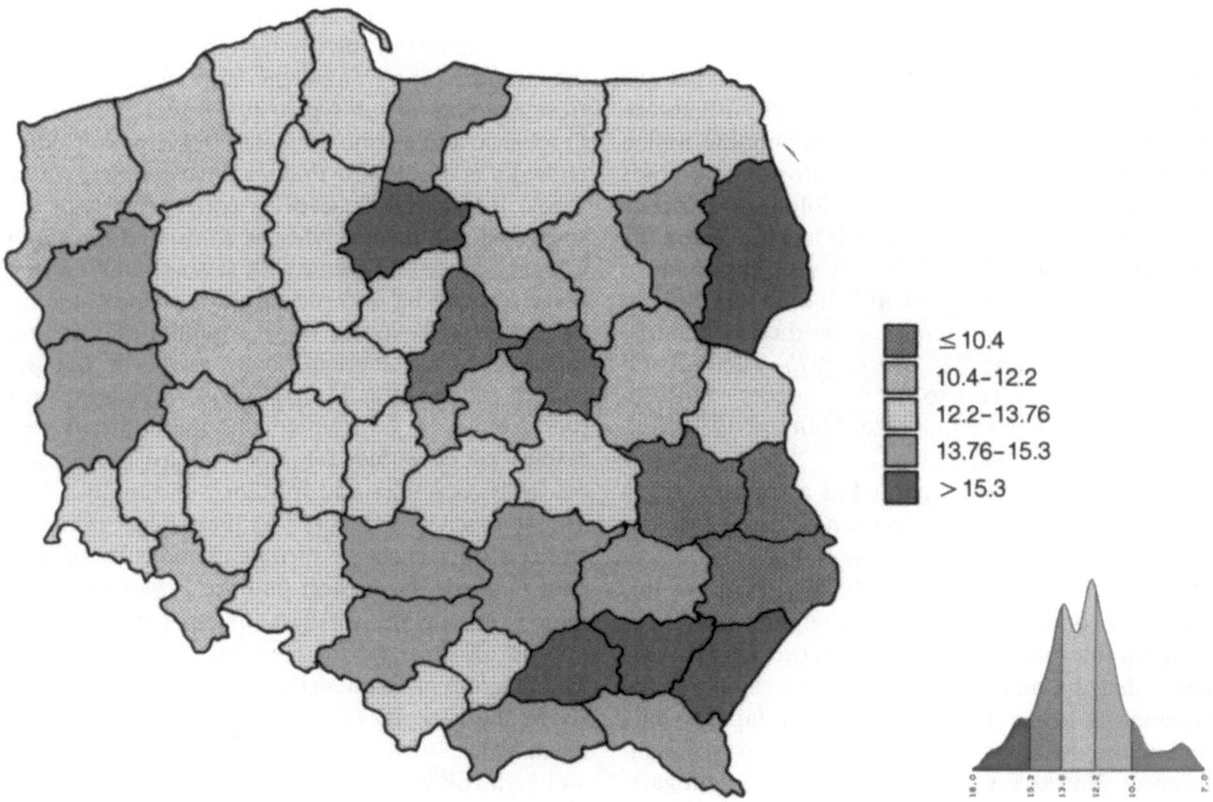
≤10.4
10.4-12.2
12.2-13.76
13.76-15.3
>15.3

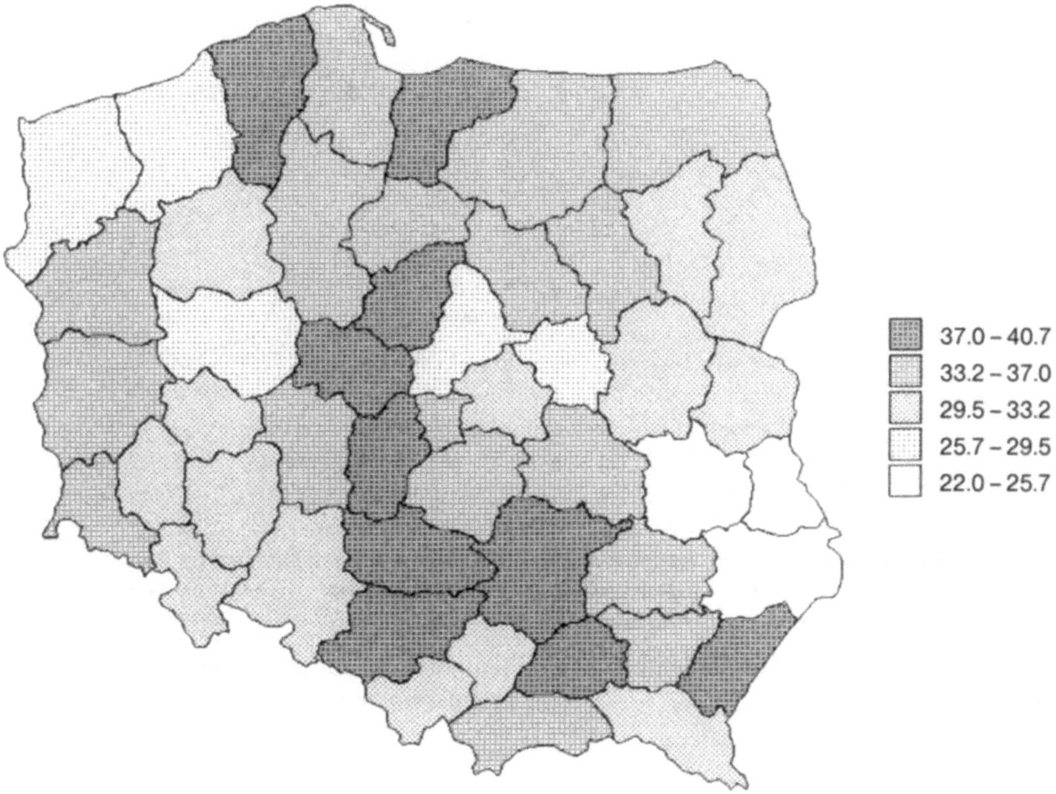
37.0 – 40.7
33.2 – 37.0
29.5 – 33.2
25.7 – 29.5
22.0 – 25.7

15.3 – 17.2
13.4 – 15.3
11.6 – 13.4
9.7 – 11.6
7.8 – 9.7

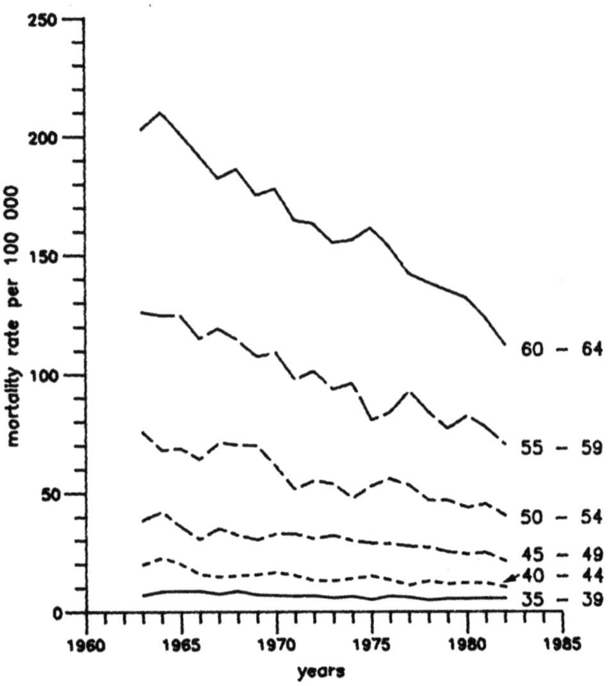

Temporal trend of mortality in individual age groups/men

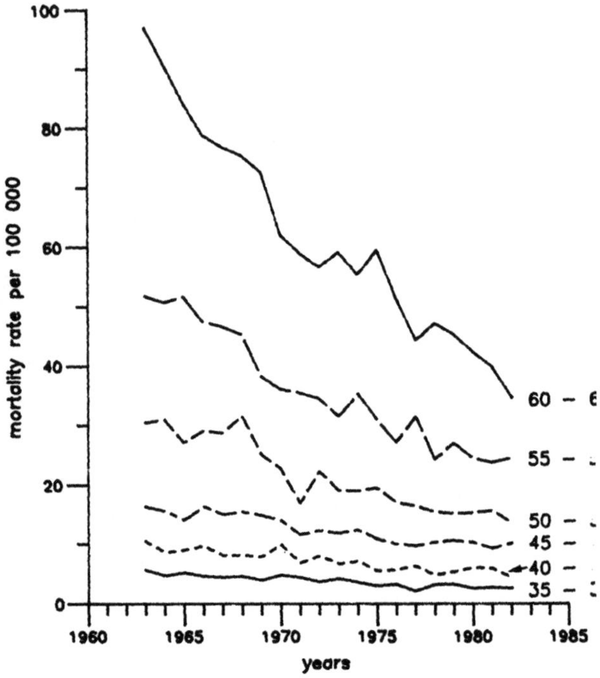

Temporal trend of mortality in individual age groups/women

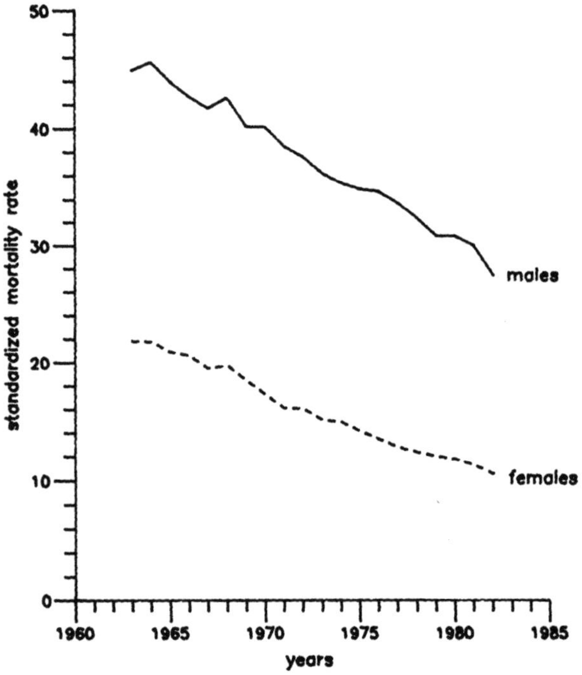

Temporal trend of the age-adjusted mortality rates for men and women

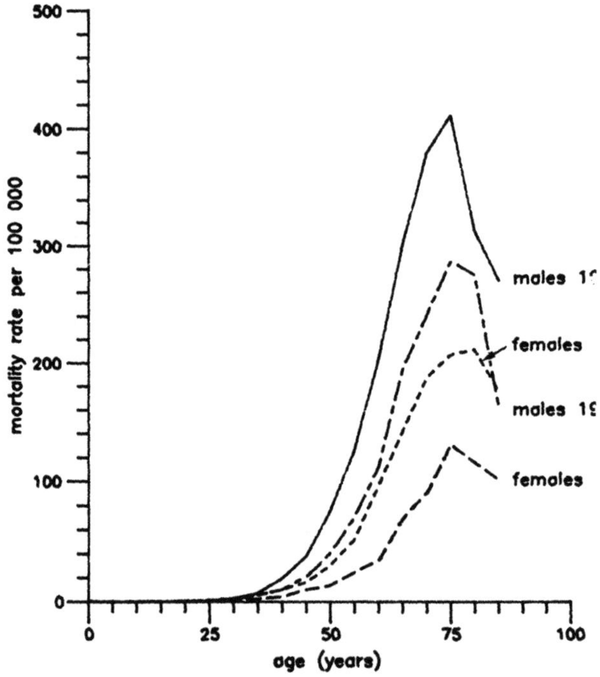

Mortality depending on age in two sample years for men and women

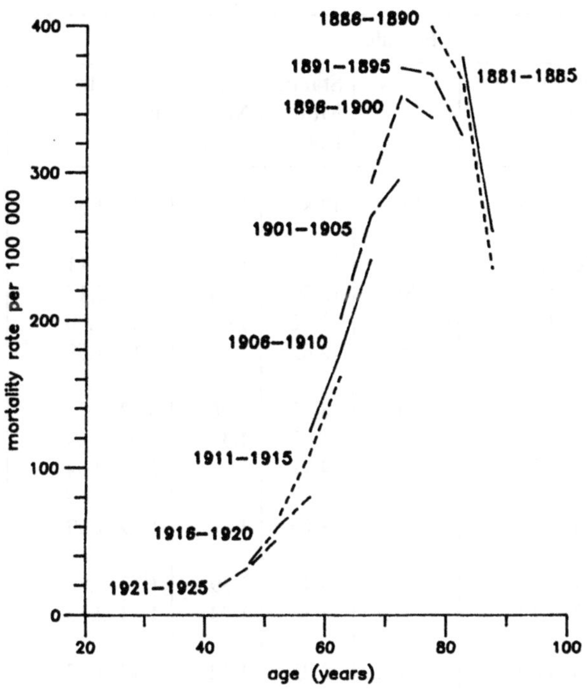

Age-dependent mortality in various birth cohorts/ men

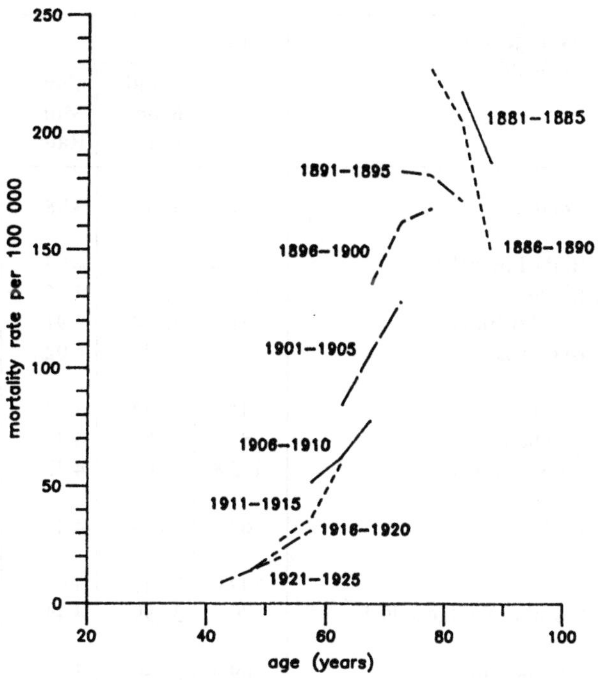

Age-dependent mortality in various birth cohorts/ women

Although there is a difference in the frequency of men and women contracting cancer of the stomach, the same provinces appear to have identical risk in both sexes. Low-risk provinces form scattered groups where both sexes are under identical risk. It is, however, difficult to find the common characteristics. The east-west trend found for other cancer sites is hardly noticeable. The provinces with the highest risk, located in southeastern Poland, are next to the provinces with the lowest risk. On the one hand, the high-risk area includes the highly industrialised area of Silesia (Katowice), and on the other, the very low-risk area comprises an urbanised place such as Warszawa, together with the rural areas of Chelm and Zamosc. The only common feature of the high-risk provinces is that they are located in the hilly south of Poland. Cancer of the stomach in other countries often shows an obvious regional character. The latest good example has been provided by an analysis of mortality related to this cancer in the Federal Republic of Germany, which points to an evident high-risk area in Bavaria (Becker et al. 1984).

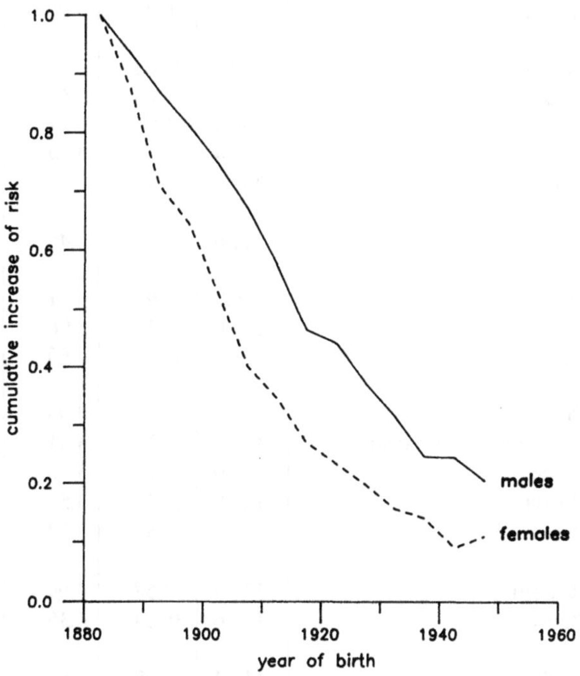

Ratios of the cumulative mortality rates for successive birth cohorts relative to the 1886–1890 cohort

Average Values 1975-1979	Males				Females			
	Cases	Stand. Mort. Rate	Cum. Mort. Rate	Confidence limits	Cases	Stand. Mort. Rate	Cum. Mort. Rate	Confidence limits
Poland	5951.6	33.18	4.08	4.01-4.15	3401.8	12.81	1.52	1.48-1.56
Biała Podlaska	57.4	31.86	4.09	3.40-4.78	32.2	13.76	1.70	1.30-2.11
Białystok	128.8	32.82	3.96	3.49-4.43	85.8	15.59	1.88	1.59-2.17
Bielsko Biała	131.2	32.14	3.91	3.45-4.37	82.2	13.62	1.65	1.39-1.90
Bydgoszcz	174.4	33.47	4.02	3.62-4.43	96.2	12.62	1.38	1.18-1.59
Chełm	31.0	22.57	3.07	2.37-3.76	16.2	8.32	0.96	0.62-1.30
Ciechanów	81.0	34.81	4.40	3.77-5.04	36.6	11.52	1.37	1.04-1.69
Częstochowa	162.8	38.01	4.72	4.24-5.20	93.6	14.71	1.78	1.52-2.04
Elbląg	67.2	38.76	4.84	4.06-5.61	32.8	13.79	1.59	1.19-1.99
Gdańsk	199.0	33.41	4.01	3.63-4.39	118.6	13.46	1.59	1.38-1.80
Gorzów Wielkopolski	70.8	35.99	4.44	3.73-5.14	37.2	14.38	1.73	1.33-2.13
Jelenia Góra	69.4	34.40	3.94	3.28-4.60	34.2	12.23	1.32	0.97-1.67
Kalisz	128.4	33.94	4.18	3.70-4.65	73.2	13.21	1.61	1.34-1.87
Katowice	637.8	38.58	4.71	4.46-4.96	401.0	14.92	1.70	1.58-1.83
Kielce	241.0	38.77	4.90	4.49-5.31	120.6	14.13	1.65	1.44-1.86
Konin	103.6	40.73	5.05	4.41-5.68	47.2	13.68	1.72	1.37-2.06
Koszalin	51.6	29.30	3.59	2.91-4.26	27.8	12.10	1.57	1.16-1.98
Kraków	172.2	30.24	3.71	3.34-4.09	121.6	13.00	1.55	1.34-1.75
Krosno	69.6	30.24	3.96	3.34-4.57	51.2	14.67	1.96	1.59-2.33
Legnica	52.8	32.02	3.66	2.95-4.37	29.0	13.44	1.47	1.07-1.87
Leszno	59.2	29.88	3.61	2.99-4.23	33.0	11.40	1.32	0.99-1.65
Lublin	109.4	21.96	2.81	2.46-3.16	55.2	7.79	0.96	0.78-1.14
Łomża	63.4	30.61	4.14	3.47-4.80	35.2	14.15	1.71	1.32-2.11
Łódź	209.0	33.71	4.05	3.68-4.42	125.0	11.87	1.32	1.14-1.49
Nowy Sącz	111.6	35.86	4.45	3.90-5.00	67.2	14.96	1.75	1.44-2.05
Olsztyn	86.2	33.92	4.21	3.61-4.81	47.6	12.83	1.30	1.01-1.59
Opole	139.0	33.11	3.96	3.50-4.42	82.8	12.48	1.41	1.18-1.63
Ostrołęka	73.6	36.96	4.65	3.95-5.35	31.2	11.68	1.54	1.18-1.91
Piła	68.2	32.71	4.03	3.38-4.67	37.8	12.59	1.39	1.05-1.73
Piotrków Trybunalski	121.2	34.85	4.41	3.91-4.92	59.8	12.30	1.50	1.24-1.77
Płock	74.0	27.23	3.36	2.86-3.86	36.2	10.04	1.18	0.91-1.45
Poznań	189.8	29.43	3.51	3.17-3.84	113.6	11.11	1.30	1.12-1.48
Przemyśl	87.2	39.32	5.12	4.42-5.81	58.8	17.20	2.19	1.79-2.59
Radom	131.4	33.58	4.04	3.57-4.50	67.2	12.42	1.57	1.31-1.83
Rzeszów	123.6	36.24	4.35	3.82-4.86	76.6	15.82	1.94	1.63-2.25
Siedlce	112.4	29.68	3.82	3.36-4.28	53.0	10.49	1.38	1.12-1.63
Sieradz	102.8	39.95	4.98	4.36-5.59	44.8	12.71	1.51	1.20-1.83
Skierniewice	75.0	31.77	3.86	3.26-4.45	37.4	11.14	1.40	1.08-1.72
Słupsk	53.8	36.98	4.80	3.94-5.66	23.6	12.33	1.32	0.92-1.72
Suwałki	64.4	33.34	4.19	3.48-4.89	35.8	13.55	1.62	1.22-2.01
Szczecin	95.4	28.48	3.61	3.09-4.12	50.8	11.40	1.45	1.17-1.73

Average Values 1975-1979	Males				Females			
	Cases	Stand. Mort. Rate	Cum. Mort. Rate	Confidence limits	Cases	Stand. Mort. Rate	Cum. Mort. Rate	Confidence limits
Tarnobrzeg	110.2	33.45	4.17	3.65-4.68	62.4	13.87	1.69	1.39-1.99
Tarnów	132.0	40.05	5.10	4.52-5.67	77.4	16.49	2.03	1.71-2.35
Toruń	106.2	36.42	4.37	3.82-4.92	71.4	15.94	1.91	1.59-2.23
Wałbrzych	97.6	32.69	3.89	3.35-4.43	48.6	11.56	1.41	1.13-1.70
Warszawa	329.0	27.62	3.28	3.03-3.52	224.6	10.33	1.13	1.01-1.25
Włocławek	82.0	37.48	4.58	3.92-5.23	40.2	12.35	1.56	1.22-1.90
Wrocław	145.4	32.36	3.79	3.35-4.23	79.8	12.33	1.46	1.22-1.70
Zamość	80.8	25.67	3.43	2.95-3.92	36.2	9.14	1.18	0.93-1.44
Zielona Góra	87.8	34.44	4.08	3.49-4.67	51.4	13.93	1.70	1.36-2.04

4 Colon – ICD 153

The ASMR for cancer of the colon in men was 3.0 in 1963 and 4.6 in 1982, while the respective figures for women were 2.8 and 3.4. The time trend for 1963–1982 was in two phases: an increase in mortality over the period 1963–1978 in males and females, and after that, in 1979–1982, a decrease for both sexes. The mortality rates increase rapidly with age starting from about 40. The extreme value for both sexes is about 45 deaths per 100000. Mortality increase with calendar time is also observed (usually by the end of the 1970s) in all single age groups and in both sexes.

In 1978 the highest rates in Europe were observed in men in the Republic of Ireland (15.2) and in Scotland (15.0). The lowest were reported in Bulgaria (3.9), Yugoslavia (4.3) and Poland (5.0). Outside Europe, the highest rates were found in New Zealand and Australia (15.7) as well as in Canada (15.3). The mortality rate was low in Japan (5.5). The women's mortality rate was very similar. Europe's highest rates were observed in the Republic of Ireland (14.2), Scotland (13.6) and Northern Ireland (13.4). The lowest were found in Yugoslavia (3.4), Bulgaria (3.9) and Poland (4.1). With rates of 5.0 for men and 4.1 for women, Poland belonged to the low-risk countries.

Analysis of Data from the Provinces 1975–1979

Malignant neoplasms of the colon were much more frequent in city dwellers than in the rural population. The town/country ratio for both sexes was 1.7. This cancer was slightly more frequent among men than women (1.2).

Men

(Mean ASMR = 4.3, Range 2.4–7.7, Standard Deviation 1.1; 2.8% of Male Cancer Mortality, Rank 10)

The maximum/minimum ratio was 3.2. Provinces with the highest rates were Warszawa (7.74), Poznan (6.27), Katowice (6.25), Lodz (5.79) and Krakow (5.72). Provinces with the lowest rates were Rzeszow (2.41), Radom (2.74), Ciechanow (2.77), Lomza (2.82) and Ostroleka (2.85). The mortality rates were fairly uniform in all provinces, with the exception of the province of Warszawa which had a very high rate (7.74) and was well ahead of the second-highest rate of 6.27. The geographical distribution ran along the east-west line: the mortality rate was low in eastern parts and increased westwards to reach medium values in central Poland and high rates in the west. Only the highly industrialised provinces, such as Warszawa, Katowice, Krakow and Poznan, defy this pattern and belong to the group of provinces with relatively high mortality rates, irrespective of their geographical situation.

Women

(Mean ASMR = 3.5, Range 2.0–6.1, Standard Deviation 0.9; 4.2% of Female Cancer Mortality Rank 9)

The highest value was 3.1 times greater than the lowest. Provinces with the highest rates were Warszawa (6.13), Lodz (5.77), Poznan (5.43), Katowice (4.89) and Leszno (4.88). Provinces with the lowest rates were Zamosc (1.95), Przemysl (1.98), Tarnobrzeg (2.14), Rzeszow (2.23) and Ostroleka (2.33). The mortality rates are symmetric over the whole range except the three very high values in the provinces of Warszawa, Lodz and Poznan. The highly urbanised provinces of Warszawa, Lodz, Poznan Katowice (Silesia) and Krakow were the ones where risk was greatest for both men and women. The only exception is the presence of the province of Leszno (where a rural population predominates) in this group of provinces with high risk for both sexes. Similarly, the low-risk provinces were usually the same for men and women. As in the case of men, the geographical alignment is of the east-west type, in which provinces with the lowest risk form two clusters in the eastern part of central Poland. The highest rates predominate in the western parts of the country.

Comments

Despite a large number of epidemiological studies, the aetiology of cancer of the colon remains unclear. It is believed that a highly refined diet rich in fats and meat is a risk factor, whereas food rich in dietary fibre is a protective factor (Zaridze 1983). Some studies also seem to suggest a possible connection with alcohol consumption (McMichael et al. 1979). Comparative studies of migrating populations, especially the classic works of Haenszel (1961; Haenszel et al. 1973) and those carried out by Staszewski (1971, 1976; Staszewski and Haenszel 1965) show that environmental differences in general dietary habits are the main element. Nutritional changes connected with the dietary habits found in the new country (USA, Australia) lead to the fact that immigrants from low-risk countries (Japan, Poland) face the same risk as indigenous people within one or two generations' time. Interestingly enough, religious groups, such as the Seventh Day Adventists or Mormons who obey specific dietary regimens, have a low risk of cancer of the colon and rectum (Enstrom 1975; Phillips 1975).

Poland had and continues to have, one of the lowest rates of mortality from the cancer of the colon in Europe. The risk is increasing steadily or at least it increased up to the end of the 1970s. The decrease in mortality rates observed over the period 1978-1982 is rather difficult to interprete. However, it is parallel in time to the decrease (starting from 1975) in the consumption of animal fats and meat.

The relationship between cancers of the colon and rectum is intriguing. In North America (USA and Canada), where the mortality rate for cancers of the lower digestive tract is very high, mortality rates for cancer of the colon are substantially higher than for rectal cancer. Rectal cancer in Japan, unlike most developed countries, is more frequent than cancer of the colon (Schottenfeld and Winawar 1982). The risk of rectal cancer in Poland is increasing much faster than the risk of cancer of the colon, which can be seen from the dynamics of the increase, especially in the analogous age groups (see section 3.5). The much more rapid increase in the mortality rate for rectal cancer has reversed the proportions of these two indices in the last two decades. Both rates were at a similar level in the early 1960s, whereas the mortality rate for rectal cancer increased much faster and was nearly twice as high as cancer of the colon at the beginning of 1980s. This is the complete opposite of the trend observed in Polish migrants to the United States. As described by Staszewski (1976) a higher proportion of cancer of the colon compared to rectal cancers occurred among Polish born persons who died in the United States.

Cancer of the colon shows the most distinct geographical pattern of all cancer sites. Well-marked divisions are observed between the low-risk area in the east, the medium-risk area in the central parts, and the high-risk area in the west. These are interspersed only by the urbanised areas which had the highest risk of all. Urbanisation in Poland closely related to many life-style factors, including diet, appears to be the most powerful factor influencing the geographical alignment of mortality from cancer of the colon.

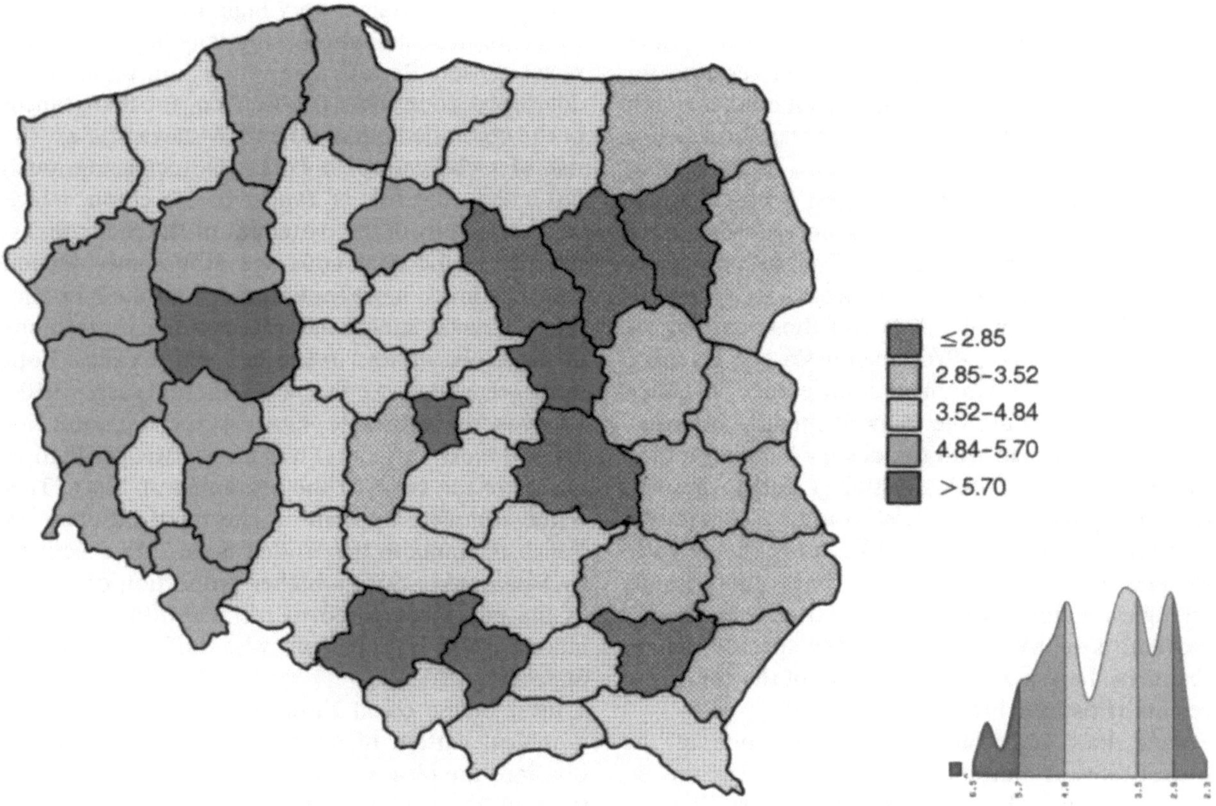
≤2.85
2.85–3.52
3.52–4.84
4.84–5.70
>5.70

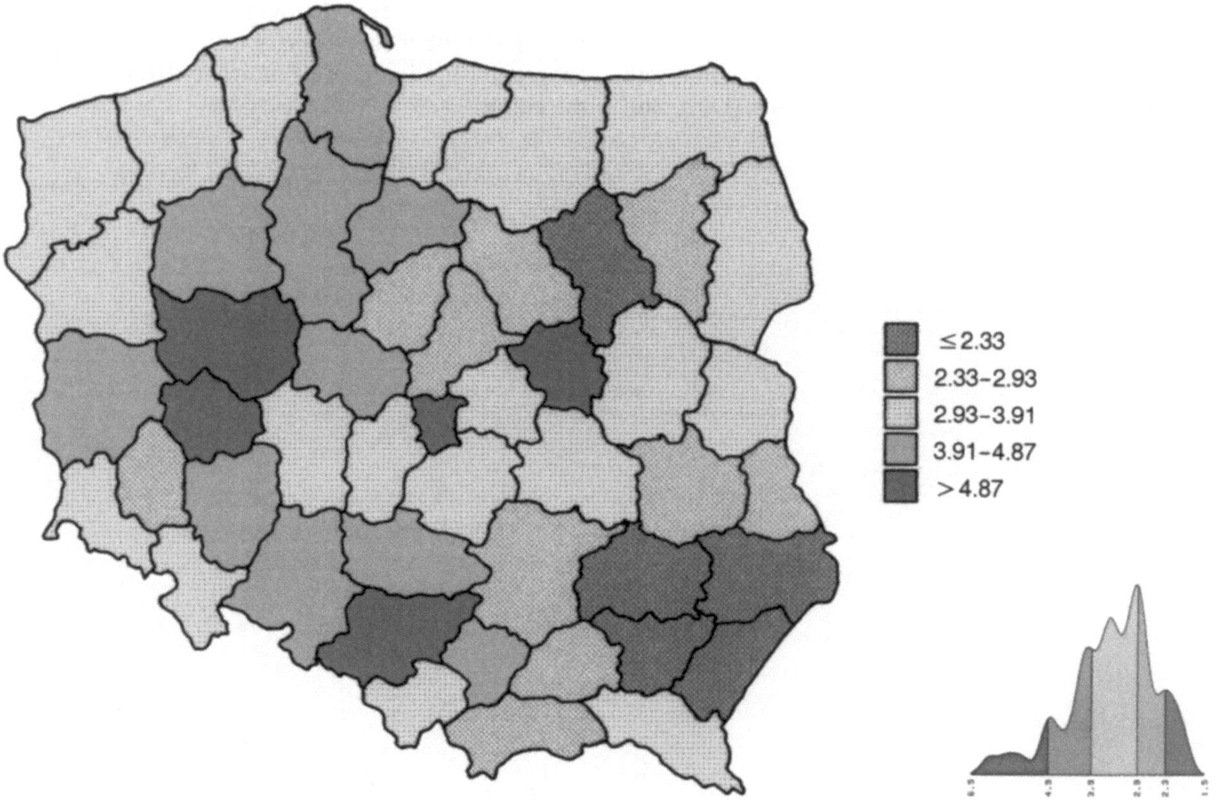
≤2.33
2.33–2.93
2.93–3.91
3.91–4.87
>4.87

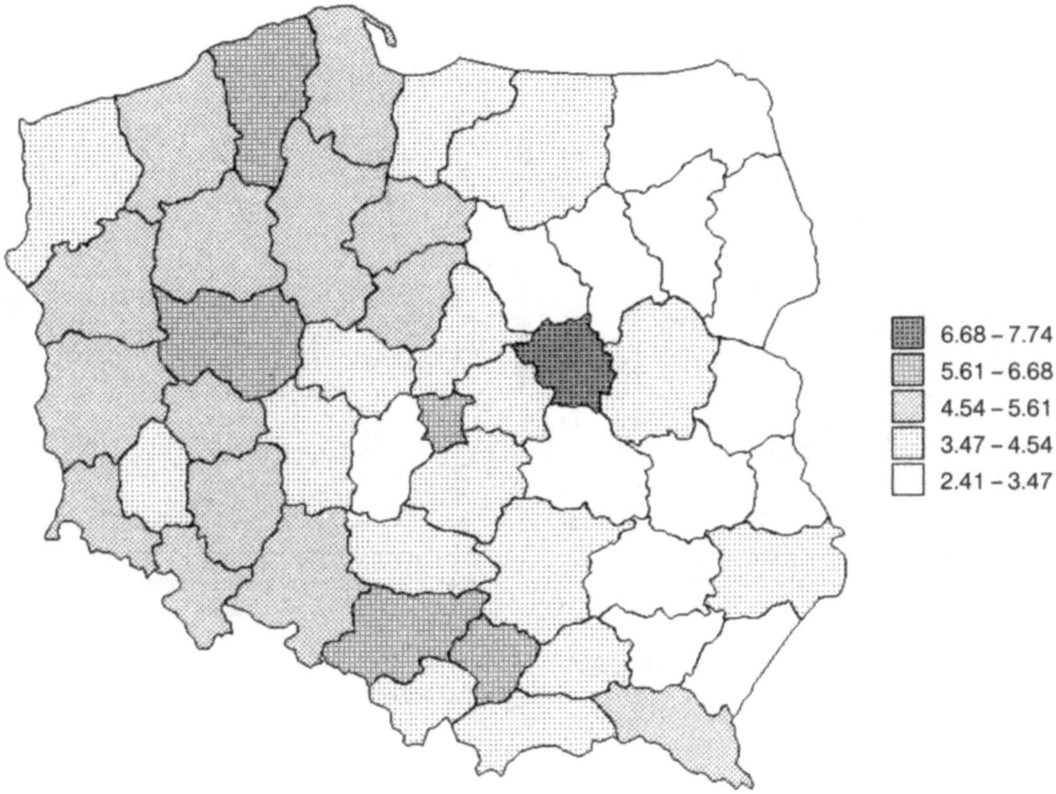
6.68 – 7.74
5.61 – 6.68
4.54 – 5.61
3.47 – 4.54
2.41 – 3.47

5.29 – 6.13
4.46 – 5.29
3.62 – 4.46
2.79 – 3.62
1.95 – 2.79

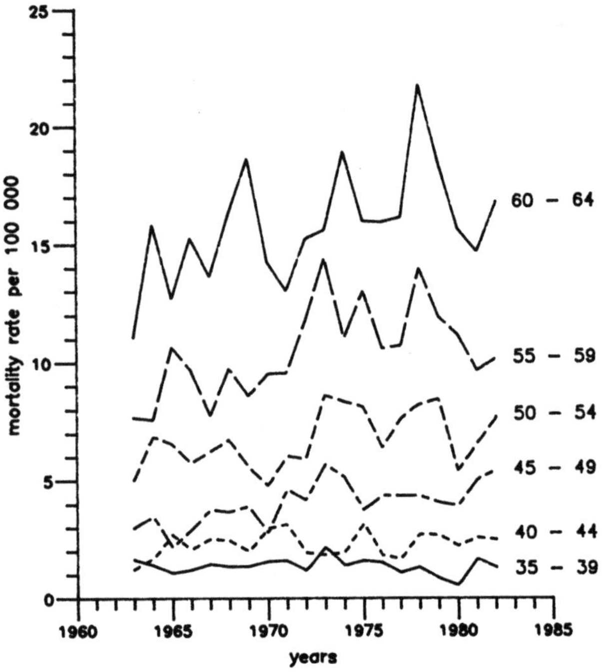

Temporal trend of mortality in individual age groups/men

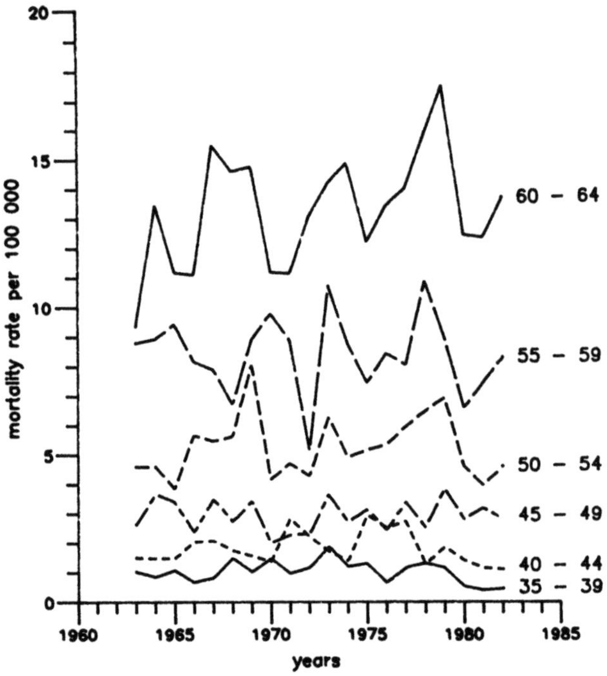

Temporal trend of mortality in individual age groups/women

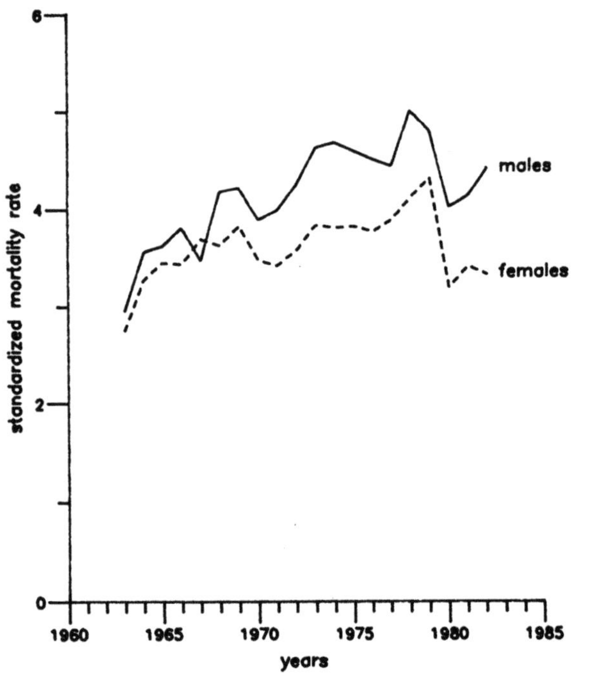

Temporal trend of the age-adjusted mortality rates for men and women

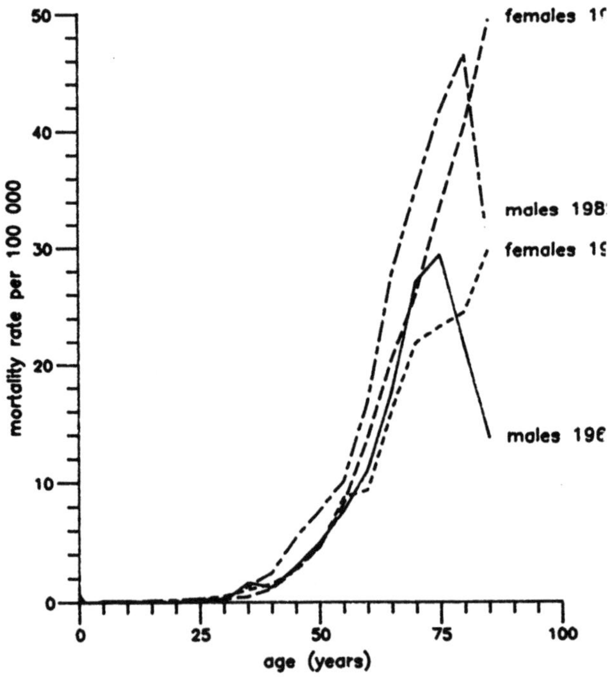

Mortality depending on age in two sample years for men and women

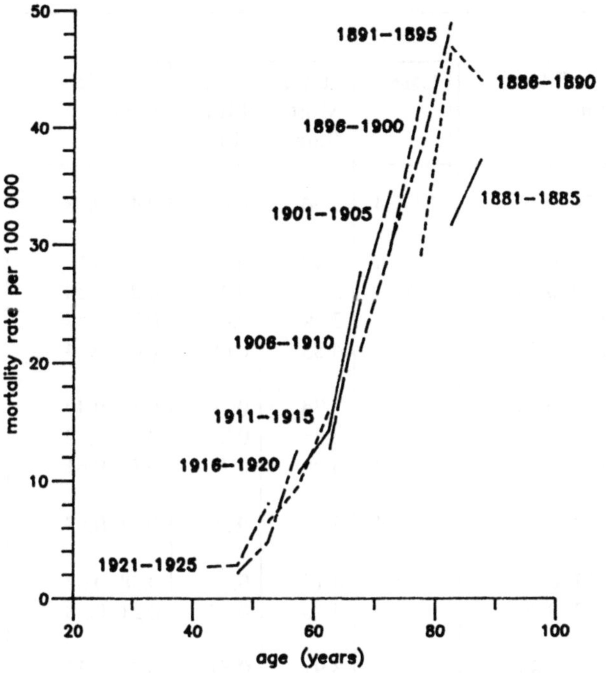

Age-dependent mortality in various birth cohorts/ men

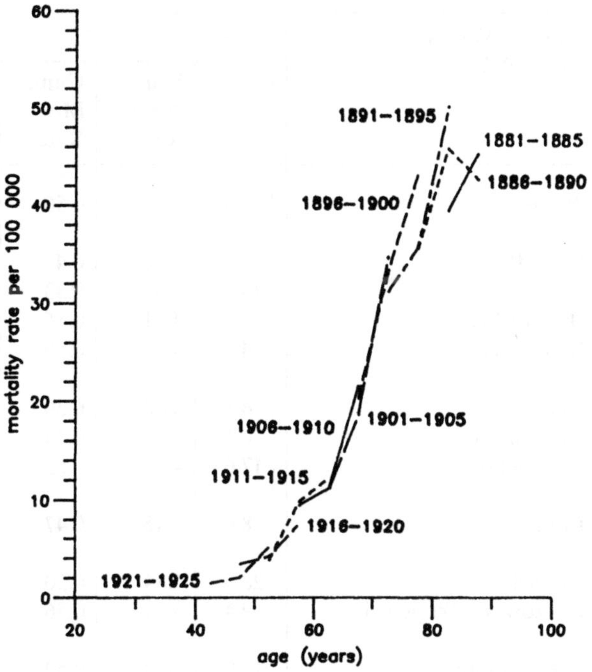

Age-dependent mortality in various birth cohorts/ women

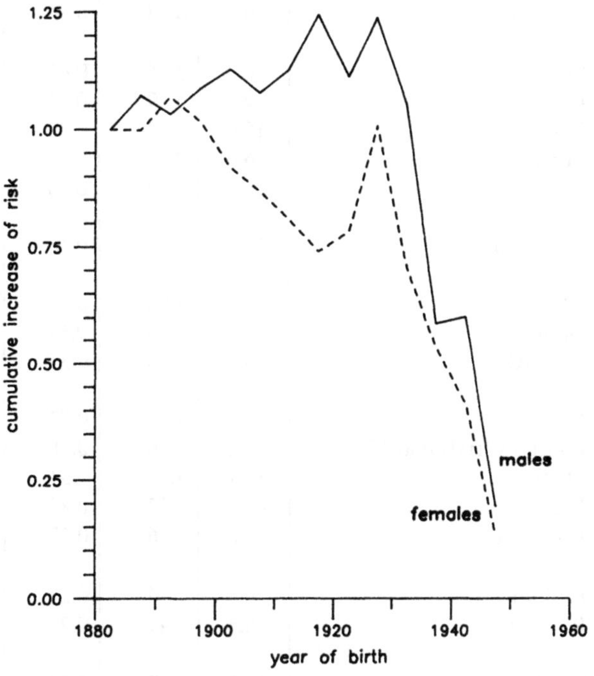

Ratios of the cumulative mortality rates for successive birth cohorts relative to the 1886–1890 cohort

Average Values 1975-1979	Males				Females			
	Cases	Stand. Mort. Rate	Cum. Mort. Rate	Confidence limits	Cases	Stand. Mort. Rate	Cum. Mort. Rate	Confidence limits
Poland	833.4	4.62	0.56	0.54-0.59	1035.4	3.94	0.46	0.44-0.48
Biała Podlaska	6.0	3.10	0.47	0.23-0.71	7.4	3.10	0.43	0.22-0.63
Białystok	13.2	3.06	0.33	0.19-0.46	16.0	3.15	0.40	0.27-0.54
Bielsko Biała	17.2	4.21	0.55	0.38-0.73	21.8	3.69	0.41	0.28-0.53
Bydgoszcz	24.6	4.73	0.59	0.43-0.75	38.0	4.83	0.60	0.46-0.74
Chełm	4.8	3.46	0.50	0.21-0.78	5.2	2.74	0.30	0.11-0.49
Ciechanów	6.4	2.77	0.34	0.16-0.51	7.6	2.55	0.28	0.13-0.42
Częstochowa	17.6	4.03	0.53	0.36-0.69	24.2	4.06	0.47	0.34-0.61
Elbląg	8.0	4.45	0.47	0.23-0.72	7.4	3.13	0.38	0.18-0.57
Gdańsk	28.0	4.84	0.50	0.37-0.64	35.8	4.17	0.50	0.38-0.62
Gorzów Wielkopolski	9.4	5.01	0.56	0.32-0.80	9.2	3.46	0.39	0.21-0.58
Jelenia Góra	11.0	5.28	0.59	0.33-0.85	11.0	3.91	0.51	0.29-0.73
Kalisz	14.0	3.75	0.47	0.31-0.64	20.8	3.57	0.41	0.27-0.54
Katowice	103.0	6.25	0.77	0.66-0.87	127.2	4.89	0.56	0.49-0.63
Kielce	22.2	3.53	0.46	0.34-0.59	19.6	2.36	0.29	0.20-0.38
Konin	8.8	3.54	0.37	0.19-0.54	13.4	3.97	0.45	0.28-0.63
Koszalin	8.8	4.63	0.54	0.27-0.80	7.4	3.15	0.44	0.22-0.66
Kraków	33.4	5.72	0.69	0.53-0.86	42.4	4.61	0.53	0.42-0.65
Krosno	10.4	4.75	0.66	0.40-0.92	12.0	3.60	0.42	0.25-0.59
Legnica	6.0	3.75	0.43	0.17-0.68	6.8	2.93	0.33	0.14-0.53
Leszno	9.6	5.39	0.58	0.33-0.83	13.4	4.88	0.59	0.37-0.81
Lublin	15.6	3.02	0.35	0.23-0.47	20.4	2.81	0.32	0.22-0.42
Łomża	6.0	2.82	0.43	0.20-0.65	7.4	2.93	0.30	0.14-0.47
Łódź	38.2	5.79	0.70	0.54-0.86	58.4	5.77	0.64	0.51-0.76
Nowy Sącz	12.2	3.83	0.46	0.28-0.63	11.8	2.43	0.28	0.16-0.41
Olsztyn	10.6	3.96	0.56	0.34-0.79	13.0	3.40	0.41	0.24-0.58
Opole	20.6	4.84	0.64	0.45-0.83	25.8	3.99	0.50	0.36-0.63
Ostrołęka	5.8	2.85	0.33	0.13-0.52	6.8	2.33	0.32	0.15-0.49
Piła	11.6	5.54	0.73	0.45-1.02	12.0	4.14	0.54	0.33-0.75
Piotrków Trybunalski	13.2	3.76	0.38	0.23-0.53	17.0	3.47	0.41	0.27-0.55
Płock	10.4	3.79	0.51	0.30-0.71	10.0	2.90	0.39	0.23-0.54
Poznań	40.6	6.27	0.82	0.65-0.99	54.6	5.43	0.60	0.48-0.72
Przemyśl	6.8	3.16	0.37	0.18-0.56	7.6	1.98	0.25	0.11-0.39
Radom	9.6	2.74	0.27	0.15-0.40	16.8	3.10	0.39	0.25-0.52
Rzeszów	8.6	2.41	0.28	0.15-0.41	11.2	2.23	0.26	0.14-0.37
Siedlce	13.2	3.52	0.44	0.28-0.59	14.8	2.96	0.31	0.19-0.44
Sieradz	8.6	3.34	0.44	0.26-0.63	12.0	3.76	0.48	0.30-0.66
Skierniewice	10.6	4.28	0.53	0.30-0.75	10.8	3.35	0.44	0.26-0.62
Słupsk	7.6	5.63	0.68	0.34-1.01	6.6	3.57	0.47	0.22-0.72
Suwałki	5.4	2.96	0.41	0.18-0.64	7.4	2.94	0.37	0.17-0.56
Szczecin	14.0	4.12	0.49	0.31-0.67	16.8	3.72	0.48	0.32-0.64

Average Values 1975-1979	Males				Females			
	Cases	Stand. Mort. Rate	Cum. Mort. Rate	Confidence limits	Cases	Stand. Mort. Rate	Cum. Mort. Rate	Confidence limits
Tarnobrzeg	8.6	2.88	0.30	0.17-0.44	10.6	2.14	0.23	0.12-0.33
Tarnów	12.6	4.00	0.53	0.34-0.72	15.0	2.90	0.34	0.21-0.48
Toruń	15.6	5.15	0.58	0.38-0.79	20.2	4.45	0.50	0.33-0.66
Wałbrzych	16.2	5.10	0.60	0.39-0.82	15.0	3.51	0.43	0.27-0.59
Warszawa	91.6	7.74	0.89	0.76-1.02	129.4	6.13	0.72	0.62-0.81
Włocławek	10.8	4.77	0.65	0.40-0.90	8.8	2.87	0.33	0.17-0.48
Wrocław	21.6	4.96	0.55	0.38-0.73	26.2	4.17	0.48	0.35-0.61
Zamość	10.4	3.50	0.43	0.26-0.60	8.0	1.95	0.22	0.11-0.33
Zielona Góra	14.4	5.30	0.62	0.40-0.84	14.4	4.17	0.56	0.36-0.76

5 Rectum - ICD 154

The ASMR in men was 3.1 in 1963 and 7.9 in 1982, while the respective figures for women were 2.2 and 5.6. The mortality rate increased rapidly in the period 1963-1982 with the annual average increase rate being 9.8% for men and 8.8% for women. This was one of the sharpest increases of all cancer sites. The mortality rate increases with age starting about the age of 30-40, to reach its maximal values of over 80 deaths per 100000 men and 60 per 100000 women. It increases with calendar time in all age groups and in both sexes. The birth cohort evaluation also shows a very significant increase of risk over the successive birth cohorts.

In 1978, the male rectal cancer mortality rate in Europe was highest in Czechoslovakia (13.0), Denmark (10.9) and Austria (10.8). In women, the highest rates were in Luxembourg (7.7), Czechoslovakia (7.5) and Hungary (6.2). The lowest rates were in Greece (0.9 in men and 0.7 in women) and in Iceland (4.0 in men and 2.7 in women). With rates of 6.1 for men and 4.3 for women, Poland is a country of medium risk.

Analysis of Data from the Provinces, 1975-1979

Cancer of the rectum is more frequent in men than in women (ratio 1.4). It is also more frequent in towns than in rural areas (ratio for men 1.5, for women 1.3).

Men

(Mean ASMR = 5.5, Range 3.2-8.9, Standard Deviation 1.2; 3.6% of Male Cancer Mortality, Rank 6)

The highest value was 2.8 times greater than the lowest. Provinces with the highest rates were Katowice (8.88), Opole (7.56), Lodz (7.17), Poznan (7.03) and Kalisz (6.98). Provinces with the lowest rates were Siedlce (3.22), Suwalki (3.32), Lomza (3.83), Biala Podlaska (4.01) and Koszalin (4.06). Except for the two extreme values recorded in the Silesia (the provinces of Katowice and Opole) the mortality rates are rather evenly distributed over the other provinces. The geographical arrangement was similar, but it was less distinct than in the case of cancer of the colon. Low mortality rates occur mainly in eastern, northern and central Poland. Western and southern regions were the areas of high risk.

Women

(Mean ASMR = 3.9, Range 2.2-6.4, Standard Deviation 0.8; 4.3% of Female Cancer Mortality, Rank 8)

The highest value was 2.9 times greater than the lowest. Provinces with the highest rates were Katowice (6.42), Lodz (5.20), Opole (5.15), Jelenia Gora (4.99) and Kielce (4.94). Provinces with the lowest rates were Siedlce (2.23), Zamosc (2.40), Koszalin (2.70) and Lublin (2.80). The distribution of the rates was very similar in all provinces, with the exception of the province of Katowice where the rate was much higher than in the other provinces. The geographical distribution was similar to that of men but less distinct. A line of provinces with a higher mortality rate was found in the south of Poland in the provinces of Jelenia Gora, Opole, Katowice and Kielce. There was a group of provinces with a lower risk in the eastern part of the country.

Comments

It is assumed that, in principle, the risk factors in rectal cancer are similar to those in cancer of the colon. They include a high-calorie diet rich in fat and meat (Schottenfeld and Winawar 1982). The risk posed by drinking beer is being discredited (Jensen 1980; Pollack et al. 1985). Cancer of the rectum has shown a great increase in Poland during the last 20 years. The rate of this increase in all age groups is one of the highest of all the cancer sites. In the 1960s, Poland was a country of low risk in Europe. The rapid increase in the mortality rate has made Poland into a country of high risk in the

1980s. Mortality rates are now similar in magnitude to those of neighbouring central European countries (Czechoslovakia, Austria, Hungary, GDR, FRG) which have the highest risk. The geographical distribution is similar to that of cancer of the colon. The same provinces usually form groups with high and low mortality rates for both cancer sites. The group with the highest risk is made up chiefly of highly urbanised provinces. The only exception is the province of Warszawa, where mortality rate for rectal cancer is below the national average for both sexes.

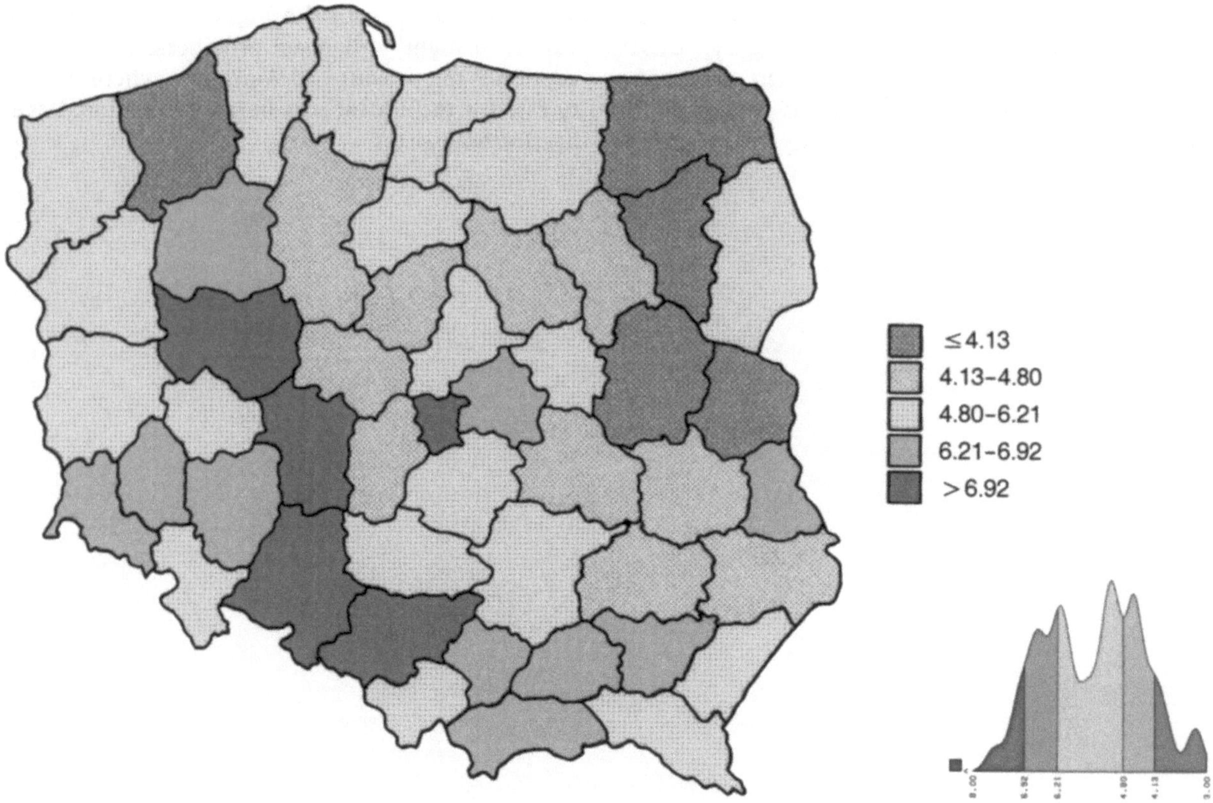
≤4.13
4.13–4.80
4.80–6.21
6.21–6.92
>6.92

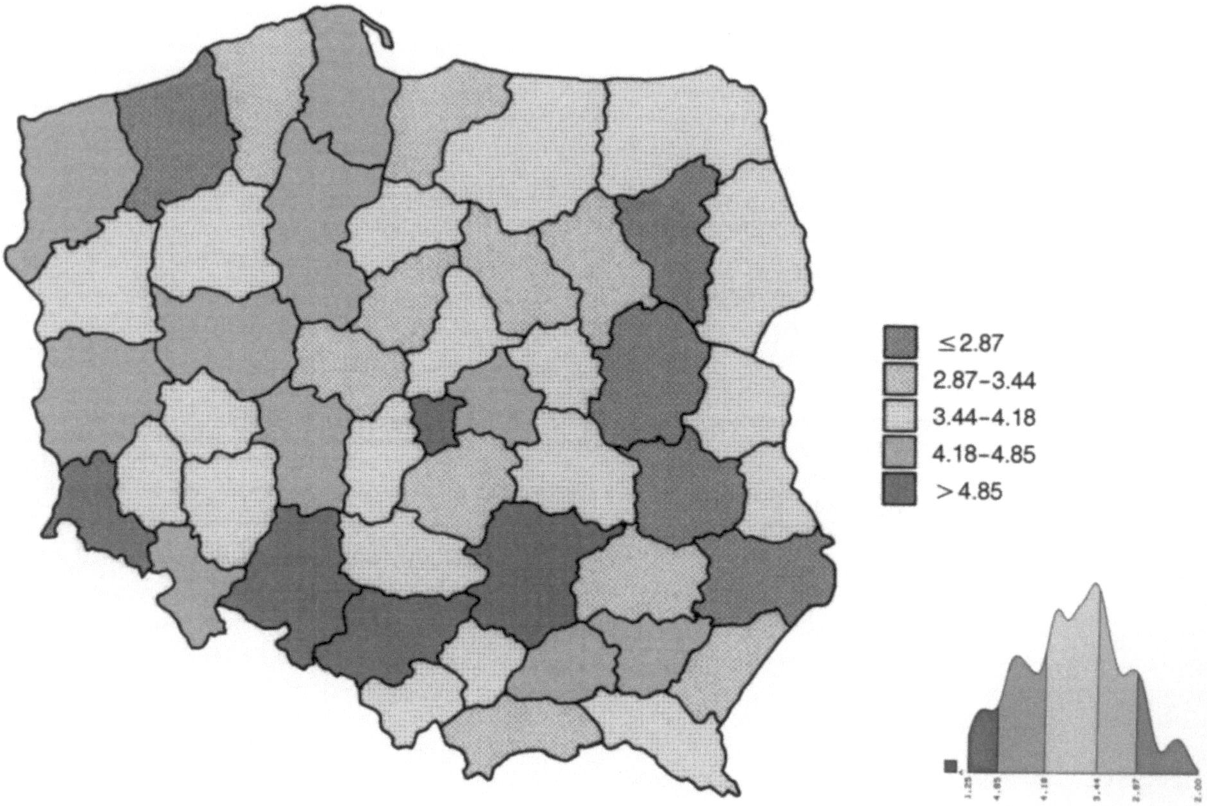
≤2.87
2.87–3.44
3.44–4.18
4.18–4.85
>4.85

7.75 – 8.88
6.62 – 7.75
5.49 – 6.62
4.35 – 5.49
3.22 – 4.35

5.58 – 6.42
4.74 – 5.58
3.90 – 4.74
3.07 – 3.90
2.23 – 3.07

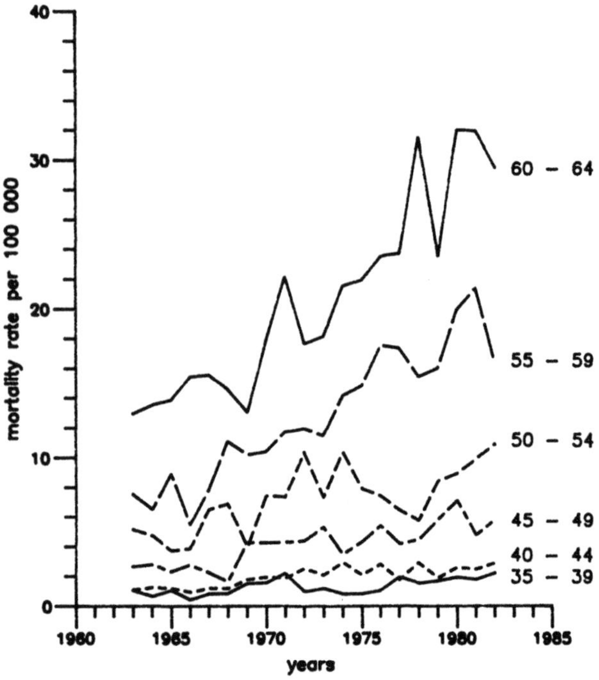

Temporal trend of mortality in individual age groups/men

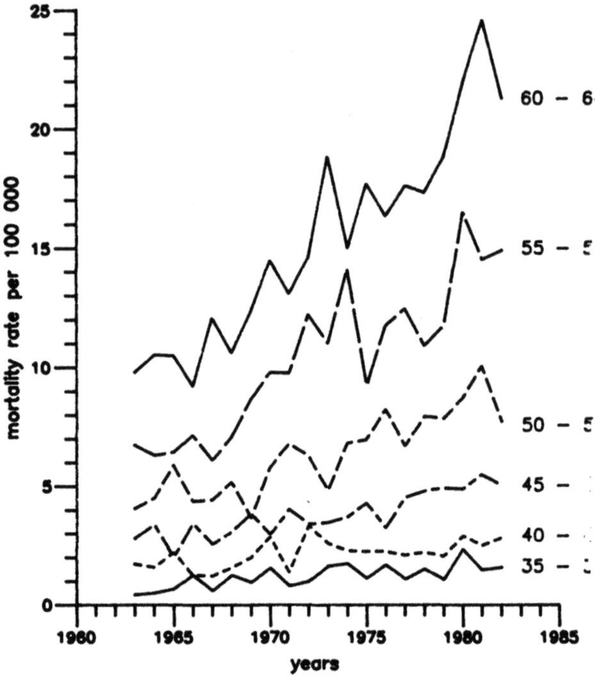

Temporal trend of mortality in individual age groups/women

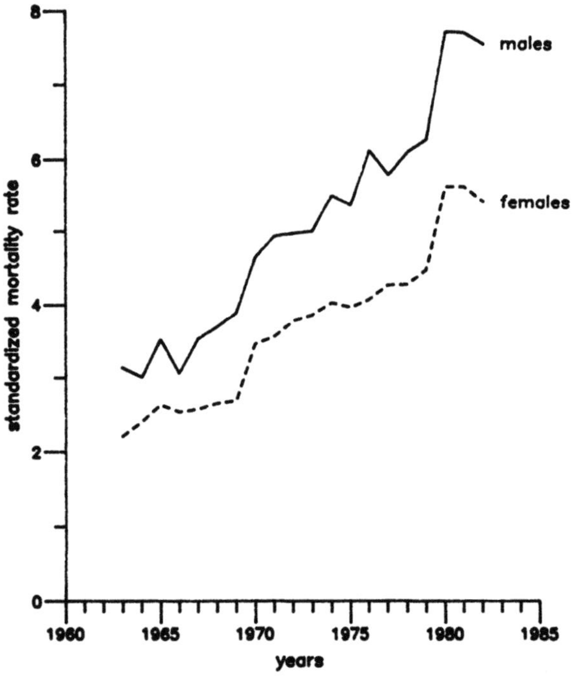

Temporal trend of the age-adjusted mortality rates for men and women

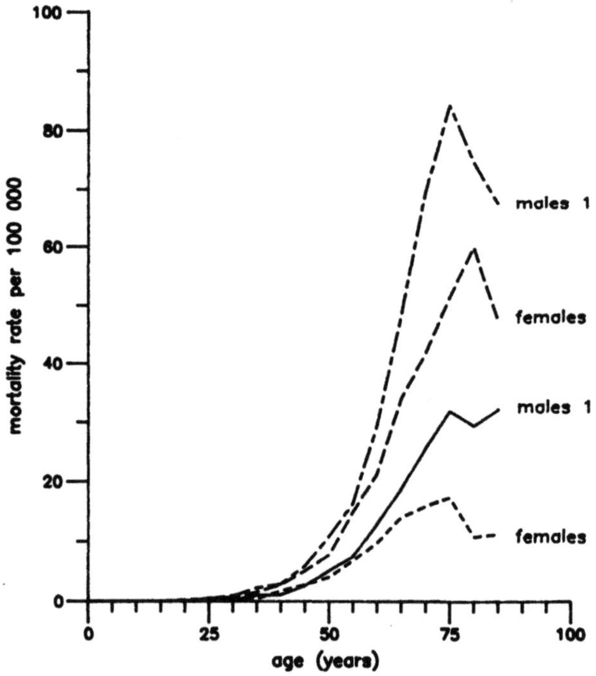

Mortality depending on age in two sample years for men and women

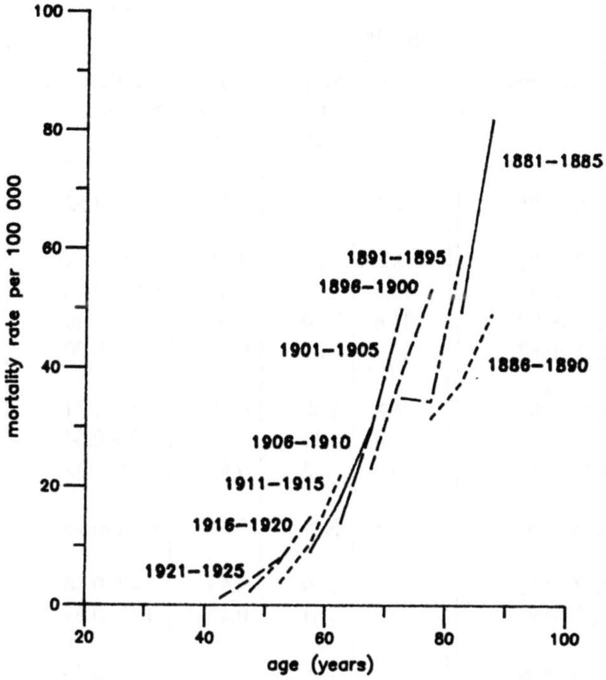

Age-dependent mortality in various birth cohorts/ men

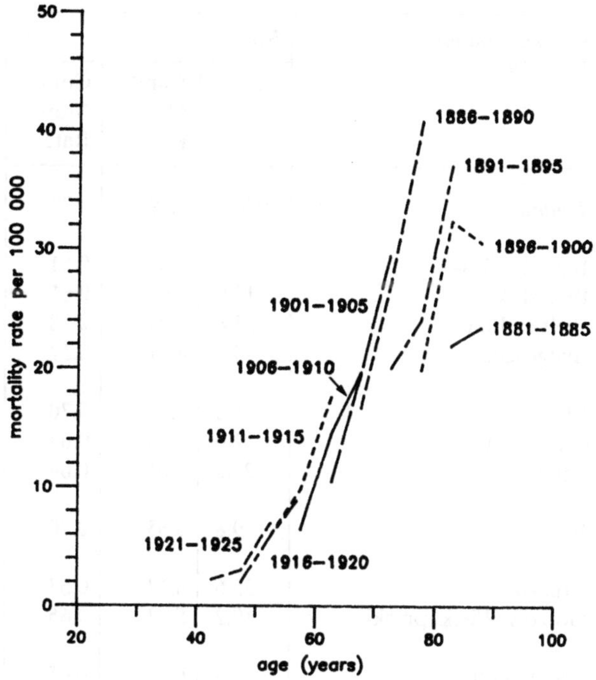

Age-dependent mortality in various birth cohorts/ women

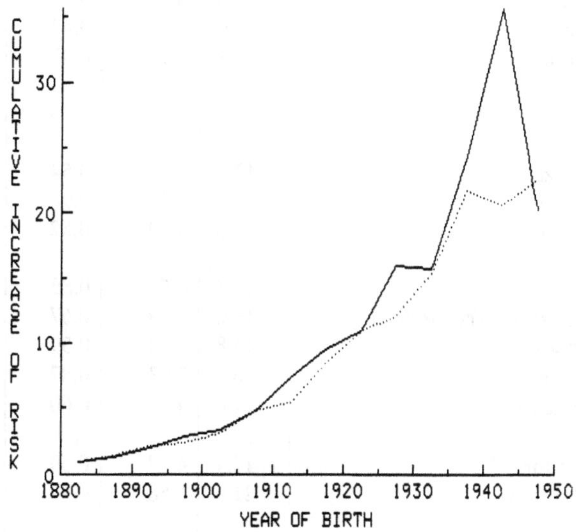

Ratios of the cumulative mortality rates for successive birth cohorts relative to the 1886–1890 cohort

Average Values 1975-1979	Males				Females			
	Cases	Stand. Mort. Rate	Cum. Mort. Rate	Confidence limits	Cases	Stand. Mort. Rate	Cum. Mort. Rate	Confidence limits
Poland	1058.2	5.89	0.72	0.69-0.75	1058.6	4.18	0.50	0.48-0.52
Biała Podlaska	8.2	4.01	0.51	0.26-0.75	8.6	3.82	0.47	0.26-0.68
Białystok	19.0	5.02	0.61	0.41-0.80	19.4	3.59	0.46	0.31-0.60
Bielsko Biała	23.8	5.99	0.78	0.57-0.99	21.6	3.74	0.46	0.32-0.60
Bydgoszcz	24.2	4.51	0.52	0.38-0.67	32.2	4.62	0.56	0.43-0.70
Chełm	8.6	6.22	0.70	0.38-1.03	6.8	3.98	0.47	0.23-0.71
Ciechanów	11.0	4.60	0.64	0.39-0.89	10.4	3.31	0.37	0.20-0.54
Częstochowa	21.2	5.01	0.64	0.46-0.83	19.8	3.53	0.41	0.28-0.53
Elbląg	9.8	5.65	0.70	0.38-1.00	6.8	3.01	0.34	0.16-0.53
Gdańsk	35.6	6.14	0.67	0.51-0.83	35.6	4.39	0.54	0.42-0.66
Gorzów Wielkopolski	10.2	5.23	0.65	0.37-0.92	9.2	3.61	0.42	0.22-0.61
Jelenia Góra	13.8	6.35	0.65	0.40-0.89	14.0	4.99	0.58	0.36-0.79
Kalisz	26.4	6.98	0.82	0.60-1.03	22.8	4.71	0.55	0.39-0.70
Katowice	147.6	8.88	1.10	0.97-1.22	161.8	6.42	0.77	0.68-0.85
Kielce	38.8	6.20	0.80	0.63-0.97	42.2	4.94	0.63	0.49-0.76
Konin	11.2	4.64	0.61	0.38-0.84	10.0	2.98	0.38	0.22-0.55
Koszalin	7.2	4.06	0.48	0.24-0.72	6.0	2.70	0.38	0.18-0.58
Kraków	39.6	6.63	0.83	0.65-1.01	33.8	3.83	0.45	0.34-0.56
Krosno	12.0	5.23	0.64	0.39-0.89	12.0	3.67	0.46	0.28-0.64
Legnica	11.2	6.77	0.90	0.53-1.27	8.6	4.12	0.47	0.25-0.70
Leszno	11.0	5.81	0.67	0.40-0.94	10.8	3.72	0.47	0.27-0.66
Lublin	22.6	4.60	0.52	0.37-0.67	20.0	2.80	0.39	0.27-0.50
Łomża	7.0	3.83	0.47	0.24-0.71	7.8	2.82	0.34	0.16-0.52
Łódź	43.8	7.17	0.90	0.72-1.08	52.4	5.20	0.61	0.49-0.72
Nowy Sącz	20.2	6.42	0.76	0.53-0.99	14.2	3.25	0.44	0.28-0.59
Olsztyn	13.4	5.01	0.54	0.32-0.76	14.4	4.04	0.45	0.28-0.63
Opole	32.2	7.56	0.98	0.75-1.21	31.0	5.15	0.62	0.47-0.77
Ostrołęka	9.0	4.20	0.52	0.28-0.75	9.2	3.42	0.41	0.22-0.60
Piła	13.8	6.66	0.85	0.55-1.14	11.4	4.06	0.50	0.30-0.69
Piotrków Trybunalski	19.0	5.09	0.67	0.47-0.87	15.0	3.12	0.40	0.26-0.53
Płock	13.8	5.12	0.59	0.38-0.81	12.4	3.45	0.44	0.27-0.61
Poznań	46.4	7.03	0.87	0.70-1.04	43.4	4.57	0.50	0.39-0.61
Przemyśl	11.0	4.95	0.60	0.35-0.85	11.8	3.42	0.40	0.23-0.58
Radom	17.4	4.57	0.59	0.41-0.78	20.6	3.92	0.44	0.30-0.57
Rzeszów	21.6	6.58	0.82	0.58-1.05	20.0	4.24	0.57	0.40-0.74
Siedlce	12.4	3.22	0.45	0.29-0.62	11.0	2.23	0.29	0.17-0.40
Sieradz	12.2	4.66	0.61	0.39-0.83	11.8	3.50	0.41	0.25-0.57
Skierniewice	14.4	6.22	0.80	0.53-1.07	13.4	4.48	0.54	0.35-0.74
Słupsk	7.0	5.09	0.58	0.26-0.90	5.2	2.92	0.41	0.18-0.64
Suwałki	6.2	3.32	0.38	0.16-0.59	9.0	3.49	0.38	0.19-0.56
Szczecin	20.0	6.05	0.67	0.45-0.90	20.4	4.42	0.54	0.37-0.71

Average Values 1975-1979	Males				Females			
	Cases	Stand. Mort. Rate	Cum. Mort. Rate	Confidence limits	Cases	Stand. Mort. Rate	Cum. Mort. Rate	Confidence limits
Tarnobrzeg	15.0	4.64	0.59	0.40-0.79	14.2	3.18	0.42	0.27-0.57
Tarnów	21.6	6.63	0.84	0.60-1.08	19.0	4.29	0.55	0.38-0.72
Toruń	16.2	5.53	0.60	0.39-0.82	18.4	4.04	0.42	0.27-0.57
Wałbrzych	19.2	6.07	0.75	0.51-0.98	20.4	4.76	0.50	0.34-0.66
Warszawa	64.2	5.30	0.65	0.54-0.76	76.2	3.77	0.43	0.36-0.50
Włocławek	10.2	4.42	0.52	0.30-0.75	9.8	3.30	0.43	0.25-0.61
Wrocław	30.4	6.86	0.81	0.60-1.02	27.0	4.09	0.48	0.34-0.61
Zamość	13.2	4.23	0.53	0.34-0.72	10.8	2.40	0.30	0.17-0.43
Zielona Góra	14.4	5.58	0.70	0.45-0.95	16.0	4.65	0.46	0.29-0.64

6 Gall Bladder - ICD 156

Because of changes in the ICD classification, we could only use data of the period after 1970 for this analysis. The ASMR for cancer of the gall bladder in men was 1.6 in 1970 and 1.7 in 1982, and 4.9 and 4.4, respectively, in women. The mortality rate in men remained at its previous level, while in women it decreased slightly. The mortality rate for cancer of the gall bladder in women increases after the age of 40 to reach its maximal value of about 50 deaths per 100000 women aged 75. In men, the rate also increases significantly with age, starting from the age of 55 and reaching a peak of 25 deaths per 100000 men aged about 80. There is no observable tendency in the time trend in the age groups of both sexes.

In 1978 the highest mortality rate for cancer of the gall bladder in European countries was in Hungary (men 3.4, women 8.4). The group of high-risk countries included Czechoslovakia (men 3.0, women 5.6), the German Democratic Republic (men) 2.8 and Iceland (women) 6.1. The lowest men's rates were in Bulgaria (0.1), Greece (0.3) and Austria (0.3), whereas the lowest women's rate was in Greece (0.6); Norway, England and Wales and Northern Ireland each had a rate of 1.3. Poland is a country of relatively high risk. The 1978 mortality rates for cancer of the gall bladder were 1.7 for men and 4.6 for women.

Analysis of Data from the Provinces 1975-1979

Women had much higher mortality rates for cancer of the gall bladder than men (ratio 2.7). Like most of the neoplasms, this cancer occurs more frequently in urban populations (ratio 1.5).

Men

(Mean ASMR = 1.6, Range 0.6-4.0, Standard Deviation 0.7; 1.0% of Male Cancer Mortality, Rank 17)

Malignant neoplasms of the gall bladder showed very strong geographical patterns. The difference between the highest and the lowest values was more than seven-fold. The mortality rates in most provinces ranged from 0.56 to 1.88. A group of provinces with a high risk included nine with rates ranging from 2.18 to 3.15 and also the province of Lodz where the mortality rate was 3.95. Provinces with the highest rates were Lodz (3.95), Warszawa (3.15), Konin (3.11), Radom (2.7) and Wroclaw (2.68). Provinces with the lowest rates were Zamosc (0.56), Suwalki (0.56), Rzeszow (0.64), Biala Podlaska (0.67) and Leszno (0.75). Generally, lower rates were found in eastern and northeastern parts of the country. Provinces in the centre of the country form the area of higher risk.

Women

(Mean ASMR = 4.2, Range 1.5-10.6, Standard Deviation 1.7; 4.9% of Female Cancer Mortality, Rank 7)

As in men, the maximal value was nearly seven times higher than the lowest (but with much higher figures). Forty-four provinces had uniformly distributed mortality rates varying from 1.50 to 5.82. Four others form a group with the greatest risk with rates between 6.72 and 7.59. In the province of Lodz, as in men, the rate is much higher at 10.58. Provinces with the highest rates were Lodz (10.58), Warszawa (7.59), Wloclawek (7.17), Radom (6.91) and Konin (6.72). Provinces with the lowest rates were Bialystok (1.5), Lomza (1.76), Biala Podlaska (1.8), Rzeszow (1.92) and Suwalki (2.2). The high- and low-risk provinces are usually the same for men and women. The geographical pattern of women's mortality rates shows an even more distinct low-risk region in the most eastern areas of the country and a region with a higher risk in central Poland.

Comments

The knowledge of risk factors related to cancer of the gall bladder is fragmentary. In recent years aetiological investigations have focused on the association with biliary calculi. Both disorders have an exceptionally similar epidemiological picture. Many studies have shown a very strong correlation to the occurrence of gallstones. For example, the high risk of cancer of the gall bladder in American Indians forms part of the endemic picture of gallstone disorders in this population (Creagan and Fraumeni 1972). Gallstones are also frequent in Latin Americans (Menck et al. 1975) and Israelis of central European descent (Hart et al. 1971).
An interesting picture of the frequency distribution of cancer of the gall bladder in the world is provided by a review of incidence rates published by Waterhouse et al. (1982). American Indians and - in central Europe - Poland, Hungary, the German Democratic Republic, the Federal Republic of Germany and also Israel, where a substantial proportion of the population originates from central Europe, have the highest incidence in both sexes. High incidence is also found in Latin American countries and Japan. The rates are lowest in the peoples of Black Africa (Heaton 1973).
Mortality from cancer of the gall bladder in Poland, especially in women, ranks high among the world records. Unfortunately, the data on gallstones are incomplete in Poland. The available publications based on hospital records show that the disease is more frequent in women than in men. The wide range between the rates in various provinces is caused mainly by high figures obtained in a small number of provinces where the risk is considerable for men and women alike. These provinces are situated in central Poland and they are usually the same for both sexes (Lodz, Warszawa, Konin, Wloclawek, Radom and Plock). Lodz has a particularly high mortality rate for this cancer in both sexes.

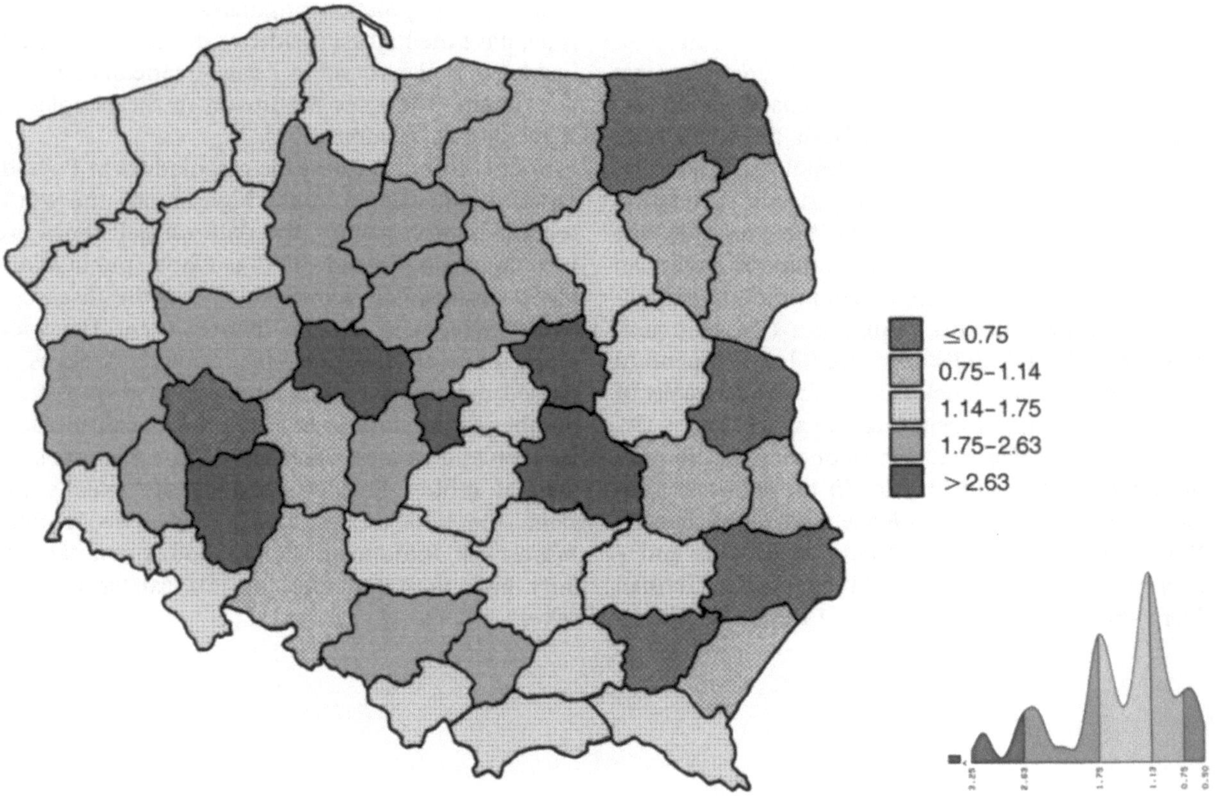
≤0.75
0.75-1.14
1.14-1.75
1.75-2.63
>2.63

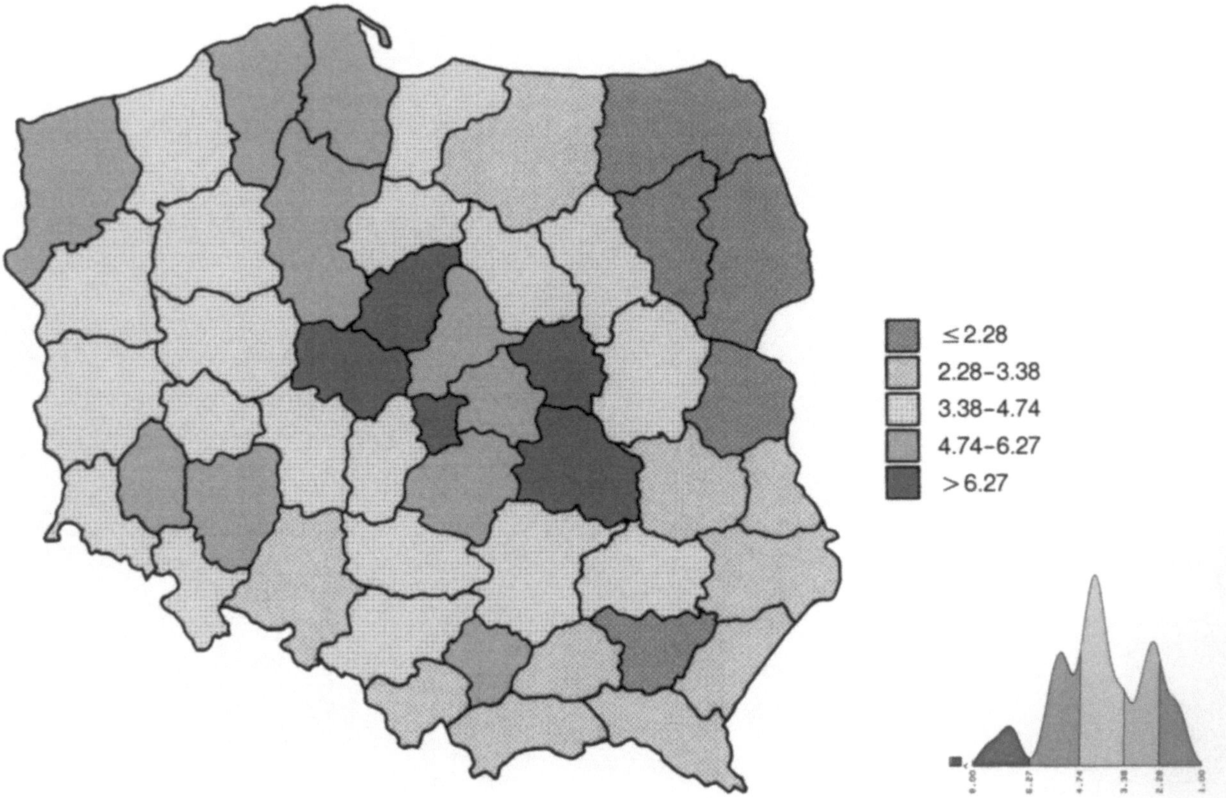
≤2.28
2.28-3.38
3.38-4.74
4.74-6.27
>6.27

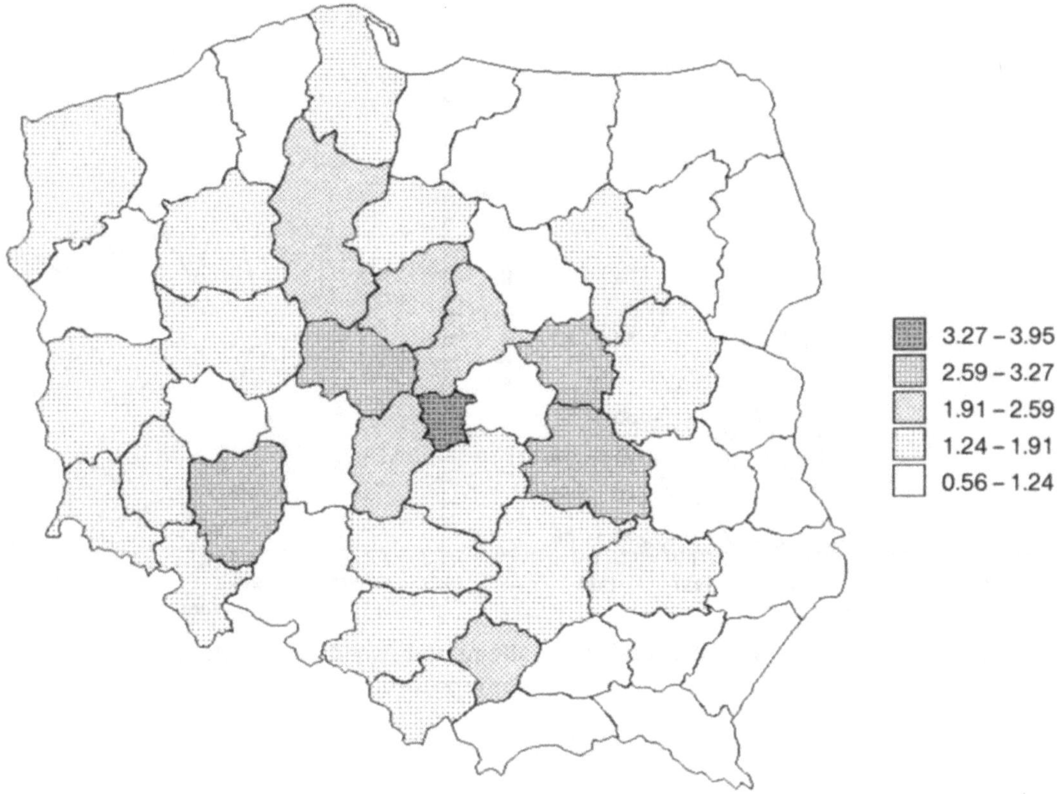
3.27 – 3.95
2.59 – 3.27
1.91 – 2.59
1.24 – 1.91
0.56 – 1.24

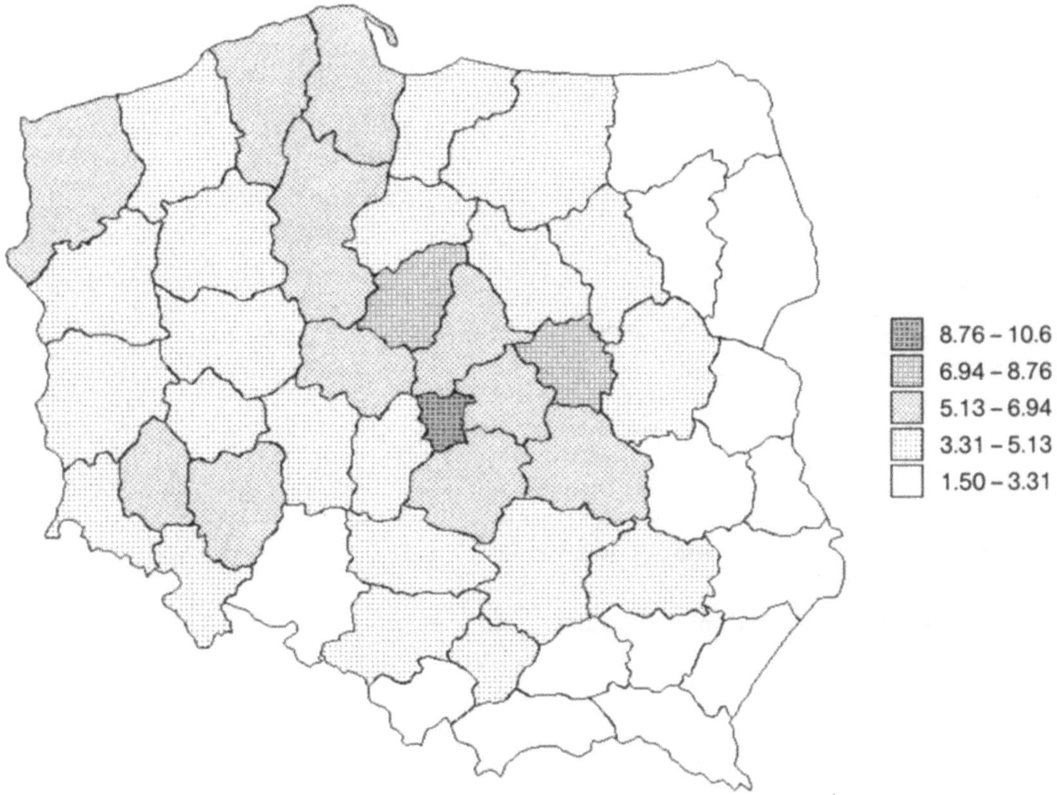
8.76 – 10.6
6.94 – 8.76
5.13 – 6.94
3.31 – 5.13
1.50 – 3.31

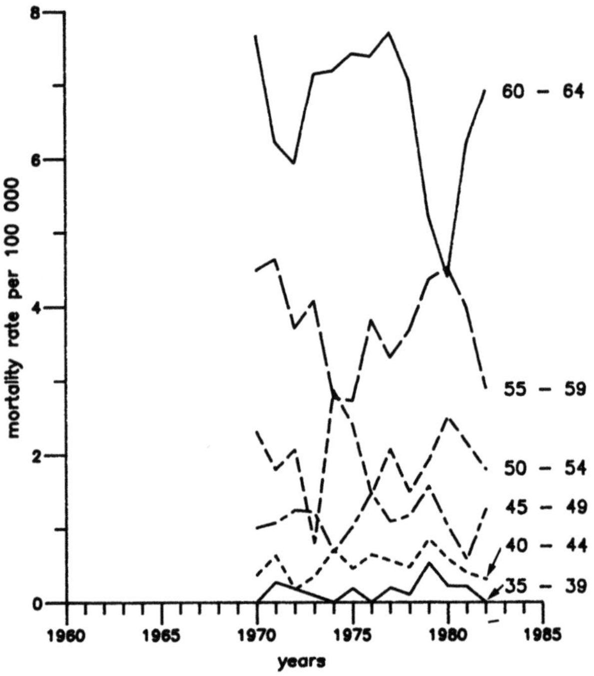

Temporal trend of mortality in individual age groups/men

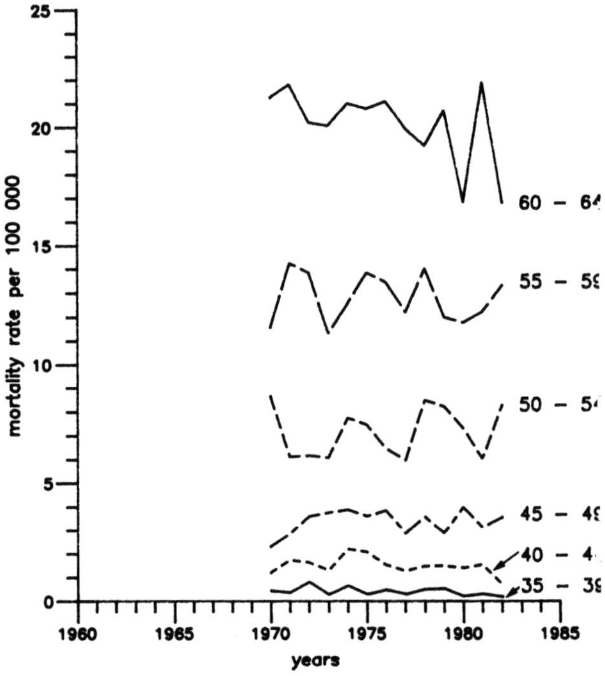

Temporal trend of mortality in individual age groups/women

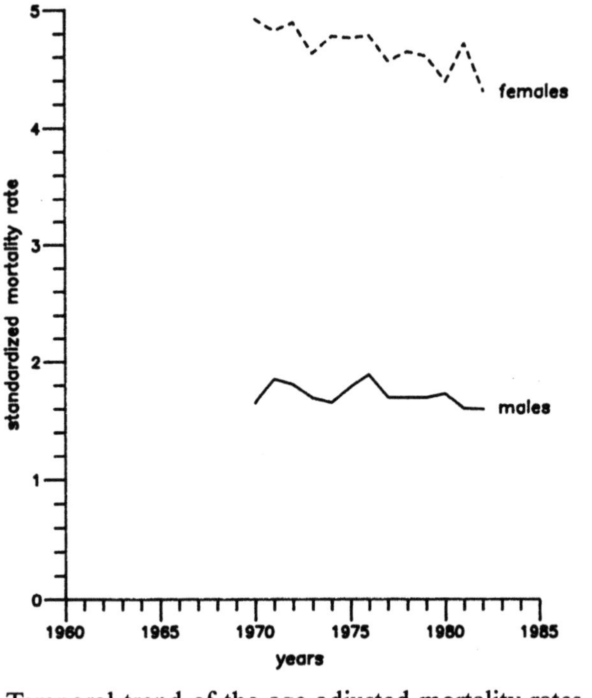

Temporal trend of the age-adjusted mortality rates for men and women

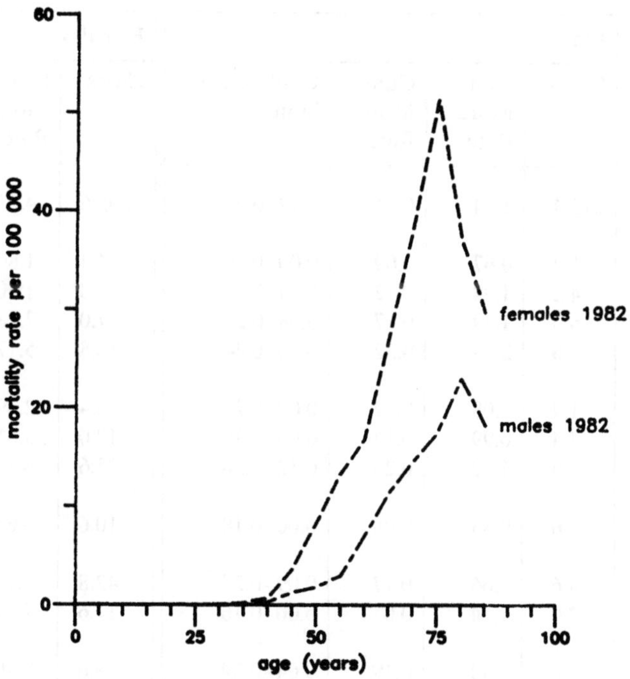

Mortality depending on age in 1982 for men and women

Average Values 1975-1979	Males				Females			
	Cases	Stand. Mort. Rate	Cum. Mort. Rate	Confidence limits	Cases	Stand. Mort. Rate	Cum. Mort. Rate	Confidence limits
Poland	312.4	1.74	0.21	0.19-0.23	1205.6	4.63	0.57	0.55-0.59
Biała Podlaska	1.2	0.67	0.09	0.00-0.19	4.4	1.80	0.23	0.08-0.37
Białystok	4.2	1.04	0.12	0.04-0.21	7.8	1.50	0.22	0.12-0.33
Bielsko Biała	6.0	1.59	0.17	0.08-0.27	17.0	2.78	0.34	0.23-0.46
Bydgoszcz	12.6	2.53	0.32	0.20-0.44	36.8	5.17	0.62	0.48-0.76
Chełm	1.4	1.08	0.12	0.00-0.25	4.4	2.49	0.32	0.12-0.52
Ciechanów	2.4	0.99	0.17	0.03-0.30	12.0	3.61	0.53	0.33-0.74
Częstochowa	7.6	1.72	0.23	0.12-0.34	25.6	4.35	0.55	0.41-0.70
Elbląg	1.6	0.83	0.08	0.00-0.18	10.6	4.65	0.60	0.34-0.85
Gdańsk	9.6	1.66	0.17	0.09-0.25	42.8	5.13	0.64	0.50-0.77
Gorzów Wielkopolski	2.0	1.14	0.07	0.00-0.16	11.6	4.37	0.56	0.33-0.78
Jelenia Góra	3.0	1.40	0.19	0.04-0.34	9.6	3.40	0.43	0.24-0.62
Kalisz	4.0	1.10	0.13	0.04-0.21	22.6	4.22	0.54	0.38-0.69
Katowice	28.0	1.77	0.21	0.15-0.26	110.6	4.22	0.50	0.44-0.57
Kielce	7.8	1.32	0.17	0.09-0.24	38.4	4.39	0.59	0.46-0.72
Konin	7.4	3.11	0.40	0.21-0.59	22.6	6.72	0.83	0.59-1.07
Koszalin	2.0	1.20	0.12	0.00-0.25	10.4	4.53	0.64	0.38-0.90
Kraków	13.8	2.42	0.33	0.22-0.45	43.8	4.75	0.56	0.44-0.69
Krosno	2.6	1.22	0.13	0.01-0.25	8.8	2.45	0.31	0.17-0.46
Legnica	3.0	1.84	0.25	0.05-0.45	12.6	5.62	0.73	0.45-1.01
Leszno	1.8	0.75	0.11	0.00-0.22	11.8	4.17	0.50	0.29-0.70
Lublin	4.0	0.75	0.10	0.03-0.16	17.6	2.36	0.28	0.18-0.37
Łomża	2.6	1.12	0.17	0.03-0.30	5.2	1.76	0.27	0.11-0.43
Łódź	25.0	3.95	0.47	0.34-0.60	108.8	10.58	1.27	1.10-1.44
Nowy Sącz	3.8	1.21	0.14	0.04-0.25	11.4	2.58	0.40	0.25-0.55
Olsztyn	2.6	1.01	0.12	0.01-0.23	12.2	3.36	0.40	0.23-0.56
Opole	3.8	0.91	0.09	0.02-0.15	20.0	2.95	0.40	0.27-0.52
Ostrołęka	2.4	1.26	0.16	0.02-0.29	12.0	4.03	0.50	0.29-0.71
Piła	3.6	1.60	0.24	0.07-0.41	10.8	3.96	0.55	0.34-0.77
Piotrków Trybunalski	5.2	1.41	0.22	0.10-0.35	26.4	5.51	0.70	0.52-0.88
Płock	6.6	2.46	0.29	0.13-0.44	20.0	5.51	0.72	0.50-0.93
Poznań	13.0	1.82	0.20	0.11-0.28	43.4	4.43	0.54	0.43-0.66
Przemyśl	1.8	1.08	0.09	0.00-0.20	10.4	2.85	0.34	0.18-0.50
Radom	11.0	2.70	0.36	0.21-0.50	37.4	6.91	0.89	0.69-1.08
Rzeszów	2.2	0.64	0.07	0.00-0.13	9.2	1.92	0.25	0.14-0.36
Siedlce	4.6	1.26	0.15	0.06-0.23	17.6	3.42	0.42	0.28-0.56
Sieradz	5.8	2.18	0.26	0.11-0.41	15.0	4.30	0.55	0.36-0.75
Skierniewice	2.6	1.17	0.15	0.03-0.27	17.4	5.45	0.68	0.46-0.90
Słupsk	1.8	1.16	0.16	0.00-0.32	9.2	5.23	0.51	0.25-0.76
Suwałki	1.0	0.56	0.06	0.00-0.15	6.0	2.20	0.30	0.12-0.47
Szczecin	5.2	1.75	0.20	0.07-0.33	26.8	5.82	0.71	0.51-0.90

Average Values 1975-1979	Males				Females			
	Cases	Stand. Mort. Rate	Cum. Mort. Rate	Confidence limits	Cases	Stand. Mort. Rate	Cum. Mort. Rate	Confidence limits
Tarnobrzeg	5.6	1.63	0.21	0.09-0.32	16.0	3.83	0.48	0.32-0.64
Tarnów	3.4	1.17	0.12	0.03-0.21	11.6	2.58	0.32	0.19-0.45
Toruń	5.8	1.88	0.22	0.09-0.35	18.0	3.97	0.50	0.33-0.66
Wałbrzych	5.2	1.71	0.28	0.11-0.44	20.2	4.72	0.62	0.43-0.81
Warszawa	38.4	3.15	0.35	0.27-0.43	158.8	7.59	0.88	0.78-0.99
Włocławek	6.0	2.58	0.32	0.13-0.51	21.4	7.17	0.89	0.63-1.15
Wrocław	11.2	2.68	0.33	0.19-0.46	33.8	5.25	0.61	0.46-0.77
Zamość	1.8	0.56	0.09	0.01-0.18	8.6	2.38	0.30	0.17-0.43
Zielona Góra	4.4	1.75	0.17	0.05-0.29	16.2	4.50	0.56	0.36-0.75

7 Pancreas - ICD 157

The ASMR for cancer of the pancreas in men was 3.2 in 1963 and 6.6 in 1982, while the respective figures for women were 2.5 and 4.4. The average annual increase in the mortality rate is 5.81% for men and 3.54% for women. The mortality rate increases with age, particularly after 50, and it reaches its highest value of about 50 per 100000 men and 42 per 100000 women (1982 figures). An increase in the mortality rate with calendar time can be seen for both sexes. The risk of dying from cancer of the pancreas increases with successive birth cohorts.
In 1978 the mortality rate for cancer of the pancreas in men fluctuated between 3.9 (Bulgaria) and 10.8 (Northern Ireland). Countries with a high risk included Finland (9.5), Denmark and Sweden (9.0), while Spain, Greece and Yugoslavia had a low risk with rates of 4.0, 4.2 and 4.5, respectively. The women's mortality rate peaked in Czechoslovakia (8.1), Iceland (7.0) and Sweden (6.9). It was lowest in Spain (2.3), Bulgaria (2.4), Greece (2.6) and Yugoslavia (2.7). Poland, with a mortality rate of 6.4 in men and 4.1 in women is among the countries with a medium risk.

Analysis of Data from the Provinces 1975-1979

Cancer of the pancreas is 1.6 times more frequent in men than in women. Like most of the malignant neoplasms, this one is more frequent in urban populations than in people in rural areas (1.4 times more in both men and women).

Men

(Mean ASMR = 6.0, Range 4.1-8.5, Standard Deviation 1.0; 3.7% of Male Cancer Mortality, Rank 5)

Regional differences between the mortality rates are not very large. The difference between the highest and the lowest figures is slightly higher than 2. Provinces with the highest rates were Elblag (8.45), Katowice (8.15), Torun (7.60), Gdansk (7.43) and Warszawa (7.19). Provinces with the lowest values were Siedlce (4.07), Konin (4.08), Lublin (4.37), Rzeszow (4.40) and Kalisz (4.51). Areas with low risk of cancer of the pancreas form a fairly clear-cut north-south line in eastern Poland. There is a higher risk in the central (north-south) strip of northern Poland and also in Silesia, Krakow and Warszawa.

Women

(Mean ASMR = 3.9, Range 2.7-5.9, Standard Deviation 0.7; 4.2% of Female Cancer Mortality, Rank 11)

The highest mortality rate was over twice as high as the lowest. Provinces with the highest rates were Legnica (5.90), Walbrzych (5.48), Bydgoszcz (5.08), Krakow (4.96) and Katowice (4.94). Provinces with the lowest rates were Olsztyn (2.70), Nowy Sacz (2.85), Siedlce (2.89), Lublin (2.90) and Rzeszow (2.94). Low-risk provinces predominate in eastern Poland. Southwestern regions have a higher risk.

Comments

Little is known about the aetiology of cancer of the pancreas. Tobacco smoking has been identified as a risk factor with values of relative risk fluctuating between 1.6 and 3.9 (IARC 1986). There are contradictory reports about the relationship between this cancer and alcohol but this association does not seem to be particularly important (Velema et al. 1986). The connection with coffee consumption, discovered by the studies of McMahon (1981), has not been confirmed by others (Mack 1982) and a later study by McMahon's group (Hsiek and McMahon 1986). There is a controversy as to whether high consumption of fats is a promoting factor (Wynder 1975). A hypothesis claiming links to diabetes has been put forward but it lacks sound evidence (Mack 1982) as is the case with the hypothesis implying occupational exposure (Mack 1982).

Cancer of the pancreas usually has a bad prognosis; only 10%-14% of patients survive 1 year after diagnosis and the rate of 5-year survivals is below 1%. The increasing number of cases combined with the bad prognosis is a special oncological problem.

Poland was a country of low risk 20 years ago. The frequency of this neoplasm is now increasing rapidly in all age groups, especially in men (the increase rate is 5.81% annually) but it still remains a country of relatively low risk of this cancer. On the other hand, cancer of the pancreas is difficult to detect and a proportion of the increase in the mortality rate has probably been caused by improved diagnostic methods. Diagnostic standards may also play a role in regional differences. This cancer is 40%-70% more frequent in town dwellers than in country people, as has been found in other countries (Mack 1982). This factor is probably responsible for the obvious tendency of provinces to form groups of lower mortality rates in rural parts of eastern Poland, while higher mortality rates were found in more urbanised regions, especially in Silesia, Krakow and Warszawa.

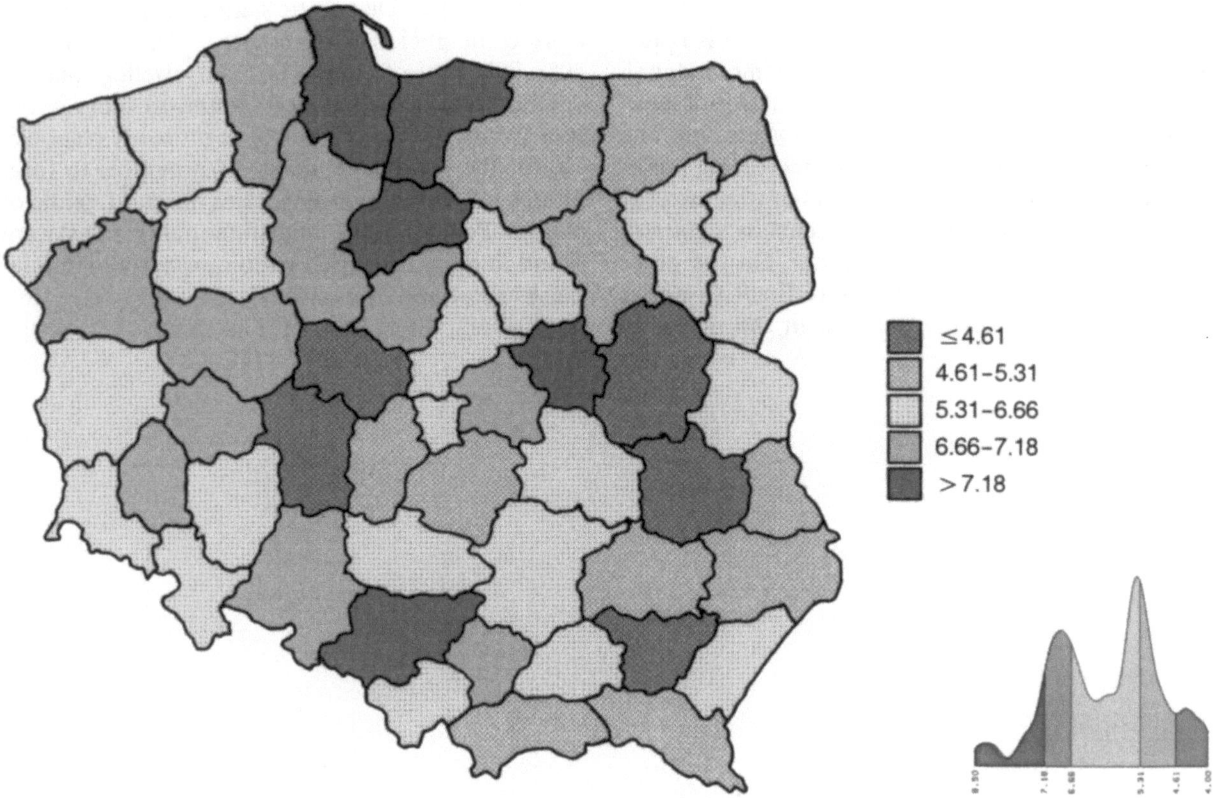
≤4.61
4.61–5.31
5.31–6.66
6.66–7.18
>7.18

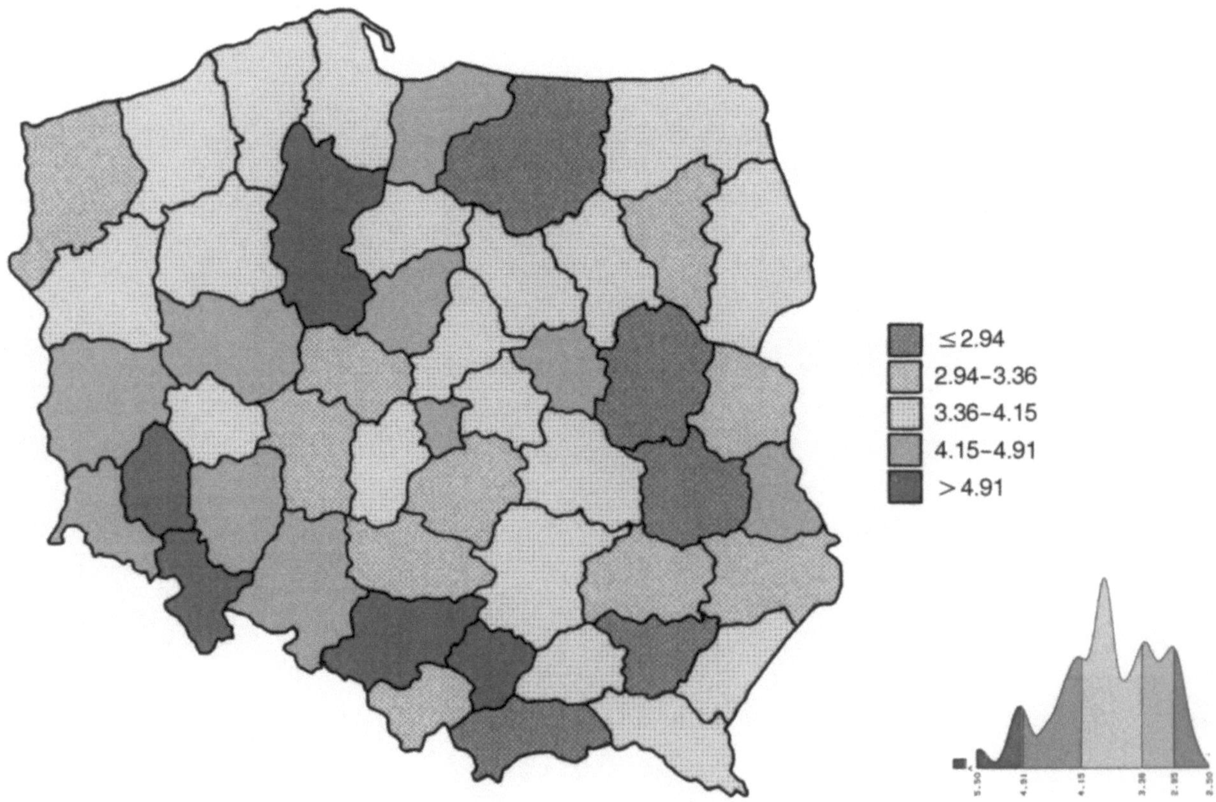
≤2.94
2.94–3.36
3.36–4.15
4.15–4.91
>4.91

7.58 – 8.45
6.70 – 7.58
5.83 – 6.70
4.95 – 5.83
4.07 – 4.95

5.26 – 5.90
4.62 – 5.26
3.98 – 4.62
3.34 – 3.98
2.70 – 3.34

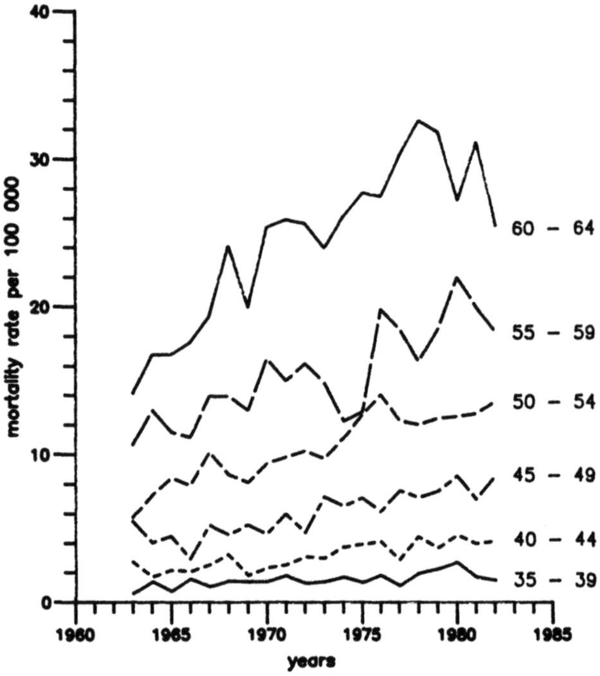

Temporal trend of mortality in individual age groups/men

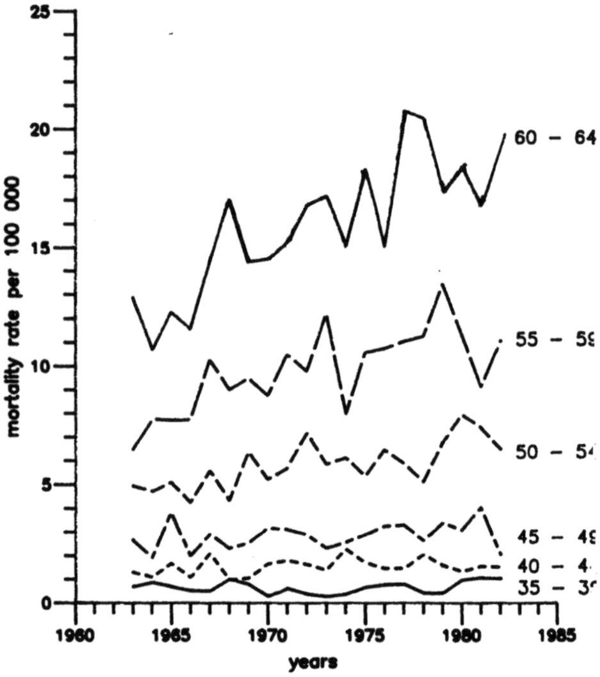

Temporal trend of mortality in individual age groups/women

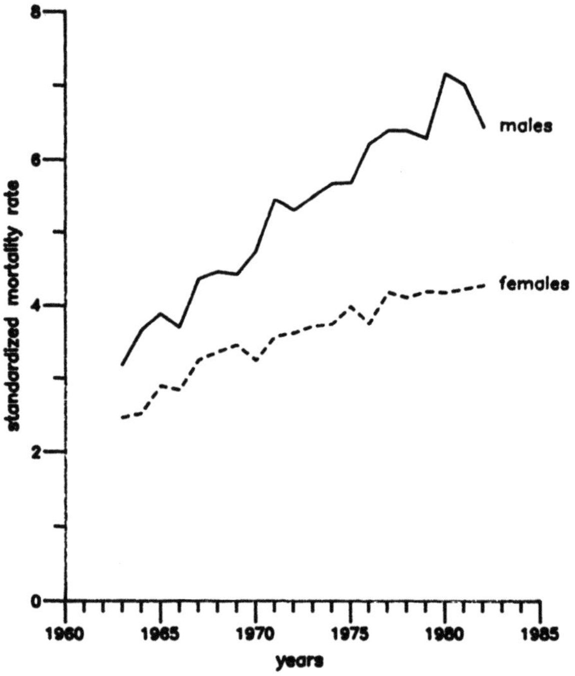

Temporal trend of the age-adjusted mortality rates for men and women

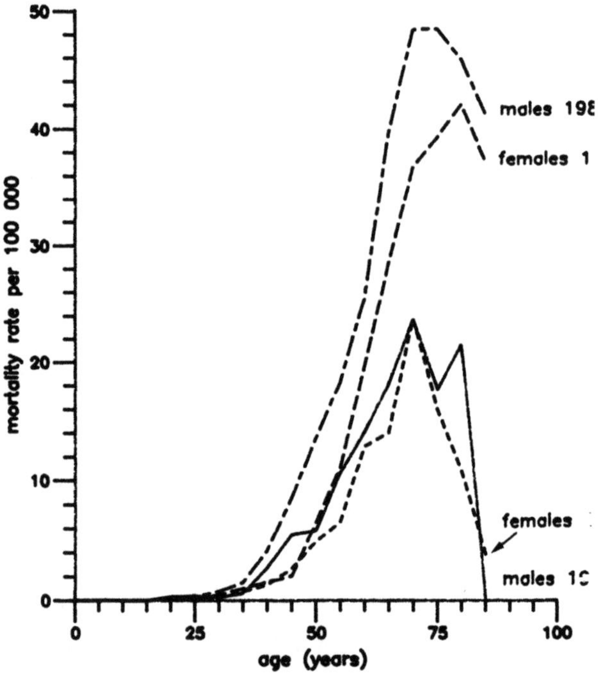

Mortality depending on age in two sample years for men and women

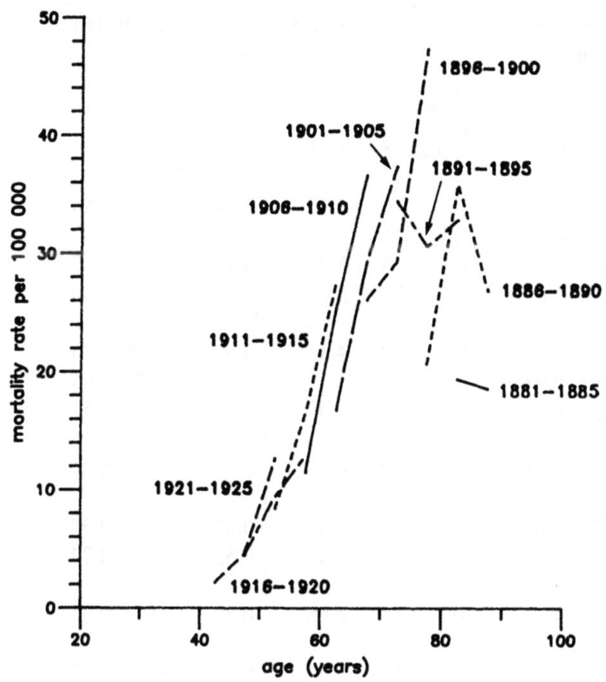

Age-dependent mortality in various birth cohorts/ men

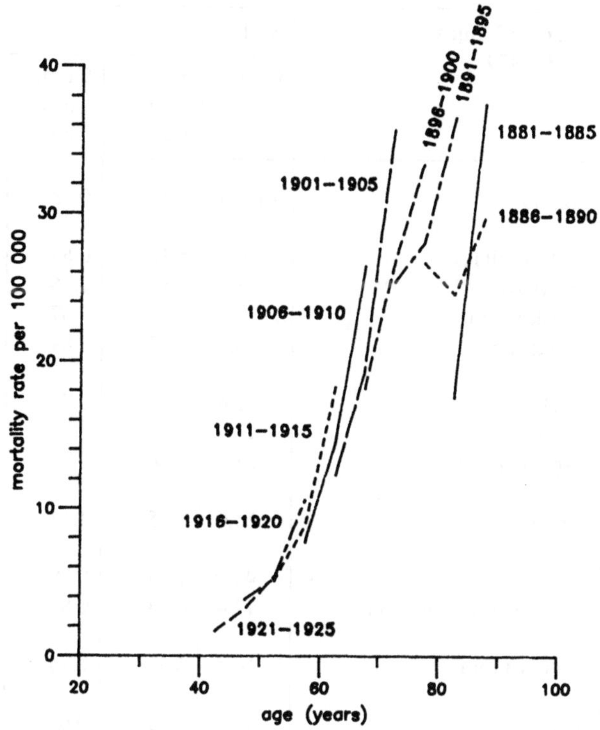

Age-dependent mortality in various birth cohorts/ women

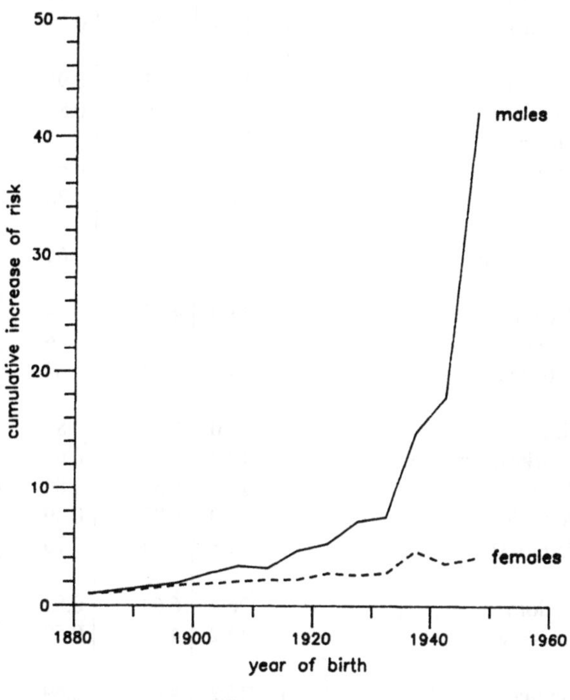

Ratios of the cumulative mortality rates for successive birth cohorts relative to the 1886–1890 cohort

Average Values 1975-1979	Males				Females			
	Cases	Stand. Mort. Rate	Cum. Mort. Rate	Confidence limits	Cases	Stand. Mort. Rate	Cum. Mort. Rate	Confidence limits
Poland	1093.4	6.18	0.78	0.75-0.81	1027.8	4.01	0.50	0.48-0.52
Biała Podlaska	9.4	5.32	0.69	0.41-0.98	8.6	3.33	0.37	0.19-0.56
Białystok	23.2	5.85	0.75	0.54-0.96	19.6	3.70	0.45	0.31-0.60
Bielsko Biała	20.2	5.46	0.67	0.47-0.86	18.8	3.21	0.45	0.32-0.59
Bydgoszcz	35.4	6.97	0.89	0.70-1.08	36.4	5.08	0.65	0.51-0.80
Chełm	7.6	5.17	0.71	0.37-1.05	8.2	4.37	0.59	0.31-0.86
Ciechanów	13.4	5.99	0.72	0.47-0.97	10.0	3.37	0.46	0.27-0.65
Częstochowa	23.2	5.66	0.71	0.52-0.89	18.2	3.08	0.39	0.27-0.51
Elbląg	15.0	8.45	1.13	0.74-1.51	9.2	4.18	0.52	0.29-0.74
Gdańsk	43.0	7.43	0.89	0.70-1.07	30.4	3.56	0.41	0.30-0.52
Gorzów Wielkopolski	12.4	6.88	0.84	0.52-1.15	10.6	3.91	0.52	0.30-0.74
Jelenia Góra	14.4	6.57	0.75	0.47-1.03	13.2	4.66	0.59	0.36-0.83
Kalisz	17.8	4.51	0.61	0.43-0.79	17.8	3.27	0.35	0.23-0.48
Katowice	133.2	8.15	1.03	0.91-1.15	127.4	4.94	0.61	0.54-0.69
Kielce	32.2	5.53	0.64	0.49-0.79	31.6	3.79	0.47	0.36-0.59
Konin	9.8	4.08	0.55	0.33-0.77	10.2	3.36	0.43	0.25-0.60
Koszalin	10.0	5.47	0.62	0.35-0.89	9.4	3.85	0.50	0.26-0.73
Kraków	41.0	7.12	0.91	0.72-1.09	44.0	4.96	0.59	0.47-0.71
Krosno	11.8	5.26	0.71	0.45-0.97	12.8	3.91	0.41	0.24-0.57
Legnica	12.0	6.97	0.95	0.58-1.31	12.8	5.90	0.74	0.45-1.03
Leszno	13.4	7.16	0.89	0.58-1.20	9.8	3.52	0.43	0.23-0.62
Lublin	21.6	4.37	0.52	0.37-0.67	19.0	2.90	0.39	0.28-0.51
Łomża	10.2	5.45	0.69	0.41-0.97	8.4	3.04	0.40	0.21-0.59
Łódź	37.8	6.08	0.78	0.62-0.94	44.0	4.41	0.56	0.45-0.68
Nowy Sącz	16.4	5.25	0.65	0.44-0.86	12.8	2.85	0.36	0.22-0.50
Olsztyn	13.0	4.88	0.59	0.37-0.81	9.4	2.70	0.33	0.18-0.48
Opole	27.2	6.68	0.86	0.64-1.07	26.4	4.23	0.51	0.37-0.65
Ostrołęka	9.2	5.09	0.63	0.36-0.89	9.4	3.57	0.48	0.28-0.68
Piła	14.0	6.52	0.85	0.55-1.14	11.0	3.80	0.49	0.29-0.70
Piotrków Trybunalski	17.2	4.85	0.61	0.42-0.80	15.8	3.33	0.42	0.28-0.56
Płock	17.0	6.31	0.86	0.60-1.12	15.6	4.07	0.51	0.33-0.69
Poznań	44.0	6.83	0.89	0.72-1.06	43.4	4.41	0.55	0.43-0.66
Przemyśl	12.8	6.24	0.76	0.48-1.04	12.6	3.89	0.51	0.31-0.70
Radom	26.4	6.64	0.83	0.62-1.05	20.0	3.84	0.48	0.34-0.62
Rzeszów	14.2	4.40	0.58	0.38-0.77	15.0	2.94	0.41	0.27-0.55
Siedlce	15.2	4.07	0.49	0.32-0.66	14.0	2.89	0.37	0.24-0.50
Sieradz	13.4	5.31	0.65	0.43-0.88	13.2	3.86	0.51	0.32-0.69
Skierniewice	16.6	7.09	0.80	0.53-1.07	13.0	3.86	0.49	0.30-0.68
Słupsk	9.8	6.84	0.87	0.50-1.24	7.2	4.12	0.47	0.23-0.72
Suwałki	9.6	5.26	0.65	0.37-0.92	9.2	4.01	0.52	0.29-0.75
Szczecin	18.6	5.52	0.72	0.49-0.96	12.8	2.95	0.39	0.24-0.54

Average Values 1975-1979	Males				Females			
	Cases	Stand. Mort. Rate	Cum. Mort. Rate	Confidence limits	Cases	Stand. Mort. Rate	Cum. Mort. Rate	Confidence limits
Tarnobrzeg	15.2	5.04	0.63	0.42-0.83	13.8	3.07	0.40	0.25-0.54
Tarnów	16.8	5.38	0.63	0.43-0.84	17.2	3.44	0.47	0.32-0.63
Toruń	21.6	7.60	0.95	0.69-1.22	17.0	3.92	0.49	0.33-0.66
Wałbrzych	20.8	6.46	0.78	0.54-1.01	24.2	5.48	0.60	0.42-0.78
Warszawa	86.2	7.19	0.93	0.79-1.06	94.6	4.57	0.56	0.47-0.64
Włocławek	15.0	6.79	0.89	0.60-1.18	15.0	4.87	0.62	0.40-0.83
Wrocław	26.8	5.90	0.71	0.53-0.90	28.0	4.25	0.51	0.37-0.65
Zamość	13.4	4.71	0.56	0.36-0.75	12.4	3.17	0.38	0.23-0.53
Zielona Góra	15.0	5.53	0.73	0.49-0.98	14.4	4.22	0.50	0.31-0.68

8 Larynx - ICD 161

Cancer of the larynx constitutes an increasingly important oncological problem in Poland. Its frequency in men has risen dramatically during the last 20 years. The ASMR for men was 2.6 in 1963 and 6.6 in 1982, while the respective figures for women were 0.3 and 0.4. The male mortality rates have increased since 1970. The increase of mortality with age reaches its peak of 35 deaths per 100000 men aged 70-75, after which the curve slopes down. The highest figure for women is 3 deaths per 100000, also at the age of 70-75. The age-specific mortality rates in males show a considerable increase with calendar years. A substantial increase of risk for men is also observable in successive birth cohorts. Women's mortality rates for laryngeal cancer were low throughout the entire study period, although an analysis of successive birth cohorts shows a small but noticeable increase in risk.

In 1978 France had the world's highest laryngeal cancer mortality rate in men (11.7). Second to France was Spain (7.8), and the other high-risk countries were Luxembourg (6.8), Italy (6.7) and Hungary (6.6). Outside Europe, high mortality rates were also observed in Uruguay (7.5). In women, the mortality rate from laryngeal cancer is much lower with rates in most countries below 1. The exceptions are Mauritius (1.7), Venezuela (1.4) and Cuba (1.3). In Europe the highest women's rates were in Northern Ireland (1.0) and Yugoslavia (0.6). The lowest values were found in Iceland (0.0) and Sweden, Switzerland, Finland, the Netherlands, Austria and Norway (0.1). Poland, with a rate of 5.2 for men, belongs to the group of high-risk countries. The risk for women was medium (0.3).

Analysis of Data from the Provinces, 1975-1979

Malignant neoplasms of the larynx occur more frequently in urban than in rural populations (ratio 1.3 for men, 2.0 for women). They are also much more frequent in men than in women. This sex ratio is the highest for all cancer sites (16.3).

Men

(Mean ASMR=4.7, Range 2.7-6.9, Standard Deviation 1.1; 2.9% of Male Cancer Mortality, Rank 9)

The highest value was 2.6 times greater than the lowest. Provinces with the highest rates were Jelenia Gora (6.88), Walbrzych (6.81), Wroclaw (6.77), Wloclawek (6.66) and Katowice (6.63). Provinces with the lowest rates are Lomza (2.69), Siedlce (2.90), Chelm (3.10), Suwalki (3.27) and Bielsko (3.29). Most of the eastern provinces have a low risk, while higher rates are found in Lower and Upper Silesia.

Women

(Mean ASMR=0.3, Range 0.0-0.7, Standard Deviation 0.1; 0.3% of Female Cancer Mortality, Rank 31)

Laryngeal cancer is rare in women. One province, Biala Podlaska, recorded not one single death from this cancer in the 5-year period under study. Provinces with the highest rates were Jelenia Gora (0.66), Walbrzych (0.54), Szczecin (0.51), Warszawa (0.5) and Slupsk (0.48). Provinces with the lowest rates were Biala Podlaska (0.00), Skierniewice (0.04), Leszno (0.06), Sieradz (0.1) and Tarnobrzeg (0.13). High mortality rates were noted, as in men, in Lower and Upper Silesia. As for many other cancer sites, eastern Poland has lower rates than central and western parts.

Comments

Many epidemiological studies leave no doubt that tobacco smoking (IARC 1986) and alcohol (Flanders and Rothman 1982) are important risk factors in the development of laryngeal cancer. It seems that a more limited role is played by occupational exposures to asbestos and nickel, though these are among the best-documented cases (Stell 1973; Pederson et al. 1973); these studies, however, did not take tobacco smoking and alcohol into consideration as possible confounders. Recent reports have postulated a protective action of diet rich in vitamins A and C (Graham et al. 1981).

Despite the large number of studies, we are still far from fully understanding the aetiology of this cancer. The influence of tobacco and alcohol alone, as well as their synergistic effects, still remain unclear. The relationship between cancer of the larynx and tobacco smoking has been known since the time of the first investigation into the epidemiological effects of tobacco smoking carried out in the 1950s. Wynder et al. (1956) determined tobacco smoking as the main risk factor in cancer of the glottis and supraglottis. A linear dependence was found between the amount of tobacco smoked and the magnitude of risk. A significant increase of risk was also found among pipe and cigar smokers although this was not as high as for cigarette smokers (Rothman et al. 1980). The Polish case-control study by Staszewski showed that tobacco smokers faced a risk which was over 40 times higher than in non-smokers (Staszewsky 1960). A comparable increase in risk was found by Herity et al. (1981) in the Republic of Ireland.

The second factor which seems to increase the risk of laryngeal cancer is alcohol. Although neither experimental models nor epidemiological work have proved that alcohol per se is a carcinogen, suggestions are being made on the grounds of several studies (Wynder et al. 1956, 1976; Jensen 1980) that alcohol increases the risk moderately even if tobacco smoking is controlled for. Rothman, however, points out methodological difficulties in ruling out the residual confounding effect between the role of tobacco and alcohol (Rothman 1980). As early as the first study, Wynder (1956) emphasised that the consumption of alcohol by smokers seems to lead primarily to a greater risk of a tumour in the supraglottis. Also Schottenfeld (1979) suggests that tumours localised in this part result from an interaction between tobacco and alcohol, while in the case of a glottic tumour the impact of alcohol seems to be much smaller.

Graham et al. (1981) described the protective action of vitamins A and C against laryngeal cancer after controlling for smoking and drinking in an extensive case-control study. It seems that the nutrient intake and the type of diet, overlooked in most surveys, may, in view of the increasing evidence of their protective action, turn out to be the third crucial element that modifies the magnitude of the risk of cancer of the larynx.

Descriptive epidemiological data constitute an interesting contribution to the discussion on the aetiology. Austin et al. (1982) draw attention to the existence of some inconsistencies in the interpretation of the data. The first unresolved problem is how much tobacco smoking alone alters the risk. Stell (1972) wrote that although lung cancer incidence had increased by 500% in the years 1900-1970 and correlated well with the increase in cigarette smoking in Great Britain, the incidence of laryngeal cancer showed no substantial changes over that time. The mortality rate for lung cancer increased by 300% in Australia over the period 1950-1970 whereas the mortality rate for laryngeal cancer remained unchanged (Atkinson 1975). McMichael (1978) suggests, on the grounds of observing the behaviour of laryngeal and oesophageal cancer mortality trends and the consumption of alcohol and tobacco in England and Australia, that the magnitude of alcohol consumption relates to laryngeal cancer more strongly than tobacco consumption. Observations made by Tuyns and Audigier (1976) in France are similar. They show dissimilarities between the frequency of lung and laryngeal cancers in many countries of Europe. The frequency of lung cancer in Scottish men is the highest in Europe although laryngeal cancer rates are relatively low in this population (Tuyns 1982).

Cancer of the larynx in Poland mainly affects the male population and is very rare in women. The sex ratio was 16.3 in the years 1975-1979 and was the highest difference in all cancer sites. The risk of laryngeal cancer is increasing rapidly. Although this increase primarily involves men, similar trends are also observed in women who live in towns. The frequency of laryngeal cancer among females living in urban areas is two times greater than among those living in rural areas. This is the biggest difference of all cancer sites in females with respect to residence. Women of the largest town, Warszawa, show rising mortality rates (0.8 per 100000 in 1963-1967 and 1.4 per 100000 in 1973-1977; Zatonski et al. 1983). Malignant neoplasms of the larynx were rare, even in men, at the beginning of the 1960s. At that time Poland was a low-risk country in Europe. Between 1972 and 1982 the risk doubled in men with an annual increase rate of 8.7%. The increase occurred in all age groups. The cohort effect is easily seen as the risk of the 1940 cohort is several dozen times greater than that threatening the cohort born in 1880.

The part of the larynx most affected in men is the supraglottis. Our population-based case-control study in Lower Silesia showed that 58% of laryngeal cancers were localised in the supraglottis, 41% in the glottis and only 1% in the subglottis. This distribution is significantly different in Poland in comparison to some other countries (Rothman 1980).

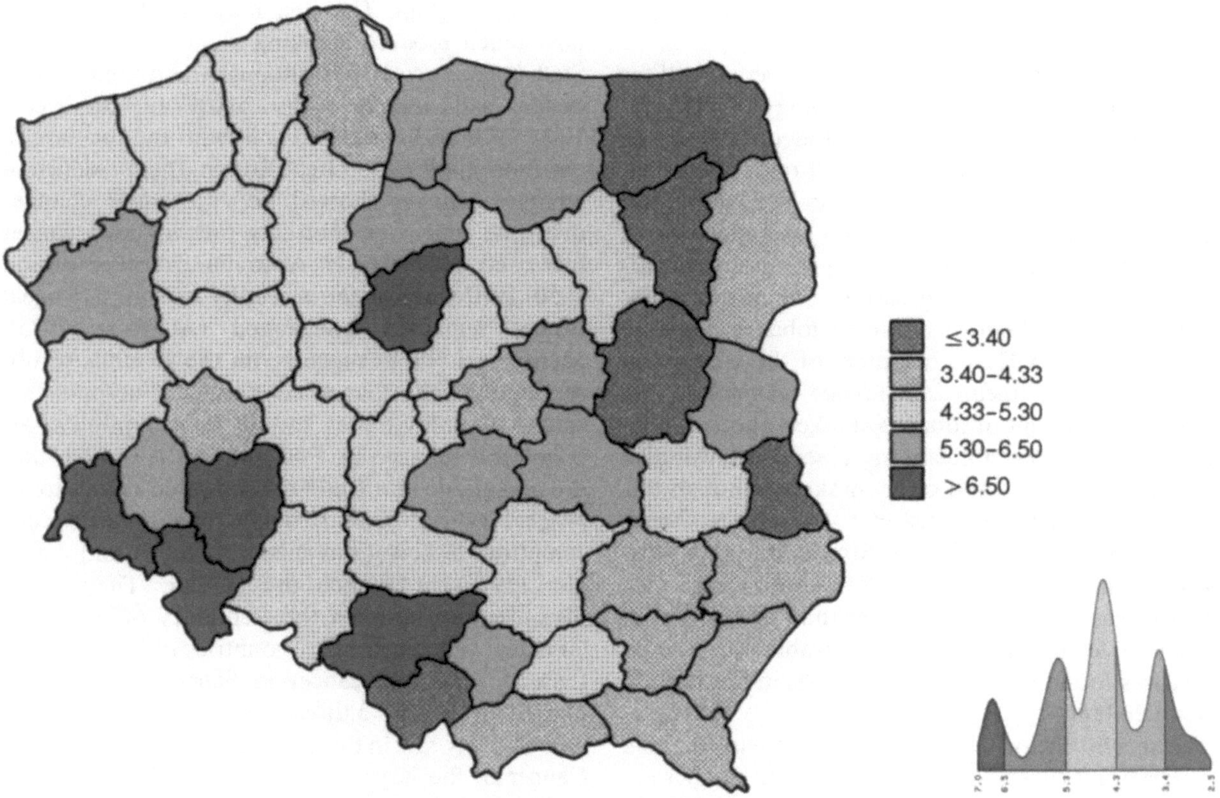
≤3.40
3.40–4.33
4.33–5.30
5.30–6.50
>6.50

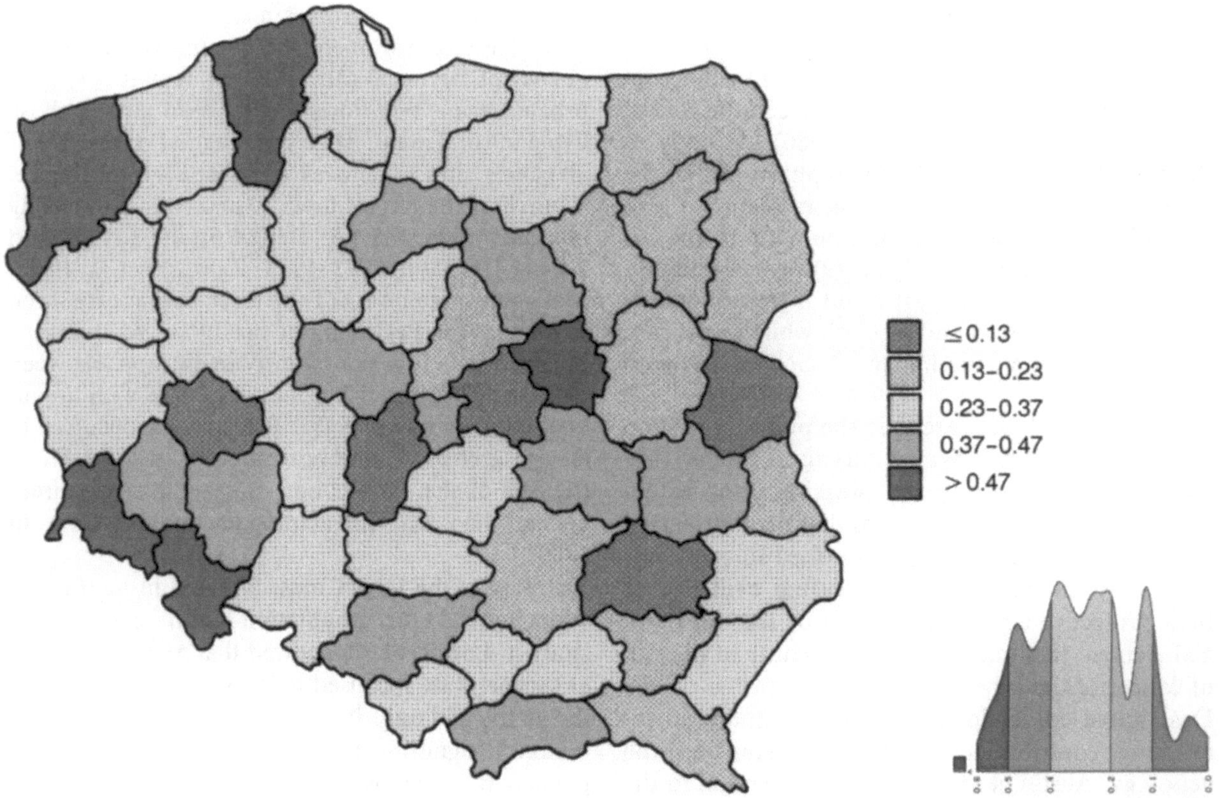
≤0.13
0.13–0.23
0.23–0.37
0.37–0.47
>0.47

6.05 – 6.88
5.21 – 6.05
4.37 – 5.21
3.53 – 4.37
2.69 – 3.53

0.53 – 0.66
0.40 – 0.53
0.26 – 0.40
0.13 – 0.26
0.00 – 0.13

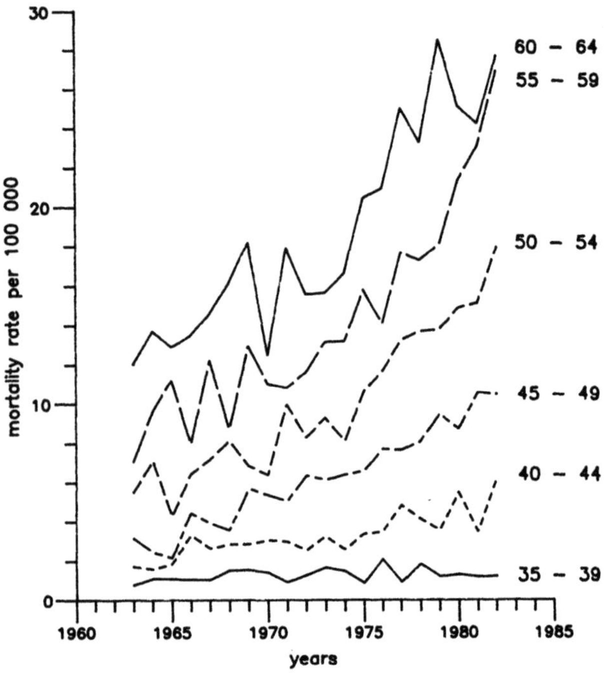

Temporal trend of mortality in individual age groups/men

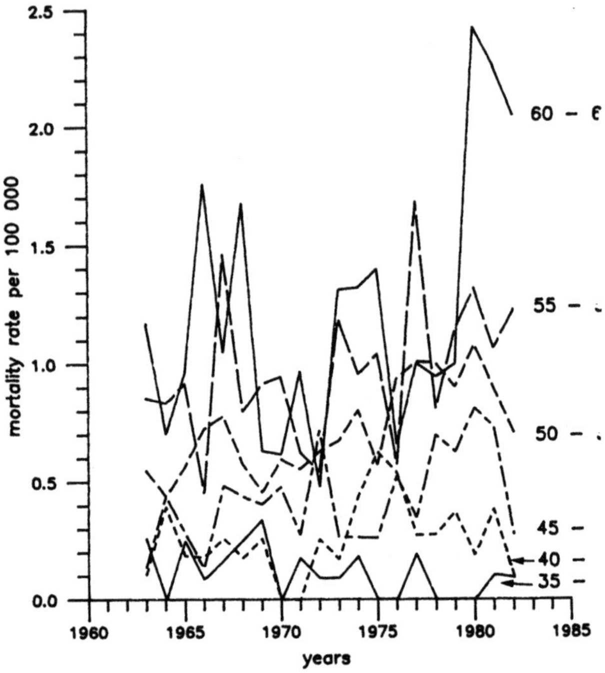

Temporal trend of mortality in individual age groups/women

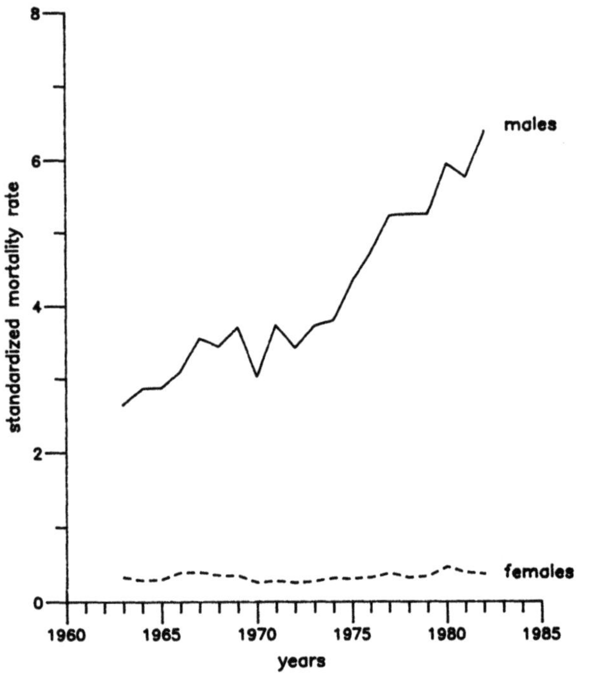

Temporal trend of the age-adjusted mortality rates for men and women

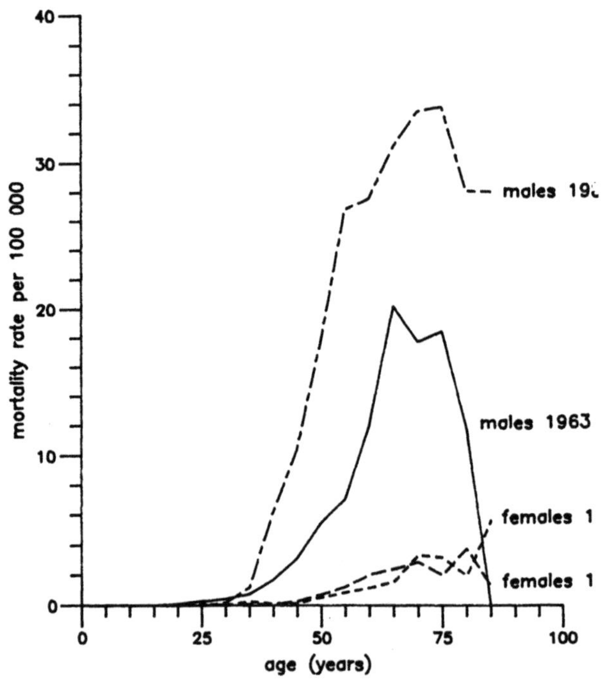

Mortality depending on age in two sample years for men and women

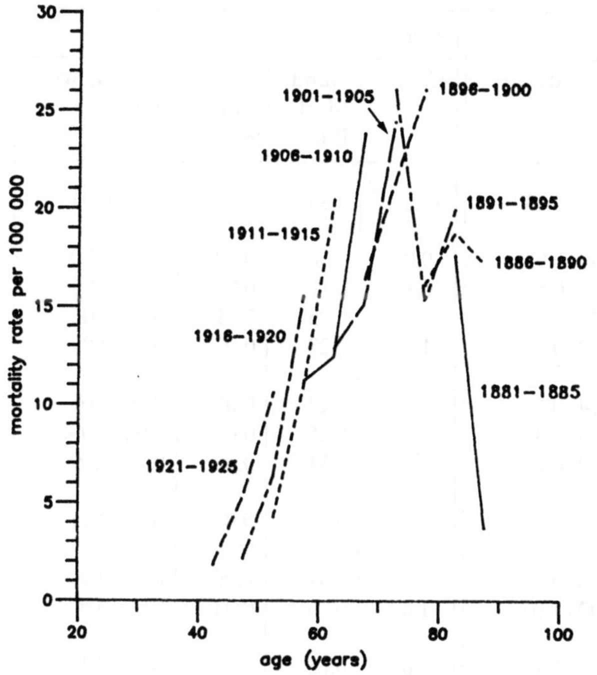

Age-dependent mortality in various birth cohorts/ men

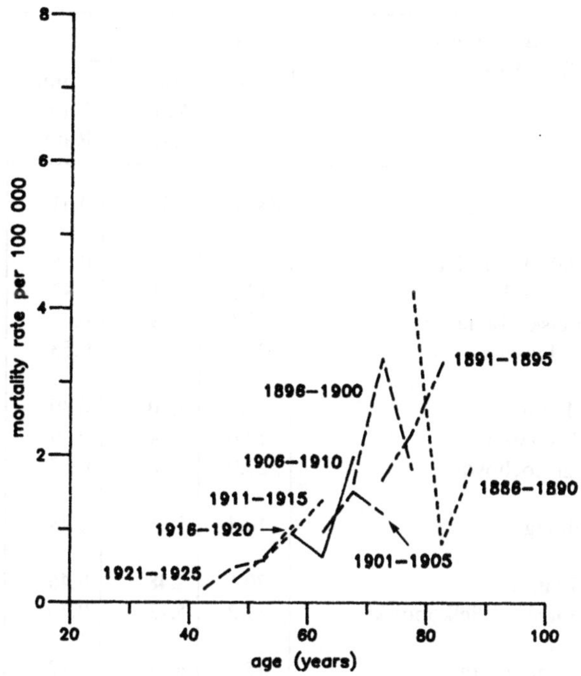

Age-dependent mortality in various birth cohorts/ women

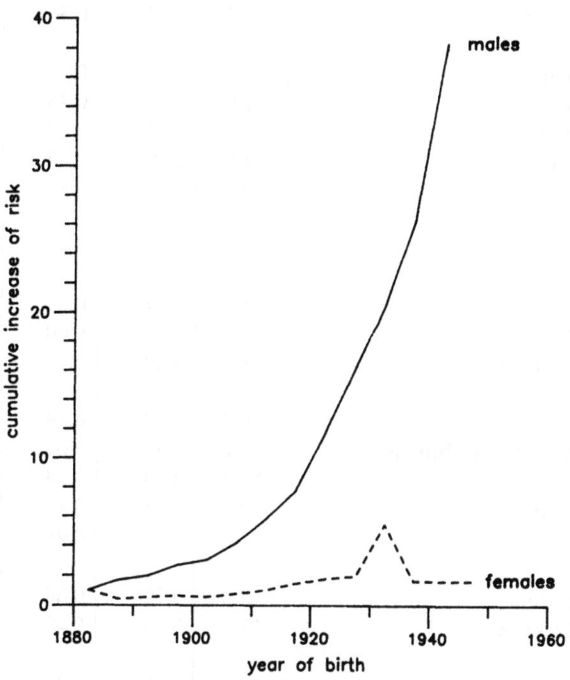

Ratios of the cumulative mortality rates for successive birth cohorts relative to the 1886–1890 cohort

Average Values 1975-1979	Males				Females			
	Cases	Stand. Mort. Rate	Cum. Mort. Rate	Confidence limits	Cases	Stand. Mort. Rate	Cum. Mort. Rate	Confidence limits
Poland	866.4	4.94	0.61	0.58-0.63	81.6	0.33	0.04	0.03-0.05
Biała Podlaska	9.8	5.69	0.68	0.40-0.95	0.0	0.00	0.00	0.00-0.00
Białystok	12.6	3.46	0.42	0.26-0.57	0.8	0.13	0.01	0.00-0.03
Bielsko Biała	13.4	3.29	0.41	0.27-0.56	1.6	0.25	0.01	0.00-0.03
Bydgoszcz	22.8	4.56	0.53	0.39-0.68	1.8	0.27	0.03	0.00-0.07
Chełm	4.0	3.10	0.39	0.14-0.63	0.4	0.23	0.01	0.00-0.05
Ciechanów	12.0	5.24	0.69	0.44-0.93	1.2	0.45	0.04	0.00-0.09
Częstochowa	22.0	5.28	0.67	0.49-0.85	1.8	0.31	0.05	0.01-0.09
Elbląg	10.4	5.56	0.78	0.46-1.11	0.6	0.29	0.04	0.00-0.11
Gdańsk	20.6	3.48	0.46	0.33-0.59	3.0	0.37	0.05	0.01-0.09
Gorzów Wielkopolski	11.2	5.73	0.76	0.47-1.06	1.0	0.36	0.04	0.00-0.09
Jelenia Góra	15.2	6.88	0.87	0.59-1.16	2.0	0.66	0.09	0.01-0.17
Kalisz	16.6	4.70	0.54	0.38-0.71	1.2	0.24	0.03	0.00-0.07
Katowice	106.2	6.63	0.83	0.72-0.93	10.0	0.42	0.04	0.02-0.06
Kielce	26.6	4.42	0.54	0.40-0.67	1.6	0.15	0.02	0.00-0.04
Konin	11.2	4.61	0.63	0.40-0.86	1.6	0.46	0.06	0.00-0.12
Koszalin	7.8	4.33	0.55	0.28-0.81	0.8	0.33	0.03	0.00-0.08
Kraków	31.4	5.54	0.66	0.50-0.81	3.2	0.36	0.04	0.01-0.07
Krosno	9.4	4.03	0.56	0.33-0.79	0.6	0.16	0.03	0.00-0.08
Legnica	10.2	5.90	0.70	0.41-1.00	0.8	0.39	0.04	0.00-0.11
Leszno	7.0	3.59	0.45	0.24-0.66	0.2	0.06	0.01	0.00-0.05
Lublin	22.6	4.63	0.57	0.42-0.72	2.6	0.40	0.05	0.01-0.09
Łomża	4.8	2.69	0.34	0.14-0.54	0.6	0.16	0.03	0.00-0.08
Łódź	29.2	4.64	0.56	0.43-0.69	4.0	0.38	0.04	0.01-0.07
Nowy Sącz	11.0	3.51	0.45	0.28-0.62	1.8	0.41	0.06	0.00-0.11
Olsztyn	15.0	5.54	0.69	0.45-0.92	1.2	0.33	0.05	0.00-0.12
Opole	19.8	4.78	0.60	0.42-0.78	2.0	0.33	0.04	0.00-0.07
Ostrołęka	8.6	4.42	0.50	0.27-0.72	0.6	0.17	0.01	0.00-0.04
Piła	9.2	4.62	0.54	0.31-0.78	1.2	0.35	0.07	0.00-0.14
Piotrków Trybunalski	18.2	5.32	0.67	0.48-0.86	1.0	0.24	0.02	0.00-0.05
Płock	12.2	4.48	0.54	0.34-0.73	0.6	0.22	0.03	0.00-0.07
Poznań	29.4	4.85	0.54	0.41-0.68	2.8	0.31	0.03	0.01-0.06
Przemyśl	7.6	3.93	0.48	0.26-0.70	0.8	0.28	0.04	0.00-0.09
Radom	20.0	5.39	0.64	0.45-0.82	2.0	0.44	0.06	0.01-0.11
Rzeszów	11.8	3.48	0.40	0.24-0.55	0.6	0.14	0.02	0.00-0.05
Siedlce	10.8	2.90	0.35	0.21-0.49	0.6	0.15	0.02	0.00-0.05
Sieradz	10.6	4.48	0.56	0.35-0.77	0.4	0.10	0.02	0.00-0.06
Skierniewice	8.4	3.56	0.48	0.27-0.69	0.2	0.04	0.00	0.00-0.00
Słupsk	7.4	4.98	0.67	0.35-0.99	1.0	0.48	0.03	0.00-0.07
Suwałki	6.4	3.27	0.39	0.18-0.59	0.6	0.22	0.02	0.00-0.07
Szczecin	17.2	4.77	0.59	0.39-0.79	2.6	0.51	0.06	0.01-0.10

Average Values 1975-1979	Males				Females			
	Cases	Stand. Mort. Rate	Cum. Mort. Rate	Confidence limits	Cases	Stand. Mort. Rate	Cum. Mort. Rate	Confidence limits
Tarnobrzeg	11.2	3.67	0.46	0.29-0.63	0.4	0.13	0.02	0.00-0.05
Tarnów	14.2	4.74	0.56	0.37-0.76	1.2	0.28	0.03	0.00-0.07
Toruń	14.2	5.42	0.63	0.41-0.84	1.8	0.47	0.06	0.00-0.12
Wałbrzych	22.0	6.81	0.73	0.51-0.94	2.2	0.54	0.07	0.01-0.14
Warszawa	74.6	6.36	0.80	0.68-0.92	8.8	0.50	0.06	0.04-0.09
Włocławek	13.8	6.66	0.84	0.56-1.12	0.8	0.27	0.02	0.00-0.05
Wrocław	31.6	6.77	0.84	0.65-1.04	2.6	0.45	0.06	0.01-0.11
Zamość	12.2	4.33	0.50	0.32-0.68	1.0	0.25	0.03	0.00-0.08
Zielona Góra	12.0	4.37	0.52	0.32-0.71	1.4	0.35	0.03	0.00-0.07

Atkinson (1975) writes that 70% of laryngeal cancers in Australia affect the glottis and 25% affect the supraglottis, while in East Yorkshire, England, the supraglottis and glottis are affected equally (about 48% each) (Williams and Beetham 1976). Clinical records on laryngeal cancers in men also show that the increase in laryngeal cancers involves mainly the supraglottis. Cancer sites in the larynx tend to "move" upwards. Clinical data collected by the Otolaryngology Clinic at the Medical Academy in Poznan show a considerable change in the laryngeal sites with the distribution changing towards the supraglottis in the period 1946-1979. This has consequences in clinical symptomatology. The first clinical symptoms do not include those of the affected glottis (hoarse voice) but in most cases the first symptom is a sore throat, painful swallowing, etc. (W. Zatonski and J. Mierzwinska, Cancer of the Larynx in Lower Silesia, unpublished data).

The increase in laryngeal cancer in men occurred in all provinces, although differences among them remain considerable (Zatonski and Didkowska 1984). The geographical pattern differs greatly from the distribution of lung cancer (see section 3.9). Tobacco smoking, which shows a very good linear relationship to the risk of lung cancer in men in various provinces, does not show correlation with the risk of laryngeal cancer in the individual provinces. The increase rate in the 1970s in men certainly belongs to the world's highest (Zatonski et al. 1982, 1983), with the result that within the last two decades Poland has become a country with one of the highest risks in Europe. Cancers of the larynx in men are found chiefly in those who smoke. In our population based case-control study in Lower Silesia, we found only 2.5% of non-smokers among all the cases while the rest had a history of long-term heavy exposure to tobacco. Of some significance must be the fact that the cigarettes smoked were almost entirely manufactured from Polish (shag-like) tobacco. It is noteworthy that Zavala and Correa (1986) believe that black tobacco is a particular risk factor for laryngeal cancer. Most of the patients in our case-control study group were also exposed to the second risk factor, alcohol. Only 1.2% of them were abstinent (never drinking alcohol), and 70% admitted heavy alcohol consumption in the form of vodka. Laryngeal cancer in Poland seems to affect only the heavy-smoking and heavy-drinking part of population.

9 Lung - ICD 162

Cancer of the lung has become the predominant form of cancer in men and a major problem for women. The ASMR in men was 23.8 in 1963 and 57.3 in 1982, while the respective figures for women were 3.9 and 7.2. The time trend calculated for the years 1963-1982 shows a mean annual increase rate of 7.26% for men and 4.1% for women. The frequency of lung cancer increases after the age of 45 years in both sexes. There is a decrease in men aged 65-70. In 1982, the curve peaked at 380 per 100000 in men and 50 per 100000 in women. Compared with 1963, the curves in 1982 had their peaks at much higher levels, whereas the shape of these curves was similar for both these periods. The age-specific rates for men show a permanent increase in risk in all age groups over successive calendar years. In women, the increase was more rapid after the 1970s, especially in the older age groups. A cohort analysis shows a steady increase in risk after the cohort born between 1901 and 1905. The frequency did not rise in the three oldest cohorts. Analysis of the successive birth cohorts shows that the 1940 cohort has a risk which is several dozen times higher in men and several times higher in women than the 1880 cohort.
Compared with other parts of the world, Europe has a very high mortality rate for lung cancer. In 1978 the highest rate in men was recorded in Scotland (85.8). Other high-risk countries were the Netherlands (78.2), England and Wales (73.0), Czechoslovakia (69.0) and Luxembourg (67.2). The lowest rates were recorded in Portugal (19.4) and Iceland (20.6). The mortality rate in women was at a much lower level, the highest being in Scotland with 22.5, England and Wales 16.4, Ireland 14.4 and Denmark 13.1. Outside Europe, the highest value was found in Hong Kong (23.7). European countries with low mortality rates were Portugal (3.1), France (3.8) and Spain (4.0). With a rate of 51.0 deaths per 100000, Poland is a high-risk country for men, while the women's rate of 6.3 makes Poland a medium-risk country.

Analysis of Data from the Provinces, 1975-1979

Lung cancer occurred more often in towns than in rural areas. The men's urban/rural ratio was 1.4 and the women's 1.7. Lung cancer was much more frequent in men than in women (8.1 times).

Men

(Mean ASMR=42.1, Range 26.9-66.9, Standard Deviation 10.4; 29.1% of Male Cancer Mortality, Rank 1)

The highest frequency rate was 2.5 times greater than the lowest. Provinces with the highest rates were Szczecin (66.90), Opole (61.39), Olsztyn (61.02), Katowice (60.96) and Elblag (60.71). Provinces with the lowest rates were Lomza (26.92), Siedlce (28.35), Bialystok (30.27), Piotrkow (30.44) and Ostroleka (31.04). The highest mortality rates were found in western and especially northwestern Poland, along the Baltic Coast and in Silesia. Eastern and eastern-central regions are at a low risk.

Women

(Mean ASMR=5.6, Range 2.8-9.9, Standard Deviation 1.8; 6.0% of Female Cancer Mortality, Rank 5)

The highest value was 3.5 times greater than the lowest. Provinces with the highest rates were Warszawa (9.94), Wroclaw (9.59), Elblag (8.96), Slupsk (8.77) and Gdansk (8.16). Provinces with the lowest rates were Lomza (2.83), Siedlce (3.42), Konin (3.45), Chelm (3.58) and Ciechanow (3.63). The geographical arrangement of lung cancer mortality rates is fairly clear-cut. A higher-risk area is in the northwest and in Lower Silesia, and it is very similar to the men's higher-risk area. The risk is low in eastern-central Poland, except for the province of Warszawa.

Comments

Since the early 1950s there has been no doubt that tobacco smoking, especially cigarettes, is the main risk factor for cancer of the lung. The agreement of epidemiological observations, the intensity of this relationship, the dose/effect relationship, biological plausibility, freezing of the risk after stopping, all these elements confirm the relationship between tobacco smoking and lung cancer. Also, the identification of dozens of carcinogens present in the tobacco smoke along with experiments on laboratory animals corroborate the above observations (IARC 1986). Thus, all the conditions required for the recognition of a causative relation have been met. There are, of course, other factors which potentially lead to lung cancer. These are usually associated with occupational exposures or air pollution. Occupational exposures, e.g. to asbestos, radon, polyaromatic hydrocarbons, are known risk factors. Doll (1978) summarised that atmospheric air pollution may have some (small) effect on the increase of the lung cancer risk, especially in smokers. Some studies also point out that a high vitamin A content in the diet can reduce risk in tobacco smokers (Bjelke 1975). However, tobacco smoke remains the principal cause of lung cancer with the other factors playing a much smaller role. It has been assumed that in industrialized countries 83%-94% of lung cancers in men and 57%-80% in women are caused by tobacco smoking (Doll and Peto 1981).

Since the 1960s Poland has had a rapid increase in the lung cancer mortality rate. It has risen exceptionally fast in men with an annual rate (7.26%) which is twice as high as in any other European country. Women too, especially those living in towns, are under a rapidly increasing risk. Incidence in Warszawa, which is distinguished by the amount of tobacco smoked by women - about 40% of Warszawa women smoked (Jokiel 1983) - is rising at a rate of 10% annually (Koszarowski et al. 1972, 1977). For the entire country the rate is 4.1%, which is similar to other European countries. Lung cancer is, as in other countries, much more frequent in men than in women. Every 17th male and every 82th female died of this tumour in 1982 (sex ratio 8.1). The relationship between the frequencies in urban and rural areas is interesting. As the frequency of exposure to tobacco smoke in rural men increases in comparison to urban men, so does the frequency of lung cancer in that population. The male urban/rural ratio was 1.74 in the years 1967-1968 (Staszewski 1976), 1.56 in 1970-1974 (Staszewski 1979), and our analysis covering the years 1975-1979 has established it at 1.4. A converse phenomenon was found in the female population. With a more rapid increase in smoking in urban women, the urban/rural ratio of lung cancer has also increased. It was 1.45 in 1967-1968 (Staszewski 1976), 1.60 in 1970-1974 (Staszewski 1979) and 1.70 in 1975-1979. Lung cancer is increasing dramatically in younger birth cohorts, corresponding with their experience in tobacco smoking.

There have been regional differences in the lung cancer mortality rate for a very long time (Staszewski 1976, 1979). All regions experienced increasing mortality rates in men after the early 1960s. The distribution of mortality rates of provinces is non-symmetrical. We observe a shift towards the higher values. The lowest- and highest-risk provinces remain the same. Regional differences in women's lung cancer mortality rates are a little greater than in men. But women too, have increasing mortality rates in all provinces, and these increases are greatest in the high-risk provinces. The distribution of provinces with regard to the mortality rates is also non-symmetrical. The values of most provinces are below the national average (see black-and-white map). As in the case of time trends, also in the geographical pattern, the epidemiological picture of lung cancer risk fits neatly into that of tobacco smoking. Differences between the mortality rates for lung cancer in the provinces can be best explained by the differences in the amount of tobacco smoked. As the correlation of lung cancer to tobacco was impossible for 1975-1979 because of the administrative reform of the whole country in 1975, we carried out an analysis of the province-related mortality rates (using the old administrative units) in the period 1970-1974 and the tobacco consumption in the provinces during the period 1958-1962. We found a highly significant positive correlation between the lung cancer mortality rate and cigarette consumption per capita in the provinces. The correlation was 0.9 for men and women. The effect of atmospheric air pollution on the mortality rate is, despite heavy pollution in many regions, still difficult to grasp. Women in the province of Katowice, who are exposed to Poland's highest air pollution, faced a lower-than-average risk both in the period 1970-1974 (Staszewski 1979) and in that covered by our analysis, i.e. 1975-1979. Indigenous men of the nearby town of Zabrze have mortality rates lower than immigrants from other regions, despite being exposed to the highest air pollution during the whole of their lives (Zemla 1984). Men living in rural areas show a greater increase in the incidence of lung cancer than those living in towns.

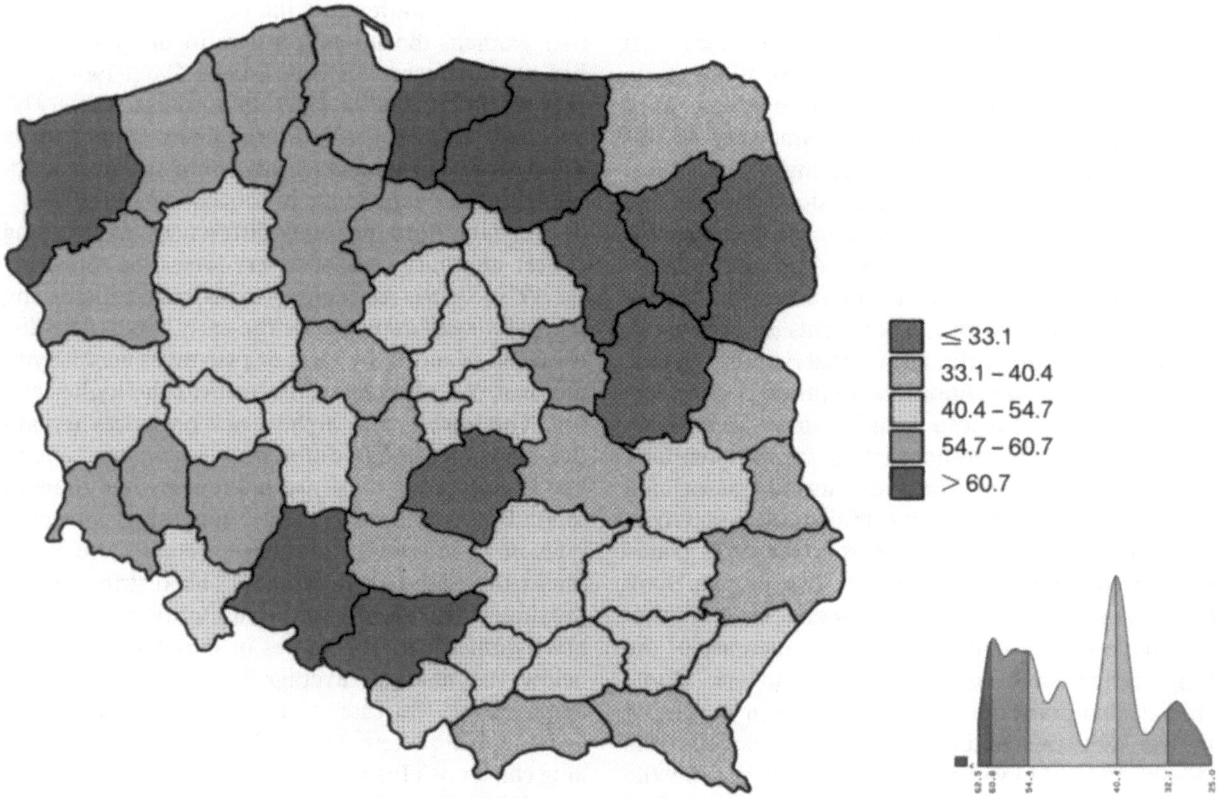
≤ 33.1
33.1 – 40.4
40.4 – 54.7
54.7 – 60.7
> 60.7

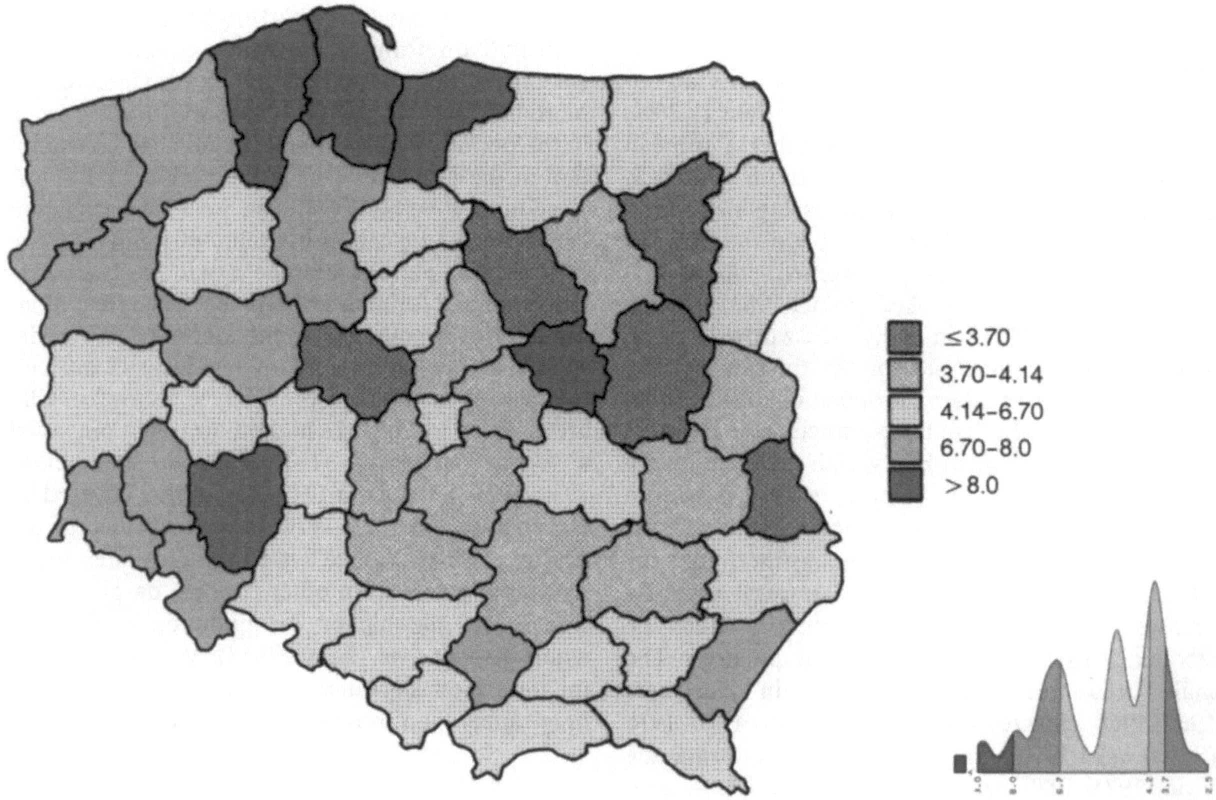
≤ 3.70
3.70–4.14
4.14–6.70
6.70–8.0
> 8.0

58.9 – 66.9
50.9 – 58.9
42.9 – 50.9
34.9 – 42.9
26.9 – 34.9

8.52 – 9.94
7.10 – 8.52
5.68 – 7.10
4.26 – 5.68
2.83 – 4.26

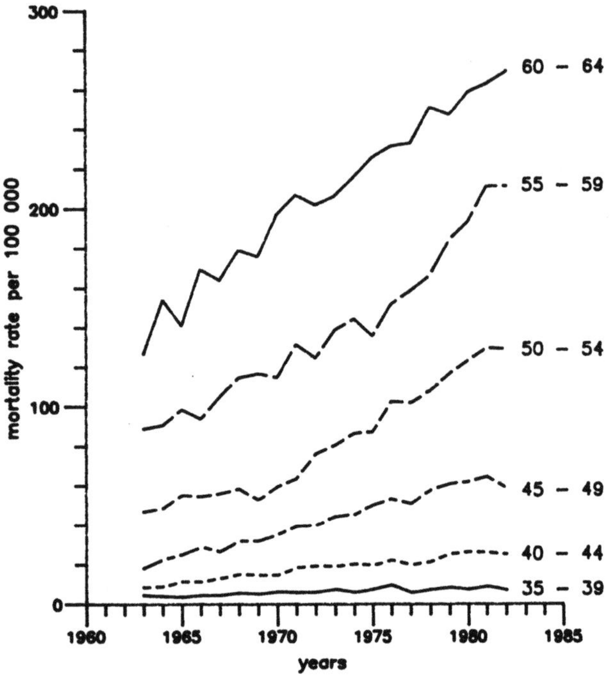

Temporal trend of mortality in individual age groups/men

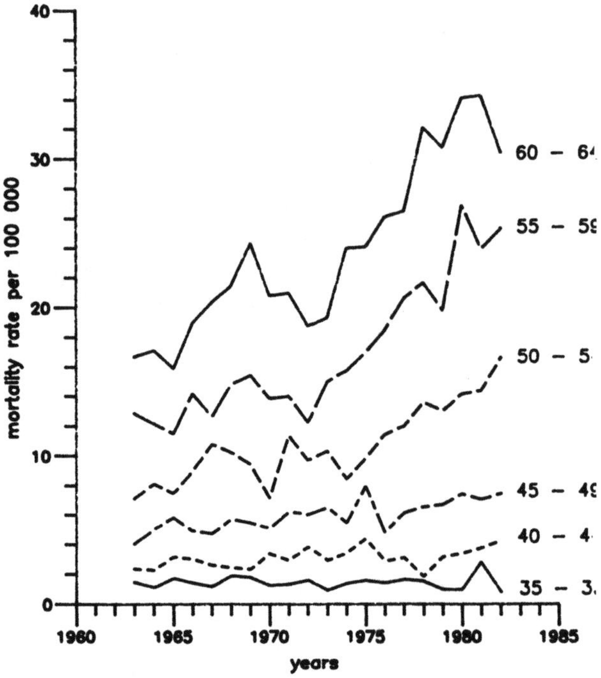

Temporal trend of mortality in individual age groups/women

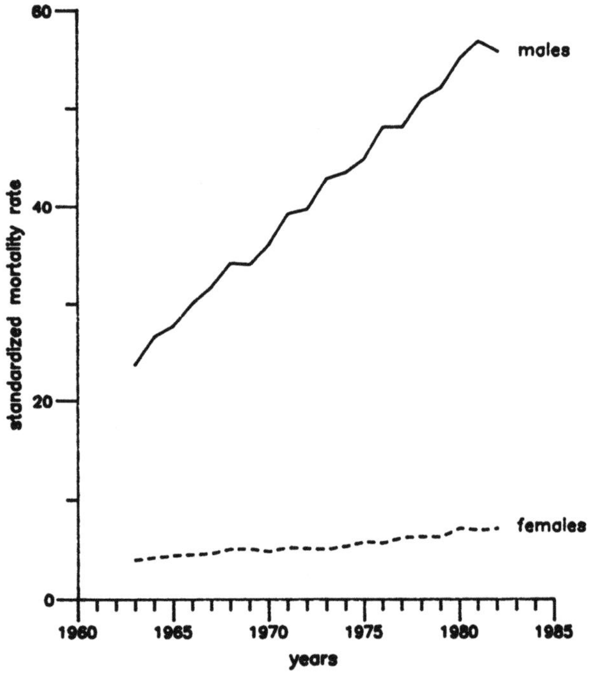

Temporal trend of the age-adjusted mortality rates for men and women

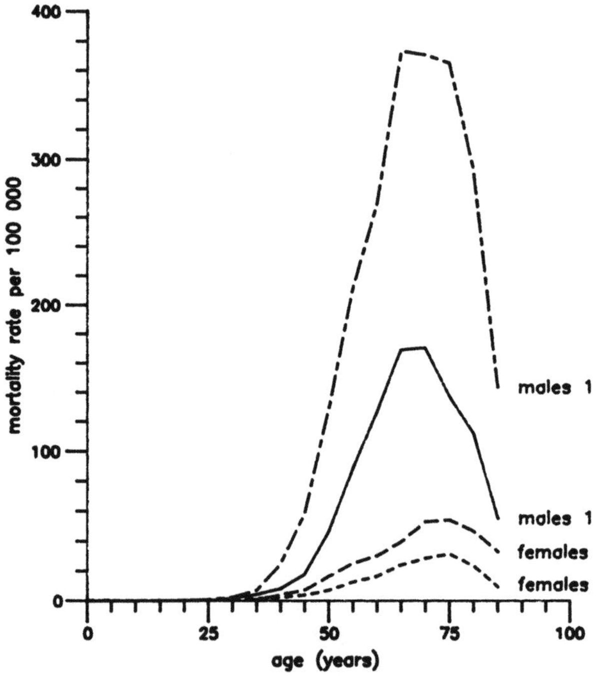

Mortality depending on age in two sample years for men and women

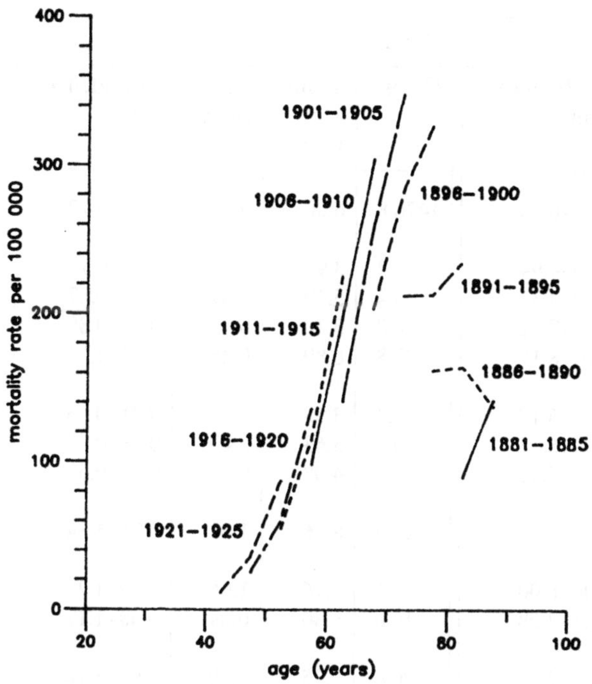

Age-dependent mortality in various birth cohorts/ men

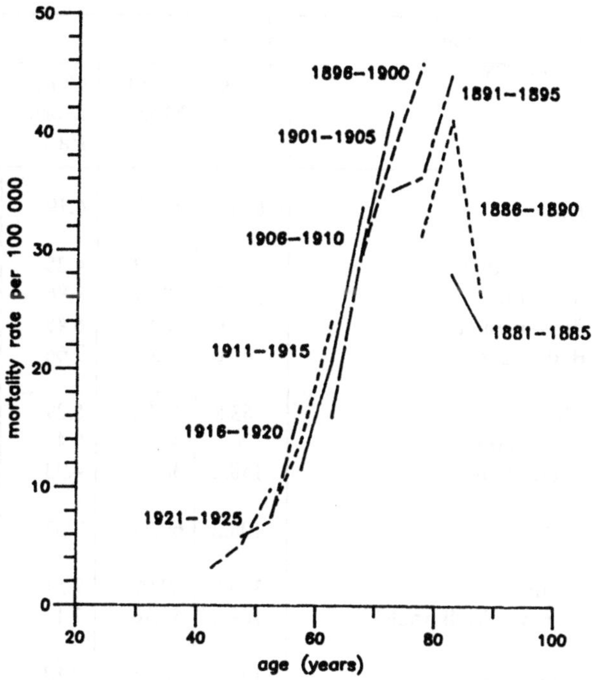

Age-dependent mortality in various birth cohorts/ women

A low-risk country in the early 1960s, Poland has one of the highest risks of lung cancer in the 1980s, especially for men. Two factors seem to be responsible for this: extremely high tobacco consumption and the very high tar content (average 24 mg per cigarette) and nicotine (average 1.8 mg per cigarette) in the black tobacco grown in Poland (Zatonski et al. 1986). There are reasons to suspect that the risk may continue to rise in the future. This is suggested by the very high mortality rates in young age groups at the beginning of this decade and a very high frequency of cigarette smoking in the same age groups: in 1982 81% of men and 57% of women in the age group 30-34 years. Epidemiological data indicate that the tobacco smoking epidemic leads to the epidemic of lung cancer. It seems that the only solution would be primary prevention in this country, too.

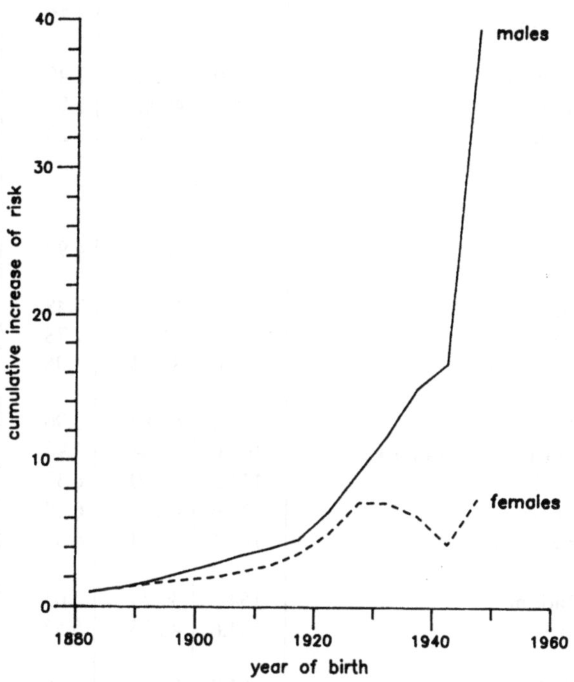

Ratios of the cumulative mortality rates for successive birth cohorts relative to the 1886-1890 cohort

Average Values 1975-1979	Males				Females			
	Cases	Stand. Mort. Rate	Cum. Mort. Rate	Confidence limits	Cases	Stand. Mort. Rate	Cum. Mort. Rate	Confidence limits
Poland	8670.2	48.77	6.19	6.11-6.28	1476.8	6.00	0.75	0.72-0.77
Biała Podlaska	58.4	33.12	4.25	3.56-4.94	9.4	3.93	0.49	0.28-0.71
Białystok	115.2	30.27	3.86	3.40-4.32	26.4	5.19	0.69	0.51-0.87
Bielsko Biała	201.0	50.82	6.46	5.88-7.02	30.8	5.10	0.64	0.49-0.80
Bydgoszcz	307.0	60.41	7.64	7.10-8.17	47.8	6.89	0.86	0.69-1.02
Chełm	53.8	39.00	5.29	4.40-6.17	6.4	3.58	0.43	0.21-0.66
Ciechanów	96.2	42.92	5.49	4.80-6.17	10.6	3.63	0.40	0.23-0.57
Częstochowa	158.2	38.16	4.93	4.45-5.41	24.4	4.08	0.53	0.39-0.67
Elbląg	108.2	60.71	7.67	6.72-8.60	20.2	8.96	1.03	0.71-1.34
Gdańsk	355.2	59.92	7.51	7.00-8.00	65.6	8.16	1.06	0.89-1.23
Gorzów Wielkopolski	108.4	56.76	7.12	6.25-7.98	16.0	6.80	0.89	0.60-1.17
Jelenia Góra	127.4	58.64	7.12	6.29-7.93	20.4	7.25	0.90	0.62-1.18
Kalisz	152.6	40.70	5.23	4.71-5.75	23.0	4.38	0.57	0.41-0.72
Katowice	996.0	60.96	7.75	7.44-8.06	146.2	5.98	0.75	0.66-0.83
Kielce	248.6	40.79	5.33	4.92-5.75	34.0	4.09	0.47	0.36-0.58
Konin	83.8	35.66	4.47	3.87-5.06	11.2	3.45	0.44	0.27-0.61
Koszalin	101.0	56.55	6.92	6.03-7.80	17.4	7.09	0.84	0.55-1.13
Kraków	311.0	54.01	6.92	6.42-7.41	67.2	7.86	1.01	0.84-1.17
Krosno	91.6	39.61	5.39	4.69-6.08	18.6	6.56	0.75	0.51-0.99
Legnica	97.0	57.45	7.40	6.43-8.37	14.6	6.90	0.82	0.53-1.11
Leszno	76.2	40.45	5.05	4.35-5.75	12.8	5.12	0.65	0.42-0.88
Lublin	203.0	41.30	5.23	4.77-5.69	27.6	4.07	0.53	0.39-0.66
Łomża	52.2	26.92	3.57	2.96-4.19	7.6	2.83	0.37	0.19-0.55
Łódź	329.6	52.24	6.63	6.17-7.08	61.8	6.60	0.82	0.68-0.96
Nowy Sącz	120.2	38.89	4.99	4.42-5.56	20.8	4.80	0.61	0.43-0.79
Olsztyn	160.8	61.02	7.48	6.72-8.24	21.0	6.31	0.81	0.58-1.05
Opole	251.0	61.39	7.78	7.15-8.40	32.4	5.06	0.65	0.50-0.80
Ostrołęka	59.6	31.04	4.06	3.41-4.70	9.6	3.80	0.50	0.29-0.71
Piła	95.4	47.14	5.96	5.21-6.71	15.8	5.36	0.68	0.45-0.92
Piotrków Trybunalski	106.0	30.44	3.98	3.50-4.46	18.8	4.08	0.45	0.31-0.59
Płock	133.6	50.10	6.35	5.68-7.02	14.8	4.12	0.52	0.34-0.69
Poznań	319.6	49.23	6.19	5.76-6.62	60.2	6.76	0.82	0.68-0.96
Przemyśl	101.4	48.44	6.08	5.32-6.85	19.8	7.25	0.82	0.57-1.08
Radom	154.2	39.79	5.03	4.52-5.53	21.0	4.19	0.55	0.39-0.70
Rzeszów	141.6	42.35	5.57	4.99-6.15	22.8	5.21	0.69	0.50-0.88
Siedlce	103.8	28.35	3.59	3.16-4.03	16.4	3.42	0.45	0.31-0.60
Sieradz	81.8	33.33	4.21	3.64-4.77	13.0	4.01	0.51	0.32-0.69
Skierniewice	96.0	43.03	5.64	4.94-6.34	11.6	3.85	0.47	0.29-0.66
Słupsk	81.4	56.96	7.28	6.24-8.30	16.2	8.77	1.11	0.73-1.48
Suwałki	75.4	40.01	5.18	4.42-5.94	9.8	4.19	0.53	0.30-0.76
Szczecin	230.2	66.90	8.10	7.39-8.81	34.8	7.18	0.90	0.69-1.12

Average Values 1975-1979	Males				Females			
	Cases	Stand. Mort. Rate	Cum. Mort. Rate	Confidence limits	Cases	Stand. Mort. Rate	Cum. Mort. Rate	Confidence limits
Tarnobrzeg	134.6	41.52	5.46	4.88-6.04	17.0	4.14	0.48	0.32-0.64
Tarnów	150.6	48.44	6.03	5.41-6.64	22.0	4.73	0.62	0.44-0.80
Toruń	173.2	59.38	7.70	6.98-8.42	26.0	6.53	0.79	0.59-0.99
Wałbrzych	173.0	54.22	6.88	6.19-7.57	33.4	7.87	0.87	0.66-1.08
Warszawa	647.8	54.67	6.75	6.41-7.09	185.6	9.94	1.25	1.13-1.37
Włocławek	115.8	53.90	6.87	6.09-7.64	15.0	4.91	0.60	0.39-0.81
Wrocław	264.6	56.67	7.00	6.43-7.57	61.0	9.59	1.14	0.93-1.34
Zamość	122.8	40.32	5.23	4.65-5.81	20.0	5.14	0.70	0.50-0.89
Zielona Góra	144.2	54.13	6.68	5.96-7.39	18.0	5.29	0.59	0.39-0.78

10 Melanoma – ICD 172

Melanoma malignum is a rare neoplasm. It caused the death of 781 men and 928 women during the period 1975-1979. Despite the small number of cases, it is a subject of particular interest because of the sharp increase in its frequency in many countries. The present analysis is based on data of the period 1963-1979.[1] The ASMR for the skin melanoma in men was 0.4, in 1963 and 1.0 in 1979, while the respective rates for women were 0.3 and 0.9. The period under study saw a considerable increase in the mortality rates in both sexes. The mean annual mortality rate increase, calculated for the years 1963-1979, was the highest of all other cancers, namely, 12.2% in men and 9.8% in women. The mortality rate increased in all age groups, both sexes and in successive birth cohorts. The cumulative mortality rate increase in the 1920 birth cohort compared with the 1880 cohort was 18 times greater in men and eight times greater in women.

In 1978 the highest mortality rates for malignant melanoma in Europe were in Iceland (3.7), Sweden (2.6) and Switzerland (2.4). The lowest rates were in Northern Ireland (0.0), Denmark (0.4) and Spain (0.4). Women had the highest rates in Iceland (2.1), Denmark (1.9) and Switzerland (1.7). Outside Europe, Australia had a high mortality rate with figures of 4.1 for men and 2.3 for women. With rates of 0.9 for men and 0.8 for women, Poland can be regarded as a medium-risk country.

Analysis of Data from the Provinces, 1975-1979

This cancer is more frequent among city dwellers than among the rural population (ratio for men 1.6, women 1.3) and it is slightly more frequent in men than in women (sex ratio 1.1).

[1] Data after 1979 are not comparable because of changes in the ICD classification.

Men

(Mean ASMR = 0.9, Range 0.1-1.8, Standard Deviation 0.4; 0.5% of Male Cancer Mortality, Rank 24)

The highest mortality rate was 12.5 times greater than the lowest figure, which is probably partly the result of the small number of deaths reported by some provinces. Provinces with the highest rates were Skierniewice (1.75), Opole (1.55), Gdansk (1.40), Poznan (1.35) and Ciechanow (1.34). Provinces with the lowest rates were Lomza (0.14), Pila (0.26), Konin (0.28), Suwalki (0.38) and Zamosc (0.40). No geographical pattern has been observed in the distribution of melanoma mortality rates.

Women

(Mean ASMR = 0.8, Range 0.0-1.5, Standard Deviation 0.3; 0.8% of Female Cancer Mortality, Rank 22)

Provinces with the highest rates were Siedlce (1.50), Bielsko Biala (1.36), Gdansk (1.33), Zielona Gora (1.23) and Leszno (1.19). One province, Biala Podlaska, had no deaths at all from this cancer in the period under study. Provinces with the lowest rates were Ciechanow (0.22), Bialystok (0.31), Rzeszow (0.39) and Lomza (0.42). As in men, there seems to be no geographical distribution pattern for this cancer.

Comments

The aetiology of malignant melanoma of the skin is both complex and incompletely understood. Sunlight seems to be the major aetiological factor in malignant skin melanoma. However, its aetiological links with sunlight are not as clear and simple as in the case of non-melanoma skin cancer where a dose/effect relationship has been identified (Holmann and Armstrong 1984; Elwood 1985). Malignant melanoma of the skin is a disease of populations with fair skin, blue eyes and light hair who have a limited melanin-forming capacity. The number of nevi may also be a risk factor (Holman and Armstrong 1984). Other hypothetical factors of presumably minor importance include air pollution (Leach et al. 1979), occupational exposure to fluorescent light (Beral et al. 1982) and oral contraceptives (Holman and Armstrong 1984).

Epidemiological studies in many countries show sharp increase in the frequency of melanoma malignum among people of the white race (Jensen and Bolender 1980). The geographical distribution of this cancer over territories populated by white populations is very interesting. It is more frequent in Caucasians living close to the equator than in those living closer to the poles. An "equatorial" type of distribution of this cancer can be seen in North America (Elwood and Lee 1974; Mason et al. 1975). Israelis of European origin face a risk that increases with the number of years spent in the new country (Anaise et al. 1978), just as it does in Britons emigrating to Australia (Holman et al. 1980). On the other hand, the settled European nations further north have a higher incidence of malignant melanoma than nations further south. There are, however, contradictory reports claiming and denying an equatorial correlation in Nordic countries (Magnus 1973, Eklund and Malec 1978, Teppo et al. 1978). The frequency of malignant skin melanoma has increased dramatically in many countries (Jensen and Bolender 1980) and it appears to be a true increase not merely an effect of improved diagnostic methods. The frequency has increased in successive birth cohorts (Boyle et al. 1983).

Poland also has a rapid increase in the frequency of deaths caused by malignant skin melanoma. This increase was the most rapid of all the cancer sites under investigation. The level and increase in the mortality rates are very similar in both sexes. The increase occurred in all age groups, and successive birth cohorts are facing an increasing risk of the malignant skin melanoma. As in the Scandinavian countries (Magnus 1973; Eklund and Malec 1978; Teppo et al. 1978), the frequency of malignant melanoma of the skin in Poland is higher in urban than in rural populations. Poland differs from other countries in that there is a slightly higher frequency of deaths in men than in women (sex ratio 1.1). Malignant melanoma of the skin has no obvious geographical pattern in Poland. As in Finland (Teppo et al. 1978) the south-north trend described in Norway and Sweden (Magnus 1973; Eklund and Malec 1978) has not been found in this country.

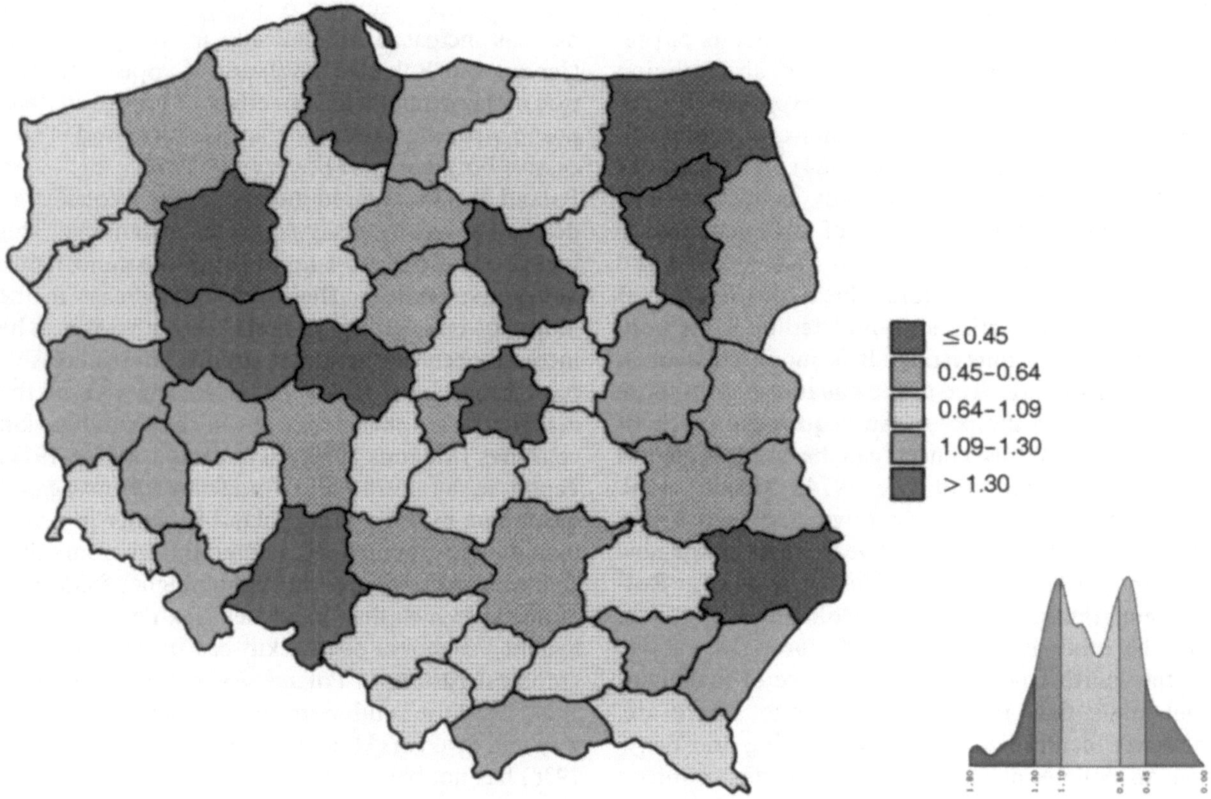
≤0.45
0.45-0.64
0.64-1.09
1.09-1.30
>1.30

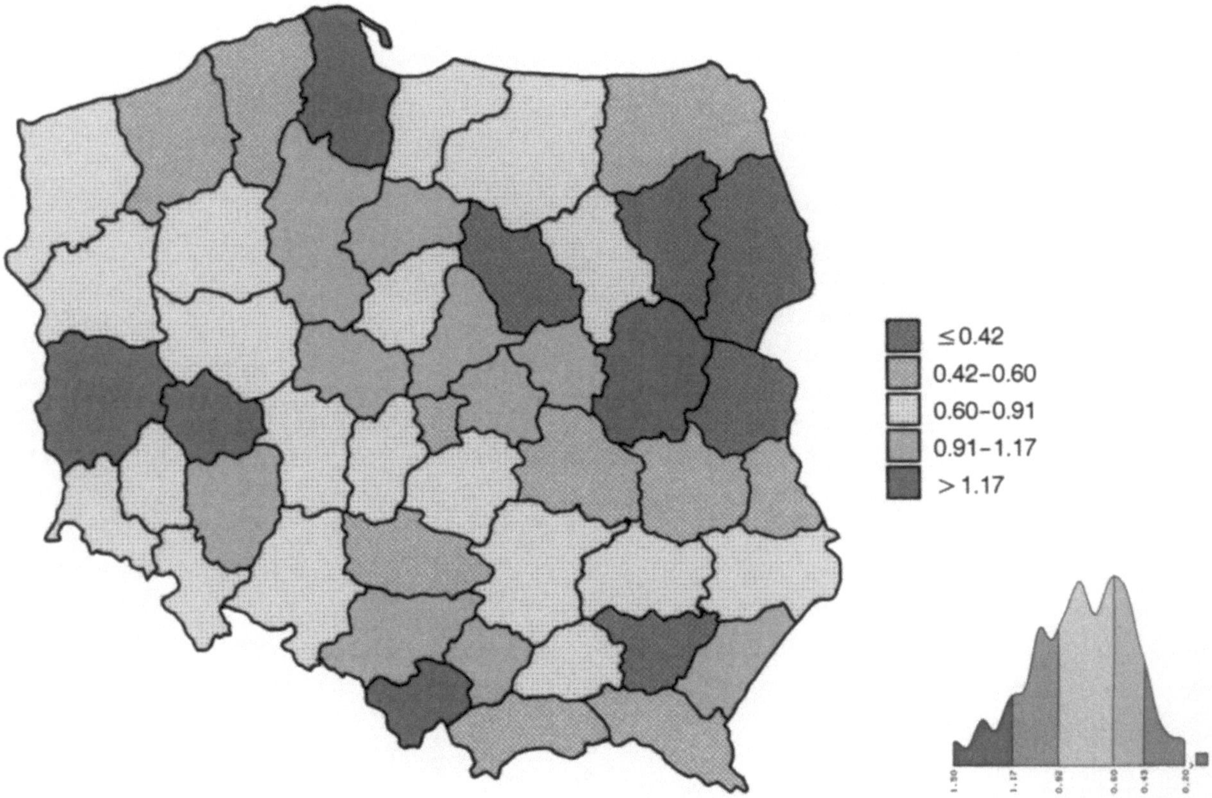
≤0.42
0.42-0.60
0.60-0.91
0.91-1.17
>1.17

1.43 – 1.75
1.11 – 1.43
0.78 – 1.11
0.46 – 0.78
0.14 – 0.46

1.20 – 1.50
0.90 – 1.20
0.60 – 0.90
0.30 – 0.60
0.00 – 0.30

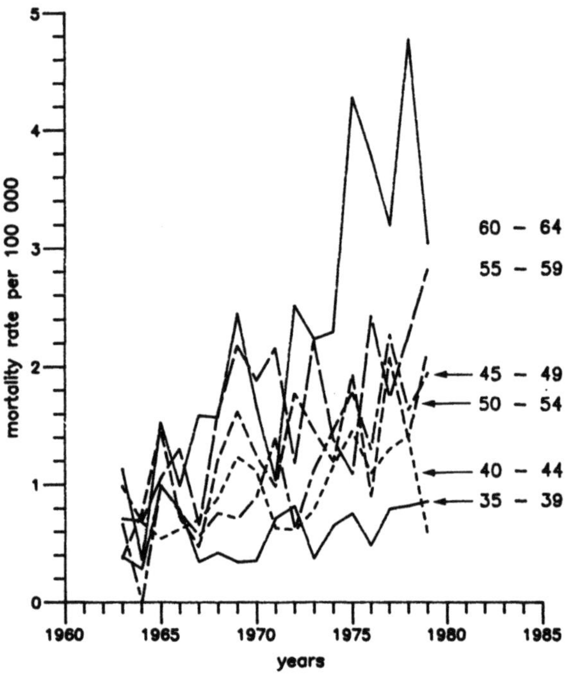

Temporal trend of mortality in individual age groups/men

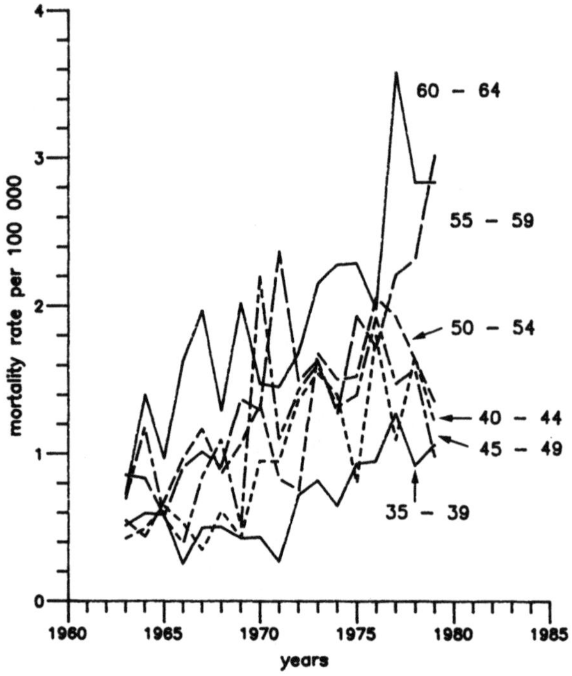

Temporal trend of mortality in individual age groups/women

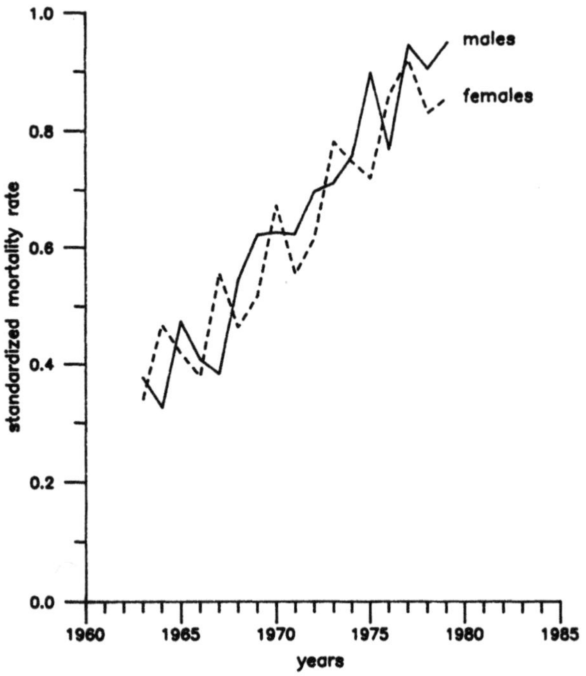

Temporal trend of the age-adjusted mortality rates for men and women

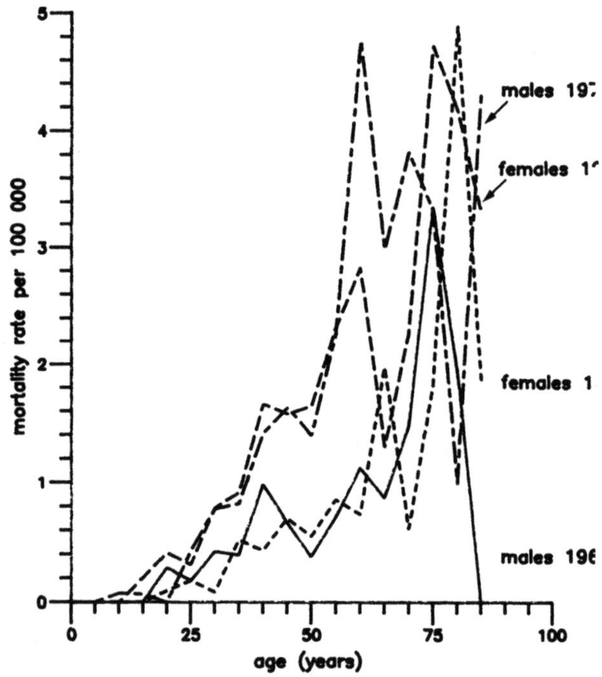

Mortality depending on age in two sample years for men and women

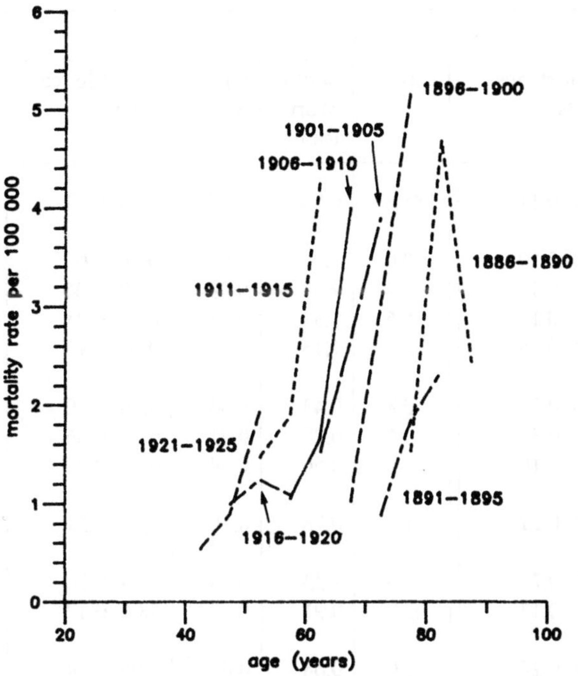

Age-dependent mortality in various birth cohorts/ men

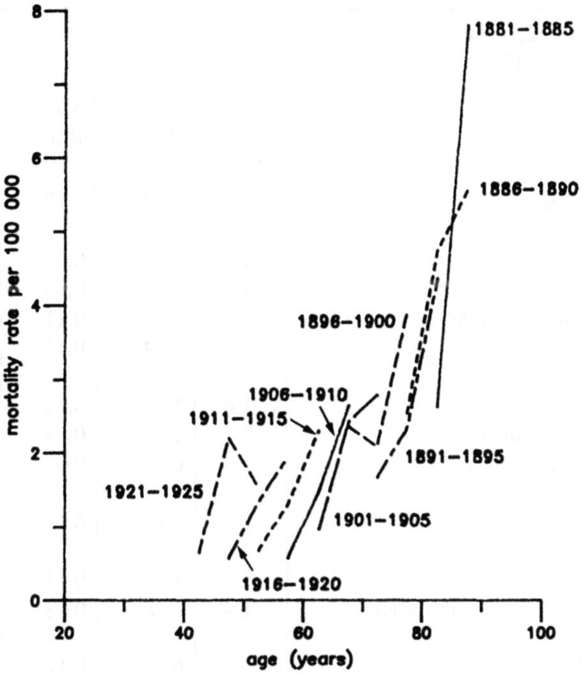

Age-dependent mortality in various birth cohorts/ women

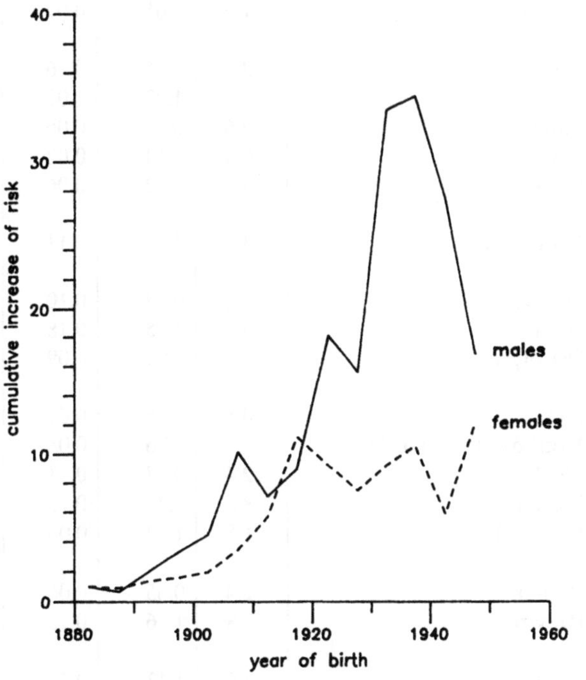

Ratios of the cumulative mortality rates for successive birth cohorts relative to the 1886-1890 cohort

Average Values 1975-1979	Males				Females			
	Cases	Stand. Mort. Rate	Cum. Mort. Rate	Confidence limits	Cases	Stand. Mort. Rate	Cum. Mort. Rate	Confidence limits
Poland	156.2	0.90	0.10	0.09-0.11	185.6	0.83	0.08	0.08-0.09
Biała Podlaska	1.0	0.61	0.09	0.00-0.19	0.0	0.00	0.00	0.00-0.00
Białystok	1.6	0.53	0.06	0.00-0.12	1.4	0.31	0.03	0.00-0.06
Bielsko Biała	4.0	1.05	0.11	0.04-0.18	6.6	1.36	0.14	0.07-0.21
Bydgoszcz	4.6	0.94	0.11	0.04-0.18	6.8	1.15	0.11	0.06-0.17
Chełm	1.4	1.10	0.12	0.00-0.25	0.8	0.43	0.04	0.00-0.10
Ciechanów	3.2	1.34	0.18	0.05-0.31	0.6	0.22	0.02	0.00-0.06
Częstochowa	2.0	0.55	0.05	0.01-0.10	2.4	0.50	0.04	0.00-0.08
Elbląg	2.2	1.12	0.14	0.02-0.27	1.8	0.78	0.10	0.00-0.21
Gdańsk	8.6	1.40	0.17	0.09-0.25	9.6	1.33	0.14	0.08-0.20
Gorzów Wielkopolski	1.4	0.78	0.08	0.00-0.17	2.2	0.91	0.09	0.01-0.17
Jelenia Góra	1.6	0.71	0.12	0.00-0.24	2.0	0.68	0.07	0.00-0.14
Kalisz	2.2	0.64	0.08	0.01-0.15	3.6	0.83	0.10	0.04-0.17
Katowice	15.8	0.91	0.09	0.06-0.13	20.0	0.92	0.09	0.06-0.12
Kielce	3.4	0.61	0.07	0.02-0.11	5.2	0.75	0.06	0.02-0.10
Konin	0.6	0.28	0.02	0.00-0.06	2.6	1.02	0.09	0.02-0.17
Koszalin	1.2	0.56	0.04	0.00-0.10	1.2	0.52	0.06	0.00-0.12
Kraków	5.0	0.96	0.11	0.05-0.17	8.6	1.12	0.12	0.07-0.17
Krosno	1.6	0.65	0.07	0.00-0.14	1.4	0.56	0.05	0.00-0.11
Legnica	2.2	1.26	0.16	0.02-0.30	2.2	0.86	0.09	0.00-0.17
Leszno	2.2	1.22	0.07	0.00-0.15	2.8	1.19	0.10	0.02-0.19
Lublin	2.6	0.55	0.06	0.01-0.10	3.6	0.60	0.06	0.02-0.11
Łomża	0.4	0.14	0.02	0.00-0.07	0.8	0.42	0.03	0.00-0.08
Łódź	3.0	0.52	0.06	0.02-0.10	5.8	0.54	0.05	0.02-0.09
Nowy Sącz	3.2	1.23	0.11	0.03-0.20	1.8	0.54	0.06	0.00-0.12
Olsztyn	2.8	0.92	0.10	0.02-0.18	2.6	0.76	0.08	0.01-0.14
Opole	6.8	1.55	0.18	0.09-0.27	5.0	0.85	0.10	0.04-0.15
Ostrołęka	1.8	0.91	0.09	0.00-0.19	1.4	0.62	0.07	0.00-0.14
Piła	0.6	0.26	0.03	0.00-0.08	2.0	0.80	0.08	0.01-0.16
Piotrków Trybunalski	2.2	0.76	0.08	0.01-0.14	2.8	0.69	0.07	0.02-0.13
Płock	2.4	0.97	0.11	0.02-0.20	2.6	1.01	0.09	0.02-0.17
Poznań	8.6	1.35	0.15	0.08-0.21	8.4	0.90	0.09	0.05-0.14
Przemyśl	1.8	1.24	0.09	0.00-0.18	1.8	0.92	0.09	0.01-0.18
Radom	2.4	0.65	0.06	0.01-0.11	2.8	0.60	0.05	0.01-0.09
Rzeszów	3.8	1.16	0.13	0.05-0.22	2.0	0.39	0.03	0.00-0.06
Siedlce	4.0	1.13	0.14	0.05-0.23	6.2	1.50	0.16	0.08-0.25
Sieradz	1.4	0.72	0.07	0.00-0.15	2.0	0.66	0.08	0.01-0.15
Skierniewice	3.8	1.75	0.20	0.07-0.32	2.8	1.06	0.10	0.02-0.18
Słupsk	1.4	0.85	0.12	0.00-0.27	0.8	0.46	0.05	0.00-0.11
Suwałki	0.8	0.38	0.03	0.00-0.08	1.2	0.52	0.07	0.00-0.14
Szczecin	2.8	0.83	0.13	0.03-0.24	2.8	0.63	0.07	0.01-0.13

Average Values 1975-1979	Males				Females			
	Cases	Stand. Mort. Rate	Cum. Mort. Rate	Confidence limits	Cases	Stand. Mort. Rate	Cum. Mort. Rate	Confidence limits
Tarnobrzeg	3.6	1.07	0.09	0.02-0.16	3.2	0.82	0.10	0.03-0.17
Tarnów	3.2	1.07	0.13	0.04-0.22	2.6	0.74	0.08	0.02-0.14
Toruń	1.4	0.55	0.06	0.00-0.12	4.0	1.03	0.11	0.04-0.18
Wałbrzych	3.6	1.11	0.12	0.04-0.20	3.0	0.68	0.06	0.01-0.11
Warszawa	12.8	1.09	0.13	0.08-0.18	17.6	1.03	0.11	0.08-0.14
Włocławek	1.2	0.49	0.05	0.00-0.12	1.6	0.61	0.08	0.00-0.16
Wrocław	3.8	0.71	0.07	0.02-0.11	6.4	0.98	0.10	0.04-0.15
Zamość	1.2	0.40	0.05	0.00-0.11	2.2	0.80	0.09	0.02-0.16
Zielona Góra	3.0	1.20	0.13	0.03-0.23	4.0	1.23	0.11	0.04-0.19

11 Breast – ICD 174

Poland is among the European countries with a low risk of breast cancer in women. Only in the 1980s has this site become the number one cause of cancer mortality in women. The ASMR was 9.3 in 1963 and 15.0 in 1982. A steady increase in the mortality rate was observed in the period 1963–1982, on average by 2.87% annually. The mortality rate increases rapidly from the age of 30 years, the curve forms a plateau at the age of about 50, after which it rises again. The highest value in 1982 was about 70 deaths per 100000 women aged 65 and over. The mortality/age curves of 1963 and 1982 differ in their steepness, especially in the age groups over 50 years. The breast cancer mortality rate is marked by a substantial increase in the age groups over time and in successive birth cohorts. The risk in the cohort born in 1940 is almost four times greater than the rates for the 1880 cohort.

In 1978 the mortality rates for malignant neoplasms of the breast in Europe were highest in the United Kingdom (28.2 in Scotland, 28.1 in England and Wales, 26.9 in Northern Ireland) and in the Republic of Ireland (26.9). The lowest rates were recorded in Yugoslavia (11.8), Romania (12.2), Bulgaria (13.4) and Spain (13.4). A mortality rate of 14.2 makes Poland a low-risk country.

Analysis of Data from the Provinces, 1975–1979

Women

(Mean ASMR = 12.6, Range 7.8–19.4, Standard Deviation 2.6; 12.7% of Female Cancer Mortality, Rank 2)

Breast cancer was 1.5 times more frequent among women living in towns than in the country. The highest value was 2.5 times greater than the lowest. Provinces with the highest rates were Poznan (19.35), Warszawa (17.76), Leszno (16.77), Bydgoszcz (16.72) and Katowice (16.66). Provinces with the lowest rates were Zamosc (7.80), Ostroleka (8.14), Slupsk (8.53), Chelm (9.06) and Koszalin (10.09). There was a region with higher mortality rates in central-western Poland covering the area o the province of Poznan and the adjacent regions Eastern provinces show a smaller risk as do those ir the northwestern corner of the country.

Comments

Breast cancer seems to be primarily associated witl the hormonal state resulting from the reproductive behaviour of women, as well as, perhaps, from the repeatedly reported influences of diet. Some relationship may also exist between these and geneti factors. As early as 1743, Ramazzini put forward a hypothesis that linked breast cancer with reproductive behaviour based on the observation that nuns in Padua had a high mortality from breast cancer From many epidemiological studies we know today that the earlier the first full pregnancy, the lower the risk of developing breast cancer. The risk of contracting breast cancer in a woman who has her firs child before the age of 18 is one-third lower than ir a woman who has her first child at over 30 years o age (MacMahon et al. 1973). The risk of breast cancer may decline with the number of children borne by a woman (Tulinius et al. 1978). For Polish women Staszewski (1971) showed an elevated risk witl earlier menarche, and Herity et al. (1975) showed that in the Republic of Ireland the risk increases with late menopause. Artificial menopause may reduce this risk (Trichopoulos et al. 1972). A pregnancy that lasts less than 5 months is associated with a higher risk of breast cancer (Choi et al. 1978). The study by Choi et al. (1978) also demonstrated tha patients suffering from this cancer more frequently have an irregular menstrual cycle. Many studies indicate that diet may have some impact on the development of the disease. Many authors believe tha diet may be particularly important in breast cance contracted by women after menopause (de Waard and Halewijn 1974).

The typical mortality/age curve with a plateau a the age of about 50 (perimenopausal) seems to be divided into pre-menopausal and post-menopausal sections (Clemmesen 1965). The post-menopausal section of the curve is significantly different in countries with high and low risk. In the high-risk countries (USA, Canada, Western Europe, Australia, New Zealand), the post-menopausal section of the curve increases more with age. In the low-risk countries (e.g. Japan) the curve decreases in the older age groups, after reaching its peak about the age of 45-55. On this basis de Waard and Halewijn (1964) postulate the existence of two aetiologically different types of breast cancer, although specialists in Iceland maintain that this is merely an effect of changing risk in successive birth cohorts (Bjarnasen et al. 1974). The curve illustrating the relationship between frequency of breast cancer and age in Poland has changed its shape over the last 20 years. This applies to both the incidence (Doll et al. 1970; Waterhouse et al. 1976, 1982) and mortality curves. The data from 1963 and 1982 illustrate the direction of the changes very well. The shape of the age-dependent mortality curves in Poland and other eastern and southern European countries has been described as intermediate between those of high- and low-risk countries (Petrakis et al. 1982). Analysis of Polish data indicates that the risk increase chiefly involves age groups over 50, resulting in a changed shape of the post-menopausal section of the mortality/age curve. This shape is today closer to the high-risk western European countries. A similar phenomenon was noted in Iceland (Bjarnason et al. 1974).

The increase observed in the mortality rate caused by this cancer corresponds with the increasing incidence reported by Polish cancer registers (Waterhouse et al. 1982). However, cancer of the breast in Poland is still not as dominant as in most European countries. The frequency of breast cancer in Poland, as in other countries, is greater in towns than in rural areas. This difference is particularly great in Poland with a ratio of about 1.5 in the years 1975-1979. It affects all age groups and increases with age (Staszewski 1979). The predominance of breast cancer in urban communities decreased in the period 1963-1982.

The geographical distribution of breast cancer in Poland differs from other cancer sites. A cluster of high-risk provinces around Poznan confirmed the observations that this province has had the highest risk over the last 20 years (Staszewski 1976, 1979). The analysis of cancer geography in smaller administrative districts in the period 1975-1979 illustrates this fact even better. Poznan and its neighbouring provinces form the area with the highest risk. Of the ten provinces with the highest risk, seven are in the area around Poznan. Apart from these, there is also a high risk in the urban provinces of Warszawa, Katowice, Lodz, Krakow and Gdansk. Rates lower than the national average are found in 35 of the 49 provinces in Poland. These are mainly the eastern provinces.

The full picture of female breast cancer, seen in time and space, appears to agree with the hypotheses claiming the influence of reproductive behaviour on the risk of breast cancer. Rural women, who have a lower risk of breast cancer, still have considerably higher parity than urban women and their first pregnancy also occurs at a younger age (GUS 1985). There are also more multiparous women in rural populations. The type of reproductive behaviour in Poland distinguishes it from other countries in that the parity of women ranks high among European figures. Compared with other countries, especially the neighbouring ones, changes in reproductive behaviour are also much slower (Lopez 1984).

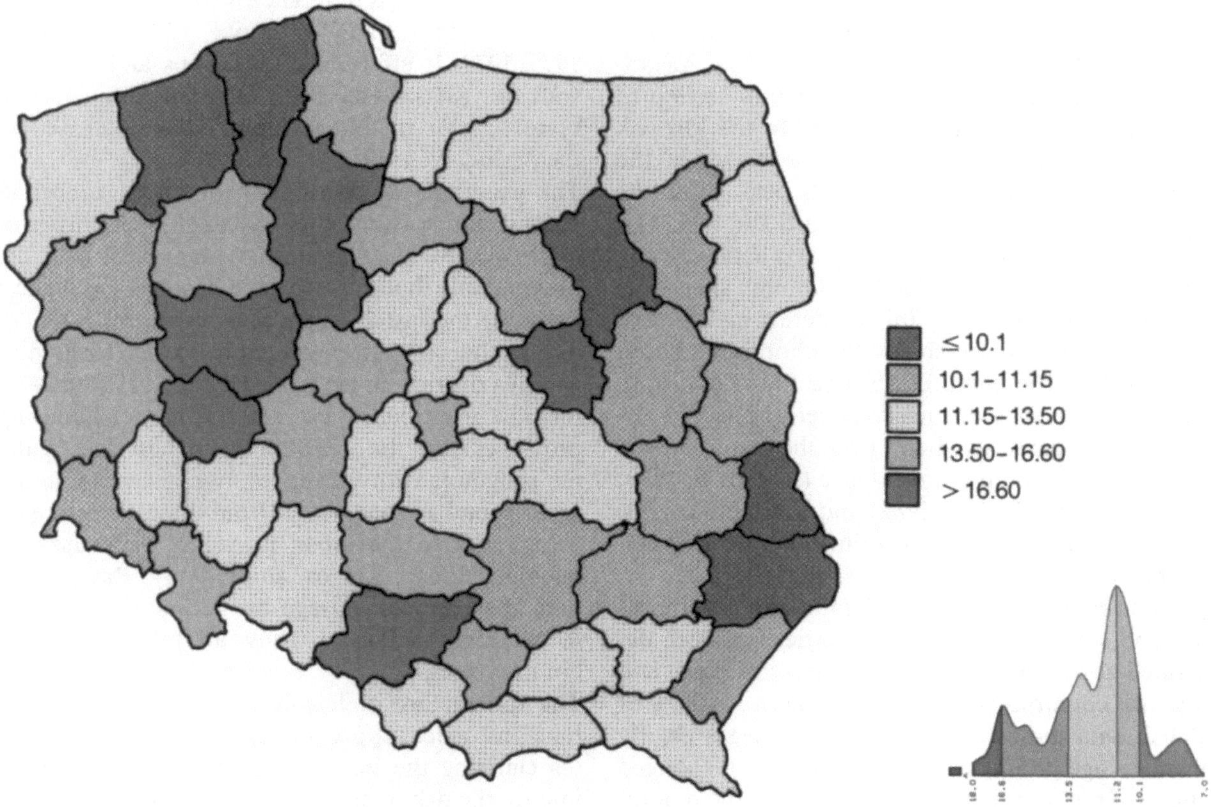
≤10.1
10.1–11.15
11.15–13.50
13.50–16.60
>16.60

17.04 – 19.35
14.73 – 17.04
12.42 – 14.73
10.11 – 12.42
7.80 – 10.11

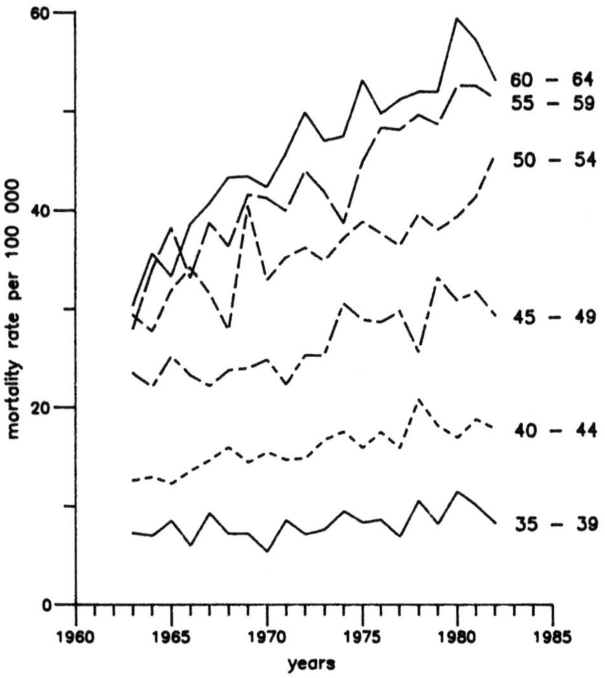

Temporal trend of mortality in individual age groups

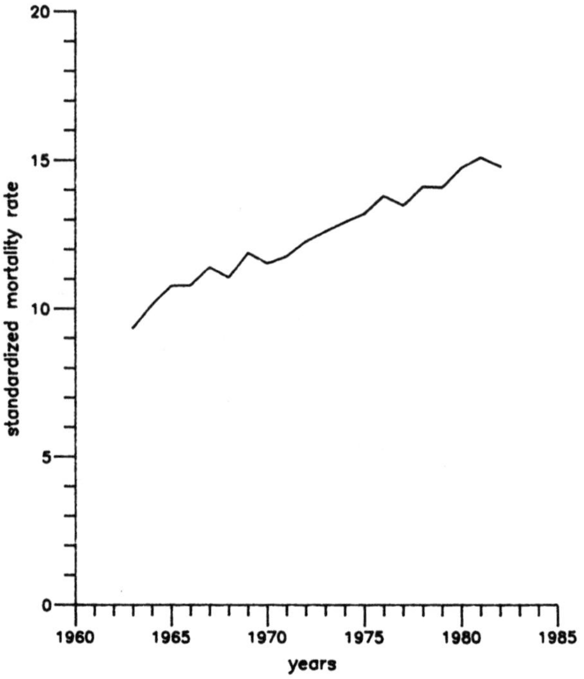

Temporal trend of the age-adjusted mortality rates

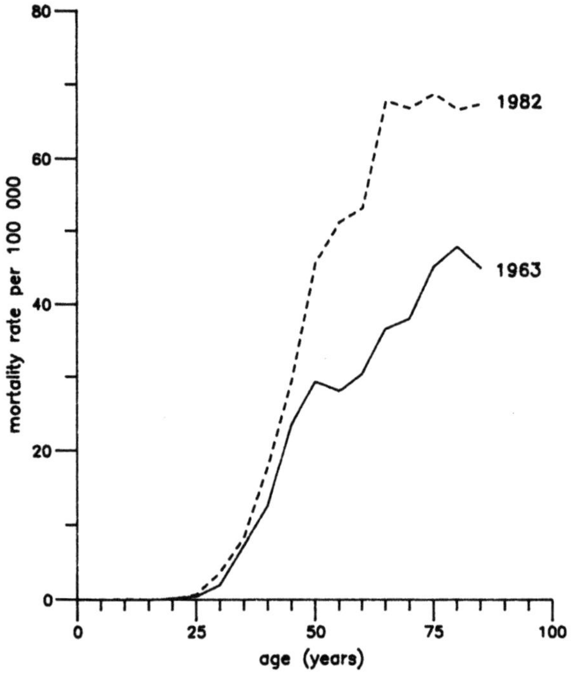

Mortality depending on age in two sample years

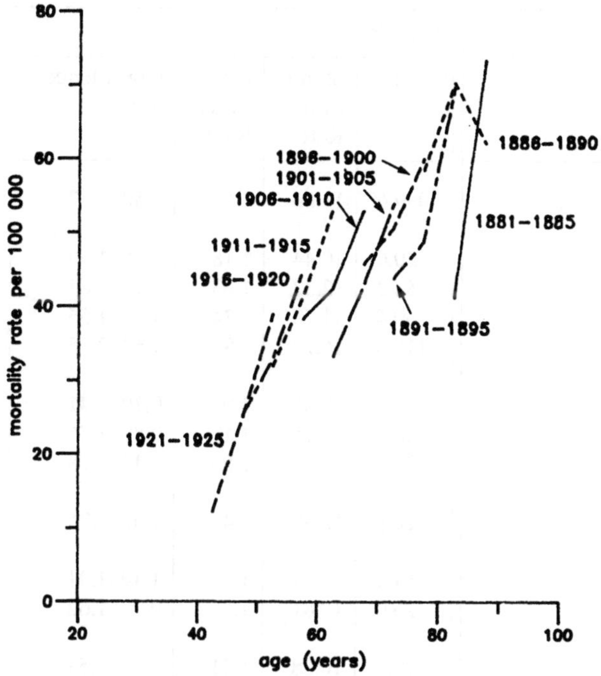

Age-dependent mortality in various birth cohorts

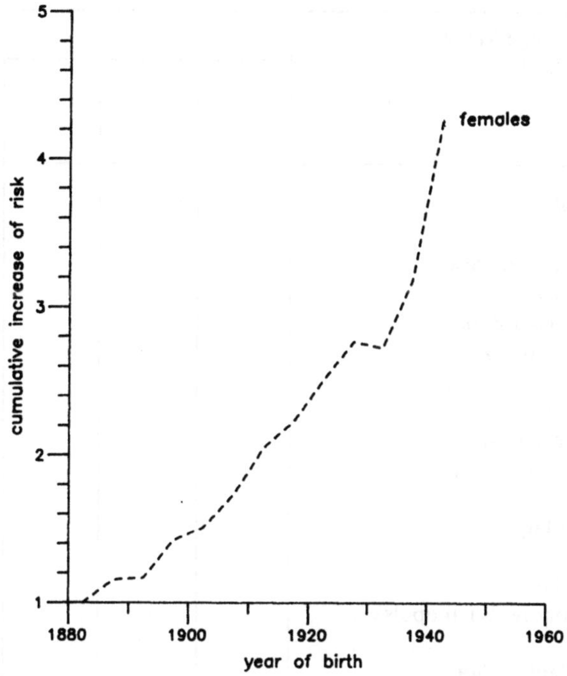

Ratios of the cumulative mortality rates for successive birth cohorts relative to the 1886-1890 cohort

Average Values 1975-1979					Females			
					Cases	Stand. Mort. Rate	Cum. Mort. Rate	Confidence limits
Poland					3099.6	13.66	1.54	1.50-1.57
Biała Podlaska					20.6	10.44	1.18	0.85-1.50
Białystok					52.2	12.32	1.43	1.18-1.67
Bielsko Biała					60.4	11.78	1.34	1.12-1.56
Bydgoszcz					110.8	16.72	1.91	1.68-2.15
Chełm					14.4	9.06	1.06	0.70-1.41
Ciechanów					26.4	10.15	1.17	0.89-1.46
Częstochowa					72.2	14.02	1.55	1.32-1.78
Elbląg					28.8	12.90	1.41	1.07-1.75
Gdańsk					114.4	15.41	1.70	1.49-1.91
Gorzów Wielkopolski					26.0	10.81	1.30	0.97-1.62
Jelenia Góra					29.6	10.68	1.21	0.92-1.51
Kalisz					72.0	16.15	1.74	1.47-2.00
Katowice					382.6	16.66	1.87	1.75-2.00
Kielce					81.6	11.15	1.26	1.08-1.44
Konin					37.4	13.84	1.53	1.22-1.84
Koszalin					23.2	10.09	1.09	0.79-1.39
Kraków					124.0	15.64	1.75	1.55-1.96
Krosno					33.4	11.49	1.31	1.02-1.60
Legnica					25.6	11.54	1.27	0.94-1.60
Leszno					39.0	16.77	1.90	1.52-2.29
Lublin					61.8	10.37	1.20	1.01-1.39
Łomża					23.0	10.66	1.17	0.86-1.48
Łódź					146.6	16.60	1.87	1.67-2.07
Nowy Sącz					48.8	12.92	1.46	1.19-1.73
Olsztyn					38.0	11.29	1.30	1.03-1.57
Opole					76.6	12.94	1.46	1.24-1.68
Ostrołęka					18.4	8.14	0.92	0.65-1.20
Piła					39.4	15.40	1.76	1.40-2.12
Piotrków Trybunalski					46.6	11.25	1.28	1.04-1.52
Płock					41.2	12.98	1.52	1.23-1.82
Poznań					158.0	19.35	2.18	1.95-2.40
Przemyśl					27.8	10.82	1.22	0.93-1.51
Radom					51.6	11.18	1.25	1.03-1.47
Rzeszów					46.6	11.38	1.34	1.10-1.59
Siedlce					44.0	10.75	1.15	0.93-1.37
Sieradz					34.8	12.44	1.36	1.07-1.65
Skierniewice					31.2	11.54	1.32	1.02-1.62
Słupsk					15.8	8.53	0.98	0.65-1.31
Suwałki					26.4	11.28	1.27	0.94-1.60
Szczecin					55.4	11.99	1.33	1.09-1.58

Average Values 1975-1979					Females			
					Cases	Stand. Mort. Rate	Cum. Mort. Rate	Confidence limits
Tarnobrzeg					36.0	10.58	1.17	0.93-1.40
Tarnów					49.2	13.36	1.45	1.19-1.71
Toruń					54.8	14.66	1.61	1.33-1.90
Wałbrzych					57.6	13.60	1.58	1.30-1.86
Warszawa					310.0	17.76	1.99	1.84-2.13
Włocławek					31.8	11.68	1.42	1.10-1.74
Wrocław					80.6	12.74	1.42	1.20-1.63
Zamość					26.4	7.80	0.87	0.66-1.08
Zielona Góra					46.6	13.93	1.58	1.28-1.88

12 Cervix Uteri - ICD 180

Mortality statistics are not the best source of information regarding the risk posed by the malignant neoplasms of the cervix uterine because the introduction of efficient screening programmes (early diagnosis and treatment) have caused a decrease in mortality rates over the last 30 years. However, taking into account the high proportion of cervical cancers, we decided to analyse the mortality statistics which are the only available epidemiological data for the whole country. The mortality statistics are, however, the basic measure of the effectiveness of early diagnosis and treatment (Hakama 1982). Our analysis of cervical cancer was based on the death statistics after 1970, that is, after the publication of the 8th Edition of the ICD.[1]

The ASMR for cancer of the uterine cervix was 8.8 in 1970 and 8.1 in 1982. The respective time trend shows a moderate decline in the same period. This decline was observed particularly in younger age groups. An exponential increase in the risk of dying from cervical cancer is observed after the age of about 30. The extreme value recorded was 35 deaths per 100000. In 1978 the mortality rates for cervical cancer in the world were highest in Fiji (21.3), Chile (14.4), Costa Rica (12.0) and Venezuela (10.6). The highest European figures were recorded in Romania (9.6), Poland (8.6) and Denmark (8.3), while the lowest ones were in Italy (1.0), Spain (1.1) and Greece (1.5).

Analysis of Data from the Provinces, 1975-1979

Women

(Mean ASMR = 8.5, Range 4.2-14.9, Standard Deviation 2.5; 7.8% of Female Cancer Mortality, Rank 4)

Cervical cancer was 1.3 times more frequent in urban than in rural women. The highest rate was 3.6 times greater than the lowest. The provinces with the highest rates were Szczecin (14.91), Walbrzych (12.99), Koszalin (12.66), Legnica (12.49) and Jelenia Gora (12.11). Provinces with the lowest rates were Lomza (4.19), Leszno (4.69), Bielsko Biala (4.86), Bialystok (4.94) and Krosno (5.53). Cancer of the cervix uteri showed a fairly strong geographical pattern. Regions with higher risk were situated mainly in the western half of the country, with the highest risk in the extreme western provinces and the northwestern corner of the country. Eastern provinces had a low risk of this cancer.

Comments

Although the aetiology of this neoplasm is not fully understood, most of the analytical studies link it to infections. Epidemiological surveys have shown that the risk is greater in women with earlier sexual experience and a greater number of sexual partners. It also seems to be connected with the husband's (partner's) sexual behaviour (Skegg et al. 1982). On the other hand, the application of barrier contraception is a protective factor (Rotkin 1967). The association between infection by the herpes genitalis virus (HSV-2) and cervical cancer was suggested many years ago (Naib et al. 1966), but has not been confirmed in other studies, particularly in a recent prospective cohort study in Czechoslovakia (Vonka et al. 1984). Zur Hausen has put forward a hypothesis that papilloma viruses induce the process of anogenital carcinogenesis (Zur Hausen 1976). Indeed, specific types of papilloma viruses are regularly found in cervical cancer biopsies. Recent molecular-biological studies suggest a causal relationship (Zur Hausen 1986) and a possible interaction between papilloma virus infections and tobacco smoking. A number of recent studies have also suggested that tobacco smoking and oral contraceptives may be risk factors (Winkelstein 1977; Vonka et al. 1984).

Cancer of the cervix uteri is, and will probably remain, a major health hazard for Polish women. Although the mortality rate for cervical cancer is de-

[1] The percentage of cervical cancers in the total number of cancers of the uterus (as in others countries, Doll and Peto 1981) was underestimated in Polish statistics until 1970, i.e. until the time the 8th revision of the ICD was introduced.

creasing moderately, Poland, together with Romania and Denmark, remains a country where the risk of death from cervical cancer is the highest in Europe. This not only points to a considerable risk of developing this disease (which is confirmed by the high incidence rates determined by Polish cancer registers (Waterhouse et al. 1982) but also to the low efficiency of screening in Poland. This seems to suggest that most of the women at the highest risk remain outside the smear test projects, whereas nationwide screening is indispensable if the mortality rate is to drop as much as it did in Finland (Hakama 1982).

The geographical distribution of cervical cancer is relatively clear-cut. Regions with a higher risk are mostly situated in western Poland with the highest risk in western and northwestern provinces (Szczecin, Walbrzych, Koszalin, Legnica, Jelenia Gora, Pila, Gorzow, Slupsk, Zielona Gora). These are the areas to which major migrations took place after 1945. Big towns and industrial agglomerations (Silesia) are also in the group of high-risk areas. Low-risk areas are mainly in eastern Poland which is more rural and less urbanised. The province of Leszno in western Poland, which is rural and inhabited by a more stable population, is also a province with a low risk.

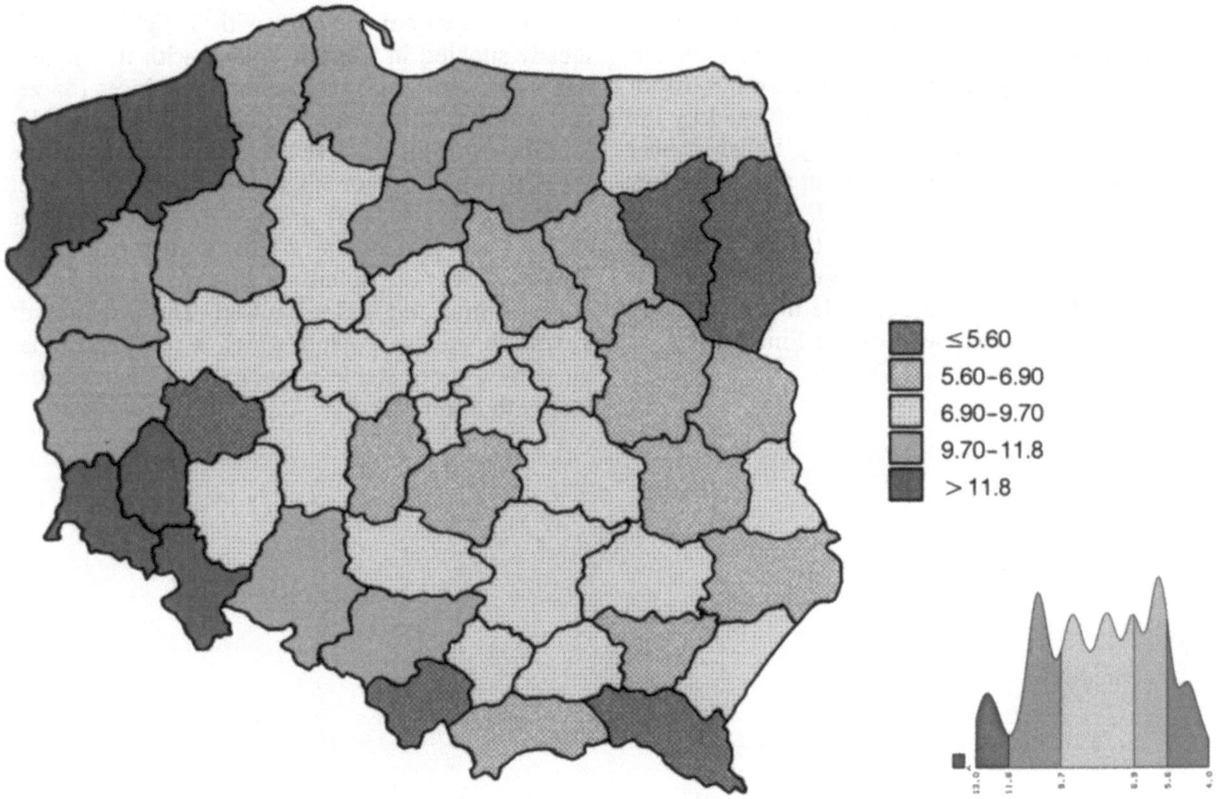
≤5.60
5.60-6.90
6.90-9.70
9.70-11.8
>11.8

12.8 – 14.9
10.6 – 12.8
8.48 – 10.6
6.33 – 8.48
4.19 – 6.33

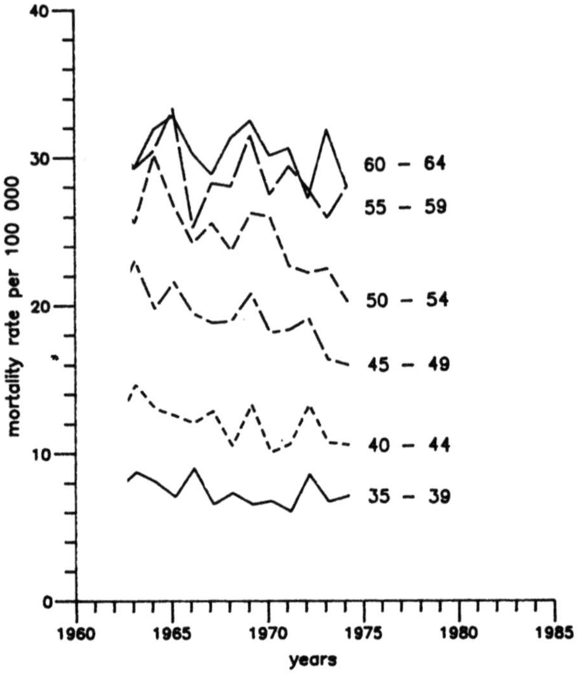

Temporal trend of mortality in individual age groups

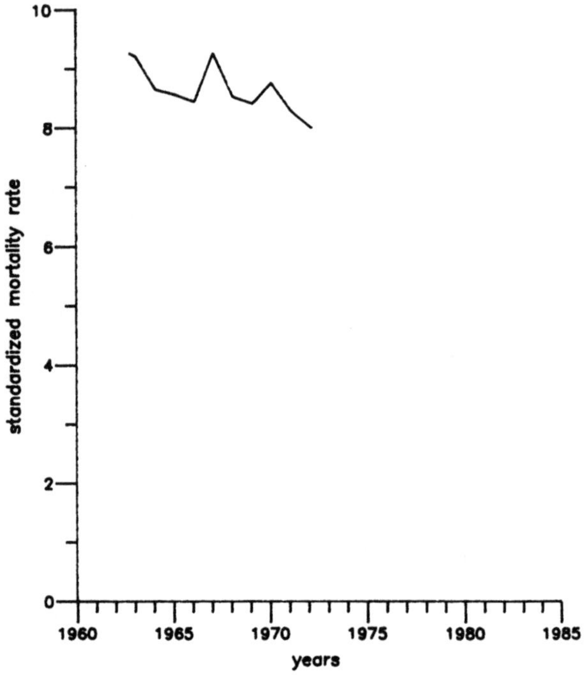

Temporal trend of the age-adjusted mortality rates

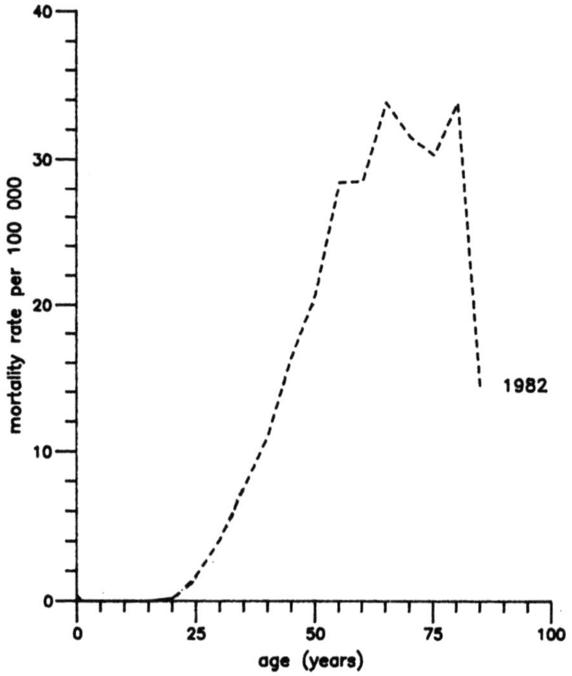

Mortality depending on age in 1982

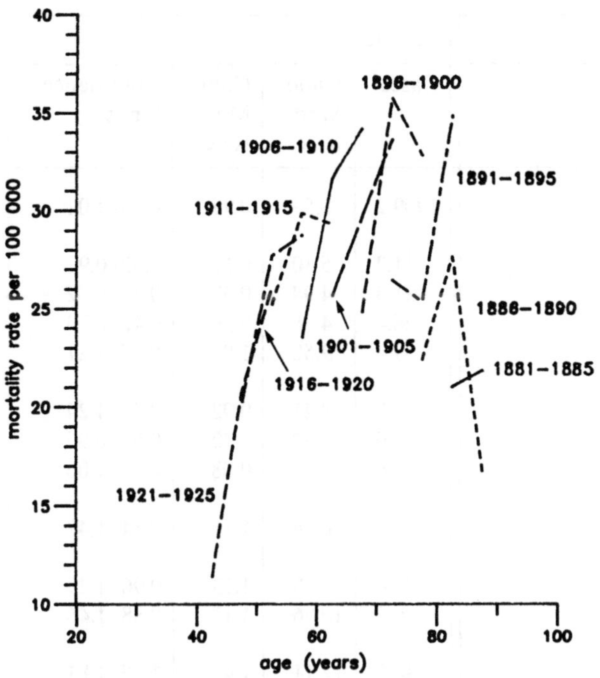

Age-dependent mortality in various birth cohorts

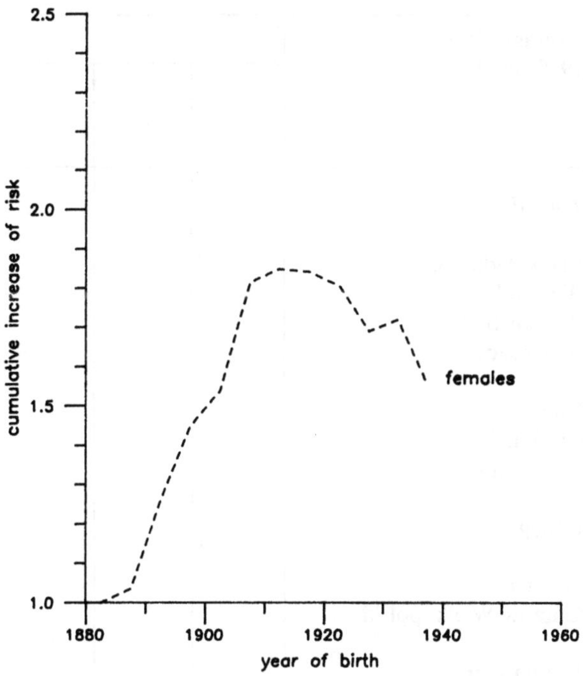

Ratios of the cumulative mortality rates for successive birth cohorts relative to the 1886–1890 cohort

Average Values 1975-1979	Females			
	Cases	Stand. Mort. Rate	Cum. Mort. Rate	Confidence limits
Poland	1909.2	8.59	0.98	0.95-1.01
Biała Podlaska	11.2	5.80	0.67	0.42-0.92
Białystok	21.4	4.94	0.57	0.41-0.72
Bielsko Biała	26.4	4.86	0.56	0.42-0.70
Bydgoszcz	59.4	9.50	1.04	0.87-1.21
Chełm	13.0	8.21	0.92	0.59-1.24
Ciechanów	17.0	6.32	0.72	0.50-0.95
Częstochowa	39.6	7.84	0.88	0.71-1.06
Elbląg	22.2	10.14	1.15	0.84-1.47
Gdańsk	73.4	9.88	1.13	0.96-1.29
Gorzów Wielkopolski	26.2	10.86	1.17	0.88-1.46
Jelenia Góra	34.0	12.11	1.48	1.15-1.81
Kalisz	32.4	7.66	0.86	0.68-1.05
Katowice	241.2	10.71	1.23	1.13-1.33
Kielce	52.6	7.70	0.86	0.71-1.01
Konin	23.2	8.77	1.03	0.77-1.28
Koszalin	28.8	12.66	1.49	1.13-1.84
Kraków	64.2	8.20	0.92	0.77-1.07
Krosno	16.4	5.53	0.71	0.49-0.93
Legnica	26.2	12.49	1.50	1.12-1.88
Leszno	10.6	4.69	0.49	0.30-0.69
Lublin	37.6	6.20	0.74	0.59-0.89
Łomża	9.6	4.19	0.50	0.29-0.70
Łódź	81.6	9.42	1.05	0.90-1.20
Nowy Sącz	24.6	6.81	0.73	0.54-0.92
Olsztyn	35.4	10.42	1.23	0.96-1.51
Opole	60.0	10.45	1.23	1.03-1.43
Ostrołęka	13.2	5.67	0.67	0.44-0.90
Piła	27.8	11.41	1.32	1.01-1.63
Piotrków Trybunalski	23.6	5.81	0.64	0.47-0.80
Płock	25.6	8.26	0.91	0.68-1.14
Poznań	57.6	7.27	0.81	0.67-0.94
Przemyśl	21.6	9.26	1.02	0.75-1.30
Radom	42.0	9.09	1.04	0.84-1.24
Rzeszów	24.6	6.02	0.68	0.50-0.86
Siedlce	26.4	6.72	0.78	0.59-0.96
Sieradz	16.0	5.87	0.70	0.49-0.91
Skierniewice	23.6	8.72	0.94	0.70-1.19
Słupsk	20.0	10.72	1.19	0.84-1.54
Suwałki	16.4	7.03	0.83	0.56-1.10
Szczecin	68.6	14.91	1.69	1.42-1.96

Average Values 1975-1979					Females			
					Cases	Stand. Mort. Rate	Cum. Mort. Rate	Confidence limits
Tarnobrzeg					28.4	7.96	0.94	0.72-1.16
Tarnów					27.2	7.02	0.80	0.61-1.00
Toruń					40.0	10.90	1.24	1.00-1.49
Wałbrzych					55.8	12.99	1.48	1.22-1.75
Warszawa					119.4	7.01	0.79	0.70-0.89
Włocławek					24.2	9.11	1.03	0.77-1.30
Wrocław					60.2	9.60	1.09	0.91-1.28
Zamość					22.2	6.17	0.77	0.56-0.97
Zielona Góra					36.6	10.64	1.27	1.00-1.54

13 Ovary - ICD 183

The ASMR for cancer of the ovary was 3.2 in 1963 and 6.0 in 1982. Mortality increased rapidly during this period with an annual increase rate of 4.2%. The frequency of ovarian cancer increases substantially from the age of 30 and reaches its maximum about 60. In 1982 the peak was much higher than in 1963, with 27 deaths per 100000. The age-specific mortality rates have increased with time in all the age groups. There is a pronounced cohort effect with a risk which is several times higher in the youngest birth cohorts. In 1978 ovarian cancer caused the highest mortality rates in Iceland (11.5) and Denmark (10.5) and the lowest in Spain (2.2) and Greece (2.6). With its rate of 5.9, Poland belongs to the medium-risk European countries.

Analysis of Data from the Provinces, 1975-1979

Women

(Mean ASMR=5.4, Range 2.8-7.8, Standard Deviation 1.2; 5.2% of Female Cancer Mortality, Rank 6)

Ovarian cancer was 1.4 times more frequent in urban than in rural women. The highest rate was 2.8 times greater than the lowest. Provinces with the highest rates were Torun (7.79), Lodz (7.17), Krakow (7.08), Katowice (7.01), Warszawa (6.81). Provinces with the lowest rates were Zamosc (2.80), Tarnobrzeg (3.32), Elblag (3.39), Chelm (3.51) and Ostroleka (3.66). Provinces with a low risk tend to be situated in eastern Poland. The high-risk provinces are the most populated ones like Lodz, Krakow, Katowice and Warszawa.

Comments

Little is known about the aetiology of ovarian cancer. Women with ovarian tumours tend to be single or to have married late, to have a history of menstrual disorder or to be subfertile (Weiss 1982). Mortality from this disease is inversely correlated with the number of children a woman has (Beral 1978). The growing risk in immigrants from low-risk countries (Haenszel and Kurihara 1968) and the low risk faced by female Seventh Day Adventists (Phillips 1975) and Mormons (Enstrom 1975) indicate the need to investigate the relationship between this cancer and diet. The risk factors are similar to those identified in breast cancer. Muir and Nectoux (1978) points out that both sites also have a similar epidemiological picture.

In Poland, however, there are no major similarities between the geographical distribution of ovarian and breast cancers. On the other hand, a considerable increase in mortality can be seen at a much higher rate than in most western European states. This is in agreement with Muir's observation (1978) that the increase is mucher higher in countries which originally had low rates. The increase affects all age groups. The growing mortality rate combined with bad prognosis is the reason why ovarian cancer is becoming an increasingly pertinent oncological problem for women.

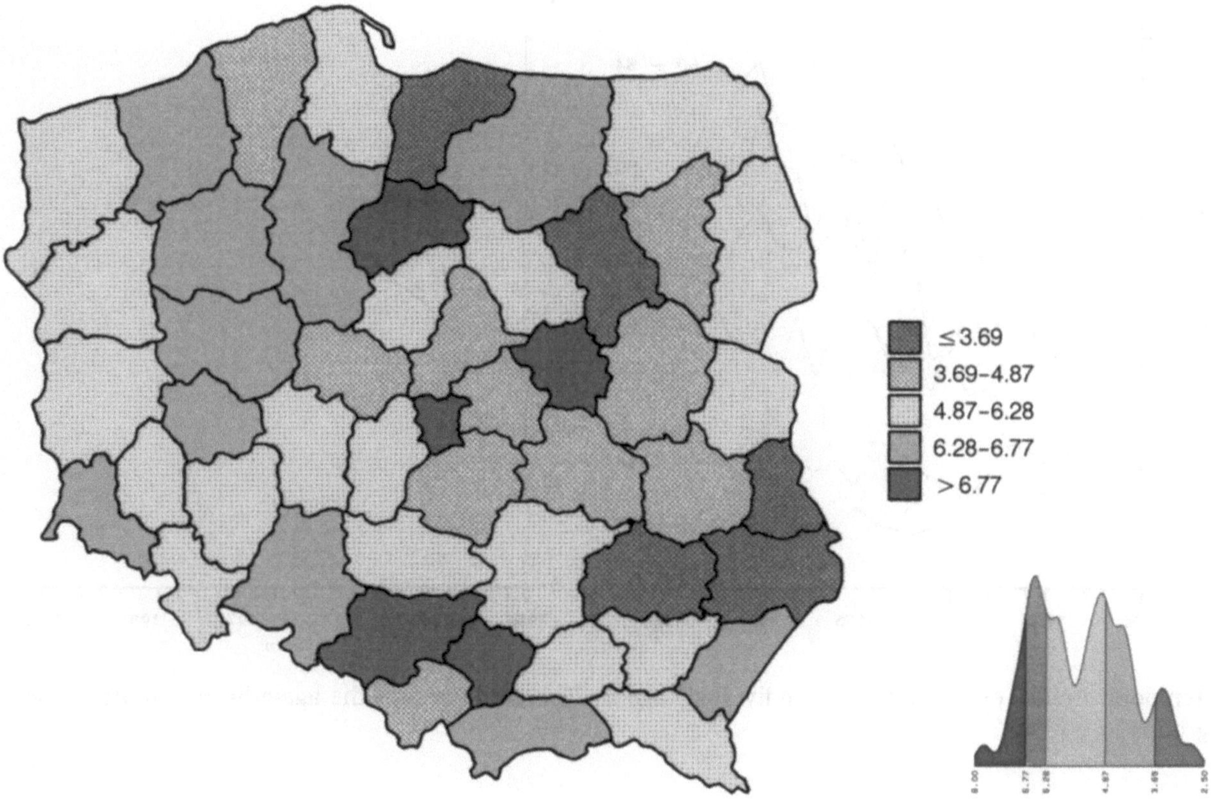
≤3.69
3.69–4.87
4.87–6.28
6.28–6.77
>6.77

6.79 – 7.79
5.79 – 6.79
4.80 – 5.79
3.80 – 4.80
2.80 – 3.80

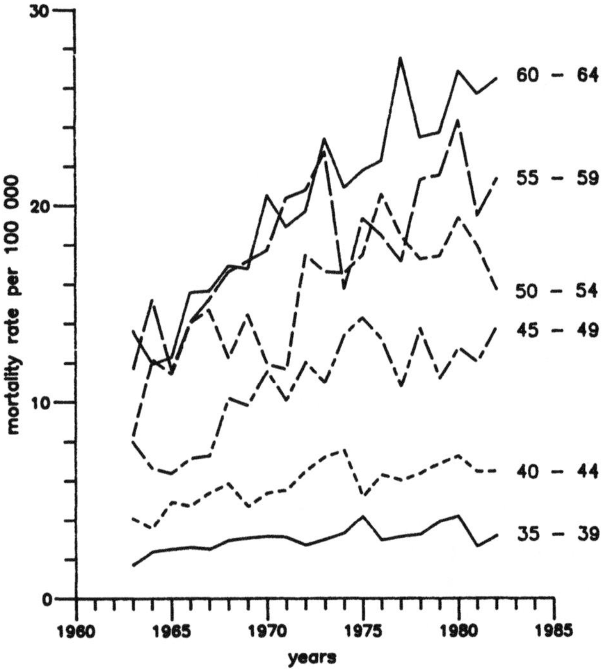

Temporal trend of mortality in individual age groups

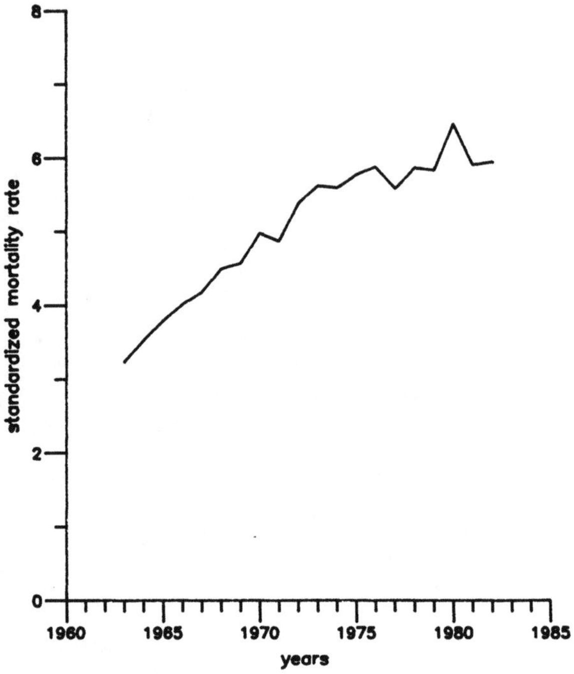

Temporal trend of the age-adjusted mortality rates

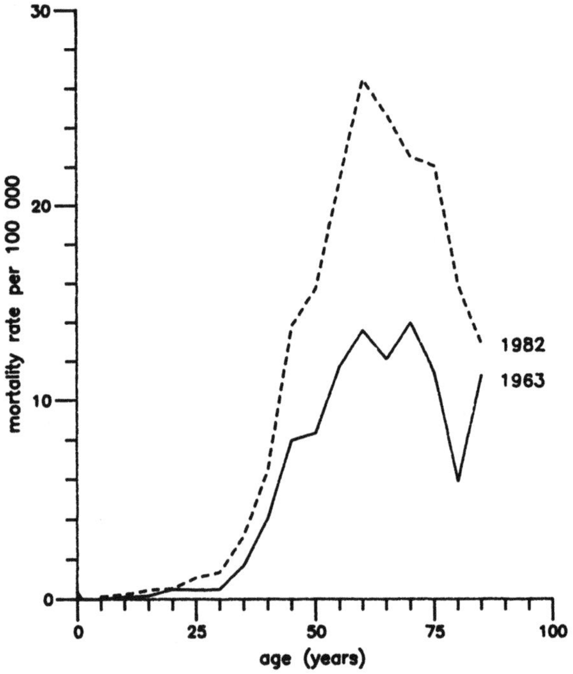

Mortality depending on age in two sample years

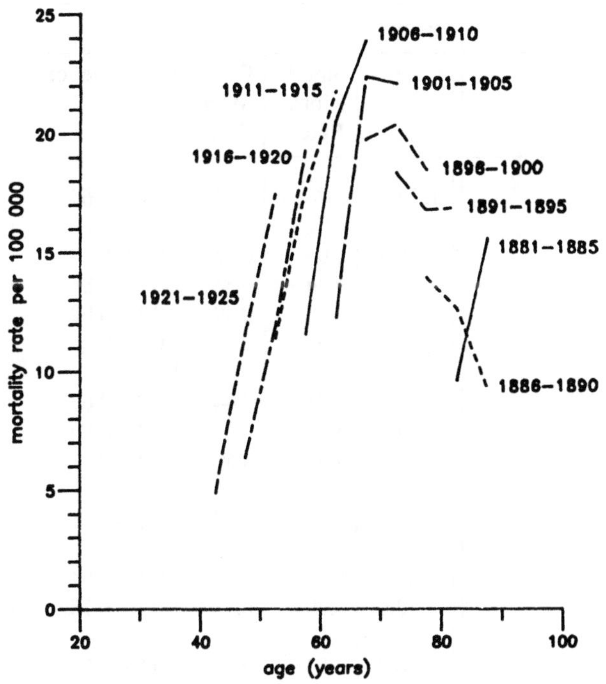

Age-dependent mortality in various birth cohorts

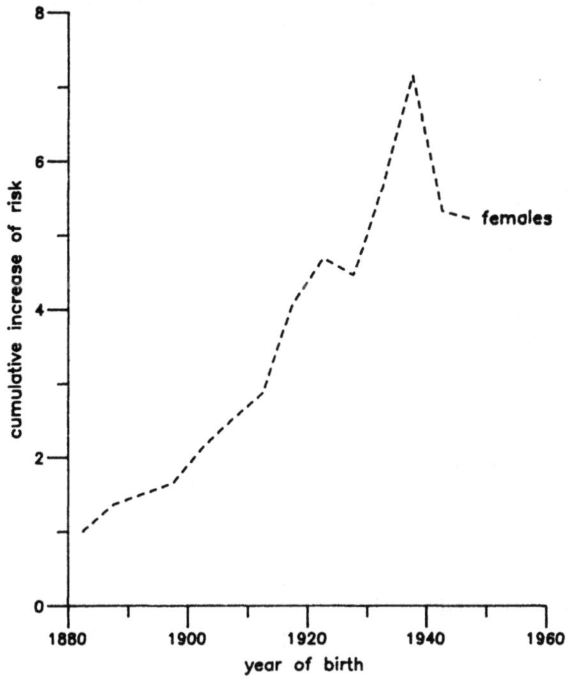

Ratios of the cumulative mortality rates for successive birth cohorts relative to the 1886-1890 cohort

Average Values 1975-1979					Females			
					Cases	Stand. Mort. Rate	Cum. Mort. Rate	Confidence limits
Poland					1271.2	5.76	0.66	0.64-0.69
Biała Podlaska					9.8	5.08	0.55	0.34-0.77
Białystok					22.6	5.44	0.66	0.49-0.83
Bielsko Biała					22.6	4.38	0.49	0.36-0.62
Bydgoszcz					40.6	6.53	0.74	0.59-0.89
Chełm					5.4	3.51	0.44	0.21-0.67
Ciechanów					14.2	6.01	0.67	0.45-0.89
Częstochowa					24.4	4.94	0.59	0.44-0.73
Elbląg					7.6	3.39	0.37	0.19-0.55
Gdańsk					44.0	5.92	0.71	0.57-0.84
Gorzów Wielkopolski					12.0	4.98	0.57	0.36-0.78
Jelenia Góra					18.0	6.53	0.79	0.55-1.04
Kalisz					21.8	5.17	0.60	0.45-0.76
Katowice					151.0	7.01	0.80	0.72-0.88
Kielce					36.0	4.91	0.55	0.44-0.67
Konin					12.6	4.67	0.52	0.34-0.70
Koszalin					15.0	6.63	0.77	0.51-1.02
Kraków					53.6	7.08	0.83	0.69-0.97
Krosno					15.6	5.69	0.67	0.45-0.88
Legnica					11.2	5.36	0.59	0.35-0.83
Leszno					15.0	6.67	0.75	0.51-1.00
Lublin					21.0	3.71	0.41	0.30-0.52
Łomża					8.8	4.39	0.45	0.25-0.64
Łódź					62.8	7.17	0.86	0.72-0.99
Nowy Sącz					24.0	6.38	0.73	0.54-0.91
Olsztyn					21.8	6.42	0.73	0.53-0.93
Opole					36.0	6.39	0.76	0.61-0.92
Ostrołęka					8.6	3.66	0.42	0.24-0.60
Piła					16.0	6.73	0.78	0.53-1.02
Piotrków Trybunalski					16.0	4.10	0.46	0.32-0.60
Płock					14.6	4.83	0.52	0.35-0.69
Poznań					54.6	6.71	0.79	0.65-0.92
Przemyśl					16.0	6.53	0.74	0.51-0.98
Radom					19.8	4.44	0.50	0.36-0.64
Rzeszów					25.6	6.18	0.73	0.54-0.91
Siedlce					17.8	4.55	0.49	0.35-0.64
Sieradz					13.0	5.00	0.60	0.41-0.80
Skierniewice					11.8	4.29	0.51	0.32-0.70
Słupsk					8.0	4.52	0.50	0.26-0.73
Suwałki					12.0	5.29	0.60	0.38-0.82
Szczecin					26.0	5.84	0.70	0.52-0.88

Average Values 1975-1979					Females			
					Cases	Stand. Mort. Rate	Cum. Mort. Rate	Confidence limits
Tarnobrzeg					12.0	3.32	0.39	0.25-0.54
Tarnów					19.8	5.30	0.56	0.39-0.72
Toruń					29.2	7.79	0.88	0.67-1.09
Wałbrzych					25.6	6.00	0.64	0.47-0.81
Warszawa					118.0	6.81	0.78	0.68-0.87
Włocławek					13.0	4.91	0.62	0.41-0.83
Wrocław					37.4	6.03	0.72	0.57-0.87
Zamość					9.4	2.80	0.35	0.22-0.49
Zielona Góra					19.6	6.10	0.71	0.51-0.92

14 Prostate Gland - ICD 185

The ASMR for cancer of the prostate was 6.4 in 1963 and 8.4 in 1982. It showed a rising trend until the early 1970s but then remained unchanged for the next decade. The time trend for the individual age groups corresponds with this picture: it increased up to 1970-1972 and hovered around the same level afterwards. The cohort data have a similar pattern. The mortality/age curves show similar shapes for 1963 and 1982. The highest value, in 1982, was around the age of 80 with about 170 cases per 100000 which was only slightly higher than in 1963.

In 1978 the mortality rate for cancer of the prostate was highest in Sweden (20.2), Norway (19.0) and Switzerland (18.4). It was lowest in Bulgaria (6.1), Greece (6.8) and Iceland (8.0). With a mortality rate of 8.5, Poland belongs to the low-risk countries.

Analysis of Data from the Provinces, 1975-1979

Men

(Mean ASMR = 8.0, Range 5.8-12.0, Standard Deviation 1.2; 5.0% of Male Cancer Mortality, Rank 3)

Cancer of the prostate was only slightly more frequent in towns than in rural areas (ratio 1.2). The highest value was twice as high as the lowest. Provinces with the highest rates were Pila (11.99), Gorzow (10.62), Poznan (10.54), Szczecin (9.65) and Bydgoszcz (9.40). Provinces with the lowest rates were Ciechanow (5.78), Bialystok (5.89), Piotrkow (6.05), Lomza (6.24) and Nowy Sacz (6.49). Provinces with the highest risk form a compact cluster in northwestern Poland, while the low-risk provinces are scattered.

Comments

In spite of the fact that the prostate is the most frequent site for cancer in some populations, the knowledge of its aetiology is poor. The finding that the incidence of this cancer is much higher in Black than in Caucasian ethnic groups in the United States leads to the assumption of genetic or life style factors. The latter seem to be more significant, according to studies of migrants which show that changes in life style habits influence the risk of developing cancer of the prostate. Major factors are assumed to be nutrition and the hormonal state controlled by sexual activity (Zaridze et al. 1984; Armstrong and Doll 1975). It must also be taken into account that the hormonal state may also be influenced by nutrition. Another aspect of the "sexual activity" factor is that it seems mainly to act as a risk factor if it corresponds with a frequent change of partners. However, venereal transmission has not been confirmed. A further interesting observation is the finding of latent carcinoma at autopsy in old men who neither contracted cancer of the prostate during their life nor died of it. The frequency of these carcinoma in situ is not much lower in countries with a low incidence then in those with a high incidence. However, the foci are smaller and they are less aggressive in countries with low incidence than in those with high incidence.

Malignant neoplasms of the prostate are rare in Poland in comparison to other countries. The level of mortality has remained practically unchanged for at least 10 years. The cluster of provinces with the highest risk in the northwestern corner of Poland is, however, intriguing, especially because this area has a high risk of breast cancer and testicular cancer.

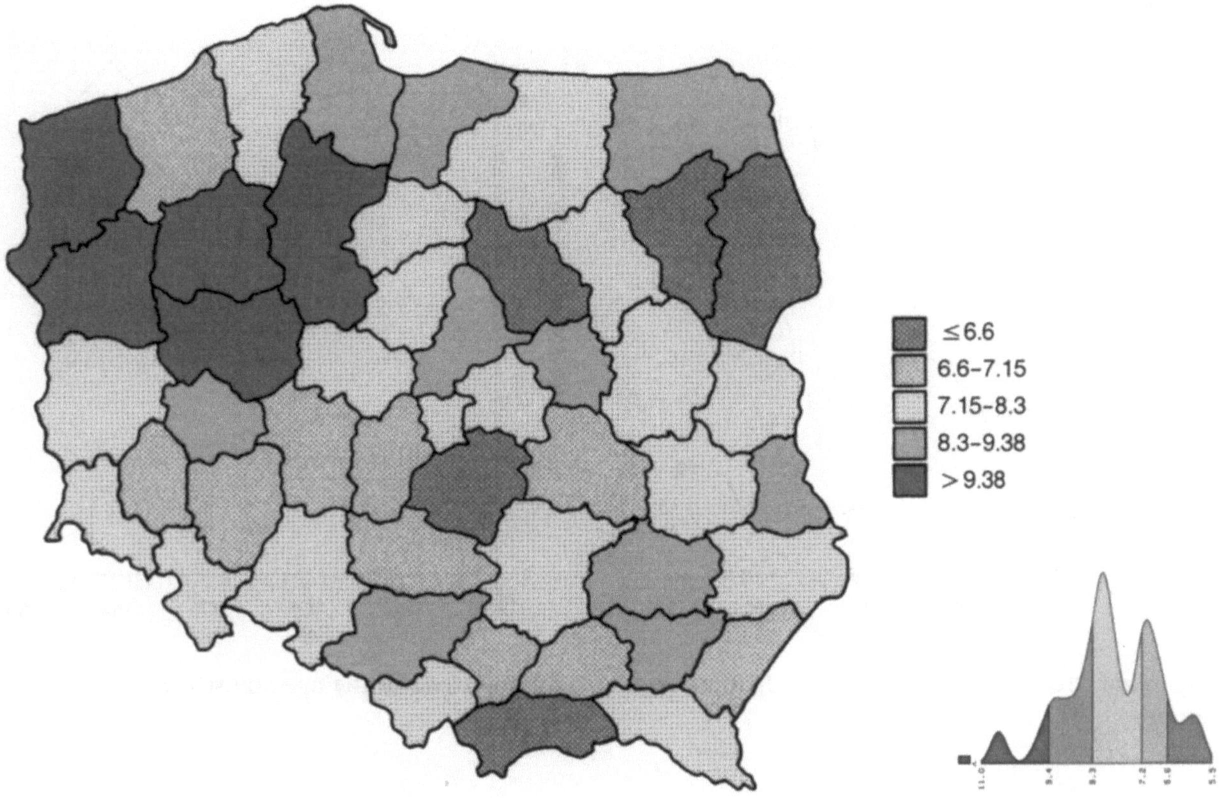
≤6.6
6.6–7.15
7.15–8.3
8.3–9.38
>9.38

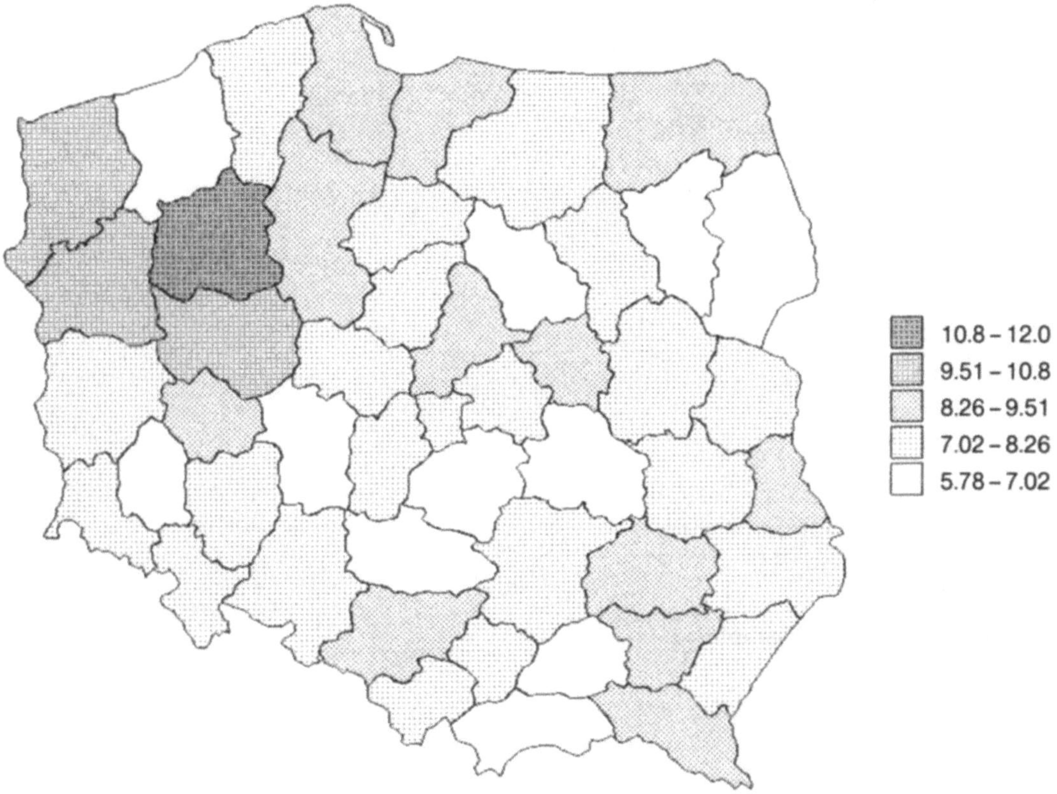
10.8 – 12.0
9.51 – 10.8
8.26 – 9.51
7.02 – 8.26
5.78 – 7.02

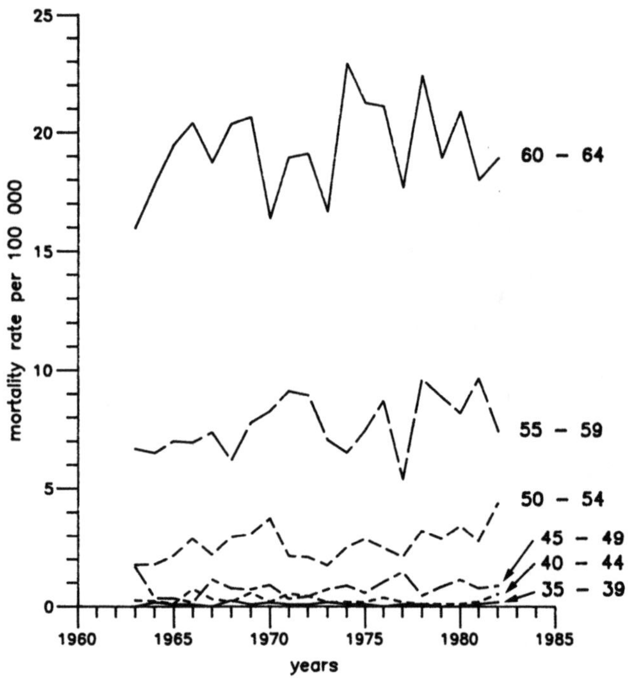

Temporal trend of mortality in individual age groups

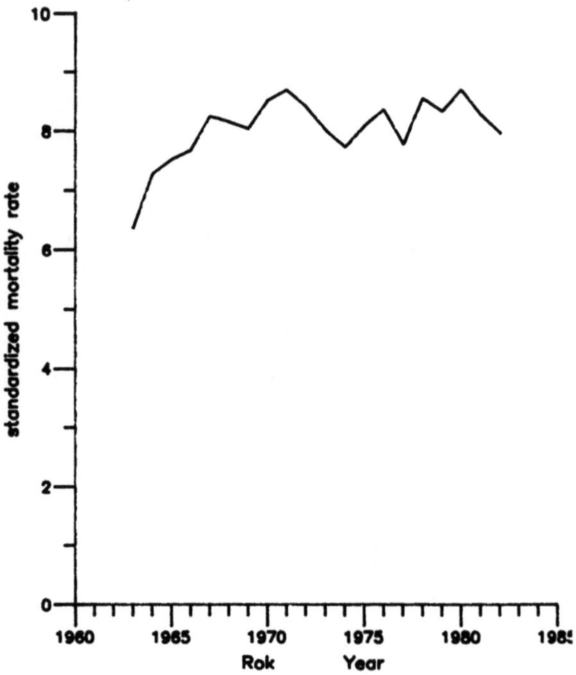

Temporal trend of the age-adjusted mortality rates

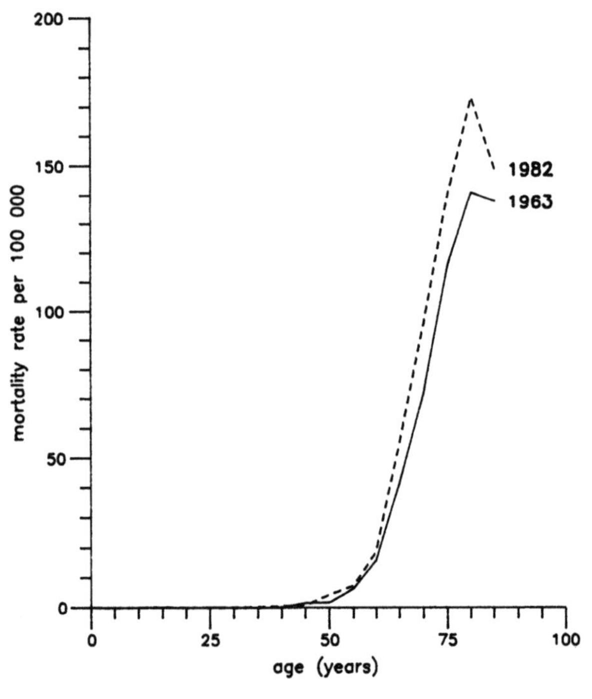

Mortality depending on age in two sample years

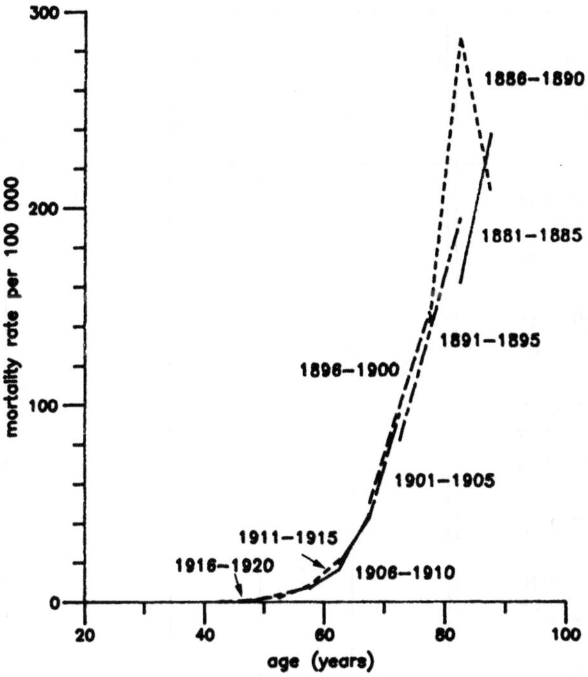

Age-dependent mortality in various birth cohorts

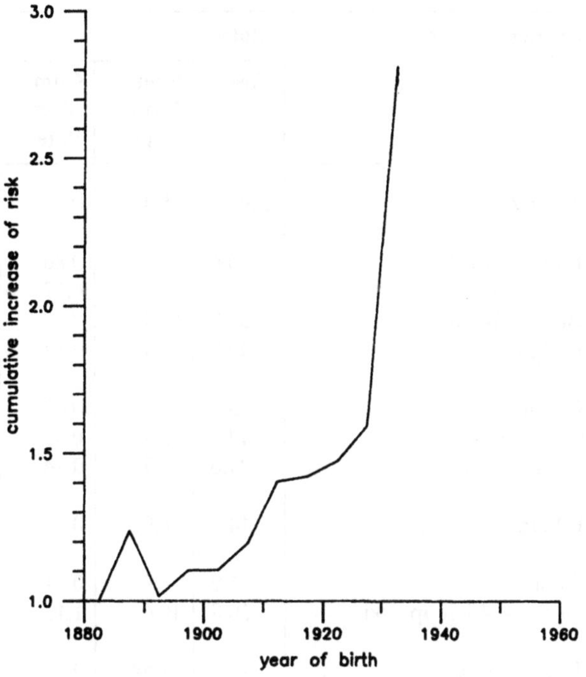

Ratios of the cumulative mortality rates for successive birth cohorts relative to the 1886–1890 cohort

Average Values 1975-1979	Males							
	Cases	Stand. Mort. Rate	Cum. Mort. Rate	Confidence limits				
Poland	1491.8	8.12	0.87	0.84-0.91				
Biała Podlaska	15.6	7.25	0.86	0.53-1.20				
Białystok	28.6	5.89	0.57	0.39-0.76				
Bielsko Biała	34.8	8.19	0.92	0.69-1.15				
Bydgoszcz	49.0	9.40	0.87	0.67-1.07				
Chełm	13.4	8.58	0.98	0.56-1.40				
Ciechanów	14.2	5.78	0.53	0.30-0.77				
Częstochowa	29.6	6.72	0.74	0.53-0.94				
Elbląg	14.2	8.92	0.87	0.52-1.23				
Gdańsk	51.2	8.93	0.91	0.72-1.10				
Gorzów Wielkopolski	20.8	10.62	1.17	0.78-1.57				
Jelenia Góra	13.8	7.54	0.89	0.54-1.23				
Kalisz	28.6	6.89	0.72	0.51-0.93				
Katowice	155.0	9.25	1.00	0.87-1.12				
Kielce	51.0	8.15	0.82	0.64-1.00				
Konin	20.4	7.70	0.78	0.51-1.06				
Koszalin	11.8	6.78	0.88	0.49-1.27				
Kraków	40.4	7.11	0.75	0.57-0.93				
Krosno	18.6	8.28	0.88	0.58-1.18				
Legnica	8.6	6.63	0.69	0.34-1.03				
Leszno	17.6	8.52	0.96	0.63-1.28				
Lublin	41.6	8.01	0.88	0.68-1.09				
Łomża	15.4	6.24	0.76	0.46-1.06				
Łódź	49.6	8.14	0.80	0.62-0.98				
Nowy Sącz	22.2	6.49	0.68	0.45-0.91				
Olsztyn	20.0	8.12	0.84	0.55-1.13				
Opole	35.6	8.07	0.95	0.71-1.19				
Ostrołęka	17.4	8.14	0.95	0.61-1.29				
Piła	26.6	11.99	1.22	0.85-1.59				
Piotrków Trybunalski	22.6	6.05	0.61	0.41-0.81				
Płock	27.6	9.38	1.17	0.85-1.49				
Poznań	71.0	10.54	1.15	0.94-1.35				
Przemyśl	16.8	7.07	0.80	0.51-1.08				
Radom	28.6	6.90	0.70	0.49-0.91				
Rzeszów	31.0	8.52	0.90	0.65-1.14				
Siedlce	30.2	7.29	0.81	0.59-1.04				
Sieradz	20.6	7.13	0.77	0.51-1.03				
Skierniewice	20.0	7.91	0.93	0.62-1.25				
Słupsk	9.6	7.79	0.73	0.36-1.11				
Suwałki	17.6	8.74	1.12	0.73-1.52				
Szczecin	27.0	9.65	1.01	0.70-1.31				

Average Values 1975-1979	Males							
	Cases	Stand. Mort. Rate	Cum. Mort. Rate	Confidence limits				
Tarnobrzeg	29.4	8.42	0.81	0.57-1.04				
Tarnów	25.0	6.97	0.79	0.55-1.03				
Toruń	24.0	7.88	0.71	0.47-0.94				
Wałbrzych	19.8	7.20	0.85	0.57-1.14				
Warszawa	108.2	9.12	0.95	0.81-1.09				
Włocławek	19.4	8.09	0.97	0.65-1.29				
Wrocław	29.4	7.10	0.70	0.49-0.90				
Zamość	27.6	7.88	1.01	0.74-1.29				
Zielona Góra	20.8	8.25	1.02	0.70-1.34				

15 Testis - ICD 186

The ASMR for cancer of the testis was 0.7 in 1970 and 0.9 in 1982. This period saw a rapid increase in the mortality rates. The annual increase of 8.57% was the third-highest of all cancer sites under study. The mortality/age curve displays a bimodal pattern. The frequency increases after the age of about 15 years to reach a first peak at the age of 25-30 after which it declines until the age of about 45. The second part of the curve increases again starting from the age of 50-55 years. The shapes of the mortality/age curves for the years 1970 and 1982 are different, especially in younger age groups. The increase in the mortality rate was faster in young age groups. In 1978, the mortality rate for testicular cancer fluctuated between 1.8 in the German Democratic Republic and 1.5 in Hungary, to 0.3 in Finland, Greece, Spain and 0.0 in Iceland. With a rate of 0.8 Poland is a medium-risk country.

Analysis of Data from the Provinces 1975-1979

Men

(Mean ASMR = 0.7, Range 0.2-1.5, Standard Deviation 0.3; 0.5% of Male Cancer Mortality, Rank 26)

Cancer of the testis was 1.1 times more frequent in the urban than in the rural populations. The highest value was 6.2 times greater than the lowest. Provinces with highest rates were Konin (1.48), Bydgoszcz (1.24), Lodz (1.23), Poznan (1.13) and Chelm (1.11). Provinces with the lowest rates were Bialystok (0.24), Rzeszow (0.24), Ostroleka (0.25), Zamosc (0.29) and Siedlce (0.31). Western Poland is an area of high risk with a strong concentration of high values in the central-western part known as the Wielkopolska. Eastern Poland has low mortality rates except for the province of Chelm where the rate is high.

Comments

The knowledge of risk factors for testicular cancer is fragmentary. The only factor which has been confirmed is the elevated risk in patients with cryptorchidism or undescended testis. Some 10% of the testicular cancers are diagnosed in patients suffering from cryptorchidism (Henderson et al. 1979). Hypotheses link this phenomenon with hormonal disorders developing during intrauterine development of the foetus or during childhood and puberty (Li and Fraumeni 1972). Other reports on risk factors are even more general, suggesting factors such as upper class origin, horse riding, bicycling (Ross et al. 1979; Coldmen et al. 1982). This limited knowledge of the aetiology of testicular cancer contrasts with the considerable increase in mortality, particularly in young men, in many countries (Clemmesen 1968; Teppo 1973; Muir and Nectoux 1979; Osterlind 1986; Boyle 1986).

The epidemiological picture in Poland is similar to that in other countries. In spite of the good prognosis, there has been a rapid increase in the number of deaths caused by testicular cancer. It is similar in towns and rural areas. The annual increase rate is 8.57% in all the age groups. As in other countries, this increase involves mainly young men aged 15-45; this age group had an annual increase rate of as much as 16%. This is the most rapid increase among all the cancer sites in this age group (Madej et al. 1984). Such sharp increase in the testicular cancer mortality rate in the younger age groups seems to indicate that some unidentified risk factor has come into existence in Poland, as well as in other countries.

The geographical distribution of testicular cancer shows a low risk in the eastern half of the country. Central-western provinces form an area of high risk which is the same as the area of high risk of breast cancer in women and cancer of the prostate in men. The aetiology of testicular cancer is far from being fully investigated, but the major improvement in the treatment, where a breakthrough was achieved in the late 1970s (Einhorn and Donohue 1977), offers a good chance of reducing the risk of mortality

(Samson 1981; Boyle 1986). This can be illustrated by the decrease in the mortality rate in Denmark, where the rate dropped by 50% in the period 1978-1982 (Osterlind 1986). A similar phenomenon has been noted in the testicular cancer mortality rate in Poland from 1983 (mortality rate in 1983 1.0, 1984 0.7, 1985 0.6).

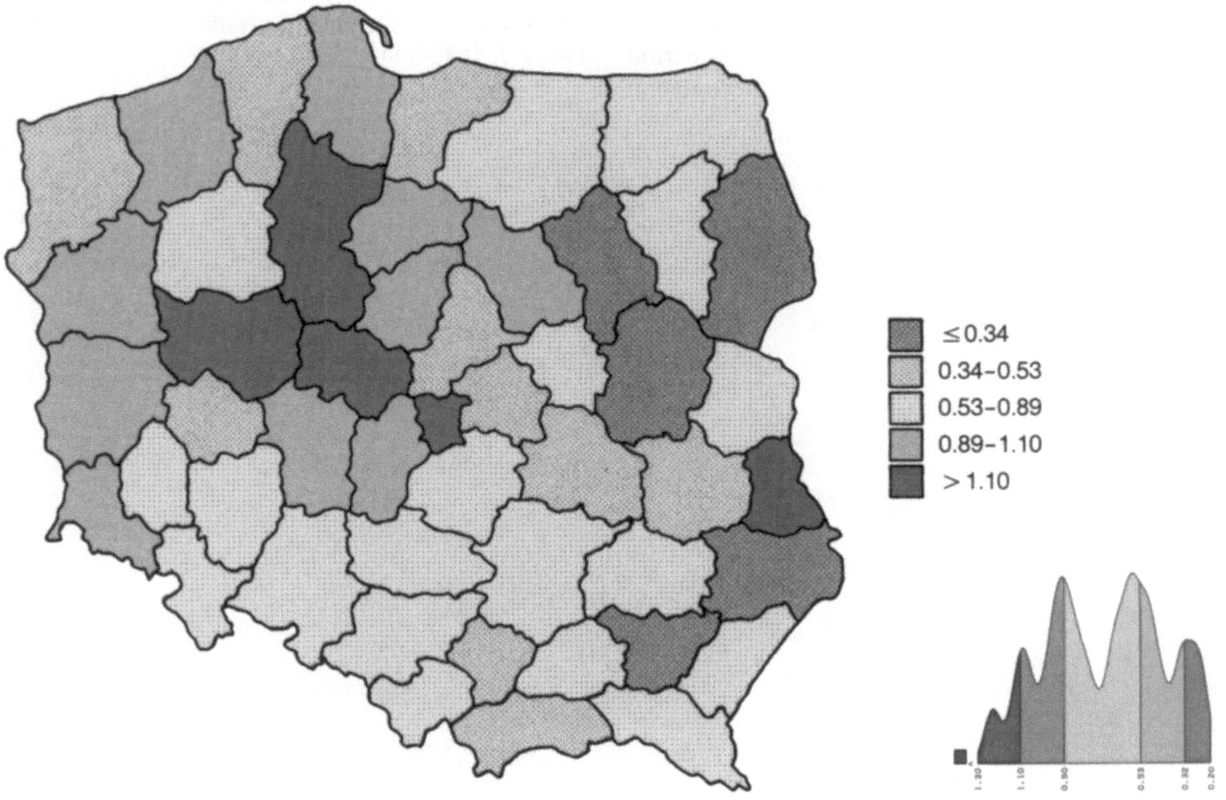
≤0.34
0.34-0.53
0.53-0.89
0.89-1.10
>1.10

Temporal trend of the age-adjusted mortality rates

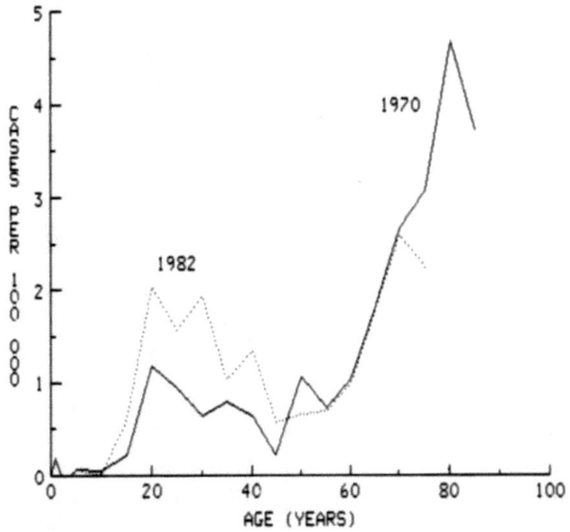

Mortality depending on age in two sample years

Average Values 1975-1979	Males			
	Cases	Stand. Mort. Rate	Cum. Mort. Rate	Confidence limits
Poland	140.0	0.74	0.06	0.06-0.07
Biała Podlaska	1.0	0.57	0.07	0.00-0.15
Białystok	1.0	0.24	0.03	0.00-0.06
Bielsko Biała	3.0	0.67	0.06	0.02-0.11
Bydgoszcz	7.0	1.24	0.09	0.04-0.13
Chełm	1.2	1.11	0.13	0.00-0.28
Ciechanów	2.0	0.93	0.09	0.01-0.17
Częstochowa	3.4	0.86	0.08	0.02-0.13
Elbląg	1.2	0.50	0.04	0.00-0.08
Gdańsk	7.2	1.01	0.09	0.04-0.14
Gorzów Wielkopolski	2.4	1.08	0.13	0.01-0.25
Jelenia Góra	2.4	0.92	0.06	0.00-0.14
Kalisz	3.0	0.90	0.07	0.01-0.12
Katowice	14.6	0.76	0.05	0.03-0.08
Kielce	3.8	0.70	0.05	0.01-0.08
Konin	3.6	1.48	0.13	0.05-0.22
Koszalin	2.6	1.06	0.10	0.00-0.20
Kraków	2.4	0.36	0.03	0.01-0.06
Krosno	1.0	0.58	0.04	0.00-0.09
Legnica	1.8	0.78	0.06	0.00-0.13
Leszno	1.0	0.51	0.04	0.00-0.08
Lublin	1.6	0.34	0.03	0.00-0.07
Łomża	0.8	0.57	0.05	0.00-0.12
Łódź	7.8	1.23	0.10	0.06-0.15
Nowy Sącz	1.6	0.50	0.04	0.00-0.07
Olsztyn	3.0	0.89	0.07	0.01-0.12
Opole	2.6	0.60	0.06	0.01-0.11
Ostrołęka	0.6	0.25	0.02	0.00-0.06
Piła	1.6	0.65	0.05	0.00-0.11
Piotrków Trybunalski	1.6	0.63	0.03	0.00-0.07
Płock	1.2	0.44	0.05	0.00-0.10
Poznań	7.6	1.13	0.10	0.05-0.14
Przemyśl	1.2	0.59	0.04	0.00-0.09
Radom	2.0	0.51	0.05	0.01-0.10
Rzeszów	0.8	0.24	0.02	0.00-0.05
Siedlce	1.0	0.31	0.02	0.00-0.05
Sieradz	2.4	1.10	0.09	0.02-0.17
Skierniewice	0.8	0.34	0.04	0.00-0.09
Słupsk	1.0	0.42	0.03	0.00-0.06
Suwałki	1.6	0.81	0.08	0.00-0.18
Szczecin	2.4	0.48	0.04	0.01-0.06

Average Values 1975-1979	Males							
	Cases	Stand. Mort. Rate	Cum. Mort. Rate	Confidence limits				
Tarnobrzeg	2.0	0.66	0.07	0.01-0.13				
Tarnów	2.6	0.89	0.06	0.02-0.11				
Toruń	3.0	0.96	0.07	0.02-0.12				
Wałbrzych	2.2	0.56	0.07	0.00-0.15				
Warszawa	10.8	0.86	0.07	0.04-0.10				
Włocławek	2.2	0.97	0.06	0.01-0.12				
Wrocław	4.2	0.82	0.07	0.02-0.13				
Zamość	1.0	0.29	0.04	0.00-0.09				
Zielona Góra	3.2	0.94	0.07	0.02-0.11				

16 Urinary Bladder - ICD 188

The ASMR for cancer of the urinary bladder in men was 4.4 in 1963 and 7.0 in 1982, while the respective figures for women were 0.9 and 1.0. The period 1963-1982 saw a steady increase in the mortality rate for this cancer in men, with a mean annual increase rate of 2.4%, while the female rate tended to remain unchanged. Men aged about 50 show a steep increase in the mortality rate while women's mortality increases only moderately with age. The cumulative increase in the risk of urinary bladder cancer in men between the 1880 and 1920 birth cohorts was significant. In 1978, the highest European mortality rate was found in Czechoslovakia (13.6 and 4.1 for men and women, respectively). Rates were also high, though much lower than in Czechoslovakia, in men in Denmark (9.2) and women in Scotland (3.0). Low mortality rates were observed in men in Iceland (1.6) and Yugoslavia (3.8) and in women in Bulgaria (0.7), Poland (0.8), Greece and Yugoslavia (1.0 each). The mortality rates for Polish men and women were low (5.9, 0.8, respectively).

Analysis of Data from the Provinces, 1975-1979

Cancer of the urinary bladder occur more often in city dwellers than in the rural population with a ratio of 1.4 for men and 1.7 for women. This form of cancer is 7.3 times more frequent in men.

Men

(Mean ASMR = 5.7, Range 2.7-8.5, Standard Deviation 1.2; 3.5% of Male Cancer Mortality, Rank 7)

The highest value was 3.2 times greater than the lowest. Provinces with the highest rates were Koszalin (8.47), Torun (8.45), Pila (7.86), Lodz (7.38) and Bydgoszcz (7.30). Provinces with the lowest rates were Siedlce (2.68), Ostroleka (3.58), Ciechanow (3.64), Piotrkow (4.0) and Biala Podlaska (4.0). As in the case of many other cancer sites, eastern Poland had lower mortality rates for cancer of the urinary bladder than the western parts. The highest rates were found in the northwestern regions and the province of Lodz.

Women

(Mean ASMR = 0.8, Range 0.3-1.6, Standard Deviation 0.3; 0.9% of Female Cancer Mortality, Rank 20)

There were great differences among the provinces: the highest rate was 5.2 times greater than the lowest. Provinces with the highest rates were Warszawa (1.60), Legnica (1.33), Jelenia Gora (1.29), Konin (1.21) and Slupsk (1.18). Provinces with the lowest rates were Leszno (0.31), Lublin (0.35), Tarnobrzeg (0.38), Zamosc (0.42) and Biala Podlaska (0.45). Provinces with a higher risk form no particular geographical pattern, while areas of low risk are found predominantly in eastern Poland plus a small area of southern and southwestern Poland in the provinces of Kalisz, Leszno, Wroclaw and Sieradz.

Comments

Tobacco smoking has long been recognised as a risk factor in cancer of the urinary bladder (Lilienfeld et al. 1956; Miller 1977; Howe et al. 1980). According to assessments, tobacco smoking is associated with 39%-56% of cases of this cancer in men, and perhaps about 30% of women are affected by the disease for the same reason (Cole et al. 1971; Miller 1977). The workplace is another major source of exposure to carcinogenic factors causing this cancer. Occupational exposure to aromatic amines, like naphthylamine and benzidine in the dye industry, is related to this tumour (Case et al. 1954). Many other occupations and industrial processes are also connected with cancer of the bladder. These include the leather, rubber, steel and textile industries, engineering, and also occupations like hairstyling and painting (Matanoski and Elliot

1981). Treatment with chlornaphazine (Thiede and Christensen 1975) and cyclophosphamide is suspected of playing a role in the development of cancer of the bladder (Selzer et al. 1978).

The time trends of the mortality rates are different in both sexes in Poland. In males, a steady increase was observed with one of the highest rates in comparison to other countries (Staszewski 1979). This is true for all age groups and birth cohorts. On the other hand, the rates remained unchanged in women over the period 1963-1982. The difference between the highest values recorded in the provinces is greater in women (5.2 times) than in men (3.2 times).

The geographical distribution of men's mortality rates is fairly even, while women in as many as 16 provinces are in the lowest range of values (see black-and-white map). The geographical distribution of cancers of the urinary bladder and lung show some similarities. Analysis of the distribution of mortality rates over the provinces showed the existence of a substantial correlation at the level of 0.61 in men. This is similar to the findings by Lea (1966), and Staszewski (1979) found a strong correlation between the mortality rates for cancer of the lung and urinary bladder in 20 countries. This similarity between the epidemiological pictures of cancer of the urinary bladder and tobacco-related lung cancer (Staszewski 1960) encourages speculation that a large proportion of bladder cancers, especially in men, are related to tobacco smoking, just as in Denmark or the United States (Jensen 1983; Cole et al. 1971). To corroborate our hypothesis, we correlated mortality rates and the number of cigarettes smoked per capita in the individual provinces (estimated for 1970-1974 vs. 1958-1964; see section 3.9). The analysis showed a good correlation in men (0.61). Similar observations were made by Fraumeni (1968) in the United States. The relationship, confirmed by analytical epidemiology, between tobacco smoking and cancer of the urinary bladder - together with the prevalence of cigarette smoking, the high tar content in Polish cigarettes, the epidemiological nature of bladder cancer, its resemblance to the geographical pattern of lung cancer, and the correlation of the mortality rate of bladder cancer and the number of cigarettes smoked per capita in the provinces seems to indicate that most malignant neoplasms of the urinary bladder, at least in men in Poland, are caused by tobacco smoking. The fact that an increase has not been observed in the mortality rate for cancer of the urinary bladder in the female population since the early 1980s may be due to the long latency of this disease (Matanoski and Elliot 1981). The frequency of smoking in women born before 1920 is 5%. The increase in the risk of bladder cancer will probably threaten the more recent female birth cohorts who smoke more frequently. For instance, in the cohort born before 1922 the proportion of female smokers is 7.5%, in the 1923-1942 birth cohort 24.2% and in the 1943-1957 birth cohort 50.0% (Zatonski et al. 1986). Thus an increasing risk of bladder cancer in women will perhaps occur when cohorts with a higher proportion of smokers reach the age when risk is the highest.

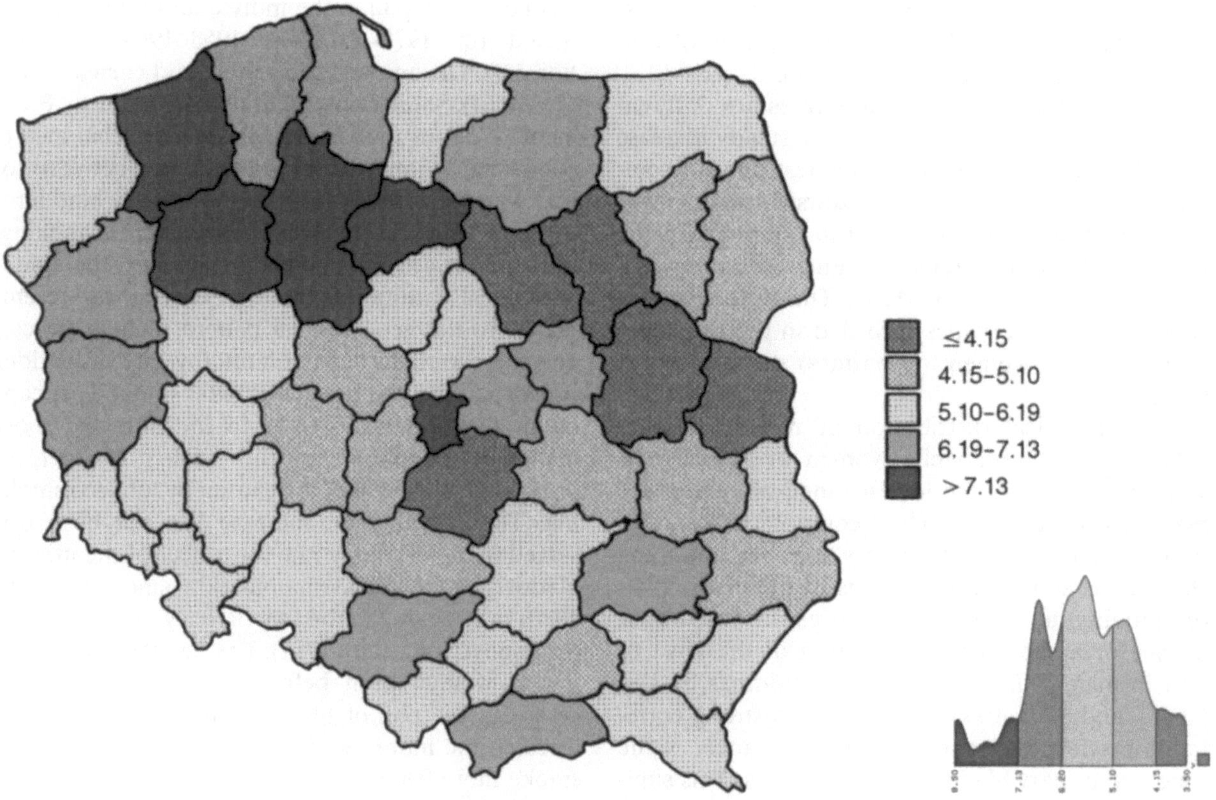
≤4.15
4.15-5.10
5.10-6.19
6.19-7.13
>7.13

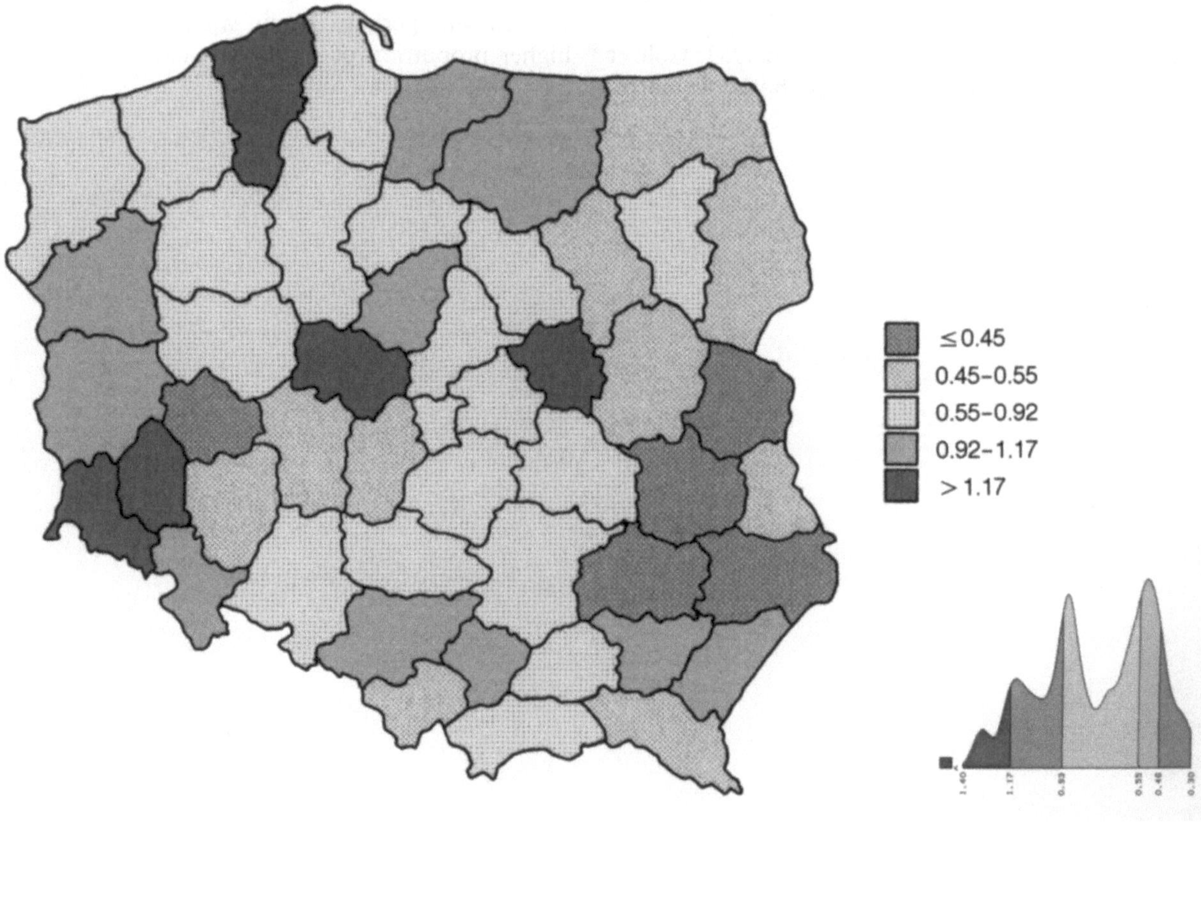
≤0.45
0.45-0.55
0.55-0.92
0.92-1.17
>1.17

7.32 – 8.47
6.16 – 7.32
5.0 – 6.16
3.84 – 5.0
2.68 – 3.84

1.34 – 1.60
1.08 – 1.34
0.82 – 1.08
0.57 – 0.82
0.31 – 0.57

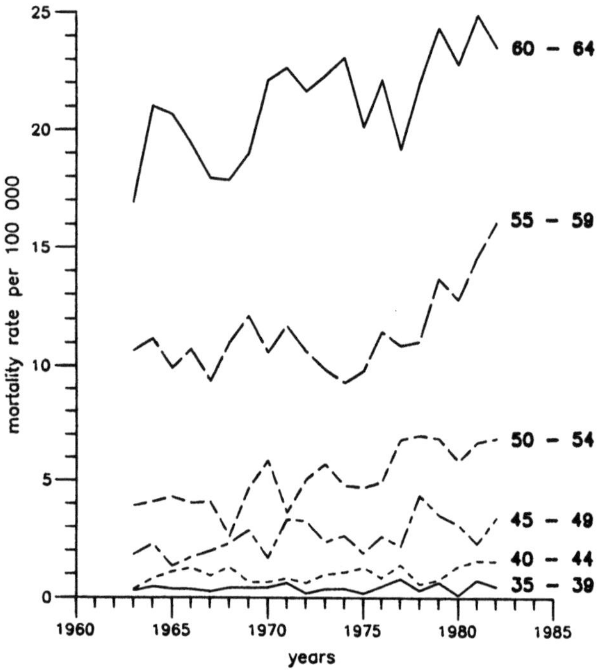

Temporal trend of mortality in individual age groups/men

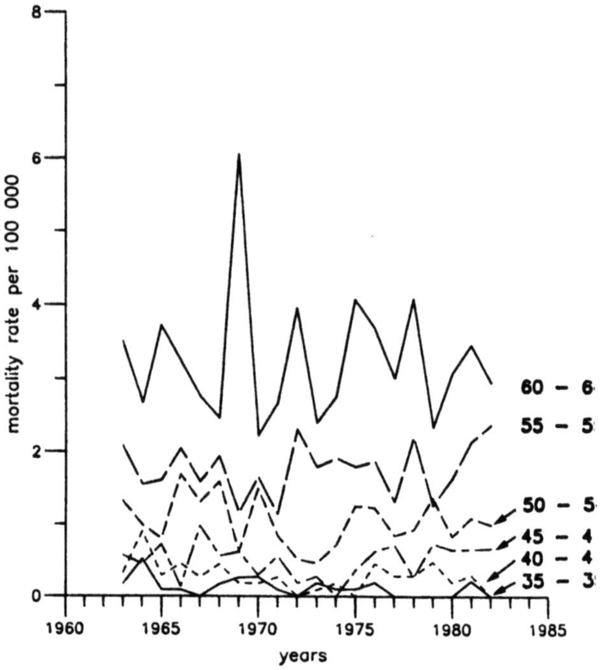

Temporal trend of mortality in individual age groups/women

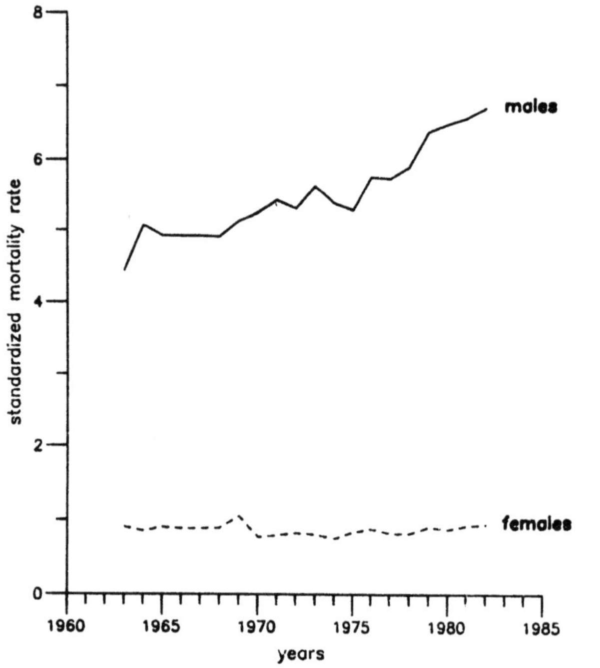

Temporal trend of the age-adjusted mortality rates for men and women

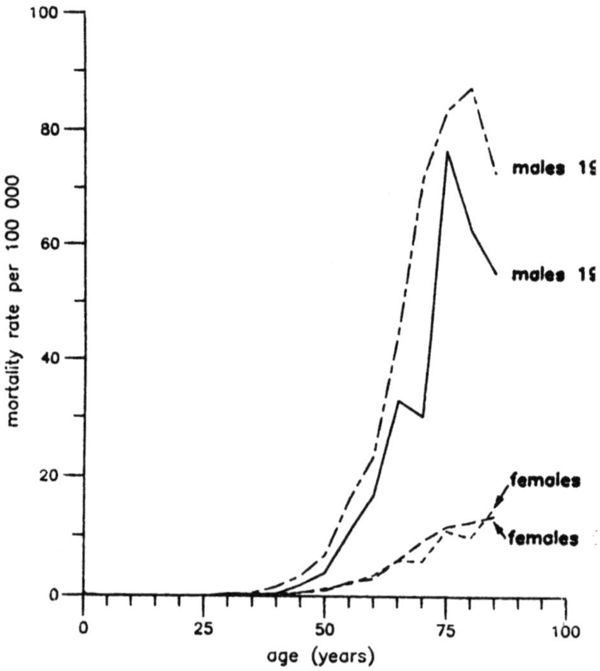

Mortality depending on age in two sample years for men and women

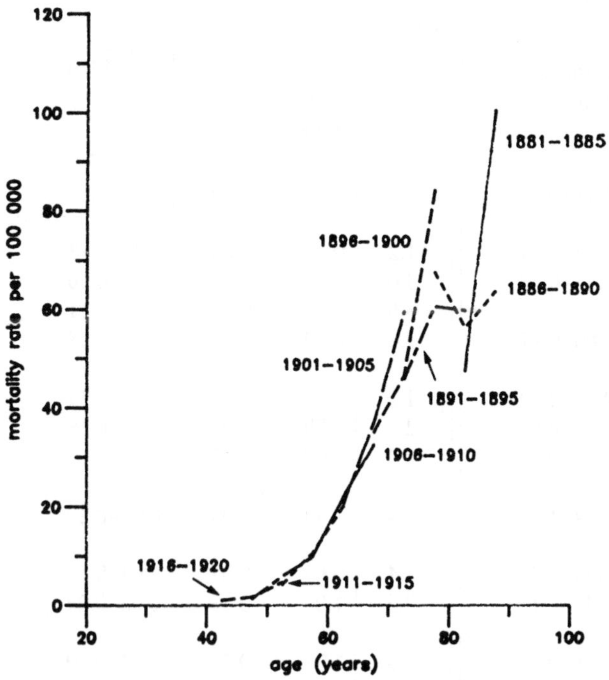

Age-dependent mortality in various birth cohorts/ men

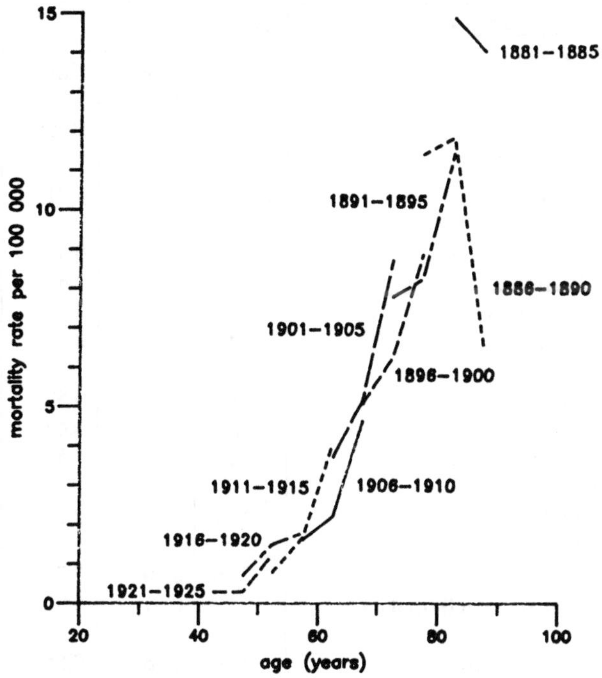

Age-dependent mortality in various birth cohorts/ women

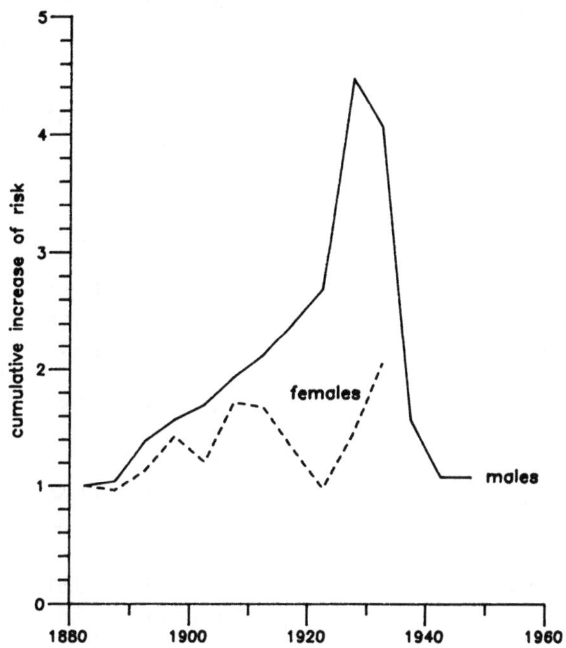

Ratios of the cumulative mortality rates for successive birth cohorts relative to the 1886–1890 cohort

Average Values 1975-1979	Males				Females			
	Cases	Stand. Mort. Rate	Cum. Mort. Rate	Confidence limits	Cases	Stand. Mort. Rate	Cum. Mort. Rate	Confidence limits
Poland	1050.2	5.77	0.71	0.68-0.74	225.4	0.84	0.10	0.09-0.11
Biała Podlaska	8.2	4.00	0.49	0.24-0.74	1.2	0.45	0.06	0.00-0.13
Białystok	19.8	4.93	0.60	0.41-0.79	3.0	0.46	0.05	0.00-0.10
Bielsko Biała	23.4	5.48	0.73	0.52-0.93	3.6	0.53	0.06	0.01-0.11
Bydgoszcz	39.4	7.30	0.78	0.60-0.97	7.2	0.90	0.12	0.05-0.18
Chełm	7.2	5.27	0.59	0.27-0.90	1.2	0.53	0.07	0.00-0.17
Ciechanów	9.0	3.64	0.46	0.25-0.67	2.4	0.70	0.09	0.01-0.18
Częstochowa	20.6	4.47	0.52	0.35-0.68	4.4	0.62	0.05	0.01-0.10
Elbląg	10.2	6.19	0.78	0.44-1.11	2.4	0.93	0.09	0.00-0.20
Gdańsk	36.0	6.20	0.73	0.56-0.90	5.4	0.63	0.07	0.03-0.12
Gorzów Wielkopolski	12.4	6.61	0.80	0.49-1.11	2.6	1.05	0.13	0.02-0.24
Jelenia Góra	12.8	5.98	0.65	0.38-0.91	3.6	1.29	0.16	0.04-0.29
Kalisz	19.8	5.10	0.63	0.44-0.83	2.8	0.52	0.06	0.01-0.12
Katowice	109.8	6.62	0.85	0.73-0.96	28.2	1.10	0.13	0.09-0.16
Kielce	32.0	5.11	0.72	0.55-0.88	7.2	0.84	0.10	0.05-0.15
Konin	11.0	4.31	0.56	0.33-0.79	3.8	1.21	0.13	0.04-0.22
Koszalin	13.8	8.47	1.08	0.68-1.47	2.2	0.92	0.07	0.00-0.17
Kraków	34.8	6.01	0.77	0.59-0.95	9.2	0.98	0.12	0.06-0.18
Krosno	15.4	6.19	0.88	0.58-1.18	2.2	0.49	0.07	0.00-0.14
Legnica	10.0	6.01	0.82	0.45-1.19	2.6	1.33	0.17	0.03-0.31
Leszno	12.0	5.65	0.69	0.42-0.97	1.0	0.31	0.02	0.00-0.06
Lublin	25.4	4.86	0.61	0.44-0.78	3.0	0.35	0.03	0.00-0.07
Łomża	9.4	4.50	0.47	0.24-0.70	1.4	0.62	0.07	0.00-0.15
Łódź	45.4	7.38	0.87	0.69-1.05	9.8	0.89	0.12	0.06-0.17
Nowy Sącz	21.0	6.73	0.87	0.61-1.12	4.0	0.90	0.11	0.03-0.18
Olsztyn	17.4	6.75	0.80	0.53-1.06	4.2	1.17	0.16	0.05-0.26
Opole	23.2	5.63	0.78	0.57-1.00	5.6	0.80	0.09	0.03-0.15
Ostrołęka	8.2	3.58	0.45	0.22-0.68	1.4	0.55	0.06	0.00-0.13
Piła	16.4	7.86	0.89	0.58-1.21	2.8	0.89	0.09	0.00-0.18
Piotrków Trybunalski	14.4	4.00	0.54	0.36-0.73	3.4	0.71	0.09	0.03-0.16
Płock	15.4	5.60	0.79	0.53-1.05	2.2	0.60	0.08	0.01-0.15
Poznań	34.2	5.23	0.66	0.51-0.81	8.4	0.91	0.11	0.05-0.16
Przemyśl	12.0	5.21	0.64	0.39-0.90	2.8	1.06	0.11	0.02-0.21
Radom	19.2	4.83	0.61	0.43-0.80	3.2	0.57	0.07	0.01-0.12
Rzeszów	20.8	5.71	0.68	0.47-0.89	5.0	0.99	0.11	0.04-0.18
Siedlce	11.2	2.68	0.33	0.19-0.47	2.6	0.46	0.04	0.00-0.08
Sieradz	12.4	4.67	0.56	0.34-0.78	2.2	0.53	0.07	0.00-0.14
Skierniewice	16.2	6.75	0.72	0.45-0.99	2.4	0.77	0.08	0.00-0.15
Słupsk	9.2	6.43	0.83	0.45-1.21	2.2	1.18	0.09	0.00-0.20
Suwałki	10.6	5.81	0.86	0.52-1.19	1.6	0.48	0.06	0.00-0.13
Szczecin	18.0	5.90	0.74	0.49-0.99	3.0	0.69	0.09	0.02-0.17

Average Values 1975-1979	Males				Females			
	Cases	Stand. Mort. Rate	Cum. Mort. Rate	Confidence limits	Cases	Stand. Mort. Rate	Cum. Mort. Rate	Confidence limits
Tarnobrzeg	23.2	6.79	0.84	0.60-1.08	1.8	0.38	0.06	0.00-0.11
Tarnów	16.4	4.76	0.59	0.38-0.79	4.0	0.85	0.12	0.04-0.20
Toruń	24.6	8.45	1.02	0.74-1.31	3.0	0.55	0.08	0.01-0.15
Wałbrzych	18.0	6.18	0.67	0.44-0.90	4.4	1.12	0.12	0.04-0.21
Warszawa	80.4	6.79	0.76	0.64-0.88	31.4	1.60	0.20	0.15-0.25
Włocławek	13.6	5.67	0.81	0.52-1.09	3.0	0.93	0.14	0.03-0.24
Wrocław	23.2	5.59	0.72	0.51-0.93	3.8	0.49	0.03	0.00-0.07
Zamość	15.0	4.72	0.56	0.36-0.76	2.4	0.42	0.07	0.00-0.13
Zielona Góra	18.2	6.97	0.80	0.52-1.07	4.2	1.14	0.15	0.05-0.25

17 Kidney - ICD 189

The ASMR for renal cancer in men was 1.6 in 1963 and 3.8 in 1982, while the respective figures for women were 1.0 and 2.0. The mortality rates increase exponentially from the age of 35-40 years to reach the highest value of 23 deaths per 100000 in men aged about 70 and 11 deaths per 100000 in women aged 70-80. The mortality rates increased throughout the period 1963-1982 at a constant mean annual rate of 8.21% in men and 4.69% in women. This increase occurred in all age groups and successive birth cohorts.

In 1978 cancer of the kidney occurred most frequently in European men in Iceland and Czechoslovakia (6.8) and in Sweden (6.6). For women, it was most frequent in Denmark (4.0) and Sweden (3.7). Men had the lowest mortality rates in Bulgaria (1.3), Greece and Yugoslavia (1.7), while women's rates were lowest in Greece (0.8), Bulgaria and Spain (1.0). With a rate of 3.3 for men and 1.8 for women Poland is a medium-risk country.

Analysis of Data from the Provinces, 1975-1979

Like most cancers, renal cancer is more frequent in urban than in rural populations (the urban/rural ratio for men 1.9, for women 1.6). The men's rate is twice as high as the women's.

Men

(Mean ASMR = 2.8, Range 1.2-5.3, Standard Deviation 0.9; 1.9% of Male Cancer Mortality, Rank 13)

The highest mortality value was 4.6 times greater than the lowest. Provinces with the highest rates were Warszawa (5.29), Szczecin (4.65), Katowice (4.47), Opole (4.06) and Torun (3.80). Provinces with the lowest rates were Konin (1.16), Piotrkow (1.46), Krosno (1.70), Lomza (1.74) and Chelm (1.79). No geographical distribution pattern was observed.

Women

(Mean ASMR = 1.5, Range 0.7-2.9, Standard Deviation 0.5; 1.5% of Female Cancer Mortality, Rank 17)

The highest mortality rate was four times greater than the lowest. Provinces with the highest rates were Pila (2.91), Koszalin (2.25), Olsztyn (2.18), Gdansk (2.18) and Poznan (2.17). Provinces with the lowest rates were Ostroleka (0.73), Suwalki (0.79), Zamosc (0.83), Siedlce (0.87) and Biala Podlaska (0.89). A low mortality rate for cancer of the kidney was observed in southeastern Poland, while the northwestern area had an increased risk of this tumour.

Comments

Aetiological studies on renal tumours have to take into account the fact that this site covers several histologically different forms of tumour which are presumably associated with quite different risk factors. The typical renal tumours of childhood are nephroblastoma (Wilms' tumours), while those of adults are predominantly sarcomas or carcinomas of the actual renal cells or of the transitional tissue of the renal pelvis and the renal duct. Thus, the only unquestionable risk factor for this cancer, tobacco smoking, seems to apply mainly to the transitional tissue.

Genetical factors have been found to be involved in relation to Wilms' tumours. Familial accumulations of these tumours in infants as well as the connection with congenital anomalies (aniridia) should be interpreted as genetic factors. Risk factors, which are still hypothetical, include certain occupational exposures (e.g. asbestos), a diet rich in fats and coffee consumption. However, fat and coffee consumption have not been confirmed as risk factors by subsequent studies. All things considered, the known or even assumed risk factors are not sufficient to explain the total incidence of renal cancer.

Like many other countries (Morrison and Cole

1982), Poland has had a steady increase in the renal cancer mortality rate over the last two decades. The increase in men was nearly two times greater than in women. This makes the difference between the frequency of this cancer in men and women much bigger. Furthermore, renal cancer is much more frequent in urban populations. The substantial increase in the risk faced by the Polish population probably stems, to some extent, from the rapid increase in the smoking of high-tar cigarettes. As indirect proof we can take the positive correlation ($r = 0.81$) of inter-provincial differences in mortality rates for kidney cancer in men and inter-provincial differences in the number of cigarettes smoked per capita over 1970-1974 as compared to 1958-1964. Fraumeni (1968) noted a similar phenomenon in the United States.

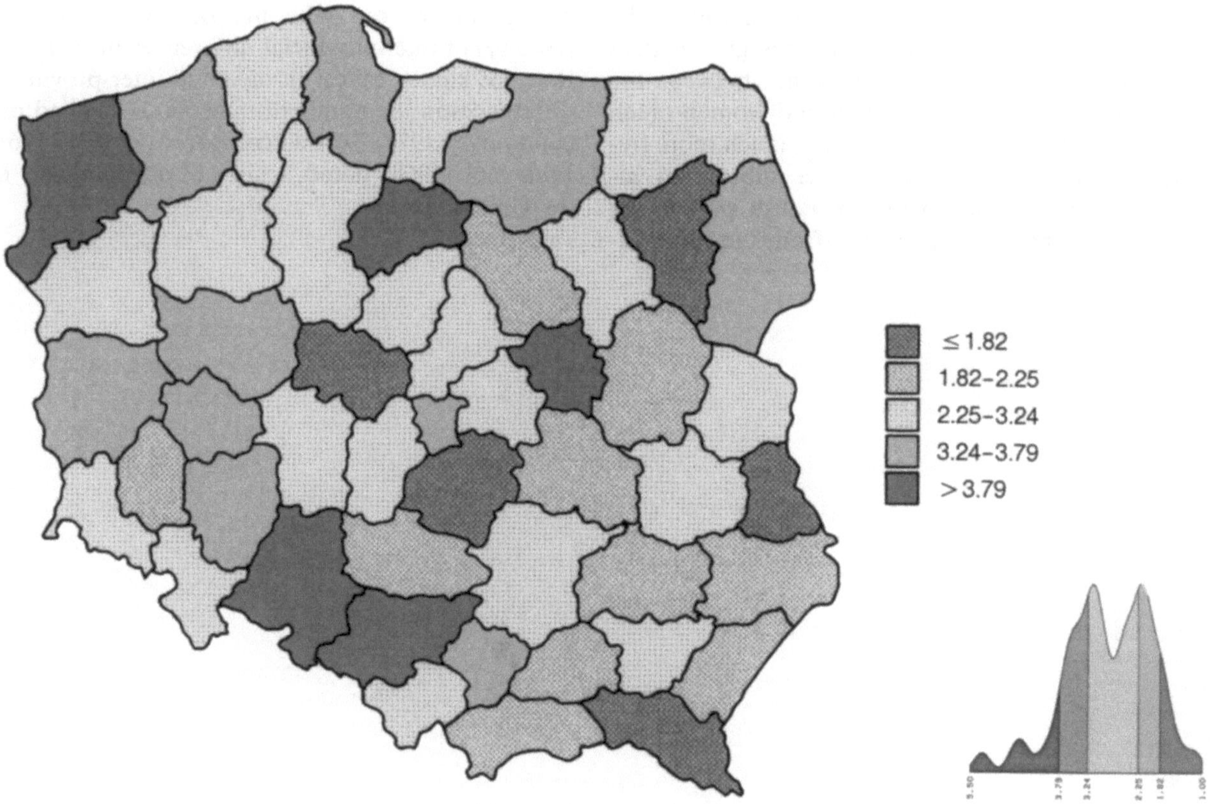
≤1.82
1.82-2.25
2.25-3.24
3.24-3.79
>3.79

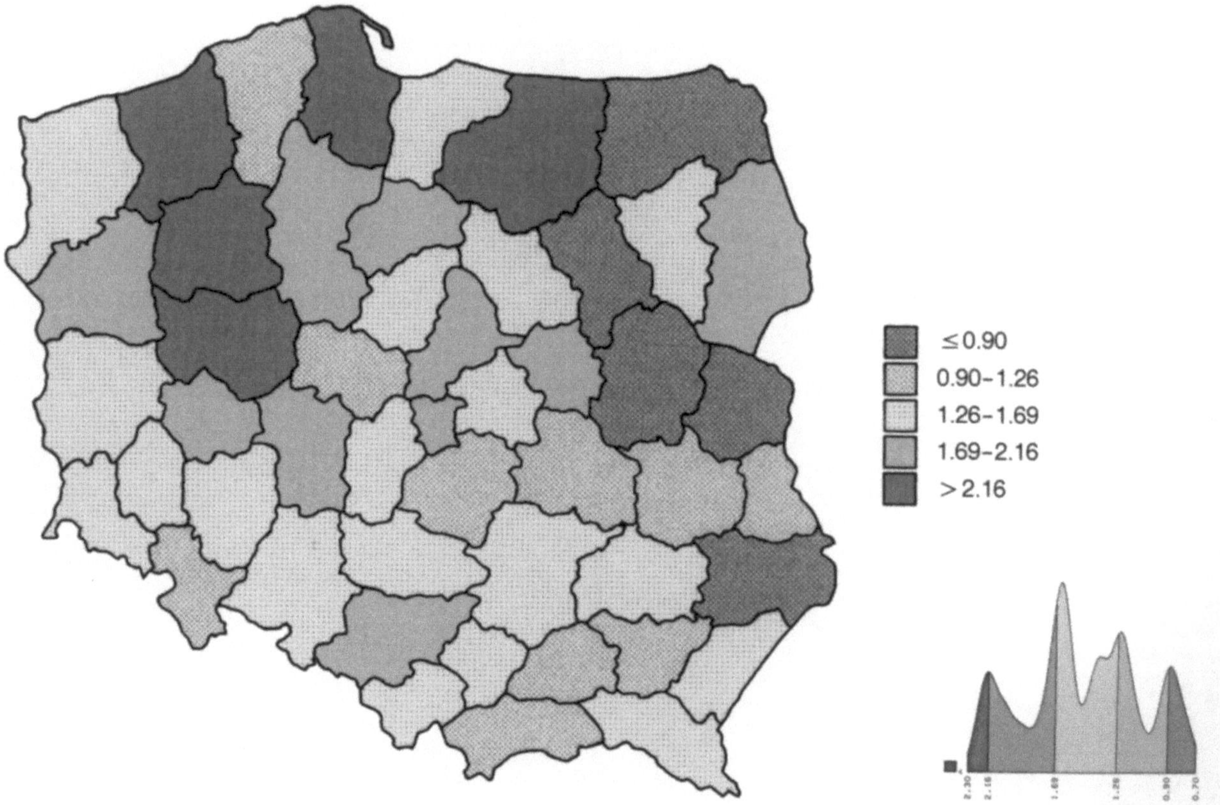
≤0.90
0.90-1.26
1.26-1.69
1.69-2.16
>2.16

4.46 – 5.29
3.64 – 4.46
2.81 – 3.64
1.98 – 2.81
1.16 – 1.98

2.47 – 2.91
2.04 – 2.47
1.60 – 2.04
1.16 – 1.60
0.73 – 1.16

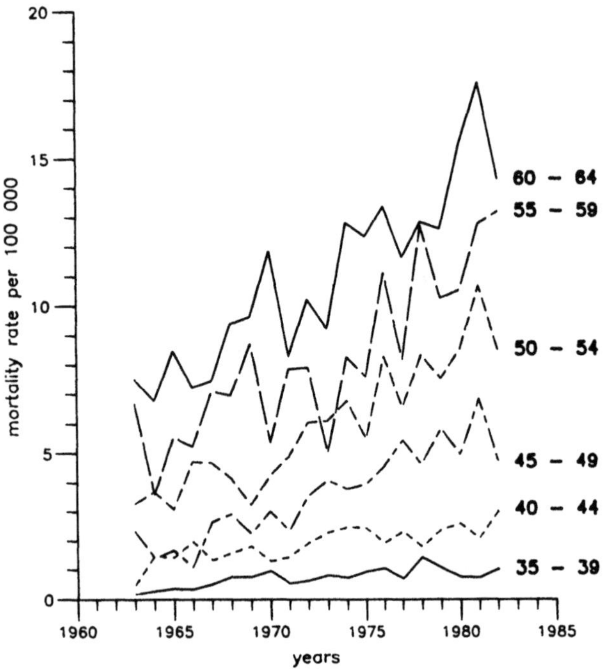

Temporal trend of mortality in individual age groups/men

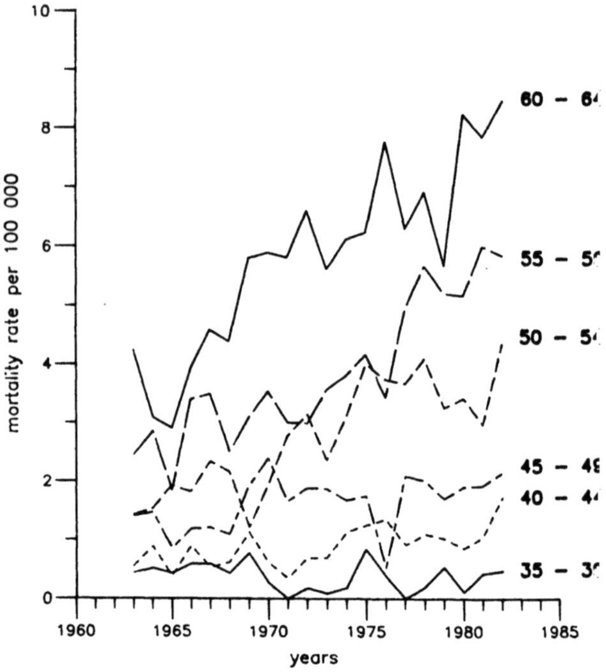

Temporal trend of mortality in individual age groups/women

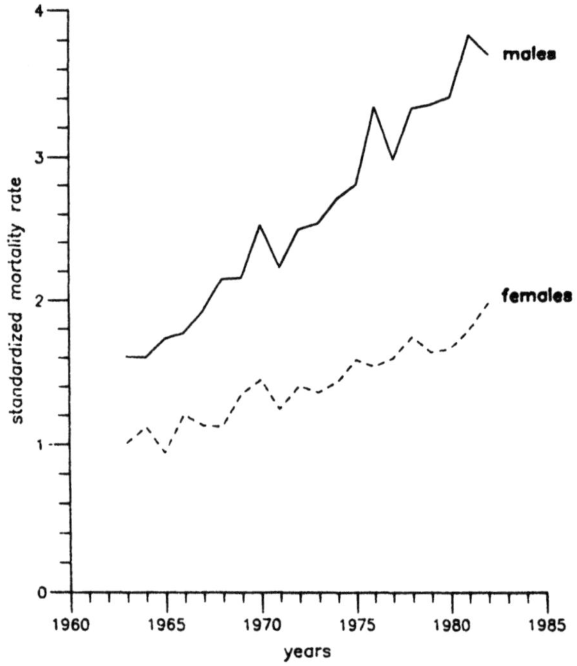

Temporal trend of the age-adjusted mortality rates for men and women

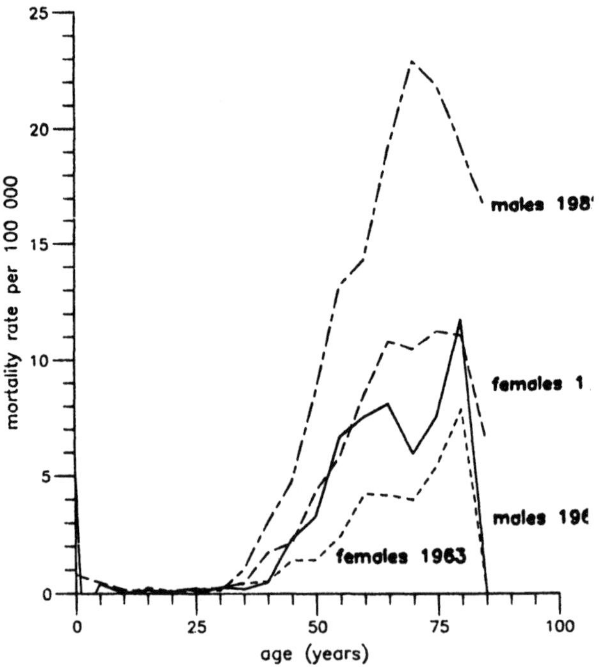

Mortality depending on age in two sample years for men and women

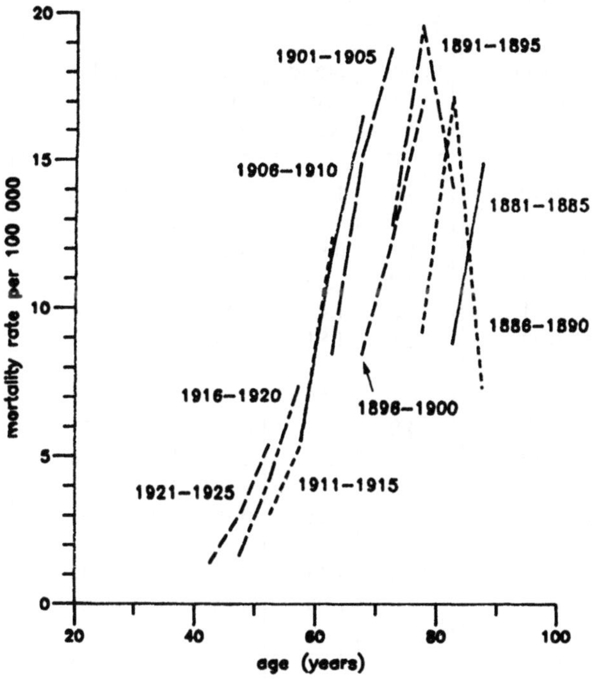

Age-dependent mortality in various birth cohorts/ men

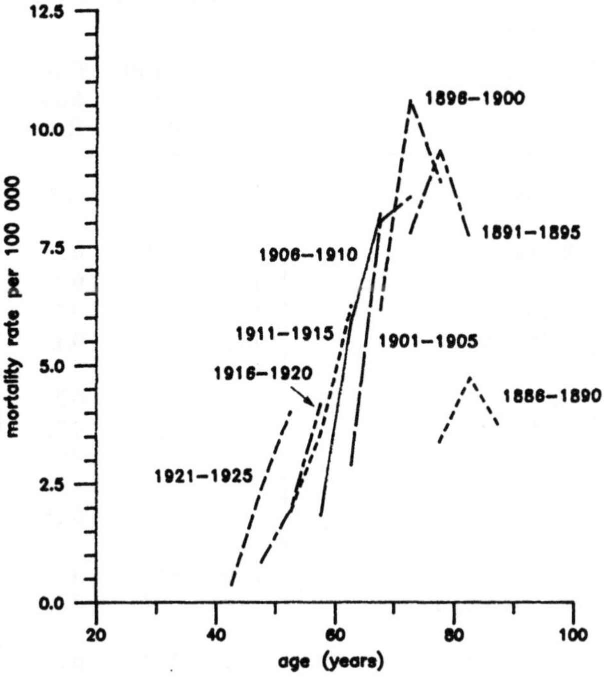

Age-dependent mortality in various birth cohorts/ women

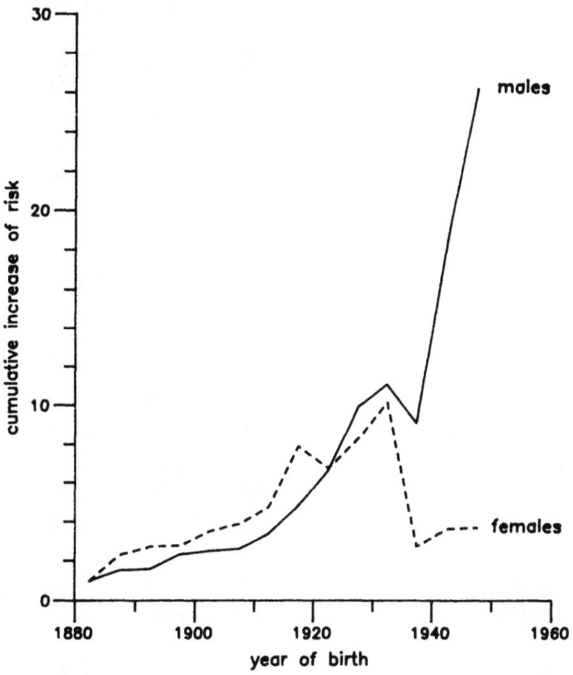

Ratios of the cumulative mortality rates for successive birth cohorts relative to the 1886–1890 cohort

Average Values 1975-1979	Males				Females			
	Cases	Stand. Mort. Rate	Cum. Mort. Rate	Confidence limits	Cases	Stand. Mort. Rate	Cum. Mort. Rate	Confidence limits
Poland	557.6	3.16	0.38	0.36-0.40	375.0	1.62	0.19	0.18-0.20
Biała Podlaska	5.0	3.05	0.36	0.16-0.57	1.6	0.89	0.08	0.00-0.17
Białystok	12.0	3.53	0.46	0.29-0.62	9.2	2.09	0.25	0.14-0.35
Bielsko Biała	10.8	2.66	0.37	0.23-0.51	7.8	1.45	0.18	0.09-0.26
Bydgoszcz	16.2	3.19	0.39	0.27-0.52	12.8	1.81	0.21	0.13-0.29
Chełm	2.4	1.79	0.23	0.05-0.40	1.8	1.25	0.14	0.01-0.27
Ciechanów	5.0	2.16	0.23	0.09-0.37	4.0	1.63	0.16	0.05-0.27
Częstochowa	9.0	2.17	0.27	0.16-0.39	7.8	1.40	0.18	0.10-0.26
Elbląg	4.2	2.26	0.28	0.09-0.47	4.2	1.68	0.19	0.06-0.32
Gdańsk	21.6	3.64	0.44	0.31-0.56	16.6	2.18	0.25	0.17-0.34
Gorzów Wielkopolski	5.8	3.02	0.38	0.18-0.58	5.0	2.05	0.25	0.10-0.41
Jelenia Góra	6.2	2.64	0.27	0.11-0.43	3.6	1.27	0.19	0.06-0.33
Kalisz	9.4	2.52	0.30	0.18-0.42	8.2	1.91	0.20	0.11-0.30
Katowice	72.8	4.47	0.53	0.45-0.61	50.2	2.15	0.25	0.21-0.30
Kielce	14.2	2.42	0.30	0.20-0.40	10.4	1.35	0.18	0.11-0.25
Konin	3.0	1.16	0.10	0.02-0.19	3.2	1.13	0.13	0.04-0.22
Koszalin	6.2	3.25	0.39	0.18-0.60	5.4	2.25	0.24	0.10-0.39
Kraków	19.8	3.35	0.38	0.27-0.50	12.0	1.65	0.19	0.12-0.26
Krosno	4.0	1.70	0.18	0.06-0.30	4.0	1.59	0.18	0.07-0.29
Legnica	3.8	2.02	0.27	0.08-0.45	3.4	1.67	0.17	0.05-0.29
Leszno	6.6	3.44	0.44	0.23-0.65	4.2	1.70	0.19	0.07-0.31
Lublin	14.4	2.98	0.36	0.24-0.48	7.0	1.15	0.14	0.07-0.21
Łomża	3.4	1.74	0.23	0.08-0.39	3.0	1.51	0.16	0.05-0.28
Łódź	23.0	3.64	0.39	0.28-0.50	15.6	1.72	0.19	0.12-0.25
Nowy Sącz	6.2	1.89	0.24	0.12-0.36	3.6	0.92	0.10	0.03-0.17
Olsztyn	9.8	3.56	0.42	0.24-0.60	7.6	2.18	0.28	0.15-0.42
Opole	16.0	4.06	0.48	0.32-0.64	7.2	1.29	0.15	0.08-0.22
Ostrołęka	4.8	2.52	0.28	0.12-0.44	1.8	0.73	0.09	0.00-0.17
Piła	5.8	3.23	0.37	0.17-0.57	7.8	2.91	0.38	0.20-0.56
Piotrków Trybunalski	4.6	1.46	0.17	0.07-0.27	4.6	0.94	0.14	0.06-0.23
Płock	6.6	2.40	0.32	0.16-0.47	4.8	1.78	0.19	0.09-0.30
Poznań	24.8	3.78	0.49	0.36-0.62	19.6	2.17	0.28	0.20-0.37
Przemyśl	4.6	2.02	0.22	0.09-0.36	3.2	1.27	0.15	0.04-0.26
Radom	8.4	2.24	0.26	0.14-0.37	4.2	0.92	0.09	0.03-0.15
Rzeszów	10.0	3.07	0.35	0.21-0.50	5.8	1.21	0.15	0.07-0.23
Siedlce	7.2	2.16	0.21	0.11-0.31	3.6	0.87	0.11	0.04-0.18
Sieradz	6.6	3.13	0.33	0.17-0.49	4.0	1.60	0.15	0.06-0.25
Skierniewice	6.2	2.82	0.36	0.17-0.54	3.6	1.44	0.16	0.06-0.27
Słupsk	4.6	2.94	0.35	0.12-0.58	2.2	1.21	0.09	0.01-0.16
Suwałki	4.8	2.66	0.32	0.13-0.52	1.8	0.79	0.12	0.01-0.22
Szczecin	16.6	4.65	0.61	0.41-0.82	8.0	1.68	0.21	0.11-0.31

Average Values 1975-1979	Males				Females			
	Cases	Stand. Mort. Rate	Cum. Mort. Rate	Confidence limits	Cases	Stand. Mort. Rate	Cum. Mort. Rate	Confidence limits
Tarnobrzeg	6.8	2.13	0.28	0.15-0.42	5.2	1.41	0.16	0.07-0.25
Tarnów	5.8	1.86	0.22	0.10-0.34	4.8	1.23	0.15	0.06-0.23
Toruń	11.4	3.80	0.41	0.24-0.57	7.6	1.95	0.25	0.13-0.36
Wałbrzych	8.0	2.41	0.32	0.17-0.46	4.2	1.05	0.14	0.05-0.23
Warszawa	61.0	5.29	0.64	0.53-0.75	37.4	2.03	0.24	0.18-0.29
Włocławek	6.4	3.10	0.38	0.19-0.56	3.4	1.37	0.13	0.04-0.22
Wrocław	16.6	3.53	0.45	0.30-0.59	10.2	1.63	0.22	0.13-0.32
Zamość	6.2	2.17	0.27	0.13-0.40	2.4	0.83	0.07	0.01-0.13
Zielona Góra	9.0	3.28	0.37	0.20-0.55	5.4	1.66	0.17	0.07-0.27

18 Brain - ICD 191

This analysis is based on data from the period 1970-1979 due to the changes in the ICD. Mortality rates analysed from a small number of cases tend to show greater annual variability. In the years mentioned, the rates remained at an unchanged level in men and women. The mortality age curve has one peak in childhood, then the mortality rate decreases until the age of about 30. The curve for men peaked with 14 deaths per 100000 and eight for women in 1979. In 1978 countries with the highest mortality rates for cancer of the brain were Greece (6.1) and Denmark (5.8) for men, and Iceland (4.5), Denmark (4.1), Sweden and Greece (3.6 each) for women. The lowest rates for both sexes were recorded in the Federal Republic of Germany (1.1, 0.7, respectively) and in Bulgaria (2.0, 1.5, respectively). The mortality in Poland was at a medium level with 3.7 and 2.5, respectively.

Analysis of Data from Provinces, 1975-1979

Cancer of the brain is slightly more frequent in city dwellers (1.1 times) and 1.6 times more frequent in men than in women.

Men

(Mean ASMR = 3.5, Range 1.7-5.8, Standard Deviation 1.0; 2.1% of Male Cancer Mortality, Rank 12)

The highest value was 3.4 times greater than the lowest. Provinces with the highest rates were Warszawa (5.79), Torun (5.06), Gdansk (5.0), Wloclawek (4.97) and Olsztyn (4.75). Provinces with the lowest rates were Lublin (1.69), Krakow (1.72), Leszno (1.8), Konin (2.0) and Wroclaw (2.1). The high- and low-risk areas were scattered, but lower mortality rates tended to occur in western Poland rather than in the east.

Women

(Mean ASMR = 2.3, Range 1.1-4.0, Standard Deviation 0.7; 1.9% of Female Cancer Mortality, Rank 15)

Provinces with the highest rates were Warszawa (4.04), Gdansk (3.65), Olsztyn (3.35), Pila (3.31) and Torun (3.03). Provinces with the lowest rates were Wroclaw (1.11), Lublin (1.11), Piotrkow (1.30), Kalisz (1.30) and Gorzow Wielkopolski (1.33). Western Poland is an area of lower risk, even more than in the case of men.

Comments

Cancers of the brain form a heterogenous group of disease from the clinical and, probably, the aetiological points of view. The knowledge of risk factors is very limited (Schoenberg 1982). Modan and his group have shown in their observations of a cohort of 11000 children, who had been exposed to radiation as treatment for tinea capitis (Modan 1974), that ionising radiation is a risk factor in brain tumours. This observation has been confirmed by other studies (Preston-Martin 1978).

Studies on occupational cancers have shown an increased risk originating from exposure during the production of rubber and synthetic fibres. Since, in the fields of production preponderantly concerned, workers are exposed to N-nitroso compounds, attention is focused on this group of substances. It is known from animal experiments that these compounds belong to the strongest carcinogens known and are capable of inducing brain tumours. Since N-nitroso compounds can occur in daily life in manifold forms, epidemiological studies currently being conducted investigate the meaning of this exposure for the incidence of human brain tumours. Pointers in this direction are also to be found in the case-control studies already mentioned, inasfar as associations are established between the consumption of meat treated with nitrite or drugs containing nitrosable amins and the incidence of brain tumours.

Other exogenic factors such as injuries and viruses are also being discussed as potential risk factors (Schoenberg 1982).
With respect to endogenic factors, familial accumulations and the association with genetic disorders (e. g. neurofibromatosis, tuberous sclerosis) suggest the involvement of genetic factors.
In Poland, cancer of the brain is very rare. It is more frequent in men than in women, but there is no significant difference between its frequency among the urban and rural population. It is somewhat less frequent in people living in the western parts of the country, especially in women, unlike most of the other cancer sites. Interestingly, most of the high- and low-risk provinces are the same for both sexes.

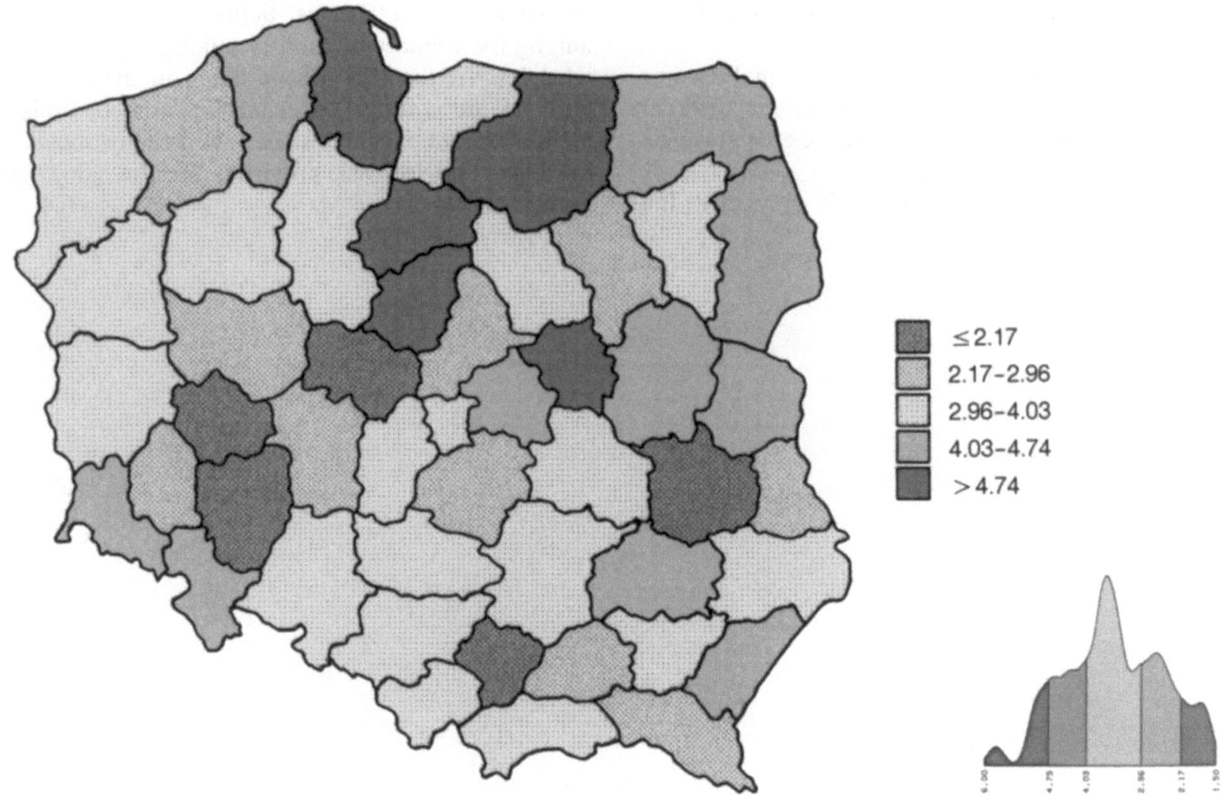
≤2.17
2.17-2.96
2.96-4.03
4.03-4.74
>4.74

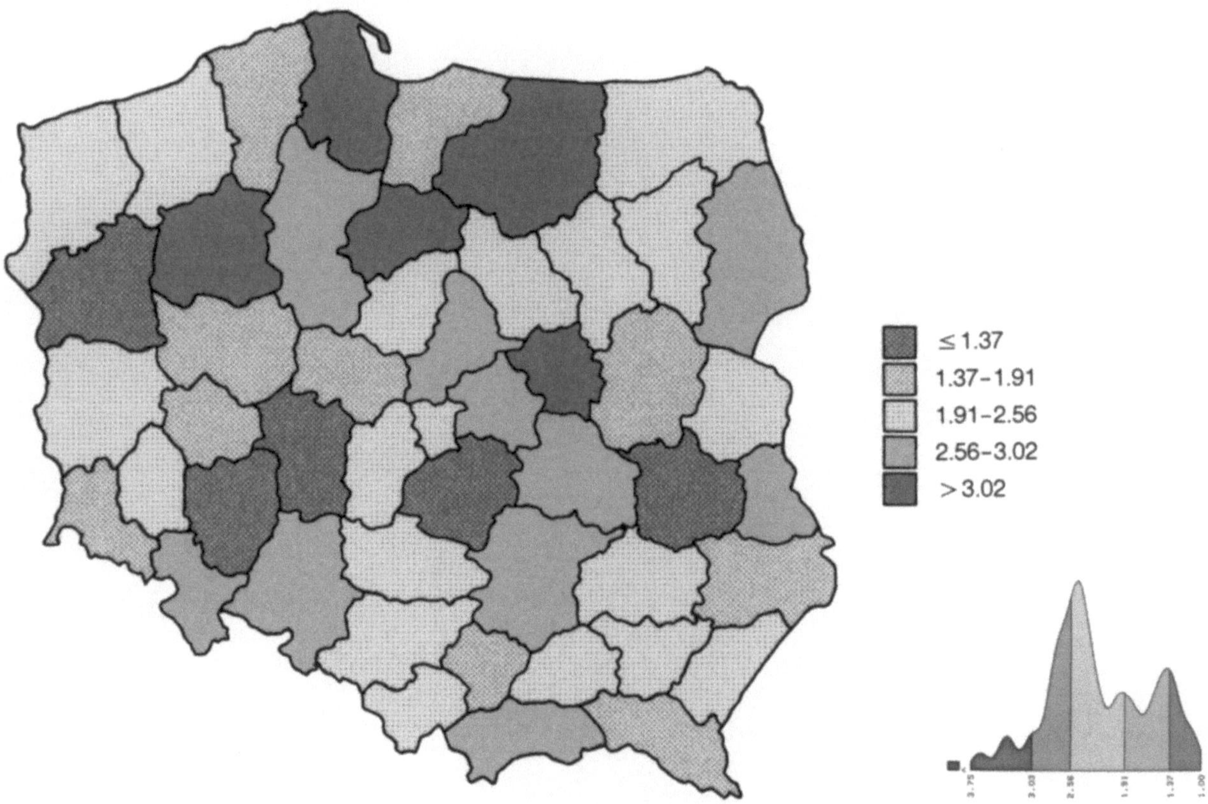
≤1.37
1.37-1.91
1.91-2.56
2.56-3.02
>3.02

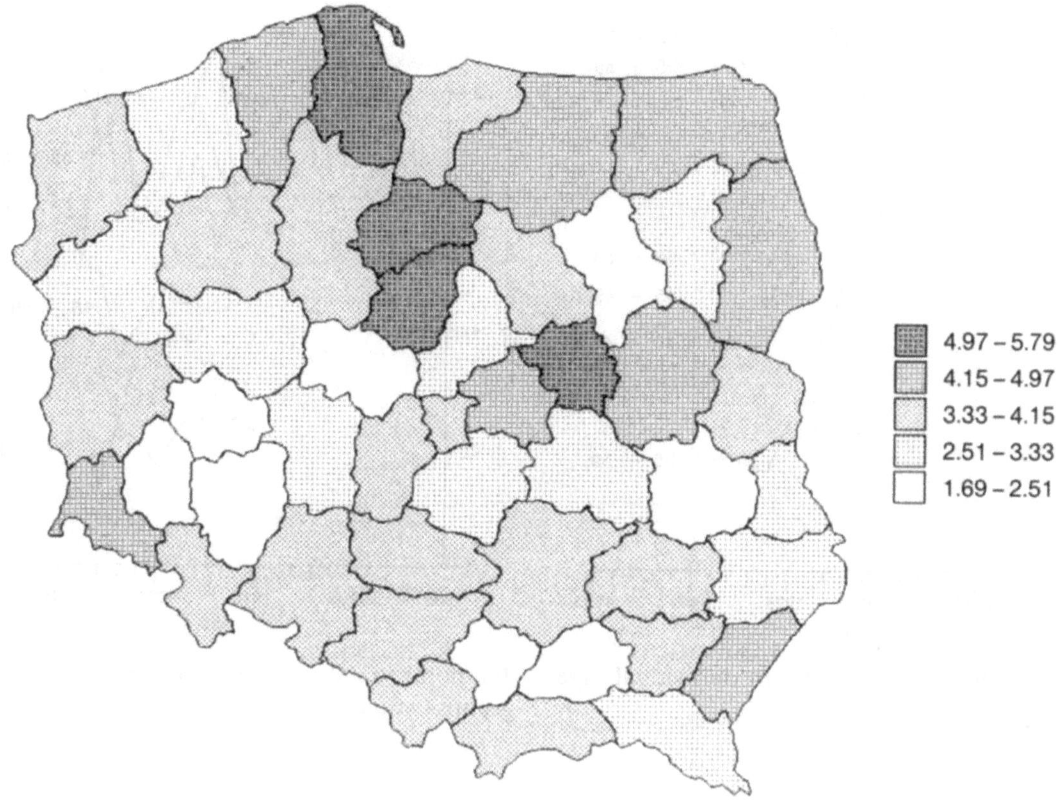
4.97 – 5.79
4.15 – 4.97
3.33 – 4.15
2.51 – 3.33
1.69 – 2.51

3.46 – 4.04
2.87 – 3.46
2.28 – 2.87
1.69 – 2.28
1.11 – 1.69

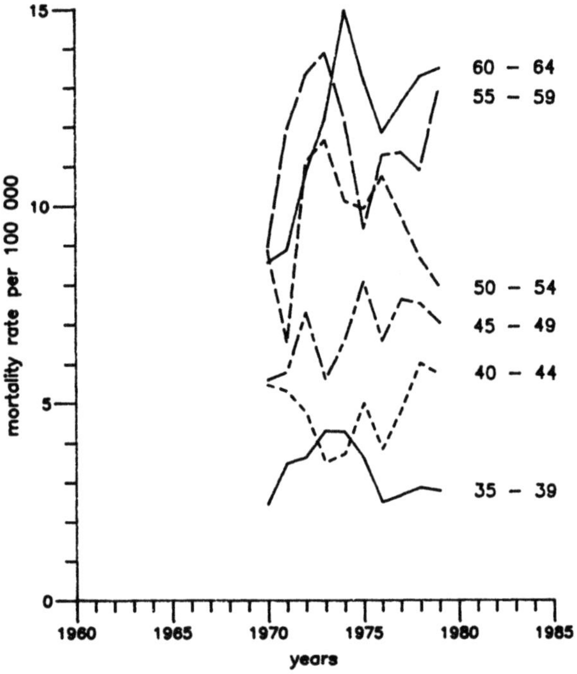

Temporal trend of mortality in individual age groups/men

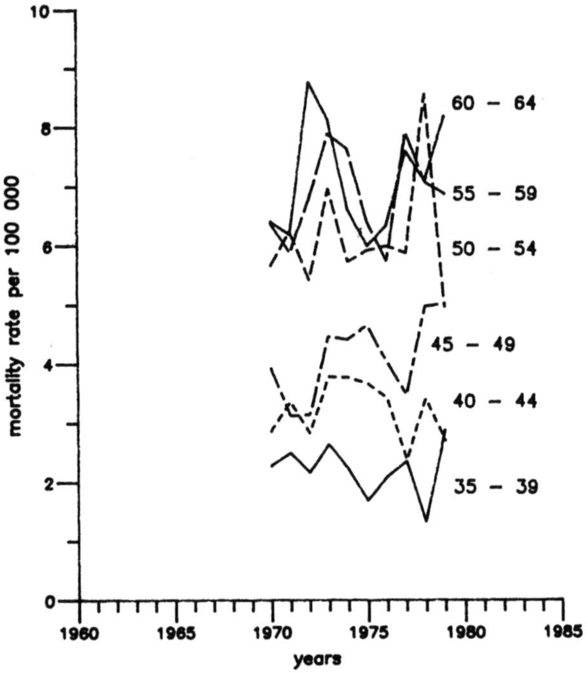

Temporal trend of mortality in individual age groups/women

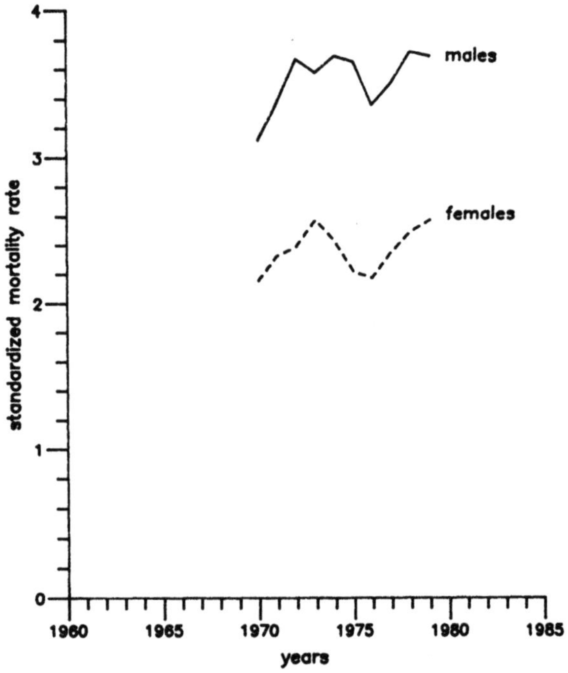

Temporal trend of the age-adjusted mortality rates for men and women

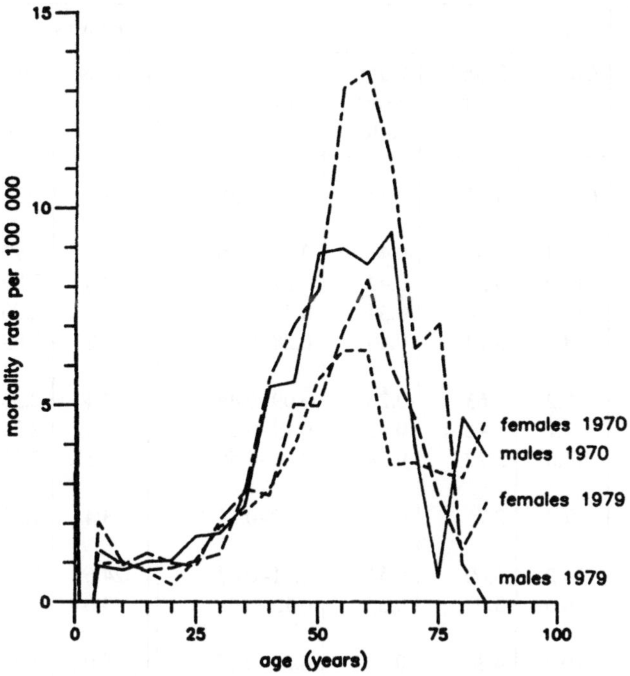

Mortality depending on age in two sample years for men and women

Average Values 1975-1979	Males				Females			
	Cases	Stand. Mort. Rate	Cum. Mort. Rate	Confidence limits	Cases	Stand. Mort. Rate	Cum. Mort. Rate	Confidence limits
Poland	611.2	3.57	0.37	0.35-0.38	457.6	2.35	0.23	0.21-0.24
Biała Podlaska	6.4	4.04	0.41	0.21-0.60	3.2	1.97	0.19	0.06-0.33
Białystok	14.0	4.32	0.44	0.29-0.59	9.8	2.80	0.28	0.17-0.39
Bielsko Biała	12.8	3.44	0.34	0.22-0.46	8.8	2.00	0.18	0.11-0.26
Bydgoszcz	18.0	3.72	0.40	0.28-0.51	14.8	2.69	0.26	0.18-0.34
Chełm	3.2	2.63	0.26	0.09-0.44	3.4	2.56	0.25	0.09-0.42
Ciechanów	7.2	3.42	0.35	0.19-0.52	5.0	2.25	0.23	0.11-0.35
Częstochowa	14.0	3.72	0.38	0.26-0.50	10.8	2.39	0.23	0.15-0.32
Elbląg	7.8	3.75	0.35	0.19-0.51	3.4	1.59	0.13	0.04-0.23
Gdańsk	30.2	5.00	0.54	0.41-0.67	24.6	3.65	0.38	0.29-0.48
Gorzów Wielkopolski	6.6	3.02	0.32	0.15-0.48	3.0	1.33	0.12	0.02-0.22
Jelenia Góra	10.2	4.30	0.40	0.24-0.57	5.0	1.79	0.17	0.07-0.27
Kalisz	9.0	2.76	0.24	0.14-0.35	4.8	1.30	0.11	0.04-0.17
Katowice	57.0	3.41	0.38	0.32-0.45	44.2	2.20	0.22	0.18-0.26
Kielce	20.0	3.70	0.38	0.27-0.48	17.8	2.80	0.28	0.20-0.36
Konin	4.2	2.00	0.17	0.07-0.28	3.0	1.40	0.13	0.04-0.21
Koszalin	5.4	2.58	0.23	0.11-0.36	4.2	2.08	0.20	0.08-0.33
Kraków	10.0	1.72	0.17	0.10-0.24	9.2	1.44	0.14	0.08-0.19
Krosno	5.0	2.51	0.29	0.13-0.45	3.6	1.55	0.14	0.05-0.22
Legnica	4.8	2.23	0.21	0.07-0.34	5.0	2.53	0.21	0.09-0.33
Leszno	3.0	1.80	0.18	0.06-0.31	3.0	1.66	0.16	0.05-0.27
Lublin	7.8	1.69	0.17	0.09-0.24	5.4	1.11	0.10	0.05-0.15
Łomża	4.8	3.11	0.31	0.12-0.50	3.8	2.37	0.21	0.08-0.33
Łódź	21.4	3.54	0.38	0.28-0.48	16.6	2.46	0.23	0.16-0.30
Nowy Sącz	10.4	3.77	0.40	0.24-0.55	8.8	2.64	0.26	0.15-0.37
Olsztyn	14.0	4.75	0.46	0.29-0.62	10.6	3.35	0.32	0.19-0.44
Opole	18.0	4.02	0.42	0.29-0.55	14.6	2.80	0.27	0.18-0.36
Ostrołęka	4.2	2.32	0.21	0.08-0.34	4.6	2.32	0.22	0.09-0.34
Piła	7.0	3.45	0.32	0.17-0.47	7.2	3.31	0.26	0.14-0.39
Piotrków Trybunalski	8.4	2.93	0.25	0.15-0.36	4.4	1.30	0.13	0.06-0.20
Płock	6.6	2.69	0.27	0.14-0.39	7.6	2.75	0.27	0.15-0.38
Poznań	16.4	2.78	0.26	0.18-0.34	9.2	1.43	0.12	0.07-0.17
Przemyśl	8.6	4.59	0.48	0.27-0.68	5.2	2.43	0.23	0.11-0.36
Radom	11.4	3.18	0.32	0.21-0.44	10.4	2.69	0.26	0.16-0.35
Rzeszów	11.2	3.59	0.36	0.23-0.49	8.6	2.49	0.23	0.14-0.33
Siedlce	14.8	4.69	0.50	0.34-0.65	6.6	1.81	0.18	0.09-0.26
Sieradz	7.8	3.73	0.39	0.22-0.55	5.0	2.54	0.21	0.10-0.33
Skierniewice	9.8	4.74	0.51	0.31-0.70	6.8	3.02	0.30	0.16-0.43
Słupsk	6.4	4.40	0.46	0.22-0.69	3.4	1.85	0.17	0.06-0.28
Suwałki	8.2	4.42	0.41	0.22-0.60	5.0	2.41	0.23	0.10-0.37
Szczecin	13.4	3.42	0.36	0.22-0.50	11.0	2.48	0.27	0.16-0.39

Average Values 1975-1979	Males				Females			
	Cases	Stand. Mort. Rate	Cum. Mort. Rate	Confidence limits	Cases	Stand. Mort. Rate	Cum. Mort. Rate	Confidence limits
Tarnobrzeg	11.0	4.05	0.38	0.24-0.53	7.4	2.47	0.23	0.13-0.33
Tarnów	7.0	2.43	0.25	0.13-0.36	6.2	1.98	0.20	0.10-0.30
Toruń	14.0	5.06	0.55	0.36-0.74	10.8	3.03	0.30	0.18-0.42
Wałbrzych	14.6	4.08	0.39	0.26-0.53	10.2	2.65	0.21	0.13-0.30
Warszawa	66.0	5.79	0.63	0.53-0.73	58.4	4.04	0.42	0.36-0.49
Włocławek	10.0	4.97	0.53	0.33-0.74	5.4	2.56	0.24	0.12-0.36
Wrocław	11.6	2.10	0.21	0.13-0.30	6.8	1.11	0.11	0.06-0.16
Zamość	7.4	2.99	0.27	0.15-0.38	4.0	1.50	0.14	0.05-0.22
Zielona Góra	10.2	3.67	0.33	0.19-0.46	7.0	2.27	0.19	0.10-0.27

19 Thyroid Gland - ICD 193

The ASMR for cancer of the thyroid gland in men was 0.4 both in 1963 and in 1982, while the respective figures for women were 0.6 and 0.7. The mortality rates show no clear increase in time either in the individual age groups or in all of them together. The mortality rate increases exponentially with age from 45-50 onwards, and the steepness of the curve is greater in women than in men.

In Europe, Austria, Finland and Switzerland had the highest mortality rates for thyroid cancer in 1978. Men in these three countries had the respective rates of 1.1, 1.0 and 1.0, while the women's rates were 1.3, 1.3 and 1.2, respectively. Greece had the lowest risk of mortality from thyroid cancer (0.1 for men and 0.4 for women). Also with low rates were Spain (0.2 and 0.4, respectively) as well as Bulgaria (men 0.2), the Republic of Ireland (men 0.2) and Northern Ireland (men 0.3 and women 0.4). With values of 0.3 for men and 0.7 for women, Poland belonged to the group of countries at low risk for men and at medium risk for women.

Analysis of Data from the Provinces, 1975-1979

Thyroid cancer in the male population was 1.3 times more frequent in towns than in rural areas. The urban/rural ratio for women was 1.0. Together with the gall bladder, the thyroid gland is a cancer site occurring more often in women than in men (sex ratio 0.6).

Men

(Mean ASMR = 0.3, Range 0.0-1.2, Standard Deviation 0.2; 0.2% of Male Cancer Mortality, Rank 36)

In absolute figures, cancer of the thyroid gland caused 317 deaths in the years 1975-1979. Provinces with highest rates were Nowy Sacz (1.19), Tarnobrzeg (0.76), Przemysl (0.68), Jelenia Gora (0.58) and Zielona Gora (0.56). Provinces with the lowest rates were Wloclawek (0.0), Elblag (0.07), Slupsk (0.12), Leszno (0.12) and Biala Podlaska (0.13). The mortality rates were lowest in the north (close to the sea) and they increased towards the hilly south. In general terms, a low mortality rate for this tumour is typical in regions situated in northern and central Poland. The highest mortality rates were found in southern provinces such as Nowy Sacz, Tarnobrzeg, Przemysl and Jelenia Gora.

Women

(Mean ASMR = 0.7, Range 0.1-1.5, Standard Deviation 0.3; 0.7% of Female Cancer Mortality, Rank 23)

The great variability, with the highest mortality rates 13.3 times greater than the lowest, is most probably caused by the low frequency of this cancer. Provinces with the highest rates were Bielsko-Biala (1.46), Nowy Sacz (1.33), Rzeszow (1.18), Walbrzych (1.15) and Tarnow (1.11). Provinces with the lowest rates were Slupsk (0.11), Siedlce (0.23), Lomza (0.28), Chelm (0.31) and Biala Podlaska (0.33). The high-risk region is in the south of Poland. Provinces with the highest mortality rates run along the foot of the mountains. Provinces with the lowest mortality rates are scattered all over the country.

Comments

Although a heterogenous groups of tumours, thyroid cancer is of necessity treated as one disease in this analysis. Thyroid cancer as a cause of death is rare. It has several histological types differing considerably in their clinical course and, frequently, in the aetiological factors promoting it. It is assumed that papillary carcinoma is related to excess iodine in the diet (Williams et al. 1977) while follicular and aplastic cancers are linked to the endemic thyroid goitre which is caused by the absence of iodine in the diet (McGill 1978). The only proven factor with a causal relationship to thyroid cancer is external radiation to the thyroid region (Colman et al. 1978).

In Poland the mortality rate for malignant neoplasms of the thyroid remained unchanged during the 20 years of observation. In a similar way to other countries (Ron and Modan 1982), the frequency of thyroid cancer was higher in women than men. The regional distribution of thyroid cancer is notable in that it is the only cancer site with north-south distribution. The cluster of provinces with the highest risk is very clear-cut, especially for women. They make up a meridional stretch of provinces running along the Carpathian and Sudeten mountain ranges. This area was known for endemic goitre before iodine salt was given to the population. The neighbouring countries, the German Democratic Republic and the Federal Republic of Germany, have the same north south distribution of thyroid cancer (sea-mountains) (Becker et al. 1984).

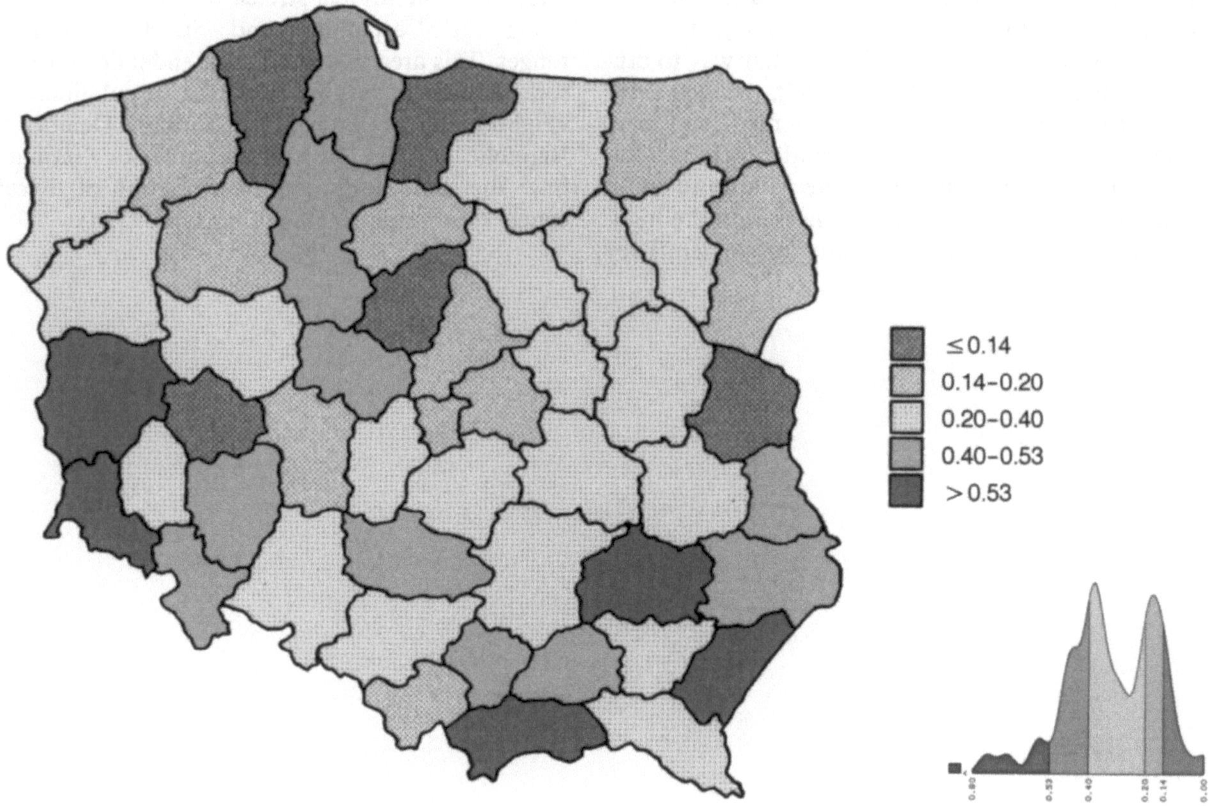
≤0.14
0.14–0.20
0.20–0.40
0.40–0.53
>0.53

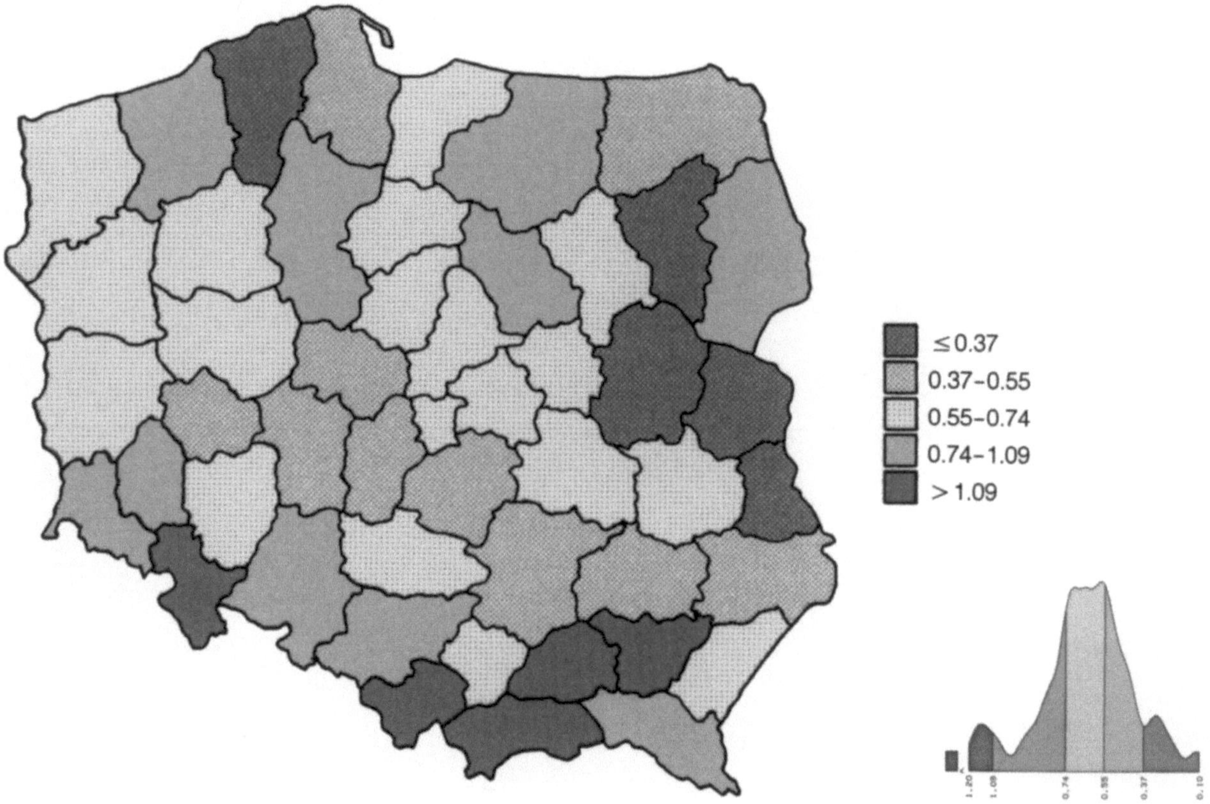
≤0.37
0.37–0.55
0.55–0.74
0.74–1.09
>1.09

0.95 - 1.19
0.71 - 0.95
0.48 - 0.71
0.24 - 0.48
0.0 - 0.24

1.19 - 1.46
0.92 - 1.19
0.65 - 0.92
0.38 - 0.65
0.11 - 0.38

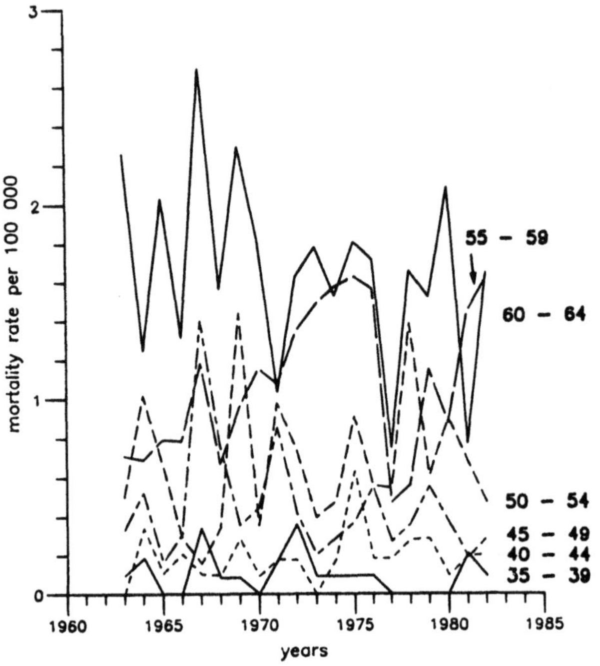

Temporal trend of mortality in individual age groups/men

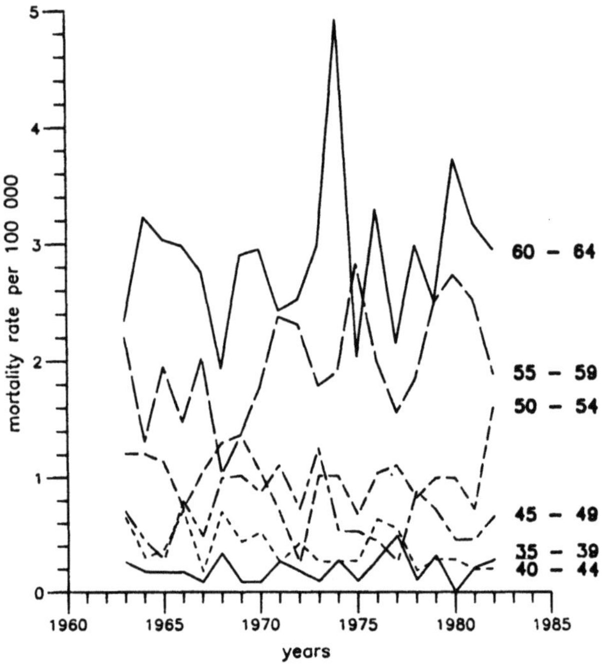

Temporal trend of mortality in individual age groups/women

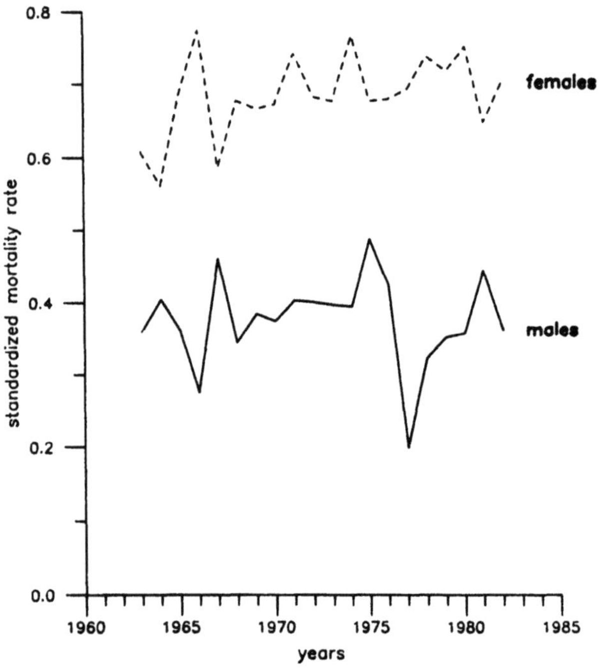

Temporal trend of the age-adjusted mortality rates for men and women

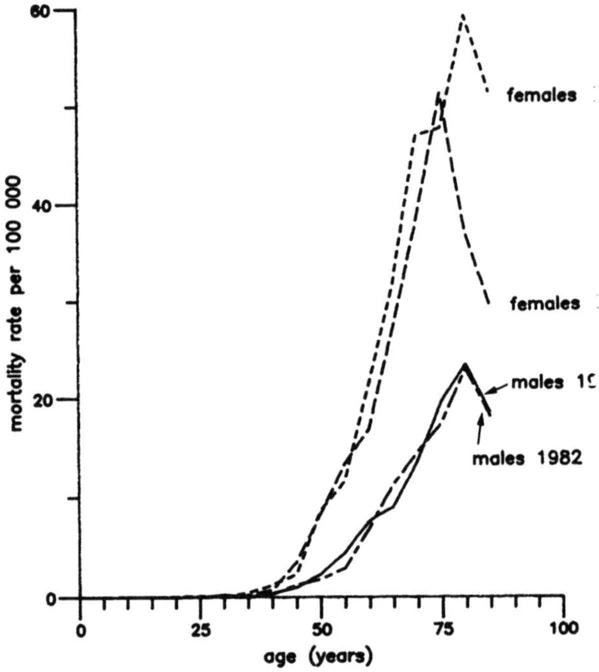

Mortality depending on age in two sample years for men and women

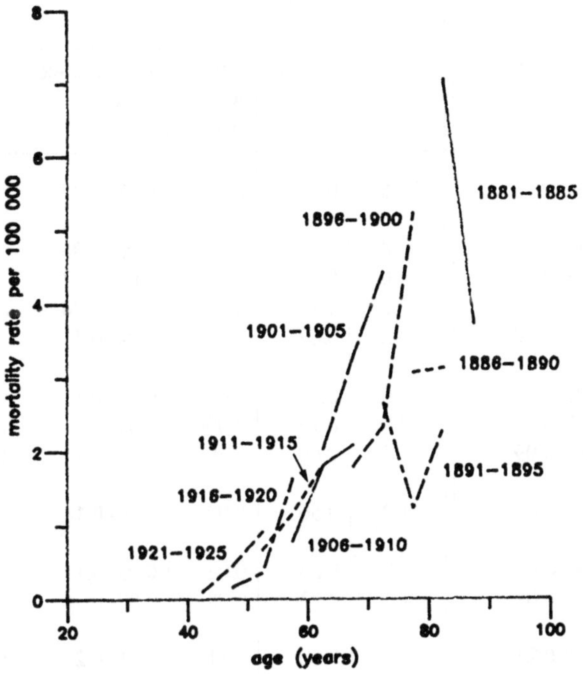

Age-dependent mortality in various birth cohorts/ men

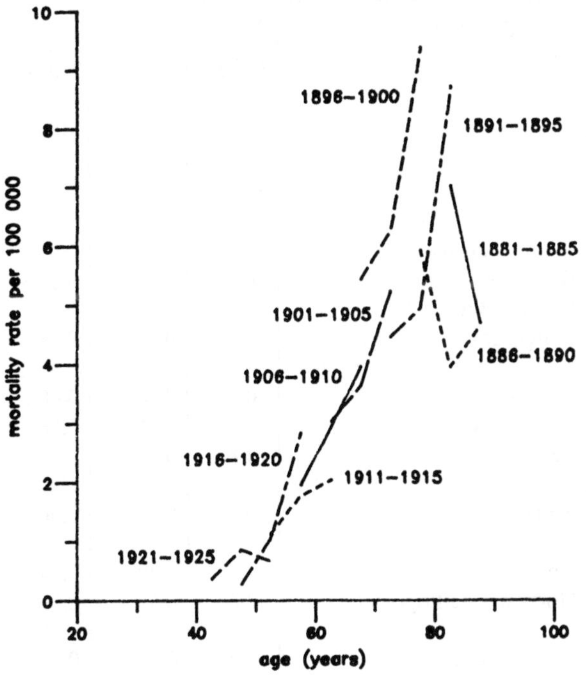

Age-dependent mortality in various birth cohorts/ women

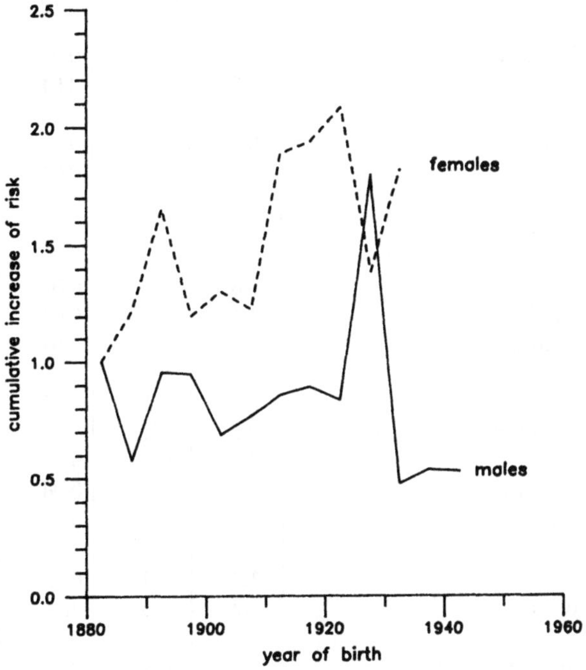

Ratios of the cumulative mortality rates for successive birth cohorts relative to the 1886–1890 cohort

Average Values 1975-1979	Males				Females			
	Cases	Stand. Mort. Rate	Cum. Mort. Rate	Confidence limits	Cases	Stand. Mort. Rate	Cum. Mort. Rate	Confidence limits
Poland	63.4	0.35	0.04	0.04-0.05	177.6	0.69	0.08	0.08-0.09
Biała Podlaska	0.2	0.13	0.01	0.00-0.04	0.8	0.33	0.02	0.00-0.06
Białystok	0.8	0.20	0.02	0.00-0.05	4.6	0.81	0.10	0.03-0.17
Bielsko Biała	0.8	0.17	0.03	0.00-0.08	8.0	1.46	0.16	0.08-0.24
Bydgoszcz	2.4	0.50	0.06	0.01-0.12	5.2	0.82	0.10	0.04-0.16
Chełm	0.6	0.46	0.08	0.00-0.19	0.6	0.31	0.04	0.00-0.11
Ciechanów	0.8	0.36	0.06	0.00-0.14	2.2	0.75	0.09	0.01-0.16
Częstochowa	1.8	0.44	0.05	0.00-0.09	3.6	0.60	0.09	0.03-0.14
Elbląg	0.2	0.07	0.00	0.00-0.02	1.2	0.56	0.09	0.00-0.18
Gdańsk	2.0	0.40	0.04	0.00-0.08	4.8	0.54	0.08	0.03-0.12
Gorzów Wielkopolski	0.8	0.35	0.03	0.00-0.08	1.6	0.73	0.08	0.00-0.16
Jelenia Góra	1.2	0.58	0.10	0.00-0.21	2.6	0.90	0.11	0.01-0.21
Kalisz	0.6	0.16	0.02	0.00-0.05	3.2	0.55	0.07	0.02-0.13
Katowice	6.6	0.38	0.05	0.03-0.08	19.8	0.74	0.10	0.07-0.13
Kielce	1.8	0.30	0.04	0.00-0.07	3.4	0.41	0.06	0.02-0.10
Konin	1.0	0.46	0.06	0.00-0.14	1.6	0.46	0.04	0.00-0.09
Koszalin	0.4	0.19	0.01	0.00-0.04	1.8	0.83	0.12	0.01-0.24
Kraków	2.6	0.48	0.05	0.01-0.09	5.6	0.57	0.07	0.02-0.11
Krosno	1.0	0.37	0.05	0.00-0.12	3.4	1.06	0.12	0.03-0.21
Legnica	0.6	0.31	0.05	0.00-0.13	2.0	0.95	0.14	0.02-0.27
Leszno	0.2	0.12	0.01	0.00-0.04	1.0	0.43	0.04	0.00-0.09
Lublin	1.2	0.23	0.03	0.00-0.07	4.6	0.71	0.09	0.04-0.14
Łomża	0.6	0.30	0.05	0.00-0.12	0.6	0.28	0.04	0.00-0.10
Łódź	1.0	0.15	0.01	0.00-0.03	6.0	0.66	0.07	0.03-0.11
Nowy Sącz	3.8	1.19	0.14	0.05-0.24	5.2	1.33	0.17	0.07-0.26
Olsztyn	0.6	0.20	0.02	0.00-0.06	2.8	0.86	0.10	0.01-0.18
Opole	1.4	0.33	0.03	0.00-0.07	4.4	0.75	0.11	0.05-0.18
Ostrołęka	0.8	0.40	0.03	0.00-0.07	1.6	0.62	0.07	0.00-0.15
Piła	0.4	0.15	0.02	0.00-0.07	1.8	0.60	0.09	0.00-0.17
Piotrków Trybunalski	0.6	0.22	0.02	0.00-0.05	2.4	0.49	0.08	0.01-0.14
Płock	0.6	0.20	0.02	0.00-0.04	2.0	0.62	0.05	0.00-0.11
Poznań	2.6	0.39	0.04	0.01-0.08	7.0	0.66	0.07	0.03-0.11
Przemyśl	1.2	0.68	0.09	0.00-0.19	2.8	0.74	0.11	0.02-0.19
Radom	1.4	0.37	0.03	0.00-0.07	3.4	0.66	0.09	0.03-0.15
Rzeszów	1.2	0.35	0.04	0.00-0.09	5.0	1.18	0.16	0.07-0.24
Siedlce	1.2	0.38	0.04	0.00-0.09	1.2	0.23	0.02	0.00-0.05
Sieradz	0.8	0.28	0.04	0.00-0.09	1.8	0.51	0.07	0.00-0.14
Skierniewice	0.4	0.16	0.03	0.00-0.08	2.2	0.64	0.08	0.00-0.16
Słupsk	0.2	0.12	0.02	0.00-0.05	0.2	0.11	0.02	0.00-0.07
Suwałki	0.4	0.20	0.02	0.00-0.06	1.4	0.53	0.05	0.00-0.11
Szczecin	0.8	0.25	0.03	0.00-0.07	3.2	0.67	0.06	0.01-0.12

Average Values 1975-1979	Males				Females			
	Cases	Stand. Mort. Rate	Cum. Mort. Rate	Confidence limits	Cases	Stand. Mort. Rate	Cum. Mort. Rate	Confidence limits
Tarnobrzeg	2.6	0.76	0.09	0.02-0.16	1.8	0.44	0.05	0.00-0.10
Tarnów	1.6	0.47	0.06	0.00-0.12	5.0	1.11	0.14	0.06-0.22
Toruń	0.6	0.17	0.04	0.00-0.10	2.4	0.57	0.05	0.00-0.11
Wałbrzych	1.6	0.48	0.07	0.00-0.14	5.0	1.15	0.15	0.05-0.24
Warszawa	4.8	0.40	0.04	0.01-0.07	15.6	0.72	0.08	0.05-0.11
Włocławek	0.0	0.00	0.00	0.00-0.00	1.8	0.56	0.08	0.00-0.16
Wrocław	2.0	0.44	0.07	0.00-0.13	4.8	0.71	0.06	0.01-0.11
Zamość	1.0	0.40	0.06	0.00-0.12	2.0	0.48	0.07	0.01-0.13
Zielona Góra	1.6	0.56	0.07	0.00-0.15	2.6	0.66	0.06	0.00-0.12

20 Non-Hodgkin's Lymphoma - ICD 200 and 202

The term "non-Hodgkin's lymphoma" covers the neoplasms of the lymphoreticular systems. The ASMR was 0.7 in 1963 and 1.1 in 1982 in men, while the respective figures for women were 0.4 and 0.4. The time trend for all age groups shows an increase in risk in the years 1963-1975, followed by a substantial decline during the years 1976-1982, which was similar, although in different ways, in both sexes. The 35-64 age group appears to have a similar time trend. Deaths from non-Hodgkin's lymphoma occur in childhood, after which its frequency declines a little until the age of 40-50 when there is another rise. The peak value in 1982 was about six deaths in men and three deaths in women, both sexes aged about 70.
In 1978 the highest European rates were found in Finland (4.3 in men and 2.1 in women). High-risk countries also included Norway (2.6 and 1.2, respectively) and the Netherlands (2.0, 1.2, respectively). For men alone, the Hungarians faced the lowest risk (0.2), followed by Sweden (0.6) and Greece (0.8). The risk was lowest for women in Iceland (0.0), Austria (0.3) and Hungary (0.3). With rates of 1.1 in men and 0.6 in women in 1978, Poland was a medium risk country.

Analysis of Data from the Provinces, 1975-1979

Non-Hodgkin's lymphoma was 2.2 times more frequent among men than among women. The urban/rural ratio was 1.3 for men and 1.2 for women.

Men

(Mean ASMR=1.2, Range 0.2-2.3, Standard Deviation 0.4; 0.9% of Male Cancer Mortality, Rank 19)

The highest mortaliy rate was 12.7 times greater than the lowest. Provinces with the highest rates were Lublin (2.29), Biala Podlaska (2.14), Zielona Gora (1.99), Gdansk (1.92) and Wroclaw (1.91). Provinces with the lowest rates were Suwalki (0.18), Ciechanow (0.43), Siedlce (0.44), Piotrkow (0.66) and Radom (0.70). Provinces with low mortality rates form a compact area in the eastern part of central Poland. Higher risk is found mainly in western Poland but also in the two southeastern provinces of Lublin and Biala Podlaska which belong to the group with the highest risk.

Women

(Mean ASMR=0.6, Range 0.1-1.3, Standard Deviation 0.3; 0.5% of Female Cancer Mortality, Rank 28)

The highest value was 12.1 times greater than the lowest. Provinces with the highest rates were Pila (1.33), Konin (1.24), Gdansk (1.13), Chelm (1.00) and Wroclaw (0.86). Provinces with the lowest rates were Ciechanow (0.11), Tarnow (0.13), Bialystok (0.20), Plock (0.22) and Wloclawek (0.26). The geographical distribution pattern is less distinct than in men. The lowest mortality rates were found in eastern and central Poland. Provinces with the highest rates were scattered over the whole country.

Comments

Non-Hodgkin's lymphoma is a heterogenous group of tumours. The mortality/age curves show a typical bimodal shape (Green 1982). Little is known about the aetiology of this group of tumours. The disease is connected with immune deficiency syndromes (Gatti and Good 1971), especially the acquired immune deficiency syndrome (AIDS) (Ziegler et al. 1984) or with therapy (Kinlen 1979). Other hypothetical risk factors include ionising radiation, chemicals (medicine) and occupational exposure (Green 1982).
Many countries have an increase in the incidence (CIFC 1982) and mortality rates for this tumour (Stalsberg 1973; Abramson 1975). Poland also had a rapid increase in the mortality rate, especially in men, in 1963-1975. The rate of increase was among the highest for all cancer sites, just as in the United

States where the rate of increase ranks very high (Cantor and Fraumeni 1980). The decline in the mortality rate noted after 1975 may be an effect of improved treatment. Non-Hodgkin's lymphoma is more frequent in men than in women (2.2 times) which is also similar to other countries (Greene 1982). The disease occurs 20%-30% more often in urban populations.

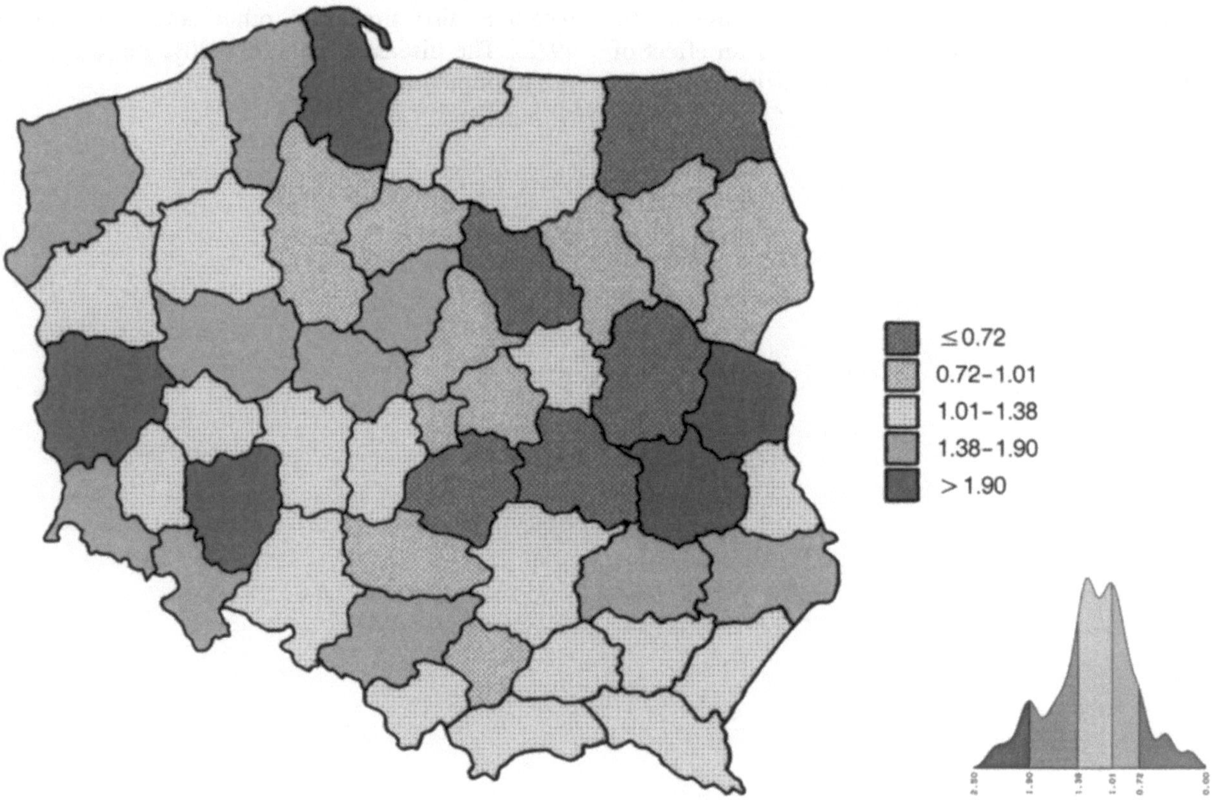
≤0.72
0.72–1.01
1.01–1.38
1.38–1.90
>1.90

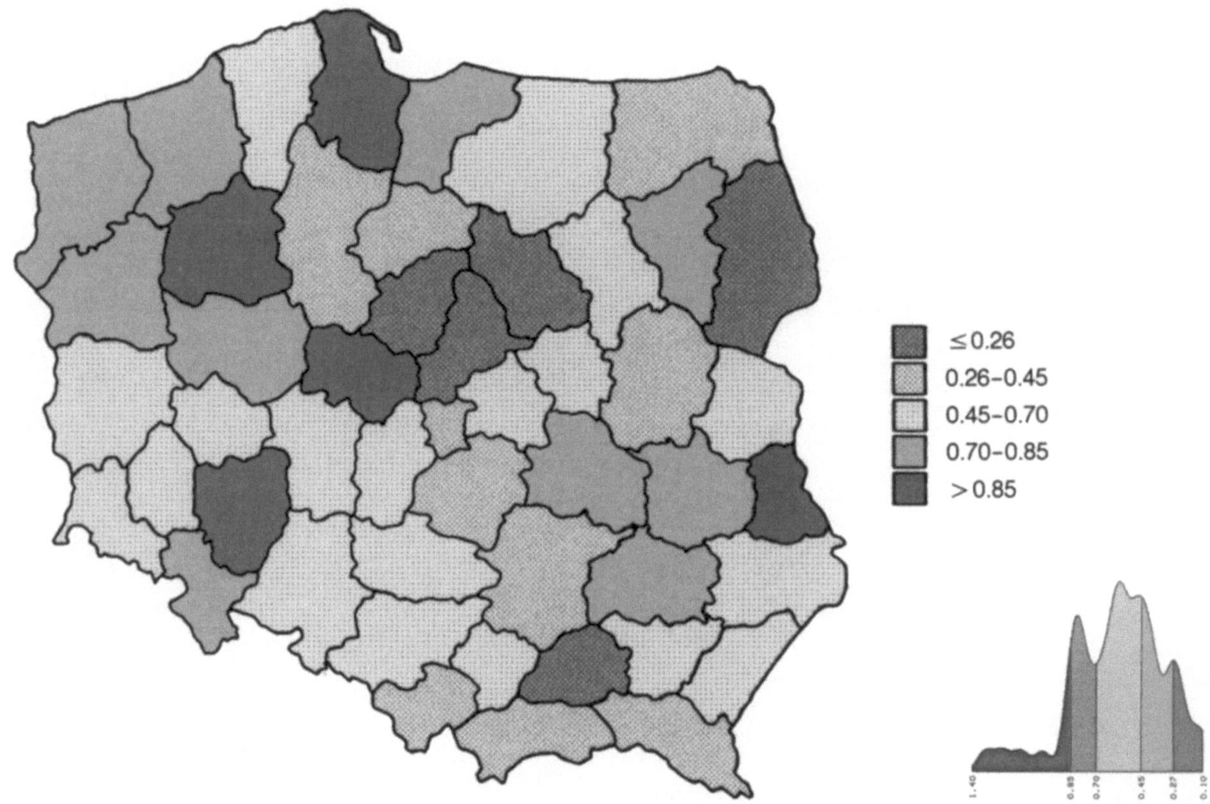
≤0.26
0.26–0.45
0.45–0.70
0.70–0.85
>0.85

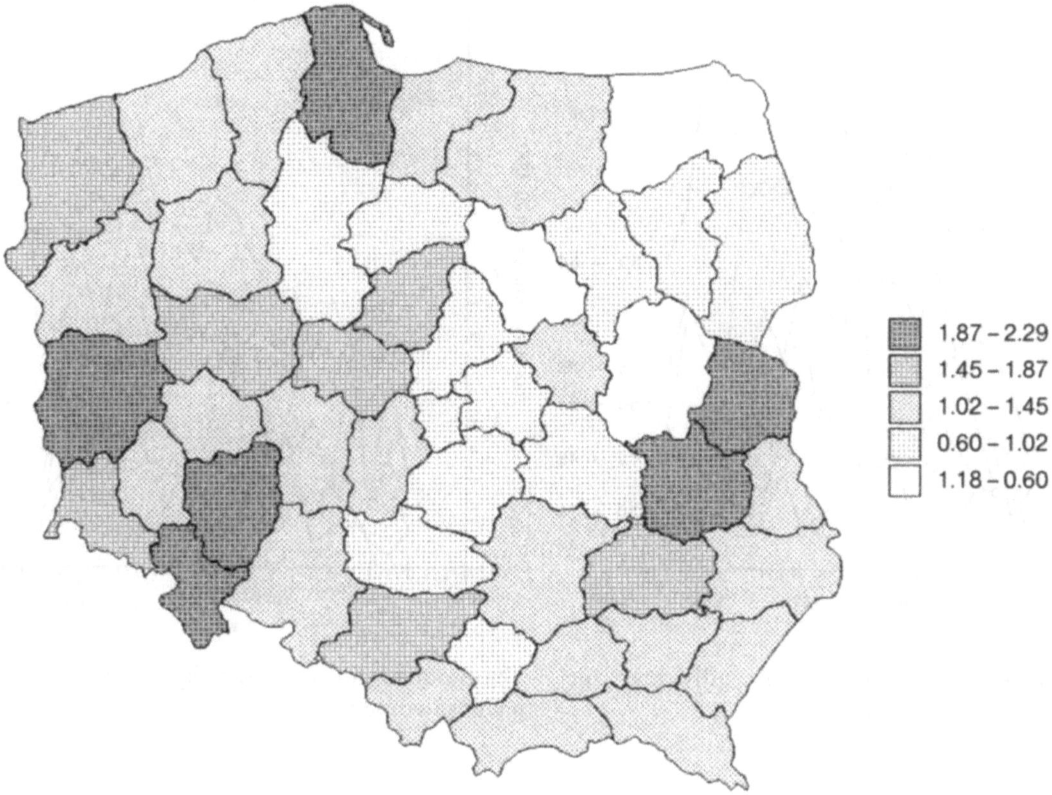
1.87 – 2.29
1.45 – 1.87
1.02 – 1.45
0.60 – 1.02
1.18 – 0.60

1.09 – 1.33
0.84 – 1.09
0.60 – 0.84
0.35 – 0.60
0.11 – 0.35

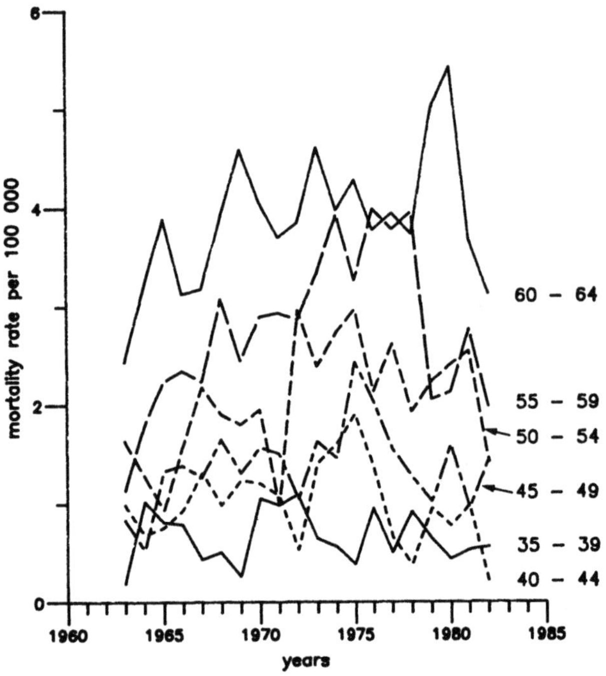

Temporal trend of mortality in individual age groups/men

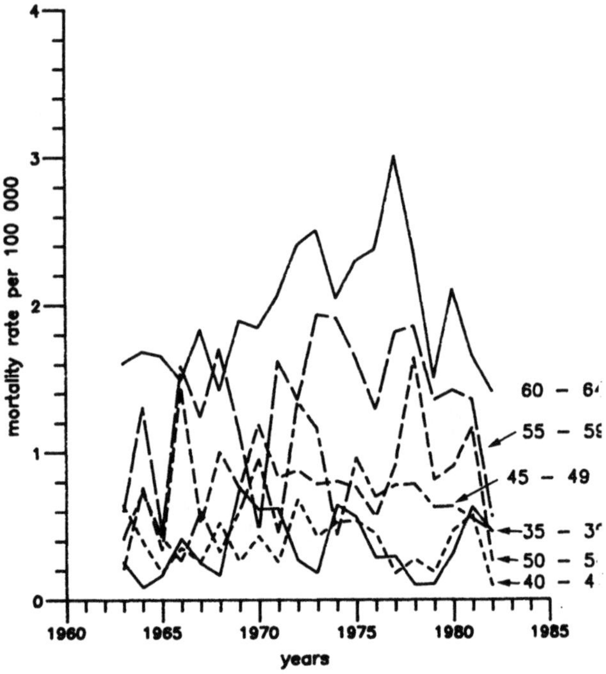

Temporal trend of mortality in individual age groups/women

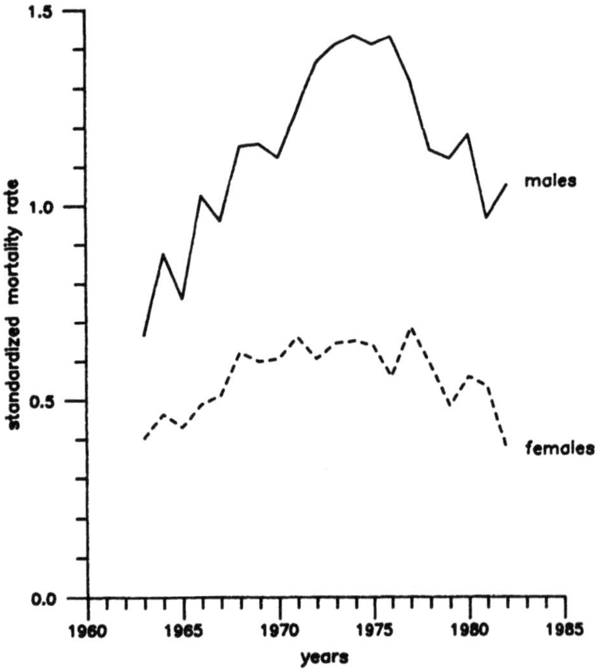

Temporal trend of the age-adjusted mortality rates for men and women

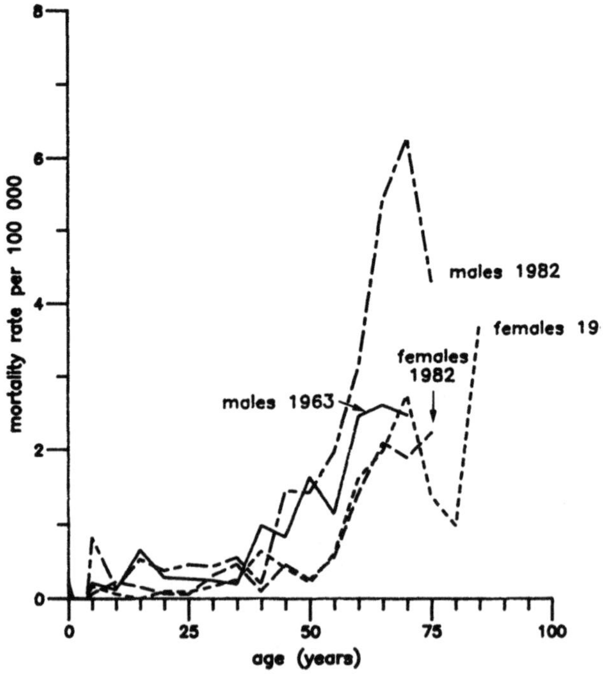

Mortality depending on age in two sample years for men and women

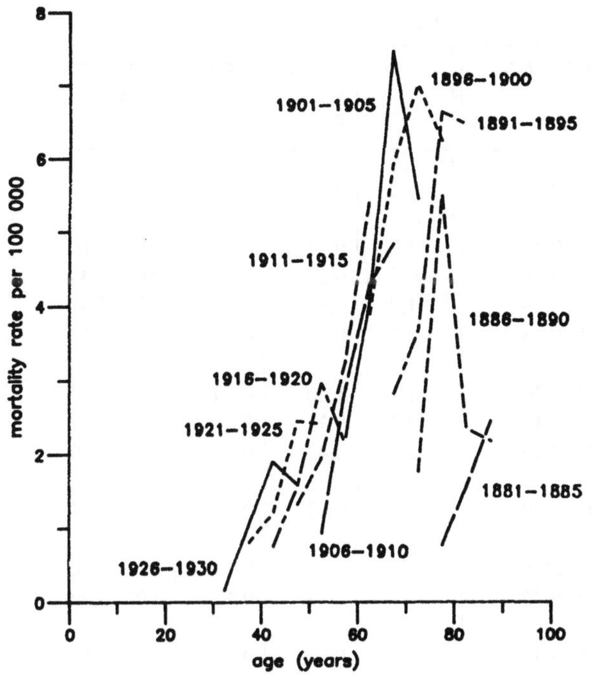

Age-dependent mortality in various birth cohorts/ men

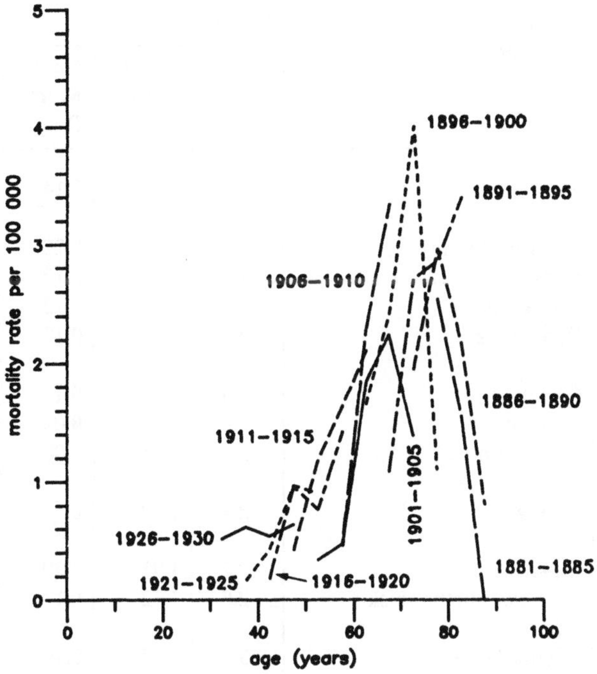

Age-dependent mortality in various birth cohorts/ women

Average Values 1975-1979	Males				Females			
	Cases	Stand. Mort. Rate	Cum. Mort. Rate	Confidence limits	Cases	Stand. Mort. Rate	Cum. Mort. Rate	Confidence limits
Poland	221.6	1.27	0.14	0.13-0.15	127.0	0.59	0.07	0.06-0.07
Biała Podlaska	3.0	2.14	0.22	0.06-0.37	1.2	0.51	0.08	0.00-0.16
Białystok	3.0	0.96	0.12	0.03-0.20	0.8	0.20	0.02	0.00-0.05
Bielsko Biała	4.2	1.03	0.12	0.04-0.19	1.8	0.42	0.04	0.00-0.07
Bydgoszcz	5.0	0.91	0.12	0.05-0.18	2.2	0.39	0.04	0.00-0.07
Chełm	1.4	1.17	0.13	0.00-0.26	1.4	1.00	0.10	0.00-0.20
Ciechanów	0.8	0.43	0.04	0.00-0.10	0.2	0.11	0.01	0.00-0.02
Częstochowa	3.2	0.81	0.08	0.02-0.14	2.0	0.45	0.05	0.01-0.10
Elbląg	2.4	1.20	0.16	0.02-0.30	1.8	0.83	0.11	0.00-0.21
Gdańsk	12.2	1.92	0.20	0.12-0.28	8.6	1.13	0.14	0.08-0.20
Gorzów Wielkopolski	2.8	1.32	0.13	0.03-0.22	1.8	0.78	0.10	0.00-0.20
Jelenia Góra	3.8	1.77	0.19	0.06-0.31	1.8	0.66	0.08	0.00-0.16
Kalisz	3.6	1.07	0.10	0.03-0.16	2.0	0.49	0.05	0.01-0.09
Katowice	27.6	1.67	0.20	0.15-0.25	15.4	0.70	0.08	0.06-0.11
Kielce	7.2	1.30	0.13	0.07-0.19	2.6	0.37	0.04	0.01-0.07
Konin	3.6	1.60	0.19	0.07-0.32	3.2	1.24	0.17	0.06-0.28
Koszalin	2.0	1.06	0.11	0.00-0.22	1.8	0.70	0.08	0.00-0.16
Kraków	5.4	0.94	0.09	0.04-0.14	3.8	0.58	0.05	0.02-0.09
Krosno	2.4	1.05	0.10	0.02-0.19	0.8	0.32	0.04	0.00-0.09
Legnica	2.6	1.30	0.13	0.02-0.24	1.4	0.62	0.07	0.00-0.14
Leszno	2.2	1.25	0.09	0.01-0.18	1.4	0.57	0.07	0.00-0.15
Lublin	10.6	2.29	0.24	0.14-0.34	4.6	0.80	0.09	0.04-0.14
Łomża	1.8	0.78	0.07	0.00-0.15	1.6	0.84	0.08	0.00-0.16
Łódź	5.6	0.92	0.10	0.04-0.15	3.4	0.45	0.04	0.01-0.07
Nowy Sącz	3.6	1.37	0.13	0.04-0.22	1.8	0.40	0.05	0.00-0.11
Olsztyn	3.6	1.29	0.15	0.04-0.25	1.6	0.48	0.04	0.00-0.09
Opole	5.4	1.29	0.16	0.07-0.25	3.4	0.60	0.07	0.02-0.12
Ostrołęka	1.4	0.73	0.07	0.00-0.14	1.2	0.56	0.06	0.00-0.13
Piła	2.8	1.23	0.16	0.03-0.29	3.2	1.33	0.15	0.05-0.25
Piotrków Trybunalski	2.0	0.66	0.06	0.00-0.12	1.6	0.40	0.05	0.00-0.09
Płock	2.4	0.95	0.09	0.01-0.16	0.6	0.22	0.02	0.00-0.05
Poznań	9.4	1.51	0.19	0.11-0.27	6.2	0.83	0.09	0.05-0.14
Przemyśl	2.4	1.08	0.13	0.03-0.23	1.6	0.62	0.07	0.01-0.14
Radom	2.8	0.70	0.08	0.01-0.14	3.6	0.84	0.09	0.03-0.15
Rzeszów	3.8	1.32	0.16	0.06-0.27	2.0	0.57	0.06	0.01-0.11
Siedlce	1.4	0.44	0.04	0.00-0.08	1.2	0.27	0.03	0.00-0.07
Sieradz	2.4	1.21	0.12	0.03-0.20	1.6	0.47	0.07	0.00-0.14
Skierniewice	1.8	0.89	0.08	0.01-0.15	1.4	0.59	0.05	0.00-0.10
Słupsk	2.4	1.39	0.13	0.01-0.25	1.4	0.66	0.08	0.00-0.18
Suwałki	0.4	0.18	0.01	0.00-0.03	0.6	0.27	0.02	0.00-0.04
Szczecin	6.2	1.65	0.18	0.08-0.27	3.4	0.79	0.09	0.02-0.16

Average Values 1975-1979	Males				Females			
	Cases	Stand. Mort. Rate	Cum. Mort. Rate	Confidence limits	Cases	Stand. Mort. Rate	Cum. Mort. Rate	Confidence limits
Tarnobrzeg	4.6	1.52	0.18	0.07-0.28	2.4	0.73	0.08	0.01-0.14
Tarnów	3.0	1.04	0.11	0.03-0.20	0.4	0.13	0.02	0.00-0.05
Toruń	2.8	0.99	0.09	0.02-0.17	1.2	0.28	0.04	0.00-0.09
Wałbrzych	6.6	1.89	0.22	0.10-0.34	2.6	0.79	0.08	0.02-0.14
Warszawa	12.4	1.11	0.12	0.07-0.16	9.6	0.55	0.07	0.04-0.10
Włocławek	3.0	1.46	0.15	0.04-0.25	0.6	0.26	0.03	0.00-0.07
Wrocław	9.4	1.91	0.22	0.12-0.32	5.2	0.86	0.10	0.04-0.16
Zamość	4.0	1.40	0.16	0.06-0.26	1.6	0.52	0.06	0.00-0.11
Zielona Góra	5.2	1.99	0.19	0.08-0.30	1.4	0.45	0.05	0.00-0.10

21 Hodgkin's Disease - ICD 201

Hodgkin's disease is a neoplasm that affects the lymphatic tissue of the body. The ASMR for Hodgkin's disease in men was 1.8 in 1963 and 1.4 in 1982, while the respective figures for women were 0.7 and 0.9. Men had slightly higher mortality rates in the period 1963-1969, but these remained unchanged in the years 1970-1982. The women's mortality rate did not change during the study period. The frequency of deaths from Hodgkin's disease increases after the first years of life. The mortality/age curve is hard to evaluate because of the small number of cases, but it seems to reveal the first peak about the age of 30, and then, after a decline, the frequency increases again. In 1982, the peak for men was 5 cases and for women 3 cases per 100000. The picture of mortality in individual age groups is hard to interpret because of the small number of cases.
In 1978 Switzerland had the highest European mortality rate for Hodgkin's disease in men and women, 3.2 and 2.3, respectively. Yugoslavia had similar rates with 3.2 for men and 1.8 for women. The lowest rates for men were reported in Bulgaria (0.3), Hungary (0.5), Scotland (0.8), Denmark (0.9). The lowest rates for women were in Iceland (0.3), Hungary (0.3), Northern Ireland (0.4) and Denmark (0.5). With a rate of 1.4 for men and 0.6 for women in 1978, Poland was a country with a medium risk of Hodgkin's disease.

Analysis of Data from the Provinces, 1975-1979

Hodgkin's disease caused a greater number of deaths in rural men over the period 1975-1979 than in men living in towns (urban/rural ratio 0.9), while there was no difference in women. The disease was 2.3 times more frequent in men than in women.

Men

(Mean ASMR = 1.4, Range 0.6-2.3, Standard Deviation 0.4; 0.8% of Male Cancer Mortality, Rank 18)

The highest mortality rate was 3.9 times greater than the lowest. Provinces with the highest rates were Wloclawek (2.32), Bydgoszcz (2.25), Leszno (2.25), Pila (2.08) and Legnica (2.04). Provinces with the lowest rates were Chelm (0.60), Sieradz (0.61), Lomza (0.79), Krosno (0.93) and Tarnow (0.99).
The central part of western Poland was found to have a high mortality rate for Hodgkin's disease. Low-risk regions do not form compact clusters but, in general terms, the rates are somewhat lower in the east.

Women

(Mean ASMR = 0.6, Range 0.2-1.2, Standard Deviation 0.2; 0.5% of Female Cancer Mortality, Rank 27)

The highest value was 6.5 times greater than the lowest. Hodgkin's disease is relatively rare in women. Provinces with the highest rates were Biala Podlaska (1.24), Legnica (1.16), Wroclaw (0.99), Sieradz (0.89) and Bydgoszcz (0.86). Provinces with the lowest rates were Suwalki (0.19), Kielce (0.31), Przemysl (0.32), Ostroleka (0.35) and Tarnobrzeg (0.36). There is no distinct geographical distribution pattern in women, but there seems to be a higher risk in western provinces. Eastern Poland mostly has rates below the national average. The provinces of Biala Podlaska, Chelm, Przemysl and Warszawa are exceptions.

Comments

Little is known about the aetiology of Hodgkin's disease. Epidemiological observations allow us tc distinguish three separate disorders: one typical ir childhood (1-14 years), one in young adults (15-34) and one in older adults (55 and over) (Gruffermar 1982). Infectious agents are suspected of playing some role in Hodgkin's disease (Vianna and Polar 1973). Previous infection with mononucleosis is a risk factor in this disease (Munoz et al. 1978). Some studies suggest a connection between this disease and occupational exposure in the timber industry and to certain chemicals (Olsson and Brandt 1979). Hodgkin's disease is rare in Poland, and, as in other countries, there have been no major changes in the mortality rates over the past 20 years. It is more frequent in men than in women, which is another similarity with other countries (Correa 1977). The shape of the mortality/age curve is different from country to country (Correa 1971). The frequency of Hodgkin's disease increases quite considerably starting from the 1st year of life. Comparisons of incidence data reported by Polish cancer registers also show that the childhood groups have a fairly high frequency of this disease (Koszarowski et al. 1977; Correa 1971). An analysis of the mortality/age curve based on a greater number of cases over several years shows the evidently bimodal character with a peak about the age group of 30-35, followed by a decline and another increase from the age of 50. The geographical pattern of Hodgkin's disease is marked by lower risk in the east and higher risk in the Poznan region and Lower Silesia. The lack of knowledge about the risk factors offers no basis for discussion of the epidemiological pattern of the disease in Poland.

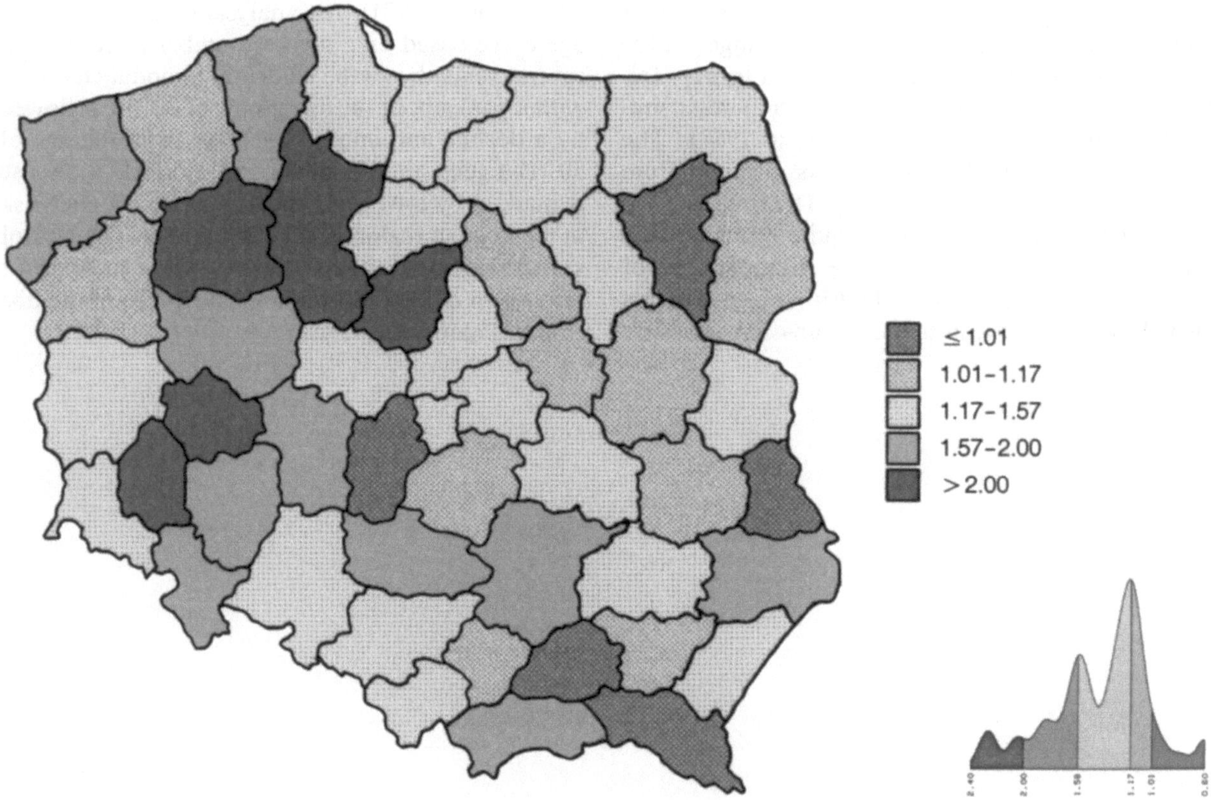
≤1.01
1.01–1.17
1.17–1.57
1.57–2.00
>2.00

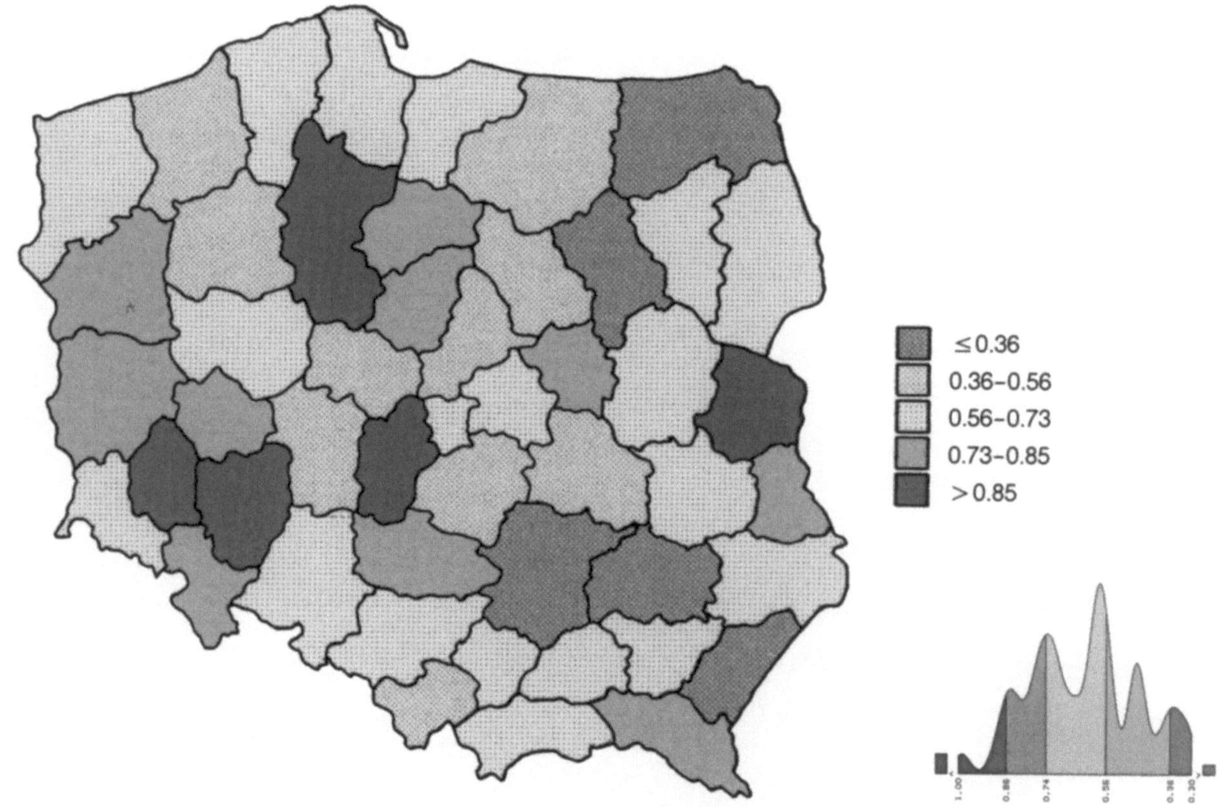
≤0.36
0.36–0.56
0.56–0.73
0.73–0.85
>0.85

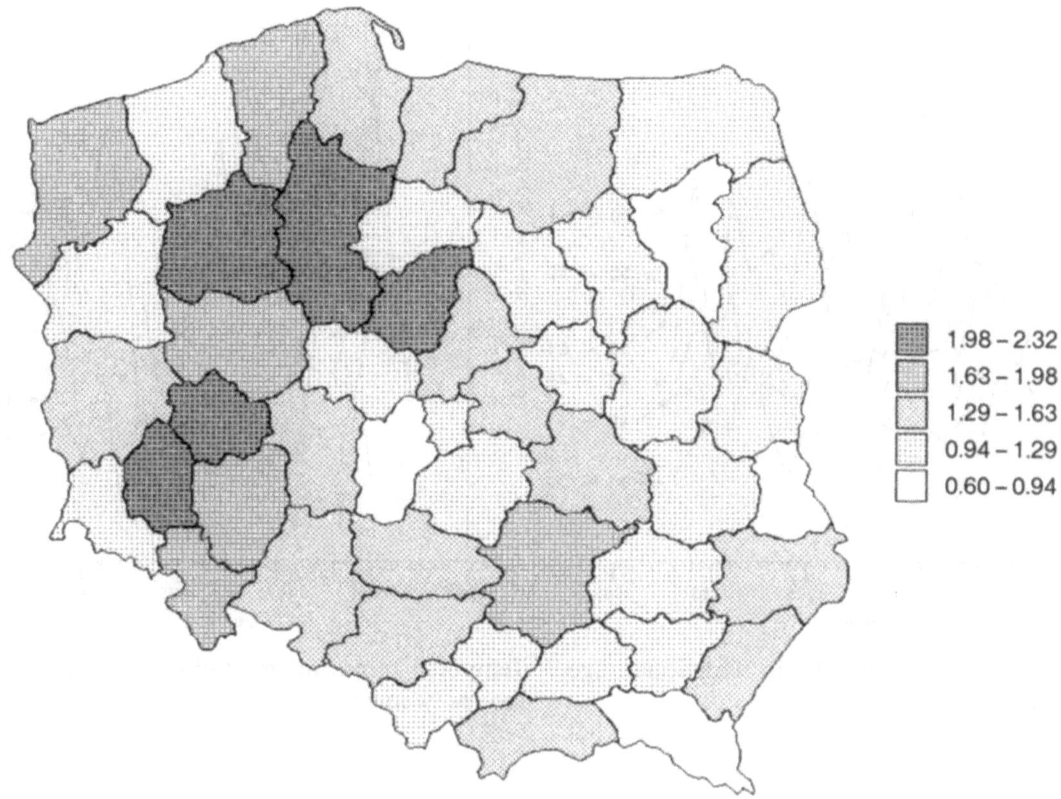
1.98 – 2.32
1.63 – 1.98
1.29 – 1.63
0.94 – 1.29
0.60 – 0.94

1.03 – 1.24
0.82 – 1.03
0.61 – 0.82
0.40 – 0.61
0.19 – 0.40

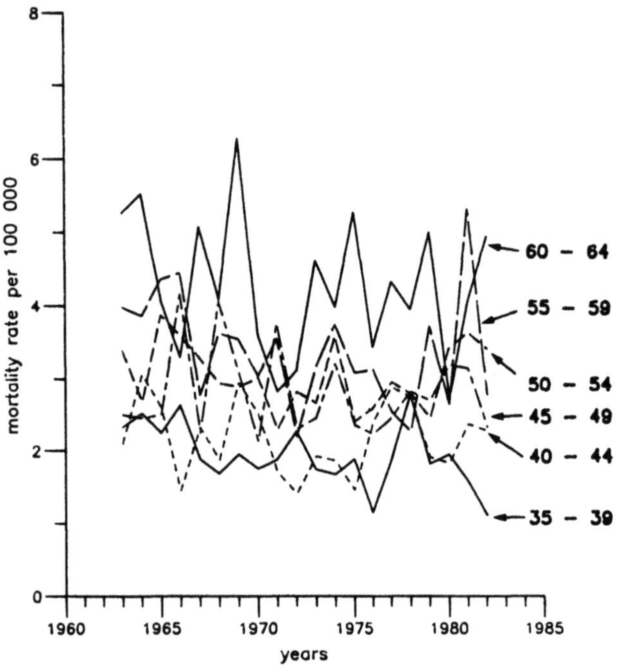

Temporal trend of mortality in individual age groups/men

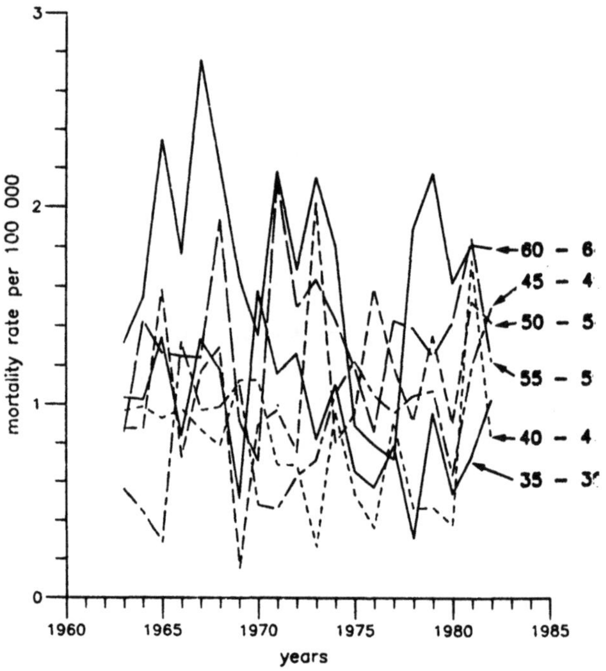

Temporal trend of mortality in individual age groups/women

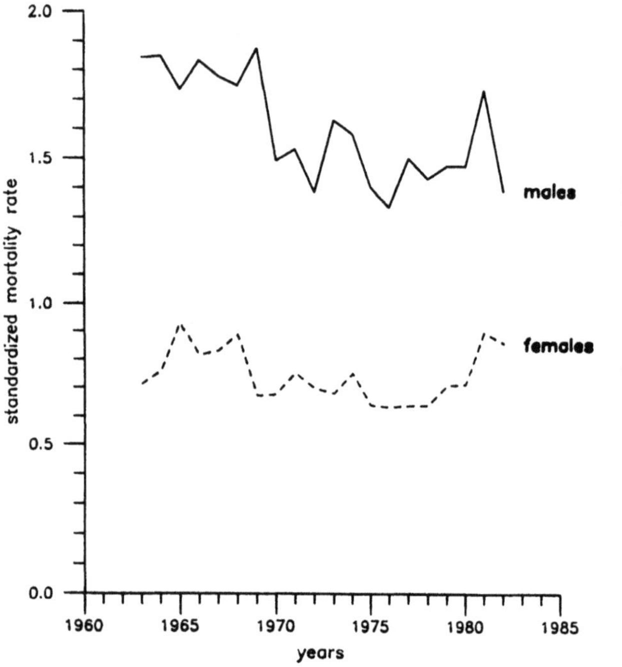

Temporal trend of the age-adjusted mortality rates for men and women

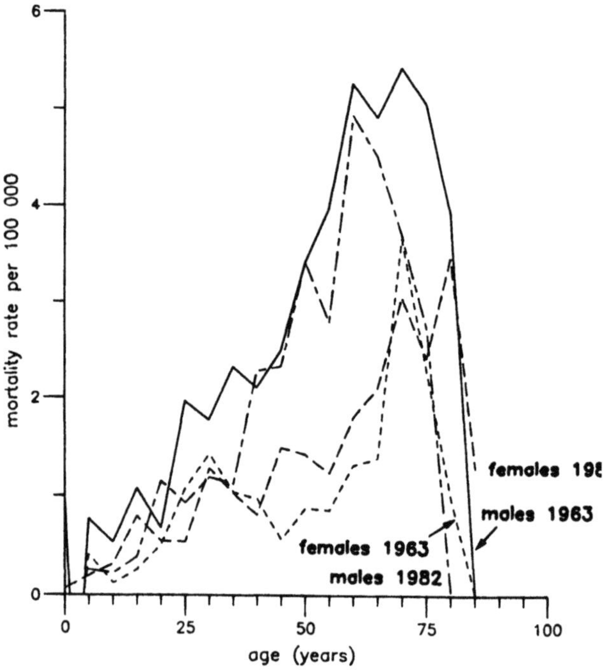

Mortality depending on age in two sample years for men and women

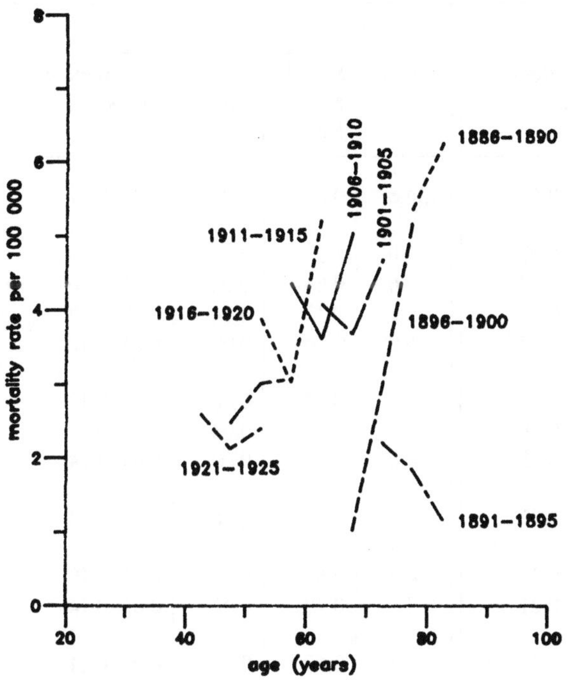

Age-dependent mortality in various birth cohorts/ men

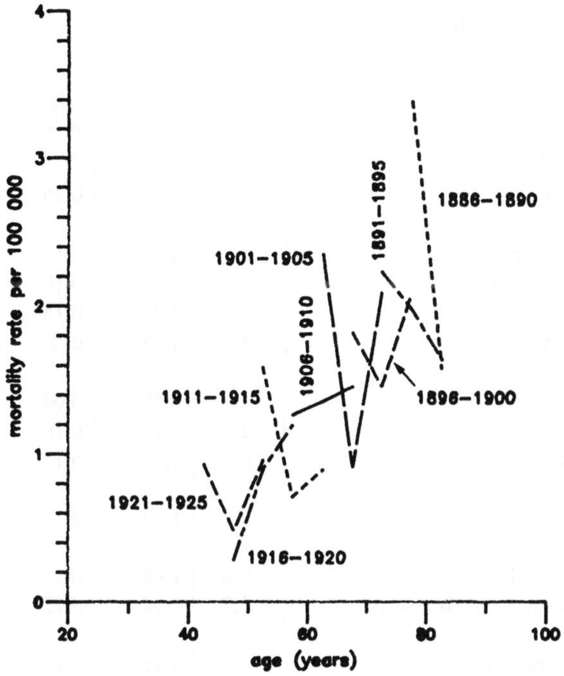

Age-dependent mortality in various birth cohorts/ women

Average Values 1975-1979	Males				Females			
	Cases	Stand. Mort. Rate	Cum. Mort. Rate	Confidence limits	Cases	Stand. Mort. Rate	Cum. Mort. Rate	Confidence limits
Poland	253.0	1.43	0.15	0.13-0.16	134.6	0.64	0.06	0.06-0.07
Biała Podlaska	2.0	1.25	0.15	0.02-0.27	2.0	1.24	0.10	0.01-0.18
Białystok	3.8	1.03	0.10	0.03-0.17	2.6	0.61	0.06	0.01-0.10
Bielsko Biała	4.8	1.23	0.13	0.05-0.20	2.0	0.37	0.04	0.00-0.08
Bydgoszcz	11.0	2.25	0.24	0.14-0.33	5.0	0.86	0.08	0.03-0.12
Chełm	0.8	0.60	0.04	0.00-0.09	1.2	0.77	0.08	0.00-0.17
Ciechanów	2.4	1.11	0.10	0.02-0.18	1.0	0.45	0.04	0.00-0.10
Częstochowa	6.4	1.60	0.17	0.09-0.25	4.2	0.81	0.09	0.03-0.14
Elbląg	3.2	1.54	0.13	0.04-0.22	1.4	0.58	0.06	0.00-0.13
Gdańsk	9.2	1.48	0.15	0.08-0.22	4.8	0.66	0.06	0.03-0.10
Gorzów Wielkopolski	2.2	1.14	0.12	0.02-0.21	2.0	0.79	0.07	0.01-0.14
Jelenia Góra	2.6	1.23	0.15	0.02-0.27	1.6	0.60	0.05	0.00-0.11
Kalisz	5.4	1.61	0.17	0.08-0.25	2.0	0.47	0.05	0.01-0.10
Katowice	27.4	1.49	0.15	0.11-0.19	13.4	0.63	0.07	0.04-0.09
Kielce	10.4	1.95	0.20	0.12-0.27	1.8	0.31	0.02	0.00-0.04
Konin	2.8	1.21	0.14	0.03-0.25	1.0	0.40	0.04	0.00-0.09
Koszalin	2.4	1.14	0.10	0.01-0.18	1.2	0.47	0.04	0.00-0.09
Kraków	6.8	1.16	0.11	0.06-0.17	4.0	0.59	0.06	0.02-0.10
Krosno	2.0	0.93	0.10	0.01-0.20	2.0	0.84	0.08	0.01-0.15
Legnica	4.2	2.04	0.20	0.06-0.35	2.8	1.16	0.12	0.02-0.22
Leszno	4.2	2.25	0.22	0.08-0.35	1.6	0.74	0.09	0.00-0.17
Lublin	5.4	1.14	0.12	0.06-0.19	3.0	0.57	0.05	0.02-0.09
Łomża	1.4	0.79	0.06	0.00-0.13	1.0	0.71	0.05	0.00-0.12
Łódź	7.0	1.18	0.10	0.05-0.15	3.8	0.58	0.05	0.02-0.09
Nowy Sącz	4.4	1.58	0.14	0.05-0.23	1.8	0.56	0.05	0.00-0.10
Olsztyn	4.2	1.35	0.13	0.04-0.22	1.8	0.47	0.04	0.00-0.08
Opole	6.2	1.36	0.14	0.06-0.22	4.0	0.73	0.07	0.02-0.11
Ostrołęka	2.2	1.21	0.12	0.01-0.22	1.0	0.35	0.05	0.00-0.11
Piła	4.4	2.08	0.22	0.09-0.35	1.2	0.46	0.07	0.00-0.15
Piotrków Trybunalski	3.6	1.07	0.12	0.04-0.20	2.2	0.55	0.06	0.01-0.10
Płock	3.2	1.30	0.13	0.04-0.22	1.6	0.56	0.05	0.00-0.09
Poznań	11.8	1.84	0.19	0.12-0.26	5.0	0.66	0.07	0.03-0.11
Przemyśl	2.8	1.51	0.17	0.05-0.29	0.8	0.32	0.04	0.00-0.08
Radom	5.6	1.56	0.15	0.07-0.23	2.0	0.47	0.04	0.00-0.08
Rzeszów	4.0	1.12	0.11	0.04-0.18	2.2	0.59	0.05	0.01-0.10
Siedlce	3.8	1.16	0.13	0.05-0.21	2.6	0.72	0.07	0.02-0.11
Sieradz	1.4	0.61	0.08	0.00-0.16	2.2	0.89	0.09	0.01-0.16
Skierniewice	2.8	1.37	0.12	0.03-0.21	1.2	0.56	0.05	0.00-0.11
Słupsk	3.0	1.73	0.17	0.04-0.29	1.4	0.68	0.06	0.00-0.13
Suwałki	2.4	1.28	0.14	0.02-0.26	0.4	0.19	0.02	0.00-0.06
Szczecin	7.2	1.85	0.20	0.09-0.32	3.2	0.70	0.07	0.01-0.13

Average Values 1975-1979	Males				Females			
	Cases	Stand. Mort. Rate	Cum. Mort. Rate	Confidence limits	Cases	Stand. Mort. Rate	Cum. Mort. Rate	Confidence limits
Tarnobrzeg	3.6	1.23	0.13	0.05-0.21	1.2	0.36	0.03	0.00-0.07
Tarnów	2.6	0.99	0.11	0.02-0.19	2.0	0.59	0.06	0.01-0.12
Toruń	3.8	1.29	0.15	0.05-0.24	3.0	0.83	0.09	0.03-0.15
Wałbrzych	6.6	1.80	0.17	0.08-0.27	3.4	0.76	0.07	0.02-0.13
Warszawa	14.0	1.15	0.13	0.08-0.17	11.6	0.74	0.08	0.05-0.10
Włocławek	4.8	2.32	0.23	0.10-0.36	2.4	0.85	0.09	0.01-0.16
Wrocław	8.0	1.69	0.19	0.10-0.29	6.2	0.99	0.10	0.05-0.15
Zamość	4.4	1.62	0.15	0.06-0.24	2.2	0.71	0.08	0.02-0.14
Zielona Góra	4.4	1.57	0.16	0.06-0.26	2.6	0.76	0.09	0.02-0.15

22 Leukaemias - ICD 204–207

The ASMR for leukaemias in 1963 was 4.8 for men and 3.5 for women, while the respective figures for 1982 were 5.8 and 3.7. A slight increase was observed in the frequency of deaths from leukaemias, especially in men, caused by the substantial increase in the mortality of people aged 55 and over. Having peaked in the first years of life, the age-specific mortality rates decline until the age of 20–30 years, and then a nearly exponential increase begins. The men's highest value in 1982 was 40 deaths per 100000 and 19 per 100000 women aged 80.
The highest mortality rates for men in European countries were recorded in Czechoslovakia (7.5), France (7.1) and Finland (7.1); the lowest in Spain (4.7), and Bulgaria (4.7). Women had the highest mortality rates in Sweden (4.6), Czechoslovakia (4.6), Greece, Norway and Denmark (4.5 each), and the lowest in Luxembourg (2.6) and Iceland (3.3). Outside Europe, high values were found in Israel (7.3 for men and 6.9 for women) and also in Costa Rica (7.0 and 5.6, respectively). With rates of 5.5 for men and 3.9 for women, Poland was among the countries with a medium risk of leukaemias.

Analysis of Data from the Provinces, 1975–1979

Leukaemias were more frequent among men than among women (ratio 1.5). They occurred almost as frequently in urban populations as in rural communities (ratios 1.1 for men and 1.0 for women).

Men

(Mean ASMR = 5.5, Range 3.9–7.7, Standard Deviation 0.8; 3.3% of Male Cancer Mortality, Rank 8)

The highest mortality rate of the individual provinces was twice as high as the lowest. Provinces with the highest rates were Tarnow (7.69), Przemysl (7.28), Warszawa (7.06), Torun (6.94) and Biala Podlaska (6.53). Provinces with the lowest rates were Chelm (3.85), Gorzow (3.87), Sieradz (3.97), Piotrkow (4.42) and Leszno (4.53). The mortality rate for leukaemias did not form a geographical distribution, with high-risk provinces scattered among the low-risk ones.

Women

(Mean ASMR = 3.7, Range 2.6–5.6, Standard Deviation 0.6; 3.2% of Female Cancer Mortality, Rank 12)

The highest rate was 2.1 times higher rate than the lowest. Provinces with the highest rates were Lomza (5.61), Zamosc (4.87), Gdansk (4.59), Zielona Gora (4.54) and Slupsk (4.53). Provinces with the lowest rates were Sieradz (2.62), Ostroleka (2.75), Ciechanow (2.89), Bydgoszcz (2.99) and Walbrzych (3.00). As in the case of men, the mortality rate shows no particular geographical distribution pattern.

Comments

Leukaemia is a group of neoplastic diseases with the common feature that all of them arise from different cell systems circulating in peripheral blood, arising, however, in large part, from common stem cells in the bone marrow. The different cell origins of the leukaemias makes it necessary to consider the different leukaemic types separately in terms of aetiology, prognosis and therapy. Leukaemias are probably caused by a wide range of factors. Apart from genetic factors, it seems that environmental factors, such as ionising radiation, chemicals and infectious agents, play a role in the aetiology of this disease. The risk increase stems primarily from heavy exposure to ionising radiation or from nuclear radiation (Beebe 1978). The role of occupational exposure to benzene in the aetiology of leukaemia has been discussed for many years. Studies by McMichael et al. (1975) seem to confirm the existence of such a connection. Other chemicals and industrial processes are also suspected risk factors (Heath 1982).

In Poland the mortality rate for leukaemias increased slightly in all age groups and especially in men during the observation period. It is hard to tell how much of it is due to improved diagnosis and how much is an effect of higher exposure to risk factors. In men, it seems that at least part of this increase is a true one. Leukaemia is yet another disease in which mortality rates are relatively high in the first years of life; a distinct childhood peak exists, rising to about 8 cases per 100000 children aged 2-4 years. Then, following a decline, another increase occurs about the age of 25. The first peak is probably related to exposure to hypothetical risk factors in utero or in infancy. A substantial increase in age groups over 50 is probably connected with exposure to risk factors during adult life. What is remarkable, is a substantial increase, especially in men, in the age group of 55-64. As in other countries (Heath 1982), Poland has a 1.5-times higher mortality rate for leukaemias in men than in women. Place of residence does not make any significant difference and the geographical distribution of the rates has no particular pattern.

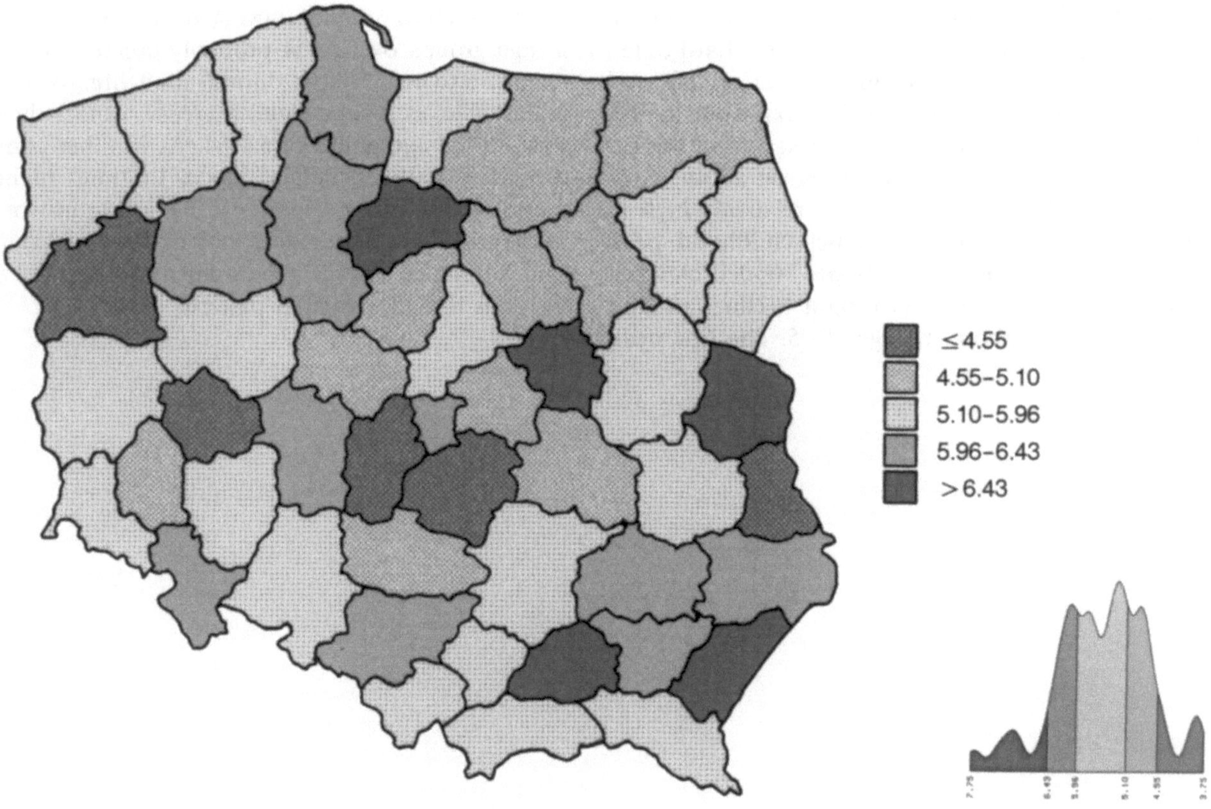
≤4.55
4.55–5.10
5.10–5.96
5.96–6.43
>6.43

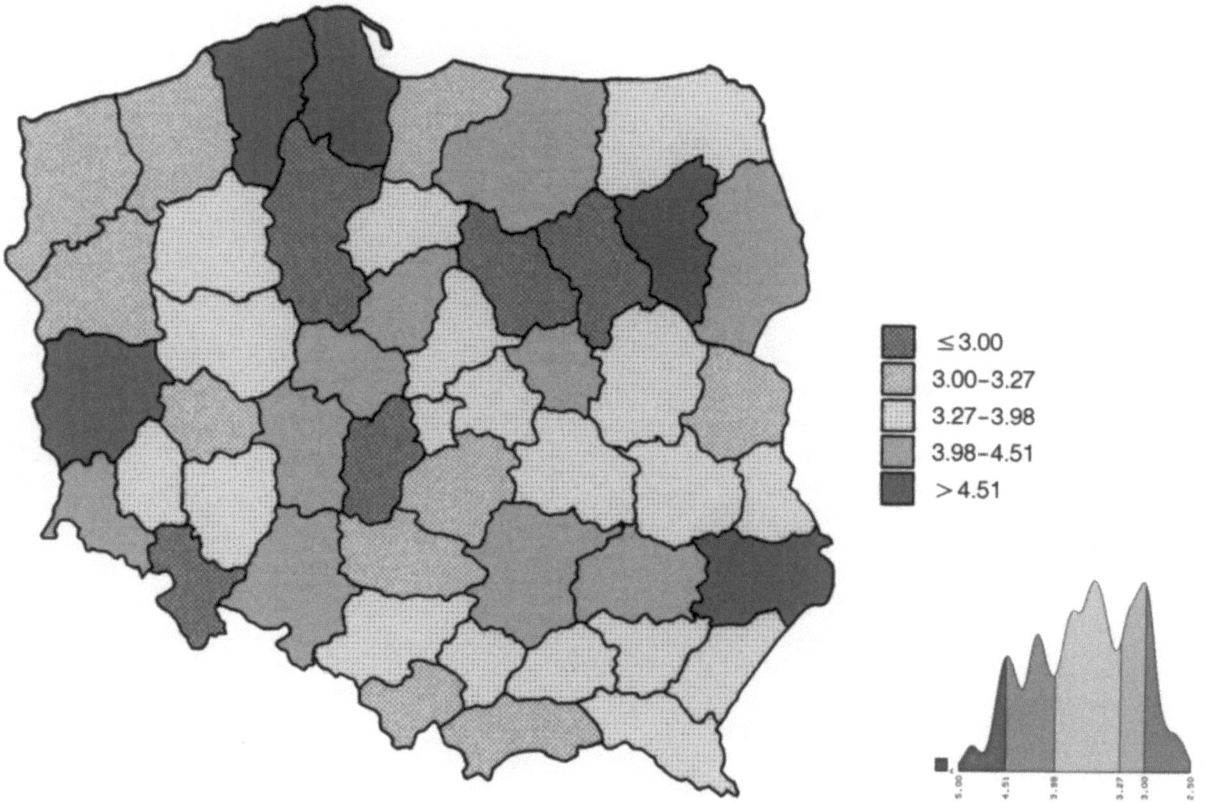
≤3.00
3.00–3.27
3.27–3.98
3.98–4.51
>4.51

6.92 – 7.69
6.15 – 6.92
5.38 – 6.15
4.62 – 5.38
3.85 – 4.62

5.01 – 5.61
4.41 – 5.01
3.81 – 4.41
3.21 – 3.81
2.61 – 3.21

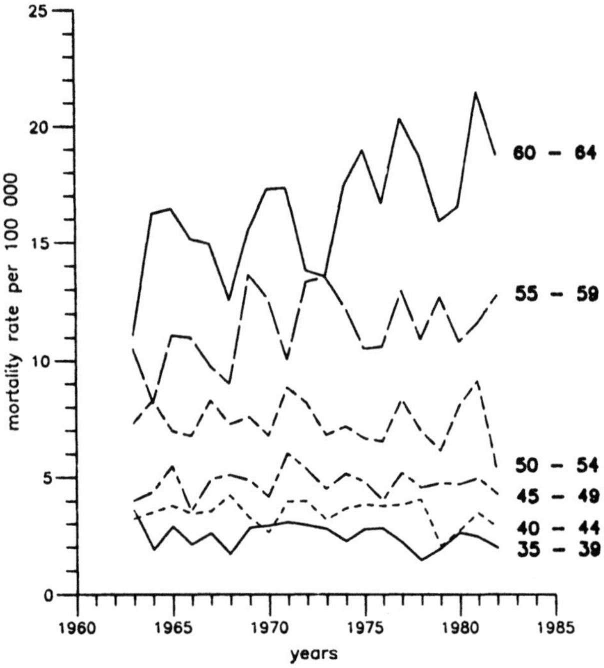

Temporal trend of mortality in individual age groups/men

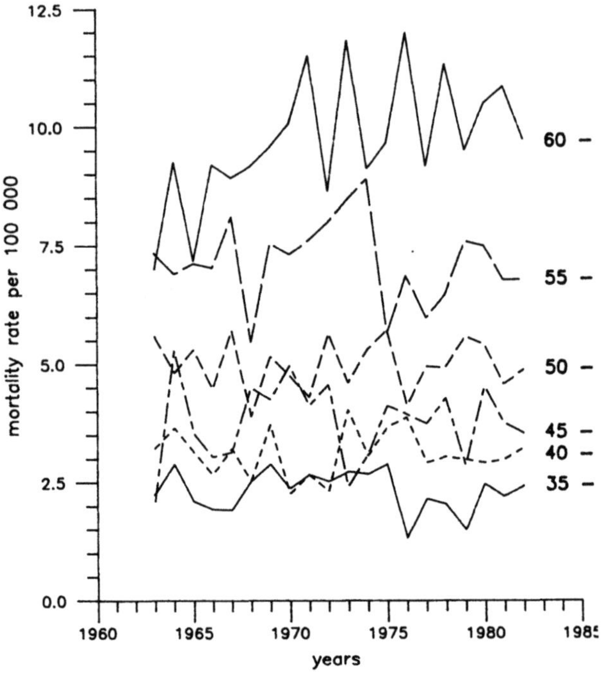

Temporal trend of mortality in individual age groups/women

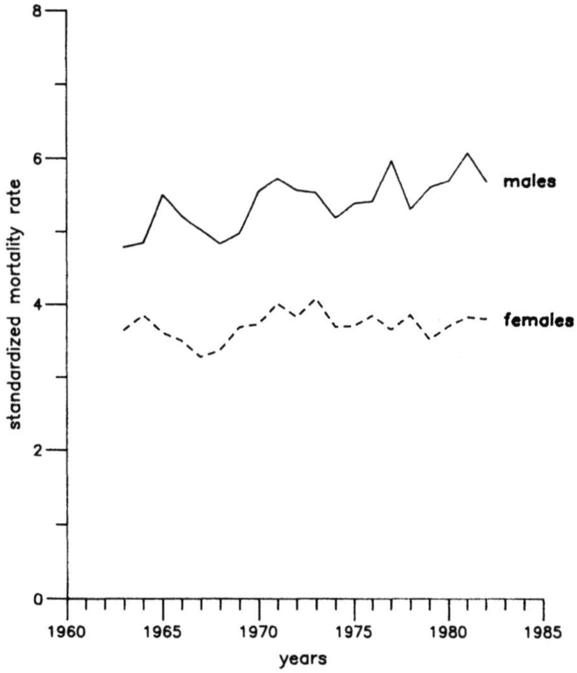

Temporal trend of the age-adjusted mortality rates for men and women

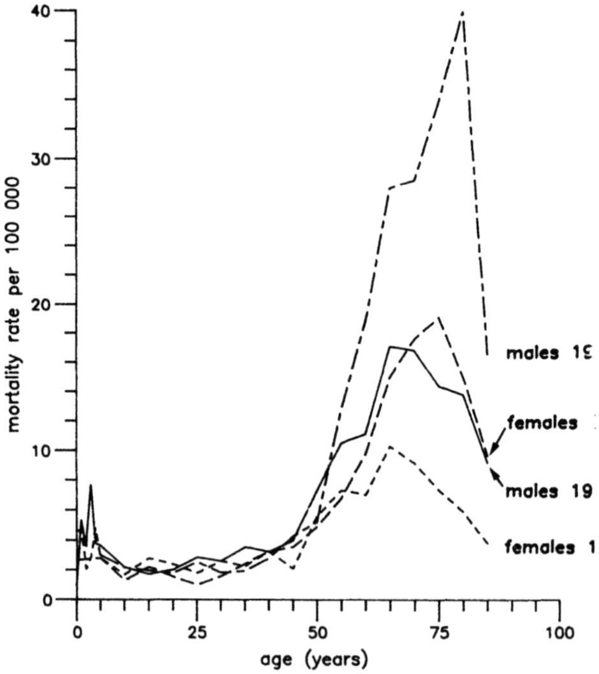

Mortality depending on age in two sample years for men and women

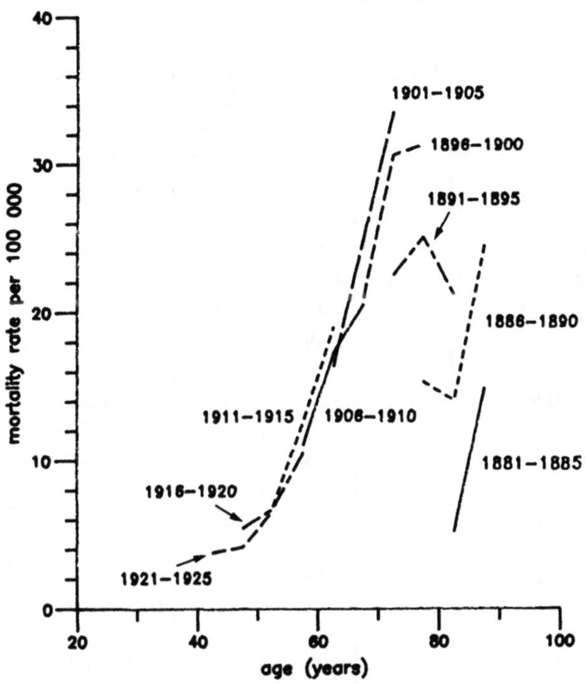

Age-dependent mortality in various birth cohorts/ men

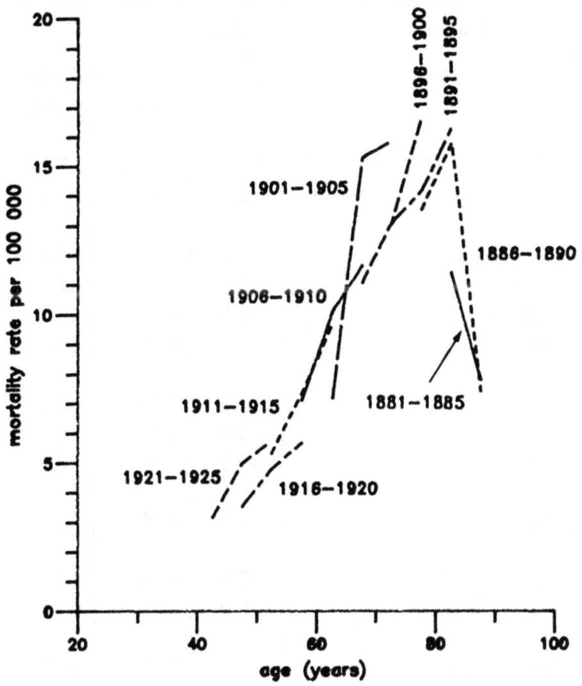

Age-dependent mortality in various birth cohorts/ women

Average Values 1975-1979	Males				Females			
	Cases	Stand. Mort. Rate	Cum. Mort. Rate	Confidence limits	Cases	Stand. Mort. Rate	Cum. Mort. Rate	Confidence limits
Poland	984.2	5.67	0.60	0.57-0.62	791.4	3.72	0.38	0.36-0.39
Biała Podlaska	10.6	6.53	0.68	0.40-0.96	6.0	3.17	0.34	0.17-0.52
Białystok	19.8	5.71	0.62	0.44-0.80	15.4	4.08	0.37	0.25-0.50
Bielsko Biała	20.8	5.27	0.64	0.46-0.83	15.6	3.17	0.31	0.21-0.41
Bydgoszcz	30.6	6.07	0.63	0.48-0.79	19.2	2.99	0.32	0.23-0.42
Chełm	4.6	3.85	0.41	0.16-0.66	5.2	3.72	0.34	0.15-0.53
Ciechanów	9.8	4.57	0.47	0.27-0.67	6.8	2.89	0.26	0.13-0.39
Częstochowa	19.2	5.00	0.51	0.36-0.66	15.8	3.23	0.35	0.24-0.47
Elbląg	9.6	5.25	0.57	0.32-0.83	6.8	3.00	0.30	0.15-0.46
Gdańsk	37.6	6.34	0.70	0.54-0.85	33.2	4.59	0.45	0.35-0.56
Gorzów Wielkopolski	8.0	3.87	0.45	0.23-0.67	7.6	3.16	0.28	0.14-0.43
Jelenia Góra	11.2	5.40	0.55	0.31-0.79	11.6	4.24	0.44	0.25-0.62
Kalisz	21.6	6.05	0.69	0.50-0.88	17.4	4.01	0.38	0.26-0.50
Katowice	100.8	6.01	0.63	0.54-0.72	75.4	3.53	0.36	0.31-0.42
Kielce	32.6	5.73	0.65	0.50-0.79	27.4	4.20	0.43	0.33-0.54
Konin	11.2	4.77	0.52	0.32-0.73	10.2	4.42	0.39	0.24-0.54
Koszalin	9.8	5.22	0.44	0.22-0.66	6.6	3.00	0.30	0.14-0.45
Kraków	31.8	5.76	0.64	0.49-0.79	26.2	3.58	0.37	0.27-0.46
Krosno	12.6	5.55	0.64	0.40-0.88	9.4	3.30	0.39	0.24-0.55
Legnica	9.8	5.06	0.47	0.23-0.70	7.6	3.63	0.41	0.21-0.61
Leszno	8.8	4.53	0.50	0.28-0.72	7.0	3.02	0.30	0.15-0.45
Lublin	26.4	5.73	0.57	0.42-0.72	18.8	3.42	0.30	0.21-0.39
Łomża	9.8	5.40	0.53	0.30-0.75	11.6	5.61	0.56	0.35-0.77
Łódź	35.4	6.05	0.59	0.46-0.73	29.0	3.56	0.35	0.27-0.44
Nowy Sącz	15.2	5.16	0.58	0.38-0.78	11.6	3.00	0.34	0.21-0.46
Olsztyn	14.8	4.89	0.51	0.32-0.71	13.6	4.20	0.43	0.27-0.58
Opole	24.2	5.48	0.62	0.44-0.79	23.0	4.20	0.47	0.34-0.60
Ostrołęka	8.8	4.82	0.50	0.29-0.72	5.6	2.75	0.28	0.13-0.43
Piła	12.4	6.06	0.63	0.39-0.87	9.2	3.43	0.41	0.23-0.59
Piotrków Trybunalski	14.6	4.42	0.48	0.32-0.65	11.8	3.12	0.34	0.22-0.47
Płock	14.0	5.41	0.59	0.38-0.79	10.6	3.84	0.34	0.20-0.47
Poznań	35.8	5.78	0.56	0.43-0.69	28.2	3.62	0.39	0.30-0.48
Przemyśl	14.0	7.28	0.73	0.48-0.99	8.8	3.68	0.32	0.17-0.47
Radom	18.4	4.84	0.58	0.40-0.76	15.8	3.81	0.39	0.27-0.51
Rzeszów	21.0	6.27	0.70	0.49-0.90	12.6	3.47	0.35	0.22-0.47
Siedlce	18.4	5.24	0.55	0.38-0.72	14.2	3.81	0.38	0.25-0.50
Sieradz	9.6	3.97	0.43	0.25-0.62	6.8	2.62	0.25	0.12-0.38
Skierniewice	10.0	4.77	0.54	0.32-0.76	8.6	3.43	0.34	0.19-0.49
Słupsk	8.2	5.23	0.60	0.31-0.90	8.2	4.53	0.50	0.26-0.75
Suwałki	9.2	4.90	0.54	0.30-0.79	8.8	3.82	0.42	0.23-0.61
Szczecin	20.0	5.71	0.52	0.34-0.70	14.6	3.24	0.31	0.20-0.43

Average Values 1975-1979	Males				Females			
	Cases	Stand. Mort. Rate	Cum. Mort. Rate	Confidence limits	Cases	Stand. Mort. Rate	Cum. Mort. Rate	Confidence limits
Tarnobrzeg	17.8	6.23	0.63	0.44-0.83	14.2	4.14	0.41	0.27-0.55
Tarnów	21.6	7.69	0.80	0.57-1.03	13.6	3.87	0.37	0.24-0.50
Toruń	19.6	6.94	0.76	0.53-0.99	14.2	3.57	0.38	0.25-0.52
Wałbrzych	20.6	6.31	0.62	0.42-0.82	12.8	3.00	0.31	0.18-0.43
Warszawa	77.2	7.06	0.70	0.59-0.81	73.0	4.49	0.44	0.37-0.51
Włocławek	10.4	4.81	0.54	0.32-0.76	10.8	4.41	0.39	0.24-0.55
Wrocław	24.4	5.14	0.52	0.37-0.68	22.2	3.95	0.40	0.29-0.52
Zamość	15.6	6.11	0.60	0.41-0.79	14.2	4.87	0.51	0.35-0.68
Zielona Góra	16.0	5.90	0.54	0.35-0.74	14.6	4.54	0.43	0.27-0.58

23 Malignant Neoplasms - ICD 140-209

The ASMR for men was 133.9 in 1963 and 183.0 in 1982. The mortality of women suffering from all malignant neoplasms in the period 1963-1982 did not change significantly and remained steady at about 100. The mortality rate increased substantially from the age of about 40. The highest value was slightly less than 1500 deaths per 100000 men aged about 75, which was much higher in 1982 than in 1963. The highest value for women was about 800 deaths per 100000 women also aged 75, but it changed little over the period 1963-1982. Mortality rates in men increased with calendar time in all the analogous age groups. The time trend for age-specific mortality rates for women does not show significant changes either. The cohort effect was observed in men, who had a greater risk of dying from any cancer in successive birth cohorts, whereas no such phenomenon was found in women.
The cancer mortality rate in Europe was rather high in comparison with countries in the rest of the world. In 1978 the highest rates in men were noted in Czechoslovakia (212.7), Luxembourg (211.1), Scotland (207.4) and Hungary (206.5). The lowest rates were observed in Iceland (110.2), Bulgaria (126.7), Yugoslavia (135.1) and Romania (135.2). In non-European countries, a very high mortality rate was observed in Uruguay (210.8). In women the highest rates were noted in Scotland (138.8), Denmark (135.1) and Hungary (130.9), while the lowest ones were found in Yugoslavia (83.5), Greece (83.6), Portugal (85.4), Spain (85.6) and Bulgaria (85.8). The highest rate outside Europe was recorded in New Zealand (123.8). With rates of 175.5 in men and 105.8 in women in 1978 Poland is a country with a medium cancer risk.

Analysis of Data from the Provinces, 1975-1979

Malignant neoplasms were more frequent in men than in women (ratio 1.7). They occurred in urban populations more frequently than in rural communities (ratios 1.2 for men and 1.3 for women).

Men

(Mean ASMR = 162.6, Range 125.3-203.2, Standard Deviation 19.5)

Provinces did not differ much in their mortality rates. The highest figure was 1.6 times greater than the lowest. The highest rates were recorded in Katowice (203.15), Gdansk (189.43), Opole (189.29), Torun (188.46) and Elblag (188.46). The lowest rates were found in the provinces of Siedlce (125.25), Lomza (125.53), Piotrkow (130.32), Lublin (130.69) and Bialystok (132.88). Geographically, the risk is quite clearly arranged along the east-west line. A strip of eastern provinces constitutes the area with the lowest risk. Western Poland generally has a higher risk and Gdansk, with the adjacent provinces of Torun and Elblag, as well as Silesia in the south (Katowice and Opole) have the highest indices.

Women

(Mean ASMR = 96.5, Range 72.6-116.9, Standard Deviation 11.5)

The highest rates were observed in the provinces of Warszawa (116.93), Katowice (116.18), Lodz (115.86), Gdansk (113.40) and Bydgoszcz (111.73). The lowest rates were found in Lublin (72.64), Zamosc (74.64), Siedlce (76.79), Ostroleka (77.72) and Lomza (78.46). The geographical pattern of risk along the east-west line is even clearer than in men. Nearly all the provinces where the risk is lower than average are situated in the eastern part of Poland. The highly urbanised provinces of Warszawa, Katowice, Lodz and Gdansk are exceptions to this geographical distribution pattern as they are the areas with the highest risk.

Comments

Aetiological consideration of all the cancer sites together is pointless. The sites usually differ in their risk factors, which sometimes act in opposite directions. The risk factors identified in the individual sites have been discussed in the respective chapters. On the other hand, a general summing up helps us to understand certain patterns in the cancer risk in Poland. This is why we have decided to close this work with a discussion of all malignant neoplasms together.

The number of cancers has increased dramatically. The disease killed 34500 people in 1963, and the number of deaths it caused in 1982 jumped to 61 729. This exceptionally rapid increase in cancer is caused by three major factors:

- A significant increase in the population (31 million in 1963, 36 million in 1982)
- Aging of the population (6.4% aged over 65 in 1963, 9.7% aged over 65 in 1982)
- An increase in the risk factors connected with environment and life style

There is a fundamental difference in the time trends of the mortality rates calculated for cancers in men and women. Malignant neoplasms are an increasingly frequent cause of death in men. In 1963 16945 cancer-related deaths were reported while in 1982 this number was already 34482. Apart from the increase and aging of the population, the increasing number of deaths in men is a result of the increasing risk which, as measured by the ASMR, was 133.9 per 100000 men in 1963 and 183.0 per 100000 in 1982.

The number of malignant neoplasms in women also increased significantly. There were 17555 cancer-related deaths among women in 1963 and as many as 27253 in 1982. The general increase in the number of deaths caused by cancer in women is primarily a consequence of the increase and aging of the population, because the risk of cancer as measured by the ASMR has not changed (in 1963 102.0 and in 1982 104.5 per 100000).

An analysis of the individual anatomical cancer sites during the years 1963-82 reveals the following significant changes in the risk:

Men

- Highly significant increase in the risk of dying from cancer of the lung, larynx and mouth
- Highly significant increase in the risk of cancer of the lower digestive tract (colon and rectum) and pancreas
- Highly significant increase in the risk of malignant skin melanoma, cancer of the testis, kidney and urinary bladder
- Decreased risk of cancer of the stomach

Women

- Highly significant increase in the risk of malignant melanoma, cancer of the rectum, pancreas and ovary
- Increasing risk of lung cancer
- Increasing risk of breast cancer
- Small decline in mortality from cancer of the cervix uteri
- Considerable decline in risk of cancer of the stomach

The increased risk of tobacco-related cancers (mouth, larynx, lung, urinary bladder, pancreas and kidney) is characteristic, especially in the male population. At the same time, the increased risk of lung and laryngeal cancers in men (of which 80%-90% strikes tobacco smokers) ranks among the world's highest rates. The lung cancer mortality rate in Polish men is increasing twice as fast as in any other European country (Brzezinski 1982). The increase in the risk of lung cancer in women is high too, although it began at a low starting point.

A growing risk of contracting cancer of the lower digestive tract (the rectum in particular) and pancreas is observed in men and women, who are also at a rapidly increasing risk of melanoma malignum. In all these cancer sites the increase began at low starting points and the risk is still not too high when compared with other European countries. This is also true of the increase in the risk of breast cancer in women. This increase is permanent, but it began at a low starting point. Poland thus remains a low-risk country for breast cancer in comparison to other Europan countries.

A sharp decline has been observed in the risk of cancer of the stomach, especially in women. The rate of decrease in the risk in men is lower and the men's risk of this disease is one of highest in Europe.

The geographical distribution of malignant neoplasms displays a clear connection between the risk of most cancers and the degree of urbanisation. Higher cancer mortality rates may be observed in the western part of Poland and lower ones in the eastern part. This geographical pattern is true for all malignant neoplasms taken as a whole, as well as for many individual cancer sites (e.g. cancer of the large intestine). However, highly urbanised provinces (e.g. Warszawa) are exceptions from this distribution pattern. For some cancer sites, especially for breast cancer in females and cancer of the prostate and testis for males, a high-risk cluster is situated in Poznan and the adjacent provinces.

Table 1. Structure of cancer in Poland

Males					
1963		1978		1982	
1. Stomach	33.2%	1. Lung	29.8%	1. Lung	31.1%
2. Lung	18.1%	2. Stomach	19.2%	2. Stomach	15.7%
3. Liver and gall bladder	6.3%	3. Colon and rectum	6.5%	3. Colon and rectum	6.9%
4. Colon and rectum	4.5%	4. Prostate	5.3%	4. Prostate	4.8%
5. Prostate	4.1%	5. Liver	4.5%	5. Urinary bladder	3.9%
6. Leukaemia	4.0%	6. Pancreas	3.7%	6. Pancreas	3.6%
7. Oesophagus	3.9%	7. Urinary bladder	3.5%	7. Larynx	3.5%
8. Urinary bladder	3.1%	8. Leukaemia	3.1%	8. Leukaemia	3.0%
9. Pancreas	2.4%	9. Larynx	3.0%	9. Oesophagus	2.6%
10. Larynx	2.0%	10. Brain	2.1%	10. Kidney	2.0%

Females					
1963		1978		1982	
1. Stomach	21.7%	1. Stomach	13.3%	1. Breast	13.4%
2. Liver and gall bladder	13.2%	2. Breast	12.9%	2. Stomach	11.4%
3. Breast	9.0%	3. Colon and rectum	8.8%	3. Colon and rectum	9.1%
4. Cervix uteri	6.0%	4. Liver	7.7%	4. Liver	7.3%
5. Colon and rectum	4.9%	5. Cervix uteri	7.7%	5. Lung	7.0%
6. Lung	3.9%	6. Lung	6.2%	6. Cervix uteri	7.0%
7. Leukaemia	3.3%	7. Ovary	5.2%	7. Ovary	5.1%
8. Ovary	3.1%	8. Gall bladder	4.3%	8. Gall bladder	4.6%
9. Pancreas	2.4%	9. Pancreas	4.2%	9. Pancreas	4.4%
10. Oesophagus	1.5%	10. Leukaemia	3.4%	10. Leukaemia	3.0%

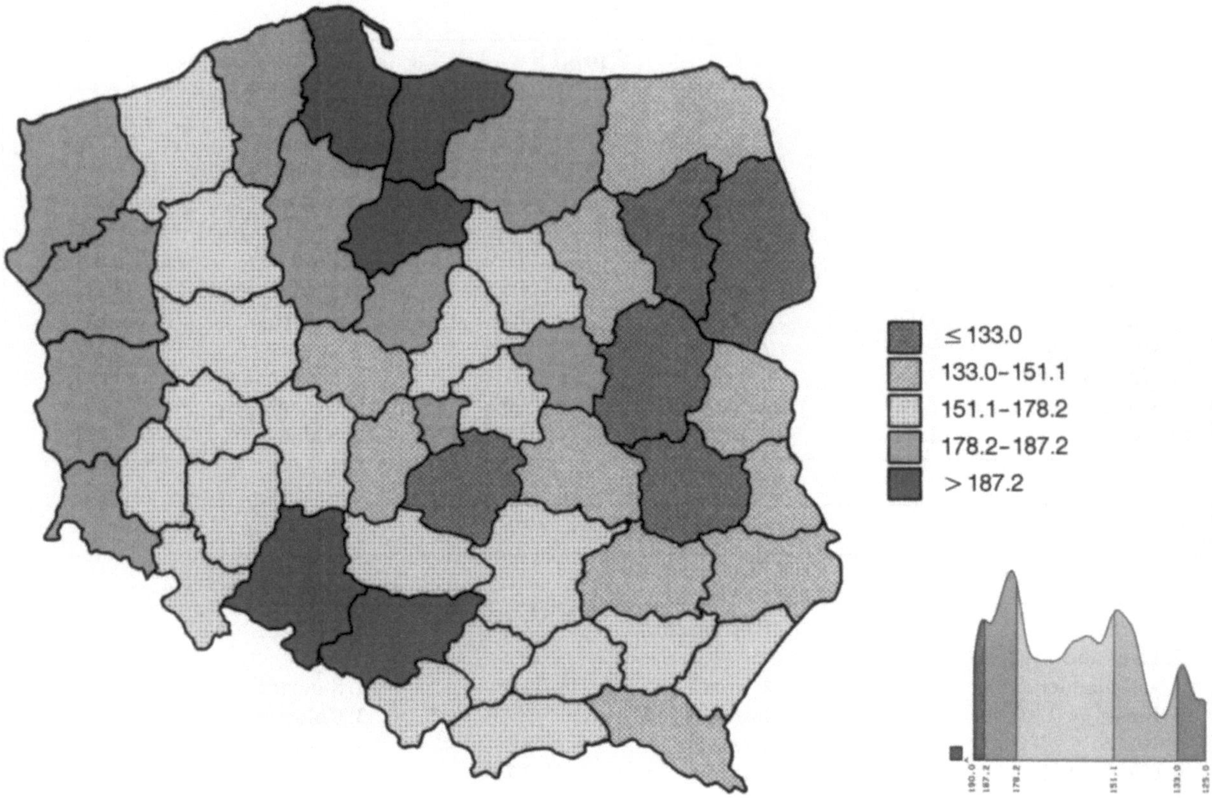
≤ 133.0
133.0–151.1
151.1–178.2
178.2–187.2
> 187.2

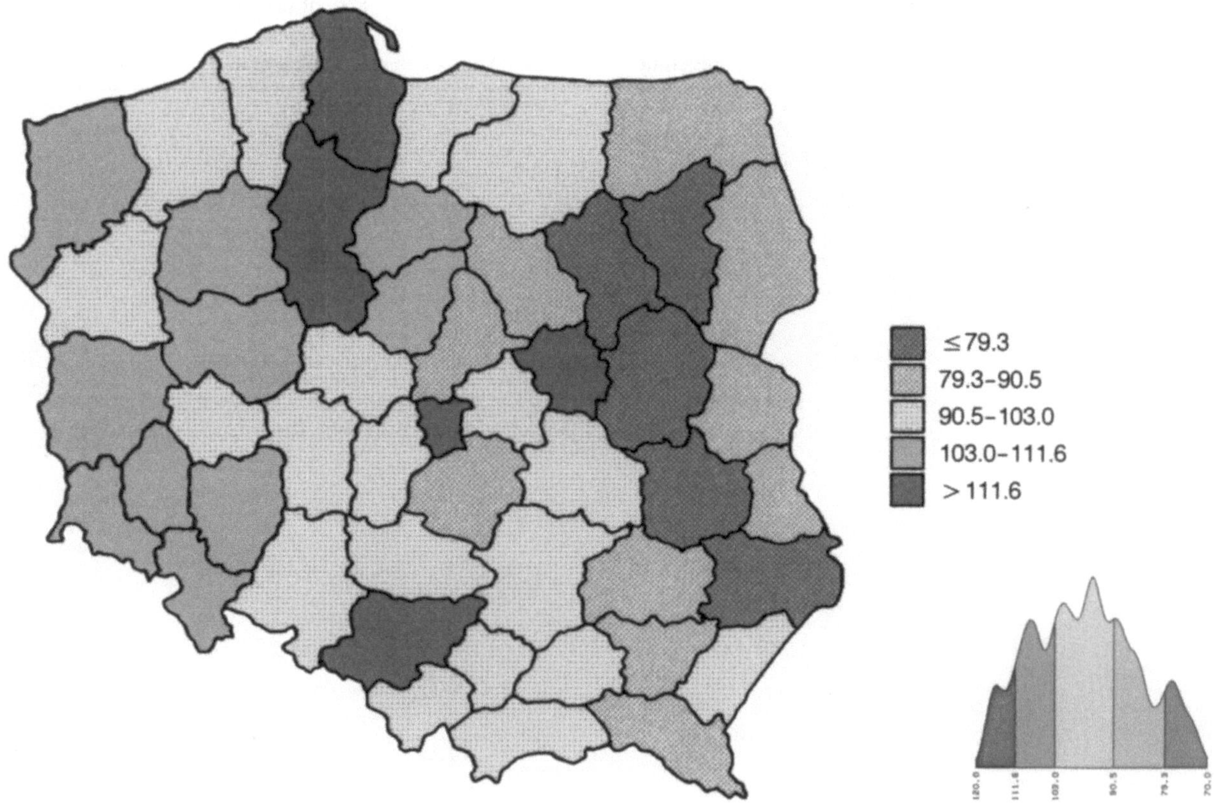
≤ 79.3
79.3–90.5
90.5–103.0
103.0–111.6
> 111.6

187.6 - 203.2
172.0 - 187.6
156.4 - 172.0
140.8 - 156.4
125.2 - 140.8

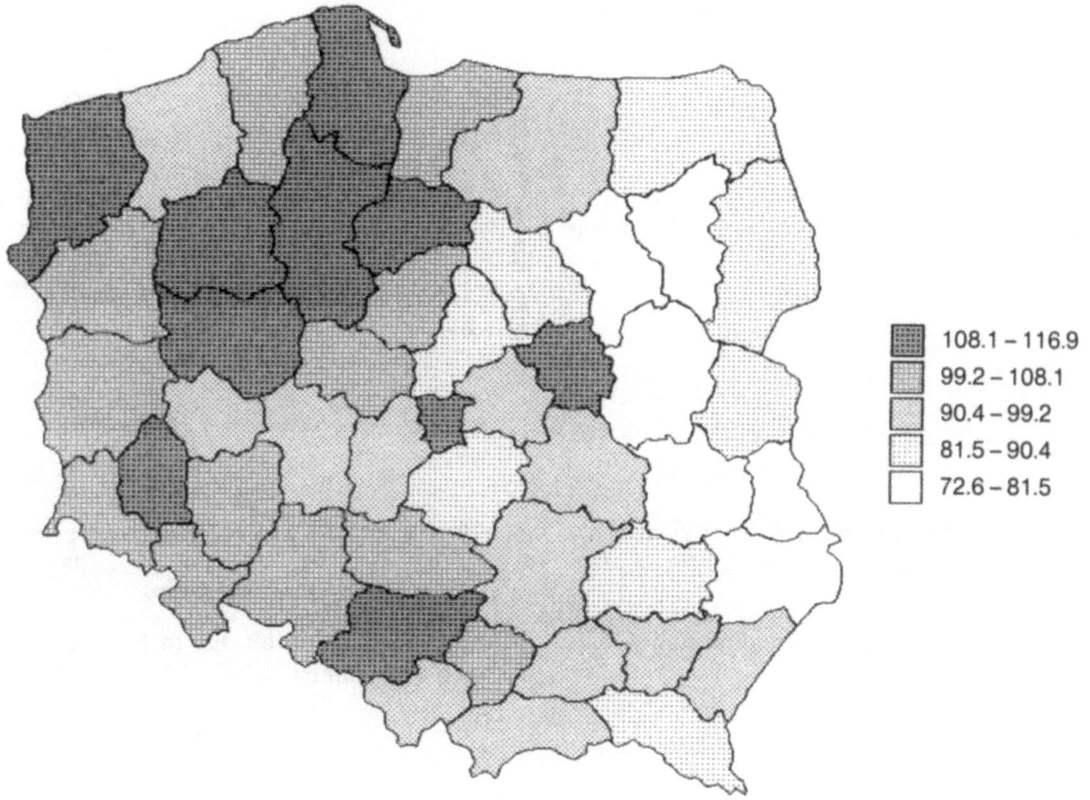
108.1 - 116.9
99.2 - 108.1
90.4 - 99.2
81.5 - 90.4
72.6 - 81.5

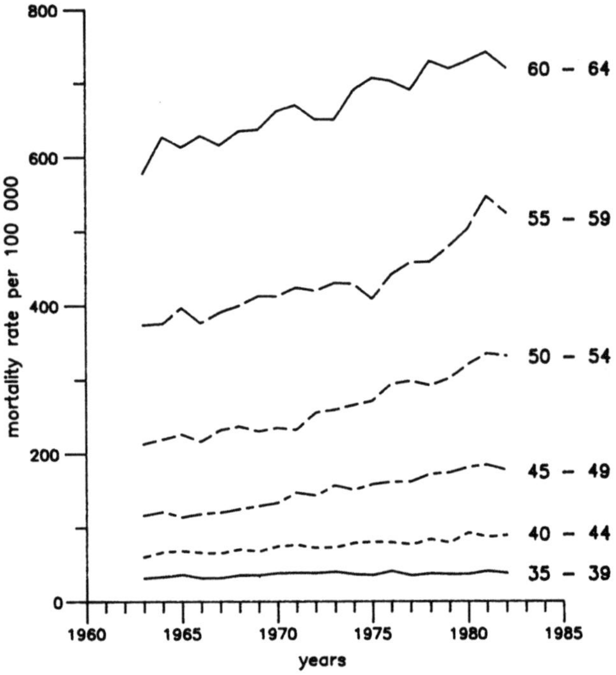

Temporal trend of mortality in individual age groups/men

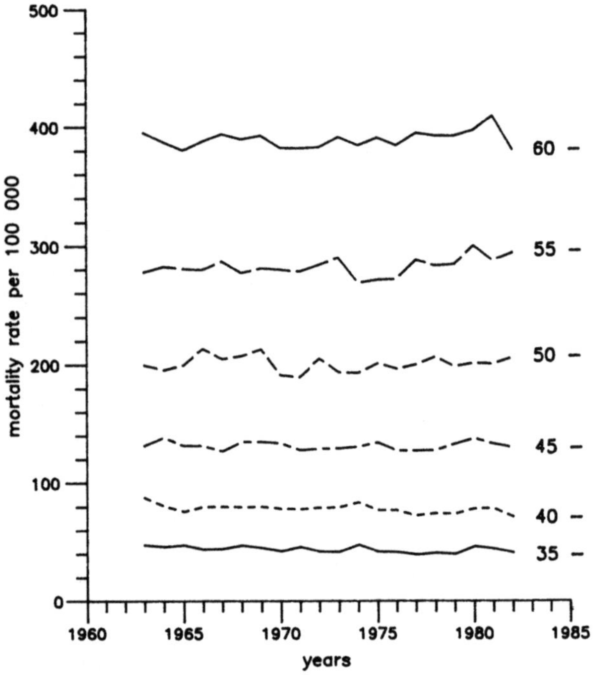

Temporal trend of mortality in individual age groups/women

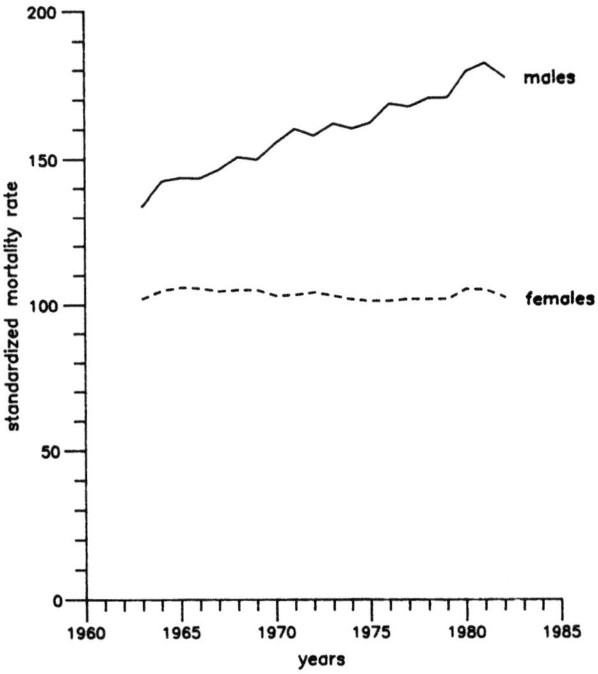

Temporal trend of the age-adjusted mortality rates for men and women

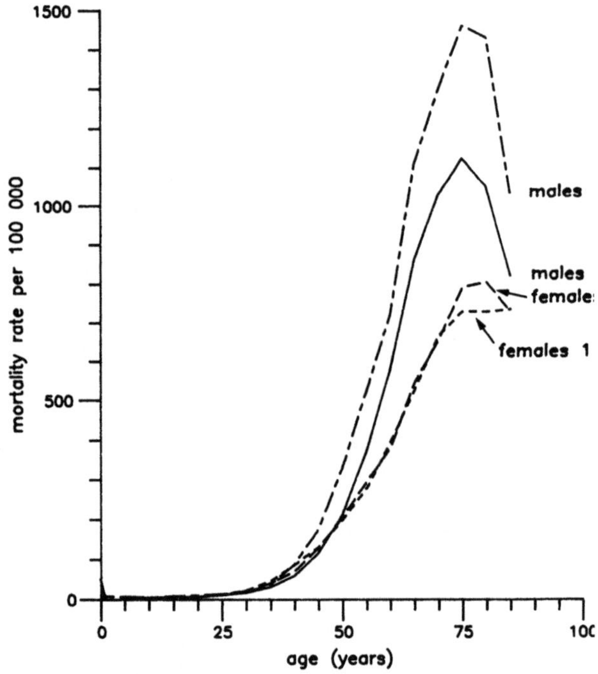

Mortality depending on age in two sample years for men and women

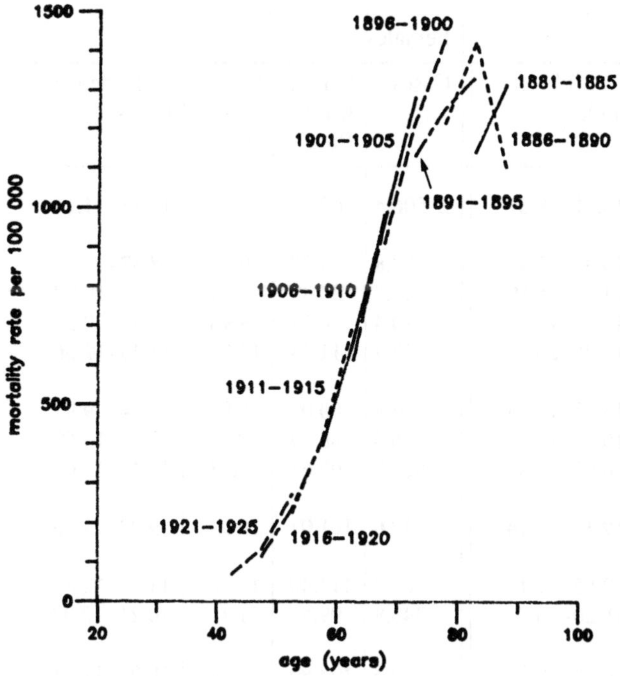

Age-dependent mortality in various birth cohorts/ men

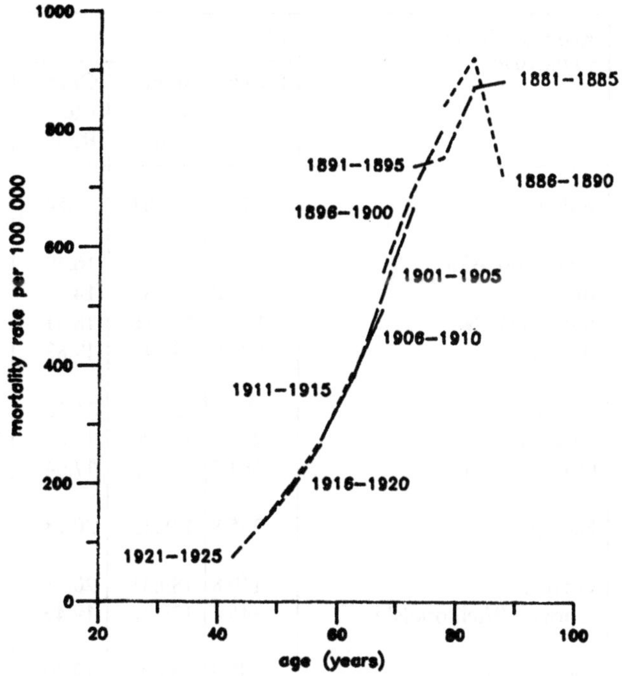

Age-dependent mortality in various birth cohorts/ women

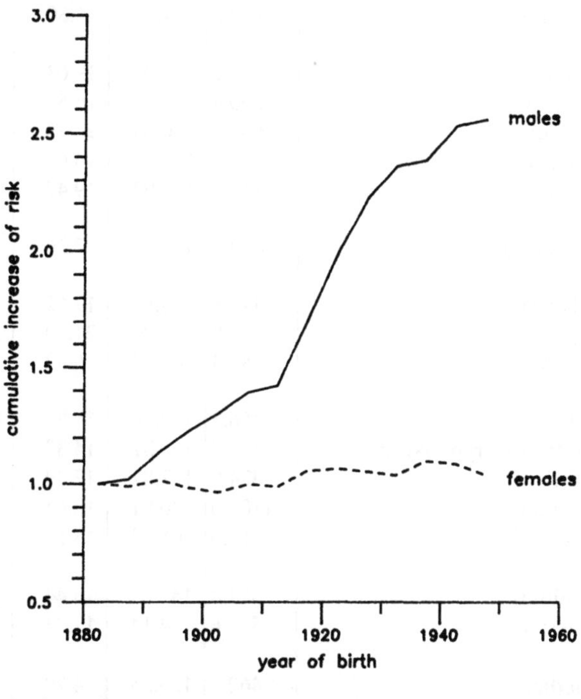

Ratios of the cumulative mortality rates for successive birth cohorts relative to the 1886-1890 cohort

Average Values 1975-1979	Males				Females			
	Cases	Stand. Mort. Rate	Cum. Mort. Rate	Confidence limits	Cases	Stand. Mort. Rate	Cum. Mort. Rate	Confidence limits
Poland	29772.2	167.07	18.54	18.41-18.67	24506.4	100.71	11.02	10.93-11.11
Biała Podlaska	251.8	141.35	16.19	14.96-17.40	187.8	84.77	9.45	8.57-10.33
Białystok	512.8	132.88	14.78	13.95-15.59	420.0	86.47	9.71	9.09-10.32
Bielsko Biała	651.0	162.86	18.41	17.54-19.27	510.4	90.52	9.98	9.41-10.56
Bydgoszcz	937.0	182.47	19.83	19.05-20.60	777.4	111.73	12.01	11.45-12.56
Chełm	182.2	133.18	15.55	14.15-16.93	136.8	80.09	9.02	8.04- 9.99
Ciechanów	359.6	157.24	17.85	16.72-18.96	256.4	88.59	9.80	9.01-10.59
Częstochowa	663.2	157.98	17.64	16.82-18.45	565.8	99.65	11.03	10.44-11.62
Elbląg	335.8	188.35	20.78	19.39-22.14	232.6	101.07	10.93	9.98-11.86
Gdańsk	1119.8	189.43	20.38	19.65-21.11	903.0	113.40	12.28	11.76-12.81
Gorzów Wielkopolski	345.6	178.32	19.49	18.20-20.76	248.8	99.57	11.12	10.21-12.02
Jelenia Góra	389.4	183.00	19.50	18.25-20.72	290.8	103.96	11.52	10.62-12.41
Kalisz	566.6	151.32	16.82	15.97-17.66	479.0	96.74	10.44	9.83-11.05
Katowice	3347.2	203.15	22.30	21.84-22.76	2833.8	116.18	12.51	12.21-12.81
Kielce	981.4	161.54	18.20	17.50-18.89	749.4	94.72	10.43	9.94-10.91
Konin	367.2	149.96	16.81	15.76-17.85	311.2	101.70	11.20	10.40-11.99
Koszalin	295.8	164.22	18.22	16.89-19.54	219.4	94.61	10.68	9.73-11.61
Kraków	967.6	168.63	19.05	18.31-19.78	869.0	102.33	11.20	10.71-11.69
Krosno	332.6	144.49	16.80	15.68-17.90	277.8	88.37	10.03	9.26-10.80
Legnica	293.2	173.43	19.03	17.61-20.41	235.2	109.28	11.74	10.73-12.74
Leszno	290.4	151.49	16.55	15.38-17.70	247.6	95.40	10.38	9.53-11.23
Lublin	645.2	130.69	14.75	14.04-15.46	474.8	72.64	8.12	7.64- 8.60
Łomża	249.6	125.53	14.61	13.47-15.74	187.8	78.46	8.59	7.77- 9.40
Łódź	1112.4	178.92	19.47	18.77-20.17	1098.2	115.86	12.47	11.98-12.96
Nowy Sącz	477.2	154.55	17.36	16.39-18.31	374.8	90.82	10.09	9.42-10.75
Olsztyn	474.8	178.85	19.52	18.41-20.62	343.4	98.16	10.55	9.79-11.30
Opole	787.8	189.29	21.00	20.08-21.90	637.6	102.90	11.31	10.73-11.88
Ostrołęka	284.4	144.28	16.32	15.14-17.49	199.2	77.72	8.85	8.04- 9.66
Piła	356.8	172.40	18.87	17.66-20.07	291.8	108.23	11.87	10.98-12.76
Piotrków Trybunalski	451.2	130.32	14.87	14.03-15.71	388.4	85.93	9.63	9.01-10.24
Płock	424.0	157.87	17.89	16.86-18.90	298.6	89.39	9.82	9.10-10.53
Poznań	1102.0	170.81	18.65	17.97-19.32	1012.2	111.44	11.98	11.49-12.46
Przemyśl	350.0	165.32	18.58	17.39-19.75	281.8	96.65	10.64	9.82-11.46
Radom	571.8	147.85	16.44	15.60-17.27	462.2	92.34	10.24	9.63-10.84
Rzeszów	522.6	154.14	17.24	16.31-18.15	401.6	90.44	10.12	9.47-10.76
Siedlce	462.6	125.25	14.29	13.48-15.09	347.8	76.79	8.49	7.91- 9.06
Sieradz	370.8	146.93	16.67	15.65-17.68	298.8	95.20	10.69	9.91-11.46
Skierniewice	367.6	160.61	17.94	16.80-19.05	277.4	93.36	10.25	9.46-11.04
Słupsk	262.2	181.62	20.28	18.74-21.79	183.6	99.74	10.79	9.74-11.84
Suwałki	278.0	146.14	16.93	15.67-18.17	207.2	84.53	9.50	8.62-10.37
Szczecin	632.2	185.99	20.43	19.39-21.45	490.8	108.45	12.05	11.34-12.75

Average Values 1975-1979	Males				Females			
	Cases	Stand. Mort. Rate	Cum. Mort. Rate	Confidence limits	Cases	Stand. Mort. Rate	Cum. Mort. Rate	Confidence limits
Tarnobrzeg	488.0	150.86	16.95	16.03-17.87	332.0	82.09	9.10	8.45- 9.73
Tarnów	533.8	167.89	18.81	17.84-19.78	407.8	94.87	10.56	9.89-11.23
Toruń	547.0	188.46	20.52	19.47-21.55	452.6	109.78	11.86	11.14-12.57
Wałbrzych	558.6	178.02	19.25	18.21-20.27	454.2	107.25	11.57	10.85-12.28
Warszawa	2187.0	185.31	19.94	19.41-20.46	2224.6	116.93	12.54	12.19-12.88
Włocławek	397.0	181.97	20.22	19.02-21.40	301.4	103.19	11.53	10.69-12.36
Wrocław	801.8	175.12	18.89	18.05-19.73	674.4	105.89	11.43	10.84-12.01
Zamość	415.8	137.71	15.90	14.98-16.82	276.8	74.64	8.61	7.97- 9.25
Zielona Góra	469.8	178.94	19.48	18.37-20.57	372.4	107.21	11.53	10.75-12.31

References

Abramson JH, Avitzour PE (1975) Mortality from lymphomas in Israel, 1950-1971: The possible role of environmental factors. Int J Epidemiol 4: 321-329

Anaise D, Steinitz R, Ben Hur N (1978) Solar radiation: a possible etiological factor in malignant melanoma in Israel. A retrospective study (1960-72). Cancer 42: 299-304

Anderson DL (1971) Cause and prevention of lip cancer. Can Dent Assoc J 37: 138-142

Armstrong B, Doll R (1975) Environmetal factors and cancer incidence and mortality in diffrent countries with special references to dietary practises. Int J Cancer 15: 617-631

Atkinson L (1975) Some features of the epidemiology of cancer of the larynx in Australia and Papua, New Guinea. Laryngoscope 85: 1173-1184

Austin DF (1982) Larynx. In: Schottenfeld D, Fraumeni JF (eds) Cancer epidemiology and prevention. Saunders, Philadelphia

Becker N, Frentzel-Beyme R, Wagner G (1984) Atlas of cancer mortality in the Federal Republic of Germany. Springer, Berlin Heidelberg New York

Beebe GW, Kato H, Land CE (1978) Studies of the mortality of A-bomb survivors. 6. Mortality and radiation dose, 1950-1974. Radiat Res 75: 138-201

Beral V, Fraser P, Chilvers C (1987) Does pregnancy protect against ovarian cancer? Lancet I: 1083-1087

Beral V, Evans S, Shaw H, Milton G (1982) Malignant melanoma and exposure to fluorescent lighting at work. Lancet II: 290-293

Bjarnsson O, Day, N, Snaedl G, Tulinius H (1974) The effect of year of birth on the breast cancer age incidence curve in Iceland. Int J Cancer 13: 689-696

Bjelke E (1975) Dietary vitamin A and human lung cancer. Int J Cancer 15: 561-565

Boyle P, Day NE, Magnus K (1983) Mathematical modelling of malignant melanoma time trends in Norway, 1953-1978. Am J Epidemiol 118: 887-896

Boyle P, Kaye S, Rebertson A (1986) Improving prognosis of testicular cancer in Scotland. IRCM Med Sci 14: 976-977

Brzezinski ZJ (1982) Mortality in the European Region. WHO, Kopenhagen

Cantor KP, Fraumeni JF (1980) Geographic and temporal patterns of non-Hodgkin's lymphoma mortality in U.S. counties, 1959-1975. Cancer Res 40: 2645-2652

Case RAM (1956) Cohort analysis of mortality rates as an historical or narrative technique. Br J Prev Soc Med 10: 159-171

Case RAM, Hosker ME, McDonald DB et al. (1954) Tumors of the urinary bladder in workmen engaged in the manufacture and use of certain dyestuff intermediates in the British chemical industry. Br J Ind Med 11: 75-104

Cassai EN, Terni M, Califano A (1974) Caratterizzazione di un virus dell'herpes simplex isolato da un tumore labiale insorto sulla sede di recidive erpetiche. Tumori 60: 325-336

Choi NW, Howe GR, Miller AB, Matthews V, Morgan RW, Munan L, Burch JD, Feather J, Jain M, Kelly A (1978) An epidemiologic study of breast cancer. Am J Epidemiol 107: 510-521

Ciechanowski S (1948) Nowotwory zlosliwe w materiale sekcyjnym zakladu Anatomii Patologicznej UJ (Cancer in the autopsy material of the Department of Pathological Anatomy of the Jagellonian University). Rozprawy Wydz Lek 9, PAU Krakow

Clemmesen J (1965) Statistical studies in the aetiology of malignant neoplasm. Vol I, Review and results. Acta Pathol Microbiol Immunol Scand [Suppl] 174

Clemmesen J (1968) A Doubling of morbidity from testis carcinoma in Copenhagen, 1943-1962. Acta pathol microbiol scand 72: 348-349

Coldman AJ, Elwood JM, Gallagher R (1982) Sports activities and risk of testicular cancer. Br J Cancer 46: 749-756

Cole P, Monson RR, Haning H et al. (1971) Smoking and cancer of the lower urinary tract. N Engl J Med 284: 129-134

Colman M, Kirsch M, Creditor M (1978) Tumours associated with medical X-ray therapy exposure in childhood. In: Late biological effects of ionizing radiation. International Atomic Energy Agency, Vienna, pp 167-180

Correa P (1977) Hodgkin's disease. International mortality patterns and time trends. World Health Stat Rep 30: 146-154

Correa P, Haenszel W, Cuello C et al (1975) A model for gastric cancer epidemiology. Lancet 2: 58-60

Correa P, O'Conor GT (1971) Epidemiologic patterns of Hodgkin's disease. Int J Cancer 8: 192-201

Creagan ET, Fraumeni JF (1972) Cancer mortality among American Indians 1950-1967. JNCI 49: 959-967

Day NE, Munoz N (1982) Esophagus. In: Schottenfeld D, Fraumeni JF (eds) Cancer epidemiology and prevention. Saunders, Philadelphia

De Waard F, Halewijn EAB (1974) A prospective study in general practise on breast-cancer risk in postmenopausal women. Int J Cancer 14: 153-160

De Waard F, Baanders-van Halewijn EA, Hurzinga J (1964) The bimodal age distribution of patients with mammary carcinoma. Evidence for the existence of two types of human breast cancer. Cancer 17: 141-151

Doll R (1978) Atmospheric pollution and lung cancer. Environ Health Perspect 22: 23-31

Doll R, Peto R (1976) Mortality in relation to smoking: 20 years observations on male British doctors. Br Med J 2: 1525-1536
Doll R, Peto R (1981) The causes of cancer. Quantative estimates of avoidable risk of cancer in the United States today. Oxford University Press, Oxford
Doll R, Muir C, Waterhouse J (eds) (1970) Cancer incidence in five continents, Vol 2. IARC, Lyon
Einhorn LH, Donohue JP (1977) Improved chemotherapy in disseminated testicular cancer. J Urol 117: 65
Eklund G, Malec E (1978) Sunlight and incidence of cutaneous malignant melanoma. Effect of latitude and domicile in Sweden. Scand J Plast Reconstr Surg 12: 231-241
Elwood JM, Lee JAH (1974) Trends in mortality from primary tumours of skin in Canada. Can Med Assoc J 110: 913-915
Elwood JM, Gallagher RP, Hill GB, Pearson JCG (1985) Cutaneous melanoma in relation to intermittent and constant sun exposure - the western Canada melanoma study. Int J Cancer 35: 427-433
Enstrom JE (1975) Cancer mortality among Mormons. Cancer 36: 825-841
Flanders WD, Rothman KJ (1982) Interaction of alcohol and tobacco in laryngeal cancer Am J Epidem 115: 3
Fraumeni JF (1968) Cigarette smoking and cancer of the urinary tract: geographic variation in the United States. JNCI 41: 1205-1211
Gatti RA, Good RA (1971) Occurrence of malignancy in immunodeficiency disease. Cancer 28: 89-98
Graham S, Mettlin C, Marshall J, Priore R, Rzepka T, Shedd D (1981) Dietary factors in the epidemiology of cancer of the larynx. Am J Epidemiol 113: 675-680
Green MH (1982) Non-Hodkin's lymphoma and mycosis fungoides. In: Schottenfeld D, Fraumeni JF (eds) Cancer epidemiology and prevention. Saunders, Philadelphia
Grufferman S (1982) Hodgkin's disease. In: Schottenfeld D, Fraumeni JF (eds) Cancer epidemiology and prevention. Saunders, Philadelphia
GUS (1925-1986) Roczniki statystyczne, Glownego Urzedu Statystycznego. (Statistical yearbooks, Central Statistical Office). Warsaw
GUS (1980-1986) Roczniki demograficzne (Demographic yearbooks). Warsaw
Haenszel W (1961) Cancer mortality among the foreign born in the United States. JNCI 26: 37-132
Haenszel W, Kurihara M (1968) Studies of Japanese migrants. I. Mortality from cancer and other diseases among Japanese in the United States. JNCI 40: 43-68
Haenszel W, Berg J, Segi M, Kurihara H, Locke F (1973) Large bowel cancer in Hawaiian Japanese. JNCI 51: 1765-1779
Hakama M (1982) Trends in the incidence of cervical cancer in the Nordic countries. In: Magnus K (ed) Trends in cancer incidence. Causes and practical implications. Hemisphere, Washington
Hart J, Modan B, Shani M (1971) Cholelithasis in the aetiology of gallbladder neoplasmas. Lancet 1: 1151-1153
Heath CW (1982) The leukemias. In: Schottenfeld D, Fraumeni JF (eds) Cancer epidemiology and prevention. Saunders, Philadelphia
Henderson BE, Benton B, Jing J, Yu MC, Pike MC (1979) Risk factors for cancer of the testis in young men. Int J Cancer 23: 598-602
Herity BA, O'Halloran MJ, Bourke GJ, Wilson-Davis K (1975) A study of breast cancer in Irish women. Br J Prev Soc Med 29: 178-181
Herity B, Moriarty M, Bourke GJ, Daly L (1981) A case-control study of head and neck cancer in the Republic of Ireland. Br J Cancer 43: 177-182
Holman CD, Armstrong BK (1984) Cutaneous malignant melanoma and indicators of total accumulated exposure to sun: an analysis separating histogenetic type. JNCI 73: 75-82
Holman CD, James IR, Gattey PH, Armstrong BK (1980) An analysis of trends of mortality from malignant melanoma of the skin in Australia. Int J Cancer 26: 703-709
Holzer JZ (1970) Demografia (Demography). PWE, Warszawa
Howe GR, Burch JD, Miller AB et al. (1980) Tobacco use, occupation, coffee, various nutriments, and bladder cancer. JNCI 64: 701-713
Howson C, Hirayama T, Wynder E (1986) The decline in gastric cancer: epidemiology of an unplanned triumph. Epidemiol Rev 8: 1-27
Hulka BS (1982) Risk factors for cervical cancer. J Chronic Dis 35: 3-11
Hsieh C-C, McMahon B, Yen S, Trichopoulos D, Warren K, Nardi G (1986) Coffee and pancreatic cancer. N Eng J Med 315: 587-589
IARC (1986) Tobacco smoking. Monographs on evaluation of the carcinogenic risk of chemicals to humans, vol 38. IARC, Lyon
Jasinski J (1984) Badania ankietowe nad spozyciem alkoholu w Polsce w roku 1980 (Surveys on alcohol consumption in Poland in 1980). Spoleczny Komitet Przeciwalkoholowy, Warsaw
Jedrychowski W, Wahrendorf J, Popiela T, Rachtan J (1986) A case-control study of dietary factors and stomach cancer risk in Poland. Int J Cancer 37: 837-842
Jensen OM (1980) Cancer morbidity and causes of death among Danish brewery workers. IARC, Lyon
Jensen OM, Bolander AM (1980) Trends in malignant melanoma of the skin. World Health Stat Q 33: 2-26
Jensen OM, Knudsen J, Sorensen B, Clemmensen J (1983) Artificial sweeteners and absence of bladder cancer risk in Copenhagen. Int J Cancer 32: 577-582
Jokiel M (1983) Struktura palenia tytoniu w Polsce (The structure of tobacco smoking in Poland). Przegl Epidemiol 37: 3-4
Keller AZ (1970) Cellular types, survival, race, nativity, occupation, habits and associated diseases in the pathogenesis of lip cancers. Am J Epidemiol 91: 486-499
Kemp I, Boyle P, Smans M, Muir C (eds) (1985) Atlas of cancer in Scotland, 1975-1980. Incidence and epidemiological perspective. IARC, Lyon
Kinlen LJ (1979) Hoover lymphomes in venal transplantation recipients; a search for clustering. Br J Cancer 40: 798
Koszarowski T, Kolodziejska H, Gadomska H, Staszewski J, Wieczorkiewicz A, Wronkowski Z, Warda B, Karewicz Z (1972) Cancer registry report in selected

areas of Poland 1965-1970. Organization of cancer control in Poland. Polish Med, Warsaw, pp 5-289
Koszarowski T, Gadomska H, Wronkowski Z, Romejko M (1977) Cancer in Poland, city of Warsaw and selected rural areas 1963-1972. Polish Med, Warsaw, pp 5-403
Koszarowski T, Gadomska H, Wronkowski Z, Romejko M (1984) Epidemiologia nowotworow zlosliwych w Polsce w latach 1952-1982 (Cancer epidemiology in Poland 1952-1982). Oncological Center Sklodowska-Curie Institute, Warsaw
Lea AJ (1966) Cigarette smoking and cancer of the lung and bladder. Lancet 1: 590-591
Lauren P (1965) The two histological main types of gastric carcinoma. Diffuse and so-called intestinal type. Acta Pathol Microbiol Immunol Scand 64: 31-49
Leach JF, Beadle PC, Pingstone AR, Aughton P (1979) Some effects of the variation of atmospheric particulates on disease in Great Britain. Aviat Space Environ Med 50: 72-79
Li FP, Fraumeni JF (1972) Testicular cancers in children: epidemiologic characteristic. JNCI 48: 1575
Lilienfeld AM, Levin ML, Moore GE (1956) The association of smoking with cancer of the urinary bladder in humans. Arch Intern Med 98: 129-135
Lindqvist C (1979) Risk factors in lip cancer: a questionnaire survey. Am J Epidemiol 109: 521-530
Lindqvist C, Teppo L (1978) Epidemiological evaluation of sunlight as a risk factor of lip cancer. Br J Cancer 37: 983-989
Lopez AD (ed) (1984) Demographic trends in the European region. WHO, Copenhagen
Lu SH, Ohshima H, Fu HM, Tian Y, Li FM, Blettner M Wahrendorf J, Bartsch H (1986) Urinary excretion of N-nitrosamine acids and nitrate by inhabitant of high and low risk areas for esophageal cancer in northern China: endogenous formation of nitrosoprolin and its inhibition by vitamin C. Cancer Res 46: 1485-1491
Mack TM (1982) Pancreas. In: Schottenfeld D, Fraumeni JF (eds) Cancer epidemiology and prevention. Saunders, Philadelphia
MacMahon B, Cole P, Brown J (1973) Etiology of human breast cancer: a review. JNCI 50: 21-42
MacMahon B, Yen S, Trichopoulos D, Warren K, Nardi G (1981) Coffee and cancer of the pancreas. N Engl J Med 304: 630-633
Madej G, Didkowska J, Zatonski W (1984) Epidemiologia nowotworow zlosliwych jadra w Polsce. Epidemiologiczna analiza umieralnosci (Epidemiology of malignant testicular tumours in Poland. Epidemiological analysis of mortality). Nowotwory 34: 245-251
Magnus K (1973) Incidence of malignant melanoma of the skin in Norway, 1955-70. Cancer 32: 1275-1286
Mason TJ, McKay FW, Hoover R, Fraumeni JF (1975) Atlas of cancer mortality for US counties: 1950-1969 (DHEW publication no 75-780). US Government Printing Office, Washington DC
Matanoski GM, Elliott EA (1981) Bladder cancer epidemiology. Epidemiol Rev 3: 203-229
Menck HR, Henersn BE, Pike MC et al. (1975) Cancer incidence in the Mexican-American. JNCI 55: 531-536
McMichael AJ (1978) Increases in laryngeal cancer in Britain and Australia in relation to alcohol and tobacco consumption trends. Lancet I: 1244-1247
McMichael AJ, Spirtas R, Kupper LL et al. (1975) Solvent exposure and leukemia among rubber workers: an epidemiologic study. J Occup Med 17: 234-239
McMichael AJ, Potter JD, Hetzel BS (1979) Time trends in colorectal cancer mortality in relation to food and alcohol consumption: United States, United Kingdom, Australia and New Zealand. Int J Epidemiol 8: 295-303
McGill PE (1978) Thyroid carcinoma in Kenya. Trop Geogr Med 30: 81-86
Miller AB (1977) The etiology of bladder cancer from the epidemiological viewpoint. Cancer Res 37: 2939-2942
Modan B, Baidatz D, Mart H et al. (1977) Radiation induced head and neck tumours. Lancet 1: 277-279
Morrison AS, Cole P (1982) Urinary tract. In: Schottenfeld D, Fraumeni JF (eds) Cancer epidemiology and prevention. Saunders, Philadelphia
Muir CS, Nectoux J (1978) Ovarian cancer. Some epidemiological features. World Health Stat Rep 31: 51-61
Muir CS, Nectoux J (1979) Epidemiology of cancer of testis and penis. Natl Cancer Inst Monogr 53: 157-164
Munoz N, Asvall J (1971) Time trends of intestinal and diffuse types of gastric cancer in Norway. Int J Cancer 8: 144
Munoz N, Connely R (1971) Time trends of intestinal and diffuse types of gastric cancer in the United States. Int J Cancer 8: 158
Munoz N, Correa P, Cuello C, Duque E (1968) Histologic types of gastric carcinoma in high and low risk areas. Int J Cancer 3: 809-818
Munoz N, Davidson RJL, Witthoff B, Ericsson J, De The G (1978) Infectious mononucleosis and Hodgkin's disease. Int J Cancer 22: 10-13
Naib ZM et al. (1966) Cytology and histopathology of cervical herpes simplex. Cancer 19: 1026-1031
Nomura A (1982) Stomach. In: Schottenfeld D, Fraumeni JF (eds) Cancer epidemiology and prevention. Saunders, Philadelphia
Olsen J, Sabroe S (1979) A follow-up study of nonretired and retired members of the Danish carpenters/cabinet makers' trade union. Int J Epidemiol 8: 375-382
Olsson H, Brandt L (1979) Occupational handling of chemicals preceding Hodgkin's disease in men. Br Med J 2: 580-581
Osterlind A (1986) Diverging trends in incidence and mortality of testicular cancer in Denmark, 1943-1982. Br J Cancer 53: 501-505
Pederson E, Hogetreit A, Anderson A (1973) Cancer of respiratory organs at a nickel refinery in Norway. Int J Cancer 12: 32-41
Petrakis N, Ernster VL, King M-C (1982) Breast. In: Schottenfeld D, Fraumeni JF (eds) Cancer epidemiology and prevention. Saunders, Philadelphia
Phillips RL (1975) Role of life-style and dietary habits in risk of cancer among Seventh-Day Adventists. Cancer Res 35: 3513-3522
Pollack ES, Nomura MY, Heilbrun LK, Stemmermann G, Green SB (1985) Prospective study of alcohol consumption and cancer. N Engl J Med 310: 617-621
Preston Martin S (1978) A case-control study of intracranial meningiomas in women (abstract). Am J Epidemiol 108: 233-234

Raineri R, Weisburger JH (1975) Reduction of gastric carcinogens with ascorbic acid. Ann NY Acad Sci 258: 181-189
Ron E, Modan B (1982) Thyroid. In: Schottenfeld D, Fraumeni JF (eds) Cancer epidemiology and prevention. Saunders, Philadelphia
Ross RK, McCurtis JW, Henderson BE, Menck HR, Mack TM, Martin SP (1979) Descriptive epidemiology of testicular and prostatic cancer in Los Angeles. Br J Cancer 39: 284-292
Rothman K, Cann CI, Flanders D, Fried MP (1980) Epidemiology of laryngeal cancer. Epidemiol Rev 2: 195-209
Rotkin JD (1967) Epidemiology of cancer of the cervix. III. Sexual characteristics of cervical cancer population. Am J Publ Health 57: 815-825
Samson MK et al. (1981) Vinblastine, bleomycin and cisdiamminedichloroplatinum in disseminated testicular cancer. Response to treatment and prognostic correlation. Eur J Cancer 16: 1359
Schoenberg BS (1982) Nervous system. In: Schottenfeld D, Fraumeni JF (eds) Cancer epidemiology and prevention. Saunders, Philadelphia
Schottenfeld D (1979) Alcohol as a co-factor in the etiology of cancer. Cancer 43: 1962-1966
Schottenfeld D, Winawer SJ (1982) Large intestine. In: Schottenfeld D, Fraumeni JF (eds) Cancer epidemiology and prevention. Saunders, Philadelphia
Segi M, Tominaga S, Aoki K, Fijimoto J (1981) Cancer mortality and morbidity statistics. Japan and the world, 1981. Japan Scientific Societies, Tokyo
Sekula W, Niedzialek Z, Liesiewicz-Cieciora H, Swistak E, Boruc T (1985) Spozycie zywnosci w Polsce w latach 1950-1983 w przeliczeniu na energie i niektore skladniki pokarmowe (Food consumption in Poland in the years 1950-1983, calculations of energy and selected food ingredients). Instytut Zywnosci i Zywienia, Warszawa
Selikoff IJ, Hammond EC, Seidman H (1979) Mortality experience of insulation workers in the United States and Canada, 1943-1976. Ann NY Acad Sci 330: 91-116
Seltzer SE, Benazzi RB, Kearney GP (1978) Cyclophosphamide and carcinoma of bladder. Urology 11: 352-356
Skegg DC, Corwin PA, Paul C, Doll R (1982) Importance of the male factor in the cancer of the cervix. Lancet 2: 581-583
Stalsberg H (1973) Lymphoreticular tumors in Norway and other European countries. JNCI 50: 1685-1702
Staszewski J (1960) Smoking and cancer in Poland. Br J Cancer 14: 419-436
Staszewski J (1971) Age at menarche and breast cancer. JNCI 47: 935
Staszewski J (1976) Epidemiology of cancer of selected sites in Poland and Polish migrants. Ballinger, Cambridge
Staszewski J (1979) Regionalne roznice umieralnosci na nowotwory zlosliwe w Polsce w latach 1970-1974 (Regional differences in cancer mortality in Poland 1970-1974). Instytut Onkologii, Gliwice, pp 2-79
Staszewski J, Haenszel W (1965) Cancer mortality among the Polish born in the United States. JNCI 35: 291
Staszewski J, McCall MG, Stenhouse NS (1971) Cancer mortality in 1962-1966 among Polish migrants to Australia. Br J Cancer 25: 599-610
Stell PM (1972) Smoking and laryngeal cancer. Lancet I: 617-618
Stell PM (1973) Asbestos and laryngeal cancer. Lancet 2: 416-417
Teppo L (1973) Testicular Cancer in Finland. Acta Path microbiol Scand Sect A [Suppl] 238
Teppo L, Pakkanen M, Hakulinen T (1978) Sunlight as a risk factor of malignant melanoma of the skin. Cancer 41: 2018-2027
Thiede T, Christensen BC (1975) Bladder tumours induced by clornafazin treatment (in Danish). Ugeskr Laeger 137: 661-666
Trichopoulos D, MacMahon B, Cole P (1972) Menopause and breast cancer risk. JNCI 48: 605-613
Tulinius H, Day NE, Johannesson G, Bjarnason O, Gonzales M (1978) Reproductive factors and risk for breast cancer in Iceland. Int J Cancer 21: 724-730
Tuyns AJ (1982) Incidence trends of laryngeal cancer in relation to national alcohol and tobacco consumption. In: Magnus K (ed) Trends in cancer incidence. Causes and practical implications. Hemisphere Publishing Corporation, Washington
Tuyns AJ, Audigier JC (1976) Double wave cohort increase for oesophageal and laryngeal cancer in France in relation to reduced alcohol consumption during the Second World War. Digestion 14: 197-208
Tuyns AJ, Pequinot G, Jensen OM (1977) Le cancer de l'oesophage en Ille-et-Vilaine en fonction des niveaux de consommation d'alcool et de tabac. Des risques qui se multiplient. Bull Cancer 64: 45-60
Velema J, Walker A, Gold E (1986) Alcohol and pancreatic cancer. Epidemiol Rev 8: 28-41
Vonka V, Kanka J, Hirsch I, Zavadova H, Krcmar M, Suchankova A, Rezacova D, Broucek J, Press M, Domorzkova E, Suoboda B, Havranova A, Jelinek J (1984) Prospective study on the relationship between cervical neoplasie and herpes simplex type-2 virus. II Herpes simplex type-2 antibody presence in sera taken at entrolment. Int J. Cancer 33: 61-66
Waterhouse J, Muir C, Correa P, Powell J (eds) (1976) Cancer incidence in five countries, vol 3. IARC, Lyon
Waterhouse J, Shanmugaratnam K, Muir C, Powell J (eds) (1982) Cancer incidence in five countries, vol 4. IARC, Lyon
Vianna NJ, Polan AK (1973) Epidemiologic evidence for transmission of Hodgkin's disease. N Engl J Med 10: 499-502
Weiss N (1982) Ovary. In: Schottenfeld D, Fraumeni J (eds) Cancer epidemiology and prevention. Saunders, Philadelphia
Williams ED, Doniach I, Bjarneson O, Michie W (1977) Thyroid cancer in an iodine-rich area: a histopathological study. Cancer 39: 215-222
Williams RG, Beetham KW (1976) Cancer of the larynx in Hull and the surrounding area of East Yorkshire. J Laryngol Otol 90: 539-653
Winkelstein W (1977) Smoking and cancer of the uterine cervix: hypothesis. Am J Epidemiol 106: 257-259
Wronkowski ZL (1985) Charakterystyka epidemiologiczno-kliniczna dwoch glownych postaci histopatologicz-

nych raka zolodka ws klasyfikacji Laurena. ("intestinal" i diffuse) (Clinico-epidemiological characteristic of two principal histopathological forms of gastric cancer acc. to Laurens' classification (intestinal and diffuse)). Nowotwory 35: 2

Wynder EL (1975) An epidemiological evaluation of the causes of cancer of the pancreas. Cancer Res 35: 2228-2233

Wynder EL, Bross IJ, Day E (1956) Epidemiological approach to etiology of cancer of the larynx. JAMA 160: 1384-1391

Wynder EL, Mabuchi K, Whitmore WF (1974) Epidemiology of adenocarcinoma of kidney. JNCI 53: 1619-1634

Wynder EL, Covey LS, Maruchi K, Mushinski M (1976) Environmental factors in cancer of the larynx. A second look. Cancer 38: 1591-1601

Zaridze DG (1983) Environmental etiology of large bowel cancer. JNCI 70: 389-399

Zaridze DG, Boyle P, Smans M (1984) The epidemiology of cancer of the prostate. Int J Cancer 33: 213-230

Zatonski W, Didkowska J, Gadomska H (1982) Cancer of the larynx in Warsaw and selected rural areas. Neoplasma 30: 379-384

Zatonski W, Didkowska J, Gadomska H (1982) Epidemiologiczna analiza umieralnosci na nowotwory zlosliwe krtani w Polsce (Epidemiological analysis of the larynx cancer mortality in Poland). Nowotwory 32: 273-279

Zatonski W, Didkowska J (1984) Geografia nowotworow zlosliwych krtani w Polsce (Geography of larynx cancer in Poland). Nowotwory 34

Zatonski W, Didkowska J (1985) Geograficzne roznice w umieralnosci na nowotwory zlosliwe krtani w Polsce w latach 1970-1981 (Geographical differences in mortality of malignant laryngeal neoplasms in Poland in the years 1970-1981). Nowotwory 35: 4, 348-354

Zatonski W, Przewozniak K, Gottesman K (1986) Zakres i nastepstwa zdrowotne palenia tytoniu w Polsce (The scale and health consequences of tobacco smoking in Poland.) In: Strzelecki Z (ed) Alkohol, narkotyki, tyton. Skutki demograficzne w Polsce (Alcohol, drugs and tobacco. Demographic effects). PAX, Warsaw

Zatonski W, Mierzwinska J (unpublished data) Cancer of the larynx in Low Silesia

Zavala D, Correa P (1986) Latin America. In: Howe GM (ed) Global geocancerology. A world geography of human cancers. Churchill Livingstone, Edinburgh

Zemla B (1984) Geografia nowotworow zlosliwych najczestszych umiejscowien wsrod mezczyzn i kobiet w swietle uprzemyslowienia i innych czynnikow ryzyka (Geography of cancer of the most frequently sites among men and women in the light of industrialization and other risk factors). Zaklad Narodowy im Ossolinskich, Wroclaw

Ziegler JL et al. (1984) Non-Hodgkin's lymphoma in 90 homosexual men. Relation to generalized lymphodenopathy and acquired immunodeficiency syndrome. N Engl J Med 311: 565-570

Zur Hausen H (1976) Condylomata acuminata and human genital cancer. Cancer Res 36: 794

Zur Hausen H (1986) Intracellular surveillance of persisting viral infections. Lancet, Vol. 2: 489-491

Słupsk
Gdańsk
Elbląg
Suwałki
Koszalin
Olsztyn
Szczecin
Bydgoszcz
Łomża
Toruń
Piła
Białystok
Ostrołęka
Gorzów Wlkp.
Ciechanów
Włocławek
Płock
Poznań
Siedlce
Warszawa
Konin
Skierniewice
Zielona Góra
Łódź
Biała Podl.
Leszno
Kalisz
Sieradz
Radom
Legnica
Piotrków Tryb.
Lublin
Wrocław
Chełm
Jelenia Góra
Częstochowa
Tarnobrzeg
Zamość
Kielce
Wałbrzych
Opole
Katowice
Rzeszów
Kraków
Przemyśl
Tarnów
Bielsko Biała

MIX
Papier aus verantwortungsvollen Quellen
Paper from responsible sources
FSC® C105338

If you have any concerns about our products,
you can contact us on
ProductSafety@springernature.com

In case Publisher is established outside the EU,
the EU authorized representative is:
Springer Nature Customer Service Center GmbH
Europaplatz 3, 69115 Heidelberg, Germany

Printed by Libri Plureos GmbH
in Hamburg, Germany